Lecture Notes in Computer Science 12189

More information about this series at http://www.springer.com/series/7409

Margherita Antona · Constantine Stephanidis (Eds.)

Universal Access in Human-Computer Interaction

Applications and Practice

14th International Conference, UAHCI 2020
Held as Part of the 22nd HCI International Conference, HCII 2020
Copenhagen, Denmark, July 19–24, 2020
Proceedings, Part II

 Springer

Editors
Margherita Antona
Foundation for Research
and Technology – Hellas (FORTH)
Heraklion, Crete, Greece

Constantine Stephanidis
University of Crete and Foundation
for Research and Technology – Hellas
(FORTH)
Heraklion, Crete, Greece

ISSN 0302-9743 ISSN 1611-3349 (electronic)
Lecture Notes in Computer Science
ISBN 978-3-030-49107-9 ISBN 978-3-030-49108-6 (eBook)
https://doi.org/10.1007/978-3-030-49108-6

LNCS Sublibrary: SL3 – Information Systems and Applications, incl. Internet/Web, and HCI

This Springer imprint is published by the registered company Springer Nature Switzerland AG
The registered company address is: Gewerbestrasse 11, 6330 Cham, Switzerland

Editors
Margherita Antona
Foundation for Research
and Technology – Hellas (FORTH)
Heraklion, Crete, Greece

Constantine Stephanidis
University of Crete and Foundation
for Research and Technology – Hellas
(FORTH)
Heraklion, Crete, Greece

ISSN 0302-9743   ISSN 1611-3349   (electronic)
Lecture Notes in Computer Science
ISBN 978-3-030-49107-9   ISBN 978-3-030-49108-6   (eBook)
https://doi.org/10.1007/978-3-030-49108-6

LNCS Sublibrary: SL3 – Information Systems and Applications, incl. Internet/Web, and HCI

This Springer imprint is published by the registered company Springer Nature Switzerland AG
The registered company address is: Gewerbestrasse 11, 6330 Cham, Switzerland

Margherita Antona · Constantine Stephanidis (Eds.)

Universal Access in Human-Computer Interaction

Applications and Practice

14th International Conference, UAHCI 2020
Held as Part of the 22nd HCI International Conference, HCII 2020
Copenhagen, Denmark, July 19–24, 2020
Proceedings, Part II

 Springer

Foreword

The 22nd International Conference on Human-Computer Interaction, HCI International 2020 (HCII 2020), was planned to be held at the AC Bella Sky Hotel and Bella Center, Copenhagen, Denmark, during July 19–24, 2020. Due to the COVID-19 coronavirus pandemic and the resolution of the Danish government not to allow events larger than 500 people to be hosted until September 1, 2020, HCII 2020 had to be held virtually. It incorporated the 21 thematic areas and affiliated conferences listed on the following page.

A total of 6,326 individuals from academia, research institutes, industry, and governmental agencies from 97 countries submitted contributions, and 1,439 papers and 238 posters were included in the conference proceedings. These contributions address the latest research and development efforts and highlight the human aspects of design and use of computing systems. The contributions thoroughly cover the entire field of human-computer interaction, addressing major advances in knowledge and effective use of computers in a variety of application areas. The volumes constituting the full set of the conference proceedings are listed in the following pages.

The HCI International (HCII) conference also offers the option of "late-breaking work" which applies both for papers and posters and the corresponding volume(s) of the proceedings will be published just after the conference. Full papers will be included in the "HCII 2020 - Late Breaking Papers" volume of the proceedings to be published in the Springer LNCS series, while poster extended abstracts will be included as short papers in the "HCII 2020 - Late Breaking Posters" volume to be published in the Springer CCIS series.

I would like to thank the program board chairs and the members of the program boards of all thematic areas and affiliated conferences for their contribution to the highest scientific quality and the overall success of the HCI International 2020 conference.

This conference would not have been possible without the continuous and unwavering support and advice of the founder, Conference General Chair Emeritus and Conference Scientific Advisor Prof. Gavriel Salvendy. For his outstanding efforts, I would like to express my appreciation to the communications chair and editor of HCI International News, Dr. Abbas Moallem.

July 2020   Constantine Stephanidis

HCI International 2020 Thematic Areas
and Affiliated Conferences

Thematic areas:

- HCI 2020: Human-Computer Interaction
- HIMI 2020: Human Interface and the Management of Information

Affiliated conferences:

- EPCE: 17th International Conference on Engineering Psychology and Cognitive Ergonomics
- UAHCI: 14th International Conference on Universal Access in Human-Computer Interaction
- VAMR: 12th International Conference on Virtual, Augmented and Mixed Reality
- CCD: 12th International Conference on Cross-Cultural Design
- SCSM: 12th International Conference on Social Computing and Social Media
- AC: 14th International Conference on Augmented Cognition
- DHM: 11th International Conference on Digital Human Modeling and Applications in Health, Safety, Ergonomics and Risk Management
- DUXU: 9th International Conference on Design, User Experience and Usability
- DAPI: 8th International Conference on Distributed, Ambient and Pervasive Interactions
- HCIBGO: 7th International Conference on HCI in Business, Government and Organizations
- LCT: 7th International Conference on Learning and Collaboration Technologies
- ITAP: 6th International Conference on Human Aspects of IT for the Aged Population
- HCI-CPT: Second International Conference on HCI for Cybersecurity, Privacy and Trust
- HCI-Games: Second International Conference on HCI in Games
- MobiTAS: Second International Conference on HCI in Mobility, Transport and Automotive Systems
- AIS: Second International Conference on Adaptive Instructional Systems
- C&C: 8th International Conference on Culture and Computing
- MOBILE: First International Conference on Design, Operation and Evaluation of Mobile Communications
- AI-HCI: First International Conference on Artificial Intelligence in HCI

Conference Proceedings Volumes Full List

1. LNCS 12181, Human-Computer Interaction: Design and User Experience (Part I), edited by Masaaki Kurosu
2. LNCS 12182, Human-Computer Interaction: Multimodal and Natural Interaction (Part II), edited by Masaaki Kurosu
3. LNCS 12183, Human-Computer Interaction: Human Values and Quality of Life (Part III), edited by Masaaki Kurosu
4. LNCS 12184, Human Interface and the Management of Information: Designing Information (Part I), edited by Sakae Yamamoto and Hirohiko Mori
5. LNCS 12185, Human Interface and the Management of Information: Interacting with Information (Part II), edited by Sakae Yamamoto and Hirohiko Mori
6. LNAI 12186, Engineering Psychology and Cognitive Ergonomics: Mental Workload, Human Physiology, and Human Energy (Part I), edited by Don Harris and Wen-Chin Li
7. LNAI 12187, Engineering Psychology and Cognitive Ergonomics: Cognition and Design (Part II), edited by Don Harris and Wen-Chin Li
8. LNCS 12188, Universal Access in Human-Computer Interaction: Design Approaches and Supporting Technologies (Part I), edited by Margherita Antona and Constantine Stephanidis
9. LNCS 12189, Universal Access in Human-Computer Interaction: Applications and Practice (Part II), edited by Margherita Antona and Constantine Stephanidis
10. LNCS 12190, Virtual, Augmented and Mixed Reality: Design and Interaction (Part I), edited by Jessie Y. C. Chen and Gino Fragomeni
11. LNCS 12191, Virtual, Augmented and Mixed Reality: Industrial and Everyday Life Applications (Part II), edited by Jessie Y. C. Chen and Gino Fragomeni
12. LNCS 12192, Cross-Cultural Design: User Experience of Products, Services, and Intelligent Environments (Part I), edited by P. L. Patrick Rau
13. LNCS 12193, Cross-Cultural Design: Applications in Health, Learning, Communication, and Creativity (Part II), edited by P. L. Patrick Rau
14. LNCS 12194, Social Computing and Social Media: Design, Ethics, User Behavior, and Social Network Analysis (Part I), edited by Gabriele Meiselwitz
15. LNCS 12195, Social Computing and Social Media: Participation, User Experience, Consumer Experience, and Applications of Social Computing (Part II), edited by Gabriele Meiselwitz
16. LNAI 12196, Augmented Cognition: Theoretical and Technological Approaches (Part I), edited by Dylan D. Schmorrow and Cali M. Fidopiastis
17. LNAI 12197, Augmented Cognition: Human Cognition and Behaviour (Part II), edited by Dylan D. Schmorrow and Cali M. Fidopiastis

38. CCIS 1224, HCI International 2020 Posters - Part I, edited by Constantine Stephanidis and Margherita Antona
39. CCIS 1225, HCI International 2020 Posters - Part II, edited by Constantine Stephanidis and Margherita Antona
40. CCIS 1226, HCI International 2020 Posters - Part III, edited by Constantine Stephanidis and Margherita Antona

http://2020.hci.international/proceedings

14th International Conference on Universal Access in Human-Computer Interaction (UAHCI 2020)

Program Board Chairs: **Margherita Antona, Foundation for Research and Technology – Hellas (FORTH), Greece, and Constantine Stephanidis, University of Crete and Foundation for Research and Technology – Hellas (FORTH), Greece**

- João Barroso, Portugal
- Rodrigo Bonacin, Brazil
- Ingo Bosse, Germany
- Laura Burzagli, Italy
- Pedro J. S. Cardoso, Portugal
- Carlos Duarte, Portugal
- Pier Luigi Emiliani, Italy
- Vagner Figueredo de Santana, Brazil
- Andrina Granic, Croatia
- Gian Maria Greco, Spain
- Simeon Keates, UK
- Georgios Kouroupetroglou, Greece
- Patrick M. Langdon, UK
- Barbara Leporini, Italy
- I. Scott MacKenzie, Canada
- John Magee, USA
- Jorge Martín-Gutiérrez, Spain
- Troy McDaniel, USA
- Silvia Mirri, Italy
- Stavroula Ntoa, Greece
- Federica Pallavicini, Italy
- Ana Isabel Paraguay, Brazil
- Hugo Paredes, Portugal
- Enrico Pontelli, USA
- João M. F. Rodrigues, Portugal
- Frode Eika Sandnes, Norway
- Volker Sorge, UK
- Hiroki Takada, Japan
- Kevin C. Tseng, Taiwan
- Gerhard Weber, Germany

The full list with the Program Board Chairs and the members of the Program Boards of all thematic areas and affiliated conferences is available online at:

http://www.hci.international/board-members-2020.php

HCI International 2021

The 23rd International Conference on Human-Computer Interaction, HCI International 2021 (HCII 2021), will be held jointly with the affiliated conferences in Washington DC, USA, at the Washington Hilton Hotel, July 24–29, 2021. It will cover a broad spectrum of themes related to Human-Computer Interaction (HCI), including theoretical issues, methods, tools, processes, and case studies in HCI design, as well as novel interaction techniques, interfaces, and applications. The proceedings will be published by Springer. More information will be available on the conference website: http://2021.hci.international/.

General Chair
Prof. Constantine Stephanidis
University of Crete and ICS-FORTH
Heraklion, Crete, Greece
Email: general_chair@hcii2021.org

http://2021.hci.international/

Contents – Part II

Universal Access to Learning and Education

Intelligent Assistive Environments

Contents – Part I

Robots in Universal Access

Technologies for Autism Spectrum Disorders

Using Augmented Reality Technology with Serial Learning Framework to Develop a Serial Social Story Situation Board Game System for Children with Autism to Improve Social Situation Understanding and Social Reciprocity Skills

Hsiu-Ting Hsu and I-Jui Lee[✉]

Department of Industrial Design,
National Taipei University of Technology, Taipei, Taiwan
tl07588030@ntut.org.tw, ericlee@mail.ntut.edu.tw

Abstract. This study adopts a Sequence Learning Strategy based on social stories and designs a sequential social story situation board game system using Augmented Reality (AR) technology (SL-ARS). In the system, the content of social stories is decomposed into social situation units with a Sequence Learning structure, different social situation judgment tasks are added into the stories, and autistic children are taught to think about the order of social events and situations that occur in their daily environment, correctly prioritize social situational states, and learn how to give appropriate social responses to others in a given situation.

This study recruited three 7–9-year-old children with autism and observed the explicit behavior of autistic children during the operation of SL-ARS by micro-behaviors for video coding. After performing the SL-ARS system in an autism case, we found that autistic children performed well in understanding social situations and responding to other people's physical behavior, as they can understand the sequence of social situations from SL-ARS, and observe the social reciprocity of social situations through the structured visual learning framework. In the process of playing, AR can improve the learning motivation and operating pleasure of autistic children to understand the social situation, and construct the relationship of social cognition and social reciprocity of autistic children into the context of social situations. This interactive learning gives them the social skills and context to develop social situations, and we believe that AR technology combined with the sequential social context is helpful to train autistic children's social reciprocal ability.

Keywords: Augmented Reality (AR) · Autism · Micro-Behaviors for Video Coding (MBV) · Non-verbal social cues · Sequence learning framework · Social context interactive board games · Social interaction skills

© Springer Nature Switzerland AG 2020
M. Antona and C. Stephanidis (Eds.): HCII 2020, LNCS 12189, pp. 3–18, 2020.
https://doi.org/10.1007/978-3-030-49108-6_1

1   Introduction

1.1   Congenital Social Deficiency in Autism

The major social deficits of autistic people are difficulty in communicating socially with others and in responding appropriately to socially reciprocal behaviors. They are unable to initiate social interaction with others or make the appropriate social reciprocal behavior with others, resulting in the inability to integrate into society and establish further social relations [1]. The main social deficit of autistic people is their lack of social communication skills, and the inability to predict social cues, body movements, and behaviors in other people's words, consequently, they are unable to make appropriate social response to others and integrate into the social relations among their peers.

The inability of autistic people to relate their emotions to the environmental elements of society and the behavior of others makes them fearful of contact with others and contributes to their social isolation [2]. Moreover, children with autistic traits are significantly visible in early childhood and do not improve with age [3]. This kind of birth defect will cause them to feel uneasy and shrink away when they interact with others in their future life, which will result in long-term negative effect. Therefore, the ability to improve social skills is the most important learning task and goal of autistic children in the learning phase, as increasing autistic people's exposure to social stimuli and training for more social behavioral changes can improve the likelihood of social interactions between autistic children and their peers [4]. Using targeted social behavior intervention training and intervention instruction can improve autistic children's social communication skills and reciprocal skills [5], encourage them to face different social situations, and be able to respond appropriately to social reciprocity.

1.2   Application of Traditional Social Story Method in Social Training of Autistic Children — Social Story Method

There have been many methods of social skill training for autistic children, and the social story has become the main social training method. Carol Gray coined the term Social Story in 1990, which stated that social stories have characters, events, and situations, thus, social stories can help autistic children learn social behaviors that are likely to occur in a social environment [6]. The training structure of a social story is suitable for autistic children to learn social cues for social environments, enhance autistic children's familiarity with social context and social characteristic cues, and provide appropriate social response, which trains and promotes autistic children's awareness and understanding of social situations [7].

1.3   The Social Story Approach Lacks Sufficient Learning Appeal and Learning Benefits for Autistic Children

Social Stories™ use simple vocabulary to narrate the content of a story and combine visual displays with text descriptions to present social situations, which can be practiced over and over [8], and thus, can help autistic children understand the social context of a social plot and improve their social skills [9]. In combination with the above advantages, social stories enable autistic children to construct the characters, events, and situations that occur in the social context, which can enhance their cognitive ability in social behavior and their mastery of social links; therefore, many teaching strategies that use social stories have been applied to actual teaching and training. The common training strategy is to use social stories as the basis of learning intervention for autistic children, such as story-based intervention and scripting [10].

However, the existing social story training strategies focus on the judgment of specific social behaviors, but have not yet been trained for the plot of social situations or the sequence of events. As a result of such teaching methods, autistic children can only understand the characteristics of social behavior described in a particular social story, but it is difficult to understand the underlying structure of social behavior, and fully clarify the relationship between the event and the story behind the content of meaning [11]. In addition, traditional social storytelling training methods are not attractive enough for autistic children, as flat images and text descriptions are not enough to give them clues to the overall social situation, which prevents them from focusing on learning and leads to poor learning outcomes [4].

2   Related Work

2.1   Using AR to Draw Autistic Children's Attention to Learning Social Story Structures

In past clinical studies, visual media and animation, such as AR, have been proved to be attractive for autistic children in learning [12, 13]. AR is an attractive learning medium that provides direct feedback to physical objects through virtual means, as it can include additional content and information that cannot be represented by the physical object; for example providing social cues, such as characters, events, and context aids that cannot be represented by the physical environment. In the process of learning social stories, AR can help autistic children to understand the appropriate social action response in a given situation by giving them timely virtual social action and situational judgment skills. Learning in this way can enhance their perception of the social environment, and help them learn to make appropriate judgments and social responses to others, as it can equip them with basic social cognitive skills and reciprocal skills in interacting with their peers, help reduce their fear of others, and enhance their interaction with their peers [14].

2.2   Using AR to Teach Autistic Children About Complex Social Concepts

In recent years, many studies have demonstrated that AR can effectively attract the attention of autistic children and be used in social teaching and training. Through the interaction of 3D virtual animation and real-life environments, AR can attract autistic children's motivation to operate and participate in social training activities, and thus, enhance the benefits of social learning. Recent studies have evaluated the use of AR, and results show that it has positive learning effect, as AR addresses the problem of the lack of attractiveness of traditional social story training for autistic children. At the same time, it brings autistic children closer to real social situations and interactions through AR simulations and visuals [15]. Despite AR technology being attractive and effective for autistic children, the rich visual effects lack a clear teaching framework and visual structure, which causes autistic children to feel confused or disturbed by the interactions. In particular, due to their social cognitive and conceptual deficits, it is difficult for them to understand the concept of operations behind different visualizations, thus, the training purposes are poorly conveyed [16, 17].

2.3   Applying the Teaching Strategy of Sequence Learning to Solve the Problems in AR Teaching — Lack of a Clear Framework for Visual Operations and Difficulty in Understanding the Complex Concepts Behind AR Interaction Interfaces

The teaching strategy of Sequence Learning is a teaching strategy with a clear teaching frame and visual structure in learning, meaning Sequence Learning is a continuous and sequential cognitive process. Learners can construct a complete concept through the Sequence Learning structure and teaching units, and understand more complex and comprehensive concepts of knowledge through the process of organization. For autistic children, the social context is a complex, abstract, and coherent concept that includes people, events, and situations, just as a social story is made up of multiple plots, while Sequence Learning is used to construct different units of this concept and situation. Thus, for autistic children, an understanding of social units contributes to a mastery and familiarity with the overall concept of social interaction. As Papert put it, "mind-size Bites", when knowledge is broken down into units the size of the mind, it is easier to convey to others, understand, and construct [18]. Breaking social stories into smaller narrative pieces and structuring their content can make it easier for autistic children to learn to construct social stories, and absorb the concepts and knowledge of stories. Every social story has its antecedents and consequences. Through systematic Sequence Learning methods, autistic children can learn the relationship between social behavior and interaction in the context, and understand each component of social interaction in the social context to give the correct social response.

2.4   Summary

The application of AR technology combined with Sequence Learning in social reciprocity training for autistic children Therefore, if we can improve autistic children's understanding of social story situations before and after, we can further enhance their ability and mastery of social interaction skills. Sequence learning is a Sequence Learning method. Through sequential situation deconstruction and arrangement, autistic children can strengthen their ability to organize social situation events. As Sequence Learning is like a social story with a sequence of events, autistic children can master and construct the sequence of social situations through sequence learning, and thus, enhance their understanding of the social environment to further enhance their social skills. For the above reasons, this study combines the advantages of AR and Sequence Learning to construct a set of board game system, as based on sequence social story situations, and uses it to improve the understanding of social situations and the mastery of social reciprocal skills in autistic children.

3   Method

This study is conducted in collaboration with the Autism Society to recruit suitable autism cases to participate in the study, where special education experts screened the autism cases. In the experimental arrangement, the research team conducted regular teaching cooperation activities and developed long-term teaching interactions with the occupational therapy classroom. Through the joint planning and deconstruction of the existing board game teaching aids by the occupational therapist and the special education teacher, the game unit components and related teaching strategies were decomposed, and then, gradually constructed into the game teaching design based on "Social Story and Sequence Learning", where the teaching strategy of Sequence Learning helps learners to understand the sequence of social situations, as well as the symbolic concepts behind them, which allows them to improve their social cognition and social skills, and finally, develop appropriate social reciprocal behaviors.

3.1   Participants

This study recruited three children aged 7–9 with high-functioning autism (2 males and 1 female; Tom, John, and Alice, which are nicknames) and a special education teacher. Through the SL-ARS system, special education teachers and researchers guided the autistic children to complete the social operation tasks, and observed the autistic participants' tiny behaviors during the game.

3.2   SL-ARS System Development

The SL-ARS system uses iClone 3D software to build 3D character models, and Maya to build the 3D character's social body movements (Fig. 1). The 3D animation model is exported into the Fbx file format and integrated with Unity for AR scenes and the character animation system (Fig. 2). The AR architecture built in this system is concatenated with Vuforia suite and the C# program, as provided by Qualcomm, and through Unity, which integrates the AR scenes with the interactive contents and situations of the game level development (Fig. 3).

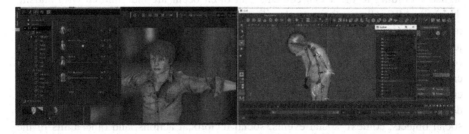

Fig. 1. Shows the iClone 3D character modeling software used to build the 3D social character models, and takes Maya for character 3D social interaction animation as the AR feedback for social interaction content, including hugging, waving, shaking hands, patting shoulders, bowing, and other basic social interaction behaviors.

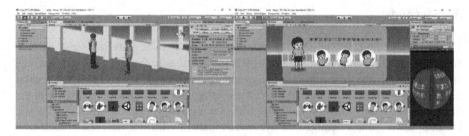

Fig. 2. Using Unity to build an AR serialized social story situation board game system scene.

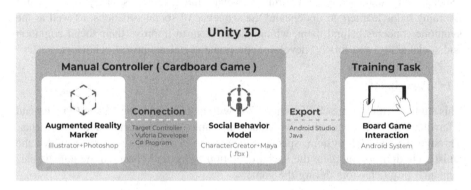

Fig. 3. The AR System architecture in SL-ARS

3.3   SL-ARS System Content Design

The design of SL-ARS system contents include (1) the relevance of social contexts and the social reciprocity behaviors behind them; (2) the interactive operations of the AR game content is the emphasis of teaching, which is strengthened by the content design. The content design of the SL-ARS system includes (1) a physical social storybook; (2) scenario cards that respond to the development of the story (Fig. 4).

The content scripts and context scripts in the physical social storybooks are designed according to the social contents that often occur around children with autism, thus, SL-ARS allows them to familiarize themselves with social content, which improves their ability to handle social problems that arise in life due to the difficulty of judging social situations. In addition, each situation unit diagram card represents a basic situation unit, and a complete social story is organized by a series of scenario cards arranged in a social context. In order to deal with the cognitive ability of autistic children and reduce the complexity of understanding, the contents of this system are designed to form a complete social situation story with 5 scenario cards, including social objects, context, social events, social reciprocal actions, and other units of the arrangement and organization. By arranging and constructing the scenario cards, autistic children can clearly understand the development of social situations, as well as the corresponding social reciprocal behaviors in the situations. The storyline is presented like a comic strip, where scenario cards consist of a series of evolving social elements, including characters, events, and situations, which form the basis of sequential instruction. Autistic children can understand the sequence of social situations through play and AR technology, which are combined with physical society storybooks and scenario cards, and the children try to make correct social reciprocal responses.

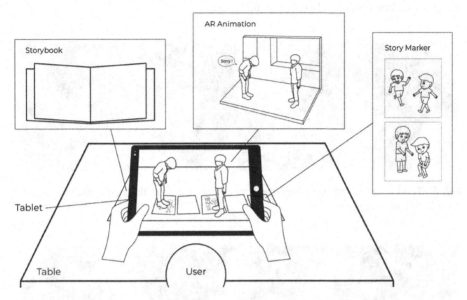

Fig. 4. SL-ARS social storybook and scenario cards

3.4   Training Phase

This study divides the training course of SL-ARS system into three phases (Table 1).

Phase 1: Understanding the social story context: to provide autistic children with a social context through a physical social storybook, and ask them to arrange the correct story cards on the storybook, in order and according to the storybook (Fig. 5).

Phase 2: Cognition of social reciprocal behavior: After arranging the entity's social scenario cards, (1) use the game interface of the SL-ARS system developed by this study, and (2) judge the social reciprocal behaviors that fit the social story context, including basic social reciprocal behaviors, such as hugging, waving, shaking hands, patting the shoulder, and bowing. When the autistic children make the correct judgment choice, (3) the special education teacher presents the SL-ARS system through a tablet, which gives the autistic children the social interaction action that the character in the situation should have done by watching the 3D social animation in AR System, and asks the autistic children to figure out and role play with the teacher to master the social interaction skills (Fig. 6).

Phase 3: The link between social context and social reciprocal behavior: After the previous intervention, the teacher will ask the autistic children to tell the whole story in the order in which it happened, and through role-playing, the children can understand the social process in the story and further engage with the teacher for (1) social reciprocity behavior practice; (2) discussing the situation will help autistic children to distinguish different states and similar situations, in order that they can develop different social cognitions and concepts (details shown in Fig. 7).

Fig. 5. Teacher asks them to arrange the correct story cards on the storybook, in order and according to the storybook.

Fig. 6. The special education teacher presents the SL-ARS system through a tablet, which gives the autistic children the social interaction action that the character in the situation should have done by watching the 3D social animation in AR System.

Table 1. The system content of SL-ARS and the purpose and extension of teaching and training at each phase

Training phase	Teaching materials and content	Teaching purpose and extended meaning
Phase 1	• Real social storybook • Several scenario cards (each social story contains 5 scenario cards)	• By arranging the cards, children can clearly understand the whole process of the social situation.

(continued)

Table 1. (*continued*)

Training phase	Teaching materials and content	Teaching purpose and extended meaning
Phase 2	• Use the SL-ARS system developed by this study • Judge the social reciprocity behavior according to the social story situation • Watch the situations of the characters presented through the 3D social interaction animation of the SL-ARS system	• By using systems to understand the body movements of social responses, and using observations to reinforce autistic children, the children can determine which social reciprocal behavior is the most appropriate social response in the present situation
Phase 3	• Social reciprocity behavior practice • Discussion and situational speculation	• To explore other possible social contexts and corresponding social reciprocal behaviors

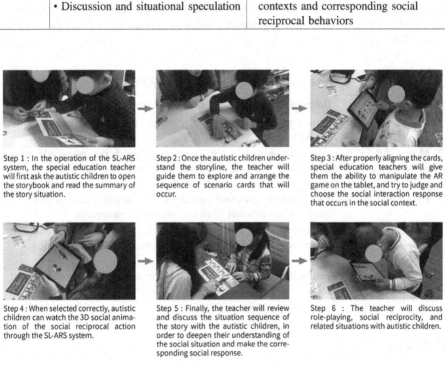

Step 1 : In the operation of the SL-ARS system, the special education teacher will first ask the autistic children to open the storybook and read the summary of the story situation.

Step 2 : Once the autistic children understand the storyline, the teacher will guide them to explore and arrange the sequence of scenario cards that will occur.

Step 3 : After properly aligning the cards, special education teachers will give them the ability to manipulate the AR game on the tablet, and try to judge and choose the social interaction response that occurs in the social context.

Step 4 : When selected correctly, autistic children can watch the 3D social animation of the social reciprocal action through the SL-ARS system.

Step 5 : Finally, the teacher will review and discuss the situation sequence of the story with the autistic children, in order to deepen their understanding of the social situation and make the corresponding social response.

Step 6 : The teacher will discuss role-playing, social reciprocity, and related situations with autistic children.

Fig. 7. SL-ARS AR System operation

3.5   Evaluation Tool Measurement

To evaluate the effect of SL-ARS on the social reciprocal behavior training of autistic children, this study refers to the observations in Micro-behaviors for video coding (MBV), as proposed by Albo-Canals et al. [19]. Five main observation aspects are selected for evaluation (Table 2), where a 7-point scale is used to indicate low participation level, while a score of 7 indicates high level of participation. Before the intervention, we observed and evaluated the behavioral responses of autistic children when operating the SL-ARS system through the traditional social storybook teaching strategy. Among the options of multiple MBV, this study redefined five micro-behavior metrics for evaluation of a specific project, including Mutual Attention, Meaningful Conversation, Response, Collaboration, and Affect Sharing. Through these five dimensions, we can observe the behavior of autistic children during play and learn the following five perspectives: (1) whether the autistic children will participate and engage in this system of learning; (2) whether the autistic children can effectively communicate with the special education teachers in the social content and context of the story during the operation, (3) whether the children can respond to the teacher's questions in terms of the social content and context of the story; (4) whether they can work with other children and think about the social context of the story as the game progresses; (5) whether they can share and explore social stories with the teacher in the context of the social content and context of the story. Regarding the scoring items, this study used the item definition in MBV to understand the behavioral responses of autistic children to SL-ARS.

Table 2. Definition and description of MBV

Micro-behavior	Behavior definition and observation focus
(1) Mutual Attention	Participants can focus on the systematic learning and operation of SL-ARS
(2) Meaningful Conversation	Participants can engage in a conversation with the special education teacher and be able to communicate the social content and context of the story
(3) Responds	Participants can respond correctly to special education teachers' questions about social situations and social reciprocity
(4) Collaboration	Participants can work with another student to complete the game task judgment of social content and situational links in the SL-ARS system
(5) Affect Sharing	Participants can share the social content and context described in the social stories with special education teachers

4   Result

4.1   Experimental Observation Orientation

This study conducted multiple game observations on 3 autistic participants to determine whether the SL-ARS intervention strategies helped children with autism to master the social situations and social reciprocal behaviors in social stories, and observe whether the SL-ARS system can effectively draw their attention to relevant social training details during the MBV game. In particular, whether the context of the social stories and social links, as shown in the social reciprocal behavior of the state, can be mastered and indirectly affect their social skills.

In the experimental arrangement, this study conducted a total of four SL-ARS teaching observations; each teaching observation is about 45–60 min, twice a week, for a total of 4 times for 2 weeks. In this study, researchers and special education experts used the five dimensions of MBV to observe the behavior of autistic children during social training with special education teachers and peers. These behaviors are related to the ability of autistic participants to effectively participate in games and to understand the social contexts and contents described in different social stories. This study used these small behavior-oriented observations to determine whether SL-ARS can help improve the abilities of autistic children to learn and understand complex social structures, which are related to the ability to focus on specific social game content, communicate with others, respond appropriately to social reciprocity, and even the ability to collaborate and share with peers.

Before the experiment, researchers observed the behavior of the three autistic participants in traditional social storybook social interaction teaching, and used MBV for seven face-to-face ratings, in order to obtain the scores for the baseline behaviors of the 3 autistic participants as a behavior baseline before the SL-ARS intervention. After the experiment, this study conducted 4 times of follow-up game teaching and intervention observations, in order to understand whether the SL-ARS system can effectively improve their social behavior and game participation learning performance, which will increase the autistic child's investment in the content and training materials, and help them to understand social situations and social interaction skills.

4.2   Overall Performances of the Micro-Behavioral Rating Scale (MBS)

After two weeks of observation, the special education teacher pointed out that the 3 autistic participants were very involved in the SL-ARS game training. These results indicate that the SL-ARS system is highly attractive to participants with autism, and has a high degree of participation in all behavioral development indicators, and such an effect would help autistic children become more involved in teaching and training, which would also be reflected in their mastery of social training.

Autistic children showed excellent scores in all aspects of the MBS system after 4 times of participation, as shown in the scoring performances focused on SL-ARS system learning, as well as its various aspects (Table 3).

(1) Mutual Attention: The three autistic participants focused on systematic learning of SL-ARS. Before the intervention, the autistic children had an average score of 2 on engagement and attention with conventional social storybook teaching strategies, the average score was 5 with systematic learning in SL-ARS (1 in SL-ARS indicates that children cannot be involved in the game, while 7 means that they can fully concentrate on the system).

(2) Meaningful conversation: Whether participants can understand the social content and context of social stories through communication. Before the intervention, the autistic children scored an average of 3.3 on social content communication and full social concept discussions in traditional social storybook teaching strategies, and the average score was 5.3 (1 in SL-ARS indicates that it is difficult to

communicate with special education teachers in terms of social content and situation, while 7 means they can communicate with teacher sufficiently).

(3) Responses: The participants were able to respond correctly to the special education teacher's questions. Before the intervention, autistic children scored an average of 3 on traditional social storytelling strategies in response to social content and contextual questions, and the average score was 5 (1 in SL-ARS indicates that it is difficult for them to respond adequately to social context problems, while 7 indicates that they can respond adequately).

(4) Collaboration: Participants completed the game content in the SL-ARS system with another peer. Before intervention, the autistic children had an average score of 1.7 on the task judgment of working with their peers to accomplish social content and situational tasks in traditional social storybook teaching strategies, and the average score was 4 (1 in SL-ARS indicates that it is difficult for them to solve social situations with peers, and 7 indicates that they can cooperate fully with peers).

(5) Affect Sharing: Participants were able to share the content of social stories with Special Education Teachers. Before the intervention, children with autism scored an average of 3 on the social content and context sharing strategies used in traditional social storytelling instruction, and the average score was 4.3 (1 in SL-ARS indicates that they find it difficult to share social stories properly, while 7 indicates that they can share social stories adequately).

Table 3. The score performance of MBV in two training strategies

Training strategy	Traditional social storybook teaching strategies	SL-ARS teaching strategy
Micro-behavior assessment orientation	Benchmark of baseline capability performance	Benchmark of intervention teaching and game performance
(1) Mutual Attention	2	5
(2) Meaningful conversation	3.3	5.3
(3) Responses	3	5
(4) Collaboration	1.7	4
(5) Affect Sharing	3	4.3
Average score	2.6	4.7

5   Discussion

Three high functioning autistic children aged 7 to 9, including two boys and one girl (Tom, John, and Alice, all named anonymously), showed curiosity and strong interest in the SL-ARS system, and enjoyed quite high investment in the SL-ARS study curriculum. We found that they were able to concentrate on reading the outline of the social story and to understand the content of the narrative under the guidance of the special education teacher. Such game content plays to the strengths of AR training over traditional storybooks, as AR can effectively increase the interest and attention of autistic children in learning, and such performance was also evident in the attention items of the MBV. Through observation, it was easy to find that the three autistic participants showed significantly higher participation in the SL-ARS game. Moreover, the Sequence Learning framework is more stable for children to master the details of each social unit and situation, which is helpful for autistic children to construct social concepts and grasp visual operations.

5.1   Feedback from the Therapist

According to the results of the interviews between the therapist and the special education teacher, Alice was able to discuss the situation and the sequence of the social story in the first phase of the training. Tom and John, with the help of the therapist, were able to consider and choose the social context following the script narration. Basically, the Sequence Learning framework can help them to clarify the sequence and development of a social situation, and to pay attention to the details and social clues of the social situation. While it is difficult to present the whole picture of the visual frame and situation of story developments in traditional social stories, the sequential teaching frame adopted in this study effectively achieved this task. Autistic children are most likely to make mistakes in the second phase. All of them had the behavior of permutation and uncertain guessing, which was due to their unfamiliarity with or difficulty in grasping the relevance of the situation, which lead to arrangement errors; however, they all got the right answer under the instruction of the special education teacher. This phase can help autistic children begin to think and organize scenario cards in a different order, which gradually builds up their understanding and learning framework for social situations.

In the final phase, the three autistic children were able to correctly sequence the situations in the story, and through the 3D animation feedback of AR, they were able to deepen their understanding of the relationship between social situations and reciprocal behaviors, and thus, strengthened their social cues for focus and interest in learning. After repeated game training, the three autistic participants were able to clearly describe the sequence of situations in the story and respond with the correct social interaction.

From the above observations, we can find that in the first and second phase, the autistic children were not sure of the correct sequence of the stories or the response action; however, in the third phase, under the guidance of the SL-ARS system and special education teacher, they had a better understanding of the development framework of social stories, as well as the corresponding social interaction behavior, by re-describing the sequence of social situations and linking them to the AR social interaction animation.

5.2 Reasons for Successful Training

After a number of training observations, this study points out that the success of SL-ARS in teaching can be attributed to the following reasons:

(1) Compared with traditional social storybooks, the SL-ARS system used in this study allows autistic children to do more than simply flip through storybooks or tell stories through teachers, but to follow and organize a clear framework of story learning and context development.
(2) Under the Sequence Learning framework, autistic children can have a clear visual framework and a comprehensive learning opportunity to deconstruct social stories through the construction of segmented storyboards.
(3) Using AR to present social reciprocal behavior can improve autistic children's attention and interactive fun in learning.
(4) The Interactive Arrangements of social story situations provide a sequence for autistic children to practice thinking, re-framing, and discussing the developments of the story.

This arrangement is followed by corresponding social responses through AR. We believe that such teaching, training, and interaction give autistic children the possibility and opportunity to master social situations and develop their social reciprocal behaviors.

6 Conclusion

This study conducted a preliminary study on autistic children's social reciprocity cognition in the context of social stories to deepen their cognition of social plots and give them correct social reciprocity behavior. We found that in the first phase of SL-ARS learning, Sequence Learning of stories can give autistic children a causal relationship to think about social situations. In the second phase, they are able to learn social interaction behavior in the AR system, and use simple and easy to carry tablet tools to achieve good interaction. In the third phase, they can quickly construct a scenario script of a social story and reach a social response that matches the situation. In the process of observation, we observed that the SL-ARS system has high teaching potential in the training of social situations and social reciprocity skills. Based on the results, we suggest that SL-ARS can be a new approach to autistic children learning social reciprocity, as it can effectively enable them to attempt to construct the con-text of social story development, and train them to judge and understand events in terms of coherent social states and more diverse social cues, and thus, make appropriate social behavioral responses through observation and reasoning. Finally, the number of autistic children who participated in the SL-ARS study was small, thus, the observational orientation has not been validated by more systematic assessments, and is not representative of a strong body of evidence; however, the results show the possibility and advantage of SL-ARS in learning and positive behavior development of autistic children, which can be used for long-term training and further experimental research in the future.

Acknowledgments. We are grateful to the Executive Yuan and Ministry of Science and Technology for funding under project No. MOST 107-2218-E-027 -013 -MY2.

References

1. American Psychiatric Association: Diagnostic and Statistical Manual of Mental Disorders, 5th edn. American Psychiatric Publishing, Arlington (2013)
2. Kanner, L.: Autistic disturbances of affective contact. Nerv. Child **2**(3), 217–250 (1943)
3. Schmidt, C., Stichter, J.P.: The use of peer-mediated interventions to promote the generalization of social competence for adolescents with high-functioning autism and Asperger's Syndrome. Exceptionality **20**(2), 94–113 (2012)
4. Bellini, S., Benner, L., Hopf, A., Peters, J.K.: A metaanalysis of school-based social skills interventions for children with autism spectrum disorders. Remedial Spec. Educ. **28**(3), 153–162 (2007)
5. Hwang, B., Hughes, C.: The effects of social interactive training on early social communicative skills of children with autism. J. Autism Dev. Disord. **30**(4), 331–343 (2000). https://doi.org/10.1023/A:1005579317085
6. Gray, C.A., Garand, J.D.: Social stories: improving responses of students with autism with accurate social information. Focus Autistic Behav. **8**(1), 1–10 (1993)
7. Sansosti, F.J., Powell-Smith, K.A., Kincaid, D.: A research synthesis of social story interventions for children with autism spectrum disorders. Focus Autism Other Dev. Disabil. **19**(4), 194–204 (2004)
8. Smith, C.: Using social stories to enhance behaviour in children with autistic spectrum difficulties. Educ. Psychol. Pract. **17**(4), 337–345 (2001)
9. Kokina, A., Kern, L.: Social Story™ interventions for students with autism spectrum disorders: A meta-analysis. J. Autism Dev. Disord. **40**(7), 812–826 (2010). https://doi.org/10.1007/s10803-009-0931-0
10. National Autism Center. https://www.nationalautismcenter.org/
11. Chen, C.H., Lee, I.J., Lin, L.Y.: Augmented reality-based video-modeling storybook of nonverbal facial cues for children with autism spectrum disorder to improve their perceptions and judgments of facial expressions and emotions. Comput. Hum. Behav. **55**, 477–485 (2016)
12. Kunda, M., Goel, A.K.: Thinking in pictures as a cognitive account of autism. J. Autism Dev. Disord. **41**(9), 1157–1177 (2011). https://doi.org/10.1007/s10803-010-1137-1
13. Lee, I.J.: Augmented reality coloring book: an interactive strategy for teaching children with autism to focus on specific nonverbal social cues to promote their social skills. Interact. Stud. **20**(2), 256–274 (2019)
14. Lee, I.J., Lin, L.Y., Chen, C.H., Chung, C.H.: How to create suitable augmented reality application to teach social skills for children with ASD. In: Mohamudally, N. (ed.) State of the Art Virtual Reality and Augmented Reality Knowhow, vol. 8, pp. 119–138. BoD – Books on Demand, Norderstedt (2018)
15. Marto, A., Almeida, H.A., Gonçalves, A.: Using augmented reality in patients with autism: a systematic review. In: Tavares, J., Natal Jorge, R. (eds.) VipIMAGE 2019. Lecture Notes in Computational Vision and Biomechanics, vol. 34, pp. 454–463. Springer, Cham (2019). https://doi.org/10.1007/978-3-030-32040-9_46

16. Chen, C.H., Lee, I.J., Lin, L.Y.: Augmented reality-based self-facial modeling to promote the emotional expression and social skills of adolescents with autism spectrum disorders. Res. Dev. Disabil. **36**, 396–403 (2015)

17. Lee, I.J., Chen, C.H., Wang, C.P., Chung, C.H.: Augmented reality plus concept map technique to teach children with ASD to use social cues when meeting and greeting. Asia-Pac. Educ. Res. **27**(3), 227–243 (2018). https://doi.org/10.1007/s40299-018-0382-5

18. Wooster, J.S., Papert, S.: Mindstorms: children, computers, and powerful ideas. Engl. J. **71**(8), 171–172 (1982)

19. Albo-Canals, J., et al.: Comparing two LEGO Robotics-based interventions for social skills training with children with ASD. In: 2013 IEEE RO-MAN, pp. 638–643 (2013)

Using Augmented Reality and Concept Mapping to Improve Ability to Master Social Relationships and Social Reciprocity for Children with Autism Spectrum Disorder

Yu-Chen Huang and I-Jui Lee[✉]

Department of Industrial Design, National Taipei University of Technology,
Taipei, Taiwan
audrey50629@gmail.com, ericlee@ntut.edu.tw

Abstract. In this study, we use augmented reality (AR) technology combined with the visual framework of the Concept Map (CM) to help children with autism spectrum disorder (ASD) apply the learned abstract social concepts and complex social relationships to the conceptual connection and establishment of social relationships in a structured and visual way. We hope to reduce the complexity and difficulty of social training for children with ASD through a teaching framework with social context and visual structure, and at the same time give children with ASD more contextual change and flexibility in teaching.

In the study, a total of four 7- to 9-year-old children with high-functioning ASD were recruited as the research subjects. They were given the AR teaching aid based on the CM design. The AR-based Concept Map (ARCM) social training system can generate corresponding 3D virtual characters and corresponding virtual social situations for different social relationships, and simultaneously give children with ASD 3D animation feedback while they watch the 3D virtual characters and social reciprocity behavior. Children with ASD can master and understand different social-relationship cognitions according to different social conditions and situations in the game. It also can be extended to the interaction state between different social objects, according to the current social context clues, through role-playing to show appropriate social reciprocity behavior. Finally, we believe that AR technology combined with the CM Framework is helpful to train autistic children's social reciprocal ability, and thus, is worth developing as a teaching strategy and training method.

Keywords: Augmented Reality (AR) · Autism Spectrum Disorder (ASD) · Concept Map (CM) · Nonverbal social cues · Social reciprocity skills · Social relationships · Tangible User Interface (TUI) · Visual framework

1 Introduction

1.1 Congenital Social Defects in Children with ASD

Children with ASD have innate social defects that make it difficult for them to maintain eye contact during social interaction with others and to make appropriate social

M. Antona and C. Stephanidis (Eds.): HCII 2020, LNCS 12189, pp. 19–37, 2020.
https://doi.org/10.1007/978-3-030-49108-6_2

reciprocal behavior judgments based on different social relationships and social situations. They also have difficulty recognizing and using other people's nonverbal social cues, such as judging others' facial expressions and body language, to understand the meaning behind these social cues. In terms of interpersonal communication, children with ASD rarely show social behaviors such as cooperation or active social relationships because they are unable to understand other people's emotions and to show appropriate social interactions. Children with ASD are typically characterized by social impairments in interacting with others, and they show social cognitive deficits and inflexible thinking. Social disorders in people with ASD include difficulties in responding to appropriate social greetings, the inability to understand other individuals' nonverbal social cues, and the inability to look into others' eyes to communicate emotionally. This makes it difficult for children with ASD to develop deep friendships, maintain social relationships, and integrate into conversations or social activities with peers.

Baron-Cohen pointed out that children with ASD have social defects in their Theory of Mind (ToM) ability [1]. That is, children with ASD cannot understand their mental state as it relates to others, so they cannot judge, identify emotions, feel emotions, understand ideas, lie, or play pretend games in social situations. ToM ability is considered to be the basis for understanding the behavior of others in social interactions. Therefore, children with ASD often have problems in understanding other people's social messages and integrating social situations, and they act inappropriately in the process of establishing, maintaining, or interacting with others [2]. These improper behaviors often cause others to be puzzled or even label them negatively (for example, giving everyone the same greeting may cause others to view them as strange). Such behaviors can also have a negative impact on the social relationships of autistic individuals with family and friends [3].

1.2   The Barriers to Social Reciprocity in Children with ASD

Children with ASD have deficiencies in understanding other people's expressions, distinguishing emotions, and ToM ability, so their social development is limited. This is one of the key issues for children with ASD because it causes them difficulty in interacting with others and prevents them from establishing further social relationships. Bellini, Peters, Benner and Hopf suggest that the main social-skill deficits of children with ASD are in the beginning stage of social communication, nonverbal communication, social reciprocity, and social cognition [2]. These abilities are important factors for deeper social interactions with other children.

Social-reciprocity ability is the most important key to these capabilities, and it is also the most important social-training project in this study. Social reciprocity refers to being able to judge a social situation, status, or other individuals' nonverbal social cues to understand others' true thoughts and intentions, and to interact with others in a socially suitable way. This ability is accompanied by comprehensive aspects such as social cognitive ability and situational-understanding ability. Because of the aforementioned defects of ASD-affected children, social skills have a great impact on the quality of life of these children, so proper-social-skills training is very important. Appropriate social training can help children with ASD to improve their social adaptation barriers, and also increase their opportunities to integrate into society and build social relationships with others.

2 Related Work

2.1 Social-Skills-Training Strategies Commonly Used in Children with ASD

Common social-skills-training strategies today include the use of role-playing or game · interaction to improve the social reciprocity of children with ASD, enhance their emotional-grasp skills, and their ability to communicate with others. Gresham, Sugai and Horner believe that the training content of social-skills training should be designed to address the social deficiencies of children with ASD, such as increasing the degree of fluency in social interaction between autistic individuals and others, or improving autistic individuals' mastery of social situations [4]. Social Stories™ is one of the most commonly used methods to help children with ASD understand and recognize social content.

Social Stories™. Social Stories™, mainly proposed by Gray and Garand, is widely used to teach children with ASD to understand social situations and social concepts to increase appropriate social reciprocity [5–7] and reduce negative behaviors in children with ASD. Social Stories™ is a special story or short scenario script written by a special education teacher from the perspective of an autistic child. Special education teachers can observe and understand the problem behaviors of children with ASD often in daily life or the types of obstacles that affect personal social development before writing social stories. Researchers use the obstacle behavior of children with ASD as the training theme.

Each social story has a clear theme and specifically describes the events, causes, time, place and participants of the story. Social stories usually use text, pictures, photos, and videos to explain how others will act, think, or feel in the same context, and point out important social cues for training [8]. The main purpose of Social Stories™ is to let children with ASD understand the skills and concepts of social reciprocity, and show appropriate social behavior in social situations. Furthermore, in addition to Social Stories™, Video Modeling (VM) has also been proven to be effective in improving strategies for children with ASD to learn social skills. The VM uses prerecording or direct shooting to target the problem behaviors or learning goals of children with ASD, and broadcasts them to children with ASD for viewing under the guidance of educators to learn social skills [9].

2.2 Applying Visual Strategies and Tangible Structured Teaching to Social Skills Training

The study found that visual strategies and tangible structured-teaching characteristics play an important key role in intervention teaching for children with ASD. Relevant past research has pointed out that social-skills-training strategies for children with ASD must be carried out through visual, tangible, and structured social-interaction scenarios.

Therefore, special educators often use Social Stories™ to conduct social training or use VMs or character play games as a strategy for social-skills training.

Traditional social-skills-training methods mostly use a single role-playing and 2D pictures and video text as scripts. Through repeated training, children with ASD can remember and recite the social meaning in the picture. Although this method of teaching can improve the social skills of children with ASD, it is often unattractive for children with ASD and easily confuses them during the learning process. It even makes it difficult to understand the complex content of training and makes them bored and impatient, which often frustrates educators.

As technology advances, interactive technologies give more choices to frontline educators. Educators can choose appropriate teaching strategies and develop assistive technology based on the uniqueness and teaching goals of children with ASD, and use games and visual media to attract the attention and improve the learning effectiveness of children with ASD. Therefore, many researchers have brought different media technologies (such as AR or VR) into social-skills courses as a medium to present their teaching strategies. In contrast, traditional 2D graphics, photos, or videos that allow children with ASD to force memory or study in a single viewing mode have become unattractive to children with ASD. Therefore, the application of interactive technology, AR, to children with ASD is an indispensable development trend for the future.

2.3 Advantages of AR in Social Training for Children with ASD

AR technology can overlay virtual materials into real environments. As a result, many studies have applied AR technology to symbolic games for children with ASD [10, 11]. For example, AR technology is used for social-reciprocity-skills training [12–15] and emotion perception [16–19]. The findings confirm the effectiveness of AR for children with ASD who have the advantage of visual learning. AR technology presents learning materials to children with ASD through visual and interactive learning methods, thereby improving the inherent motivation of children with ASD and helping them understand the learning goals and content more easily. Through AR technology, children with ASD can focus more on learning materials and make the learning process more interesting.

Related researchers have pointed out that AR technology can provide visual cues to children with ASD to maintain their focus on observing specific nonverbal social cues, such as facial emotions, body movements, and other nonverbal social cues. In addition, AR technology can provide children with ASD with abstract social-interaction situations in the form of 3D virtual interactions to reduce the predicament of children with ASD who cannot understand the social situations described by educators due to a weak imagination [20, 21]. Interacting with virtual characters through AR technology can also prevent children with ASD from facing the fear of real people in a real environment and the risk of psychological harm, and increase the likelihood that children with ASD will transfer their learned social skills to a real environment.

2.4   The Application of AR Technology in ASD Social Training Lacks a Clear Learning Framework and Organizational Structure

Although AR technology can effectively attract the attention of children with ASD in teaching and has quite a rich media effect, the 3D pictures and interaction concepts presented by AR often lack a clear learning framework and organizational structure to help ASD. Children need to sort out the teaching content behind a large amount of social concept knowledge; especially for children with ASD, it is more difficult to understand the complex social relationships and social content. Therefore, CM as a teaching tool and visualization strategy for concept presentation and contextualization is quite suitable for the understanding of social concepts in ASD-affected children; especially for children with ASD, overly complex or organizationally abstract social messages are more difficult to understand.

This study combines a CM strategy to provide a teaching framework and learning cognitive framework to help children with ASD organize complex and abstract social information for learning, as a prerequisite for the instruction of children with ASD. Knowledge is the basis for learning new ideas. Therefore, the use of AR with CM as a medium for presenting social stories to provide an environment for the contextual learning of children with ASD is a very innovative and effective teaching strategy.

2.5   CM Helps Children with ASD to Integrate and Organize Learning Content Organization

The CM method was first developed by Novak and his research team at Cornell University, USA, in 1970. CM design is based on Ausubel's cognitive learning theory [22]. In cognitive learning and constructivist epistemology, cognitive class-learning theory emphasizes that learners must first have the relevant prior knowledge framework when acquiring new knowledge. The concept is that the prior knowledge is used as the basic framework for the learner to understand the new knowledge, and the new concepts and knowledge for the learner are taught in the known-knowledge background. The learner can combine the newly learned knowledge with his original cognition, and appropriate architecture generates conceptual connections and familiarity to produce meaningful learning [23].

Ausubel believes that meaningful learning mainly occurs during the process of teaching learning materials. These processes can effectively help learners acquire a large amount of knowledge in a very short period of time [24]. The CM method is often used by educators as a teaching tool, and is widely used in teaching more complex and abstract subject areas, such as mathematics, chemistry, biology, and so on. For example, related research uses CM and AR technology as training tools to teach elementary school students' science courses to help students organize learning structures and understand ecological food chains [25]. The above related research results prove that the AR system using the CM method has a better learning effect than the AR system without CM, and CM can help students focus more on the learning goals and master the curriculum and content. The reason for this is that the CM method facilitates visualizing the patterned structure of human thinking; then, through the point-link-network, the prior knowledge and new knowledge are organized, and the visual framework is transformed into a knowledge-learning structure to help learners acquire new knowledge. At the same time, complex information and abstract concepts are presented through a visualized and structured teaching method to reduce the cognitive load on learners. In addition, the visual cognitive deficits of children with ASD make it easier to focus on specific details and ignore the interrelationships between different social contexts, content, and social objects, and children with ASD themselves have difficulty understanding abstract things. Therefore, the application of CM to decomposing complex and abstract social relationships and states is more appropriate and has research significance.

2.6   CM Helps Visual-Information Processing in Children with ASD

It is pointed out in related research that children with ASD tend to understand different abstract concepts and knowledge through vision. Cognitive load theory also shows that children with ASD who have the advantage of visual processing can use conceptual maps to reduce their cognitive load in learning tasks and help them link to learn relationships under different information concepts, thereby achieving progress in learning tasks. Related studies have also shown that the educational benefits of using visual strategies to educate children with ASD outweigh the use of written information, and that the information obtained is better retained. Roberts and Joiner also believe that children with ASD perform better in visual processing than with text [26]. Therefore, the visual-learning framework and teaching strategies of CM are very suitable for the learning needs of autistic learners. Because CM provides a link between social behavior and social-concept features, allowing children with ASD to concatenate all known details, all such teaching methods can significantly reduce the innate cognitive deficits caused by ASD symptoms.

2.7   A Case Study of the Application of CM in the Teaching of Children with ASD

In their research on CM, Roberts and Joiner teach and train autistic students with CM and require autistic students to create their own sentences according to the concept-link-concept model [26]. The results show that after CM intervention teaching, children with ASD demonstrate a positive improvement in their ability to learn and understand teaching content, which indirectly contributes to a significant improvement in learning effectiveness, and which represents four times the traditional teaching intervention [26]. This proves that CM can greatly help children with ASD in the area of organizational learning materials. In addition, some researchers have used CM and AR technology as training tools for instruction in autistic social-skills-training teaching strategies, and to teach children with ASD to focus on nonverbal social cues and recognize the social relationships of others to improve their social skills [13]. The results show that the use of CM in conjunction with AR significantly improves the cognitive ability and situational understanding of social relationships in children with ASD.

2.8   Summary

Based on the above, it can be seen that CM is of great help in teaching children with ASD to learn about abstract ideas and conceptually link abstract social information. In addition, CM can integrate learning materials into a knowledge framework. Using CM as an excellent learning and teaching framework, the educator can conduct constructive teaching of patients in a more structured manner. At the same time, learners can also use CM as a tool for meaningful learning. Therefore, this study will use the visual framework of the CM method to present different social links and social relationships in a systematic and structured way. Through the learning structure combining CM and AR, children with ASD can see the linked relationship of important concept elements in social situations and assist in the systematic presentation of social situations through the use of physical graphics cards and AR technology.

3   Method

3.1   Participants

This study mainly designed a set of ARCM social-training system based on conceptual graphics for four 7- to 9-year-old children with high-functioning ASD. Through board games, they were given structural instruction and training in social situations and relationships.

3.2   Design Purpose of the ARCM Social-Training System

The main design purpose of the ARCM social-training system is to allow children with ASD to understand social situations and relationships and show appropriate social-reciprocity behaviors. The system will simulate the full picture of real social situations and present it through 3D images to reduce the cognitive-learning load of children with ASD and attract their visual attention. The ARCM social-training system includes 3D CM, social scenes, social objects, text scripts, and dialogue voices. All content is designed based on social situations common in ASD case life to provide children with ASD with more non-spoken visual cues. These visual cues are mainly to help children with ASD to observe and understand abstract social situations and environments, and the causality of social events. The social scenes include virtual scene objects such as homes, schools, streets, and parks. The social objects include virtual characters such as family, friends, strangers, and so on. The presentation of each social-situation topic will be designed based on the social cognitive ability and level of children with ASD. The text and title content presented in the system are marked with pinyin and accompanied by a voice description, and the system will automatically determine the content selected by the autistic child and give text, voice, sound effects and visual feedback.

3.3   ARCM Social-Training-System Development

The ARCM social-training-system mainly uses the unity platform for construction and development, and combines 3Dsmax to construct the 3D space models (including homes, schools, parks, supermarkets, etc.) required for social scenes, and builds 3D character animation (including classmates, neighbors, strangers, etc.). After fine-tuning the post-production of character animation, the system uses AE to make the animation option required for the social-training response. After the system is completed, the therapists, related experts, and normal children of the same age perform operational tests and evaluations to ensure that children with ASD will not feel afraid or uncomfortable during the procedure (Fig. 1).

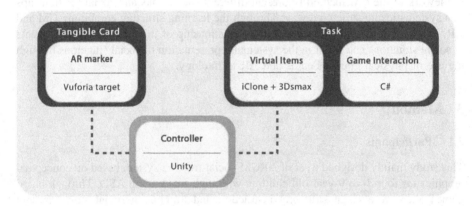

Fig. 1. ARCM social-training system-development architecture diagram

3.4 Design of ARCM Social-Training System Interface

The ARCM social-training system includes several physical cards with (1) social definitions, (2) concept boards for social situations, and (3) CM for social relationships. Those socially defined physical cards are mainly used when children with ASD operate AR systems. Children with ASD can present AR content through the ARCM social-training system developed by this institute when operating physical cards. The ARCM social-training system recognizes the physical cards with social definitions through the back-end program, and sees the 3D characters and extended social content in the game interaction from the 15-in. laptop's screen in front. Each physical card represents a specific social line of information, and a complete social situation concept board consists of several cards. The superposition of different physical cards is equivalent to the superposition of social relationships and social concepts (Fig. 2). At the same time, the cards are linked in the process, and children with ASD can clearly see the social relationships and relationship status between each social role.

3.5 Operational Design Between ARCM Social-Training System

ARCM social-training system's teaching mainly includes a series of interactions between social processes and social objects. Its design draws on the CM social-training strategies used in ASD teaching in the past, and designs social situations and content through strategies with visual structure, social relationships and specific social-training strategies.

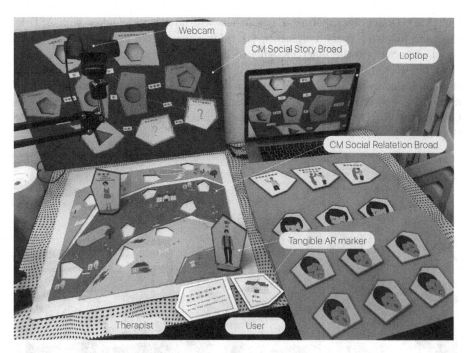

Fig. 2. The physical setup of the ARCM social-training system

The content design of ARCM social-training system teaching materials includes three sections of content and procedures: (1) the background of social events and social situations; (2) the conceptual map of the relationship between social situations and social roles; (3) a quiz to determine the individuals' emotion and social reciprocity.

The Background of Social Events and Situations. After contacting the children with ASD, the researchers understood the social-skills issues of children with ASD. Then they developed a social-story script based on the theme of social disorders that often occur in the daily lives of children with ASD, and set social-learning goals according to the abilities of children with ASD. ARCM social-training system describes and organizes social-situation problems that often occur in children with ASD through social-story strategies, and uses them as social-training tasks, and then considers the abilities of children with ASD to give them an ASD textbook. In addition, in order to ensure that the teaching content is consistent with the reading ability and social awareness of children with ASD, the teaching content was reviewed by 2 experts with experience in social-story-strategy script intervention teaching to ensure that the social-story situation script used in this research was suitable for children of that age with ASD.

Conceptual Diagram Between Social Situation and Social Relationship. The researchers deconstructed the content of the described social-story scripts into several parts, including (1) social objects, (2) situational context of social events, and (3) main social-event content. This content will be provided for the social training of children with ASD. During the experiment, researchers will further ask children with ASD to make the following social judgments: (1) judging the current emotional state of the social character; (2) the inner thoughts of the social character; (3) what the social characters should do in the context action. According to the CM strategy, the social story presented by the social process is decomposed into simple concept nodes, and the relationship between different points is communicated through link lines to establish a CM framework. The "concept-link-concept" is organized into a social situation CM (Fig. 3).

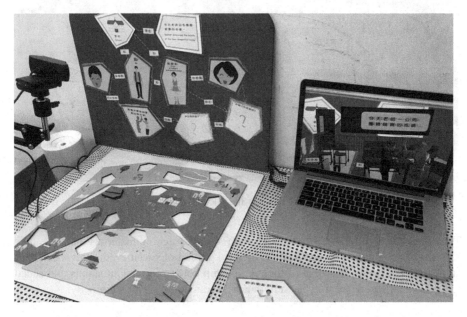

Fig. 3. Conceptual graphic design between social situations and relationships

In addition, in the CM, the social relationship between different social objects and children with ASD is constructed, and it is divided into three levels according to the degree of intimacy, including intimacy, acquaintance and strangeness. Each social object is an independent node, and the distance between the link lines between the nodes represents the relationship between the two. Through the connection between points and lines, the difference in the distance between social objects and children with ASD is also presented. The closer to the center, the closer the social relationship (Fig. 4).

In addition, this study also uses two corresponding CMs to allow children with ASD to repeatedly compare and generate conceptual relationship structures. Children with ASD can understand different social relationships and interaction structures through operations and games, and use the visual content presented in the CM to express them and make appropriate interactive content (Fig. 5).

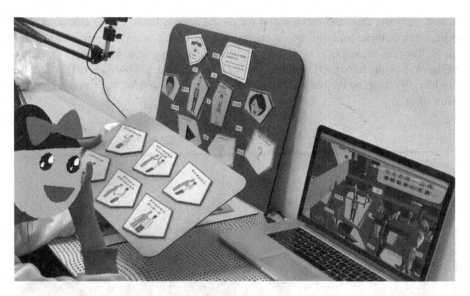

Fig. 4. Social relationship expressions and situation scenes

Fig. 5. Two corresponding CMs can allow children with ASD to repeatedly compare and generate conceptual relationship structures

Quiz to Identify Each Other's Emotions and Social Reciprocity. This research not only aims to enable children with ASD to grasp the scenes in daily life and show appropriate social-reciprocity behaviors according to different characters, but also constructs the conceptual framework emotionally. Researchers make social emotional judgments using the six major emotions defined by Ekman: happiness, anger, sadness, disgust, surprise, fear, and make social reciprocal actions based on the emotions. The formulation of these actions is based on the social greeting behaviors common in daily life in Taiwan, including: (1) waving hands, (2) nodding and smiling, (3) shaking hands, (4) holding hands, (5) hugging, (6) shaking the head, (7) bowing, (8) patting the shoulder, (9) clapping the hands, (10) placing hands on shoulders, and so on, as shown below (Fig. 6).

Fig. 6. The therapist asks the child with ASD to determine the emotional state of the subject character in the game and what social reciprocal actions should be taken

3.6   System Operation and Teaching Environment Observation

In this study, the therapists, special education teachers, and researchers observed and recorded the ASD-affected children's situation in the game and the teaching process of operating the ARCM social-training system. During the game, children with ASD must first place the social object's character graphics, field graphics, and event descriptions in the corresponding spaces according to the order arranged on the social-situation concept board. At this time, the ARCM social-training system will superimpose 3D virtual characters and virtual scenes on the physical-graphics card through the screen display, and then the social-context animation will be played when the system detects the correct graphics-card pairing. Special education teachers will require children with ASD to watch social-context animations, and put the emotion and action-graphic cards corresponding to social situations into the corresponding spaces. At the same time, the system will play subsequent social-context animation according to the physical-graphics option selected by the children with ASD. In these processes, children with ASD can see not only different social situations, but most importantly, they can see the connection between the social information represented by physical graphics. In addition, after using ARCM social-training system for children with ASD, special education teachers and researchers scored according to the learning status of children with ASD as a result of evaluating the use of the ARCM social-training system. Children with ASD must complete the following operational tasks when using ARCM social-training system for social-skills training, as shown below (Fig. 7). Those conducting this study hope that children with ASD can complete different social context tasks through the ARCM social-training system and improve their grasp of social context and reciprocity behavior during the game.

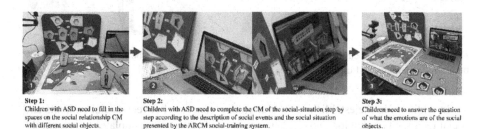

Step 1:
Children with ASD need to fill in the spaces on the social relationship CM with different social objects.

Step 2:
Children with ASD need to complete the CM of the social-situation step by step according to the description of social events and the social situation presented by the ARCM social-training system.

Step 3:
Children need to answer the question of what the emotions are of the social objects.

Step 4:
Children with ASD need to answer the question of what kind of social behavior the social objects are showing.

Step 5:
They then respond to the social actions of the social objects with appropriate social responses.

Step 6:
Finally, they perform role-playing activities with special education teachers to figure out the state of social reciprocity in this situation.

Fig. 7. ARCM social-training system social-training flowchart

Social-Training Content Covered by the ARCM Social-Training System. The social-training content covered in the ARCM social-training system mainly addresses the establishment of two main social-cognitive concepts: (1) cognitive concepts among social objects; (2) cognitive concepts between social context and social reciprocity. In the establishment of cognitive concepts among social objects, first of all, children with ASD will learn about the cards of all social objects and 4 main social environments (including their own rooms, homes, school classrooms, urban streets, etc.) in a ARCM social-training system. Then, the special education teacher will ask the children with ASD to place the social object graphic card in the corresponding social environment field space according to the problem's instructions, and then connect the links between these social objects (the line segments represent the social correspondence between themselves and others, such as close family members, friends, strangers, etc.) (Fig. 8).

Fig. 8. The ARCM social-training system line segments represent the social correspondence between themselves and others

In addition, in the establishment of cognitive concepts between social contexts and social reciprocity behaviors, researchers use social context concept plates to present the social reciprocity behaviors that should be generated in different social contexts. A total of nine spaces on the social situation CM represent different social structural units, including (1) oneself, (2) social objects, (3) the place of occurrence, (4) the event, (5) their emotions, (6) the emotions of the social object, (7) the actions of the social object, (8) the inner thoughts of the social object, and (9) the response of the social object. This series of social structural units constitutes a complete social context and corresponding social-reciprocity actions (Fig. 9).

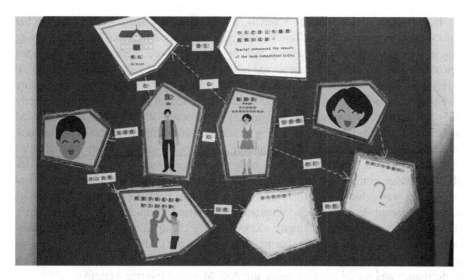

Fig. 9. The social reciprocity behavior that should be produced in different social situations

4   Results

In this study, we conducted multiple game observations with 4 children with ASD and a special education teacher and therapist to understand whether the ARCM social-training system intervention strategy would help children to grasp the social context and social reciprocity. A score of 0–7 was assigned to measure whether the child with ASD could master abstract social concepts and the structure of complex social relationships (1 means complete lack of understanding; 7 means full understanding).

Researchers also observed whether the ARCM social-training system could effectively attract their attention to the relevant social-training details during the game, especially whether they could grasp the social-context content in the social story and the state of social-reciprocity behaviors that should be displayed in social links, which indirectly would affect their social-skills improvement.

After 5 weeks of observation, this study referred to 6 aspects of Positive Technological Development (PTD) to observe the social-reciprocity behavior of children with ASD during social training with special education teachers using ARCM social-training system. (The PTD included (1) Communication; (2) Collaboration; (3) Community Building; (4) Content Creation; (5) Creativity; (6) Choice of Conduct.) Discussion and evaluation with therapists and special education teachers by recording the results of the film then followed.

After discussion and observation, the therapist pointed out that 4 children with ASD were quite invested in ARCM social-training system game training. This shows that the ARCM social-training system is quite attractive for children with ASD and performs well with respect to all six indicators. Such performance will help children with ASD be more integrated into teaching and training, and such training results are also reflected in their mastery of the social-training content.

In the observation record of 5 weeks, the therapist and special education teacher gave 4 children with ASD a different score performance on the ARCM social-training system-learning and social-training-content mastery-score performance, as listed below: (a) A score of 4.75 was achieved in the expression of social-speaking ability (0 represented lack of oral interaction and 7 represented full oral expression). (b) A score of 4 points was achieved in facial expression and emotional grasp (0 meant completely difficult to grasp, 7 meant completely grasps). (c) A score of 4.25 points was achieved in the social situation and understanding of social relationships (0 meant complete lack of understanding; 7 meant full understanding). (d) A score of 3.75 points was achieved in social behavior, understanding of body movements, social reciprocity behavior ability (0 meant completely unable to master; 7 meant fully able to master). (e) A score of 5 points was achieved for the performance of other people's social physical interaction (0 meant lack of social interaction; 7 meant frequent social interaction). (f) Sharing the relevant social situation story with the therapist earned 5 points (0 meant not happening, 7 meant actively sharing with the therapist). The above scores show that this training method is helpful and effective for ASD-affected children's learning performance and social training using the ARCM social-training system.

5   Discussion and Conclusion

Based on the above, it can be shown that the CM method is of great help in teaching children with ASD to learn about abstract social concepts and to conceptually link abstract social information. We attribute the success of the ARCM social-training system to the following:

5.1   The ARCM Social-Training System Reduces the Cognitive-Learning Load of Children with ASD and Makes Social-Skills Training More Efficient

CM provides structured teaching strategies to help children with ASD better understand and organize abstract social skills and to help educators know which areas children with ASD need to strengthen. In addition, in the past, in social-skills training, due to the imagination deficit of children with ASD, the therapist needs to spend a lot of time simulating, explaining the situation, preparing graphics or setting the environment for the unimaginative ASD child to understand social-story situations, all of which often take a lot of time or frustrate the therapist and case parents. Today, the visual process of the ARCM social-training system can quickly allow children with ASD to understand and explain social situations and relationships, so that therapists or case parents can directly teach social skills to enable children to see through the screen of the social situation.

5.2 Provide a Physical Operation Interface that Is Consistent with Past Gaming Experiences and Maintain the Attention of Children with ASD

Children with ASD are curious about technology aids. ARCM social-training system use graphics cards to display virtual social situations on the screen, so that children can keep their attention on the screen to help educators train their social skills. The operating system of the graphics card is also consistent with their previous experience in playing games, and the learning threshold is low, which can make it easier for children with ASD to understand how to use ARCM social-training system, and so no further learning is required. Compared with past images or tablet games, ARCM social-training system increases the interaction of physical board games, which enhances the fun of learning and the visual sensory stimulation.

5.3 Provide Lively Social-Teaching Situations and Protect Children with ASD from Physical and Mental Harm

Compared to the one-way VM, the ARCM social-training system can provide a variety of social situations and two-way interaction with virtual social objects, especially social situations that have not yet occurred. This is very important for children with ASD, because they often lack social situations and opportunities to learn and practice how to socialize with others in real life. In addition, the ARCM social-training system can present the role of the children with ASD in the scene when establishing the character model (the character model can be established according to the facial features of the ASD case). Children with ASD can use screens to observe their social situations with social partners. They can also zoom and rotate the lens to change the viewing angle and distance. The full picture of a social situation can be seen in the distance, along with the actions of social virtual objects and even facial expressions from a short distance. In addition, ARCM social-training system teaching has a controllable feature, which allows children with ASD to practice social skills over and over again. Even if they make mistakes, they will not be harmed, which helps to reduce the uneasiness of children with ASD.

5.4 Future Work

At present, the ARCM social-training system developed by this research institute focuses on teaching ASD-affected children's cognitive abilities in social relationships, social situations, and social reciprocity behaviors to improve their social skills. By observing the behavioral responses of children with ASD during the use of ARCM social-training system, we found that CM combined with AR-technology-aided teaching aids can better maintain the focus of children and strengthen their curiosity and interest in learning tasks by heart. Finally, our research shows that ARCM social-training system can better help children with ASD understand social situations and reduce their learning load. In addition, researchers have collected considerable first-hand information to help improve ARCM social-training system to provide more evidence-based and in-depth research in the future.

Acknowledgments. We are grateful to the Executive Yuan and Ministry of Science and Technology for funding under project No. MOST 107-2218-E-027 -013 -MY2.

References

1. Baron-Cohen, S., Leslie, A.M., Frith, U.: Does the autistic child have a "theory of mind". Cognition **21**(1), 37–46 (1985)
2. Bellini, S., Peters, J.K., Benner, L., Hopf, A.: A meta-analysis of school-based social skills interventions for children with autism spectrum disorders. Remedial Spec. Educ. **28**(3), 153–162 (2007). https://doi.org/10.1177/07419325070280030401
3. Webb, B.J., Miller, S.P., Pierce, T.B., Strawser, S., Jones, W.P.: Effects of social skill instruction for high-functioning adolescents with autism spectrum disorders. Focus Autism Other Dev. Disabil. **19**(1), 53–62 (2004)
4. Gresham, F.M., Sugai, G., Horner, R.H.: Interpreting outcomes of social skills training for students with high-incidence disabilities. Except. Child. **67**(3), 331–344 (2001)
5. Karal, M.A., Wolfe, P.S.: Social story effectiveness on social interaction for students with autism: a review of the literature. Educ. Train. Autism Dev. Disabil. **53**(1), 44–58 (2018)
6. Rao, P.A., Beidel, D.C., Murray, M.J.: Social skills interventions for children with asperger's syndrome or high-functioning autism: a review and recommendations. J. Autism Dev. Disord. **38**(2), 353–361 (2008). https://doi.org/10.1007/s10803-007-0402-4
7. Gray, C.A., Garand, J.D.: Social stories: improving responses of students with autism with accurate social information. Focus Autistic Behav. **8**(1), 1–10 (1993)
8. Coogle, C.G., Ahmed, S., Aljaffal, M.A., Alsheef, M.Y., Hamdi, H.A.: Social narrative strategies to support children with autism spectrum disorder. Early Child. Educ. J. **46**(4), 445–450 (2018). https://doi.org/10.1007/s10643-017-0873-7
9. Fitzgerald, E., et al.: Comparing the effectiveness of virtual reality and video modelling as an intervention strategy for individuals with autism spectrum disorder: brief report. Dev. Neurorehabil. **21**(3), 197–201 (2018)
10. Bai, Z., Blackwell, A.F., Coulouris, G.: Through the looking glass: pretend play for children with autism. In: 2013 IEEE International Symposium on, Mixed and Augmented Reality, ISMAR (2013)
11. Syahputra, M., et al.: Implementation of augmented reality in pretend play therapy for children with autism spectrum disorder. In: Journal of Physics: Conference Series (2019)
12. Lee, I.-J., Lin, L.-Y., Chen, C.-H., Chung, C.-H.: How to create suitable augmented reality application to teach social skills for children with ASD. In: Mohamudally, N. (ed.) State of the Art Virtual Reality and Augmented Reality Knowhow. BoD – Books on Demand, Norderstedt (2018)
13. Lee, I.-J., Chen, C.-H., Wang, C.-P., Chung, C.-H.: Augmented reality plus concept map technique to teach children with ASD to use social cues when meeting and greeting. Asia-Pac. Educ. Res. **27**(3), 227–243 (2018). https://doi.org/10.1007/s40299-018-0382-5
14. Syahputra, M., Arisandi, D., Lumbanbatu, A., Kemit, L., Nababan, E., Sheta, O.: Augmented reality social story for autism spectrum disorder. In: Journal of Physics: Conference Series (2018)
15. Lee, I.-J.: Kinect-for-windows with augmented reality in an interactive roleplay system for children with an autism spectrum disorder. Interact. Learn. Environ. 1–17 (2020)

16. Chen, C.-H., Lee, I.-J., Lin, L.-Y.: Augmented reality-based video-modeling storybook of nonverbal facial cues for children with autism spectrum disorder to improve their perceptions and judgments of facial expressions and emotions. Comput. Hum. Behav. **55**, 477–485 (2016)
17. Chen, C.-H., Lee, I.-J., Lin, L.-Y.: Augmented reality-based self-facial modeling to promote the emotional expression and social skills of adolescents with autism spectrum disorders. Res. Dev. Disabil. **36**, 396–403 (2015)
18. Ahmad, H.B.: An augmented reality system to enhance facial expressions recognision in autistic children. J. Adv. Comput. Sci. Technol. **8**(2), 46–49 (2019)
19. Lee, I.-J.: Augmented reality coloring book: an interactive strategy for teaching children with autism to focus on specific nonverbal social cues to promote their social skills. Interact. Stud. **20**(2), 256–274 (2019)
20. Lorenzo, G., Gómez-Puerta, M., Arráez-Vera, G., Lorenzo-Lledó, A.: Preliminary study of augmented reality as an instrument for improvement of social skills in children with autism spectrum disorder. Educ. Inf. Technol. **24**(1), 181–204 (2019). https://doi.org/10.1007/s10639-018-9768-5
21. Keshav, N.U., Vogt-Lowell, K., Vahabzadeh, A., Sahin, N.T.: Digital attention-related augmented-reality game: significant correlation between student game performance and validated clinical measures of attention-deficit/hyperactivity disorder (ADHD). Children **6**(6), 72 (2019)
22. Novak, J.D.: Concept mapping: a strategy for organizing knowledge. In: Glynn, S.M., Duit, R. (eds.) Learning Science in the Schools: Research Reforming Practice, 229-245. Routledge, Abingdon (1995)
23. Zheng, R.Z., Dahl, L.B.: Using concept maps to enhance students' prior knowledge in complex learning. In: Song, H., Kidd, T. (eds.) Handbook of Research on Human Performance and Instructional Technology, pp. 163–181. IGI Global, Hershey (2010)
24. Novak, J.D., Bob Gowin, D., Johansen, G.T.: The use of concept mapping and knowledge vee mapping with junior high school science students. Sci. Educ. **67**(5), 625–645 (1983)
25. Chen, C.-H., Chou, Y.-Y., Huang, C.-Y.: An augmented-reality-based concept map to support mobile learning for science. Asia-Pac. Educ. Res. **25**(4), 567–578 (2016). https://doi.org/10.1007/s40299-016-0284-3
26. Roberts, V., Joiner, R.: Investigating the efficacy of concept mapping with pupils with autistic spectrum disorder. Br. J. Spec. Educ. **34**(3), 127–135 (2007)

Applying the Game Mode and Teaching Strategies of Computational Thinking to the Improvement of Social Skills Training for Children with Autism Spectrum Disorders

I-Jui Lee[(⊠)]

Department of Industrial Design, National Taipei University of Technology,
Taipei, Taiwan
ericlee@mail.ntut.edu.tw

Abstract. The main congenital defects of children with autism spectrum disorders (ASD) are social communication barriers and behavioral defects in social reciprocity. Because it is difficult for them to distinguish the deeper social meanings or abstract situational concepts of others in the social reciprocity process, it is difficult for them to give appropriate social responses in a specific social context. Such deficiencies will make it difficult for autistic people to establish further social relationships and social interactions with others. However, with the development and maturity of media technology in recent years, the teaching strategies of interactive technology combined with games are quite common. At present, there are quite a few research applications that use computational thinking (CT) combined with games to apply interactive teaching to ordinary children and achieve good results. However, it is curious what kind of help and influence wills this teaching method have on the social skills training of autistic children. Therefore, with a goal of using CT's game intervention strategy to help children with ASD improve their skills in social reciprocity, this study will use an interactive game robot with CT concept on the market to guide children with ASD to develop different social skills and reciprocal behaviors and to construct an interactive learning framework for autistic children in social games through materialized operations and visual feedback interfaces.

Keywords: Autism spectrum disorders · Social skills · Social reciprocity · Social skills training · Computational thinking

1 Introduction

1.1 The Innate Defects in Autism

Defect in social skills are a major feature of autistic children [1], which is inherent to autistic individuals and a source of barriers to language skills and social cognition [2]. The social defects of autistic patients are variable and complex. Different individuals will face different symptoms, and the types and intensity of symptoms will be also very different, mainly reflecting in oral expression ability, speaking communication skills and interpersonal interaction. Common social deficiencies include: difficulty in

M. Antona and C. Stephanidis (Eds.): HCII 2020, LNCS 12189, pp. 38–47, 2020.
https://doi.org/10.1007/978-3-030-49108-6_3

engaging in continuous conversations with others, inability to stand in the perspective of others, difficulty in controlling the tone and the speed of speech, confusion in rising and falling inn cadence, or only enthusiasm for a particular topic, difficulty in understanding others' expressions, and difficulty in interpreting metaphors or satires in other people's conversations [3–5]. These deficiencies will directly or indirectly lead to difficulties for autistic patients to socialize and interact with others: not knowing how to start and end conversations, or difficult to understand other people's social movements and interaction with peer groups [6]. These symptoms will become more complicated as people grow older facing more complex interpersonal interactions, and the problem of social skills will become more apparent, causing helplessness and anxiety in the life of autistic patients. Therefore, social skill training is an important project involved in the training of children with ASD [7], which aims to teach specific social reciprocity skills and abilities through repeated social training. (For example, being able to judge current social situational objects and making appropriate social reciprocal behaviors, etc.) [8].

1.2   Research Objectives

In the world of autistic children, it is difficult for them to generate interest in specific social clues or interactive games of peer groups. The reason is that their innate social and attention deficits make it difficult for them to understand complex social relationships and generate appropriate social reciprocity in social relationships. Therefore, in order to improve the social problems of children with ASD, therapists often use Social Stories™ and Video Modeling (VM) with role-playing teaching strategies to enable autistic children to perform role-playing through pictures or images or try to figure out social reciprocity in different situations through imitation. However, this type of training has limited effect on children with ASD. Some researchers have put forward similar views and explanations, such as Bellini, Peters, Benner, and Hopf [9] though that the traditional Social Stories™ or VM training methods are unattractive and difficult to understand for children with ASD. The reason is that VM's continuous and complex visual structure and social content difficult to understand are often boring or lack of interest in learning for autistic children, which ultimately leads to poor training effects. The other approach, Social Stories™, is difficult to develop an extended social ability and social flexibility in different contexts because of its single material. On the contrary, it becomes another limitation of the development of social skills in children with ASD, which causes the behavior of children with ASD to be "shaped and rigid", which leads to more life problems. (For example, the child can't make a different social greeting behavior for different object situations, but only respond to all peoples with the same social greetings). Therefore, compared with VM or traditional social story method, developing a "flexible" teaching philosophy with a "clear visual framework" is a challenging and necessary attempt for social skills training for autistic children. However, the CT teaching method and game learning framework conducted in this study may enable children with ASD to develop more flexible social reciprocal behaviors and social relationships in different situations.

2   Literature Review

2.1   Structural Visual Cues and Teaching Strategies

However, children with ASD are not without academic advantages. They have special learning abilities and interests in specific learning projects. For example, the learning project having (a) structural and regular visual cues and tasks (b) programmed game strategies or (c) materialized operational tasks and (d) mathematical games with logical architecture. These learning methods and operational concepts have special appeal and learning mastery for most autistic children, and such games are easy to stimulate their motivation and interest in learning. The reason is that autistic children themselves are able to grasp the visually regular learning framework and the game themes of repeated operation tasks, and can effectively draw their attention on the learning materials. Therefore, many researchers have made good use of the specific behaviors and learning advantages of autistic people to develop different teaching strategies and achieve good teaching results. For example, TEACCH (the full name of Treatment and Education of Autistic and Communication handicapped Children) has been applied to the teaching fields and courses of many children with ASD, and has achieved good teaching results. The reason is that such a visual strategy can make autistic children more stable in learning and cognitive judgment through "structured visual cues" and "clear learning framework" and improve their concentration and mastery of task learning and operational understanding.

2.2   Teaching Method and Learning Structure of CT

Therefore, social skills training for autistic children needs to start from how to attract their limited attention and visual learning advantages. CT games, a problem-solving approach to CT and interactive game strategies, can attract learning interests and attention from children with ASD. In particular, game content combined with rich visual media and programming tasks is more attractive for children with ASD. In the game, autistic children can operate a physical robot with mathematical logic concepts [10] through a tablet computer combined with a programming game interface. Linking to different social concepts through a programming game interface gives autistic children a new attempt and teaching of social reciprocity skills [11]. In training, this approach is both flexible and ensures that they can apply the social skills of learning to real life and correctly judge the situation to make a suitable social response. Therefore, this study integrated into the "social story situation", with a view to hoping to train social skills for children with ASD through the concept of "CT game".

3   Methods

3.1   Participants

This study mainly involved 3 autistic children recruited by the Taipei Autism Society as a participant, age 7–9 (Full scale IQ (FIQ) > 80). They have three days a week in the same functional treatment clinic for after-school tutoring and social skills and language training courses, such learning conditions and teaching background facilitate researchers to conduct group game therapy and classroom observation. In addition, long-term observations and evaluation report by functional therapists in the clinic show that these three children with ASD generally lack the ability to socially reciprocate. Their performance in social behavior is often repeated and rigid, and they cannot make appropriate social reciprocal responses by judging the current social context and objects. One of their main social barriers is that they only use the same and fixed social greetings to face different social objects and situational states. For example, no matter what the occasion, they see anyone waving their hands or hugs for social greetings. However, because of their current small age, the behavioral problems at this stage are not obvious (because others will feel that children's hugs are very lovely). However, as the age increases and the frequency of contact with different social objects increases, many inappropriate social situations will occur, leading to misunderstandings and strange eyes. However, their parents and special education teachers said that there is no effective way at this stage to reverse the rigid behavior that they have established in the past, which ultimately leads to unnecessary social problems and troubles.

3.2 Training Course Content

Therefore, the social training course conducted in this study is mainly to combine the concept of "social situation" script with the game robot with programming and thinking to develop different social situation tasks, and transform the game concepts and interfaces of the programming in the existing programming game into interactive social game content. For example, adapting the program instructions to the left and right to add different social context determination options, and some key unit trigger items are transformed into social events that occur in social stories and the program unit object becomes a persona. Through the learning of different social situations, objects, and social events, and through the "programming and computing game" teaching methods and strategies, children with ASD can judge different "social situational states" through interactive teaching, problem solving and flexible teaching frameworks for programming games, and make correct "social reciprocity behaviors".

3.3 Developing Social Story Content for CT Game Systems

In the development of the content of "programming computing game", we have mastered the design conditions that should be possessed in the programming concept. For example, the programming structure of game units, bit operators, logical operators, function operators, conditional operators, and event operators. And these programming computing concepts are inherently sequential and well-defined logical rule architectures that are consistent with social contexts in everyday life. For example, different game units are like individual social situation stories, and the game task judgement performed in the content corresponding to the social content become a social content that needs to be judged in different social situations. The conditional operator echoes the choice and decision of the social reciprocal behavior, and the functional operator corresponds to what level of social performance should be done or what social performance in a particular relationship. (For example, when encountering people with different close or distant relationships in the same situation, we will have different social greeting behaviors. For example, we will hug family members who haven't seen each other for a long time, but for strangers who meet for the first time, we may just shake hands or wave). The mastery of different social links of such game logic rules became a unit component of a programming game, including the game framework between social objects, social situations, social events and social relationships. Different social story plots in the training process and the design content of the programming game will correspond to the relationship properties of CT. And these attributes are then combined with the social situational picture through the materialized programming operation card to carry out the subsequent social game interaction, and gradually integrate the social reciprocal situational story into the social skills training of the autistic children.

3.4 Measurement Materials

In this study, the Social Responsiveness Scale (SRS) was used to observe the explicit behavior performance and intrinsic social cognitive status. Of participants with autism in programming computing games, learning and the achievement of social reciprocity. During the game, SRS's assessment will be used to observe the help of "programming computing games" for children with ASD in understanding the different aspects of "social situational status" and corresponding "social reciprocity behavior" and to understand the changes for autistic children in the behavioral and social skills brought by the application of game mode and teaching strategies in computation thinking. Through long-term game intervention and observation, the performance status of children with ASD participating in social activities and operating games can be discovered.

3.5 Social Responsiveness Scale

SRS includes social speaking skills, social behavior and physical movements, facial expressions and emotional control, peer social interaction, social reciprocity, etc. It is mainly aimed at the explicit behavioral ability of children with ASD, and conducted SRS subjective assessment through the therapist's assessment observation and multiple games to understand whether autism child has achieved substantial behavioral changes during the game. In addition, the game mode and teaching strategy of computation thinking are mainly to enable the children with ASD to try to think and face the social reciprocal behaviors that should be made under different situational judgments through the process of game operation, and to develop flexible social reciprocity through the flexible teaching framework of computation thinking, thus getting rid of the institutionalized learning framework and the negative rigid behavior of traditional teaching methods.

3.6 Design

The subject of social training in this study was mainly discussed with therapists and special education teachers, and was designed in accordance with the social situations, events, objects, environmental status and life links that are common in children's daily life and use the operating framework and interface of the existing programming game, and it then link the research team's own design of the visual operation card and the discussion of the sticky notes to let autistic children quickly deconstruct different social situations and tasks through game interaction and peer discussion, and learn to express different social reciprocal behaviors and social content through problem-solving gameplay. These materials will be paired with the programmed game content to express the visual structure through the transformation of programming concepts and social concepts by means of game and interaction, which also allows children with ASD to learn more about the interrelationships between these social behaviors and the logical concepts behind.

3.7 Procedure

The experimental phase lasted for about 3 months, and there was 1.5 h of play time per week for group game therapy and social training. The experiment was divided into three phases (including three stages: baseline period, intervention period, and maintenance period) and used ABA experimental method to conduct game intervention observation. During (a) baseline period (4 weeks): allow individuals to conduct traditional social game training sessions and observe the performance of autistic children in various abilities, (b) intervention period (6 weeks): the game robot of computation thinking applied in this research was trained combined with social context scripts. (c) Maintenance period (2 weeks): return to the baseline teaching method to see if the behavior can be maintained after withdrawing training. Whether autistic children will improve their social reciprocity because of this intervention strategy can be understood through a three-stage experiment to understand. During the experiment, the researcher will work with a professional functional therapist to manipulate programming games and role-playing for social behavior evaluation observations. All three are aware of whether the social cognitive ability and behavioral performance of autistic children was improved with the intervention of this teaching strategy through the weekly group therapy treatment time at the functional treatment clinics. In the process, the researcher will discuss with the therapist and other experts in the field of special education on the content of social games and the conversion of game concepts in programming calculations in order to be closer to the individual's living conditions and behavioral needs to develop different social story script, and integrated it into the computation game.

3.8 Data Collection and Test Reliability

The data collection in the study was based on the five dimensions defined by the SRS. And the same functional therapist cooperated with the researcher to do interventional therapy for social training and make subsequent data evaluation. The researcher will also participate in the game activities and discuss with the therapist whether the learning status and performance of the case will be improved at various stages and record the data completely.

4 Results

4.1 Overall Performances of SRS

After three months of interventional observation, the therapist pointed out that the social ability of the three autistic cases in various social aspects of the SRS showed significant improvement, which was respectively shown in (a) the expression of social speaking ability between individuals with autism and others. Prior to the intervention, the baseline period score increased from 1.58 to 3.50 (1 means lack of oral interaction to 7 means adequate oral expression) and remained at 3.33 after the withdrawal of game intervention. In (b), facial expression and emotional control, before the intervention, the baseline period score increased from 1.75 to 3.28 on average (1 means completely difficult to control; 7 means complete control), and remained at 3.33 after the withdrawal of game intervention (maintenance period). In (c), the understanding of social behavior and physical movement, the average score before the intervention increased from 1.33 to 3.83 (1 means completely incomprehensible; 7 means fully understood), and remained at 3.50 after the withdrawal of game intervention (maintenance period). In (d), mastery of social reciprocity, before the intervention, the average rating increased from 1.42 to 3.56 (1 means completely impossible to master; 7 means completely master), and remained at 3.67 after the withdrawal of game intervention (maintenance period). In (e), the performance of social interaction with others, before the intervention, the score increased from 1.50 to 3.00 (1 means lack of social interaction; 7 means frequent social interaction), and remained at 3.33 after the withdrawal of game intervention (maintenance period). The above behaviors have repeatedly indicated the success of the training method and its help and effectiveness in social training for autistic children (See Table 1).

Table 1. The SRS scores of participants.

Social Responsiveness Scale Orientation		Performance of SRS (Score from 1 to 7)		
		Baseline	Intervention	Maintenance
(a)	The expression of social speaking ability	1.58	3.50	3.33
(b)	Facial expression and emotional control	1.75	3.28	3.33
(c)	The understanding of social behavior and physical movement	1.33	3.83	3.50
(d)	Mastery of social reciprocity	1.42	3.56	3.67
(e)	The performance of social interaction with others	1.50	3.00	3.33
Mean Score		1.52	3.43	3.43

5 Discussion

In this study, we observed 3 children with ASD aged 7–9 with high-functioning autism who use interactive game products with CT concept, and applied Gigo intelligent robots as a game project for children with ASD to learn social situations and story scripts. The researcher adapted and redefined the program content of the programming game, and integrated the story of "social situation" as the training background of social skills and let autistic children master the "social status" in different situations and develop appropriate social reciprocal behaviors and abilities through the "teaching characteristics" of CT and the "operational features and learning framework" in the game. In terms of assessment methods, this study used a subjective SRS, and observed the different explicit behaviors of each autism case in the game interaction, learning and the achievement of social tasks with the help of therapists. Under the evaluation of the therapist, the results of the study show that interactive game strategies with CT concepts can effectively generate learning interest in autism cases and that the teaching strategy of "programming computing game" combined with the "social story situation" helps autistic children to understand "social tasks" and "situational stories". What is more, these intervention strategies also indirectly affected the improvement of behavioral ability and social reciprocity skills in individual cases.

5.1 Feedback from the Children, Therapist, and Parents

In terms of intervention effectiveness, the therapist received a lot of help in operation training collaboratively conducted by "programming and computing game" with physical robot in autistic children. In particular, the learning interest and social skills of children with ASD have been significantly improved. Because in the teaching strategies of social stories or VM used in the past, single teaching materials lacking of interaction are often unattractive for children with ASD, which ultimately leads to poor training. Today, this type of programming robot operation, because of the interesting and structured content, invisibly enhances the learning process of their hands-on operation and computation thinking, and also stimulates their participation in the game learning and peer interaction discussion. The therapist said that this teaching method has invisibly increased autistic children's familiarity and mastery of operational tasks, and the social stories that accompany the game also help them to build and connect the relevance between different social situations, objects and events. Just as in the past research, Scratch's programming game has been used to guide children with ASD to understand the procedural concepts behind it, which has achieved good learning results. This research is to incorporate such programming concepts into the concept of social stories. The logical thinking framework of programming corresponds to the framework of social situations and becomes another learning strategy. In addition, the materialized visual structure allowed autistic children to interact with physical programming robots through a tangible visual interface with a view to driving the robot to complete different social tasks (the task content is defined by the researcher). Such thinking and feedback mechanisms invisibly transformed the concept of programming thinking into a teaching strategy that can master social skills skillfully. Because they could master the logical thinking through repeated interactions of programming games, and they were also willing to solve different social problems by discussing with their peers. Such process also helped them to master and develop more flexible social capabilities and situational concepts at the same time.

5.2   Benefits of Using the Teaching Strategies of CT

In addition, in the classroom, therapists and parents also reflect that such learning styles also reduce the frequency of past rigid behaviors of autism, and gradually develop new social resilience. Because they could master the logical thinking through repeated interactions of programming games, and they were also willing to solve different social problems by discussing with their peers. This process also helped them to master and develop more flexible social capabilities and situational concepts. Repeated and institutional greetings past are gradually decreasing, and they also classify and evolve some more appropriate social reciprocity through the programming concepts in the game to face changes in different social situations. In addition, during the interview, the therapist also indicated that the autism case will explained to the parents or teachers in different real situations what does the game character do when he is in the game (For example, how a girl in a programming game will handle such a situation) and parents also have more contexts to describe, and can use situations that have emerged in the game to guide children with ASD to make appropriate social reciprocity.

6   Conclusion

In this study, we conducted an innovative teaching strategy and experiment through the game concept of programming calculation, by linking the social reciprocity concept with the operational interface of the physical robot. After three months of game training and observation, we have confirmed that this approach is helpful for the social and contextual control of the subjects of the research, that is, three children with ASD aged 7–9 with high-functioning autism. We attributed this effectiveness to the "teaching characteristics" of programming computing and the "operational characteristics and learning framework" in social games for the learning outcomes and behavioral effects of these three autistic children. However, such concepts could be applied to many teaching subjects, and we have successfully applied this concept to the social training of children with ASD. We firmly believe that this approach contributes to the development of a more flexible learning channel for autistic children and the avoidance of rigid behaviors. In the future, we will also extend this concept to more autism-related social training and we will focus more on the special needs of children with ASD and find more innovative teaching strategies to design and develop more interesting game content and teaching applications.

Acknowledgments. We are grateful to the participants, therapists, and family members who participated in our study as well as the participants who assisted in the various phases of the study. We would also like to thank the individuals who participated in this research and the Autism & Developmental Research Center in Taiwan.

Funding. We are grateful to the Executive Yuan and Ministry of Science and Technology for funding under project No. MOST 107-2218-E-027-013-MY2.

References

1. American Psychiatric Association: Diagnostic and statistical manual of mental disorders (DSM-5®). American Psychiatric Pub., Washington, DC (2013)
2. Carter, A.S., Davis, N.O., Klin, A., Volkmar, F.R.: Social development in autism. In: Cohen, D.J., Volkmar, F.R. (eds.) Handbook of Autism and Pervasive Developmental Disorders, vol. 1, 3rd edn., pp. 312–334. Wiley, Boston (2005)
3. Kerbel, D., Grunwell, P.A.: Study of idiom comprehension in children with semantic-pragmatic difficulties Part II: between-groups results and discussion. Int. J. Lang. Commun. Disord. **33**(1), 23–44 (1998)
4. Shaked, M., Yirmiya, N.: Understanding social difficulties. In: Prior, M.R. (ed.) Learning and behavior problems in Asperger syndrome, pp. 104–125. Guilford Press, New York (2003)
5. Tager-Flusberg, H.: Effects of language and communicative deficits on learning and behavior. In: Prior, M.R. (ed.) Learning and behavior problems in Asperger syndrome, pp. 85–103. Guilford Press, New York (2003)
6. Fodstad, J.C., Matson, J.L., Hess, J., Neal, D.: Social and communication behaviours in infants and toddlers with autism and pervasive developmental disorder-not otherwise specified. Dev. Neurorehabil. **12**(3), 152–157 (2009)
7. McConnell, S.R.: Interventions to facilitate social interaction for young children with autism: Review of available research and recommendations for educational intervention and future research. J. Autism Dev. Disord. **32**(5), 351–372 (2002)
8. Elsabbagh, M., et al.: Visual orienting in the early broader autism phenotype: disengagement and facilitation. J. Child Psychol. Psychiatry **50**(5), 637–642 (2009)
9. Bellini, S., Peters, J.K., Benner, L., Hopf, A.: A meta-analysis of school-based social skills interventions for children with autism spectrum disorders. Remedial Spec. Educ. **28**(3), 153–162 (2007)
10. Pila, S., Aladé, F., Sheehan, K.J., Lauricella, A.R., Wartella, E.A.: Learning to code via tablet applications: an evaluation of daisy the dinosaur and kodable as learning tools for young children. Comput. Educ. **128**, 52–62 (2019)
11. Almeida, L.M., et al.: ALTRIRAS: a computer game for training children with autism spectrum disorder in the recognition of basic emotions. Int. J. Comput. Games Technol. **2019**, 16 (2019)

Creation Process for a Technology Design Model Promoting Active Participation of End Users with Neurodevelopmental Disorders: Achievements and Pitfalls

Dany Lussier-Desrochers[1(✉)], Marie-Ève Dupont[2(✉)],
Yves Lachapelle[1], Line Massé[1], Annie Martineau[3(✉)],
and Laurence Pépin-Beauchesne[1]

[1] Département de psychoéducation, Université du Québec à Trois-Rivières,
Trois-Rivières, QC, Canada
Dany.Lussier-Desrochers@uqtr.ca
[2] Institut de recherche d'Hydro-Québec, Shawinigan, Canada
Dupont.Marie-Eve2@ireq.ca
[3] Neuro Solutions Group©, Québec City, QC, Canada
contact@neurosolutionsgroup.com

Abstract. The promotion of social inclusion of people with neurodevelopmental disorders (e.g., intellectual disability [ID] and autism spectrum disorder [ASD]) is currently a social concern. Recent studies suggest that technologies may be beneficial when they are used by people with ID or ASD. However, for these users, digital tools often require the development of new knowledge and competencies. In addition, technologies are most of the time created and designed for mainstream users and hardly ever encompass the specific needs of people with neurodevelopmental disorders. According to some authors, participation to the designing process may promote digital inclusion. While this proposal seems common sense, no models or recommendations are currently available to guide the conduct of such collaborative work. The purpose of this research is to create a participatory conception model guiding the development of technologies intended for people with ID or ASD. This conception model involves users with ID or ASD in all the phases of technology development. To date, no such model has been proposed. This study uses a developmental research design. This method seemed the most appropriate to meet the research's goal. The Bergeron's 4-steps developmental research model (precision phase, model conceptualization, improvement of the prototype and dissemination) serves as a framework for the entire development process and highlight a series of issues (e.g., communication, work coordination, ethical issues). It is hoped that the model will support other teams in the development of future technologies.

Keywords: Participatory design · Intellectual disability · Autism

© Springer Nature Switzerland AG 2020
M. Antona and C. Stephanidis (Eds.): HCII 2020, LNCS 12189, pp. 48–57, 2020.
https://doi.org/10.1007/978-3-030-49108-6_4

1 Background

In recent years, social actors (practitioners, relatives, researchers) have been wondering about the means to promote social participation and inclusion of all individuals in society [1–3]. Despite the many actions taken, no community has yet been able to create social contexts conducive to the full and effective participation of all its citizens. Among the populations presenting the highest rates of exclusion are people with neurodevelopmental disorders (PWND) [4, 5].

2 Population with Neurodevelopmental Disorders

According to the fifth version of the Diagnostic and Statistical Manual of Mental Disorders (DSM-V), neurodevelopmental disorders are characterized by developmental delays and translate, in concrete terms, to cognitive, behavioral, and sensorimotor damage [6]. Appearing generally in early childhood before the child enters school, they comprise, notably: attention-deficit/hyperactivity disorder (ADHD), autism spectrum disorder (ASD), and intellectual disabilities (ID). People with ADHD, ASD, or ID frequently present cognitive functioning deficits (attention, executive functioning, memory, and information processing) [7–10]. Depending on the type of disorder, the damage to the executive functions will vary and will have different manifestations in the individual's life. However, because of these difficulties, the person is generally unable to respond optimally to the demands and requirements of various life settings (academic, professional, family, community, etc.) [2]. Consequently, PWND face psychosocial adjustment difficulties whose severity is proportional to the level of damage to the cognitive functions [11, 12].

2.1 Social Participation in the Digital Era

For the past 40 years, numerous initiatives have been implemented to promote social inclusion and participation of PWND [13–15]. In addition to the actions taken by associative movements, theoretical models have been developed. Scientific studies have also helped provide a better understanding of the conditions in which social inclusion and participation are optimized. However, over the last twenty-odd years, a new element has radically transformed the issues related to social participation: rapid development of the digital and artificial intelligence sector [16–18]. In just a few years, technology has changed the modes of communication and access to information. It has influenced consumption and entertainment modalities as well. Digitization has also complicated the everyday lives of several PWND, some of whom have even lost ground in terms of social participation [19, 20]. To guide the actions in the process of inclusion in the digital era, Lussier-Desrochers et al. [20] created a model presenting the factors to take into account (access to technologies, sensorimotor skills, cognitive skills, technical skills, understanding rules and conventions). This work shows notably the importance of having a holistic vision.

2.2 A Holistic Vision of Social Participation

FQCRDITED (2013) have advanced that one of the current social challenges is ensuring active participation by PWND in the development and implementation of support modalities intended for them, including technological support [21]. This vision requires a radical change in paradigm. Lachapelle and Lussier-Desrochers (2018) thus believe that the digital inclusion process should begin as soon as the first steps are taken in the design of new technological solutions [22]. Furthermore, this element is consistent with the third recommendation of the Quebec Charter and the action plan for inclusive technologies [23]. Founded on collaborative and participative development models, this vision recognizes the need to implement contexts that promote close collaboration between technology designers and PWND [24]. In addition to generating higher levels of satisfaction with the technological products that are developed, this collaboration reduces resistance to change and promotes faster and beneficial integration of technological solutions into the users' lives [25]. It also enables action on two components that influence the intention to use a new technological solution, that is, usability and perceived usefulness [26–30].

Although this proposal is relevant, no models or recommendations give concrete expression to such contexts of technological development involving the designers and the end users with neurodevelopmental disorders. Participatory design models exist [23] but are not designed to specifically involve users with this type of profile. In fact, they are designed primarily for end users with no special needs.

In this context, it is essential to first implement concrete measures promoting active involvement of PWND in the development process for new technologies. As part of the full citizenship movement, the selected approach should be based on a decompartmentalization of the disciplinary fields as well as mutual and egalitarian exchanges where the expertise of all the actors is recognized and called upon. According to the Social Sciences and Humanities Research Council (SSHRC), this "hybridization of knowledge from different actors, including end users, across various disciplines is becoming increasingly important for the optimal use of new technologies" [31]. In our opinion, it is only in this context that technology will foster true inclusion of these people in the digital society.

3   Objectives

The objective of this study is to develop a participative model for designing new technological solutions that (1) actively involves people with ID or ASD in all the steps of the design, (2) includes acceptability, acceptance, and appropriateness conditions [28–30], and (3) aims to optimize end users' satisfaction with the technology. The purpose of the study was also to validate the components of the model with designers, developers, and end users as part of the development of two applications that can be used on electronic tablets.

4   Method

In this study, a research and development process was used because it was the most appropriate method for achieving the previously stated objectives. According to Bergeron et al. [32], this process makes it possible notably to involve actors in the development of an innovation while developing scientific knowledge on the problem to solve. These authors propose a five-step research and development process. Given that the research methods and the results are closely linked and that several methods can be used successively, it was agreed that it would be simpler to present the process and the results more specifically in the same section. This will help readers better understand the process leading to the development of the design model.

5   Results - Steps in the Development of the Model

This section presents the steps followed to develop the model in accordance with the steps in Bergeron et al. [32] research and development process.

5.1   Phase 1: Specification of the Development Idea

According to Bergeron et al. [32], this first phase consists in examining the available knowledge and linking it to the target users' needs and experiences. For this step, two elements were explored (1) currently used design models that promote the end users' active involvement and (2) factors that would make a person want to use the technologies resulting from this design process.

For this step, scientific literature reviews were carried out and several models were explored. The analysis showed that although designers may rely on such an approach when developing a technological solution, they remain ill-equipped to apply it with end users who have neurodevelopmental disorders. Indeed, these people's profiles are heterogenous and require specific actions that take into account their sensorial and cognitive characteristics. For instance, for people with ID, the objective of the task must be simple and concrete. For people with ADHD, brief work sessions should be favored and consulting techniques should lead to the user's active involvement. For people with ASD, user-designer interactions could be difficult and means should be taken to promote the participants' involvement in the task to accomplish (use prototypes and icons to express satisfaction).

Furthermore, the consultation modalities and activities proposed should also take into account the PWND's profiles with respect to the executive functions (memory, cognitive flexibility, attention, time management, etc.). Our literature review also led us to the work conducted by Druin [33] defining the four main roles that end users can play in the development of technological solutions. Two of these roles give the user a passive position (user and tester) in the design process whereas the two others involve the person more actively (key informer or design partner). Also, the design phases will influence which role is given to the users. For example, for a product whose development is very advanced, the role of a tester or a user will be favored, whereas products in the prototype phase will provide the opportunity for more intense involvement of the users as key informers or even design partners. The choice of role given to the users must be thought out and be accompanied by a specific plan on how to carry out the necessary actions. In sum, the analysis of these models sensitized the research team to the importance of informing designers of the cognitive particularities and profiles of PWND as well as of the roles they can play in the design process.

In parallel, the team attempted to understand the dimensions of acceptability of the technologies for PWND from a psychosocial perspective. This step was necessary because technological solutions must be developed with a deep understanding of the individual and environmental factors that will make end users accept or refuse to use the technology designed for them. This reflection was based on the work by Dupont [27], who, through an electronic consultation conducted with 211 stakeholders in ID and ASD, identified and modeled the dimensions related to the acceptability of a new technological solution. The study results show that the intention to use a new technology is influenced by personal and environmental factors [28–30]. At the personal level, the intention to use is influenced by perceived usefulness, usability, and the end user's attitude. Additionally, the strength of the relationship between personal variables and intention are also modulated by moderating variables, such as age, gender, previous experience with technology, ethical concerns, characteristics of the technological solution, and knowledge. Environmentally, the factors associated with the intention to use a technological solution are social influences, availability, support, and time available to incorporate the technological solution into the person's everyday life.

5.2   Phase 2: Structuring Novel Solutions

This phase consists in formalizing and conceptualizing the model based on the reflections made in the first phase. A first draft of the design model was thus developed. Interviews were also conducted with designers ($n = 3$) from a company specializing in the development of technological solutions intended for people with special needs. These interviews made it possible to validate certain ideas found in the scientific literature concerning participative design models and to determine the issues that could arise. The analyses helped identify the five following issues: (1) establishment of modalities for quick and efficient communication between the collaborators; (2) the importance of informing and training designers regarding the profiles of users with neurodevelopmental disorders; (3) the need to reflect on the issues related to intellectual property and ethics; (4) identification of modalities for acknowledging the collaborators' contribution; and (5) having a precise idea of the end users' needs before developing the prototypes. The information collected served as a foundation for the development of a second version of the model, which could be used in a design experiment.

5.3   Phase 3: Development and Improvement of the Prototype

In this step, the team formalized the model and tested some components. Figure 1 presents the participative design model.

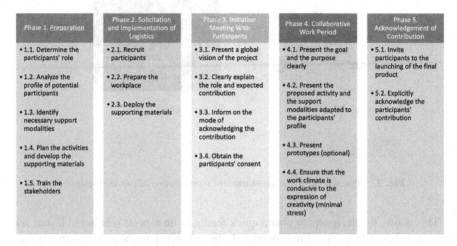

Phase 1. Preparation	Phase 2. Solicitation and Implementation of Logistics	Phase 3. Initiation Meeting With Participants	Phase 4. Collaborative Work Period	Phase 5. Acknowledgement of Contribution
• 1.1. Determine the participants' role	• 2.1. Recruit participants	• 3.1. Present a global vision of the project	• 4.1. Present the goal and the purpose clearly	• 5.1. Invite participants to the launching of the final product
• 1.2. Analyze the profile of potential participants	• 2.2. Prepare the workplace	• 3.2. Clearly explain the role and expected contribution	• 4.2. Present the proposed activity and the support modalities adapted to the participants' profile	• 5.2. Explicitly acknowledge the participants' contribution
• 1.3. Identify necessary support modalities	• 2.3. Deploy supporting materials	• 3.3. Inform on the mode of acknowledging the contribution	• 4.3. Present prototypes (optional)	
• 1.4. Plan the activities and develop the supporting materials		• 3.4. Obtain the participants' consent	• 4.4. Ensure that the work climate is conducive to the expression of creativity (minimal stress)	
• 1.5. Train the stakeholders				

Fig. 1.   Participative design model

In parallel, accompanying files were also developed so that useful information could be presented, for each of the sub-steps of each of the phases, to ensure a successful deployment of the participative design model. For instance, for Step 1.1, a two-page file in non-scientific language, intended for the designers, describes the roles that end users can play in the design process. For Step 1.2, a series of files present the various profiles of users with neurodevelopmental disorders as well as recommendations for optimizing the benefits of their involvement. An additional file presents the ethical issues associated with these people's involvement. Other files present non-scientific content on the executive functions. These files were given to the designers who then made their comments. It seems that this participative design model was appreciated and supplementary files will be developed for all the steps and phases.

Phases of the participative design models were also implemented as part of the development of the two applications notably intended for PWND. The first one was the Sequence application designed for people with ID. In concrete terms, this application presents like an assistant for performing tasks in the workplace. When the participative design model was being developed, this application was in the ideation phase. It was thus possible to test the modalities for consulting on the requirements analysis and to collect comments on prototypes. For example, the design team developed an electronic questionnaire for conducting a series of consultations for the development of prototypes (Fig. 2).

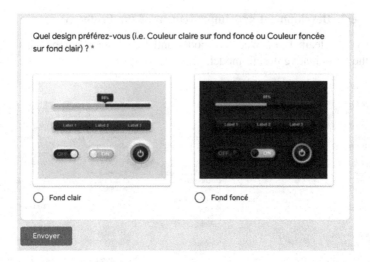

Fig. 2. Screen shot of the questionnaire (consultation about the design)

This allows the designers to obtain quick feedback on aspects relating to layout and functions of the application. For this project, the role given to the participants was key informer. Second, some components of the models were applied for the development of a video game to help children with ASD or ADHD perform their routines. Given that this project was more advanced and that the beta versions were available before the model was developed, the participants were asked to play the role of testers.

In sum, for this phase, the model was progressively applied. Other consultation modalities are also planned. They include test groups with users to obtain their opinions on certain functionalities that could be incorporated into the technological solutions developed. The process will be documented through qualitative and quantitative studies to create the final version of the collaborative design model.

5.4 Phase 4: Dissemination of the Products and of the Research Results

This last phase will be completed in the next year. The model and files will be finalized and the validation process will continue as part of the development of the two technological solutions. The deliverable is expected to be in the form of a tool box (process illustrated with supporting material) intended for designers who want to use a participative development approach involving PWND. This final version of the participative design model will be made available in 2021.

6 Discussion

The article presents the steps in the development of a participative design model for involving PWND in the creation of technological products intended for them. This study shows that the research and development process proposed by Bergeron et al. [29] applies to the development of such modeling. Phase 3, improvement of the prototype, proved very important in our process. Indeed, this phase enabled consultations with the actors concerned and active involvement of end users in the development of two technological solutions.

It is also important to mention that the partners who were designing and developing technological solutions already believed in the value of involving PWND in the development process. In fact, this element is at the core of their company's mission. Nonetheless, the model development process was marked by issues related notably to communications and to the coordination of the work processes (research team and design group). One central element is linked to the company's situation. Being in the startup stage, it must generate financing modalities to support its growth and its position on the market. In this regard, the company believes that the use of a participative design process constitutes an added value. Moreover, the research process also enables the company to give concrete expression to its mission.

It should also be noted that this study, as well as the creation process for the two technological products, received funding from several government agencies. This slightly reduced the company's financial risk but also greatly facilitated the model development process. However, in a subsequent phase, it would be important to test the model in companies that know nothing about the target audience or that have not yet incorporated participative methods into the development of their product.

7 Conclusion

In conclusion, this study allowed the implementation of concrete measures valuing the end user's role in a design process. Hopefully, the model will support other teams in the development of applications but also of other types of technological solutions, such as ergonomic peripherals or connected objects.

References

1. Boulet, M., Vincent, M.-J.: Leur histoire... notre histoire. De 1960 à nos jours. Centre de réadaptation en déficience intellectuelle et en troubles envahissants du développement de la Mauricie et du Centre-du-Québec – Institut universitaire, Trois-Rivières (2015)
2. Office des personnes handicapées du Québec: À part entière: pour un véritable exercice du droit à l'égalité. Gouvernement du Québec, Drummondville (2009)
3. Tremblay, M.: De l'exclusion à la participation démocratique des «personnes présentant une déficience intellectuelle». In: Gagnier, J.-P., Lachapelle, R. (eds.) Pratiques émergentes en déficience intellectuelle: participation plurielle et nouveaux rapports, pp. 17–38. Presses de l'Université du Québec, Sainte-Foy (2002)
4. École d'études sociales et pédagogiques: Participation sociale des personnes avec troubles neurodéveloppementaux (Neurodev) (2019). https://www.eesp.ch/organisation/reseaux-de-competences/neurodev/. Accessed 18 Feb 2020
5. Ministère de la Santé et des Services sociaux: Bilan des orientations ministérielles en déficience intellectuelle et actions structurantes pour le programme-services en déficience intellectuelle et en trouble du spectre de l'autisme. Gouvernement du Québec, Québec (2016)

6. American Psychiatric Association: Diagnostic and Statistical Manual of Mental Disorders. American Psychiatric Pub, Arlington (2013)
7. Association québécoise des neurospychologues: Les fonctions cognitives (2019). https://aqnp.ca/la-neuropsychologie/les-fonctions-cognitives/. Accessed 18 Feb 2020
8. Balle, M.: Autodétermination et autorégulation chez des adolescents présentant une déficience intellectuelle: entre caractéristiques environnementales et individuelles. L'apport des fonctions exécutives. Dissertation, Université de Charles de Gaulle (2017)
9. Nader, A.-M., Soulières, I.: Une revue systématique et méta-analyse des fonctions exécutives dans le Trouble du spectre de l'autisme (2016). http://content.pqm.net/rnted/pdf/rnetsa_2282.pdf. Accessed 18 Feb 2020
10. Simard, M.-H.: Le TDAH: définition, traitements et ressources universitaires (2019). https://www.aide.ulaval.ca/apprentissage-et-reussite/textes-et-outils/difficultes-frequentes-en-cours-d-apprentissage/le-tdah-definition-traitements-et-ressources-universitaires/. Accessed 18 Feb 2020
11. Gagné, P.-P., Leblanc, N., Rousseau, A.: Apprendre… une question de stratégies. Chenelière Éducation, Montréal (2009)
12. Portail enfance et familles: Troubles du spectre de l'autisme (TSA) (2019). http://www.portailenfance.ca/wp/modules/troubles-du-developpement/volet-2/troubles-du-spectre-de-lautisme/. Accessed 18 Feb 2020
13. Bélanger, M.: Les approches adaptatives et inclusives visant l'intégration scolaire, professionnelle et sociale des personnes handicapées. Office des personnes handicapées du Québec, Drummondville (2006)
14. Gouvernement du Québec: Plan 2015–2019 des engagements gouvernementaux (2015). https://www.ophq.gouv.qc.ca/fileadmin/centre_documentaire/Documents_administratifs/Politique_a_part_entiere_Acc.pdf. Accessed 18 Feb 2020
15. Bellefeuille, É., Labbé, L.: Inclusion sociale et déficience intellectuelle: où en est le Québec? Empan. Prendre la mesure de l'humain. **104**, 97–105 (2016)
16. Lussier-Desrochers, D., Godin-Tremblay, V., Simonato, I., Lachapelle, Y., Normand, C.L., Romero-Torres, A.: Développement et évaluation des effets d'un programme d'intervention favorisant la participation sociale des personnes présentant une déficience intellectuelle (DI) dans la société du numérique. Centre de partage d'expertise en intervention technoclinique, Trois-Rivières (2019)
17. Lussier-Desrochers, D., et al.: L'accès au milieu résidentiel par les personnes présentant une déficience intellectuelle: des solutions numériques à portée de main!. Centre de partage d'expertise en intervention technoclinique, Trois-Rivières (2020)
18. Lachapelle, Y., Dupont, M.-È., Lussier-Desrochers, D., Therrien-Bélec, M., Pépin-Beauchesne, L., Bilodeau, P.: L'intervention technoclinique dans le secteur des services sociaux: considérations théoriques et applications cliniques. In: Lussier-Desrochers, D. (ed.) Intervention technoclinique dans le secteur des services sociaux : enjeux cliniques et organisationnels, pp. 5–19. Presse de l'université du Québec, Trois-Rivières (2017)
19. Lussier-Desrochers, D., et al.: Bridging the digital divide for people with ID. Cyberpsychology J. Psychosoc. Res. Cyberspace **11**(1) (2017). Article 1
20. Lussier-Desrochers, D., et al.: Modélisation soutenant l'inclusion numérique des personnes présentant une DI ou un TSA. Revue francophone de la déficience intellectuelle **27**, 5–24 (2016)
21. Fédération québécoise des Centres de réadaptation en déficience intellectuelle et troubles envahissants du développement (FQCRDITED): La participation sociale des personnes présentant une déficience intellectuelle ou un trouble envahissant du développement : du discours à une action concertée (2013). http://laressource.ca/images/ressources/Participation-sociale.pdf. Accessed 18 Feb 2020

22. Lachapelle, Y., Lussier-Desrochers, D.: Supporting digital inclusion of people with intellectual disability or autism spectrum disorder: the inclusive technologies action plan. In: #PTI2022! Paper presented at the 23 Annual CyberPsychology, CyberTherapy & Social Networking Conference, Gatineau, June 2018

23. #CTI: Charte pour des technologies inclusives (2016). https://cestsaprod.blob.core.windows.net/media/1284/charte_techo_inclusives.pdf. Accessed 18 Feb 2020

24. #PTI: Plan d'action quinquennal pour des technologies inclusives 2017-20122 – Synthèse PTI2022. Collections de l'Institut universitaire en DI et en TSA, Trois-Rivières (2017)

25. ISO: Ergonomics of human-system interaction–Part 210: Human-centred design for interactive systems, Swiss (2010)

26. Romero, A., Bendavid-Castro, L., de Marcellis-Warin, N.: Mettre l'utilisateur au centre du cycle de développement des innovations technologiques pour assurer la sensibilité des projets technologiques. In: Aubry, M., Vidot-Delerue, H., Rahali, H. (eds.) Cahier de recherche Les enjeux actuels de la gestion de projet, pp. 8–14. Chaire de de gestion de projet, Montréal (2016)

27. Dupont, M.-È.: Évaluation des déterminants individuels et organisationnels liés à l'acceptabilité du robot social pour soutenir l'intervention technoclinique dans les programmes spécialisés en déficience intellectuelle et trouble du spectre de l'autisme des centres intégrés en santé et services sociaux du Québec. Dissertation, Université du Québec à Trois-Rivières (2020, in process)

28. Davis, F.D., Bagozzi, R.P., Warshaw, P.R.: User acceptance of computer technology: a comparison of two theoretical models. Manage. Sci. 35(8), 982–1003 (1989)

29. Venkatesh, V., Morris, M.G., Davis, G.B., Davis, F.D.: User acceptance of information technology: toward a unified view. MIS Quarterly 27(3), 425–478 (2003)

30. BenVenkatesh, V., Bala, H.: Technology acceptance model 3 and a research agenda on interventions. Decis. Sci. 39(2), 273–315 (2008)

31. Social Sciences and Humanities Research Council's: Advancing knowledge on how emerging technologies can be leveraged to benefit Canadians. https://www.sshrc-crsh.gc.ca/society-societe/community-communite/ifca-iac/05-emerging_technologies_report-technologies_emergente_rapport-eng.pdf. Accessed 18 Feb 2020

32. Bergeron, L., Rousseau, N., Dumont, M., Dalton-Deschênes, J.: La proposition d'une démarche de recherche-développement. In: Bergeron, L., Rousseau, N. (eds.) La pleine reconnaissance de la valeur de la recherche-développement comme activité productrice de connaissances de recherche. Presses de l'Université du Québec, Québec (2020)

33. Druin, A.: The role of children in the design of new technology. Behav. Inf. Technol. 21(1), 1–35 (2001)

The STORM Project: Using Video Game to Promote Completion of Morning Routine for Children with Attention Deficit Hyperactivity Disorder and Autism Spectrum Disorder

Laurence Pépin-Beauchesne[1]([envelope]), Dany Lussier-Desrochers[1]([envelope]),
Annie-Claude Villeneuve[1], Marie-Ève Dupont[1], Line Massé[1],
and Annie Martineau[2]([envelope])

[1] Département de psychoéducation, Université du Québec à Trois-Rivières,
Trois-Rivières, QC, Canada
{Laurence.pepin-beauchesne,
Dany.Lussier-Desrochers}@uqtr.ca
[2] Neuro Solutions Group©, Québec City, QC, Canada
contact@neurosolutionsgroup.com

Abstract. Morning routines can be challenging for children with Attention Deficit Hyperactivity Disorder (ADHD) or Autism Spectrum Disorder (ASD) [1, 2]. To support their children, parents must use daily monitoring and frequent reinforcement that can be grueling and exhausting with time [3]. Therefore, this pilot study (STORM project) aims the development of a digital solution supporting the completion of morning routine. Precisely, the daily basis use on morning routine, and the acceptance level and perception of the prototype by the children and parents were documented. A descriptive mixed design was used with five families (children aged 6–12 with ASD or ADHD) for a 2-week period. Semi-structured interviews were conducted and the French version of The Before School Functioning Questionnaire (BSFQ) [4, 5] was administered to parents before and after the STORM implementation. As results, the majority of parents believed and observed that STORM had many positive effects like it facilitating morning routine, fostering motivation, decreasing supervision and repetition. Children also said it helped they acknowledge their time management. For the BSFQ, all children scores decreased after the use of the STORM. However, the sample is too small to observe significant differences. Still, it showed that using the prototype has the potential to help parents and their children to promote completion of morning routine. In fact, a second phase of this project is underway, and a larger sample, longer study and group comparisons will be used to see if results can be significant.

Keywords: Autism · Attention Deficit Hyperactivity Disorder · Morning routine · Video game · Technology

© Springer Nature Switzerland AG 2020
M. Antona and C. Stephanidis (Eds.): HCII 2020, LNCS 12189, pp. 58–70, 2020.
https://doi.org/10.1007/978-3-030-49108-6_5

1 Introduction

Performing morning routines represents a considerable challenge for children with neurodevelopmental disorders, such as ADHD or ASD [1, 6]. ADHD is characterized by attention and/or impulsivity and hyperactivity difficulties that affect various spheres of life (social, academic, etc.) [7]. As for autistic people, significant difficulties in communication and social interaction are observed, as well as restricted or repetitive behaviors, interests, and activities [8]. Both children with ADHD or ASD frequently exhibit deficits in executive functions, working memory, or emotional and behavioral self-regulation, which can lead to serious difficulties when it comes to performing morning routines [1, 2, 9]. More specifically, those deficits may reduce children's 1) ability to plan a routine coherently, 2) motivation to engage in or continue the routine and 3) tolerance for delayed gratification. Moreover, working memory can affect the execution of the routine, notably when the child forgets to perform some steps or loses track of what he/she is doing [10].

Consequently, for these children, performing morning routines requires considerable daily supervision by the parents. They must provide consistent instructions and frequent reinforcement to support their child. However, these interventions can require substantial energy and be burdensome for many families [1]. Parents thus feel overwhelmed and exhausted when performing these routines. In fact, Johnston and Mash [11] demonstrated that parental stress may affect parent-child relationship, notably because of a decrease in positive interactions and an increase in negative comments toward children.

To support children and their parents, several traditional intervention tools, such as token systems and visual schedules, are currently used. Though, Bimbrahw et al. [3] reported that these strategies are not effective for all children and still require large investments of time by the parents. In this regard, technology may represent a promising and novel solution to support interventions with children who have ADHD or ASD [3, 12, 13]. Technology may help improve their development, provide new learning opportunities, and increase their autonomy [14]. Actually, few educational technologies are available to help children with ADHD or ASD perform their daily activities.

2 Objectives

This pilot study aimed at developing a digital solution to support children with ADHD or ASD in performing morning routines. To help empower children, a Beta version of the STORM prototype was given to each family. Three objectives were pursued to describe parents and their child's experience of using the prototype:

1. Identify the acceptance level of the STORM prototype, including perceived usefulness and user-friendliness;
2. Explore the children's and their parents' perceptions of the effects of using the prototype on the completion of morning routines;
3. Document the frequency of everyday use of the prototype as per the proposed approach.

3   Method

For these objectives to be met, a descriptive mixed design was used. Because this research sector is relatively new, qualitative research tools were appropriate for learning about the users' perceptions regarding the effects of the game but also of its user-friendliness. The addition of quantitative data collection tools made it possible to quantify the effects of using the product but also to see if its use in a real-life setting matched the designers' predictions. The various methodological aspects of the study are presented in the following subsections.

3.1   Sample

Purposive sampling was used to recruit participants through a private clinic near researchers' city. To participate, children had to meet the following inclusion criteria:

- Be diagnosed with ADHD and/or high-level ASD;
- Be between 6 and 12 years old;
- Attend a regular school;
- Have two parents living at the same address or one parent with exclusive custody of the child;
- Speak French.

Five families with children between 6 and 12 years old with a diagnosis of ASD or ADHD were recruited to use the prototype each morning for a two-week period.

3.2   Materials and Intervention Process

During the study, parents and children had to use the STORM prototype each morning on a two-week period. The prototype included: 1) a digital tablet that contained the video game for the child and the morning routine management interface for the parent, and 2) a smart watch for the child. On the watch, an avatar would appear at the beginning of the morning routine to inform the tasks he/she had to perform (e.g., eat, brush his/her teeth). The child then had to "check off" the accomplished tasks on the watch and the parent had to confirm its completion on the tablet. If the child completed 80% of the routine and the parent approved it, the child was then rewarded with a power that allowed him/her to access a new mission in the video game. This procedure was intended to make the morning routines more pleasant for the child by making him/her part of the mission, and also for the parents, by reducing negative interactions by giving them more of a motivator role where he/she would be encouraging their child. Throughout the process, the parent received technical assistance to make sure the prototype was working properly.

3.3   Measuring Instruments

For these objectives to be met, various measuring instruments were used. Four semi-structured interview canvases were created and used with parents and children. In separated rooms, the interviews were conducted before and after the testing of the solution. They pertained notably to the conduct of the morning routines and the experience of using the solution. The BSFQ [4, 5] was also administered to the parents before and after the test. Total score varied between 0 (absence of dysfunction in the child during the performance of the morning routine) and 60 (high level of dysfunction during the performance of the morning routine). Finally, for the third objective, analytics was installed within the game to collect information on the child's playing habits (e.g., tasks performed by the child, duration of the game sessions, timing of usage).

3.4   Analyses

The qualitative interviews were transcribed into verbatim and then analyzed using NVivo software to extract emerging categories. For the quantitative analysis, descriptive-type statistical analyses were used to analyze the analytics data and a Wilcoxon test was conducted for the BSFQ results in order to verify if any improvements or changes in the child's behaviors were observed during the performance of the morning routine.

4   Results

Results obtained within this study are presented into five sections: 1) Participants description; 2) Conduct of the morning routine during the test; 3) Factors influencing the conduct of the routine during testing; 4) Results of the BSFQ; and 5) User experience.

4.1   Participant's Description

Five families participated in this research project. The average age of participating children is 7.8 years old. They all had been diagnosed with ADHD, and two had ASD as well (see Table 1 for more details). All participating parents mentioned using technology at least two hours per day in their personal lives. They thus felt that they had the necessary skills to use the technology and said they were comfortable doing so. According to their perceptions, the children used technology daily at varying frequencies.

Table 1. Characteristics of the participating children

Family (#)	Gender	Age (years)	Diagnosis/Diagnoses
F1	Male	7	ADHD
F2	Male	7	ADHD
F3	Male	7	ADHD and ASD
F4	Male	8	ADHD and ASD
F5	Female	10	ADHD

4.2   Conduct of the Morning Routine During the Test

All the parents who tested the prototype during the two-week period (F1, F2, F3, F4) spoke of several positive effects. They reported that the tasks were better performed (F2), and the sequence was followed correctly by their child (F2, F3, F4). Two families also said that the routine was executed more quickly (F2, F4; e.g., earlier departure in the morning). However, one of them (F4) specified that certain tasks were sometimes performed *too* quickly by the child, who was eager to carry out his/her mission.

> *I remember...let's say that he was brushing his teeth, well, sometimes he would go a bit fast, because he was excited, he was anxious to go play. ... If the game stimulated him to do it a little bit longer, it would be even better. (Father, Family 4)*

In fact, all the families reported a reduction in parental supervision, notably in the number of repetitions required during the morning routine (F1, F2, F3, F4). They all found the child more cooperative (F1, F2) and felt less need to get angry with him/her during the morning routine (F2, F4).

> *And he is extremely cooperative, and I don't know if it's the effect of the watch or of the game, but he is very cooperative; when I would say something, he would say, "Yes, Mom." And he would go. (Mother, Family 2)*

Furthermore, the parents noticed a reduction in negative interactions as well as an increase in positive interactions within some families (more time to discuss and reinforce the child's desired behaviors). All the families thus reported that the test had helped improve the family atmosphere (F1, F2, F3, F4) and reduce fatigue for the parents. Regarding the effects on the child, three families mentioned an increase in the child's enthusiasm and motivation during the morning routine (F1, F3, F4). All the parents (F1, F2, F3, F4) found that their child had demonstrated considerable autonomy because he/she was able to choose the order in which to perform the tasks (F1).

> *He had the choice, but not the choice; he knows that that's what the routine is, but he was doing it in the order he wanted. That opened up opportunities for him. (Mother, Family 1)*

Some parents noted that their child had a better capacity for attention in the morning. According to two families (F1, F3), the introduction of STORM led to major changes in their child at home and at school alike:

> *From the first week, it was a complete change. Laurent [fictional name] had his watch all the time and he would do his whole routine. We didn't have to repeat anything... He would say to me: "This is fun, Mom; you don't have to repeat things to me." (Mother, Family 2)*

All the children found that using the STORM had a positive impact on the performance of the morning routine. Some said the routine was easier to do (F1, F3, F4), it carried out the tasks more quickly (F2, F3), and was able to do more tasks (F2).

I felt good, let's say, when the watch told me...and when it was my mother, I was like more stressed, so I would give up a little bit. (Children, Family 3)

4.3   Factors Influencing the Conduct of the Routine During Testing

According to the parents, many factors motivated the child during the study. Two families reported that gaining powers was a major motivator (F1, F4). Another said the video game in itself was an effective motivator for their child, while a second one stated that their child was more motivated by the watch than by the video game and the powers.

He was more motivated, because there was a game at the end. He was in the category of people who are perfect for that; it affected him right away... He would really try to have his privilege; he really wanted the reward that the game would give him. (Father, Family 1)

4.4   Results of the BSFQ

Table 2 presents the participants' total BSFQ scores by measurement time at the Wilcoxon test. For all the participants, the BSFQ scores decreased an average of 22 points between pre-intervention and post-intervention. This result shows an overall improvement of the children functioning in the performance of their morning routine. However, it should be noted that Family 5 encountered technical issues when using the solution (details in the next section) so they made little use of the prototype. In fact, the lowest decrease was in this family, whereas Family 4 had the most notable improvement.

Table 2. Families' total BSFQ scores by measurement time

Family (#)	Total score (Pre-intervention)	Total score (Post-intervention)	Difference
F1	32	21	−11
F2	46	10	−36
F3	37	22	−15
F4	44	5	−39
F5	47	38	−9

4.5   User Experience

The results of this pilot study showed that the parents and children had a good perception of the video game application and the avatar in the STORM prototype. Parents said they appreciated that the STORM prototype worked almost on its own and did not entail supplementary management of the morning routine, contrary to traditional methods (e.g., token system), which can be demanding and require a considerable amount of their time. Nonetheless, despite positive comments from parents and children, the use of qualitative and quantitative data provided a better understanding of the context of use of the prototype. Indeed, the data collected by the analytics showed that some families did not use STORM the way the designers and researchers had originally recommended. A diversity of product usage experiences by the five families was observed. This can be explained notably by the presence of technical glitches that influenced the usage. However, some usage patterns could still be observed. The results showed that three of the five families (F1, F3, and F4) used the STORM application in accordance with the proposed procedure. Figures 1, 2, 3, 4, 5, 6, 7, 8 and 9 presents the results for each of the five families.

Family 4 adhered perfectly to the expected usage. Four tasks were thus performed by the child and validated by the parent every day, as shown in Fig. 1. In fact, this was the family that reported the most positive effects on their child during the study. For playing time, peaks were observed (more than 20 min of playing time per day) at the mid-point and at the end (Fig. 2). A slight increase in playing time was also observed in the second week. It thus seems that the first week was a time to get a grasp on the game related to the routines.

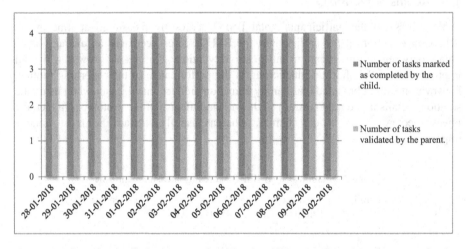

Fig. 1. Number of tasks marked as completed by the child and validated by the parent for the Family 4.

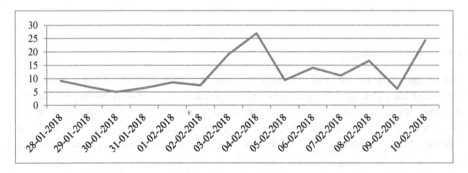

Fig. 2. Total child's play time (in minutes) of Family 4

For Family 1, the child performed routines as expected most of the time. Even if he didn't systematically mark tasks as completed, parents validated them for him. However, parents also omitted the validation during two days of the experimentation, but they caught up in the delayed validation the following day (Fig. 3). In the interviews, the parents explained this situation notably by the presence of technical issues related to the prototype. For this family, there was substantial variability in playing time, with a 60-minute peak during the second week (Fig. 4).

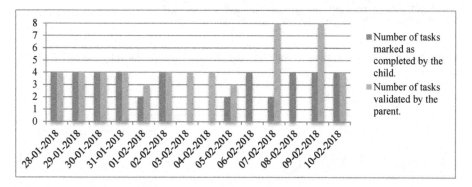

Fig. 3. Number of tasks marked as completed by the child and validated by the parent for the Family 1.

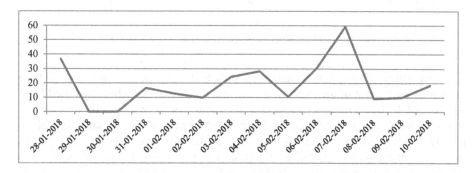

Fig. 4. Total child's play time (in minutes) of Family 1

For Family 3, there was a high level of adherence at the beginning of the test and then a gradual decline in tasks marked as completed by the child and validated by the parent in the second week (see Fig. 5). So, despite performing his routines daily, the child did not systematically enter their execution in the application. A gradual decrease in playing time was also observed (see Fig. 6). In the interview, the parent specified that this drop-in interest was attributable to technical issues.

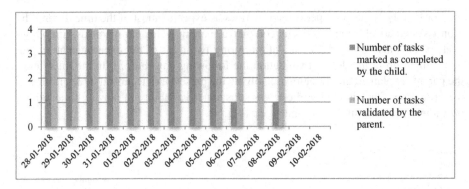

Fig. 5. Number of tasks marked as completed by the child and validated by the parent for the Family 3.

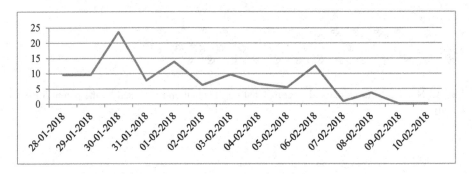

Fig. 6. Total child's play time (in minutes) of Family 3

The profile of Family 5 was characterized by high usage at the beginning and then disinterest for the rest of the experiment. In total, the prototype hadn't been used for 9 days out of 14 (see Fig. 7). According to the family, positive effects on routine performance were seen at first. However, due to the short time of use, the same difficulties usually encountered resurfaced not long after. In the interview, they said they had to stop using the prototype because of technical issues, the presence of an atypical schedule during those weeks and their child's lack interest in the type of video game chosen by the designers. Due to these issues, no play time data were provided for this family.

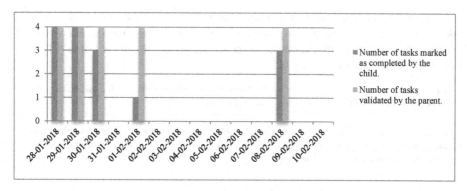

Fig. 7. Number of tasks marked as completed by the child and validated by the parent for the Family 5.

Finally, for Family 2, the data analysis by the analytics showed low adherence to the implementation of the STORM prototype (see Fig. 8). Yet, the post-intervention interviews with the parents suggested the opposite. In fact, the parents reported not having validated the tasks when their child performed them due to a lack of time in the morning. Furthermore, they said the child was very interested in the watch and less so in the video game (see Fig. 9).

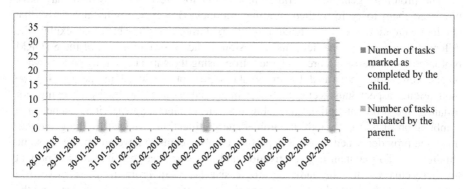

Fig. 8. Number of tasks marked as completed by the child and validated by the parent for the Family 2.

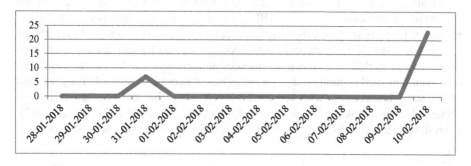

Fig. 9. Total child's play time (in minutes) of Family 2

In the interview, the child mentioned preferring to wait until the end of the study to ask his parent to unblock all the powers gained over the two weeks. This explains notably why the average playing time was concentrated mainly on the last day. Here is what the parents said in this regard:

> He started having fun yesterday. He said: "I must have some powers...." But me, during the week, he didn't ask me for it. (Parent, Family 2)

> It's funny because I didn't see him playing so much on the STORM game; I saw him playing a lot; it's like the watch was just enough to be drawn into it. He didn't talk that much about unblocking powers. (Parent, Family 2)

5 Discussion/Conclusion

Given the exploratory nature of the study, it was not possible to conduct in-depth statistical analyses for the BSFQ scores and thus quantify whether the gains observed were significant. However, all parents noticed positive effects on their family morning routines when using the prototype. This study showed that the STORM prototype may be a tool with interesting potential for helping children with ASD or ADHD on their morning routines. A study, currently underway with more than 200 families, will make it possible to overcome this limitation and to test the second version of the prototype.

The prototype generated extrinsic motivation for the children, which may have prompted them to perform their morning routines. However, results also show that children were motivated by different reinforcers during the test, which may explain the differences between the participants' adhesion to the prescribed usage of the STORM prototype. Some derived more enjoyment from using the game or gaining powers while others were more motivated by the avatar's prompts included in the watch. The motivational aspect thus seems to be an important issue to assess by checking, for instance, the different options available into the product (watch, video game, or a combination of both). Though, the immediate gratification provided by the game that the game provided when a task was performed also seems to have an impact on some children [2]. To maintain their motivation and the novelty aspect, it is thus important for these children that the game be progressive [15, 16]. From the perspective of a longitudinal study, it would also be interesting to document the process of learning the routine, notably when motivation transitions from extrinsic to intrinsic. It would also be interesting to examine the variations in the participants' gains by type of tool.

Finally, it is possible to believe that perceived usefulness had an impact on the perception of the effects of the STORM prototype and on adherence to its implementation [17]. As shown in the results, the parents who deemed the tool favorable at the pre-test meeting were the ones who reported the most positive effects and who adhered most faithfully to the recommended implementation procedure. Moreover, they even remained committed despite the technical issues encountered. They reported taking steps immediately with technical support when this situation arose. Interest decreased when the second issue occurred; however, usage did not stop completely. Interestingly, a comparison of the results obtained regarding the perceived usefulness of the STORM prototype showed that, of the four families reporting technical issues, only the one having expressed great reluctance quit the testing. It is thus possible to believe that the initial perception of the product influenced the family's involvement during the study. In fact, this is an important factor in the process of acceptability, acceptance, and adoption of a product. This element shows the importance of limiting the number of technical issues to make sure the participants adhere to the prototype and remain motivated. The product must not be an additional element to manage in the family routine.

References

1. Sallee, F.R.: Early morning functioning in stimulant-treated children and adolescents with attention-deficit/hyperactivity disorder, and its impact on caregivers. J. Child Adolesc. Psychopharmacol. **25**(7), 558–565 (2015). https://doi.org/10.1089/cap.2014.0160
2. Réseau national d'expertise en TSA: Une revue systématique et méta- analyse des fonctions exécutives dans le Trouble du spectre de l'autisme. Université du Québec à Montréal, Montréal (2016)
3. Bimbrahw, J., Boger, J., Mihailidis, A.: Investigating the efficacy of a computerized prompting device to assist children with autism spectrum disorder with activities of daily living. Assist. Technol. **24**(4), 286–298 (2012). https://doi.org/10.1080/10400435.2012.680661
4. Wilens, T.E., Hammerness, P., Martelon, M., Brodziak, K., Utzinger, L., Wong, P.: A controlled trial of the methylphenidate transdermal system on before-school functioning in children with attention-deficit/hyperactivity disorder. J. Clin. Psychiatry **71**(5), 548–556 (2010)
5. Faraone, S.V., Hammerness, P.G., Wilens, T.E.: Reliability and validity of the before-school functioning scale in children with ADHD. J. Atten. Disord. **22**(11), 1040–1048 (2018)
6. Fombonne, E., Couture, M.: Étude longitudinale de l'impact des habiletés sensori-motrices sur l'indépendance fonctionnelle dans les activités de la vie quotidienne des enfants avec trouble envahissant du développement. Université de McGill, Montréal (2008)
7. Hébert, A.: TDA/H: la boîte à outils Stratégies et techniques pour gérer le TDA/H. Éditions de Mortagne, Boucherville (2015)
8. American Psychiatric Association: Manuel diagnostique et statistique des troubles mentaux. Elsevier-Masson, Paris (2015)
9. Sinzig, J., Vinzelberg, I., Evers, D., Lehmkuhl, G.: Executive function and attention profiles in preschool and elementary school children with autism spectrum disorders or ADHD. Int. J. Dev. Disabil. **60**(3), 144–154 (2014)
10. Gagné, P.-P., Leblanc, N., Rousseau, A.: Apprendre… une question de stratégies. Chenelière Éducation, Montréal (2009)
11. Johnston, C., Mash, E.: Families of children with attention deficit hyperactivity disorder: Review and recommendations for future research. Clin. Child. Fam. Psychol. Rev. **4**(3), 183–207 (2001). https://doi.org/10.1023/A:1017592030434
12. Goodwin, M.S.: Enhancing and accelerating the pace of autism research and treatment: the promise of developing innovative technology. Focus Autism Other Dev. Disabil. **23**(2), 125–128 (2008)
13. Lussier-Desrochers, L.: Intervention technoclinique dans le secteur des services sociaux Enjeux cliniques et organisationnels. Presse de l'Université du Québec, Trois-Rivières (2017)

14. Sandall, S.R.: DEC recommended practices a comprehensive guide for practical application in early intervention/early childhood special education. Sopris West, Missoula (2005)
15. Zosh, J., Hirsh-Pasek, K., Michnick Golinkoff, R., Parish-Morris, J.: Apprendre à l'ère numérique: réintroduire l'éducation dans les applications éducatives pour jeunes enfants (2016). http://www.enfant-encyclopedie.com/sites/default/files/textes-experts/fr/4818/apprendre-a-lere-numerique-reintroduire-leducation-dans-les-applications-educatives-pour-jeunes-enfants.pdf. Accessed 16 Jan 2019
16. Courage, M.L., Troseth, G.L.: L'apprentissage à partir de médias électroniques chez les jeunes enfants (2016). http://www.enfant-encyclopedie.com/sites/default/files/textes-experts/fr/4818/lapprentissage-a-partir-de-medias-electroniques-chez-les-jeunes-enfants-.pdf. Accessed 16 Jan 2019
17. Quiguer, S.: Acceptabilité, acceptation et appropriation des systèmes de transport intelligents : élaboration d'un canevas de co-conception multidimensionnelle orientée par l'activité. Dissertation, Université Rennes 2 (2013)

Technologies for Deaf Users

A Case Study About Usability, User Experience and Accessibility Problems of Deaf Users with Assistive Technologies

Tatiany X. de Godoi$^{(\boxtimes)}$, Deógenes P. da Silva Junior,
and Natasha M. Costa Valentim

Federal University of Paraná, Curitiba, PR, Brazil
tatianyxdg@gmail.com, deogenesj@gmail.com,
valentimnatasha@gmail.com

Abstract. Interaction with mobile devices allows users to have advantages such as flexibility, mobility, and wireless communication. However, challenges have emerged in this interaction context, due to the smaller size of its screens, the new usage contexts, and the limited performance capacity. Usability, User Experience (UX) and Accessibility are quality perspectives used to improve user interaction with mobile devices. Mobile device users include the Deaf community, but some of them can have difficulties when using technologies. Therefore, Assistive Technologies (ATs) (including mobile devices) are inserted in society as important tools to enable better living conditions for their users. Moreover, it is relevant that technologies provide good interaction and help Deaf users to deal with their daily tasks. However, some available ATs have Usability, UX and Accessibility problems, such as displeasure and failures in the operational part of the ATs. We report an exploratory study with the purpose to investigate (a) if Deaf people use ATs when using mobile devices, and if so, what ATs they use; (b) what difficulties Deaf people encounter when using ATs; and c) how to overcome difficulties when using ATs. The study followed a qualitative research methodology where the data were obtained through questionnaires and observation of users performing tasks in ATs. Through the Grounded Theory method, it was possible to identify difficulties and barriers from the Usability, UX and Accessibility perspectives.

Keywords: Assistive Technology · Deaf Community · Accessibility · Usability · User Experience

1 Introduction

Mobile devices and their applications have several advantages. Nathan et al. [19] say that independence in the use of the application, in terms of flexibility and mobility, has been the main reason for people to choose mobile applications to assist them in their daily tasks. Also, the easy download and installation, to be used anywhere at any time, involved the most diverse people to use mobile applications.

Mobile devices are also a context for Assistive Technologies (AT) operation. ATs can help people with their daily tasks, thus appropriating the characteristics of a mobile

M. Antona and C. Stephanidis (Eds.): HCII 2020, LNCS 12189, pp. 73–91, 2020.
https://doi.org/10.1007/978-3-030-49108-6_6

device. As the use of mobile devices becomes more disseminated, ATs become more relevant to permit that people, to the greatest extent possible, can use and be independent with technology. However, ATs can also have problems and present barriers to their users.

Many factors influence the abandonment of an AT [31]. To deal with these factors, the Accessibility, User Experience (UX), and Usability aspects are used, to provide higher quality to assistive devices and technologies. Some steps taken in these three perspectives can be pointed out, such as reducing the amount of information to be transmitted, avoiding unnecessary actions and elements for the application, prioritizing the mobile layout, reducing the effort and time spent, and providing a pleasant UX [17].

However, there is much work to ATs have spread popularity with their users. In the Deaf community, for example, these applications have not yet gained much popularity, due to the applications' failures to achieve their expectations. Studies indicate that many advantages can be obtained, but user satisfaction with the interface usability can be one of the effects of the lower popularity of these applications [12, 29].

In Brazil, the Decree No. 5,296 [7] conceptualizes the hearing loss as "bilateral, partial or total loss, of forty-one decibels (dB) or more, measured by audiogram in the frequencies of 500 Hz, 1,000 Hz, 2,000 Hz and 3,000 Hz". In this research, the term Deaf was used, because the term "hearing impairment" always implies something incomplete or defective, which negatively differentiates the person with a disability from the normal ones. Deaf people see themselves without this deficit because their hearing is visual and they have shown us another way to apprehend the world, using a communication system that is older than oral-auditory languages [9]. Deaf culture (or Deaf community) is the term applied to the social movement that understands deafness as a difference in human experience (including the right to use Sign Language as natural language) rather than a deficiency [11].

Therefore, this paper presents a case study on the barriers of using assistive technology on a mobile device, from the Deaf perspective. More and more mobile devices have been used by the Deaf community; however, many assistive technologies are not developed with the needs of this audience in mind. This paper describes how the study was planned, executed and analyzed, to provide information that can contribute to development teams for ATs understanding and evaluation, making these technologies more accessible, providing a better experience for the user and increasingly meeting the perspectives Usability, UX e Accessibility.

As a result of this study, it was possible to identify that the participants were able to perform tasks in the AT but encountered some difficulties. Through the GT method, categories of difficulties were identified, such as "Difficulty of understanding", positive points such as "Ease of use", and other aspects of the user's interaction with the AT, such as "Exploration of the environment", "Way of smartphone use" and "Deaf community characteristic". Evidence was found that problems of a Usability, UX and Accessibility nature can affect the adoption of AT by a Deaf user, who has their characteristics and ways of using the device.

The rest of this paper is organized as follows: Sect. 2 presents the theoretical concepts of the work. Section 3 deals with the research method used. Section 4 describes the results and discussions of the study. And Sect. 5 presents the final considerations.

2 Theoretical Background

Mobile devices became a common object in people's lives. A survey by the National Association of the Deaf [6] found that 75% of Deaf users are using instant messaging and 97% are using emails daily. This fact shows that, even though there are challenges and limitations in these applications, Deaf people are trying to adopt technologies, especially telecommunication technology [22].

Among the barriers and difficulties encountered when using mobile devices, we can highlight that not all Deaf people are prone to know how to use sign languages [5, 10, 24]. However, many Deaf people prefer to communicate with sign languages [32] which lead to communication barrier when signing is used with hearing people [18].

To facilitate and generate autonomy for users, there are Assistive Technologies (ATs), which promote independence, quality of life, accessibility and social inclusion through the expansion of the user functional skills. CAT [8] and Bersch [4] define AT as an interdisciplinary area of knowledge that encompasses products, resources, methodologies, strategies, practices, and services that aim to promote functionality related to the activity and participation of people with disabilities or reduced mobility.

However, ATs can present problems that need to be overcome to reduce user abandonment. Wessels et al. [31] highlight four main factors related to the abandonment of an AT:

1. Personal factors: age, sex, diagnosis, self-expectations and expectations of the social circle, acceptance of the disability, emotional maturity/internal motivation, progression of the disability, the severity of the disability, changes in the severity of the disability and use of multiple devices;
2. Factors related to the assistive device: device quality and appearance;
3. Factors related to the use environment: support to the social circle, physical barriers, presence of opportunities and market procedures for the devices;
4. Factors related to professional intervention: user opinions, instruction and training, provision and correct installation process, length of the delivery period and follow-up service.

Given the above, various factors can influence the abandonment of an AT. AT should be assessed more comprehensively, analyzing different perspectives, such as Usability, UX and Accessibility, which are important concepts when it comes to software quality.

Accessibility is defined by ISO 25010 [14] as "the degree to which a product or system can be used by people with a wide range of characteristics and capabilities to achieve a particular objective in a specific use context". Thus, accessibility contributes as a facilitator in the AT use. Another important quality criterion to consider in TAs is Usability, defined by ISO 25010 [14] as the "extent to which a product can be used by specific users to achieve specific goals with effectiveness, efficiency, and satisfaction in a specific context of use". An AT with good usability provides greater user satisfaction concerning the product. Lastly, UX emerged as a new way to understand and study the quality in the use of interactive products [2]. UX "is considered as the user's emotions and expectations with the context of use, where emotional factors and personal experiences stand out" [1]. Positive UX is paramount to the successful adoption and acceptance of an AT.

Usability, UX and Accessibility are correlated perspectives. For some researchers, Usability is considered as part of UX [28]. According to the definition of WAI [30], Accessibility appears as a subset of Usability [26]. However, this vision can indicate that Usability should be prioritized over Accessibility. For example, a Usability assessment alone is not sufficient to meet Accessibility requirements. The definition of ISO 9241 [15] suggests that Usability is a subset of Accessibility [26]. This vision also can lead to an understanding that it is only necessary to make technologies accessible, but without aspects of ease of use, learning, among others. Interaction barriers can be resolved by Accessibility, but there may still be an impediment when technologies are difficult to use.

In this paper, we believed that, regardless of which perspective encompasses the other, Usability, UX and Accessibility must be considered together. We believed that Usability, UX and Accessibility form an intersection and, if these three perspectives are taken into account in an AT assessment, it is possible to meet most of the users' requirements, avoid a greater number of failures and imply in less chance of AT abandonment by users. Also, measuring user satisfaction with ATs is made difficult by the lack of well-validated instruments [23].

Siebra et al. [25] present a set of requirements for mobile applications considering Accessibility with Usability for several types of user impairments (visually, hearing and motor). These requirements were identified through a literature review and an observation analysis of real users, capturing how they used mobile apps, and which were the main problems regarding this use. Although some problems were mentioned, these were mostly of Usability and Accessibility types, without a broad discussion of UX problems and its relations with other quality aspects of interaction.

Considering the problems and barriers that AT suffers, the abandonment of AT by users and the necessity of a broad view of the three perspectives for ATs, a case study was planned and executed.

3   Case Study

A case study was planned and executed to know the barriers, positive and negative aspects of mobile devices. Case study is an empirical method that aims to investigate contemporary phenomena in their context [33] and it enables a researcher to closely examine the data within a specific context and explore any phenomenon in the data which serves as a point of interest to the researcher [34]. Therefore, the goal of this case study, using the paradigm GQM [3], is presented in Table 1.

Table 1. Goal of the case study using the GQM paradigm.

Analyze	Deaf using ATs
With the purpose of	To evaluate
With respect of	Perspectives of Usability, UX, and Accessibility
From the perspective of	HCI researchers
In the context of	Use of AT in mobile devices

3.1 Context

The study was carried out with a real app, named Hand Talk, with the principal functionality of translation: an avatar called Hugo translate text or audio to Libras (Brazilian Sign Language). The app also has functionalities for Libras learning and training, such as a dictionary of Brazilian signs and videos of Libras classes.

3.2 Selection of Participants

In total three Deaf participants signed an Informed Consent Form (ICF). Then they filled a Characterization Form to know: i) their knowledge about Brazilian Portuguese and Libras; ii) frequency of use and what are the assistive devices and apps that they used; iii) difficulties and positive aspects when using mobile devices; iv) if in some aspect they need help of other people to use mobile devices and if they feel harm in any way from not being able to access some content.

The experiment was conducted with Deaf users of mobile devices who were contacted and agreed to participate in the study. Deaf users used devices in their general activities in daily life. In these interactions with apps and mobile devices, we could investigate questions about Accessibility, UX, and Usability.

A characterization questionnaire was applied to the participants. The results of this questionnaire are shown in Table 2.

Table 2. Participants characterization data

Question	Participant A	Participant B	Participant C
Frequency of mobile devices use	Three times a week	Every day	Every day
Frequency of AT use	Every day	Never	Every day
Used applications in mobile devices	WhatsApp, Facebook, Google, Clock, Calendar, and Calculator	WhatsApp, Facebook, Google, Instagram	WhatsApp, Facebook, Instagram, YouTube (with caption or people signaling), Netflix, iFood, Gallery, Camera, Google duo, Transcriber, Sinalário (Libras dictionary), Uber, Spotify (vibration only)

(continued)

Table 2. (*continued*)

Question	Participant A	Participant B	Participant C
Used assistive technologies	Hearing aid	Does not use	Transcriber, Sinalário and hearing aid (hears only loud noises)
Most impacting difficulties when using mobile devices	He feels some difficulties	Has no difficulties	Call, technical assistance, video on YouTube without subtitles and signage, subtitles are horrible (sometimes they take too long to appear, they appear too fast, the wrong words appear, or there is nothing to do with what they said), small print
Due to deafness, do you feel impaired from not being able to access any content? What could be done to change that?	He doesn't feel harmed. Had no bad experience with the smartphone	Yes, because without the application you are unable to communicate in emergency or fainting situations, for example, you also need an interpreter	Spotify, Hand Talk app another translating app, which translates better, which did not translate from Portuguese to Libras word by word

All participants considered that they could understand and interpret sign language without difficulty. Regarding the Portuguese language, participants A and C said that they can read and write with difficulty. Participant B mentioned that he can read and write without difficulty.

Regarding the participants' characterization data, participant A uses the application less frequently (three times a week) and has difficulty with the Portuguese language. Participant C mentioned the largest number of applications, pointing out several examples. The factors of the frequency of mobile device use, in addition to the number of apps used, were influential at least for the execution of the activity and the results found, both in the ease of performing the tasks and in the quantified errors.

3.3   Instrumentation

Many artifacts were defined to support the study: characterization form, ICF, instructions and specification of the study tasks, where a short scenario contextualized the tasks. Besides, the tasks were done in the AT named 'Hand Talk© App', for Libras translation. Figure 1 shows the main screen of Hand Talk, used to make text or audio translation to Libras.

Fig. 1. Translation screen of the Hand Talk

3.4 Execution

To realize the study, we first carried out the planning, material preparation, and selection of subjects. ICF was used to ensure the confidentiality and privacy of the data collected.

The study was executed with one participant at a time, with three participants in total. First, the ICF was presented to the participants and it was asked for them to sign. After that, they were asked to complete the characterization questionnaire.

The next step was to instruct the participants to read the activity and a scenario. The scenario provided a greater context for the activities to be executed. The scenario was:

"Pedro, a Deaf man who was not feeling well, decided to go to the medical clinic of his friend Rafael, who is also Deaf. When describing his symptoms, Pedro is having trouble remembering the hand signaling of his symptoms. Therefore, he decides to use the Hand Talk application to assist him in his conversation with Rafael. Pedro needs to translate the following: I have a headache and shortness of breath".

After reading the scenario, the participant was asked to start the activities:

1. Try to simulate the task that Pedro needs to perform in the Hand Talk App, translating the phrase "I have a headache and shortness of breath".
2. Change the speed of translation reproduction to slow.
3. Change the speed of translation reproduction to fast.
4. Change the speed of translation reproduction to normal.
5. Press to play the translation again (replay).

With the smartphone in hand and the Hand Talk open, the participant began to interact with the app. After the end of the last activity, thanks were given, and the study ended. Video recordings were made only when the participant was using the AT. Two researchers conducted the study in the field.

4 Results and Discussion

The results of the study will be presented together with quantitative and qualitative analysis. Some participants mentioned that they knew Hand Talk App, but they did not use the app.

4.1 Quantitative Analysis

Two researchers analyzed the case study results and another one validated the results. To assess Usability, UX and Accessibility of the AT, we quantify the number of attempts made by the participants to perform a given activity, the participants' emotions on a sentiment scale in each activity, the number of times the user has not found an option, the number of interruptions (advertisements, notifications from other apps) that appeared during the use of the AT and the amount of difficulties that participants were not able to overcome without asking for help.

Percentage of Success
The success of the activity is measured by the number of attempts made by the participants to perform a given activity. The activity criteria used in this test are: (a) Easy Success: the user completed the activity on the first attempt, without problems; (b) Difficult Success: the user completed the activity with great difficulty; (c) Failure: the user was unable to complete the activity or gave up.

Table 3 presents the results of the success of each activity for each participant. All participants were able to carry out the five activities, and only participant A found it difficult to carry them out.

Table 3. Activities success per participants

Activities	Participant A	Participant B	Participant C
1. Phrase translation	Easy Success	Easy Success	Easy Success
2. Change to slow speed	Difficult Success	Easy Success	Easy Success
3. Change to fast speed	Difficult Success	Easy Success	Easy Success
4. Change to normal speed	Easy Success	Easy Success	Easy Success
5. Replay	Difficult Success	Easy Success	Easy Success

Participants Emotions
The participants' emotions in each activity were observed and quantified on scale that consists of the following emotions: (a) Joy: he/she willing to continue doing activities; (b) Anxious: he/she trying to stay focused and/or by having a hard time staying on task; (c) Frustrated: he/she is not getting it. He/she is showing signs of stress; (d) Overwhelmed: he/she is losing control and need to leave the environment; and (e) Angry: he/she has lost control. He/she is not paying attention. The results found are presented in Table 4.

Table 4. Participants results in the scale of emotion classification

	Participant 1	Participant 2	Participant 3
Activity 1	Joy	Joy	Joy
Activity 2	Joy	Joy	Joy
Activity 3	Frustrated	Joy	Joy
Activity 4	Overwhelmed	Joy	Joy
Activity 5	Joy	Joy	Joy

Participant A showed frustration and that he felt overwhelmed. The causes could be the setbacks that arose and some activities that became repetitive, where the participant showed signs that he was in a hurry to leave and to finish the study. Participants B and C demonstrated that they were happy and interested when conducting the study.

Option Not Found
This factor measures the number of times the participant went to perform a task and did not find a certain option. As can be seen in Table 5, only participant A had difficulties in finding some options, namely: a) finding the back button, and b) showing translation options.

Table 5. Resource or option not found by participants

Difficulty	Participant A	Participant B	Participant C
Finding the back button	2	0	0
Showing translation options	1	0	0

Quantity of Interruptions
This factor expresses the number of interruptions that the system presented during the use of the AT. Table 6 shows the number of interruptions that appeared during the study for each participant. Among the interruptions, we can highlight the advertisements, application notification and tutorial screen. All participants experienced interruptions during the use of AT, even in a short period of application.

Table 6. Interruptions found in the interaction of the participants

Difficulty	Participant A	Participant B	Participant C
Advertisements	2	0	0
Application notification	0	1	0
Tutorial screen	0	2	2

Asking for Help

This factor expresses the amount of difficulties participants were not able to overcome without asking for help from the researchers. Table 7 shows that only participant A needed help. It is worth mentioning that the researchers sought to interfere as little as possible during the time that users were using the AT.

Table 7. Number of times that help was asked

Difficulty	Participant A	Participant B	Participant C
Ask for help	1	0	0

4.2   Qualitative Analysis

For qualitative analysis, Deaf interaction videos with the AT were analyzed using the Grounded Theory (GT) method [27]. The video coding procedures were performed according to the recommendations of Lazar et al. [16] for the analysis of multimedia content.

The GT analysis followed using a subset of the stages of the coding process suggested by Strauss and Corbin [27] for the GT method: the open (1st stage) and axial (2nd stage) codifications. When analyzing the videos of the participants' interactions during the activities, codes (relevant concepts about the user's interaction with AT) were created related to the participants' actions, expressions and clicks on the mobile device, hand movements, and AT behavior during the interaction- open coding. Afterward, the codes were grouped according to their properties, forming concepts that represent categories and subcategories. Finally, these were related to each other- axial coding. The open and axial coding, as well as all the proposed codes and categories, were reviewed and adjusted by two other coders.

In this qualitative analysis, we seek to answer the following question: How is the interaction of the Deaf using ATs on mobile devices? The purpose of this analysis was to understand the possible difficulties, barriers, positives aspects and other relevant phenomena in the interaction of the Deaf user with an AT. Considering this question and objective, the GT procedures aim at more in-depth analysis, by comparing and analyzing the relationship between these concepts.

As it was not intended to create a theory in this regard, selective coding was not carried out (3rd phase of the GT method). The steps of open and axial coding were enough to know and understand the phenomena that arose in the interaction.

As the recorded videos focus on the interaction of the Deaf user with the AT during activities, the content of the codes was mostly about the AT behavior and descriptions of the participant's actions, behaviors, and expressions, rather than speeches and opinions expressed or stated.

Difficulty of Understanding

The category "Difficulty of Understanding" present moments when the participants demonstrated difficulty in understanding the tasks and a barrier in their understanding of the AT, in which there was no fluid and intuitive interaction.

The participants mentioned doubts regarding the execution of the activity. For example, the participant A showed an initial question before pressing the 'ok' button on the keyboard, indicating a doubt whether he was doing the correct action, before performing his first translation in the AT. After confirmation by the researchers, the participant continued their activity. The participant C expressed doubt about how the sentence to be translated in the activity should be written. The researchers indicated that it should be written in the literal mode of the text scenario. Other difficulties showed up, such as confusion about the 'remove advertisements' screen, as he was unable to translate. These difficulties are related to the emergence of new information on the screen, which might not be expected: an advertising screen appears, a black screen appears also related to advertising and a percentage loading screen appears without user expectation.

Some codes also indicate that the difficulty in understanding can affect the feeling of security, which can be a UX factor. If the user does not feel secure or confident about the technology, he may feel discouraged to use and feel intimidated to explore the application, as more errors or unexpected actions may appear in the interaction. In previous uses with ATs who lacks accessibility, if that user has many negative experiences then possibly the use of a new AT will carry these negative experiences, implying in an existing insecurity even before the use of the new technology.

After a participant's first translation, a screen related to AT advertising appeared on the app. The participant A showed confusion or discontent, shaking his head negatively when he saw the advertising screen above the translation screen. This confusion is related to the screen to remove advertisements, as he was unable to perform the translation. So participant A had to deal with an unexpected factor that hindered his understanding again, due to the appearance of advertisements, reaffirming the lack of understanding and lack of intuitive and fluid use of the AT.

Insecurity
The "Insecurity" category represents moments when there was insecurity that prevented the participant to continue in the activity. For example, the participant A demonstrated [with gestures and actions] 'I don't know' repeatedly and handed the smartphone to the researchers to do an action for him [return to the translator screen]. The participant A tried to point out that the reason for not being able to return to the translation screen was due to his lack of knowledge about the AT. However, participant A did not show the motivation to learn, indicating a possible barrier that would prevent him from continuing using the AT. This action, of another user performing an activity in AT in place of the Deaf, can be an indication that an AT barrier does not lead only to insecurity, but to a feeling of frustration for not being able to have autonomy in their actions.

Dissatisfaction
The "Dissatisfaction" category indicates that the participant showed dissatisfaction and impatience with a percentage loading screen, as it was necessary to wait. The participant, to leave that wait, clicks elsewhere on the mobile device interface. This loading action was unexpected, due to an inaccurate user click.

System Inconsistencies

Related to AT problems, it was observed the disappearance of speed control options, which have been hidden from the phone by an imprecise click of the participant. Also, while the participant was typing on the screen, when a smartphone notification appeared, the text being typed disappeared. In both cases, it refers to a feature that disappears from the AT, without the user realizing where the originated action came from.

A resource of the AT that disappears leads to a new effort to understand the system, as it was not an intuitive search to return the option to the screen. Also, like the speed control and translation options have been hidden from the smartphone screen, there is a system action that prevents the participant from continuing his activity, leading to a repetitive effort, in which the participant had to retype the text. So, there is not only a barrier to the interaction but the implication in an additional effort by the participant. In this way, the resources that were initially created to facilitate or "assist" the user's life has led to a dull and unstable experience due to inconsistencies in the AT.

Browsability Error

Also, a system problem, the category "Browsability error" was created. The errors are related to inaccurate clicks from the participants, which took them to a new action or an unexpected screen, for example when the participant clicks on a share button when it was needed to click on the speed button. The participant A also clicked and explored the side menu, looking for an option, but not finding it.

Repetition of Action

The "Repetition of Action" category was created. Related, there is the "Difference of devices" subcategory, referring to a repetitive action when participants searched for buttons on an Android device while using an iOS device. This "Repetition of Action" also indicates proximity to the "Inconsistency of the system" category, as the inconsistency led to an additional effort to the same extent that repetition in this category is an additional effort of the user, which would not be necessary.

It was observed the same behavior with different participants: repeating the action of typing the text for translation. In the 2–4 tasks, it was necessary to change the translation speed and repeat the translation with the new speed. The participants typed the text again when it was necessary only to click in the repeat button to repeat the translation with the new speed. In the AT, however, when a translation is performed, the text field is showed empty, leading the participants to think that they needed to type the text again.

In this way, translation has become probably a tedious and repetitive activity. One of the causes of this repetition may have been the lack of knowledge of the 'repeat translation' button. Another more serious cause concerning the visibility aspect of the system is that information typed disappears from the text box. Considering that a participant types a text and then forgets what he typed, he would have to click on the translation button again to remember the action he just performed, because the text field is empty, and it may even give the impression that nothing was typed. Thus, concerning typing after a translation, there is no visibility.

The repetition also seemed to be associated with a participant's desire to do some action with the AT, but without knowledge. In this case, repetition comes close to an exploration purpose, to discover what the function could be by repeatedly clicking on the same button or location on the AT screen. For example, it was observed two actions of clicking in the speed button repeatedly (3 and 11 times, respectively), for the participants to see the existing speeds and to be able to select the desired speed. Therefore, these indicate that the participants make several actions and clicks on the AT not with the direct intention of the action, but often to know the AT. An AT must take this nature into account, for example by preventing the exploratory clicks from causing errors or leading to places in the AT where the participant can no longer leave. These are requirements related to usability, such as "User control and freedom" and "Error prevention" [20].

Exploration of the Environment

The category "Exploration of the environment" is related to participants' navigation or clicks to learn and think about AT options. This category is different from "Repetition of Action" because, in the exploration, interactions are carried out successfully, without repetition because of errors.

Participants explored the AT with clicks and other interaction metaphors, such as scroll-down and finger-scroll. Participants also explored the buttons and fields of AT. The activities tasks are performed only on the initial translation screen. So, in some cases, such as when participants opened the side menu, the exploration occurred as a result of an unexpected action by AT, leading the participant trying to return to the central translation option. Therefore, we can indicate that, in addition to exploring AT to understand it, participants may have explored to return to the home screen because there was a change in context caused by AT, mainly by displaying advertisements.

The subcategory of "Text execution" deals with the action of translating a text that has been typed. There were two buttons available for translation: a blue confirm button on the keyboard operating system and an orange button in the application itself. One participant, for example, used only the keyboard button in all translations. Another participant, in turn, used the application button. This was a demonstration of the flexibility of the AT as a positive feature.

Form of Using the Smartphone

Next to the "Text execution", which was diverse by the users, the category of "Form of using the smartphone" deals with how the participants held the device for the inter-action. One of the participants supported the smartphone on the table and typed with the fingers of both hands as if he was "pinching characters" during typing. Another participant typed with both hands holding the smartphone. Finally, one participant typed with just one hand.

Each participant then had a personalized way of using the smartphone, indicating a nature of individual use that the device and system must adapt. When the participants wanted to communicate with the researchers, it was necessary to release the smartphone from their hands to make gestures for communication. This is a direct implication of the relationship between the Deaf and the way he uses the smartphone, as his hands and expressions are means of communication, which need to be free to effectively pass the message. Thus, the way of using the smartphone affected even this communicative issue, for example, one participant, as he already had his smartphone resting on the table, had his hands free to gesture and talk to the researchers.

Characteristic of the Deaf Community

This category "Characteristic of the Deaf Community" indicates that there is a different form or structure of Deaf writing. One participant, when writing the text of the task, started to write a sentence different from the original sentence written in the scenario.

The way of holding the smartphone and typing the text indicates a different form of interaction, be it in the software part or the hardware (physical) part of the device. Therefore, this different structure is an indication of other behaviors and actions that are different between the Deaf and non-Deaf user.

Ease of Use

The "Ease of Use" category presents positive points of the interaction. Ease of use comes close to Nielsen's [20] "Consistency and Standards" heuristic. These facilities take advantage of patterns and metaphors of applications known to the Deaf, such as WhatsApp (which all participants mentioned using).

Other resources, such as a tutorial that shows the buttons and main functionalities of the AT, and word suggestions on the keyboard, may also have facilitated the interaction of the participant in the execution of the task. The tutorial, for example, has a presentation mode that focuses on specific actions (for example, action to change speed), showing on the screen only the button related to that action. So, the resources related to the tutorial and word suggestion, which appear on-screen to help the user, apparently were successful to help users in their interactions. Considering ATs design, it is an opportunity to investigate metaphors known to Deaf users, to provide greater familiarity and intuitive interaction through mental models built on previous interactions.

5   Discussion

In the difficulty of options not found, participant A showed more difficulties, but was the participant with the least amount of experience with mobile devices. In turn, the difficulty of interruption occurred for the three participants. Participant B had the highest number (three) of interruptions in its use. Still, on the interruption, participants B and C had better results, leaving the interruption without difficulties. Only participant A asked the researchers for help to get out of an interruption.

In addition to the lower mention of apps used, the lower frequency of use of ATs and mobile devices, the fact that the participant A asked for help is related to the difficulty of understanding, with a repetition of the exploratory action, in which there was no success. In this case, the identified facilities of use were not able to help the user to get out of an unwanted state, caused by the inconsistency of the AT itself or by a participant's navigability error.

Regarding emotion, time may have been an influencing factor. In the case of participant A, as his interaction time became longer, it may have been the factor that made him feel anxious and desirous for the study finish. In the case of participant A, a hypothesis for the long execution time is the difficulty in dealing with the interruptions that took away the main focus of the activity. These interruptions were the advertisements and the options that were hidden. Also, participant A demonstrated a desire to teach researchers a few words in Libras, taking away the continued use of the AT. For participants B and C, they felt happy during the activity, and the execution time was short. The categories of "Insecurity" and "Dissatisfaction" are related to participant A's emotion that the study should finish soon.

Related to these emotion categories, there is also the reason that users do not use the AT translation because the product is not useful, insofar as it does not deliver a translation that is useful for the Deaf community. In this way, ATs may not even deliver a pragmatic aspect of UX to the Deaf community. If there is no pragmatic aspect, the hedonic aspect may have been left out even more. Features that negatively affect the hedonic aspect were identified, such as the advertisements that appear on the main translation screen and their continuous interruptions during the use of the AT.

The UX aspect could be influenced by the previous uses of similar ATs. Users mentioned that, in previous uses of Hand Talk, the experience was worse than they had during the study. But despite the apparent improvement in the Hand Talk, it was still not fully meeting their needs, both due to the app's expectations (hedonic aspect) and the delivery of the translation results (pragmatic aspect). In this way, it is possible to indicate that, from the perspective of UX, translation ATs may be on an initial path of trying to meet the wishes of the Deaf community in a pragmatic aspect, but without success, considering the opinion of three participants belonging to the Brazilian Deaf community.

Given the above, it was possible to observe a difference with the statement that the pragmatic aspect may increase over time [13]. As there may be an abandonment of ATs, the pragmatic aspect has no room to grow or increase. It is not the case, for example, that the AT is difficult to use, but after a while, a user learns how to interact and perform actions. In this case, in addition to the existing difficulties, the main function of the AT is not delivered and is therefore abandoned.

Participants mentioned requirements for the pragmatic and hedonic dimensions. In the pragmatic dimension, they said that the translation needs to consider the semantic diversity of words (they cited the "bank" example: in Portuguese "bank" can be "seat" and "bank"), whereas the AT apparently did not consider this diversity. In the hedonic aspect, the participants would prefer a human avatar, with all the richness of expressions and body movements in communication, instead of a virtual avatar.

Given the above, the question of this qualitative analysis can be answered: how is the interaction of the Deaf using ATs on mobile devices? The participants had many difficulties, like the categories found of "Difficulty of understanding", "Insecurity" and "Dissatisfaction". Also, there were problems directly related to the AT, such as categories of "Inconsistency", "Navigability error", "Repetition of the action" and "Device difference". Furthermore, categories of positive points in the interaction were found, such as "Ease of use". Lastly, the remaining categories are related to characteristics of the participant's interaction with the AT, like the categories of "Exploration of the environment", "Text execution", "Way of using the smartphone" and "Deaf community characteristic".

In general, in contrast to positive aspects, more barriers and problems were found. This is an implication that more solutions must be investigated to minimize these barriers. Problems of navigability error and system inconsistency is related to the Usability perspective. In its turn, Insecurity is an aspect related to the UX perspective. And the Interruptions are related to the Accessibility perspective. So, if a broad perspective of quality aspects is taken, more problems of different types can be found, and more positive aspects of the interaction can be proposed in the AT interaction.

The remaining aspects impact the AT interaction. For example, related to the category of "Way of using the smartphone" one must think that the Deaf use both hands in his communication, the same hands that he uses for interaction with the smartphone. Therefore, in some environments, the user may not have a place to support the smartphone, for example, if it needs to communicate while using the smartphone. These characteristics are an indication that the Deaf community may have its way of interacting with mobile devices.

6 Conclusions

In this paper, we presented a case study to explore the difficulties and positive aspects of Deaf interaction when using Assistive Technology. We did a quantitative and qualitative analysis and we conclude that the difficulties encountered are related to different perspectives of Usability, UX and Accessibility. The difficulties encountered in this study, in addition to the TAs being presented in their second language (Portuguese), are indications of barriers that users may encounter in their daily lives.

Despite the difficulties and additional effort in some cases, all participants were able to carry out the activities proposed in the study. On the one hand, the activities were relatively easy, indicating well-defined operations and related to the main activities within the AT. This is an indication that, at least concerning the Hand Talk app, most Deaf users would be able to perform the task. On the other hand, it was an application that the participants knew but had not knowledge nor had mastery about how to use it, and even with simple activities, errors and barriers appeared. This is also an indication that, due to the apparent difficulties, the Deaf people would not continue with the use of the AT and would keep, about it, memories of incomplete, exhausting or negative experiences, possibly not recommending other Deaf people to use the AT.

In the characterization questionnaire, participants mentioned the use of WhatsApp, some demonstrating using WhatsApp daily. In WhatsApp and other communication apps, several existing metaphors are associated with Hand Talk, such as the keyboard for typing messages and the symbol for sending messages and translating. There are also differences in metaphors, such as the keyboard button in WhatsApp creating a new paragraph and in Hand Talk serving for translation.

The way the user expects the system to work is related to a mental model created by the user. In the case of the Deaf user, there may be a negative mental model about ATs, if other ATs used had not usability, or they had not accessibility features and carried a negative expectation. All participants mentioned that they did not like or not use translation applications, such as Hand Talk. Thus, on the one hand, the interaction with the AT may carry a negative expectation by the Deaf user, who is unsure about the application. On the other hand, there is an opportunity to use metaphors known to the Deaf, based on apps that these users use in their daily lives, making ATs work similarly to the apps that the Deaf use most. However, this use of metaphors must also consider the aspects of Usability, UX and Accessibility.

Usability, for example, could help to solve the difficulties when participants were not able to leave a part of the system, it could provide greater visibility to the text that was written, provide visibility on the functions that disappear, help to deal with inaccurate click errors, among others. Thus, considering these Usability corrections, the ease of use identified in the AT would be enhanced.

However, Usability factors do not seem to be able to account for all the complexity involved in the Deaf interaction with ATs. Negative user experience with AT, as was the case with all participants saying that they do not like or use translation ATs, cannot be treated only with the dimensions of learnability, efficiency, memorability, and errors [21]. The satisfaction dimension, which deals with how pleasurable it is to use the design, comes close to the user's experience, but in a more simplified way, without representing the complexity of experiences and feelings that the user can have to an AT.

About Accessibility, some participants mentioned that the AT translation was not understandable and that its structure was not the same as what a Deaf would translate. Thus, the translation functionality would have to be optimized for the real needs of the Deaf to this aspect of Accessibility. From a positive aspect of Accessibility, providing resources to control speed is something that provides flexibility for the user and greater accessibility to AT. Although users did not mention this aspect, it was observed that this feature of speed control allowed better handling of the translation. The repeat translation button is also a positive aspect of Accessibility, as it provides, without additional effort, more or enough time for users to understand a translation. Finally, in the app's tutorial, was positive the visible focus for the options that were being shown on screen, concentrating the focus on teaching only one resource at a time.

The category "Insecurity" is related to the UX aspect. This problem is related to a sentiment and emotion of the users and can impact ATs abandonment. Pragmatic and hedonic aspects must be balanced, delivering both utility and engaging experiences for the Deaf community.

An initial landscape of AT was defined by identifying all these positive and negative aspects, as well as problems, barriers, and characteristics of Deaf interaction with ATs. It was possible to identify that the problems and barriers affect the AT quality, but this quality can be improved by considering the perspectives of Usability, UX and Accessibility.

References

1. Arhippainen, L.: Capturing user experience for product design. The 26th, pp. 1–10 (2003)
2. Bargas-Avila, J.A., Hornbæk, K.: Old wine in new bottles or novel challenges: a critical analysis of empirical studies of user experience. In: Proceedings of the SIGCHI Conference on Human Factors in Computing Systems, pp. 2689–2698 (2011)
3. Basili, V.R., Rombach, H.D.: The TAME project: towards improvement-oriented software environments. IEEE Trans. Software Eng. **14**(6), 758–773 (1988)
4. Bersch, R.: Introdução à tecnologia assistiva. CEDI, 21, Porto Alegre (2008)

5. Boulares, M., Jemni, M.: Mobile sign language translation system for deaf community. In: Proceedings of the International Cross-Disciplinary Conference on Web Accessibility, pp. 1–4 (2012)
6. Bowe, F.G.: Deaf and hard-of-hearing Americans' IM and e-mail use: a national survey. Am. Ann. Deaf **147**, 6–10 (2002)
7. Brasil: Decreto n° 5296, de 2 de dezembro de 2004. Dispõe sobre as Leis n° 10.048, de 8 de novembro de 2000, en° 10.098, de 19 de dezembro de 2000 e dá outras providências. Diário Oficial [da] República Federativa do Brasil (2004)
8. CAT: Ata da reunião vii, de dezembro de 2007 do comitê de ajudas técnicas. Secretaria Especial dos Direitos Humanos da Presidência da República (CORDE/SEDH/PR) (2007)
9. Felipe, T.A.: Diferentes Políticas e Diferentes Contextos Educacionais: Educação Bilíngue para Educandos Surdos X Educação Bilíngue Inclusiva. Revista Espaço, n. 49 (2018)
10. Fen, W.X., Cheng, W.J.: Using mobile learning way to support learning of the deaf. In: 2nd International Conference on Education Technology and Computer, vol. 2. IEEE (2010)
11. Guimarães, C., Antunes, D.R., García, L.S., Guedes, A.L.P., Fernandes, S.: Conceptual meta-environment for deaf children literacy challenge: how to design effective artifacts for bilingualism construction. In: 2012 Sixth International Conference on Research Challenges in Information Science (RCIS), pp. 1–12. IEEE (2012)
12. Harrison, R., Flood, D., Duce, D.: Usability of mobile applications: literature review and rationale for a new usability model. J. Interact. Sci. **1**(1), 1 (2013). https://doi.org/10.1186/2194-0827-1-1
13. Hassenzahl, M.: The hedonic/pragmatic model of user experience. In: Towards a UX Manifesto, p. 10 (2007)
14. International Organization for Standardization: ISO 25010: Systems and software engineering - square -software product quality requirements and evaluation: system and software quality models. ISO/IEC Standard, 25010 (2011)
15. International Organization for Standardization: ISO 9241-11: Ergonomic requirements for office work with visual display terminals (VDTs): Part 11: Guidance on usability (1998)
16. Lazar, J., Feng, J.H., Hochheiser, H.: Research Methods in Human-Computer Interaction. Morgan Kaufmann, San Francisco (2017)
17. Lee, S.-H.: Users' satisfaction with assistive devices in South Korea. J. Phys. Ther. Sci. **26**(4), 509–512 (2014)
18. Nathan, S.S., Hussain, A., Hashim, N.L.: Studies on deaf mobile application: need for functionalities and requirements. J. Telecommun. Electron. Comput. Eng. (JTEC) **8**(8), 47–50 (2016)
19. Nathan, A., et al.: Flexible electronics: the next ubiquitous platform. In: Proceedings of the IEEE 100. Special Centennial Issue, pp. 1486–1517 (2012)
20. Nielsen, J.: 10 usability heuristics for user interface design. Nielsen Norman Group 1.1 (1995)
21. Nielsen, J.: Usability 101: introduction to usability. Nielsen Norman Group (2012)
22. Power, M.R., Power, D.: Everyone here speaks TXT: deaf people using SMS in Australia and the rest of the world. J. Deaf Stud. Deaf Educ. **9**(3), 333–343 (2004)
23. Scherer, M.J.: Assistive technology: matching device and consumer for successful rehabilitation. American Psychological Association (2002)
24. Shaffiei, Z.A., Aziz, N., Mutalib, A.A., Jaafar, M.S.: Assistive courseware for hearing impaired learners in Malaysia based on theory of multiple intelligences (MI). Int. J. Comput. Sci. Emerg. Technol. **2**(6), 370 (2011)
25. Siebra, C., et al.: Toward accessibility with usability: understanding the requirements of impaired uses in the mobile context. In: Proceedings of the 11th International Conference on Ubiquitous Information Management and Communication. ACM (2017)

26. Stephanidis, C.: The Universal Access Handbook. CRC Press, Boca Raton (2009)
27. Strauss, A., Corbin, J.: Basics of Qualitative Research Techniques. Sage Publications, Thousand Oaks (1998)
28. Vermeeren, A.P., Law, E.L.C., Roto, V., Obrist, M., Hoonhout, J., Väänänen-Vainio-Mattila, K.: User experience evaluation methods: current state and development needs. In: Proceedings of the 6th Nordic Conference on Human-Computer Interaction: Extending Boundaries (2010)
29. Yeratziotis, G., Van Greunen, D.: Making ICT accessible for the deaf. In: IST-Africa Conference & Exhibition. IEEE (2013)
30. Web Accessibility Initiative (WAI): Introduction to Web Accessibility (2006). http://www.w3.org/WAI/intro/accessibility.php
31. Wessels, R., Dijcks, B., Soede, M., Gelderblom, G.J., De Witte, L.: Non-use of provided assistive technology devices, a literature overview. Technol. Disabil. 15(4), 231–238 (2003)
32. Wheatley, M., Pabsch, A.: Sign language legislation in the European Union. European Union of the Deaf (2010)
33. Wohlin, C., Runeson, P., Höst, M., Ohlsson, M.C., Regnell, B., Wesslén, A.: Experimentation in Software Engineering. Springer, Heidelberg (2012). https://doi.org/10.1007/978-3-642-29044-2
34. Zainal, Z.: Case study as a research method. J. Kemanusiaan 5(1), 1–6 (2007)

ArSign: Toward a Mobile Based Arabic Sign Language Translator Using LMC

Slim Kammoun[1,2(✉)], Dawlat Darwish[1], Hanan Althubeany[1],
and Reem Alfull[1]

[1] Information System Department, Taibah University, Medina, Saudi Arabia
{Skammoun,Dawlat,hanan.ther,
Reem-alfull}@taibahu.edu.sa
[2] Research Laboratory of Technologies of Information and Communication
and Electrical Engineering, University of Tunis, Tunis, Tunisia

Abstract. Communication connects people by allowing them to exchange messages, to express their feelings either verbally or non-verbally. To communicate with their surroundings, hearing impaired people or deaf use sign language. Unfortunately, practicing sign language is not common among society witch make barriers between peoples. In this work we propose a new system to convert Arabic sign language from gesture to written text. To do that we propose a system based on three main components: 1) The Leap motion controller as gesture recognition device to capture hand and finger movements. 2) A processing module to convert recognized gesture to alphabet using a comparison algorithm working on a predefined dataset of gesture. 3) A user interface to display the text or to convert it to speech through text to speech engine. The proposed system is implemented as a mobile application running into an android based device.

Keywords: Sign language recognition · Arabic Sign Language · Leap motion · Gesture recognition

1 Introduction

The language is the most essential way of communication and interacting with the society, and it is the only way humans can understand each other and express their feelings in words. According to the World Health Organization, there are around 466 million people worldwide who are deaf, including 34 million children. Studies show that by 2050 the number of people with hearing impairment will increase to more than 900 million people, including genetic causes, complications at birth, some infectious diseases or chronic ear infections. For Deaf community Sign Language (SL) is the most used from many different languages that help hearing impaired individuals to communicate and to be understood by their peers and the rest of the community.

In this paper we will present ArSign for Arabic Sign Language Translator using Leap Motion Controller (LMC) in mobile situation. The proposed system allow to translate sign language produced by hand gestures to a written text to help individuals understanding hearing impaired people without knowing sign language rules and\or specific alphabet. We think that using the Arabic Sign Language (ASL) translator can make deaf interaction more easier and faster.

© Springer Nature Switzerland AG 2020
M. Antona and C. Stephanidis (Eds.): HCII 2020, LNCS 12189, pp. 92–101, 2020.
https://doi.org/10.1007/978-3-030-49108-6_7

The remaining of this paper is organized into three sections. The next one describe background research and the most recent related studies presented into three subsections: Sensors based systems, vision based systems and advance in sign language recognition for Arabic alphabet. Section 3 presents the proposed system and discuss design choices. Conclusion will summarize the presented work and discuss future research directions.

2 Related Works

Sign language is not standardized around the world, some examples of sign languages are American Sign Language (ASL), Arabic Sign Language (ArSL), Greek Sign Language (GSL), or Korean Sign Language (KSL). During the last decades, several research projects have been conducted dealing with sign language recognition. Methods used for recognizing sign language can be classified into two main categories: sensors and vision-based approaches. The sensor-based approach is based on various sensors attached to the hands to capture 3D hand movements and generally relies on gloves. On the other hand, vision-based approaches utilizes one or more visual sensors to track hand movements and analyzes performed gestures based on motion algorithms.

2.1 Sensors Based Approaches

Sensor-based system employs variety of electromechanical devices that are incorporated with many sensors to recognize signs into gloves [1]. In 2018, Ahmed et al. [2] present a review on systems-based sensory gloves for sign language recognition between 2007 and 2017 with more than 20 proposed system such as [3–5]. Glove-based recognition system are composed by three main module (see Fig. 1). Sensors are used to detect finger movements and hand orientation. Preetham et al. [6] proposed a simple gloves with five flex sensors attached to the fingers. The used glove log the finger displacement and translate it to characters. Shukor et al. [27] developed a wearable smart glove using an embedded accelerometer placed on the back of the palm to capture the hand motion and 10 tilt sensors to measure the fingers' motion. This system was tested with American sign language and results reported an average accuracy rate of 89%. [7] designed a new solution based on a microcontroller board with a Bluetooth connection and 5 accelerometer sensors placed in each fingers. An android application connected to the glove have been implemented. The board send recognized hand movement to the android application witch display correspondent worlds. Authors report promising results when evaluating this prototype. Lee et al. [8] in their prototype propose to add pressure sensors in a smart hand device for recognizing American sign language alphabets. The wearable device is composed by 5 flex sensors placed in fingers, a three-axis inertial motion on the back of the palm, and 2 pressure sensors on the middle finger. The fusion of signal provided by flex and pressure sensors showed an improvement in the accuracy rate increasing from 65.7% (with only flex sensors) to 98.2% (with the fusion of signal from flex and pressure sensors). Another recent work presented by [9] for the Indonesian sign language based on an android application. The proposed system is dedicated for hearing impaired peoples. In this system a Bluetooth based glove was developed within an accelerometer mounted on the index finger and five flex sensors mounted in each finger. An Arduino Nano board collect finger movement and through a mapping algorithm identify Indonesian letters from recognized gestures. Preliminary results of the proposed system was interesting, and authors report a very high recognition rate.

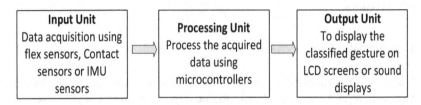

Fig. 1. The main components used by glove-based systems adapted from [2]

In addition to gloves, the Leap Motion Controller (LMC) was also widely used as input sensor for sign language recognition. [10] present a system based two Leap Motion sensors for collecting hand states from different viewing angle. This system allow recognizing digits (0–9). The achieved recognition accuracy using both sensors was 93.14%.

From the above, we can see that sensor based approaches for SLR was widely studied during last decades and results was promising to help researcher in order to propose a more accurate system for SLR.

2.2 Vision Based Approaches

Vision-based systems use cameras as primary tools to obtain the necessary input data. So, it removes the need for sensors in sensory gloves and reduces costs of such systems because cameras less expensive than sophisticated sensors, and become available with most smartphones and laptops. However, using embedded vision present various problems such as high computational costs needed to image processing, the limited and difference field of view according each capturing device and the need for stereo cameras to obtain good results.

Vision based solutions uses monocular or stereo vision to capture the gesture and analyzes the movement with certain motion algorithms [11–13]. Several works were performed in order to translate signs to written text using vision based systems. [14] utilized the Kinect system, which is proposed by Microsoft, to capture the body skeleton and the 3D trajectory of the motion of both hands to recognize word and sentence. Also [15–18] propose to use the kinect as a low coast capture device for vision based systems. [19] have presented a new dynamic Bayesian network model achieving the highest accuracy of 94.6% using a five-state hidden node for 48 ASL signs. Kang et al. [20] used depth sensors to recognize 31 Americans sign language using a convolutional neural network with an accuracy rate from 83.58% to 85.49% obtained without training and for new users.

For the Japanese Sign Language (JSL), More and Sattar [28] propose to use the scale invariance Fourier transform (SIFT) to detect the dynamic hand gestures by searching the matched key points between the input image and images stored in a database. In another work proposed by [21], authors propose to recognize Indian sign language through a webcam. The hand recognized in the image frames is segmented and the state of fingers was used to recognize the alphabet. To do that, the number of fingers fully opened, closed or semi closed and angle made between fingers are used as interesting features for recognition (Fig. 2).

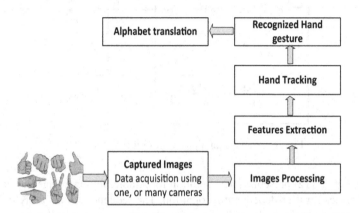

Fig. 2. Processing steps used in vision based sign recognition system adapted from [2]

The effectiveness of vision-based approaches is highly affected by the images processing issues (e.g. image filtering, background cancellation, color segmentation, and boundary detection, etc.). For instance, uncontrolled background images can greatly decrease movement detection. Hence, as presented in this section, several evaluations of vision based systems demonstrate that such system present hand occlusion problems and suffer from confusing gestures recognition.

2.3   Arabic Sign Language Translators

Sign language recognition for Arabic alphabets (see Fig. 3 for Arabic Sign language alphabets) was also studied, both approaches (i.e. Sensors and vision) was also used in order to help deaf people to communicate. A review of recent work in Arabic SLR was presented in [22]. Ibrahim et al. [11] presents SLRS an automatic visual Sign Language Recognition System that translates Arabic words signs into text. The proposed system was composed by four steps: 1) hand segmentation, 2) hand tracking, 3) feature extraction and 4) gesture classification. For hand segmentation, a dynamic skin detector is used. To evaluate the proposed solution, a preliminary evaluation was performed within a dataset of 30 isolated Arabic words. Words were chosen taking into consideration different occlusion states. Experimental results indicate that the proposed system has a recognition rate of 97% in signer-independent mode.

Fig. 3. Arabic sign alphabets as proposed by [23]

El-Jaber et al. [12] presents a new solution for Arabic Sign language gestures using disparity images for user-dependent recognition. The sequences of disparity images are used to segment out the body of the user from a non-stationary background in video based gestures. The spatiotemporal features in the sequence of images are represented in two images by accumulating the prediction errors of consecutive segmented images according to the directionality of motion. The assessment of such methodology is performed by collecting 50 repetitions of 23 gestures from 4 different users using Bumblebee XB3 camera. A classification rate of 96.8%, and an improvement of 62% are reported for the described methodology. This solution is adapted for solving the occlusion states. Hidden Markov Models (HMV) [24] and conventional neural networks [25] was also used in order to improve the recognition rate of gesture for Arabic sign language.

In 2018, a fully labeled dataset of Arabic Sign Language (ArSL) images was implemented [26]. The proposed dataset contain a large number of gesture for all Arabic letters. The authors aim to help researcher to investigate and develop automated systems for the impaired hearing people using sensors based or vision based approaches and deep learning algorithms.

3   The Proposed System

To recognize performed gestures, we use the Leap Motion Controller (LMC) which is 3D non-contact motion sensor which can tracks and detects hands, fingers, bones and finger-like objects. The LMC Application Programming Interface (API) include different features for bones, gestures, hand and fingers. The LMC is placed in front of the user connected to the device throw OTG connector. The overall architecture of the proposed system is presented by Fig. 4 and it consists on three modules, namely, the sensor to capture hand movements, processing to extract the meaning of gestures, and output modules to display or translate the recognized gestures.

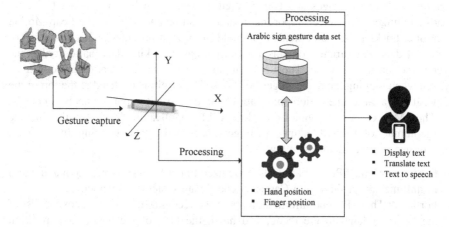

Fig. 4. The overall system architecture

Gestures will be captured through the LMC. The three-axis hand palm position and the five fingertips position will be accurately defined and will be sent to the processing unit. Once gestures recognized, a simple algorithm will perform comparison with a dataset containing 28 Arabic sign language gesture recorded by the user.

3.1 Data Acquisition and Features Extraction

Data acquisition is one of the most important process in such systems. As discussed in the literature review section, we will use a sensor based approach based on the Leap Motion Controller (LMC) to capture hand movements (see Fig. 5).

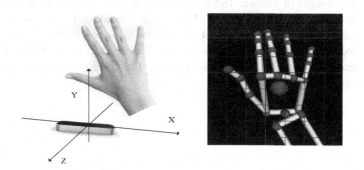

Fig. 5. A hand representation when recognized by the LMC

The LMC is a small USB peripheral device developed by Leap Motion Company[1] and designed to be placed on a physical desktop, facing upward or attach to a head-mounted display for Virtual Reality (VR) applications. The LMC is based three LEDs to capture hand information when it is into his active rang but does not provide any pictures of detected images and two infrared cameras with high precision. It detects hands and fingers like objects reporting discrete position and motion. The Leap Motion Controller tracks fingers and hands in its field of view, it provides updates as a set, or frames of data. Each frame contains a list of the basic tracking data that describes the overall motion in the scene. The LMC employs a right-handed Cartesian coordinate system when logging hand and finger positions. The origin is centered at the top of the LMC. It has a large interaction space above the device with approximately 60 cm.

The LMC company provide a complete API for application developers that include a large number of adapted features for fingers, hand and gesture tracking. In this work we will use some of them as follow:

- For fingers: The API send for each recognized finger his direction, length and width in millimeters, position in a Cartesian coordinate system and velocity.
- For hand: The API send information about the recognized hand as fellow: A list of the fingers related to the recognized hand, the type of the hand, hand position relative to the center point of the palm in millimeters, hand velocity.
- For gestures: Some gesture are already recognized such as for instance a circle gesture when a finger trace a circle in the space. A swipe gesture when linear movement of a finger is detected. A key Tap gesture is recognized if a downward tapping movement by a finger or a tool is performed.

Based on these information we can build a framework to capture hands and fingers movements and understand the meaning of gestures.

3.2   System Implementation

The proposed system is composed by three components as shown in Fig. 4. The first one is the LMC to capture hand and fingers movements. The second a processing module to convert gesture to alphabets based on an algorithm that compare recognized gesture with a dataset of gesture. The third module display recognized alphabets on a screen or through a Text To Speech (TTS) engine. An android based application is implemented for that. As presented by Fig. 6, when the user start the application, the user is asked to connect the LMC through an OTG connector. After that the main interface recognize the hand and begin to write the corresponding text according recognized gestures.

---
[1] https://www.ultraleap.com/product/leap-motion-controller/.

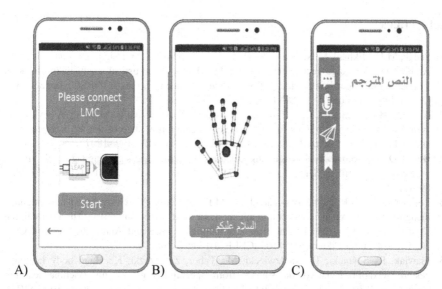

Fig. 6. A) In this interface the user is asked to connect the LMC to start interaction. B) The LMC recognize the hand and finger movements' and translate it into a text. C) The user can save the input text or send it through social media (e.g. Twitter, Facebook, Instagram, etc.) or convert it to a voice mail through a Text To Speech (TTS) engine.

4   Conclusions and Discussion

In this paper a large state of the art was presented for both sensors and vision based approaches for sign language recognition systems. Indeed vision based system suffer from image processing issues such as image filtering, background colors, segmentation, and boundary detection, etc. However researcher tries to overhead these limitation via more sensitive cameras or new image processing algorithms. Consequently, a non-vision based method is an alternative approach.

In this paper, we propose to use Leap Motion Controller within an android based application to convert Arabic sign language to written text. To do that we proposed a system with three independent module to capture gesture, recognize sign and display message. The LMC will be connected to the Smartphone via an USB connector (e.g. OTG adapter). We think that we can recognize 28 letters composing the Arabic alphabet and 10 digits. The proposed solution present a set of functions including Arabic sign recognition, a Text To Speech (TTS) translation using an android based text synthesizer engine and also social media option that allow users to directly share translated text in their social media account.

References

1. Sadek, M.I., Mikhael, M.N., Mansour, H.A.: A new approach for designing a smart glove for Arabic sign language recognition system based on the statistical analysis of the sign language. In: Proceedings of the National Radio Science Conference (NRSC), pp. 380–388 (2017). https://doi.org/10.1109/NRSC.2017.7893499
2. Ahmed, M.A., Zaidan, B.B., Zaidan, A.A., Salih, M.M., Lakulu, M.M.B.: A review on systems-based sensory gloves for sign language recognition state of the art between 2007 and 2017. Sensors (Switzerland) 18 (2018). https://doi.org/10.3390/s18072208
3. Bui, T.D., Nguyen, L.T.: Recognizing postures in Vietnamese sign language with MEMS accelerometers. IEEE Sens. J. 7, 707–712 (2007). https://doi.org/10.1109/JSEN.2007.894132
4. López-Noriega, J.E., Fernández-Valladares, M.I., Uc-Cetina, V.: Glove-based sign language recognition solution to assist communication for deaf users. In: 2014 11th International Conference on Electrical Engineering, Computing Science and Automatic Control, CCE 2014 (2014). https://doi.org/10.1109/ICEEE.2014.6978268
5. Pławiak, P., Sośnicki, T., Niedźwiecki, M., Tabor, Z., Rzecki, K.: Hand body language gesture recognition based on signals from specialized glove and machine learning algorithms. IEEE Trans. Industr. Inf. 12, 1104–1113 (2016). https://doi.org/10.1109/TII.2016.2550528
6. Preetham, C., Ramakrishnan, G., Kumar, S., Tamse, A., Krishnapura, N.: Hand talk-implementation of a gesture recognizing glove. In: Proceedings - 2013 Texas Instruments India Educators' Conference, TIIEC 2013, pp. 328–331 (2013). https://doi.org/10.1109/TIIEC.2013.65
7. Sriram, N., Nithiyanandham, M.: A hand gesture recognition based communication system for silent speakers. In: 2013 International Conference on Human Computer Interactions, ICHCI 2013, pp. 1–5 (2013). https://doi.org/10.1109/ICHCI-IEEE.2013.6887815
8. Lee, B.G., Lee, S.M.: Smart wearable hand device for sign language interpretation system with sensors fusion. IEEE Sens. J. 18, 1224–1232 (2018). https://doi.org/10.1109/JSEN.2017.2779466
9. Haq, E.S., Suwardiyanto, D., Huda, M.: Indonesian sign language recognition application for two-way communication deaf-mute people. In: Proceedings - 2018 3rd International Conference on Information Technology, Information System and Electrical Engineering, ICITISEE 2018, pp. 313–318 (2018). https://doi.org/10.1109/ICITISEE.2018.8720982
10. Fok, K.Y., Ganganath, N., Cheng, C.T., Tse, C.K.: A real-time ASL recognition system using leap motion sensors. In: Proceedings - 2015 International Conference on Cyber-Enabled Distributed Computing and Knowledge Discovery, CyberC 2015, pp. 411–414 (2015). https://doi.org/10.1109/CyberC.2015.81
11. Ibrahim, N.B., Selim, M.M., Zayed, H.H.: An automatic Arabic sign language recognition system (ArSLRS). J. King Saud Univ. Comput. Inf. Sci. 30, 470–477 (2018). https://doi.org/10.1016/j.jksuci.2017.09.007
12. El-Jaber, M., Assaleh, K.: ISMA10-1 ISMA10-2. In: 7th International Symposium on Mechatronics and its Applications, pp. 1–4 (2010)
13. Nikam, A.S., Ambekar, A.G.: Bilingual sign recognition using image based hand gesture technique for hearing and speech impaired people. In: Proceedings - 2nd International Conference on Computing Communication Control and automation, ICCUBEA 2016, pp. 1–6 (2017). https://doi.org/10.1109/ICCUBEA.2016.7860057

14. Lang, S., Block, M., Rojas, R.: Sign language recognition using kinect. In: Rutkowski, L., Korytkowski, M., Scherer, R., Tadeusiewicz, R., Zadeh, L.A., Zurada, J.M. (eds.) ICAISC 2012. LNCS (LNAI), vol. 7267, pp. 394–402. Springer, Heidelberg (2012). https://doi.org/10.1007/978-3-642-29347-4_46

15. Ahmed, M., Idrees, M., Ul Abideen, Z., Mumtaz, R., Khalique, S.: Deaf talk using 3D animated sign language: a sign language interpreter using Microsoft's kinect v2. In: Proceedings of the 2016 SAI Computing Conference, SAI 2016, pp. 330–335 (2016). https://doi.org/10.1109/SAI.2016.7556002

16. Verma, H.V., Aggarwal, E., Chandra, S.: Gesture recognition using kinect for sign language translation. In: 2013 IEEE 2nd International Conference on Image Information Processing, ICIIP 2013, pp. 96–100. IEEE (2013). https://doi.org/10.1109/ICIIP.2013.6707563

17. Unutmaz, B., Karaca, A.C., Güllü, M.K.: Kinect İ skelet ve Evri ş imsel Sinir A ğ ları ile Türkçe İş aret Dili Tanıma Turkish Sign Language Recognition Using Kinect Skeleton and Convolutional Neural Network, pp. 2–5 (2019)

18. Bessa Carneiro, S., De Santos, E.D.F.M., De Barbosa, T.M.A., Ferreira, J.O., Alcalá, S.G.S., Da Rocha, A.F.: Static gestures recognition for Brazilian sign language with kinect sensor. In: Proceedings of the IEEE Sensors (2017). https://doi.org/10.1109/ICSENS.2016.7808522

19. Roh, M.-C., Lee, S.-W.: Human gesture recognition using a simplified dynamic Bayesian network. Multimedia Syst. **21**(6), 557–568 (2014). https://doi.org/10.1007/s00530-014-0414-9

20. Kang, B., Tripathi, S., Nguyen, T.Q.: Real-time sign language fingerspelling recognition using convolutional neural networks from depth map. In: Proceedings - 3rd IAPR Asian Conference on Pattern Recognition, ACPR 2015, pp. 136–140 (2016). https://doi.org/10.1109/ACPR.2015.7486481

21. Shangeetha, R.K., Valliammai, V., Padmavathi, S.: Computer vision based approach for Indian sign language character recognition. In: 2012 International Conference on Machine Vision and Image Processing, MVIP 2012, pp. 181–184 (2012). https://doi.org/10.1109/MVIP.2012.6428790

22. Mohandes, M., Deriche, M., Liu, J.: Image-based and sensor-based approaches to Arabic sign language recognition. IEEE Trans. Hum.-Mach. Syst. **44**, 551–557 (2014). https://doi.org/10.1109/THMS.2014.2318280

23. ZakiAbdo, M., Mahmoud Hamdy, A., Abd El-Rahman Salem, S., Mostafa Saad, E.-S.: Arabic sign language recognition. Int. J. Comput. Appl. **89**, 19–26 (2014). https://doi.org/10.5120/15747-4523

24. Ahmed, A.A., Aly, S.: Appearance-based Arabic sign language recognition using hidden Markov models. In: ICET 2014 – 2nd International Conference on Engineering and Technology (2015). https://doi.org/10.1109/ICEngTechnol.2014.7016804

25. Hayani, S., Benaddy, M., El Meslouhi, O., Kardouchi, M.: Arab Sign language recognition with convolutional neural networks. In: Proceedings of the 2019 International Conference of Computer Science and Renewable Energies, ICCSRE 2019, pp. 1–4 (2019). https://doi.org/10.1109/ICCSRE.2019.8807586

26. Latif, G., Mohammad, N., Alghazo, J., AlKhalaf, R., AlKhalaf, R.: ArASL: Arabic alphabets sign language dataset. Data Brief **23**, 103777 (2019). https://doi.org/10.1016/j.dib.2019.103777

27. Shukor, A.Z., et al.: A new data glove approach for Malaysian sign language detection. Procedia Comput. Sci. **76**, 60–67 (2015).https://doi.org/10.1016/j.procs.2015.12.276

28. More, S.P., Sattar, A.: Hand gesture recognition system using image processing. In:2016 International Conference on Electrical, Electronics, and Optimization Techniques(ICEEOT), Chennai, pp. 671–675 (2016). https://doi.org/10.1109/ICEEOT.2016.7754766

Digital Accessibility in the Education of the Deaf in Greece

Vassilis Kourbetis[1]([⊠]), Spyridoula Karipi[2],
and Konstantinos Boukouras[3]

[1] Ministry of Education and Religious Affairs, Athens, Greece
vkourmpetis@minedu.gov.gr
[2] University of Western Macedonia, Florina, Greece
skaripi78@gmail.com
[3] Institute of Educational Policy, Athens, Greece
kboukouras@iep.edu.gr

Abstract. This article begins with an introduction to the digital accessibility as a human right followed by the presentation of the educational needs of deaf children and the challenge to fight the linguistic and cultural deprivation they are faced with. We present the project "Universal Design and Development of Accessible Digital Educational Material" and the steps and procedures for development and production of our open accessible digital educational materials for deaf students. We present the Digital Multimedia Library, the Online Dictionary, the multimedia accessible e-Books in detail within the bilingual context, the Curriculum-based Assessment instruments and the newly developed application for testing expressive sign language skills. The initial results from the implementation of these ongoing research and development project, suggest that our project is cohesive and successful pedagogical practice for accessible bilingual education and for learning of deaf children in Greece with great possibilities to be applied in any Signed Language of the world. We conclude that the use of interactive accessible digital material supports the documentation, development and use of GSL and provides deaf students a communicative tool that helps prevent linguistic and cultural deprivation.

Keywords: Open educational resources · Digital accessibility · Greek sign language · Universal Design · Multimedia bilingual e-Books

1 Introduction

Digital accessibility in the education of the Deaf in Greece, as it is in countries all over the world, has been a challenge for educators, the assistive technology sector, governments, and world organizations [1]. Accessibility is a human rights issue that the United Nations has addressed. The United Nations Convention on the Rights of Persons with Disabilities (CRPD) [2] established that accessibility is a prerequisite to enjoying the rest of the rights enshrined in the Convention.

The CRPD, the first international treaty that explicitly mentions sign language, is a human rights instrument with great importance for deaf people. Article 24 (Education) (3b), mandates that State Parties shall *"Facilitat[e] the learning of sign language and the promotion of the linguistic identity of the deaf community."*

© Springer Nature Switzerland AG 2020
M. Antona and C. Stephanidis (Eds.): HCII 2020, LNCS 12189, pp. 102–119, 2020.
https://doi.org/10.1007/978-3-030-49108-6_8

The 2030 agenda for the sustainable development of the United Nations [3] is a broad and universal policy with broad principles and commitments. These commitments include providing access to a quality education, fostering a sense of inclusion and equality, and creating the opportunity for lifelong learning.

The principles of the Universal Design for Learning (UDL) [4] should be accessible to all students [5]. Educational systems must provide each student with the opportunity to evolve using individually tailored methodologies, tools, and materials [6].

A recent study that systematically reviewed 31 relevant papers provided insights about accessibility and functional diversity within open educational resources [7]. The study concluded that only nine (9) countries (Ecuador, Spain, UK, Greece, Ireland, Turkey, Uruguay, Tunisia, and Italy, in order of published papers per country) were involved in the investigation of the use of Open Educational Resources (OER) and Open Educational Practices (OEP) for accessible learning.

2 Deaf Children and Educational Challenges

Over 90% of deaf children in Greece are born to hearing parents who do not know or use a natural Sign Language (SL). This phenomenon is not unique to Greece. Thus, the majority of deaf children in the world have little to no receptive experience with any language. Deaf children's lack of exposure to an accessible SL impacts language fluency and proficiency throughout their lives [8–11].

In most cases, deaf children lack exposure and access to a natural language in early childhood until they come in contact with other deaf children through sign language in school [8, 12–14] among others). It has been shown that delayed exposure to a first language in childhood affects all subsequent language acquisition in all modalities [14, 15].

International studies demonstrate that academic progress, in addition to social and emotional growth, in deaf children is directly related to the acquisition of sign language as a first language. Furthermore, empirical findings on the acquisition of sign languages by deaf children of deaf parents who learn a sign language naturally have been shown to follow the same developmental path as hearing children learning spoken languages [8, 9, 16–20].

Theoretical and practical findings alike demonstrate that early exposure to SL through proper teaching techniques improves deaf children's written literacy [8, 16, 18, 21, 22].

The work of Mirus and Napoli [23] noted the effectiveness of using Bimodal-Bilingual eBooks for both deaf children and hearing adults. Specifically, they stressed the increasing need for bimodal-bilingual eBooks for pleasure—to develop pre-literacy skills—and the need for pedagogical eBooks designed specifically for acquiring academic knowledge. Mirus and Napoli [23] concluded by acknowledging the unfortunate shortage of such eBooks.

For deaf students, technological solutions can be particularly effective for enhancing learning in many subject areas, such as language development and literacy, world knowledge, and communication [24–27]. ICT facilitates deaf students' access to communication, interaction, and information because it presents information visually. A visual approach is most effective for deaf students because they rely on sight alone to develop language and thought. Deaf students comprehend the world through sight [9, 28]. Consequently, we take advantage of ICT by presenting information via Signed Language, which allows deaf students to visually access the data that already exists in written form. Employing this technique makes academic content fully accessible to deaf students. The next section discusses the creation of teaching and assessment materials that will deliver previously inaccessible content to deaf students.

3   The Universal Design Project

In the context of the project "Universal Design and Development of Accessible Digital Educational Material," bearing the acronym "Prosvasimo," we will present the instructional materials (e.g., creating, adopting, and adapting teaching materials) that we developed for the last five years in Greece. The final products of Prosvasimo are, first, Open Educational Resources and, second, resources for students with various disabilities that attend mainstream schools. All material is publicly available on project's site: http://prosvasimo.iep.edu.gr/el/.

The development and production of our open digital, educational materials for deaf students follow the basic accessibility technological requirements proposed by Kouroupetroglou [29]. Since that study, Zhang et al. [7] also have recommended four accessibility attributes that researchers should focus on when providing Open Educational Resources (OER):

Perceivable Content: Information should be presented to users in modalities they can perceive—in Greek Sign Language, in written Greek, or in a natural voice (for deaf children that can perceive information acoustically with the sound amplification devices). We use professional narrators who are native Greek speakers, instead of the recommended Automated Reading Devices (ARD) or Text-to-Speech systems [29], which are too expensive and time consuming to meet the receptive needs of hard of hearing students.

Operable Platform and Software: The interface components, navigation, browsing and searching require simple interaction that deaf children can easily perform.
Understandable Content: Content should be fully understandable and tested with curriculum-based assessments. The levels of content must be differentiated to meet the needs of all language users.

Robust Content: The material should be complete from Kindergarten through Fifth Grade, along with five additional levels of content teaching GSL as a first language. All interfaces should be interrelated, open, and accessible to a wide variety of users, including parents and teachers.

In the present article, due to size limitations, we will focus on only materials designed for bilingual education of deaf children with the use of sign language. Specifically, we will present 1) the interactive Digital Multimedia Library, 2) the Open Online Sign Language Dictionary, 3) the fully Accessible, Multimodal e-Books for bilingual instruction, and 4) the Curriculum-Based Sign Language Assessment instruments.

4   Methodology

The methodology for the development and production of our open, accessible digital educational materials for deaf students is presented in accordance with the four steps and procedures proposed by Ruemer, Kouroupetroglou, Murillo-Morales, and Miesenberger [30]: the source, the conversion, the presentation, and the workflow, in addition to the evaluation of the end result by teachers.

4.1   The Source

The source of our academic content (Modern Greek, Greek literature, History, Math, Social-Environmental studies and Religion affairs) is the official printed textbooks used in general education developed by the Department of Education from K - 12. The source consists of 43 books with a total of 4601 pages making it the largest accessible digital educational materials ever produced in Greece for the education of deaf students.

The source of Greek Sign Language as a first language is developed by the first author and Marianna Hatzopoulou (4th Grade). It covers, so far, five levels (grades K-4th).

4.2   The Conversion

All printed source materials are available in PDF or enriched HTML format at the official website of the Publishing House of the Department of Education "ITYE Dio-fantos" http://ebooks.edu.gr/new/allmaterial.php. All content of the text books is divided into meaningful units from a word level (single vocabulary items or terms) to a sentence level for voicing, presenting in GSL, and for integrating interactive subtitles.

The materials for teaching GSL as a first language are transcribed using simple GLOSSING and written Greek. Glossing is a transcription system of signs in a written form that uses capital letters (and other indicators of pointing signs, classifiers etc.) for writing the meaning of each sign in order of appearance following GSL syntax [31]. We follow the same methodology for the fairytales, oral stories, and picture stories.

4.3   The Presentation

The procedure of the presentation of the sources in GSL is the most innovative, expensive, time-consuming, and demanding part of the production. We used only native signers when developing our digital material [8] of all GSL data, interactive signed stories, signed lexical items, and signed assessment tools. Native signers come in two forms. First, they can be Deaf adults that have Deaf parents and learned GSL as a first language. Second, they can also be Deaf adults that learned GSL as a first language at a residential school for the Deaf, are active members of the Deaf Community, and/or teach GSL as a first or second language. In all production processes native signers collaborated with professional GSL interpreters and active members of the Deaf Community.

4.4 The Workflow

The efficient production of accessible educational materials involves management of human, financial, and technical resources to deliver robust and understandable content that will be used in an operable platform and/or software. This was a significant challenge.

4.5 The Evaluation

Two groups of teachers of the Deaf (fifty-one in total) evaluated the effectiveness of the applications we developed. The first group was comprised of twenty-three (23) teachers of the Deaf in five (5) day schools of the Deaf (K - 12). These teachers completed the assessments after school. The second group was comprised of twenty-eight (28) teachers in twenty one (21) inclusive educational setting serving deaf children. This group completed a seven-section online quantitative and qualitative evaluation.

Most participants (44) were female, and most participants (40) were hearing. Thirty-two (32) evaluators were below forty years old and nineteen (19) were above forty years old. The majority of the participants work on the mainland (46); only five work on the islands.

The methodology and the tools used to develop the applications are presented in each separately due to the unique character of each tools used.

5 Open Accessible Applications

In this section we will present the Digital Multimedia Library, the Online Dictionary, the Curriculum-based Assessment instruments, the newly-developed application for testing expressive sign language skills, and, finally, the e-books that cover the educational needs of deaf children in Greece. We have been developing and refining these projects since 2010. All of the digital material is designed to meet the needs of learners who use Sign Language as a first language (L1) or as a second language (L2).

5.1 The Digital Multimedia Library (DML)

The Digital Multimedia Library (DML) for bilingual education (SL and Print) is a platform for teaching signed language as a school subject and also general content teaching, such as Written Greek Literature (Fig. 1). (http://multimedia-library.prosvasimo.gr/DZ/player/E). The DML is based on the pan.do/ra platform (http://pan.do/ra) and the javascript OxJS library (https://oxjs.org/#doc) and is implemented, using the PostgreSQL database. The Digital Multimedia Library is installed in Ubuntu OS 14.04 LTS 64 bit, runs on nginx web server and is able to accept various video formats (.mp4, .webm, .mpeg) all of which are easily converted into .webm format during the uploading. The signed stories can be viewed in many different ways to meet the pedagogical and communicative needs of the users.

Fig. 1. Partial display of Written Greek Literature content in the DML

The Digital Multimedia Library (DML) for bilingual education (SL and Print) (Fig. 1) is an independent platform that contains signed stories from the digital e-Books. It is continuously updated with newly-developed content (http://multimedia-library.prosvasimo.gr/DZ/player/E).

The DML does not allow the user to upload videos of their own. The administrator of the project can upload such videos if she chooses. Video downloading is available to anyone through the platform's web graphical interface. The interactive video subtitles are generated automatically using the graphical interface or by uploading subtitle files (.srt files) using the platform's video upload interface.

The Digital Library includes signed stories ranging from 38 s to 35 min in length. A GSL corpus of more than forty-thousand signed videos has been constructed and is open to all, making it the largest trove for GSL available. Part of the open data has been used for a PhD thesis at the University of Western Macedonia, Kozani, Greece, and for developing sign language applications in a European funded research project "aRTI-FICIAL iNTELLIGENCE for the Deaf" (https://aideaf.eu/) at the University of Technology, Limassol, Cyprus.

This multisensory (visual: SL & print, plus audio: spoken translation) approach may be used in a bilingual environment to motivate students. An increase in motivation will result in an increase in their participation in classrooms; as information becomes more accessible, students will better comprehend the material. These applications support teaching and learning GSL (L1) and written Greek (L2) [8, 19, 22, 31].

The signed stories can be viewed in many different ways to meet the pedagogical needs of the users. Users are able to sort the video clips by title, program name, subtitle number, duration, resolution, video size, etc. An example will be illustrative. Students can choose to view video clips like they would view a story, or they can view it as a grid that displays the video as a cover page (like a book cover) along with screenshots of individual frames (Fig. 1), with a visual time line presenting the duration of the video under the video window (Fig. 2, D). All these display modes are depicted in the drop-down menu.

The videos can also be viewed in various resolutions, from a low resolution of 240p to a high resolution of 1080p (high definition), to meet the hardware needs or preferences of the user.

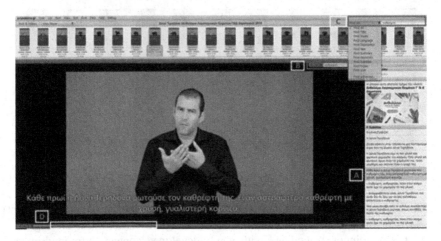

Fig. 2. Playback of educational material with interactive video subtitles. *Note.* Sections: A. Browse video using subtitles, B. Search in subtitles of the video being played, C. Search in subtitles in all of the videos of the platform, D. Visual presentation of the timeline of the video

The interactive subtitles are a useful tool that allows the user to browse the video by searching for various words (see Fig. 2, Section A). The user is able to search for words and phrases included in the subtitles. When a phrase is selected, a signed playback of the segment identified will occur in the large window on the left of the screen (Fig. 2, Section B).

The total number of search results are tabulated and may also be displayed (Fig. 2, Section B). It is also possible for users to search subtitle content within and across all videos (Fig. 2, Section C) of the platform. In the timeline (Fig. 2, Section D), it shows at what times the signed word appears in the video. Clicking the highlighted areas of the timeline moves the video to the corresponding scene.

The platform features an advanced search engine, which allows the user to search for words (transcribed signs) or phrases across the entire platform, so the user can view and compare all the available video clips matching the searched word or phrase. This is a useful tool for students, teachers, and parents with varying sign language skills. Users can download the presented videos in a WebM format, which is not space demanding, using direct download or torrent software.

Another feature is the ability to identify and save the URL address of the video as it is being played in a specific time range. For example, if someone is interested in a specific portion of a video, they can copy the URL of that specific segment. The URL address of the video (with or without subtitles), in its entirety (or merely a segment) can be saved and later used for homework assignments, for self-evaluation, or for formal assessment or research.

The videos are stored and played on a local server and do not depend on a central video service like YouTube. The entire application can be installed in traditional schools, in locations which do not have internet access but have computing units (with good processing power and storage options), or in schools whose computers are connected to a local area network.

The innovative search engine used for the development of the DML enables the user to search for a signed segment in the digital sign language database, something that until recently was impossible in the language training of deaf students [31]. The DML is also linked to the Open Online Dictionary, which we turn to now.

5.2 The Open Online Dictionary

The Open Online Dictionary is the largest fully-accessible, interactive online dictionary for Greek Sign Language. It contains more than 3,500 signed lexical entries (lemmas), sorted into 38 categories. It also includes 1,815 phrases and sentences categorized according to the 5 types of sentences: questions, statements, negation, simple, and conjoined. It is enriched with content from educational material that is currently being developed by project "Prosvasimo", which makes textbooks accessible with the use of Greek Sin Language.

There are presently two existing online dictionaries for sign language (http://lexiko. sign1st.eu/ and http://prosvasimo.iep.edu.gr/el/onlne-lexiko-ennoiwn). After completion of the debugging process the two dictionaries will merged into one Uniform Resource Locator (URL) under the auspices of the Institute of Educational Policy: http://prosvasimo.iep.edu.gr/dblexiko/.

The new database will include signs from native signers or from other available signed sources. The signs will be presented in different styles to account for regional variations (Fig. 3). The user is able to search for Greek words or phrases in the database (GSL Lexicon) using several filters and selections from display menus (see Fig. 3, left).

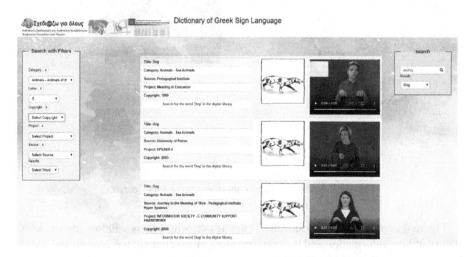

Fig. 3. A search for the word – sign "DOG" in the dictionary.

Lexical items can be identified by alphabetic search, by the source of the GSL data, or by a scroll down list. To search using Signed Language properties, one will search by handshape or by location of the signs, a feature currently under development.

Because students can not learn a language from a dictionary, which presents words out of context, our main goal has been to connect the dictionary to the Digital Multimedia Library (DML). Connecting the dictionaries database to the DML permits students to access signs in meaningful contexts. All GSL content in the DML and the GSL Lexicon is drawn from native signers, providing access to more meaningful and useful content. This visual presentation of information is now accessible for the many deaf children who have limited access to native signed languages.

An example will be useful: A search in the dictionary for the word/sign "DOG" is presented in Fig. 3. The results show that there are three variations of the sign for "DOG." The signs are signed by different signers, which allows deaf students to view variations of signs used by the Deaf community of Greece. In addition, if someone wants more context, she can also search the DML. The DML search will locate signed stories that contain the sign for "DOG." The dictionary and DML were tested in three schools for the Deaf in Greece. Professionals who participated in the beta testing reported that the DL search functionality was found to be a valuable teaching tool.

The GSL Lexicon contains 1,815 phrases, which are categorized by their type (e.g., question, negation, or statement), their content, (e.g., Wh-YES/NO questions) and their structure (Simple or Conjoined). When the user selects a type of phrase from the menu available (Fig. 4), the remaining filters are, by default, available. The search results are shown at the bottom of the search column.

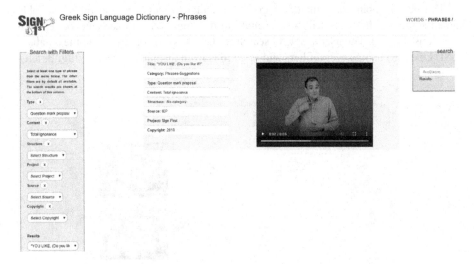

Fig. 4. Results for Yes/No question phrase type search.

Figure 4 depicts three components: 1) the Search with Filters window (on the left), 2) the resulting information and the corresponding video clips (in the center), and 3) the Text Search window (on the right).

In addition to searching by category, users can search the database by typing a single word in the Text Search window (on the right).

5.3 The Multimodal Accessible e-Books

The multimedia form of the accessible e-books (either in the form of a single copy or a web application) combines the presentation of the original printed book in GSL, the text in subtitles underneath the videotaped presentation in the GSL video, and the voice translation of the text.

Recent technology used by the Masaryk University known as "Hybrid Book" [32] was used for the creation of study materials aimed at users with different disabilities. We also followed the proposed system for delivery of accessible e-Books by Pino, Kouroupetroglou and Riga [33] to create e-Books for deaf students. The format we created was developed following the text of the national curriculum textbooks. The electronic form of the e-Books (either in the form of a single copy or a web application) combines the presentation of the original printed book in GSL, the text in subtitles underneath the videotaped presentation in the GSL video, and the voice translation of the text. The components of this app are presented in Fig. 5. The multimedia data are shown in PDF, video, and audio files, and are now available as independent files for other uses.

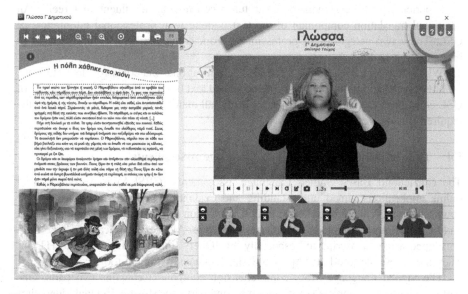

Fig. 5. Screen from a Multimodal Accessible e-Book book (Modern Greek, 3rd grade) whose accessible interface presents the text with the use of Greek Sign Language. There are three separate sections: A. The video window (Upper right corner), B. The boxes of individual frame captures of video clips (Lower right corner), and C. The story as it appears in the printed text book (Left part of the screen).

Our application allows students to view the GSL translation either continuously or in parts.

The user is able to view the story at different speeds, in full screen mode or in reduced screen size, and with or without subtitles (Fig. 5, Section A). But most importantly (educationally), the user is able to take snapshots (still frames) of the signed videos. The user can use the snapshots alone or can connect the still frame to text, (Fig. 5, Section B). The user can then print them and/or develop tests, homework, or presentation with them.

The end result of this application entails creating textbooks to be used in the first four grades of elementary school. The textbooks will feature written, spoken, and signed Greek. Emphasis was placed on the relationship between the printed and signed concept. Accessibility critically depends on the quality of the text in GSL. The translation of a printed text in GSL can closely parallel the original content or may be more flexible to reflect an adaptation. Using the National curriculum textbooks, the native signers either focus on content comprehension or on learning vocabulary, Modern Greek grammar, or the acquisition of phonological awareness.

If the objective is to understand the meaning of the text, then the Deaf native signers will not follow the text word for word, as that would severely inhibit comprehension. If the objective is to foster grammatical skill or phonological awareness, then interpretation mostly follows the original source. It is clear that signing Greek texts is an extremely demanding and difficult task [26]. The signing of the texts is done by experienced native signers or Deaf tutors/consultants (all fluent in Greek). An additional translation component of the text is done with professional interpreters of GSL. These two categories of professionals work collaboratively to form a team of bilingual translators.

While converting textbooks to accessible educational materials for deaf students, we have placed additional emphasis on the signed text because the efficient, clear use of GSL constitutes the core of the project. Finally, all material developed aim to fulfil the requirements of Design-for-All.

5.4   The Curriculum Based Signed Language Assessments

The Curriculum Based Signed Language assessments (CBSLA) is a collection of online applications aimed understanding and evaluating of Signed Language story comprehension skills (Examples are in GSL), question formation in GSL, phonological and syntactic structures, and vocabulary knowledge. All these applications have been developed using Javascript and especially the JQuery library, PHP, CSS and HTML. They are accessible to all at: http://www.sign1st.eu/en/assesment-tools/.

The Signed Language Story comprehension component contains two parts. One part is a video of a complete story and the second part consists of individual video clips of the story selected from the full video. Two rows of up to eight (8) individual clips of a story are contained in this application (Fig. 6). In the first row, the video clips of a signed language story are presented in a random order. The second row contains empty boxes. Two approaches may be implemented. First, the user can start by viewing the full story (by clicking the box on the upper left corner) and then work to arrange the story sequence clips in the correct order. Second, the user can begin with the story sequence clips and put them in the order they think is correct.

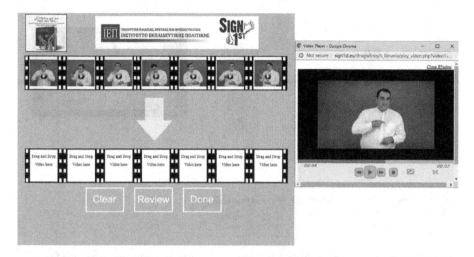

Fig. 6. Interactive application of sign language story comprehension "The Punishment" ("I Tomoria")

The video clips are presented in a sequence that may not make sense or flow correctly. The user watches the individual video clips in the first row. When the user decides on the flow of the story, they drag and drop the videos into the empty boxes in the second row. The user then examines the clips to decide if the sequence is appropriate. The expectation is that the student will rearrange the individual clips into the correct sequence of the story by dragging them into the boxes in the second row. At any point they can click "Review" and watch the videos in the sequence they have chosen. If the user is not satisfied, they can drag and drop the videos again and place them in another position. When satisfied, they click "Done." When the "Done" box is clicked, the application evaluates the user's choices. If all the choices are correct, then the user sees a positive message. If the sequence is not correct, then the user is referred back to the initial page. The user is then prompted to rearrange the videos in the correct order. If the correct sequence is created this time, a positive message occurs; if another incorrect sequence is submitted, the student will repeat the exercise until they find the correct sequence of videos.

After implementing these applications in two schools for the Deaf, we concluded that this design helps students by positively reinforcing their correct choices, minimizing their frustration, enhancing their memory, and, most importantly, supporting their story sequence skills. The application presented here is for Greek Sign Language Stories. However, it can easily be adapted to other signed languages as well. The application is able to connect and retrieve stories from a database using any Signed Language story as a template.

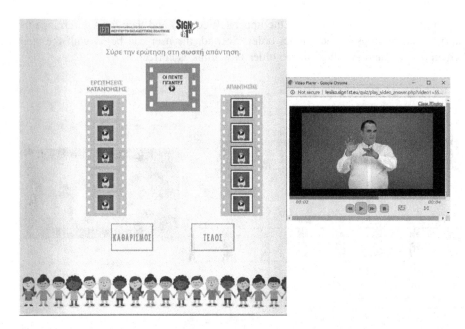

Fig. 7. Sign language video evaluation test matching questions – answers "The Five Giants".

Two columns of videos and a story window are depicted in Fig. 7. The column on the left contains questions from the story. After watching a signed video of the story, the user matches the videos with the questions in the left column by selecting the correct answer box in the right column. The example shown in Fig. 7 is for the Greek sign language story *"The Five Giants"* "Oi Pente Gigantes". This application can easily be adapted to other Signed Languages as well.

This playful test is an informal, child-centered activity that can help teachers collect evidence of story comprehension. This information can then, in turn, be used to structure teaching strategies, develop individualized educational plans, and produce reports. We found that students greatly enjoyed interacting with this application. All of the above assessment instruments are receptive. Expressive assessment instruments in web-based or stand-alone applications are challenging to develop. We will next present our first Expressive Sign Language Test application in detail.

5.5   The Expressive Sign Language Test Application

Despite the need for sign language fluency tests, there are presently no standard measures of SL competency readily available. Most instruments are available via only the authors [34, 35]. Recognizing this need, we have developed the Expressive Sign Language Test application. This application was designed by the second author for data collection for her PhD thesis. The third author developed the application. All authors collaborated in all stages of development.

This online, interactive application has been developed using PHP, CSS and Javascript. It is a test where the students are asked to find the question of an answer and express it using sign language. The student is able to record the answer using her computer camera and the recorded video starts to play automatically when the recording ends. This allows the student to quickly check her response and correct it, if needed. The recorded video is available for download in HTML5 (webm) format. No special setup is needed, the application starts to record as soon as the record button is pressed. The recording application has been developed using the WebRTC Javascript library. It is an open source library which has been developed and supported by Google, Mozilla and Opera and provides browsers and mobile applications with Real-Time Communications (RTC) capabilities via simple Application Programming Interfaces. In order to correctly operate it requires a web server with PHP version 7 enabled.

Fig. 8. The Expressive Sign Language Test application. Illustrations used with permission of Super Duper Publications, www.superduperinc.com.

The four visible interactive response features (Fig. 8) of the application are:

1. (Upper left corner) A signed video containing the test instructions
2. (Lower left corner) The statement part of the Phrase ("When I am sick," in a picture and in a video recorded in sign language)
3. (Lower right corner) The answer part of the phrase ("the Doctor" in a picture and in a video recorded in sign language)
4. (Upper right corner) The window for video recording the participant's responses. (Expected answer: Where do you go when you are sick?)

The current test has 25 items, but there is no limit to how many items the test can have. The application can be and will be developed for all types of expressive sign language data collection. The video recording can offer the user the possibility to view her answer, and, if need be, she can change it and record another one. The administrator can have immediate access to the results without any additional recording devices. This allows the application to be self-administered. Alternatively, the application can be used with a test-administrator. Participant responses can either be saved on a designated folder on a computer or on a secure server to be evaluated.

6 Results

The initial results from the implementation of this project suggest that it is a cohesive and successful pedagogical method for teaching the grammatical structures of GSL as an L1. We believe this holistic approach to be effective in the bilingual, bicultural education of deaf children [9]. Learning about the grammar and increasing vocabulary knowledge in GSL will support learning written Greek as an L2 [10].

Access to curricula and materials for teaching GSL as an L1, as reported by teachers themselves, has helped teachers who are not proficient in SL in four critical ways: 1) by providing teachers with all of the fully accessible visual materials—especially pre-recorded video narratives by native signers, 2) by providing interactive and accessible curriculum-based assessment material in both GSL and printed Greek, 3) by providing teachers with access to video narratives by native signers to improve their learning of GSL in a supportive way, and 4) by providing them with curriculum-based assessment essential for their teaching practices.

The deliverables of the project presented are perceivable and meet the receptive and expressive linguistic and educational needs of deaf and hard of hearing students, are stored in an operable platform and software for deaf children, have a fully understandable content and include a robust content that meets the educational needs of deaf children up to 4th grade.

The main request of most teachers was the need for continues training and support ether by in school training or online distant learning.

7 Conclusions

The benefits of the presented applications are numerous; they apply to students, teachers, and parents alike. If these projects are implemented, deaf students will have the opportunity to acquire knowledge and information at a much earlier age. The use of interactive, digital material supports the documentation, development, and use of GSL. Finally, and most importantly, these resources provide deaf students with a communicative tool that helps prevent linguistic and cultural deprivation.

The development of accessible interfaces in digital resources for bilingual education of deaf students using information technology offers solutions to support deaf students' learning to the maximum. We argue that using digital, open and accessible resources will enhance inclusive, effective and accessible learning in a bilingual education of deaf environment. Training of educators of the deaf remains a challenge. We are in the proses of developing and we will soon present Massive Open Online Courses (MOOCs) (www.iepX.gr) based on the Open Edx platform of Harvard and MIT (www.edx.org) to tackle this challenge.

Credits, Acknowledgments. This work is co-financed: By Greece and the European Union (European Social Fund - ESF) through the Operational Program "Human Resources Development, Education and Lifelong Learning 2014-2020" in the context of the project "Universal Design and Development of Accessible Digital Educational Material" bearing the Acronym title "Prosvasimo" and code number MIS 5001313.

By the European Programme Erasmus+, KA2 – Cooperation for Innovation and the Exchange of Good Practices, Strategic Partnerships for school education, in the context of the project "Teaching European Sign Languages as a First Language" bearing the Acronym title "Sign First" and code number 2016-1-EL01-KA201-023513. The State Scholarship Foundations (IKY) is the National Agency of the Erasmus+ Programme.

We like to thank Janey Greenwald and John Czubek for their valuable comments, suggestions and proof reading.

References

1. WDR. https://www.worldbank.org/en/publication/wdr2016. Accessed 24 Oct 2019
2. Convention on the Rights of Persons with Disabilities Homepage. http://www.refworld.org/docid/45f973632.html. Accessed 24 Oct 2019
3. United Nations, Transforming our world: The 2030 agenda for sustainable development. https://www.un.org/ga/search/view_doc.asp?symbol=A/RES/70/1&Lang=E. Accessed 12 Dec 2019
4. CAST: Universal Design for Learning Guidelines (version 2.0). Author, Wakefield, MA (2011)
5. Izzo, M., Bauer, W.: Universal design for learning: enhancing achievement and employment of STEM students with disabilities. Univ. Access Inf. Soc. **14**(1), 17–27 (2015)
6. Tomlinson, C.: How to Differentiate Instruction in Mixed-Ability Classrooms, 2nd edn. Association for Supervision and Curriculum Development (ASCD), Alexandria (2001)
7. Zhang, X., et al.: Accessibility within open educational resources and practices for disabled learners: a systematic literature review. Smart Learn. Environ. **7**(1), 1–19 (2020). https://doi.org/10.1186/s40561-019-0113-2
8. Hoffmeister, R., Caldwell-Harris, C.: Acquiring English as a second language via print: the task for deaf children. Cognition **132**(2), 229–242 (2014). https://doi.org/10.1016/j.cognition.2014.03.014
9. Kourbetis, V., Hatzopoulou, M.: Mporó kai me ta mátia mou, [I can do it with my eyes as well, In Greek]. Kastaniotis Editions, Athens (2010)
10. Morford, J., Hänel-Faulhaber, B.: Homesigners as late learners: connecting the dots from delayed acquisition in childhood to sign language processing in adulthood. Lang. Linguist. Compass **5**(8), 525–537 (2011)
11. Woll, B., Ladd, P.: Deaf communities. In: Marschark, M., Spencer, P. (eds.) Oxford Handbook of Deaf Studies, Language, and Education, pp. 151–163. Oxford University Press, New York (2003)
12. Lane, H., Hoffmeister, R., Bahan, B.: A Journey into the Deaf-World. Dawn Sign Press, San Diego (1996)

13. Mayberry, R.: First-language acquisition after childhood differs from second-language acquisition: the case of American Sign Language. J. Speech Hear. Res. **36**(6), 1258–1270 (1994)
14. Mayberry, R., Lock, E.: Age constraints on first versus second language acquisition: evidence for linguistic plasticity and epigenesis. Brain Lang. **87**(3), 369–384 (2003)
15. Boudreault, P., Mayberry, R.: Grammatical processing in American Sign Language: Age of first-language acquisition effects in relation to syntactic structure. Lang. Cognitive Process. **21**(5), 608–635 (2007)
16. Hatzopoulou, M.: Acquisition of Reference to Self and Others in Greek Sign Language. From Pointing Gesture to Pronominal Pointing Signs. Stockholm University, Stockholm (2008)
17. Hoffmeister, R.: A piece of the puzzle: ASL and reading comprehension in deaf children. In: Chamberlain, C., Morford, J., Mayberry, R. (eds.) Language acquisition by eye, pp. 143–163. Lawrence Erlbaum Associates, Mahwah (2000)
18. Hrastinski, I., Wilbur, R.: Academic achievement of deaf and hard-of-hearing students in an ASL/English Bilingual Program. J. Deaf Stud. Deaf Educ. **21**(2), 156–170 (2016). https://doi.org/10.1093/deafed/env072
19. Niederberger, N.: Does the knowledge of a natural sign language facilitate deaf children's learning to read and write? Insights from French Sign Language and written French data. In: Plaza-Pust, C., Morales-Lopeze, E. (eds.) Sign Bilingualism. John Benjamins Publishing Company, Philadelphia (2008)
20. Woll, B.: The development of signed and spoken language. In: Gregory, S., Knight, P., McCracken, W., Powers, S., Watson, L. (eds.) Issues in Deaf Education, pp. 58–69. Fulton, London (1998)
21. Albertini, J.A., Schley, S.: Writing: characteristics, instruction, and assessment. In: Marschark, M., Spencer, P. (eds.) Oxford Handbook of Deaf Studies, Language, and Education, pp. 123–135. Oxford University Press, New York (2003)
22. Scott, J., Hoffmeister, R.: American Sign Language and Academic English: factors influencing the reading of bilingual secondary school deaf and hard of hearing students. J. Deaf Stud. Deaf Educ. **22**(1), 59–71 (2017). https://doi.org/10.1093/deafed/enw065
23. Mirus, G., Napoli, D.J.: Developing language and (pre)literacy skills in deaf preschoolers through shared reading activities with bimodal-bilingual eBooks. J. Multilingual Educ. Res. **8**(1), 75–110 (2018)
24. Burnett, C.: Technology and literacy in early childhood educational settings: a review of research. J. Early Child. Lit. **10**(3), 247–270 (2010)
25. Gentry, M., Chinn, K., Moulton, R.: Effectiveness of multimedia reading materials when used with children who are deaf. Am. Ann. Deaf **149**(5), 394–403 (2005)
26. Kourbetis, V.: Design and development of accessible educational and teaching material for deaf students in Greece. In: Stephanidis, C., Antona, M. (eds.) UAHCI 2013. LNCS, vol. 8011, pp. 172–178. Springer, Heidelberg (2013). https://doi.org/10.1007/978-3-642-39194-1_20
27. Mich, O., Pianta, E., Mana, N.: Interactive stories and exercises with dynamic feedback for improving reading comprehension skills in deaf children. Comput. Educ. **65**, 34–44 (2013)
28. Ferreira, M.A.M., Bueno, J., Bonacin, R.: Using computational resources on bilingual deaf literacy: an analysis of benefits, perspectives and challenges. In: Antona, M., Stephanidis, C. (eds.) UAHCI 2015. LNCS, vol. 9176, pp. 362–372. Springer, Cham (2015). https://doi.org/10.1007/978-3-319-20681-3_34
29. Kouroupetroglou, G.: Accessibility of documents. In: Encyclopedia of Information Science and Technology, 3d edn., pp. 563–571. IGI Global, Hershey (2015). https://doi.org/10.4018/978-1-4666-5888-2.ch437

30. Ruemer, R., Kouroupetroglou, G., Murillo-Morales, T., Miesenberger, K.: Standards, tools and procedures in accessible eBook production. In: Miesenberger, K., et al. (eds.) ICCHP 2016, Part I. LNCS, 9758, pp. 378–380. Springer, Heidelberg (2016)

31. Kourbetis, V., Hatzopoulou, M., Karipi S., Boukouras K., Gelastopoulou, M.: Teaching European Sign Languages as a first language: can they be taught without the use of ICT? Paper presented at the international conference on information, communication technologies in education, Rhodes, Greece (2017)

32. Hladík, P., Gůra, T.: The hybrid book – one document for all in the latest development. In: Miesenberger, K., Karshmer, A., Penaz, P., Zagler, W. (eds.) ICCHP 2012, Part I. LNCS, vol. 7382, pp. 18–24. Springer, Heidelberg (2012)

33. Pino, A., Kouroupetroglou, G., Riga, P.: HERMOPHILOS: a web-based information system for the workflow management and delivery of accessible eTextbooks. In: Miesenberger, K., Bühler, C., Penaz, P. (eds.) ICCHP 2016. LNCS, vol. 9758, pp. 409–416. Springer, Cham (2016). https://doi.org/10.1007/978-3-319-41264-1_56

34. Hauser, P., Paludneviciene, R., Riddle, W., Kurz, K., Emmorey, K., Contreras, J.: American sign language comprehension test: a tool for sign language researchers. J. Deaf Stud. Deaf Educ. **21**(1), 64–69 (2016)

35. Haug, T.: Use of information and communication technologies in sign language test development: results of an international survey. Deafness Educ. Int. **17**(1), 33–48 (2015). https://doi.org/10.1179/1557069X14Y.0000000041

Participatory Design Workshops for Adapting a Form for Deaf Respondents

Angelina Sales[1]($\boxtimes$), Yuska Paola Costa Aguiar[2]($\boxtimes$), and Tiago Maritan U. de Araujo[1]($\boxtimes$)

[1] Federal University of Paraiba, João Pessoa, Brazil
{angelina.sales,tiagomaritan}@lavid.ufpb.br
[2] Federal University of Paraiba, Rio Tinto, Brazil
yuska@dcx.ufpb.br

Abstract. With the guidelines and inclusion laws of Assistive Technology (TA) features have been developed to promote accessibility. As well as for other interactive products, these must pass to usability evaluations that consider the perspective of the real users. In the traditional approaches of observation of the interaction it is common the use of questionnaires to identify the profile, satisfaction and emotional state of the participants. However, these instruments may be inadequate when their respondents are deaf, not fluent in the Portuguese language. Aiming to promote autonomy for deaf users in the evaluation process of TA resources, this paper describes the planning and conduction of 2 Participatory Design workshops to adapt forms to be answered by deaf people in the context of usability tests. The workshops were held with 2 interpreters of Libras and 20 deaf people, at FUNAD - located in João Pessoa. The results of workshops indicate how appropriate the use of multimedia elements for the questions and answers of the form, such as: videos, animations, images, etc.

Keywords: Participatory design · Assistive Technology · Form for deaf

1 Introduction

According to the statistics of the last Census carried out in 2010 by IBGE [1], 45 million people declared to have at least one of the deficiencies investigated. At the time, the declared visual, motor, hearing and intellectual deficiencies corresponded to 23.9% of the Brazilian population. Visual impairment is the most representative and affects 18.8% of Brazilians, physical disability is the second most frequent and summarizes 7.0% of the population, followed by hearing (5.1%) and intellectual (1.4%).

Considering that people with disabilities represents the largest minority in the world and that the definition of laws that aim to promote accessibility and inclusion, as Law No. 13,136/15, Law No. 10.436/02, Law No. 12.319/10, etc.

© Springer Nature Switzerland AG 2020
M. Antona and C. Stephanidis (Eds.): HCII 2020, LNCS 12189, pp. 120–131, 2020.
https://doi.org/10.1007/978-3-030-49108-6_9

it is a reality, it is necessary to ensure for this portion of the population rights such as adequate access to services, products, information, etc. In addition, to include them in society in its various segments (educational, cultural, health, etc.), allowing them to participate actively, with as few restrictions as possible, is a necessity.

However, historically, people with disabilities (sensory, physical, cognitive, etc.) were left out of society [2], with the mistaken conclusion, even in the Middle Ages, that deaf people were not "educable" [3]. Although advances are noticeable in the way society has been dealing with the desire for inclusion, the educational gap in this portion of the population is still significant. Also according to the 2010 Census [1], the low level of education and training of people over 15 and who declared themselves to be disabled, corresponds to 61.1% of the population (have no education or have only the incomplete elementary school). On the other hand, this percentage is 38.2% for people without disabilities, in the same age group.

When the focus is directed to people with hearing impairment (deaf) it is necessary to understand that the absence of phonetic perception (sounds) hinders the process of literacy in the Portuguese language [4]. Therefore, the teaching of Libras (Brazilian Sign Language), regulated by law No. 10,436/02, makes this the mother tongue of most deaf people. When the deaf has Libras as their first language, there is a difficulty in understanding the text written in Portuguese, as the mental process for interpreting these two languages is different [2].

Therefore, when the presentation of information is primarily textual, in Portuguese, the difficulty of understanding the content, on the part of the deaf, is evident. As alternatives to minimize this problem, Assistive Technology resources have been developed to allow the translation between Portuguese and Libras, like the ProDeaf[1], HandTalk[2], FaLibras[3], VLibras[4], etc. applications.

However, when considering the need to assess the usability of these AT resources with its target audience (deaf people), difficulties are faced by the evaluation team with regard to data collection. Usually the interaction observation sessions are supported by the application of questionnaires to obtain information about the participants' profile, their level of subjective satisfaction and their emotional state when interacting with the product under evaluation [5,6]. The questionnaires adopted have, for the most part, presentation of primarily textual information (questions and answer options). As examples, it is possible to mention: POCUS (Objective and Cognitive User Profile) [9]; SUMI (Software Usability Measurement Inventory) [7], SUS (System Usability Scale) [8], GEW (Geneva Emotion Wheel) [5].

In order to make usability assessments also inclusive, in which means In order to make the usability assessments of AT resources intended for deaf users inclusive, it is necessary that test participants can answer the questionnaires

---

[1] Available at: http://www.prodeaf.net/.

[2] Available at: https://www.handtalk.me/.

[3] Available at: http://www.ufal.edu.br/aedhesp/falibras.

[4] Available at: (http://www.vlibras.gov.br/.

applied autonomously. Therefore, the questionnaires that are commonly adopted in this context of evaluation need to be adapted so that the representation of information (questions and answers) prioritizes Libras. This article describes, therefore, the planning, conduct and results of a set of Participatory Design workshops [10] conducted at the *Fundação Centro Integrado de Apoio ao Portador de Deficiência* (FUNAD), with the participation of two Libras interpreters and 20 deaf people, literate or in the process of literacy in Libras. The results of the workshops will serve as a basis for the collaborative design of TUTAForm (Assistive Technology Usability Test - Form). This resource consists of an online, multimedia form and adapted for deaf respondents who communicate in Libras. With TUTAForm, the aim is to allow deaf respondents to be autonomous during the data collection performed. Via form, in usability tests of targeted assistive technology resources and this audience of users. From TUTAForm it is possible to obtain data on the profile of respondents, the survey of their subjective satisfaction and their emotional state when interacting with the resource under evaluation.

This article is organized into six sections, including this one. Section 2 presents some proposals for adapting questionnaires in order to make them accessible to the public of respondents with some types of disability. Section 3 details the methodology adopted for planning, conducting and verifying the results of the Participatory Design workshops conducted within the scope of this research. In Sect. 4 there is a description of the Participatory Design workshops, including the decisions made on the creation of TUTAForm. In Sect. 5 the results of the DP workshops held with a group of potential users are presented. Finally, in Sect. 6, the conclusions and potential for expanding this work is presented.

2   Related Works

There are a number of instruments that can be used to support data collection when assessing the usability of products and systems. These are mostly self-reported (questionnaires, interviews, checklist, etc.) and seek to highlight the perception of participating users about the product being evaluated. These instruments favor the measurement of subjective satisfaction levels, or emotional state and their intensities. Questionnaires are still adopted that allow to outline the profile of the participating users.

Prietch and Filgueiras [11] carried out a mapping of data collection instruments used in usability assessments to investigate their suitability for deaf respondents. The authors highlighted, after analysis that the gap in adequate instruments for respondents with hearing impairment is evident. Since they rely on predominantly textual information and the use of value scales (Table 1). In both cases, understanding is not evident for deaf respondents, literate in Libras and illiterate in Portuguese. Although the authors have identified some initiatives that use multimedia resources, not exclusively textual ones, to represent the content of the questionnaires. None of them was developed targeting the specific audience of deaf respondents.

Table 1. Analysis of allaboutux.org UX methods.

Question	Yes	No
Does it offer an avatar expressing emotions?	7%	93%
Does it offer video expressing emotions?	0%	100%
Does it offer levels of intensity of emotions?	9%	91%
Does it use sign language or does it mention deaf users?	0%	100%
Does your format mention bipolar dimensions (negative x positive)?	19,5%	80,5%

However, in a literature review, it was possible to identify two propositions of questionnaires adapted for deaf respondents: SignQUOTE [12] and Emotion-Libras [11].

SignQUOTE [12] is a tool to support remote usability assessment data collection. This aims to maintain the advantages of remote tests (scheduling flexibility and reduced cost) and enable the participation of deaf users. For this, all information and instructions available in the tool (from the consent form to the post-test questionnaire) are presented in American Sign Language (ASL). The questions and answers available on SignQUOTE consist of videos previously recorded by interpreters with knowledge of the sign language. Considering the particularities of each assessment and the need for specific questions, the configuration of Sign-QUOTE is recurrent. Adopting this strategy for the production of ASL content can be costly considering the cost of interpreter participation. Furthermore, the adaptation of this tool to be used with Libras is not evident.

Emotion-Libras [11] is a questionnaire to be used in the context of evaluating the user's experience in the face of interaction with a specific interactive product. Its objective is to allow the deaf user to express his emotional state without the help of third parties, therefore, in a more independent way. The participant can indicate, in addition to the emotions felt, the respective intensities. At Emotion-Libras, emotions and intensities are presented from videos previously recorded with interpreters. The fact that the tool does not have an Open Source license limits its configuration, restricting the amount of emotions covered in the questionnaire. In addition, for the participants' profile and subjective satisfaction data (commonly collected during the assessments of this nature) the deaf respondent continues to depend on third parties.

In view of the scarcity of adapted questionnaires for deaf respondents. When developers of AT resources need to evaluate their solutions with real users, they prepare adapted questionnaires, in an ad hoc manner. This strategy was adopted for the evaluation of CineLibras [4] and VLibras [13]. On both occasions, an interpreter participated to translate the questions to be recorded on video and hosted on an online form creation platform. The problem of adapting the collection instruments used in an ad hoc manner (without the participation of users who will be real respondents) is that it often leads to doubt when questionnaires are applied, and interpreter interference is still necessary, implying expenses additional. According to the Translators' Union, hiring an interpreter costs around R$ 300.00 to R$ 3,000.00 depending on the context and the hours required.

As the elaboration of research contents carried out in an ad hoc manner also requires an interpreter to translate the contents in real-time or in previously recorded video, workshops for Participatory Design were proposed for the elicitation of the system requirements. The construction of a tool through DP workshops results in a product with the lowest possible failure rate [10].

The decisions taken to meet the requirements mentioned and the preparation of the workshops are described in the following section with the methodological steps adopted.

3   Methodology

As can be seen in the analysis of Table 1, the existing assessment methods do not include the deaf as the assessor and have no or little visual illustration, presenting most of their content still in written language. The few evaluation methods that present the possibility of using visual aids, have limitations that make it impossible to use them in the context of the proposition. To this end, the methodology of the work is divided into two stages: bibliographic survey and its data collection instruments, where an analysis of the existing data collection tools is made for possible adaptation; analysis of similar works in which a study of the existing data collection tools is carried out in order to analyze the possible improvements to apply to the proposed tool; analysis of questionnaires to survey the content, in which the analysis of contents in common between the existing questionnaires already applied is done; elaboration and execution of participatory design workshops, where the complete script of the experience is elaborated, and describes the results obtained in them.

Usability test is and what user information needs to be recorded for analysis [6,15]. It was possible to conclude that for a good usability test, three types of information should be obtained and evaluated. They are: User Profile Characteristics, Satisfaction Test and Emotional State.

Therefore, the two proposals mentioned above are not adequate to support the data collection in Assistive Technology Usability Tests. Whose users are deaf, Brazilian, literate or in LIBRAS literacy process since neither meets the set of requirements listed below:

1. To be for LIBRAS, given that the target audience is deaf Brazilians literacy (or in process of) in LIBRAS;
2. Do not depend on the active participation of interpreters to generate the questionnaire content or its application, aiming at reducing the cost of production and the autonomy of the respondents;
3. Not based on primarily textual representation. However, multimedia, based on the use of images, animated gifs and videos made with an avatar in order to facilitate the understanding of the content covered;
4. Be made available online, allowing respondents to use the service simultaneously and not in person (if necessary);

5. Contemplate items related to the respondents' profile, their level of subjective satisfaction and emotional state after interaction with the product under evaluation.

A practice that can be used to collect, analyze and project information in this process is participatory design, which covers the participation of all those interested in this process as developers, users, employees and partners [10]. The role of all those involved in the process (organizing, implementing and executing an inclusive environment) is to perceive differences, listen to the different ones and establish involvement strategies [16]. That in turn enable each one to influence the organization's destinies, building the sense of belonging.

4 Participatory Design Workshop as an Involvement Strategy in Adapting Communication

In this stage, a survey of the number of tools was carried out from the point of view of usability that have an adaptive interface. Aiming to evaluate the existing tools and realize the possibility of taking advantage of some types of result already obtained. Subsequently, an evaluation of the usability testing methods was also carried out from the perspective of the needs of the deaf. Verifying whether the tools have more visual content than textual, in order to be able to use some devices and adapt them to the context of the proposal.

4.1 Choice of Items for the Form

As a guide for the definition of the elements that would compose the analysis section of the user profile that will use TUTAForm, the profile adopted by POCUs - Objective and Cognitive User Profile [9], was chosen, which originated from the profiles [4,14].

In addition to the model adopted by the POCUs, others profiles was also considered [13,14]. Since, it was noticed that some specific elements related to disability contemplated in the study should be added and that some adaptations should be made to the context. Some works were applied in tests with deaf people [13,14].

On the other hand, the set of information requested in the POCUs contains 76 items and obtaining all this information by the user would end up being an overly tiring task, in addition to those that would be added due to the context. Thus, the inverse filtering was performed, considering in the first instance the information presented in the models [13,14] and analyzed which ones were in the POCUs and which ones are not and are relevant to the context, without making it very large section. Due to having other questions that should be analyzed and it would not be interesting to leave the user tired from the beginning of the questionnaire.

A comparative analysis was carried out and it was noticed that some information was presented in the same way in the three profiles. Others had to be adapted, so that they were common to the analyzed profiles.

Based on this filtering, it was concluded that the user information that would be relevant to the context of the proposed form are:

- Genre;
- Age;
- Deafness level;
- Educational stage;
- Level of understanding of Portuguese;
- Level of understanding in LIBRAS;
- Frequency of smart phone use;
- Frequency of computer use.

For each of the items analyzed, some items were collected from the literature that could illustrate each of them in a self-explanatory way, either through a static or mobile figure, video, typing and also in written text.

For the items of satisfaction and usability, among the instruments analyzed, the SUMI - Software Usability Measurement Inventory, a questionnaire of 50 items of the likert type, seemed to be very complete and suitable for the context, it is online, it can be applied in systems under development: functional or market prototype and can be applied to web services. On the other hand, as it consists of a vast amount of questions, it would tire the user a lot.

Another instrument that appeared in the form of a questionnaire and seemed to fit the context of TUTAForm, was the SUS - System Usability Scale, a 10-item questionnaire, which, in addition to being quick, can be online and applied to any product.

In comparative studies, most scores on usability questionnaires are highly correlated somewhere. This means that on most items, they actually measure the same thing. Where it can be several points can be evaluated. For example, what users feel about the efficiency of a software, what they will say it is if they liked it or not. Thus, as the two types of questionnaires presented seem to fit in the context. A comparative analysis of the two was carried out in order to arrive at a set of items in common in both.

Some items are directly linked to the context, others had to have their structure adapted, in the form of a direct question and without presenting bipolar information. The emotional state in the usability analysis, the existence of bipolar emotions in opposite ends caused confusion in understanding the relationship between them [11]. And the same can be received when composing a questionnaire with bipolar reactions, where there may be results of an inverse scale.

With the result of this analysis and adaptation, the following set of items was reached:

- Would you use this system more often?
- Did you find the system easy to use?
- Would you recommend the system to your friends?
- Did you need help from someone to use the system?
- Were you able to understand all the functions of the system?

- Did you think that the system had many errors?
- Did you find it easy to learn how to use the system?
- Did you find the system organized?
- Did you feel confident using the system?
- Did you need to learn new things to use the system?

As for the type of response of the items, SUMI and SUS are based on scale. The SUMI scale consists of three options: Agree-Undecided-Disagree. The SUS scale, for each item, the user must evaluate on a scale of one to five how much he agrees with the statement, being 1 - Totally Disagree and 5 - Totally Agree. Among these, it was chosen to keep SUMI's, with three options. Since in the same study by [16] it was noticed that the deaf is confused when there is a lot of choice between "Yes" and "No", since for them there are no intermediate options.

When the answer options were presented only with the numbers five to one, there was a lack of understanding about their meaning [11]. And as a possible solution one could use illustrations indicating the meaning of the answers. It was also considered to add illustrations to the answers, whether they are textual, static and mobile figurative, typing or video.

For the items that would make up the emotional state section, from the instruments listed on allaboutux.org, none of them had adaptation for the sign language, some had images or animations and users need to check answer options informing about the emotions felt. Only the Brazilian tool Emotion-Libras provides support for the deaf to understand, taking into account that it was developed considering the deaf as their target audience.

However, for the creation of videos expressing emotions, a person is required, whether an interpreter or a deaf person. And the idea is that TUTAForm is automatic and does not depend on third parties to compose the content.

For the generation of the videos, a translation application was used. Due to experience with the tool, the application chosen was VLibras. And the emotions assessed are only positive [11], bipolar emotions represented in the same scenario, caused confusion in understanding. The emotions assessed are:

- Cheered up;
- Confident;
- Scared;
- Interested;
- Pleased.

4.2   Workshop Planning

Before giving the workshops, there was a planning stage. And it was taking into consideration: (i) the infrastructure of the place where the workshops would be; (ii) the availability of an interpreter to accompany the sessions; (iii) the organization of the workshop; (iv) preparation of the material to be evaluated; (v) script; and, (vi) the role of the evaluator and other helpers and the evaluation method.

At the end of the planning stage, the place where the workshops would be held was defined, at FUNAD. And how the evaluation team would be composed:

1. An evaluator, with no experience in Libras, responsible for running the workshop in a way that followed the previously prepared script. In addition, he was responsible for distributing and collecting the questionnaires in due course during the tests.
2. A Libras interpreter, responsible for passing on the evaluator's information to the participants.
3. An observer, responsible for recording the personal information of the deaf participants. Where such as the interpreter, the role is making notes on the behavior of the deaf and everything else that she found relevant for further analysis. He was also responsible for photographing the workshops during the experiment.

The sessions were divided into two days and subdivided into four sessions.

4.3 Conducting the Workshops

The execution of the workshop was divided into three phases and will be exhibited in just one day, they are:

1. Presentation of the different ways to display a question;
2. Representation of possible responses for collecting user profile data;
3. Scale representation, which aims to measure the degree of satisfaction of usability questions.

The sessions were divided into two days and had the participation of 20 deaf employees, who proposed to analyze the material voluntarily. Each of them lasts 15–30 min, depending on the number of participants in each one. All had the same infrastructure: a projector, a computer and the answer sheets that were given to the participants.

The workshop was conducted as follows:

1. Delivery of the answer book to the participants, where each page of the answer book has three until six options of items. These items v vary according to the objective of the question, in which he would have to choose among them which he liked best.
2. Previous explanation of its purpose. The options were designed and the deaf was instructed to choose the option that pleased him most among those displayed. Or maybe to suggest one that was not present in the material.
3. Display of each set of options presented on the slide. In a class board was presented all the available options, just like the answer book. Each option contains a corresponding color, in order to facilitate the interpretation of participants who do not have knowledge in Portuguese and keep data consistent.

The participants were between 14 and 54 years old and their educational level ranged from the 5th year of elementary school to complete higher education.

5 Results

The final result of the workshops together with the result of the interviews was analyzed. The conclusion was that to present the questions the video with an interpreter would be ideal, in the opinion of the deaf. In contrast, the pending of having an interpreter in the construction of the questionnaire is not a valid option. Due the fact the scope of the proposal is to grant greater independence while the research participants answer it. Without the need for assistance from third parties, besides, there would be no freedom to add and edit the questions and there would be additional expenses with the interpreter.

Dactylology was chosen as the best or one of the best options to represent several items of the questionnaire. However, this option was disregarded, based on the report of the teachers who participated in the workshops. In these cases, the second most voted option was chosen to compose the questionnaire.

Resulting in the following representations:

- Personal profile:
  - Genre: Illustration similar to bathroom gender plates;
  - Age: Numerical illustration;
  - Deafness Level: Video using the VLibras automatic translator;
  - Education: Video using the VLibras automatic translator;
  - Yes or No options: Like/Dislike illustration;
- Subjective satisfaction:
  - Agree-Undecided-Disagree option: illustration by emoji for agreement, neutrality and disagreement.
- Emotional state:
  - Video with avatar translated by VLibras converted into gif to represent emotions (excited, confident, surprised, interested and satisfied).

6 Conclusion

After the approval of Law 13.146/15, there were many change by the public authorities in general and public service concessionaires. Wherever it became mandatory to provide institutionalized ways to support the use and diffusion of Libras as an objective means of communication.

Thus, the production of products, equipment, devices, resources, methodologies, strategies, practices and services that aim to promote functionality, related to the activity and participation of people with disabilities or reduced mobility have become more frequent.

Such products need to be evaluated by consumers. However, none of the data collection instruments is presented in a way that considers the deaf to be a potential user. They usually have content in Portuguese with little or no visual illustration. Without aiming at their autonomy, independence, quality of life and social inclusion.

Therefore, it was perceived the need to create a technological solution that enables the autonomous participation of deaf people in Usability Tests of Assistive Technology resources. Usability tests which they are potential users, regarding the filling of questionnaires/forms usually adopted. Participatory Design workshops were adopted as a strategy for obtaining system requirements. Since by involving people who can use the system later, the system can be more accepted by end users and consequently more accessible and usable.

The proposal of TUTAForm is to allow the deaf to access a data collection instrument whose information is in their natural language of communication (Libras) and with representations that they understand at first (video, images, animations), avoiding the use of Portuguese terms. And that your design is fully collaborative.

Finally, this work presented the first phase of creation of TUTAForm, which is the definition of the media items that will compose it. The media representations of the questions and answers were obtained through the Participatory Design workshops and counted with the collaboration of 20 literate deaf people or in the process of literacy in Libras and two Libras teachers. The workshops were held at FUNAD and were subdivided into four sessions.

The results of the workshops were analyzed and a set of media was reached. Which, in the opinion of the participants, would be the best representations to illustrate the topics presented. Such results are the basis for consolidating the design of the tool.

As a perspective for future work, we intend to apply the results obtained in the DP workshops in the creation of TUTAForm. Then that it can support the data collection in usability tests by deaf respondents.

References

1. IBGE. Censo Demográfico do Brasil (2010)
2. Avelar, T.F., Freitas, K.P.: Português como Segunda Língua na Formação do Aluno Surdo. Revista Sinalizar **1**(1), 12–24 (2016)
3. Lacerda, C.B.F.: Um pouco da história das diferentes abordagens na educação dos surdos. Cadernos Cedes **19**, 68 (1998)
4. Domingues, L.A., et al.: CineLibras: automatic generation and distribution of librastracks for digital cinema platforms. J. Inf. Data Manag. **6**(2), 144 (2016)
5. Sacharin, V., Schlegel, K., Scherer, K.: Geneva emotion wheel rating study. Center for Person, Kommunikation, Aalborg University, NCCR Affective Sciences, Technical report (2012)
6. Nielsen, J.: Usability Engineering. Elsevier, London (1994)
7. Kirakowski, J., Corbett, M.: SUMI: The software usability measurement inventory. Br. J. Educ. Technol. **24**(3), 210–212 (1993)
8. Brooke, J.: SUS-a quick and dirty usability scale. Usability Eval. Ind. **189**(194), 4–7 (1996)
9. Scherer, K.R.: What are emotions? And how can they be measured? Soc. Sci. Inf. **44**(4), 695–729 (2005)
10. de Araújo, C.L.S., Fazani, A.J.: Explorando o design participativo como prática de desenvolvimento de sistemas de informação. InCID: Revista De Ciência Da Informação E Documentação **5**(1), 138–150 (2014)

11. Prietch, S.S., Filgueiras, L.V.L.: Emotional quality evaluation method for interviewing deaf persons (Emotion-LIBRAS). In: Proceedings of the IADIS International Conference Interfaces and Human Computer Interaction (ICHI), Portugal (2012)
12. Schnepp, J., Shiver, B.: Improving deaf accessibility in remote usability testing. In: The Proceedings of the 13th International ACM SIGACCESS Conference on Computers and Accessibility. ACM (2011)
13. Guimarães, A.P.N., Tavares, A.T.: Anais Estendidos do XX Simpósio Brasileiro de Sistemas Multimídia e Web. Avaliação de Interfaces de Usuário voltada à Acessibilidade em Dispositivos Móveis: Boas práticas para experiência de usuário. SBC, Brasil (2014)
14. Lima, M.A.C.B.: Tradução Automática com Adequação Sintático-Semântica para LIBRAS. Dissertação (Mestre em Informática). Universidade Federal da Paraíba, João Pessoa (2015)
15. Preece, J., Rogers, Y., Sharp, H.: Design de interação. Bookman (2005)
16. Silva, S.: Educação Especial: entre a técnica pedagógica e a política educacional (2008)

A Methodology for Assessing Translation Quality Generated by Sign Language Machine Translators: A Case Study with VLibras

Luana Silva Reis[1]([✉]), Tiago Maritan U. de Araujo[1],
Yuska Paola Costa Aguiar[2], and Manuella Aschoff C. B. Lima[1]

[1] Federal University of Paraiba, João Pessoa, Brazil
luanasreis@live.com, {tiagomaritan,manuella.lima}@lavid.ufpb.br
[2] Federal University of Paraiba, Rio Tinto, Brazil
yuska@dcx.ufpb.br

Abstract. Machine translation tools for sign languages are developed to reduce barriers to access to information for deaf people. However, these technologies have some limitations related to the difficulty of dealing with some specific grammatical aspects of sign languages, which can negatively influence the experience of deaf users. To address this problem, we developed a methodology for assessing the quality of the translation of machine translators from Brazilian Portuguese (PT-BR) to the Brazilian Sign Language (Libras). We apply the evaluation methodology as a study case with Libras, a Brazilian machine translate to Libras. In this experiment, some Brazilian human interpreters evaluated the treatment of some specific grammatical aspects in the application. As a result, we observed significant limitations in the translations performed by this application, indicating the need to improve the treatment of these grammatical aspects. Thus, the proposed methodology can be used by researchers and developers in the field to identify limitations and points of improvement in the process of translating a spoken-to- sign language machine translator.

Keywords: Machine translation · Deaf user · Quality of translation

1 Introduction

Some Assistive Technology (AT) resources have been developed in recent years to promote accessibility to digital and non-digital content, as well as to facilitate communication between deaf and hearing people. These resources can be valuable in the construction of knowledge and the autonomy of the deaf community. An example of this type of AT is the machine translators to sign languages, which are designed to reduce barriers to access to information for deaf people by allowing them to view content in sign languages on the web, mobile devices, TV, movies, among others.

M. Antona and C. Stephanidis (Eds.): HCII 2020, LNCS 12189, pp. 132–146, 2020.
https://doi.org/10.1007/978-3-030-49108-6_10

In the scientific literature, we have several works addressing the machine translation of content in spoken languages into sign languages [1,3–5,11–15, 17–19], etc. Araujo [1], for example, describes an architecture for the machine translation of the Brazilian Portuguese into Brazilian Sign Language (Libras) in real-time for TV. The system called LibrasTV[1] receives a text as input and generates a window with an avatar signing the information in Libras. Zhao and Huenerfauth [11] presented a solution for the machine translation of English into American Sign Language (ASL), considering questions related to syntactic, grammatical, and morphological aspects of the sign language. Li et. al [12] and Xu and Gao [19] present a machine translation of Chinese texts into Chinese Sign Language (CSL), considering the context of the sentence.

For the Brazilian Sign Language (Libras), we also have some machine translation solutions, such as VLibras[2] proposed by Araujo [1], HandTalk[3], Rybená[4], among others. These applications perform the machine translation of digital content, such as texts, audios, and videos, to Libras through a 3D animated avatar, allowing deaf and hearing people to access digital content in Libras.

According to Eco [8], during a translation process, there may be loss of information between the source and the target language since there is no total equivalence in many cases between the terms of the two languages. As a result, the use of these machine translation has divided opinions of deaf and hearing users, especially sign language interpreters [5]. The controversy is based on the fact that sign languages are natural languages, independent of spoken languages, and have their own grammatical structure [7,16]. Moreover, like all-natural languages, the sign languages represented in a digital interface presents some limitations [4,5,17]. One example is the inability of the deaf person to ask about some aspect of the translation context, which usually occurs in the case in a real-life sign language interpretation. Thus, the translation must generate the best translation possible, reducing doubts and ambiguities, since this doubting function is not yet available in these machine translators.

Thus, considering the relevance of ensuring the quality of translation generated by applications of this nature, in this work, we propose a methodology for evaluating sign language machine translators and perform a case study to evaluate VLibras, an open-source machine translator for Brazilian Sign Language (Libras). The case study was applied in the mobile version of the application, but the methodology could also be applied in a web or desktop version. This methodology aims to assist developers and researchers in this area to evaluate if they are adequately treating the grammatical aspects during the translation process. Besides, it could also be used to identify points of improvement in these tools.

The rest of the paper is organized as follows. In Sect. 2, works related to the theme of this research are presented. In Sect. 3, the evaluation methodology

---

[1] http://lavid.ufpb.br/index.php/2015/09/28/libras-tv/.

[2] http://www.vlibras.gov.br/.

[3] https://www.handtalk.me.

[4] http://portal.rybena.com.br/site-rybena.

proposed by this research is presented. Section 4 presents the case study carried out to validate the proposed evaluation methodology. Then, in Sect. 5, the results obtained with the case study are presented. Finally, Sect. 6 presents the final considerations and future work.

2   Related Works

In the scientific literature, some works aim to evaluate the quality of the machine translation of sentences from PT-BR to Libras (e.g., HandTalk, ProDeaf, Rybená, and VLibras). In Colling and Boscarioli [3], the authors evaluated the HandTalk, ProDeaf, and Rybená machine translation tools to Libras with deaf children. The children presented sentences according to their understanding of the translation generated by the applications, and a Libras specialist translated these sentences into Brazilian Portuguese for further evaluation. The authors identified that the children had difficulties in understanding the translations generated by these tools.

Vieira et al. [18] present a study where deaf and hearing users have elaborated 29 narratives using the HandTalk and ProDeaf to analyze their use of "Non-Manual Expressions". As a result, the participants indicated that the avatars did not sign non-manual expressions, which are fundamental for the characterization and understanding of several semantic and syntactic elements in Libras.

Lima [13] identify fifteen problems related to the treatment of context in the process of translating PT-BR to Libras in the VLibras. To address this problem, she proposed a solution that treats some problems such as adequacy of syntactic analysis, tense verbal treatment, treatment of nouns of two genera, qualified elimination of articles and prepositions, among others. Then, she implemented and integrated a new version of the translation component, besides the creation of a language of description for translation rules and a grammar containing rules that dealt with these aspects. Afterward, she evaluated with users and noted an improvement in the quality of translation.

Despite a large number of research evaluating the quality of translations generated by machine translations from spoken languages to sign language, currently, it has not been possible to identify a structured methodology for assessing the quality of these machine translators. Thus, the methodology proposed in this research emerges as a guide that developers can use to evaluate spoken-to-sign language machine translators. The proposed methodology has three parts: Planning, Conduction, and Analysis, which we describe in Sect. 3.

3   Evaluation Methodology

According to Fig. 1, a proposed methodology is structured in 3 steps: The Planning that is realized in five parts (the definition of grammatical aspects to be evaluated, the selection of sentences that are used in the evaluation of grammatical aspects, the selection of automatic translators for evaluation, the selection of the profile of the evaluators and definition of the evaluation strategy used);

Conduction, where the evaluation is performed and is obtained the data collection; and Analysis of the results obtained. Each of the process steps is detailed below.

As mentioned in Sect. 2, we structure the proposed methodology in three steps: (1) Planning, (2) Conduction, and (3) Analysis (see Fig. 1). Initially, the users of the methodology (e.g., the developers) must plan the assessment in five parts (Planning step): the definition of grammatical aspects to be evaluated, the selection of sentences used in the evaluation of grammatical aspects, the selection of the machine translators for evaluation, the selection of the profile of the evaluators and definition of the evaluation strategy. Afterward, they must perform the evaluation (Conduction step) and analyze the data obtained (Analysis step). We detail these process steps in Sects. 3.1, 3.2, and 3.3.

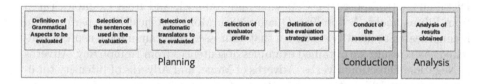

Fig. 1. Translation quality assessment methodology

3.1   Planning

Definition of the Grammatical Aspects to Be Evaluated. Initially, it is essential to perform a literature review to identify the particularities involved in the translation of the source language to the target language and their impact on the machine translation process. The grammatical aspects considered relevant and whose inadequate treatment may interfere in the comprehension of the translated sentences by the users should be considered when carrying out the evaluation process.

In the case study we have carried out with VLibras to validate the methodology, initially, we conduct a literature review with the participation of a Libras expert to identify the grammatical aspects which are essential in the PT-BR to Libras translation context and their impact on the machine translation process. The result of the review can assist developers or testers of Brazilian sign language machine translators, and it is one of the contributions of this work.

In this review, we identify that the Libras grammatical aspects whose inadequate treatment may interfere in the comprehension by the Brazilian deaf users are: (i) homonym; (ii) adverbs of intensity; (iii) adverbs of mode; (iv) adverbs of negation; (v) directional verbs; (vi) verbs that agree with the location; (vii) classifier verb; (viii) regionalisms (differentiation of signs of the same word according to region); (ix) crossover (positioning of characters in space); (x) interrogative sentences; and (xi) exclamation sentences.

From these identified grammatical aspects, the developers of sign language machine translators can select all or a subset of them according to their convenience and time available for the assessment.

Sentence Selection Used for Evaluation. After the definition of the grammatical aspects that should be evaluated, in the second step of the planning process, we suggest the selection of the corpus of sentences (e.g., examples of translations) that will be used in the evaluation.

In this step, we suggested using examples of translations from the literature, since it exempts the author of the research from the creation of sentences that can positively or negatively influence the final result of the evaluation. A suggestion would be to use an official sign language dictionary that will be evaluated to identify the sentences used and/or to search the official sign language literature, which will provide examples of sentences used in sign language grammar learning, as used in case study applied in this research.

The process of selection the Corpus of Sentences[5] used in our case study presented came from an analysis of Libras' Trilingual Illustrated Encyclopedic Dictionary [2] proposed by Capovilla and Raphael, and from examples taken from Libras books (Felipe [9] e Quadros [6]). More specifically, we performed a manual search to identify sentences that addressed the grammatical aspects evaluated. As a result, we obtained examples of sentences from Homonymy, Adverbs of Negation, Directional Verbs, Adverbs of Mode, and Adverbs of Intensity totaling more than 527 sentence examples that address these grammatical aspects. The corpus of sentences available in this research can be used as auxiliary material to perform the assessments of machine translators from PT-BR to Libras. The sentences that will be used in the evaluation with users can be randomly selected from this corpus.

Some consideration should be made regarding the number of sentences evaluated for each grammatical aspect along the expected execution time of the evaluation. This analysis is important because an excessive number of sentences can make the user exhausted (in the case of evaluation with the user) and a reduced number may imply an unsatisfactory amount of data for the final analysis. In the case study presented in this paper, we evaluated 24 sentences addressing the grammatical aspects considered relevant for evaluation.

Selection of the Machine Translator(s) to Be Evaluated. The choice of the machine translator(s) to be evaluated should be made according to the need of the research. If only one specific translator is selected, the methodological scheme should be carried out only with this application. However, whether we have more than one translator for evaluation, one sentence must not be evaluated by the same user in more than one application, since the evaluation of the translation in a first application can influence the evaluation of the second one. Thus, it is suggested that the same sentence applied to two translators (for example) should be evaluated by two different participants.

Evaluator Profile Selection. The selection of the profile of the evaluators should be defined according to the purpose of the research. We recommend that

---

[5] Corpus of Sentences available at https://tinyurl.com/CorpusOfSentences.

the number of participants is appropriate since if the number of participants is too small, we can not have a reasonable conclusion, or the results obtained can be inferred. For example, getting only one answer per assessed sentence is not appropriate because no conclusion can be drawn on the evaluated question.

We also recommend that deaf users make use of accessible technologies for sign language or human sign language interpreters.

When we use human sign language interpreters, for example, an interesting approach is to compare the output produced by machine translators with the output produced by human interpreters, since the sign language interpreter knows both languages involved (source language and target language). Besides, another option is to ask the sign language interpreters to record videos with their translation of the sentences used in the experiment. Thus, it is possible to identify similarities and discrepancies in the translations evaluated.

When we evaluate the translator with deaf users, one option is to assess whether the target audience of the solution understands the output generated by the machine translator. In addition, the participant can analyze points for improvement in the translation process.

Definition of the Evaluation Strategy Used. There are different procedures for performing data collection, which vary according to the need of the research or the type of investigation. Some of them are interview, form, observation, questionnaire, among others.

This evaluation methodology proposes the use of questionnaires as a direct tool to obtain the information observed by the participants. In the proposed methodology, we suggest that a video with the translation of the sentences evaluated by the machine translator be presented in the questionnaire. Then, for each of the evaluated sentences, the participating respondent could indicate their evaluation for (i) grammatical correctness of the translation (Is the translation grammatically correct?); (ii) understanding of the translation generated (Is the generated translation understandable?), and (iii) the overall quality of the translation (Is the overall quality of the translation adequate?). We also suggest that the answers considered an even scale (e.g., a six-point scale (1 = poor and 6 = perfect)). We suggest this type of scale because it avoids mostly neutral evaluations [14] and has already been used in works of the same type [1,15]. An example of a questionnaire used in the case study can be seen in Fig. 2.

In addition to the applied questionnaire, it is suggested that the signaling of the sentences be filmed by the participating interpreters since these videos can be used as auxiliary material in the analysis of the results obtained.

During to the application of the questionnaire, it is advisable to make notes of the participants' voluntary opinion, as well as to record (with prior authorization) the signing of the evaluated sentences (whether the participants are sign language interpreters), since this information can assist in the analysis of the results.

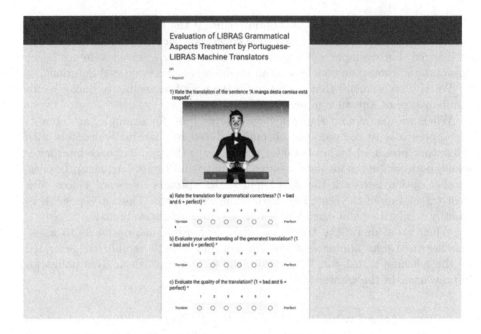

Fig. 2. Evaluation questionnaire example

3.2 Conducting the Evaluation

The preparation of the assessment environment should be done by positioning cameras for audio and video capture (if necessary), followed by the consent form by participants, who should be instructed on the evaluation procedures. The assessment should be done individually and not overlapping.

In addition, opinion and improvement points may be questioned to participants at this time. It is essential to obtain the participant's opinion to assist in the analysis of the data obtained in the answers to the questionnaires.

3.3 Data Analysis

In the Data Analysis step, the evaluators should analyze the grades attributed by the users to the translation of the sentences, including information related to the correctness, comprehension, and quality of the translation. Besides, they should also consider the statements collected during the evaluation process. In addition, complimentary audios and/or videos should be analyzed for similarities and discrepancies with the machine translations performed, helping to understand the data obtained.

Thus, the answers to the questionnaires should be tabulated and analyzed. The information obtained should allow associating, by application, the grammatical aspects of interest, the participants' evaluation of its correctness, the understanding of the sentence, and its overall quality.

4   Case Study: VLibras

This case study presented the applicability of a methodology for evaluating the quality of machine translation for sign languages that can be applied by developers and scholars in the field. To validate the proposed methodology, we performed a case study to investigate the correctness, comprehension, and quality of the translation generated by VLibras, a Brazilian Portuguese to Libras machine translator.

In this case study, we evaluate the content generated by VLibras with Libras interpreters, and the ratings generated by them were also compared with the video translations performed by each of the participants.

In the Planning phase, we study and identify the grammatical aspects to be addressed; define the corpus of sentences to be considered for the translations and the strategy for evaluation of the quality of the sentences; prepared the questionnaires, among others. In the Conduction phase, we asked Libras specialists to generate the translation of the sentences from Pt-Br to Libras (human translation) and to evaluate the quality of the translation of the same sentences by the VLibras. Finally, in the Analysis, we analyze and identify similarities and discrepancies of the translations generated by the machine translators and the translation performed by the human interpreters, analyzed the testimonies collected during the evaluation process and notes attributed to the correctness, among others.

We performed these three steps in sequential order, and it is important to point out that the conduction of the experiment was performed with each Libras interpreter individually, not superimposed, avoiding or making it difficult for an evaluator's opinion for a given aspect influence the opinion of the others.

To favor the participation of a higher number of interpreters, we performed evaluations in Brazilian educational institutions (Municipal, State and Federal). Thus, all the Libras interpreters performed the evaluation in their work environment.

4.1   Planning

Initially, to understand the context of the research, we carried out a literature review identifying the peculiarities of the translation of Pt-Br to Libras and their impact on the process of machine translation. We carried out this literature review with the support of a Libras specialist, who assisted in the identification of the grammatical aspects whose inadequate treatment can interfere in the comprehension of the deaf users. In this step, the following aspects were identified according to the grammatical aspects presented in the book Language of Signs Brazilian (Linguistic Studies) [7]: (i) disambiguation or homonymy (homophones, homographs and perfect); (ii) adverbs of negation; (iii) directional verbs; (iv) interrogative phrases; (v) exclamatory phrases; (vi) adverbs of mode; and (vii) adverbs of intensity.

For each grammatical aspect, we randomly selected three sentences, resulting in twenty-four sentences in total (see Table 1). The sentences will be presented in Portuguese with English translation in parentheses. It is important to mention that the number of sentences evaluated was similar to the number of sentences previously used in other works related to sign language machine translation [10].

Additionally, since we had several aspects of being evaluated, and to avoid making the evaluation tiresome for the participants, which could impact the results of the evaluations, we divided the evaluation into two stages (groups):

- Group 1: Evaluate the Homonymy, Adverbs of Negation and Directional Verbs aspects;
- Group 2: Evaluate the Adverbs of Mode, Adverbs of Intensity, Interrogative Phrases and Exclamatory Phrases aspects;

In the next step of the Planning step, which involves the selection of machine translators, we just selected the VLibras tool.

In the fourth stage of the Planing step, we selected the profile of the users. Initially, we selected Libras interpreters since they know both languages (Pt-Br and Libras). Besides, this choice would allow a comparative analysis between the human (made by the interpreter) and the machine translation (made by the applications), as well as the access to the professional opinion about the quality of the machine translation. Thus, it is possible to identify the problems and try to propose improvements, more concretely.

4.2 Conduction

The preparation of the evaluation environment consisted of the positioning of cameras to capture audio and video, followed by the signature of the Free and Informed Consent Term by the Libras interpreters, and instruction of the users about the evaluation procedures.

To favor the participation of a more significant number of interpreters, we carried out the evaluation in Brazilian educational institutions (Municipal, State and Federal). We performed the evaluation with 10 (ten) Libras interpreters, where 2 were men and 8 were women, aged 23 to 40 years. All interpreters performed the experiment in their work environment.

We conducted the evaluation individually and not parallel to each participant. The evaluator followed the execution of the tasks performed by the interpreters, taking note of the aspects relevant to the analysis. We instructed each participant to make the translation and signing of all the sentences used in the study and recorded these translations for later comparison with those generated automatically by the VLibras.

Each interpreter then answered one of the evaluation questionnaires. They access the videos generated by VLibras for the 24 sentences, in each round of the experiment (Group 1 and Group 2). For each of the sentences, the participating interpreter indicated his assessment for (i) grammatical correctness of the translation, (ii) understanding of the translation generated, and (iii) overall quality of the translation. Answers considered a six-point scale (1 = poor and 6 = perfect).

Table 1. Sentences selected for search evaluation.

Grammatical aspects	Sentences
Homonymous words	Sentence 1: A manga desta camisa está rasgada (The **sleeve** of this shirt is torn) Sentence 2: O menino escalou o muro para fugir do cachorro (The boy **climbed** the wall to escape the dog) Sentence 3: A ação do governo não conseguiu combater às drogas (Government action has failed to **combat** drugs) Sentence 4: A manga é uma fruta típica do verão (The **mango** is a typical summer fruit) Sentence 5: O diretor do hospital escalou o médico para o plantão (The hospital director **chose** the doctor to the on duty) Sentence 6: Os países decidiram dar uma trágua no combate (The countries decided to give a truce in **combat**)
Adverbs of negation	Sentence 7: Não adianta gritar, ele não ouve (Do not scream, he **does not listen**) Sentence 8: Não gosto desse seu jeito de agir (I **do not like** the way you act) Sentence 9: Não posso atendê-lo (I **can not** attend him)
Directional verbs	Sentence 10: Eu pergunto para você (I ask you) Sentence 11: Eu disse à vocês (I told you) Sentence 12: Ele deu para mim (He gave to me)
Interrogative phrases	Sentence 13: Qual é o seu nome? (What is your name?) Sentence 14: Você é casado? (Are you married?) Sentence 15: Você quer água? (You want water?)
Exclamation phrases	Sentence 16: Carro bonito! (Beautiful car!) Sentence 17: Conheci muitos surdos! (I met many deaf people!) Sentence 18: Saudades, você sumiu! (I miss you, you disappeared!)
Adverbs of mode	Sentence 19: O homem lê o livro rapidamente (The man reads the book quickly) Sentence 20: A mulher escova os dentes lentamente (The woman brushes her teeth slowly) Sentence 21: Este método vai ser melhor que o anterior (This method will be better than the previous one)
Adverbs of intensity	Sentence 22: Ela é pouco inteligente (She is little intelligent) Sentence 23: Ela está mais gorda do que eu (She's more fat than me) Sentence 24: O carnaval é muito alegre (The carnival is very joyful)

The users took, on average, 15 min to answer the questionnaire, and the participant can stop or leave the evaluation at any time. We also recorded the comments made freely by the interpreters during the process for further analysis.

It is essential to point out that we have performed all test sessions in full, without abandoning the participants or interrupting the evaluators. Besides, there was no objection from the participants to signing the Free and Informed Consent Term, to recording the translation and signing of the sentences or to answering the questionnaire. Thus, we considered all the data collected during the sessions in the analysis.

4.3   Data Analysis

The process of data analysis consisted of identifying the similarities and discrepancies between the translation performed by the interpreters (human) and the translations generated by the machine translation applications. The annotations made by the users during the observation (opinion and comments of the interpreters), associated with the audio and video records, were useful to help understand the data obtained.

Then, we tabulated and analyzed the responses to the questionnaires. The information obtained allowed to associate the grammatical aspects of interest (homonyms words, adverbs of negation, directional verbs, interrogative phrases, exclamatory phrases, adverbs of mode, and adverbs of intensity), to the interpretation of the correctness, comprehension and general quality of translation.

The study had 5 answers to the questionnaires of the first group of grammatical aspects evaluated and 5 answers to the questionnaires of the second group of grammatical aspects evaluated. The information obtained allowed us to list a set of identified grammatical problems and to propose suggestions for improvement - for each one of the contemplated applications.

4.4   Evaluation Results

Figure 3 illustrates the overall average test result for all evaluated grammatical aspects.

According to Fig. 3, we can observe that VLibras obtained a mean score value of 3.37 with a standard deviation of 0.92. In the evaluations of Group 1 of interpreters, they highlight inadequacies for the contextual treatment of the grammatical aspects of Homonyms Words, Adverbs of Negation, and Directional Verbs.

For the Homonymous Words considered in the study (MANGA, ESCALAR, COMBATER), the VLibras has adequately presented the translation for only one of the two meanings of the homonymous words. Thus, it was not possible to identify the treatment of this grammatical aspect in the translator. The result can be seen in Fig. 4, where evaluations obtained resulted in an average of 3 points.

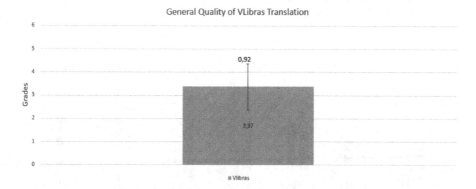

Fig. 3. General quality of VLibras translation

For the Adverbs of Negation (NOT LISTEN, NOT LIKE and NOT CAN), the VLibras application presents the appropriate treatment only for the "NOT LISTEN" negation adverb, thus presenting a partial treatment of this grammatical aspect. The result can be observed in Fig. 4, where the evaluations for this grammatical aspect presented the lowest averages among the evaluated grammatical aspects.

For the Directional Verbs evaluated, the application presented a partial treatment of this grammatical aspect. The VLibras translator doesn't present the adequacy of the "PERGUNTAR" (ASK) and "DAR" (GIVE), directional verbs. For the directional verb "DIZER" (SAY), the translator presented the incorporation of the directional verb correctly, consistent with the translations performed by all the interpreters. Figure 4 presents an average result, slightly above 3 points, for evaluations of this grammatical aspect.

In the evaluations of Group 2 of interpreters, they highlight inadequacies for the contextual treatment of the grammatical aspects of Adverbs of Mode and Adverbs of Intensity. In the evaluation of Interrogative Phrases and Exclamation Phrases, the VLibras presented adequacy for this grammatical aspect for all sentences evaluated. These results can be seen in Fig. 4, where the two grammatical aspects presented the highest averages among the evaluated grammatical aspects.

In the evaluation of two Adverbs of Mode ("QUICKLY" and "BEST"), the translator incorporates the adverb of intensity similar to the interpretations presented by the professional interpreters. However, for the evaluation of the adverb of intensity "SLOWLY", we can not identify the adequacy of this grammatical aspect in the translation generated by the application. Thus, we can infer that the translator presents partial adequacy of the evaluated grammatical aspect.

In the evaluation of the "LOW" Adverbs of Intensity, the translator presented the adequacy of this grammatical aspect in the translation process. As for the adverb of "MORE" and "VERY" intensity, the translator doesn't present correct intensification treatment for this adverb in the sentence studied. Thus, we can infer a partial treatment of this grammatical aspect by the translator. The averages of the obtained results can be observed in Fig. 4.

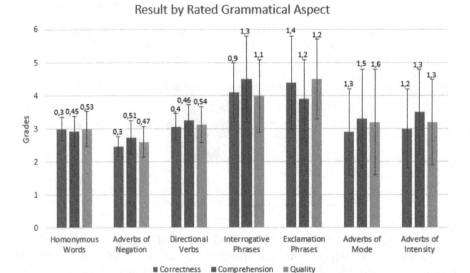

Fig. 4. Average assessment results by grammar aspect evaluated

It is noteworthy that the grammatical aspects of Adverbs of Mode and Intensity presented the highest standard deviations between the evaluations performed. Although the correctness of the translations presented in these grammatical aspects obtained marks below 3 points, they presented averages above 3 points for comprehension.

We can observe that none of the evaluated grammatical aspects presented maximum grade for correctness, comprehension, and quality of the translation. Thus, the methodology was able to identify weaknesses in the translation process of this translator, regarding the evaluated grammatical aspects.

5   Final Remarks

Machine translation of spoken languages into sign languages (or sign language machine translation) is a complex and non-trivial task, as different grammatical aspects need to be considered to minimize information loss and to promote understanding of the content generated by the translation.

This research had its scope defined around the proposal of a methodology for evaluation of the quality of the translation generated by sign language machine tic translators.

To evaluate the proposed methodology, we carried out a case study where we analyze seven grammatical aspects in one Libras machine translation tool. Grammatical aspects that need proper treatment in the translation process were selected because, if not treated correctly in these tools, they may impact the quality, comprehension, and correctness of the translations performed. The evaluated aspects were: Homonymous Words, Adverse Negation, Directional Verbs, Interrogative Phrases, Exclamative Phrases, Mode Adverbs, and Intensity Adverbs. As a result, we were able to identify weaknesses in the adequacy of the translation of the evaluated grammatical aspects, which makes it necessary to improve the translation quality of these aspects.

The methodology proposes an evaluation scheme using the participation of users (sign language interpreters or deaf users). Initially, the signing of the sentences evaluated by the sign language interpreters is recorded, addressing the defined grammatical aspects. The interpreters then evaluate the same sentences for Correction, Understanding, and Quality of the translations generated by the machine translator. Subsequently, interpreter signing videos, machine-generated translation, and results of interpreter translation evaluations are analyzed to identify similarities and discrepancies between human interpretation and machine translation.

As future work, we intend to extend the methodology for assessing translation quality without the participation of users, so that developers and/or researchers can apply this methodology without the need to recruit human interpreters, for example. In addition, we also intend to extend the evaluation methodology with the participation of deaf users, since it is essential to understand the needs of these users, in the evaluation process of these applications, in the search for continuous improvement of the translation process.

References

1. Araújo, T.M.U.: Uma solucção para geração automática de trilhas em Língua Brasileira de Sinais em conteúdos multimídia. Universidade Federal do Rio Grande do Norte (2012)
2. Capovilla, F.C., Raphael, W.D., Mauricio, A.C.: Novo dicionário enciclopédico ilustrado trilíngue da Língua de Sinais Brasileira (Novo Deit-Libras). Transtornos de aprendizagem: da avaliação à reabilitação, pp. 165–177 (2008)
3. Colling, J.P., Boscarioli, C.: Avaliação de tecnologias de tradução Português-Libras visando o uso no ensino de crianças surdas. RENOTE 12(2), 5–8 (2014)
4. Corrêa, Y., Vieira, M.C., Santarosa, L.M.C., Biasuz, M.C.V.: Tecnologia Assistiva: a inserção de aplicativos de tradução na promoção de uma melhor comunicação entre surdos e ouvintes. RENOTE 12(1), 5–6 (2014)
5. Corrêa, Y., Vieira, M.C., Santarosa, L.M.C., Biasuz, M.C.V.: Aplicativos de tradução para Libras e a busca pela validade social da Tecnologia Assistiva. In Brazilian Symposium on Computers in Education (Simpósio Brasileiro de Informática na Educação-SBIE), vol. 25, no. 1, p. 164 (2014)
6. de Quadros, R.M.: Educação de surdos: a aquisição da linguagem. Artmed Editora (2009)
7. de Quadros, R.M., Karnopp, L.B.: Língua de sinais brasileira: estudos linguísticos. Artmed Editora (2009)
8. Eco, U.: Quase a mesma coisa. Editora Record (2007)
9. Felipe, T.A.: Libras em contexto: curso básico: livro do estudante (2007)
10. Huenerfauth, M., Lu, P., Rosenberg, A. Evaluating importance of facial expression in American sign language and pidgin signed English animations. In: The proceedings of the 13th International ACM SIGACCESS Conference on Computers and Accessibility, pp. 99–106. ACM (2011)

11. Huenerfauth, M., Zhao, L., Gu, E., Allbeck, J.: Evaluating American Sign Language generation through the participation of native ASL signers. In: Proceedings of the 9th International ACM SIGACCESS Conference on Computers and Accessibility, pp. 211–218. ACM (2017)
12. Li, J., Yin, B., Wang, L., Kong, D.: Chinese Sign Language animation generation considering context. Multimed. Tools Appl. **71**(2), 469–483 (2014). https://doi.org/10.1007/s11042-013-1541-6
13. Lima, M.A., de Araújo, T.M., Oliveira, E.S.D.: Incorporation of syntactic-semantic aspects in a libras machine translation service to multimedia platforms. In: Proceedings of the 21st Brazilian Symposium on Multimedia and the Web, pp. 133–140. ACM (2015)
14. Morrissey, S.: Data-driven machine translation for sign languages. Doctoral dissertation, Dublin City University (2008)
15. San-Segundo, R., et al.: Design, development and field evaluation of a Spanish into sign language translation system. Pattern Anal. Appl. **15**(2), 203–224 (2012)
16. Santana, A. P. Surdez e linguagem: aspectos e implicações neurolinguísticas. Plexus Editora (2019)
17. Vieira, M.C., Corrêa, Y., Cheiran, J.F.P., Santarosa, L.M.C., Biasuz, M.C.V.: Contribuições da Teoria da Aprendizagem Multimídia e da Usabilidade para aprendizagem de Libras e Língua Portuguesa por meio de aplicativos móveis. RENOTE **12**(2), 7–8 (2014)
18. Vieira, M.C., Corrêa, Y., Santarosa, L.M., Biazus, M.: Análise de expressões não-manuais em avatares tradutores de Língua Portuguesa para Libras. In XIX Conferência Internacional sobre Informática na Educação-TISE, vol. 10 (2014)
19. Xu, L., Gao, W.: Study on translating Chinese into Chinese sign language. J. Comput. Sci. Technol. **15**(5), 485–490 (2000). https://doi.org/10.1007/BF02950413

Interest and Requirements for Sound-Awareness Technologies Among Deaf and Hard-of-Hearing Users of Assistive Listening Devices

Peter Yeung, Oliver Alonzo, and Matt Huenerfauth[✉]

Rochester Institute of Technology, Rochester, NY 14623, USA
{pxy9548,oa7652,matt.huenerfauth}@rit.edu

Abstract. Environmental sounds can provide important information about surrounding activity, yet recognizing sounds can be challenging for Deaf and Hard-of-Hearing (DHH) individuals. Prior work has examined the preferences of DHH users for various sound-awareness methods. However, these preferences have been observed to vary along some demographic factors. Thus, in this study we investigate the preferences of a specific group of DHH users: current assistive listening devices users. Through a survey of 38 participants, we investigated their challenges and requirements for sound-awareness applications, as well as which type of sounds and what aspects of the sounds are of importance to them. We found that users of assistive listening devices still often miss sounds and rely on other people to obtain information about them. Participants indicated that the importance of awareness of different types of sounds varied according to the environment and the form factor of the sound-awareness technology. Congruent with prior work, participants reported that the location and urgency of the sound were of importance, as well as the confidence of the technology in its identification of that sound.

Keywords: Sound-awareness technologies · Deaf and Hard-of-Hearing Users · Assistive listening devices users

1 Introduction

Environmental sounds can provide important information about surrounding activity, e.g. on a city street or in the workplace. Sounds are often part of societal conventions for conveying important information, such as drivers honking to alert another driver, alarms that indicate important times and emergencies, and announcements broadcast through loudspeakers at airports [1]. In addition, the activity and presence of other people may be sensed through sound, and many electronic devices (e.g. home appliances) may indicate their status through sound [7]. Recognizing many of these sounds, however, can be challenging for Deaf and Hard-of-Hearing (DHH) individuals. In this study, we expand upon prior work by investigating the perceptions of users of assistive listening devices in regard to the importance of sound awareness in various settings.

M. Antona and C. Stephanidis (Eds.): HCII 2020, LNCS 12189, pp. 147–158, 2020.
https://doi.org/10.1007/978-3-030-49108-6_11

Many assistive technologies for DHH individuals have been optimized for speech sounds to support verbal communication, including assistive listening devices such as hearing aids and cochlear implants [7]. However, even for speech related sounds, there is high variability in the effectiveness of those devices, which may be influenced by a number of demographic factors such as the age in which the wearer first obtains the device [2]. In addition, extensive training may be required to obtain a benefit [4]. Furthermore, users of assistive listening devices, e.g. hearing aids, often report challenges in interpreting sound direction, report sensitivity to background noise, or report missing sounds coming from specific directions [2].

In addition to assistive listening devices, specific techniques – such as devices which can trigger flashing lights when the sound of an infant crying or doorbell ringing is detected – can be used to increase awareness of specific sounds. However, prior work has found that these technologies that are specific to one sound are not widely adopted for various reasons, e.g. the monetary cost of purchasing many devices each for one specific sound [7]. Thus, researchers have suggested the use of applications for existing personal devices (e.g. smartphones and smartwatches) that could provide awareness for an array of non-speech sounds [1, 4, 7].

Various prior work has examined the preferences of DHH individuals for different aspects of such applications, including the form factor [3, 7] and the importance of identifying different types of sounds in those environments [1, 3, 7]. Notably, prior work has revealed that DHH users' perception of sound awareness technologies often varies along some demographic factors, e.g. the individual's preferred method of communication [3]. Thus, motivated by these prior findings and the limitations of assistive listening devices outlined above, in this work we focus on the preferences of a specific group of DHH users for sound-awareness technology: current users of assistive listening devices. In particular, we investigate what challenges and requirements they report for identifying sounds, which types of sounds they are interested in being aware of in different environments, and what information or properties of these sounds they are interested in knowing, e.g. where it comes from or how loud it is.

The contributions of this work include empirical information about challenges, needs, and requirements in regard to sound awareness technologies for this specific sub-group of DHH individuals. Furthermore, our work extends prior research by identifying user preferences as to the design of these technologies, e.g. which types or aspects of sounds DHH users care about, and whether the setting or form factor influences their preferences.

2   Prior Work

There has been prior work on the preferences of DHH users for various methods of obtaining sound awareness [e.g. 5–8]. Prior work has also explored various form factors for such technology (e.g. smartphones, smartwatches, head-mounted displays) and notification methods (e.g. haptic, visual). Prior researchers have investigated not only which sounds may be of interest [1, 7], but whether the environment or social context influences these preferences [1, 3]. Notably, prior work has revealed that DHH users' perception of sound awareness technologies may vary along some demographic factors, e.g. users' preferred method of communication [3].

2.1 Form Factors

Early work by [7] had explored different form factors including stationary (e.g. PC screen) and mobile ones (e.g. PDAs). In this early work, participants indicated preferring smaller form factors, such as a PDA or using only part of a PC screen. However, with the emergence of mobile technologies such as head-mounted displays (HMD), smartphones and smartwatches, more recent research has focused on the use of these technologies [1, 3, 6–8]. Jain et al. found enthusiasm for the use of HMD for sound-awareness [6]. However, more recent work by Findlater et al. found that smartphones and smartwatches score higher on social acceptability, usefulness and overall preferability than HMD, while HMD scored higher for captions (for transcribing speech) and easiness to glance [3]. Because in this work we are focused on non-speech sounds, we excluded HMD when asking users to imagine sound-awareness technologies and focused only on smartphones and smart-watches.

2.2 Environments

The early work of [7] had identified different environments in which sound-awareness may be desirable for DHH individuals. Environments that were identified were the home, the workplace, but perhaps most importantly, when someone is mobile (either when walking or when driving). Expanding on the findings of [7], the preferences of DHH individuals have been further investigated in [1], suggesting that DHH users' interest in different types of sounds varies according to the setting. The importance of these environments in the overall interest of DHH individuals in sound-awareness technologies in general has been further highlighted in [3], who found that this interest is also influenced by what other people are present in each environment. Thus, in this work, we focus on how various environments affect users' preferences.

2.3 Demographic Factors

In addition to the environment, prior work has also identified how different demographic factors influence the preferences of DHH individuals for sound-awareness technologies. For instance, researchers in [1] had identified that an individual's identity (i.e. as deaf or as hard-of-hearing) influenced which sounds they would be interested in. Furthermore, researchers in [3] identified that their participants' preferred mode of communication (i.e. oral, sign language, or both) also influenced their preferences. Thus, in this work, we focus on another key demographic sub-group of DHH users, namely individuals who currently use assistive listening devices.

3 Research Questions

Focusing on people who are DHH and who are current users of assistive listening devices, we investigate:

(1) What are the challenges and requirements for identifying sounds, as reported by DHH users of assistive listening devices?

(2) In various environments or settings, which types of sounds do DHH users of assistive listening devices report as being most important?
(3) What information about sounds are important to DHH users of assistive listening devices and how should that information be conveyed?

4 Methodology

To investigate our research questions, we conducted an online survey with DHH participants, all of whom regularly wore cochlear implants and/or hearing aids. The survey consisted of five sections, containing a mix of closed-ended and open-ended questions. The first section focused on demographic questions about their DHH identity, gender, age, and the number of hours a day they used their assistive listening devices. The second section consisted of open-ended questions focusing on their use of assistive technologies, the challenges they face when identifying sounds and features they would expect from a technology that provides information about sounds. The third section consisted of closed-ended questions focused on how they typically obtain information about the environment and how often they miss sounds in different environments (e.g. home, school). The fourth section contained Likert-type questions asking participants to indicate how much they cared about sound-awareness in different environments and multiple choice questions in which participants selected which sounds they cared about in those environments from a list identified in [1], along with a write-in "other" option. Lastly, a fifth and final section asked participants to indicate which aspects of sounds were of importance to them using a 6-point scale.

4.1 Procedure

The survey was hosted using Qualtrics and took approximately 15 min to complete. Participants in this IRB-approved study were first provided with an informed consent form. After this form, participants were taken through the five sections of the survey. At the end of the survey, participants were offered an opportunity to enter a raffle to receive a $100 gift card as a compensation for participating in the survey.

4.2 Participants and Recruitment

Participants were recruited by word of mouth, social media posts on Facebook community pages, and posters in bulletin boards across the Rochester Institute of Technology, the National Technical Institute for the Deaf, and the surrounding community. A total of 38 participants were recruited. Participants' ages ranged from 19 to 50 ($\mu = 24.6$). Twenty-three participants identified as deaf/Deaf, while the other 15 identified as Hard-of-Hearing. All participants regularly wore cochlear implants and/or hearing aids. Participants reported that they used these devices between 2 to 24 h per day ($\mu = 10.5$).

4.3   Data Analysis

The results of the open-ended questions were analyzed through a coding system shown in Table 1 and through affinity diagraming. During the coding stage, the first author identified themes in the data, later developing categories based on the resulting themes. Then, the data was organized using an affinity diagram (Fig. 1), sorting it based on the categories generated through the previous step. The results of the closed-ended questions, in turn, were analyzed through descriptive statistics, providing percentages for the scale-based questions and counts for the multiple-choice ones.

Table 1. Coding system used in our analysis.

Naming types	Description or examples
Challenges	What challenges participants report in identifying sounds (e.g., identifying sound location, specific issues with high- or low-pitch sounds, loudness, sound clarity) **Subgroups: Pitch and frequency and Location**
Requirements	What features participants wanted in a future app (e.g. vibrations, flashing screens, notifications) **Subgroups: Forms of Visual Representations, Forms of Notifications for Sound Awareness, and Usability**
Assistive technologies	What assistive technology participants have currently? **Subgroups: Cochlear Implants and Hearing Aids**
How well they can hear sounds in their environment currently	Examples: I listen to sounds outside, hears the dialogue

5   Results and Discussion

In this section, we present and discuss the results of the survey, and we report the data from all 38 respondents. This section is organized by first discussing the open-ended response data, which is followed by the results from the closed-ended items.

Two of the categories identified from the open-ended data included how well participants could hear sounds in their environment currently, how their assistive technologies improved their hearing of such sounds, and any remaining challenges they faced. These categories are summarized in the affinity diagram shown in Fig. 1.

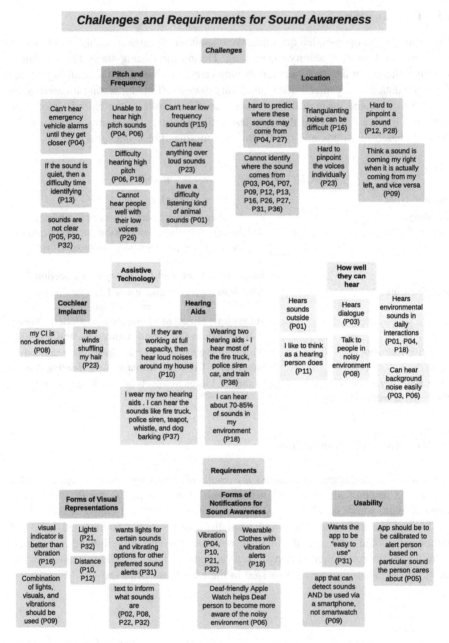

Fig. 1. Affinity Diagram summarizing open-ended responses from the survey

We noted a wide diversity in the responses for how well users reported being able to hear sounds in their environment, and in the challenges they currently face when recognizing sounds. Some participants reported being able to hear all environmental sounds when using their assistive listening devices. For example, participants discussed their hearing abilities when using assistive listening devices in terms of what percentage of the sounds in the environment or which sounds they can hear:

"Wearing hearing aids, I can hear about 70–85% of sounds in my environment." (P18)

"I wearing my two hearing aids and can hearing the sound most of the fire truck, police siren car, train, teapot whistle, and a dog barking." (P37)

In turn, as shown in Fig. 1, the major challenges discussed by participants could be grouped into some comments relating to the location of a sound or relating to the pitch/frequency of a sound. For instance, some participants indicated specific difficulty with high-frequency sounds, and others commented on difficulties they experienced in identifying the location of sounds or in pinpointing individual voices when in a group of people. For instance:

"Moderate difficulty. Sometimes I can identify the noise from a location, but if it's quieter, I have a hard time to identify." (P13)

"Always. It's difficult for me to pinpoint the location a sound is being made." (P28)

Participants were presented with the idea that future technology may be able to detect sounds in their environment and make them aware of such sounds and their characteristics. Participants were asked about their requirements for such future sound-awareness applications, as shown in the final category included in the affinity diagram shown in Fig. 1. For instance, participants discussed their requirements in regard to the usability of such an application; they also provided recommendations about the type of form-factor for such a device (e.g. smartphone, smartwatch) or the different forms of feedback such an application could incorporate (e.g. haptic or visual). Users also indicated that they were interested in being able to personalize which sounds they would be notified about – this finding was in accordance to the results in [3], which had found that users wanted the ability to "filter" being notified about certain sounds. Some comments from participants illustrating these requirements include:

"Create an app that can detect sounds AND be used via a smartPHONE ... not just limited to a smartwatch. Combination of lights, visuals, and vibrations should be used otherwise the user may mistake it for a random text message, email alert, etc." (P09)

"I would love the app to be 'easy to use' and set up - you could have lights for certain sounds (e.g. for alarms) or vibrating options for other preferred sound alerts." (P31)

"Vibration and Lights are important. So, the app should feature these..." (P21)

The remainder of this section focusses on responses from participants to closed-ended question items on the survey. As shown in Fig. 2, when asked about how they currently obtain information about sounds in their environment, 53% of participants reported using hearing aids "all the time" and 32% reported using cochlear implants "all the time." Perhaps surprisingly, given that our participants were regular users of assistive listening devices, our participants reported that they still often asked friends, family, or other people to inform them about environmental sounds. Relatively few

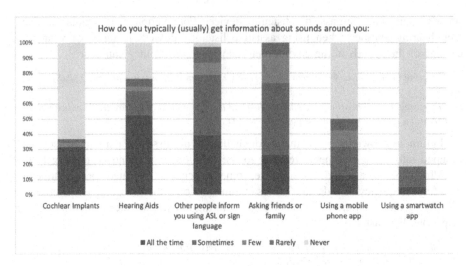

Fig. 2. How often participants used various sound-awareness methods

users indicated that they currently used mobile-phone applications or smartwatch applications to receive notifications about sounds in their environment.

We next asked participants about how often they believed that they missed important sound information, in various settings. The majority of participants reported missing important sounds at least once per day when: mobile and looking at their phone, at work/school, or at home, as shown in Fig. 3. Of course, various factors may affect which types of sounds participants miss most often: For instance, in open-ended comments (summarized in Fig. 1), participants reported having particular difficulty in identifying sounds at certain frequencies (e.g. high or low) or in determining the location of sounds.

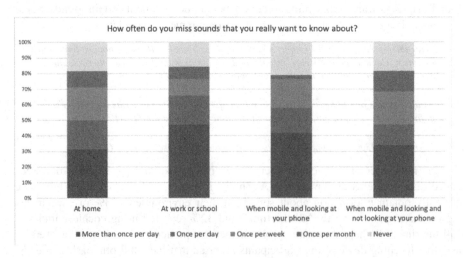

Fig. 3. How often participants missed sounds of interest

Participants also indicated how important it is to be aware of sounds in the environment in various settings, including: when at home, when at work/school, when mobile (e.g. in a city), or when at a restaurant. Figure 4 indicates that our participants reported greater interest in being aware of sounds at home, at work/school, or when mobile.

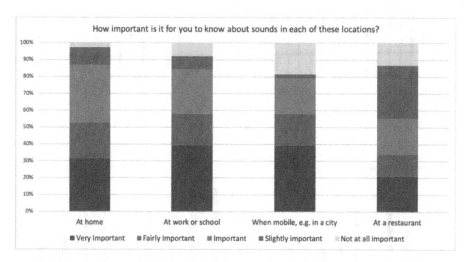

Fig. 4. The importance of sounds in different environments

For various settings (home, work/school, when driving/walking), we asked participants to indicate which sounds they would be most interested in being aware of (as shown in Fig. 5). Given prior research on DHH users' interest in smartphones and smartwatches [3], for the driving/walking setting, we also asked participants to rate their interest in being notified about sounds, when using each of those form-factors (smartphone or smartwatch). Having this information about user interest in various form-factors may be useful for future researchers, especially since our participants' open-ended responses, congruent with prior work [3], revealed that DHH users may want to filter which sounds an app recognizes. However, this filtering may depend upon which form factor is being used.

Finally, we asked participants which aspects of sound were of greatest interest to them (e.g. loudness, location) and how they would want to receive such information (Fig. 6). Since sound-awareness technologies may be able to provide users with information about some of these properties, it is therefore important to identify which are of greatest interest to users. Congruent with the prior findings of [1] and [3], most of our participants wanted to know where sounds come from, how urgent a particular sound is, and how certain the sound-awareness technology was about the sound.

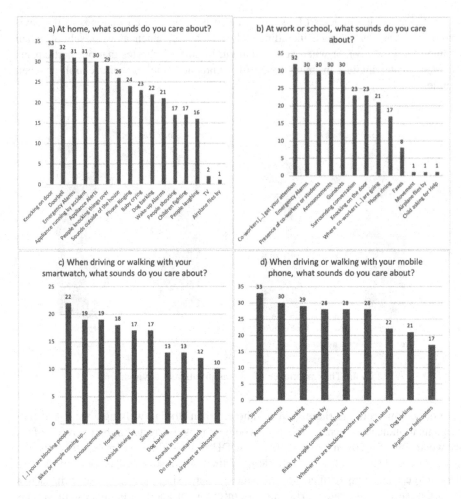

Fig. 5. Sounds of interest sorted from highest to lowest at a) home, b) work or school, c) when driving or walking with sound-notification via smartwatch, d) when driving or walking with sound-notification via smartphone

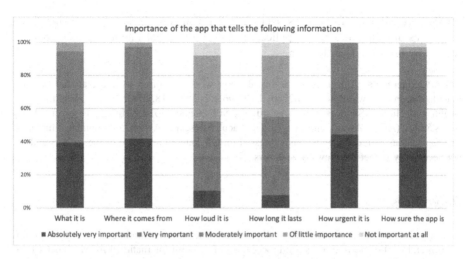

Fig. 6. Importance of different aspects of a sound when the app detects one

6   Discussion, Limitations, and Future Work

This paper has presented an online survey among 38 DHH users of assistive listening devices, to understand their interests and requirements in regard to sound-awareness technologies. The findings of our study are largely congruent with those of prior work, e.g. [1, 3]. Our work extends on this prior research by focusing on a specific sub-group of DHH users: individuals who currently use assistive listening devices. Since prior work had found that interest in sound-awareness varies along some demographic characteristics [3], studies of this nature that focus on a particular subset of the DHH population are valuable for confirming whether findings hold true among particular groups.

Our study found that participants reported often missing sounds in their environment, and they reported that they often relied on other people to obtain information about such sounds. The degree to which our participants assigned importance to being aware of specific sounds varied according to the environment and the form factor of the sound-awareness application. Lastly, our participants indicated that both the location of a sound and urgency of that sound were of particular interest to them, and they also indicated that they wanted to know the confidence of the sound-detection application – findings that are congruent with prior work in this area [1, 3].

There were three main limitations of our work. First, we only looked at users of assistive listening devices. Future work may include a comparison of both users assistive listening devices and people who are DHH who choose not to use these devices, which may help determine whether the decision of using assistive listening devices influences their preferences for other sound-awareness technologies. Second, our study may not have been sufficiently powered to determine whether there were any statistically significant differences in our data. Lastly, while we obtained some initial data about preferences for an application that would provide sound-awareness, we had asked users to imagine such an application. In future work, we may obtain more detailed requirements from users using assistive listening devices by showing them prototypes of sound-awareness applications informed by our findings in this work, as well as by prior work in the area.

Acknowledgements. This material is based upon work supported by the National Science Foundation under Award Nos. 1462280, 1540396, 1763569, 1822747; by the Department of Health and Human Services under Award No. 90DPCP0002-01-00; by a Microsoft AI for Accessibility (AI4A) Award; and by a Google Faculty Research Award. Any opinions, findings, and conclusions or recommendations expressed in this material are those of the authors and do not necessarily reflect the views of sponsors.

References

1. Bragg, D., Huynh, N., Ladner, R.E.: A personalizable mobile sound detector app design for deaf and hard-of-hearing users. In: Proceedings of the 18th International ACM SIGACCESS Conference on Computers and Accessibility (ASSETS 2016), pp. 3–13. ACM, New York (2016). https://doi.org/10.1145/2982142.2982171
2. Cochlear Implants: American Speech-Language-Hearing Association. https://www.asha.org/public/hearing/Cochlear-Implant/. Accessed 16 Jan 2020
3. Findlater, L., Chinh, B., Jain, D., Froehlich, J., Kushalnagar, R., Lin, A.C.: Deaf and hard-of-hearing individuals' preferences for wearable and mobile sound awareness technologies. In: Proceedings of the 2019 CHI Conference on Human Factors in Computing Systems (CHI 2019), Paper 46, p. 13. ACM, New York (2019). https://doi.org/10.1145/3290605.3300276
4. Fu, Q.-J., Galvin, J.J.: Maximizing cochlear implant patients' performance with advanced speech training procedures. Hear. Res. **242**(1–2), 198–208 (2008). https://doi.org/10.1016/j.heares.2007.11.010
5. Ho-Ching, F.W., Mankoff, J., Landay, J.A.: Can you see what I hear? The design and evaluation of a peripheral sound display for the deaf. In: Proceedings of the SIGCHI Conference on Human Factors in Computing Systems (CHI 2003), pp. 161–168. ACM, New York (2003). https://doi.org/10.1145/642611.642641
6. Jain, D., et al.: Head-mounted display visualizations to support sound awareness for the deaf and hard of hearing. In: Proceedings of the 33rd Annual ACM Conference on Human Factors in Computing Systems (CHI 2015), pp. 241–250. ACM, New York. https://doi.org/10.1145/2702123.2702393
7. Matthews, T., Fong, J., Mankoff, J.: Visualizing non-speech sounds for the deaf. In: Proceedings of the 7th International ACM SIGACCESS Conference on Computers and Accessibility (Assets 2005), pp. 52–59. ACM, New York (2005). https://doi.org/10.1145/1090785.1090797
8. Mielke, M., Brück, R.: A pilot study about the smartwatch as assistive device for deaf people. In: Proceedings of the 17th International ACM SIGACCESS Conference on Computers & Accessibility (ASSETS 2015), pp. 301–302. ACM, New York (2015). https://doi.org/10.1145/2700648.2811347

Universal Access to Learning and Education

Providing a Tangible and Visual Feedback of Affective States Self-expressions

Eliana Alves Moreira[1,2]([✉]), Julián Alberto Herrera[3],
and M. Cecília C. Baranauskas[2]

[1] Federal Institute of Education, Science and Technology of São Paulo (IFSP),
Guarulhos, SP, Brazil
eliana.moreira@ifsp.edu.br
[2] Institute of Computing, University of Campinas (UNICAMP),
Campinas, SP, Brazil
cecilia@ic.unicamp.br
[3] Eldorado Research Institute, Campinas, SP, Brazil
julian.herrera@eldorado.org.br

Abstract. Understanding people's emotion and affective states in educational environments is relevant given the intrinsic relationship between emotion and learning. In this work, we designed artefacts that use tangible technologies to provide manikins to report the person's affective states in three dimensions: pleasure, arousal and dominance. In a school environment, the tangible artefacts can joyfully trigger the self-expression of affective states in the students and in the teachers' practice. In order to raise the school's awareness about the self-assessment practice of expressing affective states, a joyful data presentation using a LED board was proposed as a visual feedback, which was named SAMLight. The LEDs light up according to the assessment results of the affective states of the students in different classes in the school. To evaluate the system, we carried out sessions with students of eight different classes. The results show that the visual feedback was very illustrative to both students and teachers, leading them to reflect about the subject concerning the classes and school environments.

Keywords: Affective states · Tangible interaction · Visual feedback · Inclusive educational environment

1 Introduction

Understanding people's emotion and affective states in educational environments is relevant given the intrinsic relationship between emotion and learning. Several authors have shown the importance of considering students' emotional aspects in their learning experiences and teaching relation [1, 2]. Schmidt [3] discussed in his study that harnessing the positive powers of emotion in learning is as important as mentioning some of the challenging aspects, since emotion also has the power to significantly disrupt learning.

A brief literature review shows that several authors have proposed tools aiming at helping children learn about their emotional expressions. Marshall, Rogers, & Scaife [4]

© Springer Nature Switzerland AG 2020
M. Antona and C. Stephanidis (Eds.): HCII 2020, LNCS 12189, pp. 161–172, 2020.
https://doi.org/10.1007/978-3-030-49108-6_12

proposed the "PUPPET System", which allows children to play multiple roles in an interactive narrative, as they role-play a character and reason about the character's emotional states and goals. "Storyfaces" [5] is a composition and storytelling tool for children to explore the role of emotional expressions in their narrative. The authors use the concept of working on and composing stories by using a pre-recorded video of one's facial expressions.

The purpose of these works is to make the agents think over the characters' affective states. In our approach, artefacts that use tangible technologies were created so that children express themselves by choosing a tangible manikin representing affective states. These artefacts represent in a concrete and three-dimensional way the two-dimensional manikins of the Self-Assessment Manikin (SAM), proposed by Bradley & Lang [6]. SAM is an assessment instrument that allows to express emotions regarding the activity being performed. Three dimensions of affective states are addressed: pleasure, arousal and dominance. In a school environment, the tangible artefacts can joyfully promote the self-expression of affective states in the students and lead to reflections in the teachers' practice.

In previous studies, we used these tangible artefacts so that the students self-expressed their affective states throughout the class. A graphical representation of affective states may be useful for analysis by the teacher. When teachers have the children's affective states expressed, they may reflect and adjust their working practices with the children. For providing the children with access to the data regarding the whole class affective states, this paper focusses on the process of developing this visual feedback. In addition, it also presents the results of its use with students of eight different inclusive classes.

This paper is structured as follows: Sect. 1 introduces context, some related work, the research problem and objectives; Sect. 2 presents the research methodology and workshops conducted; Sect. 3 presents the design of the artefact and its implementation; Sect. 4 reports the obtained results and discusses the findings; Sect. 5 presents conclusions and future work.

2   Research Background and Methodology

Bradley & Lang [6] proposed the Self-Assessment Manikin (SAM), a pictorial instrument of self-evaluation of pleasure, arousal and dominance concerning the affective state. SAM was originally proposed as an interactive computational program and later expanded to a paper and pen version, in which the person has a scale of nine possible choices for each dimension. It uses two-dimensional representative figures of manikins and expressions to indicate affective states on a scale for each dimension. For instance, the Pleasure dimension ranges from smiling (happy) figures to unhappy-looking figures. To represent the dimension of Arousal, figures ranging from very enthusiastic (with a big chest burst and wide eyes) to a disinterested figure (with a tiny chest burst and sleepy, with closed eyes). The Dominance dimension refers to the degree of control over the situation, represented by changes in the size of the SAM representative figure: a large figure indicates maximum control over the situation/activity. When expressing their affective state, people can select one of the five figures for each dimension, or the state "between" two figures.

According to Ishii [7], tangible interfaces technologies physically shape digital information by using physical artefacts that work as representations and controls for computational media. They provide a direct user interaction with interactive systems that are generally not identifiable as "computers" (author's highlight) *per se*. This led us to believe that an assessment artefact featuring these tangibility characteristics could be useful for children.

In previous studies, we used tangible artefacts [8–11] and we noticed that children were very interested in the interaction with tangible computational objects. Therefore, we proposed a tangible version of the SAM, named TangiSAM, which contains sets of three-dimensional manikins for each dimension (*cf.* (a), (b), and (c) in Fig. 1 for the Pleasure, Arousal and Dominance dimensions, respectively). The TangiSAM has a scale of five possible choices of manikins for each dimension.

(a)

(b)

(c)

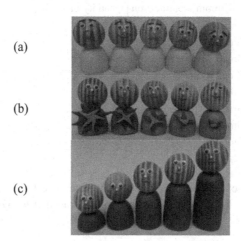

Fig. 1. Representation of the TangiSAM for the three dimensions of the affective state: yellow, red and green bodies represent the sets for the dimensions of Pleasure (a), Arousal (b) and Dominance (c), respectively. (Color figure online)

We used the TangiSAM in an educational context so that the students could self-express their affective states, by selecting one manikin in each dimension. When having the data of all students, we presented the results in charts as visual feedback. The design of the latter and an example of its application will be fully presented throughout this paper.

2.1 Context of Study, Participants and Gathered Data

We carried out eight sessions of using this system in different classes in collaboration with the Inclusive Education Program of the municipal education system of Amparo city, in the state of São Paulo, Brazil [12]. In Amparo's schools, all the regular classes with special education students have regular and assistant teachers, aiming at the collaborative teaching in class and the follow-up of students who attend the special education. Moreover, special education teachers personalize resources for students with complex communication needs, providing complementary pedagogical practices to help the students succeed in elementary school.

The number of students that answered the self-assessment of affective states is shown in Table 1. Each group represents students of a class. The groups are inclusive and have children with disability, such as hard of hearing students, others with autism, intellectual and motor disability. The users' participation was anonymous, and the data were gathered in two days. The activities were approved by the Ethics Committee on Research from the University of Campinas (UNICAMP), under the number 55678316.4.0000.5404.

Table 1. Groups of students.

Classroom identification	Quantity of participants
Group 1	15
Group 2	20
Group 3	22
Group 4	25
Group 5	14
Group 6	15
Group 7	12
Group 8	21

Each student self-expressed once his/her affective state by choosing three Tangi-SAM's manikins: one for Pleasure, one for Arousal and one for Dominance.

3 The SAMLight Artefact

In order to raise the school's awareness about the self-assessment of affective states practice, a joyful data presentation using a LED board was proposed as a visual feedback, which was named SAMLight. The LEDs light up according to the assessment results of the affective states of the students in different classes in the school.

We developed a mobile application, named SAMobile, which is the technological environment to run the proposed tools. The mobile device must feature Near-Field Communication (NFC) technology, Bluetooth technology and run Android™ operating system.

3.1 Design Rationale of SAMLight

The SAMobile app provides charts for each class containing the information chosen by the participants on their affective states. There are several types of charts and graphics with information related to the activities and the participants. While the professionals in education may find it easy to deal with the charts, the children may not fully understand them because the complexity of the information is not suitable for their age.

We believe that a suitable information for the children could be to know which manikin was the most chosen in the class. Therefore, we idealized a visual feedback using a board with LEDs that would light up according to the choices on the children's affective states.

In previous works, we analyzed the results of people's self-expressions of their affective states by rating the choices for each dimension according to the number of options available [8, 9, 11]. For example, in TangiSAM the choices are rated on a scale from 1 to 5, where five is very motivated, very satisfied or with high dominance in an activity, and one is little motivated, little satisfied and with low dominance in an activity. Rating the manikins on a scale from 1 to 5 is similar to the scoring system in games. The children can associate the scores with each manikin, so the manikins very unhappy, very unmotivated and very hard would have the score 1.

As the manikins are rated from 1 to 5 in each dimension, the artifact features 15 LEDs to represent the three dimensions for each group, with five LEDs for each dimension. The number of LEDs that will light up for each class/dimension is the mode value of the answers in the class. For example, if the manikin rated 4 appears most often in the answers for the Dominance dimension, then four LEDs light up to represent the result of the Dominance dimension in this class. The colors of the LEDs refer to each dimension according to the predominant colors in the manikins used for the choices, where yellow is for Pleasure, red is for Arousal, and green is for Dominance. Figure 2 shows the SAMLight prototype.

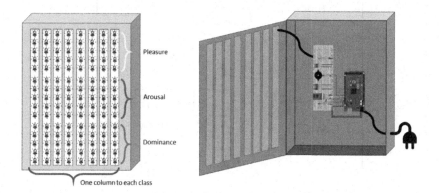

Fig. 2. SAMLight prototype. To the left, the external part, with the LEDs; to the right, Arduino Processor in the internal part. (Color figure online)

There are two types of information in our visual feedback display: (a) the manikin for each dimension who was the most chosen by the students; (b) the manikin among all dimensions who was the most chosen by the students.

3.2   Technical Structure

SAMLight is composed of eight columns with 15 LEDs each. Each column has five LEDs to represent each of the three dimensions in the tangible artefact. The result received from the application triggers the number of LEDs that will be light up.

The LED bar circuit was implemented around the open-source Arduino system, (https://www.arduino.cc/), a popular and easy to use electronics platform with an extensive ecosystem of peripherals and an active community of users around it.

Figure 3 shows the schematic diagram of the circuit, which uses an Arduino Mega 2560 (Rev. 3) board as its controller. The LED bars (columns) are made of segments of RGB LED strips, as shown in the wiring diagram of Fig. 4. There are eight LED columns, each with fifteen LEDs. The columns are connected in sequence: the DOUT signal coming out of the last LED of a column is routed to the DIN signal of the first LED of the next column. The power supply lines to the LED columns (GND and VCC) follow the same connection pattern, for convenience. The microcontroller in the Arduino board drives the DIN signal of the LED strips through the LED_STRIP_DATA serial data signal.

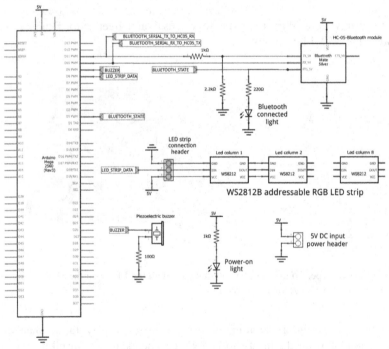

Fig. 3. Schematic diagram of the LED bar circuit.

In this project, we used the ubiquitous 5-volt WS2812B addressable LED strip, which is made of RGB LEDs connected in cascade. Each LED can be addressed individually via a serial interface, granting control of a virtually unlimited number of LEDs through a single wire. The LEDs are configured by setting the intensities of their red, green and blue components separately. Each component accepts 256 values of intensity from dark to maximum intensity, for a total of over 16 million possible colors. At its maximum brightness, a LED will drain around 60 mA. This translates to a peak current demand of 7.2 A if all the 120 LEDs are fully lit.

The configuration of the color and brightness of the LEDs follows commands received via a Bluetooth link, provided by the popular and easy-to-use HC-05 Bluetooth module. This module supports the Bluetooth Serial Port Profile (SPP) and thus provides a simple serial interface for bidirectional data transmission between two devices. In our circuit, the Bluetooth module connects to the board via two signal paths; one for data received wirelessly from a remote client (BLUETOOTH_SERIAL_RX_TO_HC05_TX) and the other for data transmitted back to the client (BLUETOOTH_SERIAL_TX_TO_HC05_RX). Since the Bluetooth module uses 3.3 V signals, the 5 V data signal coming from the Arduino board must be shifted down in order to avoid damaging the module's inputs; this is done by the voltage divider formed by the R1 and R2 resistors.

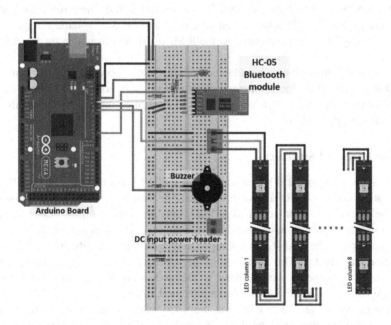

Fig. 4. Wiring diagram of the LED bar circuit. Made with the fritzing open-source EDA application (https://fritzing.org/).

In our application, the Bluetooth module is used as a Slave. Upon power up, the module will sit listening for connection requests. Upon accepting a connection from a client (a Master device) it will assert the BLUETOOTH_STATE line, informing the Arduino that a connection has been established. The *Bluetooth-connected light* will also light up to indicate this condition.

The circuit features a piezoelectric buzzer that provides acoustic feedback for the commands received by the unit. The buzzer is controlled by a pulse-width modulated (PWM) signal coming from the BUZZER pin. The 100 Ω resistor connected in series prevents overloading of the sensitive piezoelectric element. The buzzer will emit audible beeps when a connection to a client is established or tore down and when a new configuration command is received.

The circuit is powered by a regular 5 V AC to DC wall adapter. We found that an adapter capable of supplying a current of 5 A is enough for our purposes since, in most use cases, the LEDs won't be lit at their highest brightness, so the 7.2 A peak current demand won't be reached.

The Arduino device was programmed using the online Arduino Editor (https://create.arduino.cc/). The main loop of the program will wait for incoming data from the Bluetooth module. The data is structured ASCII text representing a command to the device. The microcontroller will parse the text commands and perform the respective actions (for example, setting the color of a specific LED), returning to the listening state afterwards. We rely on the Adafruit NeoPixel library (available at https://github.com/adafruit/Adafruit_NeoPixel) to control the WS2812B LED strips. Each LED requires three bytes of SRAM to store the intensity values for each of the three color components, thus, the entire LED columns consume only 360 bytes of volatile storage, which is almost negligible when compared to the 8 kB of SRAM available on the Arduino Mega.

The system can probably be adapted to run from a conventional Arduino Uno board, but we settled for the comparatively expensive Arduino Mega 2560 because the Mega's larger program, EEPROM and SRAM memories opened the possibility for more complex applications.

3.3   Architectural Structure

In our system, each manikin has an associated RFID tag containing a unique-10-digit identification code. The RFID numeric codes are sent to the SAMobile application when the manikin is approached to an NFC reader, which communicates with the system to register the self-assessments. These data are stored in a database.

To implement the SAMLight solution, a specific functionality in the SAMobile application was created. This functionality digests data of the affective states, using a 1-to-5 range to rate the chosen manikins, so the mode value for each dimension/class is found. Figure 5 shows the SAMLight architectural structure.

When the values are already known, the SAMobile app creates a text file with a .TXT file extension that must be manually saved by the user. This text file contains commands that will lead the Arduino application to decide which LEDs will light up. As each column has 15 LEDs, each line in the file will reference one of the LEDs in the artefact. Figure 6 represents a sequence of commands in a .TXT file created by SAMobile. The first line in the file shows the $CA command, which turns off all the LEDs. The remaining lines show the command in the $SL: CC,RR,HH format, where CC refers to the number of the column (01 to 08, left to right); RR refers to the number of the LED line (01 to 15, bottom to top); HH refers to the RGB value in the hexadecimal color that the LED will show (for example, FF,00,00 is for red). The file contains up to 121 command lines, which correspond to the initial line and the line of each one of the 15 LEDs for each one of the eight different groups.

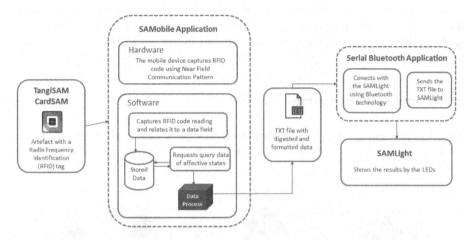

Fig. 5. SAMLight architectural structure functionality.

```
$CA
$SL:01,15,FF,FF,00
$SL:01,06,FF,00,00
$SL:01,07,FF,00,00
$SL:01,08,FF,00,00
$SL:01,09,FF,00,00
$SL:01,10,FF,00,00
$SL:01,01,00,FF,00
$SL:01,02
```

Fig. 6. Example of a sequence of commands in the file for the application in the Arduino to light up the LEDs.

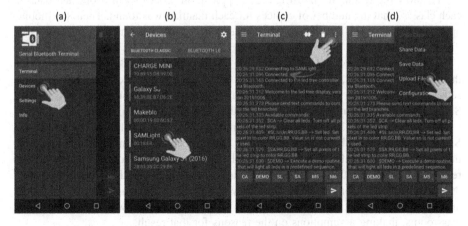

Fig. 7. Performing the serial bluetooth.

The data of the .TXT file are sent via Bluetooth to the Arduino processor, which controls the LED lights according to what it receives. The Serial Bluetooth app (Fig. 7) is used to send the data to Arduino, and it must be installed in the mobile device that the .TXT file is saved. The Bluetooth connection must be done with the SAMLight when running the app. (*cf.* (a), (b) and (c) in Fig. 7). Then, the .TXT file with the data generated by the SAMobile app must be uploaded so that the LEDs show the results (*cf.* (d) in Fig. 7).

4   Results and Discussion

Sessions were carried out with the TangiSAM in eight inclusive classes where some children with disabilities were enrolled. Figure 8 shows some moments of these sessions.

Fig. 8. Sessions moments with children choosing the manikins.

To show the results in SAMLight, the application processed the collected data of each class so that the number of choices for each manikin was found. Then, the mobile application processed the data of each classroom so that the mode value for each dimension was found.

Before running the SAMLight, the value (1 to 5) of each manikin was recalled with the students. After that, the SAMLight with the visual result of the mode values of the self-assessed affective states was presented. Figure 9 shows some moments of the SAMLight presentation with the results of the students' affective states.

We observed that the children were interested in the results presented by the SAMLight. They asked questions about how the numbers had been chosen. In addition, they reflected on the affective state of the class for each dimension and discussed the reasons why they had that result (for example, they reported that the Dominance rating 3 means a Regular Dominance because they had performed the assessment right after an exam). We also noticed that the students were curious to know the results of other classrooms, making assumptions on the reasons for that result.

The teacher also showed interest in the results even though they have access to more complete data using the SAMobile functionalities. The teachers talked with the students during the result presentation and asked the students to reflect on the data.

Fig. 9. Presentation moments of the SAMLight results for the students.

The awareness of students' affective states in the class is important because it may directly influence and affect the teaching-learning process. Moreover, with this information, the professional of education (teacher, pedagogical coordination, principal) may adjust different teaching situations so that the student does not have disadvantages in his/her learning in relation to the other students.

This awareness must exceed the field of professionals in education and reach the students so that they have a feedback on their affective states. However, the feedback with two-dimensional charts may be rather abstract. Therefore, the visual feedback of self-assessments with SAMLight is an engaging and playful way to raise children's awareness about their affective states, not exposing directly their individual responses, although affecting the group he/she belongs to.

Furthermore, the assessment feedback of affective states not only is used for indicating negative aspects, but it also provides a great opportunity to talk with the students reflecting on their feeling on learning, their personal and collective development. The awareness demands long-term changes in the culture of the schools and the reinforcement of positive aspects of approaching the affective states of students as the professionals in education can take actions towards a healthy educational environment.

5   Conclusion

The assessment of people's affective states has been addressed in several academic works. The assessment feedbacks are often done by using two-dimensional charts representations. In this work, we presented SAMLight, an artifact for a visual assessment feedback of affective states to help children understand and situate their affective states in the affective state of the whole class. The results of SAMLight practical applications in the classes observed indicated that both children and professionals of education showed interest in the subject and this type of feedback. In future works, we would like to use the artefact throughout a semester in a school, in order to conduct a thoroughly study on the changes in the children's affective states along their quotidian school life.

Acknowledgements. This work was supported by the Federal Institute of São Paulo, National Council of Technological and Scientific Development - CNPq - (#306272/2017-2), São Paulo Research Foundation (FAPESP, grant #2015/16528-0) and Institute of Computing at University of Campinas (UNICAMP). Special thanks to the Education Secretariat of city of Amparo/São Paulo/Brazil.

References

1. Balaam, M., Fitzpatrick, G., Good, J., Luckin, R.: Exploring affective technologies for the classroom with the subtle stone. In: Conference on Human Factors in Computing Systems (CHI 2010) (2010)
2. Worsley, M., Blikstein, P.: Using learning analytics to study cognitive disequilibrium in a complex learning environment. In: International Conference on Learning Analytics and Knowledge, pp. 426–427 (2015)
3. Schmidt, S.J.: Embracing and harnessing the intimate connection between emotion and cognition to help students learn. Food Sci. Educ. **2**, 1–10 (2019)
4. Marshall, P., Rogers, Y., Scaife, M.: PUPPET : a virtual environment for children to act and direct interactive narratives. In: International Workshop on Narrative and Interactive Learning Environments, pp. 6–9 (2002)
5. Ryokai, K., Raffle, H., Kowalski, R.: StoryFaces: pretend-play with ebooks to support social-emotional storytelling. In: Interaction Design and Children, pp. 125–133 (2012)
6. Bradley, M.M., Lang, P.J.: Measuring emotion: the self-assessment manikin and the semantic differential. J. Behav. Ther. Exp. Psychiatry **25**(1), 49–59 (1994)
7. Ishii, H.: Tangible bits: beyond pixels. In: International Conference on Tangible and Embedded Interaction (TEI 2008), no. November, pp. 15–25 (2008)
8. Moreira, E.A., Baranauskas, M.C.C.: Investigando processos de comunicação alternativa via tecnologia tangível: um estudo exploratório. In: Brazilian Symposium on Computers in Education, pp. 856–865 (2016)
9. Moreira, E.A., Carbajal, M.L., Baranauskas, M.C.C.: Creative learning and artefacts making: promises and challenges in practice. In: Zaphiris, P., Ioannou, A. (eds.) Learning and Collaboration Technologies. Designing Learning Experiences. HCII 2019. Lecture Notes in Computer Science, vol. 11590, pp. 856–865. Springer, Cham (2019). https://doi.org/10.1007/978-3-030-21814-0_24
10. Moreira, E.A., et al.: Explorando a Utilização de Storyboard em um Ambiente Tangível de Apoio à Comunicação Alternativa e Aumentativa. In: Brazilian Symposium on Computers in Education, pp. 1083–1092 (2018)
11. Moreira, E.A., Baranauskas, M.C.C.: Alice das Coisas: entendendo a comunicação entre objetos na construção de ambientes de aprendizagem. In: Anais do XXVIII Simpósio Brasileiro de Informática na Educação (SBIE 2017), vol. 1, no. Cbie, p. 1017 (2017)
12. Amparo: Secretaria Municipal de Educação. Programa de Educação Inclusiva : A educação tem muitas faces – Educando e aprendendo na diversidade Secretaria Municipal de Educação, Amparo (2016)

Accessible Computer Science for K-12 Students with Hearing Impairments

Meenakshi Das[1], Daniela Marghitu[1(✉)], Fatemeh Jamshidi[1],
Mahender Mandala[2], and Ayanna Howard[2]

[1] Auburn University, Auburn, AL 36830, USA
marghda@auburn.edu
[2] Georgia Institute of Technology, Atlanta, GA 30332, USA

Abstract. An inclusive science, technology, engineering and mathematics (STEM) workforce is needed to maintain America's leadership in the scientific enterprise. Increasing the participation of underrepresented groups in STEM, including persons with disabilities, requires national attention to fully engage the nation's citizens in transforming its STEM enterprise. To address this need, a number of initiatives, such as AccessCSforALL, Bootstrap, and CSforAll, are making efforts to make Computer Science inclusive to the 7.4 million K-12 students with disabilities in the U.S. Of special interest to our project are those K-12 students with hearing impairments. American Sign Language (ASL) is the primary means of communication for an estimated 500,000 people in the United States, yet there are limited online resources providing Computer Science instruction in ASL. This paper introduces a new project designed to support Deaf/Hard of Hearing (D/HH) K-12 students and sign interpreters in acquiring knowledge of complex Computer Science concepts. We discuss the motivation for the project and an early design of the accessible block-based Computer Science curriculum to engage D/HH students in hands-on computing education.

Keywords: Accessibility · American Sign Language · Block-based coding

1 Introduction

Accessibility of STEM topics is a topic that has actively engaged the Human-Computer Interaction (HCI) research community, which aims to ensure that STEM applications and services can be used on an equal basis by users with disabilities and underrepresented groups [1]. Initiatives such as AccessCSforALL [2], Bootstrap [3] and CSforAll [4] are active projects focused on engaging students with disabilities in Computer Science (CS) educational opportunities. For the deaf and hard of hearing (D/HH) community, initiatives such as ASLCORE [5] from the National Technical Institute for the Deaf (NTID) at the Rochester Institute of Technology (RIT) and ASLClear [6] are working on creating ASL signs for STEM disciplines.

American Sign Language (ASL) is a language very distinct from English and contains "all the fundamental features of language, with its own rules for pronunciation, word formation, and word order" [7]. A study by Heunerfauth and Hanson revealed that Deaf individuals often acquire sign language as their first language, and

© Springer Nature Switzerland AG 2020
M. Antona and C. Stephanidis (Eds.): HCII 2020, LNCS 12189, pp. 173–183, 2020.
https://doi.org/10.1007/978-3-030-49108-6_13

they are most fluent and comfortable in it [8]. They stated that sign language interfaces are a necessity for such D/HH individuals. Websites such as YouTube provide closed-captioning features for videos, but the captions are often inaccurate, and the reading level of this text is sometimes too complex and difficult for deaf individuals. Half of deaf students pass from secondary school with a fourth-grade reading level or less [9]. Another study stated that the frequently reported low literacy levels among students with severe hearing disability were partly due to the discrepancy between their "incomplete spoken language system and the demands of reading a speech-based system" [10]. This illustrates the need of providing coding instruction in ASL. D/HH students are at a high risk of unemployment or chronic underemployment at a rate of 70% or more nationally [11]. The number of tech job openings in the country is growing exponentially and hence, by encouraging D/HH students to learn CS concepts and tackle programming challenges from the middle school level using accessible coding instruction, we can help to lower the unemployment rate.

To address this need, in this paper, we discuss a project designed to 1) bridge the gap between K-12 D/HH students and an active block-based coding learning environment, 2) expose students to CS topics within a supportive and fun environment, including robots, and 3) provide age-appropriate ASL video resources for K-12 students while encouraging independent learning and creative problem solving.

2 Related Work

Despite the fact that human signing videos are expensive and hence difficult to update, there is a need to produce sign language content explaining core computer programming concepts which don't require frequent updating. For example, in the CS field, ASLCORE has produced signs and definitions for vocabulary and concepts such as "Recursion", "Debugger", "Linked List" and "Variable". In this way, CS jargon is being made accessible to older students who are D/HH, who have to otherwise rely on fingerspelling while communicating with this vocabulary. Apple has also recently released seven videos [12] explaining computer programming concepts in ASL. On the other hand, Drag and Drop coding applications such as MIT's Scratch [13] are popularly used to teach younger students to code. Our project aims to make CS principles, using Block-based coding interfaces, a more inclusive experience for D/HH students since many students' first experience with programming is through such coding interfaces.

A number of ambitious projects (e.g. automatic sign language recognition, animated 3D humanlike characters who perform sign language, and reading assistance technologies) are being developed to make web content more accessible to D/HH students. Although substantial work [8] is being done in creating this animated sign language using avatars, which automatically converts a body of text into avatars signing them, the majority of the work is still in the research phase. Our project does not aim to create sign language videos for every content related to CS on the web; automated virtual human sign technologies, when fully developed, are a better fit for this purpose. Instead, our objective is to create engaging human signing videos for core computing science concepts and common data structures in the context of a block-based programming environment. There are two primary reasons for doing this:

1. **To increase *pre-lingual* deaf students' excitement about CS**

According to the Communication Services for the Deaf, "98% of deaf people do not receive education in sign language" [14]. Lisa Harrod, a former sign language interpreter, mentions that captioning is simply the written form of spoken words which can be very difficult for D/HH who struggle with English as a second language [15]. Pre-lingual individuals (born with deafness or became deaf very young) who learned ASL as their first language will more likely be interested to learn coding through ASL, rather than just reading paragraphs of text or captioned videos explaining computer programming concepts. Therefore, this project tries to provide a more promising and engaging learning environment for these students that possibly their second language could not. In addition, we hypothesize that a student's sense of inclusion will increase with the knowledge that computer programming is being taught in a language that addresses their needs.

2. **To improve *post-lingual* deaf students comfort level with common CS ASL signs**

For post-lingual students who learned ASL later in life and are not very comfortable with it, web applications should provide captioning and/or transcripts for every ASL video, so that they do not have to solely depend on ASL. However, our plan is to familiarize post-lingual deaf students with the basic ASL signs for programming concepts, so they may use it to communicate with other deaf students, in addition to providing captioning in videos.

3 Project Conceptual Details

This project is part of a larger research initiative which aims to develop an accessible block-based web application for middle school students with disabilities. The app aims to provide accessibility features for students who are either blind/visually impaired, D/HH, have physical, and/or cognitive disabilities. This paper particularly focuses on the accessibility considerations for the D/HH audience, which is further divided into two parts. The first part discusses the development considerations for videos explaining core CS concepts in ASL, which will be embedded as part of the curriculum for the accessible web application project. The signs for STEM terminologies will be based on ASLCORE to ensure technical accuracy. Our ASL videos explain the following programming concepts with real-life application examples: **a.** Introduction to CS & Programming **b.** Pseudocode & Algorithms **c.** Commands **d.** Conditional Statements &

Event Driven Development. **e.** Loops **f.** Variables **g.** Functions **h.** Debugging. **i.** Object-Oriented Programming. These concepts are inspired by materials from CS Teachers Association's K-12 CS Standards, and the CS4ALL curriculum developed for an inclusive robot camp at Auburn University [16].

It is proven that D/HH individuals are visual learners [17], hence every video will demonstrate application of the particular programming concept through a block-based coding interface. Videos for other CS concepts which explain the social aspect of computing, such as cybersecurity, bias in computing, accessibility, and careers in computing, are also being filmed. We have received a SIGCSE special projects grant [18] to produce these videos. Hence, we have partnered with the non-profit organization Deaf Kids Code [11] to recruit D/HH STEM teachers and successful deaf technologists to star in these videos. Another key reason to specifically produce these computing videos in ASL is to avoid the denotation and connotation confusion of English words [19], which D/HH individuals sometimes experience. For example, the word 'call' in English has the most common meaning of contacting someone or giving someone a name. However, in the CS context, it means to execute a subroutine or a function. Young D/HH kids, especially those in middle school, may not have the contextual knowledge to compensate for these informational gaps [19], hence explaining and clarifying these contextual differences through ASL videos would be extremely helpful for D/HH middle-schoolers. Additionally, research shows that the majority of teachers for the D/HH are hearing. 2,575 K-12 D/HH teachers were surveyed and it was found that less than 22% were deaf [20]. Only 38% of D/HH teachers believed that "their expressive sign skills were on par with their expressive spoken English" [20]. This suggests that only a few D/HH K-12 individuals have access to teachers who communicate with them using ASL, let alone using appropriate signs for STEM terminologies. Hence, our videos can be used by STEM teachers in their classrooms to introduce students to CS concepts.

The second part of this project is developing built-in accessibility features for D/HH audience for the Block-based coding web application. The web application consists of some programming tutorials similar to Activity Guides [21] in MIT's Scratch. Additionally, it consists of an extensive robot platform where students can use programming blocks to control a robot. The benefits of learning CS through robotics are well researched [22]. In this sense, several robotic environments are being proposed to facilitate programming teaching, such as Lego Mindstorms [23] and NaoBlocks [24]. The Finch robot designed to align with the learning goals and concepts taught in introductory CS courses is extremely popular [25]. Our robot, which is designed at the Georgia Institute of Technology, is cost-effective and visually appealing to middle schoolers. It also has the capability to produce sounds which can serve as feedback for blind/visually impaired individuals. The robot has a wireless connection and commands to control it, via blocks, can be sent through Bluetooth from the web application.

Figure 1 is a picture of the top-view of our robot.

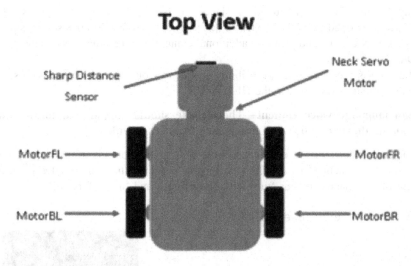

Fig. 1. Top view of the robot showing the Sharp Distance Sensor, Neck Servo Motor, Front-left Motor, Back-left Motor, Front-right Motor & Back-right Motor.

Figure 2 is a picture of the bottom-view of our robot.

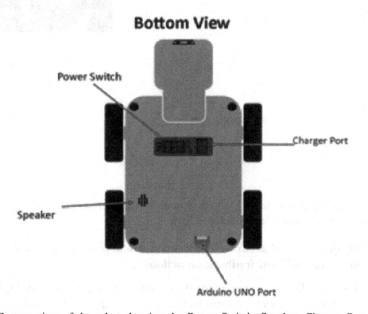

Fig. 2. Bottom view of the robot showing the Power Switch, Speaker, Charger Port and the Arduino UNO Port.

The guidelines for the heuristic evaluation for Deaf Web User Experience (HE4DWUX) were used to develop a product requirements list for D/HH accessible web application [26]. This heuristic evaluation is based on the well-known usability heuristics developed by Jakob Nielsen [27]. The HE4DWUX consists of similar heuristics as Nielson's and provides additional context with regards to accessibility for the D/HH.

We discuss the following accessibility features of our app with regards to seven relevant heuristics described in the HE4DWUX.

1. **Sign language video content—The website should support captioned video content, alternative text and make use of signers in videos**

The ASL videos will be embedded in the web application. Figure 3 is a prototype of this feature in action. The ASL video for this particular tutorial would explain the concept of commands such as 'turn left', 'turn right', and 'move forward'.

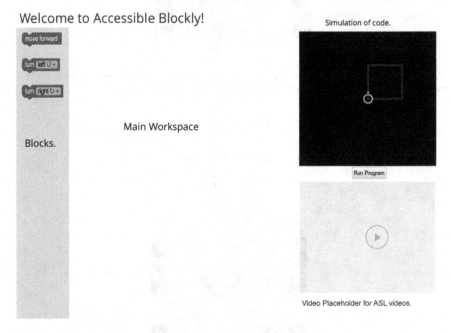

Fig. 3. Under-development block coding interface showing Placeholder for ASL videos. Block and simulation images taken from Blockly Games.

2. **Visibility of status and actions—The website should provide users who are deaf with timely visual-based feedback on actions**

Good visual feedback is very important to ensure web accessibility for D/HH. For example, when a user clicks on the run button to execute their code, it is necessary to provide clear visual cues such as text or graphics on screen, which can convey that the program has been run, as opposed to just audio cues. Some other examples of visual-based feedback in consideration are ensuring that content changes are indicated near the area of interest, using alternatives to static and textual forms of feedback, and text with icons for better navigation [26].

3. **Match between website and the world of the Deaf—The website should be aligned with language and concepts from Deaf culture**

Our signs for programming concepts are heavily based on the work done by ASLCORE [5] since they have done extensive research in creating signs for technical programming terms such as "IF", "WHILE" and "FOR". Our partnership with Deaf Kids code allows us to understand the needs and expectations of D/HH students. ASLCORE recruits a 4-person all Deaf translation team who have strong and intuitive knowledge of ASL [28]. Similarly, only ASL experts will participate in the making of our videos to ensure authenticity and correctness. The web application also provides a feedback form so that users may let us know of any potential issues in the videos.

4. **User control and freedom—The website should make users who are deaf feel in control of their experience**

Users are able to control the speed of ASL videos and increase the size of captions. ASL signs/videos for every drag and droppable 'block' like "IF-ELSE" or "WHILE", are displayed as *tooltips* for a block. Tooltip is a common graphical user interface element. It is used jointly with a cursor, commonly a pointer [29]. A research study conducted with 15 deaf users found that sign language and picture tooltips were very positively rated as opposed to only text-based tooltips or a human speaking-based tooltip (used for lip-reading) [30]. In our web application, once a user hovers their cursor over a block, it will play the sign for the block in ASL. Figure 4 is a prototype of this feature in action.

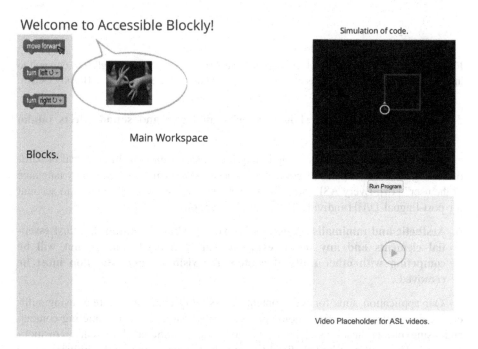

Fig. 4. Under-development block coding interface displaying tooltips in ASL as a user hover over a block. Block and simulation images taken from Blockly Games. Handshape image taken from Calliope Interpreters.

However, if the user would prefer text as tooltips instead of ASL, they have the option to change to text view as well. This ensures users have control on the features of the web application. Figure 5 is a prototype of this feature in action.

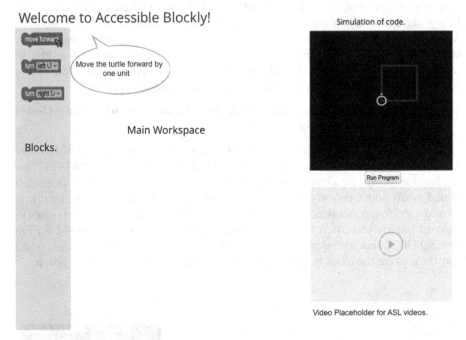

Fig. 5. Under-development block coding interface displaying tooltips in English as opposed to in ASL, if user prefers English instead. Block and simulation images taken from Blockly Games.

5. **Captions—The website should describe dialogue and sound effects (audio content)**

Lisa Harrod also mentions, "Captioning is perfect for the post-lingual deaf or hard-of hearing audience; it presents content in an accessible format, in the primary language of the user" [15]. Every ASL video in our web application includes captions to account for post-lingual D/HH individuals who prefer captions.

6. **Aesthetic and minimalist design—The website should contain the most essential elements and any non-relevant or rarely needed content that will be competing with other units of content for visibility and attention must be removed**

Our application aims for web content accessibility conformance (e.g. using sufficient color contrast, allowing zooming, minimizing distracting and cluttering content, and using proper headings). Hence, visual noise is eliminated to reduce memory overload. This will also be beneficial to individuals with cognitive disabilities.

7. **Personal skills—The website should support the skills and background knowledge of users who are deaf and not replace these**

We incorporate multimodal learning in our app which is beneficial to D/HH individuals. Multimodal approaches "involve the use of multimedia along with the content text and encourage the use of interactive literacy practices between the instructor and the students". Lacina and Mathews researched how multimodal learning tools affect the learning process, and "found that it provided a pleasant experience, captured students' attention, increased their motivation of reading, and enhanced their literacy skills" [31]. Deaf explore the world mostly by the sense of sight and vision. "Graphics, pictures, videos, and the different forms of multimedia can facilitate learning of complex theories and generalizations, which are usually challenging for deaf students that do not know how to use sign language" [32]. Involving multiple representations of the educational materials can help in decreasing the loss of the received data. "These multimodal representations for deaf students can combine text and sign language, or visual displays (e.g., pictures or videos) along with sign language subtitles" [32]. There is a diversity of learning styles among normal students, they could be verbal, visual or a different type of learners. Therefore, it's crucial to include all possible learning styles for deaf students' e-learning techniques [33, 34].

4 Future Work

We are currently in ongoing conversations with ASL subject matter experts from Deaf Kids Code and working on our video scripts and storyboarding. We plan to start producing these videos in March 2020 and finish them by mid-May 2020. After the videos are ready, we will conduct a study with a middle-school deaf population to extensively examine the impact of ASL videos in learning CS. We understand not every deaf student has access to an ASL teacher familiar with CS. Therefore, we will release our videos online so any deaf student can access it. In addition, we plan to partner with more schools for deaf in the United States to share our work and conduct similar workshops. In addition to this, work is being done on the above-mentioned block-based web application. We are currently surveying teachers of students with blind/visually impairments, D/HH, physical and cognitive disabilities to establish and validate the appropriate accessibility requirements for the various disabilities.

References

1. Stephanidis, C., et al.: Seven HCI grand challenges. Int. J. Hum. Comput. Interact. (2019). https://doi.org/10.1080/10447318.2019.1619259
2. AccessCSforAll. https://www.washington.edu/accesscomputing/accesscsforall. Accessed 28 Dec 2019
3. Bootstrap World. https://www.bootstrapworld.org. Accessed 28 Dec 2019
4. CSforALL Accessibility Pledge. https://www.csforall.org/projects_and_programs/accessibility-pledge/. Accessed 28 Dec 2019
5. ASLCORE CS. https://aslcore.org/computerscience/. Accessed 28 Dec 2019

6. ASLClear. https://clear.aslstem.com/app/#/. Accessed 28 Dec 2019
7. The National Institutes of Health, American Sign Language. https://www.nidcd.nih.gov/health/american-sign-language. Accessed 28 Dec 2019
8. Huenerfauth, M., Hanson, V.: Sign language in the interface: access for deaf signers. In: Stephanidis, C. (ed.) The Universal Access Handbook, Chapter 38, pp. 1–18. CRC Press, Boca Raton (2009)
9. Traxler, C.: The Stanford achievement test, 9th edition: national norming and performance standards for deaf and hard-of-hearing students. J. Deaf Stud. Deaf Educ. 5(4), 337–348 (2000)
10. Geers, A.: Spoken language in children with cochlear implants. In: Spencer, P., Marschark, M. (eds.) Advances in Spoken Language Development of Deaf and Hard of Hearing Children, pp. 244–270. Oxford University Press, New York (2006)
11. Deaf Kids Code Mission. https://www.deafkidscode.org/mission. Accessed 28 Dec 2019
12. Apple ASL Videos. https://developer.apple.com/asl-videos/. Accessed 28 Dec 2019
13. MIT Scratch. https://scratch.mit.edu/. Accessed 28 Dec 2019
14. ASL Day 2019: Everything You Need To Know About American Sign Language. https://www.newsweek.com/asl-day-2019-american-sign-language-1394695. Accessed 28 Dec 2019
15. Deafness and the User Experience. https://alistapart.com/article/deafnessandtheuserexperience/. Accessed 28 Dec 2019
16. Marghitu, D., Ben Brahim, T., Weaver, J., Rawajfih, Y.: Auburn university robo camp K-12 inclusive outreach program: a three-step model of effective introducing middle school students to computer programming and robotics, AACE SITE, New Orleans, LA (2013)
17. Luckner, J., Bowen, S., Carter, K.: Visual teaching strategies for students who are deaf or hard of hearing. Teach. Except. Child. 33(3), 38–44 (2001)
18. SIGCSE Special Projects Grants 2019. https://sigcse.org/sigcse/programs/special/2019.html. Accessed 28 Dec 2019
19. Reis, J., Solovey, E.T., Henner, J., Johnson, K., Hoffmeister, R.: ASL CLeaR: STEM education tools for deaf students. In: Proceedings of the 17th International ACM SIGACCESS Conference on Computers & Accessibility (ASSETS 2015), pp. 441–442. ACM, New York (2015)
20. Beal-Alvarez, J., Huston, S.G.: Emerging evidence for instructional practice: repeated viewings of sign language models. Commun. Disord. Q. 2, 93–102 (2014)
21. MIT Scratch Ideas. https://scratch.mit.edu/ideas. Accessed 28 Dec 2019
22. Leonard, J., et al.: Preparing teachers to engage rural students in computational thinking through robotics, game design, and culturally responsive teaching. J. Teach. Educ. 69(4), 386–407 (2018). https://doi.org/10.1177/0022487117732317
23. Patterson-McNeill, H., Binkerd, C.: Resources for using lego mindstorms. In: Proceedings of the Twelfth Annual CCSC South Central Conference on the Journal of Computing in Small Colleges, pp. 48–55 (2001)
24. Sutherland, C.J., MacDonald, B.A.: NaoBlocks: a case study of developing a children's robot programming environment. In: International Conference on Ubiquitous Robots, pp. 431–436 (2018)
25. Lauwers, T., Nourbakhsh, I.: Designing the finch: creating a robot aligned to CS concepts. In: AAAI Symposium on Educational Advances in Artificial Intelligence (2010)
26. Yeratziotis, A., Zaphiris, P.: A heuristic evaluation for deaf web user experience (HE4DWUX). Int. J. Hum. Comput. Interact. 34(3), 195–217 (2018)
27. Ten Usability Heuristics. https://www.nngroup.com/articles/ten-usability-heuristics/. Accessed 28 Dec 2019
28. ASLCORE CS FAQ. https://aslcore.org/faq/. Accessed 28 Dec 2019

29. Wikipedia Tooltip. https://en.wikipedia.org/wiki/Tooltip. Accessed 28 Dec 2019
30. Petrie, H., Fisher, W., Weimann, K., Weber, G.: Augmenting icons for deaf computer users. In: CHI 2004 Extended Abstracts on Human Factors in Computing Systems, pp. 1131–1134. ACM Press, New York (2004)
31. Lacina, J., Mathews, S.: Using online storybooks to build comprehension. Child. Educ. **88** (3), 155–161 (2012). https://doi.org/10.1080/00094056.2012.682547
32. Kourbetis, V., Boukouras, K., Gelastopoulou, M.: Multimodal accessibility for deaf students using interactive video, digital repository and hybrid books. In: Antona, M., Stephanidis, C. (eds.) UAHCI 2016. LNCS, vol. 9739, pp. 93–102. Springer, Cham (2016). https://doi.org/10.1007/978-3-319-40238-3_10
33. Marschark, M., et al.: Don't assume deaf students are visual learners. J. Dev. Phys. Disabil. **29**(1), 153–171 (2017). https://doi.org/10.1007/s10882-016-9494-0
34. AlShammari, A., Alsumait, A., Faisal M.: Building an interactive e-learning tool for deaf children: interaction design process framework. In: 2018 IEEE Conference on e-Learning, e-Management and e-Services (IC3e) (2018)

Competencies for Educators in Delivering Digital Accessibility in Higher Education

John Gilligan[✉]

Technological University, Dublin, Ireland
john.gilligan@tudublin.ie

Abstract. The aim of this paper is to critically review the capabilities of the European Framework for the Digital Competence of Educators (DigCompEdu) and the UNESCO ICT Competency Framework for in delivering greater accessibility for students with disabilities in a Higher Education landscape undergoing Digital Transformation. These frameworks describe what it means for educators to be digitally competent. However are there other competencies required to deliver Digital Accessibility in education. The particular focus of this paper is the role of the teachers in delivering Digital Accessibility in higher education. What should be expected of them and what are the required competencies to meet these expectations? Is it fair for example to expect teachers to cross boundaries where the effectiveness of general accessibility strategies such as UDL end for particular groups of students for example blind students in STEM subjects and where there is a need for individualised accommodations?

Keywords: Digital Accessibility · Competency frameworks · Digital transformation in education

1 Introduction

1.1 Digital technology

Digital technology, whether in the form of computing, the internet, mobile phones, digital TVs, smart technology and lately the Internet of Things, has emerged as a pervasive ubiquitous feature of modern life. Emerging technologies will necessitate a constant evolution of ways of working, systems and processes across the system, with the aim of adding value to the users, [1]. There are many responses to this challenge. The European Digital Strategy is one for example. [2] There are wide ranging programmes underway, from Building a European Data Economy to investing in Information and Communications Technology (ICT) Research and Development.

Higher education is no different. It must embrace Digital Transformation in a strategic cohesive way. However in the face of the rapidly changing landscape of digital technology in education there is an uneven response to the challenges. The European Higher Education Area in 2018 report provides an overview of the situation regarding national strategies and policies on the use of new technologies in teaching and learning across the European Higher Education Area, [3]. Of fifty countries aligned to the European Higher Education area, three have a strategy on the use of new

© Springer Nature Switzerland AG 2020
M. Antona and C. Stephanidis (Eds.): HCII 2020, LNCS 12189, pp. 184–199, 2020.
https://doi.org/10.1007/978-3-030-49108-6_14

technologies in education. Eighteen have broader national strategies which include technologies in education. Seventeen do not have national strategies but have policy measures to encourage progress and twelve have neither strategy or policy. Of the thirty eight countries that had strategies or policies in place the three main areas identified for allocation of additional funding to support digital transformation in higher education were: digital infrastructure; the development of skills of higher education staff to use digitally-based methods in their teaching; and, improving student's digital skills.

In November 2017, at the Gothenburg Summit, the European Parliament, the Council and the Commission reaffirmed the right to high-quality and inclusive education, training and life-long learning. [4] In response the EU's European Education Area initiative, has in 2018 developed a Digital Education Action Plan, which includes 11 actions to support technology-use and digital competence development from primary to third level education, [5]. Actions are grouped into three main areas, namely: making better use of digital technology for teaching and learning; developing digital competences and skills; and, improving education through better data analysis and foresight. One of the key actions in relation to higher education will be the creation of an EU-wide online platform will be created to support Higher Education institutions (HEIs) in using digital technologies to improve the quality and relevance of learning and teaching, to facilitate internationalization and support greater cooperation between HEIs across Europe.

The focus of this paper is Digital Competencies and accessibility. Digital technology can be an enabler of accessibility. The provision of electronic notes in the form of presentations and PDF can provide ready access to course notes in advance of lectures. Videos and Podcasts can provide interesting alternative ways to present course material and demonstrate skills and techniques. Good websites can be invaluable sources of information. Virtual Learning Environments offer useful learning dissemination and management environments. Indeed the role of the teacher/lecturer has evolved to be a content provider across these multiple technologies.

Rapid advances in ICTs have provided the opportunity to create entirely new learning environments by significantly increasing the range and sophistication of possible instructional activities in both conventional and e-learning settings, [6]. A wide diversity of powerful and readily available technological tools offer myriad opportunities for transforming pedagogy through the adoption of learner-centered instructional approaches. Multimedia tools such as YouTube, blogs, wikis, podcasts, social networks such as Facebook and Twitter, virtual worlds, RSS feeds, social bookmarking, etc. can offer novel and creative ways of teaching that can address a variety of learning styles. They can inspire innovative teaching methods that stimulate collaboration among learners, creation and sharing of information, and development of online learning communities. In order to affect Accessible Digital Transformation in education educators must have the necessary competences.

Digital Competence has been at the centre of European policy for many years. For example, digital competence was identified as one of the eight key competences for lifelong learning for EU citizens in 2006, [7]. More recently in January 2018, a set of recommendations for improving digital competence was published, extending its definition to cover coding and cybersecurity, [8].

Since 2014, the European Commission's working group on Digital and Online Learning (DOL, 2014–15) and the subsequent working group on Digital Skills and Competence (DSC, 2016–18) have been responsible for supporting policy actions aimed at the digital innovation of education in the EU, contributing to the development of the following tools:

European reference frameworks and related tools to support the development of DSC for citizens (DigComp 2.1), [9], teachers (DigCompEdu), [10] and educational organisations (DigCompOrg), [11].

The specific focus of this paper is the participation of students with disability in higher education and the need to build competency frameworks around digital accessibility to support this. We will look at how digital competence frameworks for educators such as the DigCompEdu and the UN ICT Competency Framework for Teachers, [12] can be used as the basis for describing a framework of digital accessibility competences for educators.

1.2 Digital Competency Frameworks for Educators

The UNESCO ICT Competency Framework of 2018 (ICT CFT Version3) is the third version of the framework building on earlier works in 2008 and 2011. It provides a comprehensive set of competencies necessary for teachers to integrate technology to facilitate students' achievement of curriculum goals, [12].

The ICT CFT Version 3 takes into account the Agenda 2030 for Sustainable Development, [13]. ICTs are critical for progress towards the achievement of all 17 Sustainable Development Goals (SDGs). ICT related targets are addressed specifically in a number of the goals for example in Goal 9, Infrastructure and Goal 10, Reduced inequalities within and across countries. Goal 4 Quality education is of obvious interest here. Technology has the innovative potential to enable learners to access information and knowledge and to more fully participate in education like never before. This in turn enables digital citizenship - the ability and ethical values to participate in society online – which is a central aspect of modern life.

The ICT CFT consists of 18 competencies organized according to the six aspects of teachers' professional practice, over three levels of teachers' pedagogical use of ICT. The six aspects of a teacher's professional practice addressed are:

1. Understanding ICT in Education Policy;
2. Curriculum and Assessment;
3. Pedagogy;
4. Application of Digital Skills;
5. Organization and Administration; and
6. Teacher Professional Learning.

These are considered over three levels, namely Knowledge Acquisition, Knowledge Deepening and Knowledge Creation. Examples of the competences include Policy Understanding at the Knowledge Acquisition level of the Understanding ICT in Education aspect to Knowledge Society skills at the Knowledge Creation level for Curriculum and Assessment, [12].

Like the UNESCO ICT CFT Version 3 framework the European Framework for the Digital Competence of Educators (DigCompEdu) was also was published in 2018. The DigCompEdu study is based on the previous work carried out to define the Digital Competence of the citizens, in general and the Digitally Competent Education Organisations (DigCompOrg), [10]. It contributes to the Commission's recently endorsed Skills Agenda for Europe.

DigCompEdu provides a general reference frame to support the development of educator-specific digital competences in Europe It is directed towards educators at all levels of education, from early childhood to higher and adult education. DigCompEdu details 22 competences organised in six competency areas. These are:

1. Professional Engagement
2. Digital Resources
3. Teaching and Learning
4. Assessment
5. Empowering Learners
6. Facilitating Learners' Digital Competence

These are defined over six levels of proficiency from newcomer to pioneer. Examples of the competences outlined Creating and Modifying in the Digital resources competence area to the provision of Feedback and Planning in the Assessment area.

There isn't direct alignment for the most part, between the competency aspects of the UNESCO Framework and the competency areas of the DigCompEdu framework. In some cases there is a strong correlation. For example Aspect II of the UNESCO framework Curriculum and Assessment which explores how ICT might support the specific objectives as identified in the curriculum, and play a role in supporting assessment aligns well with DigCompEdu competency area of Assessment which considers the use of digital technologies and strategies to enhance assessment.

Contrast this with Aspect 1 Understanding ICT in Education Policy which encourages teachers to be aware of how ICT might be aligned to national education priorities or Aspect VI: Teacher Professional Learning which could both be aligned with all of the competency areas of the DigCompEdu because policy and Teacher Education should embrace all aspects of digital technology in education. Other aspects of the UNESCO Framework dovetail to a strong degree with different competence areas of the DigCompEdu. For example Aspect IV Pedagogy links in with at least Area 3 Teaching and Learning and Area 6 Facilitating Learners Digital Competence and the Differentiated Learning Strategies considered in Area 5 Empowering learners However some elements of the DigCompEdu Framework are considered as Cross-cutting principles of the UNESCO framework and are outside the scope of the specified Aspects.

While both frameworks recognize the requirement that all competences need to consider accessibility and provide examples of the necessary skills required but they do not provide the necessary detail to demonstrate how each competency in the framework can be augmented with accessibility. In the following sections the requirements for a digital competence framework which considers digital accessibility will be explored.

2 Towards a Digital Accessibility Competency Frameworks for Educators

The rise of digital technologies in Higher Education leads to the question of how all this transformation impacts students with disabilities. Despite issues with evidence gathering, [14] people with disability are an increasing presence in higher education and this demands an appropriate response to ensure accessibility and inclusion.

From the 1994 UNESCO Salamanca declaration which advocated the mainstream education of people with disabilities, [15] through to the 2006 United Nations Convention on the Rights of People with Disability, [16] and beyond, the issue of the inclusion of people with disability in higher education has been insisted on as a right. The Agenda for Sustainable development of the UN of 2013 embraces inclusive education under Goal 4, [17]: "Ensure inclusive and equitable quality education and promote lifelong learning opportunities for all", which includes "build and upgrade education facilities that are child, disability and gender sensitive and provide safe, non-violent, inclusive and effective learning environments for all".

In spite of this, the relative numbers and rates of students with disabilities in higher education according to Academic Network of European Disability experts (ANED), [18] is still very low compared to their nondisabled peers. For example, in Ireland between 2000 and 2006, while the rate of participation for disabled students increased by 2.6%, the overall rate of access to tertiary education rose at a much higher rate, namely 8%.

Digital technologies can be critical enablers of education, opening new avenues for learning and transforming the learning experience. Digital technology too can facilitate inclusion. Nevertheless, these rapidly changing scenarios present unique challenges to the participation of people with disabilities in Higher Education. Content must be accessible. It must be usable with the variety of Assistive Technologies such as screen readers that are used. Digital competences now become a vital part of the education of learners with disabilities as more and more technology is used in the classrooms and lecture halls. The diversity of learning requirements insists on flexible and innovative curricula and assessment strategies to meet this variety of needs.

The consequence of not embracing these challenges presents real difficulties for many people. The 2016 European Network for Technology Enhanced Learning in an Inclusive Society (ENTELIS) white paper on Digital Inclusion highlights the potential of a digital divide where certain groups are left behind as technological innovation grows due to unforeseen barriers that arise, [6]. With regard to digital content and technology these barriers may manifest themselves as inaccessible content, poorly designed applications, inflexible curricula, unsuitable learning and teaching strategies and lack of training is. As the number of students with disabilities grows there has been a response.

2.1 Initiatives at European Level

There are a number of efforts at a European level which look at the participation of people with disabilities in education. None are focused specifically on the participation of people with disabilities in higher education in this age of Digital Transformation.

They address elements of this but not in its entirety. They are either focused on levels other than higher education or have some other focus. For example the goal of UDLnet-Universal Design for Learning project is to establish a network for promoting the principles of UDL in the primary and secondary education across Europe, [19].

Some address a wide range of policy issues from Employment to Health and include Education as part of their brief. Education is considered as one element of many. These wide ranging networks include the Academic Network of European Disability experts (ANED), [20]. The aim of ANED is to establish and maintain a pan-European academic network in the disability field that will support policy development in collaboration with the Commission's Disability Unit.

Others concentrate on participation in education but consider primary and secondary school and not higher education. The focus of the Network of Experts working on the Social dimension of Education and Training (NESET), [21] is on the social dimension of education which refers to the potential of education and training systems to reduce poverty and enhance equity and social inclusion, laying foundations for the development of more prosperous and more cohesive European societies.

None addresses the specific context of Accessible Digital Transformation in Higher Education. Some aspects of this are considered but not all. The DLEARN network considers Digital Learning and not necessarily how this impacts people with disability, [22]. The European Network for Technology Enhanced Learning in an Inclusive Society (ENTELIS) is a network of organisations with different backgrounds (education, social care, technology, research, advocacy, etc.) committed to full digital inclusion of persons with disabilities and older adults, [23].

There are some projects that consider inclusion in higher education in a wider sense than just people with disability, for example the ACCESS4ALL project, whose aim is to promote the educational and social inclusion of under-represented groups as well as of non-traditional learners, [24]. This reflects the approach of the European University Association who consider people with disability under the wider diversity and inclusion umbrella, [25].

The 2011 report of the Organisation for Economic Co-operation and Development (OECD) points out that tertiary education institutions have been increasingly designing a diverse array of admissions and support strategies for students with disabilities, [26]. However, countries differ in measures to provide pathways to higher education for specified groups including students with disabilities and the way they monitor these pathways, [27]. According to the ENTELIS White paper in line with the social model of disability, inclusive education perceives diversity as part of human nature, and as such the school (and not the student) has to change dramatically in order to provide quality education for all. Typical supports include but are not limited to assistive technology, examination & assessment accommodations, library supports, respite rooms, and supports such as the provision of scribes and signers, [6]. In the next section the nature of these supports and accommodations is explored further.

3 Responding to the Challenge

3.1 An Approach to Inclusive Education

The 2018 Digital Education Action plan which sets out how education and training systems can make "better use of innovation and digital technology and support the development of relevant digital competences needed for life and work in an age of rapid digital change", [5]. It further states that "Digital technology enriches learning in a variety of ways and offers learning opportunities, which must be accessible to all", [5]. The accessibility of learning programs which use digital content and technology is the central concern here. This paper considers the challenges of participation of people with disability in University Education as the use of digital technology grows.

Outside of the legal mandate of providing reasonable accommodation recent initiatives focus on embedding an inclusive education approach into the business practices of higher education. Accessibility is duly considered it in cornerstone activities such as curriculum design, learning processes and content provision. Guidelines such as the Web Content Accessibility Guidelines (WCAG) 2.1 are promoted as best practice, [28]. These Guidelines show how web content can avoid potential accessibility barriers. They specify the requirements of providing alternatives for potentially inaccessible content such as images and audio, the need for properly formed code and the requirement to work with assistive technologies among other recommendations. The guidelines are organised across the four principles of Perceivable, Operable, Understanding and Robust (POUR).

For inclusive course design and delivery approaches such as universal design for learning (UDL) are considered, [29, 30]. UDL provides a blueprint around three principles of Engagement, Representation and Expression for designing strategies, materials, assessments, and tools to reach and teach students with diverse needs.

Engagement is about providing multiple means of engagement to reach high academic goals. This means producing innovative and interesting courses that are flexible enough to engage users in ways that suit the full spectrum of learners to keep them interested and motivated in their chosen studies. Examples of Engagement: Flexible Learning Programs, Negotiated Learning, Multi Pathway Programs, Differentiated Learning.

Expression is about providing alternative ways of demonstrating acquired learning in ways that allow students to showcase their talents in the best ways possible. Examples of Expression: Practical Assessments, Recognition of Prior Learning (RPL), Multiple Forms of Assessment, Group Work, Off-Campus Initiatives (e.g. Students Learning with Communities), Problem Based Learning, Professional Practice.

Representation is about producing inclusive learning materials that typically adhere to Accessibility guidelines and standards such as WCAG 2.1, [28] and provide learners multiple ways of accessing these materials. Examples of Representation: Captioned Videos for Blended Learning, Accessible Websites, Alternative Text across all images.

Universal Design for Learning (UDL) can help educators customise curriculum to serve all learners, regardless of ability, disability, age, gender, or cultural and linguistic background. UDL has been referenced and endorsed by US educational policy and legislation such as the National Educational Technology Plan 2010, [31] and especially the "Every Student Succeeds" Act (ESSA) of 2015 which specifically endorses UDL, [32].

UDL has created a framework based on research in the learning sciences, including cognitive neuroscience, that guides the development of flexible learning environments that can accommodate individual learning differences, [29, 30]. However, UDL has not directly addressed the extensive use of digital technologies in education, particularly university education.

3.2 The Need for a Digital Accessibility Competency Framework in Higher Education

However, these resources are usually aimed at those with considerable technical knowledge and are often not useful to teachers and other staff in universities who lack the technical background and need resources tailored to their particular contexts of use.

While the introduction of digital technologies in university education has created barriers for students with disabilities, digital technologies can also create new opportunities for these students to improve their access to university education. In terms of teaching, for example, there are now ways to take output from a digital whiteboard and make it available to a screen-reader for blind students, overcoming the problem of not being able to read what a teacher is writing on a blackboard.

There have also been many developments, especially in relation to mobile technology which have increased access to assistive technology in a robust affordable way. Examples of such technology include voice recognition and text to speech available as standard on smart phones. Unfortunately, teachers in university education are often not aware of the possibilities which could improve the learning and assessment experiences of their students with disabilities.

Indeed, a general lack of awareness of the requirements of students with disabilities among faculty staff has been highlighted as a barrier to participation. Van Jaarsveldt and Ndeya-Ndereya have stated, "beyond legislation and institutional policies relating to students with disabilities, academics should accept responsibility for and have an understanding of accessibility and the establishment of inclusive learning", [33].

This begs the question what competences should educators have to effect accessibility in higher education as Digital Transformation takes hold. As a starting point in order to address this question this paper proposes to look at how accessibility may be considered across the competences of the DigCompEdu competency framework.

4 DigCompEdu as the Basis for a Digital Accessibility Competence Framework for Educators

Both digital competency frameworks have a strong commitment to accessibility as a crosscutting requirement of all competence areas. The UNESCO ICT CFT Version 3 framework insists on inclusive learning in its mission statement but does not have an specific accessibility competence defined. In contrast, the DigCompEdu framework has an accessibility competence in its Empowering Learners area. Table 1 provides a comparison of the different approaches to Accessibility.

Table 1. Comparison of framework approaches to accessibility

Accessibility consideration	UNESCO ICT Competency framework for teachers competence areas	DigCompEdu
Commitment to accessibility	Recognised in mission statement Promotes universal design for learning Commits to relevant UN sustainability goals Insists on inclusive learning No child left behind	Recognises its significance by making it a key strand of its empowering learners competence area
Scope of accessibility competencies	Recognised as a traversal cross-cutting requirement of all areas	Recognised as a traversal cross-cutting requirement of all areas
Specific accessibility competencies defined	A number of accessibility related objectives and examples are described for specified competencies e.g. for the Infusion Competency which is in the application of digital skills area	Specific accessibility competencies defined for all six levels in the empowering learners accessibility area

4.1   Extending the DigCompEdu Framework

As stated previously the DigCompEdu framework has an accessibility competence in its Empowering Learners area However while identifying this competence as a requirement across all other competences it needs to show how this may be done. The approach here is to augment existing competences with consideration of accessibility.

In some competences it is simply a matter of extending their reach to include accessibility. For example in the Professional Engagement competence area it is sufficient to extend say Reflective Practice competences to consider how accessible digital technology is or when pursuing Continuous Professional Development in digital skills that Certification in Digital Accessibility is also pursued.

In other competence areas different aspects of UDL need to be embedded into competences. There is strong alignment for example between the UDL Engagement principle Guidelines and the Teaching and Learning Competencies. Assessment Competences are the concern across all three UDL principles, [29, 30]. And there are direct correlations between the objectives of both the Differentiation and Personalization and the Actively Engaging Learners Competences and the UDL Principles of Representation and Engagement respectively, [29, 30].

For other competence areas the WCAG principles, [28] could form the basis of extending the competences to embrace Digital Accessibility. For example the Content Creation competence of the Facilitating Learners Digital Competence Area. The following table summarises possible extensions to the DigCompEdu framework to include Digital Accessibility.

Table 2. European framework for the digital competence of educators.

Areas	Competencies		
Professional engagement	Organisational communication (W) Digital CPD (X)	Professional collaboration (X)	Reflective practice (X)
Digital resources	Selecting (X)	Creating and modifying (U)	Managing protecting and sharing (X)
Teaching and learning	Teaching (U1) Self-regulated learning (U1)	Guidance (U1)	Collaborative learning (U1)
Assessment	Assessment strategies (U)	Analysing evidence (X)	Feedback and planning (U)
Empowering learners	Accessibility & inclusion	Differentiation and personalization (U2)	Actively engaging learners (U1)
Facilitating learners Digital competence	Information and media literacy (W) Responsible use (X)	Communication (DX) Problem solving (DX)	Content creation (W)
Codes	**W** - WCAG compliance **U2** - UDL representation **DX** - Device knowledge	**U** - UDL **U3** - UDL action & expression	**U1** - UDL engagement **X** - Extend to include accessibility

In summary, Table 2 shows at a high level the general augmentations that would be necessary to extend this out to include accessibility across all dimensions. However it is not meant to be definitive. Much more work is required to identify at a detailed level the competencies required for true digital accessibility. It is not a trivial challenge. In the next section two case studies are presented that show the scope of this task.

4.2   The Use of Colour Backgrounds in Digital Content

Meares-Irlen Syndrome is a perceptual processing disorder characterized by symptoms of visual stress and visual perceptual distortions that are alleviated by using individually prescribed coloured filters, [34]. Unlike dyslexia, it is not a language-based disorder but it is comorbid with dyslexia. Patients susceptible to pattern glare, perceptual distortions and discomfort from patterns, may have Meares-Irlen syndrome and are likely to find coloured filters useful [35].

Using a cream coloured background can enhance reading performance of those with dyslexia and has been recommended by institutions such as the British Dyslexia Association [36]. Given that the colour of the background may impact students, should all teachers be made aware of issues such as this and should the institute make recommendations on the design of content for learning. This knowledge should be the basis of the Content Creation Competency in Facilitating Learners Digital Competence. The question of which competence level it should be pitched at now arises.

4.3   Accessible Learning Programs

Mathematics is traditionally presented as a highly visual subject which is reliant on symbols and spatial arrangements to convey meaning. Many mathematicians still use chalk and blackboards to teach mathematics [37]. Say a blind student is enrolled in the classroom of one of these teachers. The challenges facing both are very significant.

How does an accommodation take place. Is it the responsibility of the teacher or a disability office in the school? Clearly the class notes need to be transformed. Who is responsible for this? What is an appropriate format? The student may have used Nemeth Braille Code previously for studying mathematics, [38].

Does the school have to acquire a Braille device for the student? They may use a screenreader in which case converting to the Mathematical Markup Language MathML, [39] is appropriate.

However in this example it goes way beyond the scope of the content creation competence. It involves policy. Who will undertake the conversion? It involves Teaching. Does the pedagogy change? It involves Assessment. How should the student be assessed?. If an alternative but equivalent accessible assessment process is determined, how is equivalence determined?

Again the question arises as to which competence level these issues need to be included in the framework. These are advanced skills. MathML, for example is considered to be an advanced Web Accessibility skill by the Web Accessibility Initiative, [40].

4.4   Multi-level Frameworks

The next stage in the development of a Competency Framework must consider different levels across the competency areas. Both frameworks under consideration specify levels of competency. The UNESCO ICT framework has three and the DigCompEdu has six. Again the question arises as to which competence level these issues need to be included. Proficiency levels of competency is a common feature of frameworks. The EU eCompetence Framework has five levels, [41].

The Web Accessibility Initiative, which is central to this work has recently specified three, basic, Intermediate and advanced [40]. Developing a detailed Digital Accessibility competency framework across all levels will be a complex task. There are 22 competences in the DigCompEdu Framework across six levels of proficiency, that is 132 skills and competences across all levels. Even to specify examples across the three levels of the UNESCO ICT framework for some of the aspects as shown in Table 3 is time consuming and is not definitive.

It is beyond the scope of this work to define these fully and these examples are only included to indicate the detailed future work that is involved here.

Table 3. Examples at different proficiency levels.

UNESCO ICT Competency framework for teachers competence areas	Knowledge Acquisition	Knowledge Deepening	Knowledge Creation
Understanding ICT in education	**Policy understanding** Knowing accessibility and equality legislation relevant to education	**Policy application** Creating digital accessibility strategies, conducing compliance audits and implementing best practise	**Policy innovation** Building a framework for digital accessibility in education
Application of digital skills	**Application** Audit accessible digital resources	**Infusion** Create and develop accessible learning objects	**Transformation** Design and implement a digital mathematics strategy for a screen reader user

5 Accessible Learning Programs

5.1 The Experiences of Two Digital Accessibility Courses

While efforts to establish competency frameworks with respect to digital transformation in education are to be lauded and their commitment to digital accessibility is noteworthy, the challenge ahead should not be underestimated. It is one thing identifying Digital Accessibility competencies, it is another to impart that knowledge to educators.

The author has many years experience of teaching topics in Universal Design and assistive ICT to computer science students and has also participated in the recently completed Massive Open Online Course for Accessibility Partnership project (MOO-CAP), funded by the ERASMUS+ Key Action 2 (KA2) grant program of the European Union, [42]. This had the twin aims of establishing a strategic partnership around the promotion of Universal Design and Accessibility for ICT professionals and of developing a suite of Open Educational Resources (OERS) in this domain. Both of these initiatives have digital accessibility as a common learning goal, reflecting the reported need to promote accessibility considerations amongst ICT professionals. There have been some interesting experiences on both of these initiatives which have relevance for this discussion.

5.2 The Universal Design and Assistive ICT Courses and on the MOOCAP Digital Accessibility Course

When computer science students were surveyed prior to the Universal Design and Assistive ICT courses they mostly responded that they had little knowledge of digital accessibility. The fact that these are computer science students where accessibility should be part of their core knowledge since it is mandated by law and EU directives, probably points to a wider awareness issue. The implication for Digital Accessibility competency frameworks is that there is likely to be low awareness of these topics. It is also important to pitch Digital Accessibility competences in an appropriate manner for educators.

This was an interesting feature of the MOOCAP project. This was originally targeted at ICT professionals as envisaged by the CEN Community Workshop Agreement (CWA) Curriculum for training ICT Professionals in Universal Design, CWA 16266 [43]. These were software developers, ICT managers and others working in the ICT professions. However of those who completed the pre-course survey only 19% were from IT backgrounds. Anecdotal evidence provided in the discussion fora indicated that many from ICT were content providers rather than programmers or developers. The largest group (25%) were from Teaching and Education backgrounds. This had a significant impact on the delivery of the course.

If the topic involved computer science subject matter such as where the Web Content Accessibility Guidelines, [28] were presented in technical HTML terms, students responded through online fora that this was difficult subject matter for them. The consequence of this for a competence framework is that if the content is very technical then the intended audience may be lost.

Based on both of these experiences it is essential to deliver competency education in Digital Accessibility in clear terms pitched at the right level. Do not assume prior knowledge on behalf of participants. Based on personal teaching experience it is important to root Digital Accessibility knowledge in personal experiences. For example not being able to see a poorly contrasted app on a phone when the sun is shining is an experience that many have had. By highlighting this digital accessibility is framed in terms of barriers they have personally encountered and leads to a greater engagement with the topic. This would have been borne out by animated discussions around certain topics such as online banking in the MOOCAP Digital Accessibility course, [44].

5.3 Conclusions

It is essential to promote digital accessibility knowledge amongst the educators at the front line of the Digital Transformation. While competency frameworks consider accessibility it is necessary to elaborate on this dimension. This is a considerable challenge in its own right. There are many competences already defined for Digital Technology in education. These need to be augmented with the broad knowledge of competences ranging from Content Accessibility knowledge such as WCAG, [28] to the many dimensions of UDL, [29, 30]. Many other topics including the accessibility of devices need also be considered.

The development of a Digital Accessibility Competence Framework must be met with urgency. It must be acknowledged that this will not be a trivial task. It will involve a detailed analysis of the competences required across many levels of proficiency. However this challenge must be met.

If the full opportunity of Digital Technology is to be taken, then this must be backed up by the knowledge and skills of the educators. Without the necessary competences the Digital Divide as envisaged by ENTELIS will grow as the Digital Transformation in education grows, [6].

References

1. Higher Education Authority (HEA): Digital Transformation and Empowering Technologies in Higher Discussion Paper (2019). http://hea.ie/assets/uploads/2017/04/190212_FutureFocus_Digital-Transformation_Discussion-Paper.pdf. Accessed 22 Feb 2020
2. European Digital Strategy. https://ec.europa.eu/digital-single-market/. Accessed 22 Feb 2020
3. European Commission/EACEA/Eurydice. The European Higher Education Area in 2018: Bologna Process Implementation Report. Publications Office of the European Union, Luxembourg (2018)
4. European Commission Communication 'Strengthening European Identity through Education and Culture', Gothenberg (2017): https://ec.europa.eu/commission/sites/beta-political/files/communication-strengthening-european-identity-education-culture_en.pdf. Accessed 22 Feb 2020
5. European Commission, Digital Education Plan (2018). https://ec.europa.eu/education/sites/education/files/digital-education-action-plan.pdf. Accessed 22 Feb 2020
6. Hoogerwerf, E.-J., et al.: Digital inclusion. a white paper (2016). https://www.entelis.net/en/node/349. Accessed 22 Feb 2020
7. European Parliament, Recommendation of the European Parliament and of the Council of 18 December 2006 on key competences for lifelong learning (2006). https://eur-lex.europa.eu/legal-content/EN/TXT/?uri=CELEX%3A32006H0962. Accessed 22 Feb 2020
8. European Commission, Council Recommendation on Key Competences for Lifelong Learning (2018). https://ec.europa.eu/education/sites/education/files/recommendation-key-competences-lifelong-learning.pdf. Accessed 22 Feb 2020
9. Carretero Gomez, S., Vuorkari, R., Punie, Y.: DigComp 2.1: The Digital Competence Framework for Citizens with eight proficiency levels and examples of use (2017). https://ec.europa.eu/jrc/en/publication/eur-scientific-and-technical-research-reports/digcomp-21-digital-competence-framework-citizens-eight-proficiency-levels-and-examples-use. Accessed 22 Feb 2020
10. Redecker, R., Punie, Y.: European Framework for the Digital Competence of Educators: DigCompEdu (2017). https://ec.europa.eu/jrc/en/digcompedu. Accessed 22 Feb 2020
11. Kampylis, P., Punie, Y., Devine, J.: Promoting Effective Digital-Age Learning: A European Framework for Digitally-Competent Educational Organisations (2015). https://ec.europa.eu/jrc/en/digcomporg/framework. Accessed 22 Feb 2020
12. UNESCO ICT Competency Framework for Teachers, version 3 (2018). https://unesdoc.unesco.org/ark:/48223/pf0000213475. Accessed 22 Feb 2020
13. United nations (UN) resolution, Transforming our world: the 2030 Agenda for Sustainable Development (2015). http://www.un.org/ga/search/view_doc.asp?symbol=A/RES/70/1&Lang=E. Accessed 22 Feb 2020
14. Ridell, S.: The inclusion of disabled students in higher education in Europe: Progress and challenges. In: UNIversal Inclusion Rights and Opportunities for Persons with Disabilities in the Academic Context Conference, Italian University Conference of Delegates for Disabilities in collaboration with the Università degli Studi di Torino, the Politecnico di Torino, and the Università degli Studi del Piemonte Orientale, Turin (2016)
15. UNESCO: The Salamanca Declaration and Framework for Action on Special Needs Education (1994). https://unesdoc.unesco.org/ark:/48223/pf0000098427. Accessed 22 Feb 2020
16. UN-CRPD: Convention on the rights of persons with disabilities. United Nations, New York (2006)

17. UN Sustainable Development Goal 4. https://sustainabledevelopment.un.org/sdg4. Accessed 22 Feb 2020
18. Ebersold, S., Schmitt, M.J., Priestley, M.: Inclusive Education for Young Disabled People in Europe: Trends, Issues and Challenges: A Synthesis of Evidence from ANED Country Reports and Additional Sources (2011). http://www.disability-europe.net/. Accessed 07 July 2019
19. UDLnet-Universal Design for Learning. http://www.udlnet-project.eu/. Accessed 22 Feb 2020
20. Academic Network of European Disability Experts (ANED). https://www.disability-europe.net/. Accessed 22 Feb 2020
21. Network of Experts working on the Social dimension of Education and Training (NESET). https://nesetweb.eu/en/about-us/. Accessed 22 Feb 2020
22. European Digital Learning Network (DLEARN). http://dlearn.eu/. Accessed 22 Feb 2020
23. European Network for Technology Enhanced Learning in an Inclusive Society (ENTELIS) https://www.entelis.net/en. Accessed 22 Feb 2020
24. ACCESS4ALL project. https://access4allproject.eu. Accessed 22 Feb 2020
25. European University Association. https://eua.eu/. Accessed 22 Feb 2020
26. The Organisation for Economic Co-operation and Development (OECD), Inclusion of Students with Disabilities in Tertiary Education and Employment, Education and Training Policy. OECD, Paris (2011)
27. Commission/EACEA/Eurydice, European Commission, Modernisation of Higher Education in Europe: Access, Retention and Employability, Eurydice report (2014). http://eacea.ec.europa.eu/education/eurydice/documents/thematic_reports/165EN.pdf. Accessed 22 Feb 2020
28. Web Content Accessibility Guidelines (WCAG) 2.1. https://www.w3.org/TR/WCAG21/. Accessed 22 Feb 2020
29. Universal Design for Learning (UDL) guidelines. http://udlguidelines.cast.org/. Accessed 22 Feb 2020
30. Universal Design for Learning (UDL). https://www.ahead.ie/udl. Accessed 22 Feb 2020
31. U.S. Department of Education, Office of Educational Technology, Transforming American Education: Learning Powered by Technology, Washington, D.C. (2010). https://www.ed.gov/sites/default/files/netp2010.pdf, http://udlguidelines.cast.org/. Accessed 22 Feb 2020
32. Every Student Succeeds: Act (ESSA) (2015). http://www.everystudentsucceedsact.org/. Accessed 22 Feb 2020
33. Jaarsveldt, D., Ndeya-Ndereya, C.: 'It's not my problem': exploring lecturers' distancing behaviour towards students with disabilities. Disabil. Soc. **30**, 1–14 (2015). https://doi.org/10.1080/09687599.2014.994701
34. Rello, L., Bigham, J.: Good background colors for readers: a study of people with and without Dyslexia. In: ASSETS 2017: Proceedings of the 19th International ACM SIGACCESS Conference on Computers and Accessibility, October 2017, pp. 72–80 (2017). https://doi.org/10.1145/3132525
35. Evans, B.J., Cook, A., Richards, I.L., Drasdo, N.: Effect of pattern glare and colored overlays on a simulated-reading task in dyslexics and normal readers. Optom. Vis. Sci. **71** (10), 619–628 (1994)
36. British Dyslexia Association: Dyslexia style guide (2012). http://www.bdadyslexia.org.uk/
37. Billman, A., Harding, A., Engelbrecht, J.: Does the chalkboard still hold its own against modern technology in teaching mathematics? A case study. Int. J. Math. Educ. Sci. Technol. **49**(6), 809–823 (2018). https://doi.org/10.1080/0020739X.2018.1431852

38. American Association of Workers for the Blind, Association for Education of the Visually Handicapped, and the National Braille Association, The Nemeth Braille Code for Mathematics and Science Notation 1972 Revision. http://www.brailleauthority.org/mathscience/nemeth1972.pdf. Accessed 22 Feb 2020
39. MathML. https://www.w3.org/Math/. Accessed 22 Feb 2020
40. Web Accessibility Initiative (WAI) curricula. https://www.w3.org/WAI/curricula/. Accessed 22 Feb 2020
41. European eCompetence Framework. https://www.ecompetences.eu/. Accessed 22 Feb 2020
42. MOOCs for Accessibility Partnership (MOOCAP). https://moocap.gpii.eu/. Accessed 22 Feb 2020
43. Comite Europeen de Normailisation (CEN) Community Workshop Agreement (CWA) Curriculum for training ICT Professionals in Universal Design, CWA 16266 (2011)
44. Gilligan, J., Chen, W., Darzentas, J.: Using MOOCs to promote digital accessibility and universal design, the MOOCAP experience. Stud. Health Technol. Inform. **256**, 78–86 (2018)

MyA+ Math: Teaching Math to Students with Vision Impairment

Abhishek Jariwala, Daniela Marghitu$^{(\boxtimes)}$, and Richard Chapman

Department of Computer Science and Software Engineering,
Auburn University, Auburn, USA
{avj0003,marghda,chapmro}@auburn.edu

Abstract. The study of Human-Computer Interaction (HCI) is a study of how users interact with the application. The goal of HCI research is to make systems versatile, easy to use, and accessible for the majority of people. With the accelerating growth of the Internet in the last decade, e-learning has become an effective learning mechanism for students around the globe. While computer technologies have successfully remodeled and improved the learning process, the potential promised by these technologies has not become the reality for visually impaired students. Also, the knowledge of math is crucial in any Science, Technology, Engineering and, Math (STEM) career. Due to the lack of interactive e-learning platforms for students with disabilities and the inability to process complex mathematical formulas and visual cues, students with vision-impairment are at a disadvantage. The motivation of this paper is to introduce a prototype of the web application, MyA+ Math that will help students with vision-impairment learn and understand math concepts. We hope that the use and further development of our prototype shall open doors towards universal education.

Keywords: Human Computer Interaction · Vision-impaired students · Teaching mathematics · Accessibility · Speech recognition

1 Introduction

In a matter of a few years, the Internet has become one of the widely used technologies that has changed the way we communicate, learn or do business [1]. A 2019 report by Internet World Stats shows that the number of internet users has increased by almost 1150% since 2000 [3], and 4.39 billion active internet users in 2019 [2].

Human-Computer Interaction (HCI) is a study of design, implementation, and evaluation of an interactive computing system for human use and for studying the major phenomena surrounding them [9,12]. The accelerating growth of the Internet and the technology boom has lead a number of schools and universities to provide courses and degree programs via distance education. With the evolution of HCI, developers have also been able to explore new ways to make the interaction between humans and computer easier [12].

© Springer Nature Switzerland AG 2020
M. Antona and C. Stephanidis (Eds.): HCII 2020, LNCS 12189, pp. 200–211, 2020.
https://doi.org/10.1007/978-3-030-49108-6_15

Recent findings from the 2015 International Agency for the Prevention of Blindness (IAPB) data established that 253 million people in the world are visually impaired [10]. According to the 2017 National Health Interview Survey (NHIS), an estimated 26.9 million adult Americans (about 10% of all adult Americans) have trouble seeing even when wearing glasses or contact lenses, or they are blind, or unable to see at all [4].

It is scientifically proven that the retention of information is higher when it is delivered both visually and verbally. While computer technologies have successfully remodeled and improved the learning process, the potential promised by these technologies has not become the reality for visually impaired students because of inability to process visual elements. This disadvantage leads to a big knowledge gap between students with vision-impairment and students without disabilities. Additionally, the knowledge of math is crucial in any Science, Technology, Engineering, and Math (STEM) career. For some of us, a full understanding of complex mathematical concepts is only achieved through a lifetime of practice. But for students with visual impairment, the process is further hindered by the inability to process complex mathematical formulas or visual cues.

The points mentioned above illustrate a need to implement an interactive application for visually impaired students to learn high school mathematics concepts. We present the prototype of our web application, MyA+ Math that helps students learn high school mathematics. The prototype of the web application was developed with the following features:

– Provide an easy to learn interaction mechanism to the students for clear communication with the application.
– Implement an algorithm that solves the math problems and provides step-by-step solutions to students.
– Integrate a highly interactive text-to-speech library that gives speech control to the student.

2 Background and Related Work

In the mid-twentieth century, *barrier-free design* and *accessible design* terms were introduced to illustrate efforts to remove physical barriers to people with disabilities [6,11,15]. Over the years with the technology advancements, there have been many improvements on how information is being presented to students with vision-impairment, Screen readers being the dominant mechanism.

A screen reader is a software application that converts text and/or images from a screen to the speech format that visually impaired people can understand and interact with. Many screen readers are also compatible with the websites developed under accessibility standards. The main disadvantage of screen readers as mentioned in [16] is that blind users need to go through an abundance of irrelevant content before they find what they were looking for. This problem can be resolved by using an interactive JavaScript text-to-speech library that gives the speech control of the application to the user.

Braille is a tactile system used by visually impaired students to read and write by raising dots within Braille cells. While Braille is suitable for the text representation, mathematical equations are multidimensional, and they may contain fractions, algebra, series, logs, and exponentiation. Also, 6-dot Braille can represent only alphanumeric characters and a small set of special characters by the 64 combinations of possible dot placements. Thus, by extending the 6-dot Braille system to the 8-dot Braille system, 64 possible combinations can be extended to 256 combinations. This is an excellent choice for a certain context, but by today's digital standards, the use of Braille is not applicable in a tech-driven industry [14].

NavTap [7] is a text-entry method that enables blind users to input text in a keypad-based mobile devices. It rearranges the alphabet so that users can tap four keys (2, 4, 6, and 8) on the keypad to navigate through the letters using vowels as anchors. The advantage of this method, as mentioned in [7] is that the user does not need to remember each key associated with the letter.

Another useful approach, Process-Driven Math [8] was introduced to help blind students to be successful in college mathematics. Process-Driven Math is an auditory method that frees up students' working memory while solving equations by hiding complex numbers and symbols behind the layers of mathematical vocabulary. For example, the mathematical formula, "$x^2 + 2x + 1$" will be presented to the student as "term + term + constant", freeing students' working memory and preparing the student to listen to the *"elements"* one by one. In this approach, the student is highly dependent on the trained reader-scribe for the information which can be eliminated by developing an application that acts as a reader-scribe.

3 System Description

We designed MyA+ Math with the following objectives:

- Provide clean and easy to understand user interface to the professors to add mathematical questions to the website.
- Enable navigation through voice commands for the students to explore different features of the application.
- Provide basic knowledge of each math topic and easy to understand step-by-step solutions for each question.
- Provide end-of-chapter practice questions and help students solve those by providing audio help/guidance when required.

3.1 Technologies Used

MyA+ Math is implemented using Hypertext Markup Language (HTML), Cascading Style Sheets (CSS), and JavaScript as front-end, and Java Server Pages (JSP) as back-end language. The MySQL database is used for storing important user information such as name, email, encrypted password, and user role like 'professor' or 'student' and question information. It also uses other open-source JavaScript libraries mentioned below:

Wiris MathType Editor: Wiris MathType Editor [18] is embedded on web pages for the professor to add math questions. Math formulas can be exported to multiple formats and are compatible with LaTex and MathML. These questions with other important details such as, question points, math topic, description of the math topic, math question in MathML format, and question description, etc. are stored in a secure MySQL database.

Annyang.js: Annyang [5] is an open-source JavaScript Speech Recognition library used for voice navigation on the website. Custom voice commands and actions can be programmed on a website to make voice interaction possible for visually impaired students.

ResponsiveVoice.js: ResponsiveVoice [17] is an open-source text-to-speech library written in JavaScript, offering an easy way of adding voice to any website or application. The main advantage of using a JavaScript library over traditional screen readers is the ability to personalize the text-to-speech mechanism based on how and when the user would interact with the page. In other words, the web application would provide a brief audio description of menus, links, buttons and text entry fields when user hovers the pointer over it. The web application also provides a brief description of a web page when the user lands on it.

mXparser: mXparser [13] is an open-source mathematical expressions parser and evaluator that provides the ability to solve mathematical expressions. We modified mXparser in a way that would read math questions MathML from the MySQL database, covert it to a mathematical formula and provide a step-by-step solution to users that would help them learn the math concept effectively.

3.2   MyA+ Math Architecture

The web application consists of four sub-systems: one devoted to translating mathematical formulas to a structured and less ambiguous MathML and storing it to the database, a speech recognition module that listens commands from user for voice navigation and providing hints, a teaching module that provides math questions with step-by-step solutions to users for a better understanding, and finally a practice module to help students solve mathematical problems by providing audio help/guidance when required. In the following, we detail the implementation of each module.

Translating and Storing Mathematical Formulas. MyA+ Math uses Wiris MathType Editor to add and convert mathematical questions to MathML. Figure 1 shows the MathType editor embedded on a website.

According to the Wiris, the embedding is compound by two steps. The first one is displaying the editor itself and the second one is calling the editor Application programming interface (API) to retrieve the MathML.

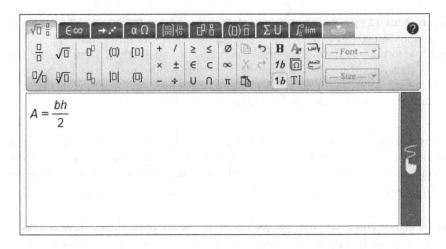

Fig. 1. MathType Editor.

Wiris MathType Editor allows the professor to add one question at a time. The question then is converted to MathML to store the question efficiently. MathML allows complex equations to be stored as structured XML text rather than images. The example of the math formulas and corresponding MathML is shown below:

$$A = \frac{1}{2}(b * h)$$ (1)

```
<?xml version="1.0" encoding="UTF-8"?>
<math xmlns="http://www.w3.org/1998/Math/MathML">
    <mi>A</mi>
    <mo>=</mo>
    <mfrac>
        <mrow>
            <mi>b</mi>
            <mi>h</mi>
        </mrow>
        <mn>2</mn>
    </mfrac>
    <mo> </mo>
</math>
```

This MathML is then stored in MySQL database with other important details related to questions such as math topic, description of math topic, number of points, and answer.

Speech Recognition Module. Annyang is an open-source JavaScript Speech Recognition library that makes adding voice commands to any website simple. Annyang works with all browsers that support speech recognition and supports multiple languages. Annyang understands commands with named variables, splats, and optional words. Table 1 shows a few of the voice commands supported by the current version of the application. With Annyang, more custom commands can be added in the future to extend the scope of the project.

Table 1. Voice commands list

Voice commands	Action
'new user'	Redirect to the registration page
'login'	Redirect to login page
'learn math'	Redirect to learning page
'options'	Speaks math topics one by one available to learn
'hints'	Provides hints while practicing math questions
'log out'	Logs out of the system

Teaching Module. The teaching module is responsible for teaching the mathematical topic selected by the student. This process is divided into four steps: The first step is to retrieve the brief description of the topic from the database and provide it to the student. This is implemented using ResponsiveVoice.js text-to-speech library. The second step is to select questions one at a time for the selected math topic from the database. Then, the math parser will take the question as an input and determines the steps to find the solution. Once the student is ready to practice questions, the student will be redirected to practice questions page. If the student encounters any issues, the student can say terms such as "hints" or "repeat question".

The current version of the math parser support the following types of math problems: solving a linear equation with one variable, simplifying linear equations, plane geometry, and user defined functions.

One example for solving linear equation questions with step-by-step solution is shown below:

Solve for x,

$$x^2 + 4(x + 1) = 1 \qquad (2)$$

$x^2 + 4(x + 1) = 1$
$x^2 + 4x + 4 = 1$.........(Multiply parentheses by 4)
$x^2 + 4x + 4 - 1 = 0$...(Move constant to the left)
$x^2 + 4x + 3 = 0$.........(Subtract)
$x^2 + 3x + x + 3 = 0$...(Factor the expression)
$x(x + 3) + x + 3 = 0$..(Factor the expression)
$(x + 3)(x + 1) = 0$......(Split into possible cases)
$x = -3, x = -1$.........(Solve the equation)

Practice Module. Once the student is ready to attempt the practice questions, the student will be redirected to the practice questions page. Upon landing on a page, the student will be given brief information about the practice module such as topic and question information, the navigation and hint commands to use when necessary. The student can start the practice module by saying terms such as "attempt first" or "attempt random".

3.3 User's View

The following are screenshots of some of the pages that have been developed. In the future, these pages will be modified, as appropriate, based on information and feedback from the students.

The web application is developed with the intent of improving the math learning experience for visually impaired high school students using voice interaction. The web application has two user groups: the professor and the student. The user will be redirected based on the user roles stored in the MySQL database.

An example scenario of the application flow is mentioned in Fig. 7.

The Professor's View. Since the professor will be responsible for adding questions and supervising student activities, the professor module is not accessible for visually impaired users. Several web pages are designed for the professor to add questions, add math topics, and to check the list of students. The following are the list of web pages with the features implemented for the professor module. Only the professor has access to these web pages.

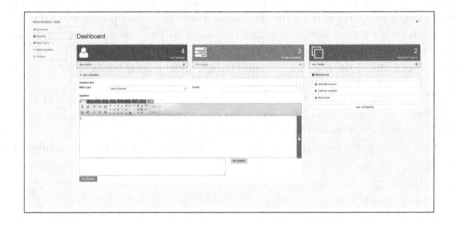

Fig. 2. The dashboard for the professor.

- Professor Dashboard Page: This web page is a dashboard for the professor to quickly access the menu to view the number of questions added, the number of students registered and links to navigate to math questions, math topics or the student page where the professor can find details about each module. Figure 2 shows the dashboard web page for the professor.

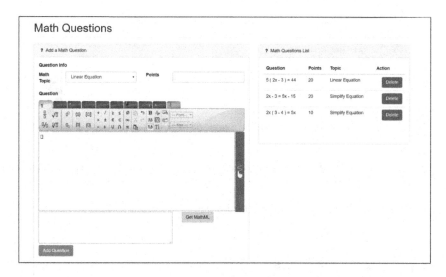

Fig. 3. The math questions page for the professor.

- Math Questions Page: The MathType editor is embedded on the page with other input fields to add questions and details. The professor will have an option to select the related math topic for the question. The questions will be stored as practice questions for the math topic. The math formulas will be converted to MathML and stored in the MySQL database. Figure 3 shows the math questions web page for the professor.
- Math Topics Page: This web page has an option for the professor to add math topics and topic-related information that the student can use to learn. This information can be anything such as a math formula or a brief text to help the student understand the topic.

The Student's View. Since the students are an important entity in this project, all the web pages students can access have voice navigation enabled. The following are the list of web pages with the features implemented for the student module. Only the student has access to these web pages.

- Student Dashboard Page: A web page for the student to access links to navigate to the math learning page or to practice questions for any math topic from the menu. A welcome speech will introduce students to all the available links. Students can use voice navigation to navigate to any web page.
- Learn Math Topics Page: This page lists all the math topics available for the student to learn. The welcome speech will give options to pick any math topic of choice to start from. Figure 4 shows the learn math topics page for the student.

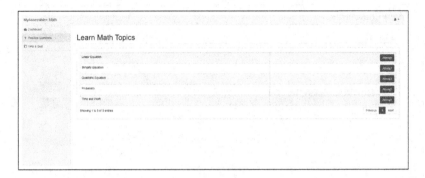

Fig. 4. Learn math topics page for the student.

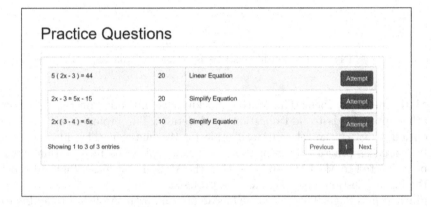

Fig. 5. The practice questions page for the student.

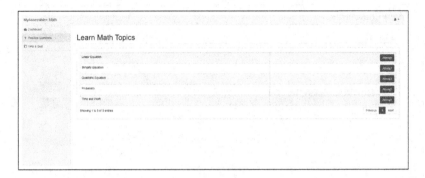

Fig. 6. Practice each question page for the student.

Student Actions	Student ⟶ Website (Voice Commands) Student ⟵ Website (Text-to-Speech)	Website Actions
The student lands on homepage of the application.		
	"Welcome to MyA+ web application. If you are new to the site say, 'New User'. If you want to login to your account, please enter your username and password"	Activates Welcome speech.
The student enters username and password and click Login.		Authenticating user.
	"Welcome back, [first name]! Say 'Practice' if you want to practice questions, say 'Learn' if you want to learn a new math topic, say 'Help' if you need any help"	Detects a student login.
The student decides to practice questions.	"Practice"	
	"You are on a practice page. You have {n} questions on a page. Say 'Attempt random' to start the practice, say 'Help' if you need any help"	Recognizes the speech and redirects to practice questions page.
The student wants to start the practice.	"Attempt random"	
		Recognizes the speech, selects the question and redirects to question page.
	"You are on a question page. Say "repeat please' if you want to listen to the question again. Say 'hints' if you need any guidance in solving problem. Are you ready?"	
The student is ready.	"Yes"	Fetches question information from database and finds the solution.
	"For a triangle with base 12 and height 5, what is the area of the triangle?"	Getting back to the student with more information.
The student needs help.	"Hints"	Recognizes the speech.
The student calculates using the formula.	"Multiple the base and the height and divide the result by 2"	Getting back to the student with hints.
The student confirms the answer with the application.	"The answer is 30"	Confirms the answer.

Fig. 7. An example scenario of the application flow.

- Practice Math Questions Page: This page lists all the practice questions the student can attempt. Students also have an option to pick random questions from the list by saying "attempt random". Figure 5 shows the practice questions web page for the student.
- Practice Each Question Page: The student will land on this page upon selecting the question to attempt. Figure 6 shows the solution for simplifying a linear equation. The left-hand side shows the question and the text-to-speech

module will read the question aloud and confirm that the student is ready to attempt the question. Based on the question, the algorithm will solve the question and provide the steps to find the solution. The right-hand side shows the hints that are hidden for the student. If the student asks for the hint, the text-to-speech module reads and shows the hint on the web page.

4   Future Work and Conclusion

Education is one space that still has the potential to be transformed by technology. Though this web application is still under development, it has great potential not only for improving the education of students with visual impairment but also for inspiring the next generation of engineers and scientists.

This prototype is developed to improve math education for visually impaired high school students. The following improvements could be added in the future release of the work:

– Collecting feedback is valuable in the development process for products such as software or a web application, as it enables the future enhancement of the application. We are planning to conduct a study at Auburn University with 15 visually impaired students enrolled in a program to evaluate the usability and efficiency of the application. We aim to assess how comfortable and adequate is the interaction with MyA+ Math application in our study.
– Upon release, the application will be open-source and will be free to use to learn and understand the mathematical concepts.
– The application will have an option to create a parent account and connect it with the student account. This will help parents keep track of students' activities and progress in mathematics.
– The current version only supports English as a primary language. In the future release, the application will be improved to support multiple languages.

References

1. Miniwatts Marketing Group. Internet World Stats: Internet Growth Statistics. https://www.internetworldstats.com/emarketing.htm. Accessed 22 Feb 2020
2. We are Social Inc.: Digital 2019: Global Internet Use Accelerates. https://wearesocial.com/blog/2019/01/digital-2019-global-internet-use-accelerates. Accessed 22 Feb 2020
3. Miniwatts Marketing Group: Internet Usage Statistics: The Internet Big Picture World Internet Users and Population Stats (2019). https://www.internetworldstats.com/stats.htm Last accessed 22 Feb 2020
4. Statistical Snapshots from the American Foundation for the Blind. https://www.afb.org/research-and-initiatives/statistics. Accessed 22 Feb 2020
5. https://www.talater.com/annyang/ . Accessed 22 Feb 2020
6. Burgstahler, S.E., Cory, R.C.: Universal Design in Higher Education. Universal Design in Higher Education: From Principles to Practice, pp. 3–20 (2008)

7. Guerreiro, T., Nicolau, H., Jorge, J., Gonçalves, D.: NavTap: a long term study with excluded blind users. In: Proceedings of the 11th International ACM SIGACCESS Conference on Computers and Accessibility, pp. 99–106 (2009)

8. Gulley, A.P., Smith, L.A.C., Price, J.A., Prickett, L.C., Ragland, M.F.: Process-driven math: an auditory method of mathematics instruction and assessment for students who are blind or have low vision (2017)

9. Hewett, T.T., et al.: ACM SIGCHI curricula for human-computer interaction. Technical report, New York, NY, USA (1992)

10. The Global Burden of Vision Impairment (2015). http://atlas.iapb.org/global-burden-vision-impairment/. Accessed 22 Feb 2020

11. Iwarsson, S., Ståhl, A.: Accessibility, usability and universal design–positioning and definition of concepts describing person-environment relationships. Disabil. Rehabil. **25**(2), 57–66 (2003)

12. Lawrence, D.O., Ashleigh, M.: Impact of human-computer interaction (HCI) on users in higher educational system: Southampton university as a case study. Int. J. Manag. Technol. **6**(3), 1–12 (2019)

13. mXparser - math expressions parser for JAVA android C#.NET/MONO/Xamarin - mathematical formula parser/evaluator library. http://mathparser.org/. Accessed 22 Feb 2020

14. Nazemi, A., Murray, I., Mohammadi, N.: Mathspeak: an audio method for presenting mathematical formulae to blind students. In: 2012 5th International Conference on Human System Interactions, pp. 48–52. IEEE (2012)

15. Ostroff, E.: Universal design: an evolving paradigm. Univ. Design Handb. **2**, 34–42 (2011)

16. Ramakrishnan, I.V., Ashok, V., Billah, S.M.: Non-visual web browsing: beyond web accessibility. In: Antona, M., Stephanidis, C. (eds.) UAHCI 2017. LNCS, vol. 10278, pp. 322–334. Springer, Cham (2017). https://doi.org/10.1007/978-3-319-58703-5_24

17. https://responsivevoice.org/. Accessed 22 Feb 2020

18. http://www.wiris.com/editor/demo/en/developers. Accessed 22 Feb 2020

Video Games to Foster Empathy: A Critical Analysis of the Potential of *Detroit: Become Human* and *the Walking Dead*

Federica Pallavicini[1(⊠)], Alessandro Pepe[1],
Chiara Carmela Caragnano[2], and Fabrizia Mantovani[1]

[1] Department of Human Sciences for Education "Riccardo Massa", University of
Milan-Bicocca, Piazza dell'Ateneo Nuovo 1, 2016 Milan, Italy
`federica.pallavicini@unimib.it`
[2] Department of Psychology, University of Milan-Bicocca, Piazza dell'Ateneo
Nuovo 1, 2016 Milan, Italy

Abstract. Empathy, defined as "the ability to understand and share another's
emotional state or context," is absolutely essential to human interactions at both
the individual and societal levels as it enables people to share and understand
other people's feelings. If empathy is indeed such an important facet of
humanity, the question of how it can be learned and taught is crucial. Today,
new methods and tools to help individuals foster their empathic abilities are
available, including information and communication technologies. Within this
context, video games appear to be an interesting new approach for developing
empathy since they provide situated, action-oriented, and embodied experiences
that allow individuals to "step into someone else's shoes." Furthermore, computer games are low cost and widespread among the population and, if effective,
could have a wide impact on promoting a more empathic society. Considering
this perspective, a critical analysis of the potential of two recent best-selling
video games – *Detroit: Become Human* and *The Walking Dead* – is discussed,
with the aim to offer insights and practical applications for the adoption of these
games to promote empathy-related abilities, in players.

Keywords: Video games · Empathy · Detroit: Become Human · The Walking
Dead

1 Introduction

Since their emergence in the 1970s, video games have quickly become one of the most
important sectors of the entertainment industry, with a profound impact on people's
daily lives and habits. Computer games are a daily activity for a high percentage of the
adult population: about 2.6 billion people worldwide play video games every day [1].
In contrast to stereotypes that project men and teenagers as the typical gamers, women
account for about 41% of total players, and the average player is 34 years old [1]. Total
consumer spending on the video game industry was 36 billion USD in 2017 and 43
billion USD in 2018, a 17% increase in just one year [1], rivaling cinema as the most
popular entertainment medium [2].

M. Antona and C. Stephanidis (Eds.): HCII 2020, LNCS 12189, pp. 212–228, 2020.
https://doi.org/10.1007/978-3-030-49108-6_16

Overcoming the typical "good-bad" dichotomy in video game research [3], and the idea of video games as "a neglected media" [4], interest is increasing toward a deep understanding of the positive effects of video games on people's health and well-being (e.g., [5–7]), as well as their potential to promote prosocial causes (e.g., [8, 9]) and foster empathy (e.g., [10–12]). Given the unique features of video games in terms of their ability to provide situated, action-oriented, and embodied experiences and to allow individuals to "step into someone's else shoes," they appear to be an interesting new approach for developing empathy, and some studies have recently been conducted to investigate their efficacy in this regard (e.g., [10, 11]).

In this chapter, after a theoretical overview of empathy, previous research on computer games to foster empathy is described, focusing both on commercial and non-commercial games. Then, a critical analysis of the potential of two recent best-selling video games – *Detroit: Become Human* and *The Walking Dead* – is proposed, with the aim to offer insights and practical applications for the adoption of these games to foster empathy in players.

2 What Is Empathy and Why It Is so Important?

2.1 Definitions of Empathy

Empathy is a complex and multidimensional construct [13–16] that in social sciences research literature is generally defined as "the ability to understand and share another's emotional state or context" [17]. Empathy consists of a set of separated but related constructs [18], and it has been broadly divided in two main categories [19, 20]:

- **Cognitive empathy (or "perspective-taking")** refers to the conscious, intellectual process of trying to interpret the emotional state of another person or to take another person's point of view [19, 21, 22].
- **Emotional empathy (or "empathic concern")** is described as the unconscious, affective response to another's emotional state [23, 24]. It is defined as the drive to recognize and respond affectively to another's emotional state [21]; this affective dimension of empathy tends to motivate altruistic, "other-oriented" feelings and behaviors [25, 26].

Recent advances in social neuroscience have provided important new insights into the brain basis of empathy [13, 15, 27, 28], changing the perception of empathy from a soft skill to a neurobiology-based competence [28–30]. Using mainly functional magnetic resonance imaging (fMRI), several studies have reported that observing affective states in others activates brain networks also involved in the direct experience of these states, suggesting that empathy is, in part, based on shared representations of firsthand and vicarious experiences of affective states [13, 15]. As stated by the psychologist and science journalist Daniel Goleman:

"To understand another, we become like the other — at least a bit. We understand others by translating their actions into the neural language that prepares us for the same actions and lets us experience alike" [31] (p. 70).

2.2 Empathy as an Essential Component of "What It Means to Be Human"

Empathy is absolutely essential to human interactions at both the individual and societal levels [28, 32, 33] as it enables people to share and understand other people's feelings, therefore making cooperation easier [19, 34, 35]. As such, empathy forms the basis for developing the shared understandings, respect for differing perspectives, and cross-cultural competency necessary for meaningful participation in a pluralistic society [31].

As pointed out for the first time by Charles Darwin (1872–1965), empathy represents a key survival skill, as animals – like humans and other mammals – who sense and seek to aid each other when in distress tend to flourish though the process of natural selection [36]. In addition to representing a fundamental ability to support interpersonal relationships, empathy has been shown to be the *condition sine qua non* for compassionate actions [31]. In fact, empathy has a close connection to prosocial behaviors [27], defined as "any voluntary actions that intentionally benefit others, regardless of whether oneself is benefited from such actions" [35, 37]. A large body of research has examined the relationship between empathy and prosocial behavior, especially with regard to:

- **Altruistic helping behavior:** Several studies have found a positive correlation between empathy and helping behavior toward humans in general [38, 39]. For example, dispositional empathy (i.e., the tendency for individuals to imagine and experience the feelings and experiences of others) [40] has been associated with numerous positive behaviors, such as constructive and non-aggressive conflict resolution [41, 42], assistance for emotionally troubled peers [43], and student helpfulness [44]. Similarly, it has been discovered that dispositional empathy is associated with differential involvement of cognitive and affective aspects of empathy in memory formation [45], thus supporting the idea that empathy is involved in modulating both lower-ordered and higher-ordered psychological aspects. Furthermore, it has been reported that students who were induced to empathize volunteered more time to assist prospective students [46, 47]. On the contrary, a lack of dispositional empathy has been reported in many aggressive and antisocial behaviors [48], including child abuse [49], sexual aggression [50], and alcohol-related aggression [51].
- **Pro-environmental behavior:** In addition to improving attitudes and motivating prosocial behavior toward humans, empathy has positive effects on pro-environmental behavior, defined as "all the actions through which people can impact on energy savings, in order to consciously seek to minimize the negative impact of one's actions on the natural and built world (e.g., minimize resource and energy consumption, use of non-toxic substances, reduce waste production)" [52]. In this case, many authors referred to the concept of dispositional empathy with regard to nature [53, 54]; for example, it has been reported that inducing both cognitive and emotional empathy toward animals and plants could increase people's pro-environmental behaviors and induce stronger feelings of moral obligation to help animals, plants, and nature as a whole [55].

- **Prejudice and stereotype reduction:** As noted by Darwin (and many others since), human beings are more likely to feel empathy – and thus, to act on it –for those whom they consider similar to themselves [19, 31, 36]. Practicing empathy breaks down differences and leads individuals to recognize similarities, and "facilitating a perceived similarity between groups may be one of the most powerful mechanisms through which empathy reduces prejudice" [10]. For example, it has been reported that individuals who participated in cognitive perspective-taking exercises may come to believe that there are fewer differences between themselves and the targets of their prejudice than they had previously believed [19]. Emotional empathy may also serve as a catalyst in prejudice reduction as well: experiencing a visceral empathic response to another group's plight may transform the "emotional lens" through which one views the other group [21].

Recently, there has been a public discussion of a societal "empathy deficit" [56, 57]. In particular, as stated by the psychologist researcher Danah Henriksen:

> "In the globally-connected contemporary world there is a paradoxical contrast between, on the one hand, the massively enhanced interpersonal contacts through social media and, on the other hand, the increasingly superficial nature of real interpersonal relationships" [58] (p. 44).

If empathy is indeed such an important facet of humanity, the question of how empathy can be learned and taught is crucial [58]. This question is even more relevant since – as stated by the *Differentiated Model of Giftedness and Talent* [59] – one individual may have the potential to be empathic, but this natural ability does not necessarily flourish spontaneously [60]. In order to support the development of empathy, several existing training strategies – such as Social and Emotional Learning (SEL) [61] and constructivism approaches [62] – focus on stimulating learners to develop (or enhance) specific empathy-related skills, such as perspective-taking, compassion practices, self-regulatory methods, and reflexive thinking [60].

Today, new methods and tools to help individuals foster their empathic abilities are available, including information and communication technologies (ICT). Within this context, video games are one of the most appealing technological instruments for developing empathy, thanks to their unique abilities especially in terms of immersion and interactivity, as well as their widespread use among populations all over the world.

3   Empathy at Play: Previous Research on Video Games to Enhance Empathy

Even if video games may not fully address the complexity of the human empathy experience, they are still an interesting approach to the promotion of empathy-related skills as characterized by particular features, especially in terms of immersion [63, 64] and interactivity [65, 66], which make them potentially effective both at encouraging cognitive perspective-taking and eliciting affective empathy [10, 58].

Over ten years ago, in one of the first published studies on the potential of video games for training empathy, a set of heuristic principles to design video games for empathy – adapted from recommendations for creating empathy in intergroup programs [19] – were proposed [10]. From that moment on, some studies have provided evidence about the efficacy of different types of video games, both non-commercial (i.e., developed ad hoc by researchers for the training of specific individuals' skills, often also called "serious games" or "advanced games") and commercial for fostering empathic abilities.

Regarding non-commercial computer games, for example, a recent study discussed the general aspects and methodology adopted for the development of an ad hoc video game intended to complement cognitive behavioral therapy (CBT) for patients with Asperger syndrome. This study contributes valuable information on empathy performance related to facial recognition and exercises for social disabilities [12]. Furthermore, a non-commercial video game (i.e., *Crystals of Kaydor,* a story-based iPad game developed to train empathy in youths) has been found to be effective at increasing empathic accuracy, producing behaviorally relevant and functional neural changes in less than six hours of gameplay in adolescents [11].

With regard to commercial video games, recent studies have explored the potentiality of different types of games to train empathic abilities. One of the most interesting types appears to be "newsgames," defined as "a broad body of work produced at the intersection of video games and journalism" [67] and considered to be a form of "enhanced journalism" [68]. In 2010, the potentiality of three video games of this genre – in particular *PeaceMaker* (ImpactGames, 2007), *Hush* (Jamie Antonisse, 2008), and *Layoff* (Tiltfactor Lab, 2010) – were being discussed, especially regarding their capacity to engage players' empathy in innovative and exemplary ways [10]. As highlighted by other recent studies, this type of video game that puts players into roles that propel the development of their empathic thinking can help audiences to understand political events of global concern, social issues, and more [58, 68].

Another interesting category of commercial video games in relation to the training of empathic abilities is action-adventure, defined as games with a mix of elements from action games and adventure games [69]. Action-adventure games require many of the same physical skills as action games but also offer a storyline, numerous characters, an inventory system, dialogue, and other features of adventure games [70]. Recent studies have reported the efficacy of a point-and-click adventure game called *That Dragon, Cancer* (Numinous Games, 2016) – an autobiographical game based on the Greens' experience of raising their son Joel, who was diagnosed with terminal cancer at twelve months old – at improving empathy among third-year medical students [71]. In addition, another recent study has shown that playing *Assassin's Creed III* (Ubisoft, 2012), a famous action-adventure video game from the *Assassin's Creed* series with a historical setting, not only gives students a sense of immediate access to history that contrasts with school-based learning, but also a sense of human connection to people in the past, increasing their perception of multiple perspectives in history [72].

4   Case Studies

In the 1970s and '80s, "Choose Your Own Adventure" books became wildly popular, especially among young readers. These stories were interactive and choice-driven because the reader could make decisions that impacted the story, shaping the narrative and the character development. Today, many video game companies are utilizing this idea to develop games that have both immersive stories and gameplay, described as convergence culture [73] and defined in several ways as "narrative games," "interactive story games," or "real-time adventure games."

The main characteristics of this type of video game are a strong emphasis on narrative and the ability to adapt to the choices made by the player, as decisions have severe consequences, sometimes with cross-chapter impacts. Because of their choice-driven narratives and the consequences that follow, these games have high replayability factors because in most cases you cannot see all the content in a single playthrough of the game. In this type of video game, there are action scenes, often in the form of quick time events (QTEs), but the main focus of the gameplay revolves around managing interpersonal relationships, mediating conflicts, and making difficult decisions, often with highly moral implications. The choices made during the game are presented to the player in a flowchart at the end of each chapter, along with aggregated decision behavior of all players worldwide who have already played the chapter.

The following paragraphs will discuss two video games with these characteristics that seem particularly interesting in relation to training empathy-related abilities: *Detroit: Become Human* (Sony Interactive Media, 2018) and *The Walking Dead* (Telltale Games and Skybound Games, 2012–2019).

4.1 Detroit: Become Human

Detroit: Become Human is an adventure game developed by Quantic Dream and published by Sony Interactive Media, released for the PlayStation 4 in May 2018 and Microsoft Windows in December 2019. The game is played from a third-person point of view and is divided into 32 chapters. The video game was written and directed by David Cage, who is famous for being the author of several video games praised by both the public and critics for their strong emphasis on the narrative and branching story-lines, such as *Fahrenheit* (2005), *Heavy Rain* (2010), and *Beyond: Two Souls* (2013) [74].

The game is set in the year 2038 in a near-future dystopian version of Detroit, a city that has become the center of production and distribution of human-like androids, created by a corporation called CyberLife. Androids have been established on the mass market to collaborate with and serve human beings in jobs considered unattractive or dangerous, such as cleaners, household help, and sexual escorts. They are programmed to follow the "Three Laws of Robotics" [75] in order to make them obedient and harmless to their human owners. However, in response to human violence and abuse, some of them find a way to develop beyond their programming, becoming so-called "deviants." The main topic of the video game – the opposition and blurring of the boundaries between the human and the nonhuman in the face of changes caused by technological development – draws several cues from science fiction literature, most notably Isaac Asimov's "I, Robot" [75] and Philip K. Dick's "Do Androids Dream of Electric Sheep?" [76]. The similarities between these works don't seem to be a coincidence; as stated by postmodern theorist Scott Bukatman, the sci-fi genre appears best suited to "narrate [this] new subject" [77].

During the game, the player alternates control of three "deviant" androids whose stories are independent at the beginning but then intertwine with each other: Connor, an investigation android whose job is to support police detectives from the Detroit Police Department and help them solve crimes involving "deviants"; Markus, an android caretaker at the service of an elderly artist confined to a wheelchair, who will play a role of primary importance as he will guide the androids in trying to assert their rights in a more or less peaceful way depending on the choices that will be made by the player; and Kara, a housekeeper android working in an infamous house for Todd, an unemployed, drugged, violent, always-drunk father, and little Alice, who tries to endure her father's harassment and for whom Kara will become a "deviant" in order to protect her.

Below are the ways in which *Detroit: Become Human* stimulates players' empathy-related abilities, both from a cognitive and affective point of view:

- **Perspective-taking and reflexive thinking:** This video game stimulates the players' perspective-taking, reflexive thinking, and compassion by encouraging them to assume the point of view of the game's androids, who represent victims of abuse. David Cage himself, director and lead game designer of the video game, said (Fig. 1):

Fig. 1. A screenshot from *Detroit: Become Human* representing Connor (Quantic Dream and Sony Interactive Media, 2018).

"We wanted to talk about our society, about segregation, discrimination, domestic violence, the right to be different, humanism. Could a video game talk about such serious things?" [78].

In the game, "deviants" serve as analogs of victims of historical oppression, thus becoming an allegory for minorities [79, 80]. For example, they are forced to wear custom clothes, an echo of the system used to oppress Jews in 1930s and '40s

Germany. They also have their own separate seats at the backs of buses, just as African Americans did in the '50s and '60s. Their sexual mistreatment, moreover, is a sad reminder of the modern scourge of sex trafficking. Also, Detroit, the city in which the game is set, is a reference to important American historical and political events involving minorities, such as Martin Luther King Jr.'s speech during the Walk to Freedom March in 1963, the precursor of the famous "I Have a Dream" speech he later gave in Washington [79]. Furthermore, through the continuous alternation of control of the three protagonists, players are forced to enact multiple perspectives at once, making decisions informed by what they know about the characters' backgrounds and taking their predilections and values into account, in a form similar to role play.

- **Empathic concern and emotion recognition**: The story in general and many chapters of *Detroit: Become Human* are constructed on a graphic and narrative level to induce intense emotions and empathic concern in the player. For example, in the 21st chapter "The Pirates' Cove," the strong emotional bond between Kara and Alice is underlined both through the setting (i.e., a park where they find an old carousel surprisingly still working) and dialogue between the two characters, which are particularly emotionally touching. Furthermore, in *Detroit: Become Human*, an important role from the emotional point of view is played by Chloe, a fully animated and voiced android who serves as the player's guide to the game's menu system. Whenever the players return to the main menu, Chloe breaks the fourth wall and speaks directly to them, emotionally reacting to the player's in-game decisions and events and even occasionally asking questions about some of the game's blunt philosophical issues [81]. Finally, in this video game, some of the greatest emotional impacts come from the very advanced graphics, in particular with respect to the facial expressions of the characters, which are extremely realistic. The bodies of over 250 actors were first scanned in 3D using a full performance capture rig and later rendered in extremely high polygon counts. A key element of *Detroit: Become Human* is the extreme attention devoted to the eyes of the characters, with a bespoke eye shader, movement mapped to the performance capture data, and a unique, perceptible difference between androids and "deviants" [82].

4.2   The Walking Dead

The Walking Dead is an episodic graphic adventure video game series developed and published by Telltale Games and Skybound Games, which consists of four main episode seasons: *Season One* (2012), *Season Two* (2013–2014), *Season Three: A New Frontier* (2016–2017), and *Season Four: The Final Season* (2018–2019). The game is based on *The Walking Dead* comic book series written by Robert Kirkman and illustrated by Tony Moore and Charlie Adlard, which also inspired the television series of the same name. Each season of the game consists of five episodes – four in the case of the final season - each lasting about two and a half hours.

The game series starts in present-day Georgia at the onset of a zombie apocalypse, where a virus has caused dead humans to become undead "walkers" that feed on the living, quickly overwhelming most of the population. Following the tradition of many of the best zombie-themed media such as *The Walking Dead* TV series and Danny Boyle's *28 Days Later*, zombies in *The Walking Dead* game series are not the primary antagonists. Instead, they exacerbate tension among survivors, thus exposing the barbarism of human beings toward one another when they are put in life-threatening situations [83].

In *The Walking Dead: Season One*, the player takes control of Lee Everett, an African-American university professor who soon meets Clementine (Clem for short), an eight-year-old girl whose parents are missing and later revealed to be (un)dead. Lee dedicates himself to looking after Clem, becoming a father figure toward her, until he is bitten by a walker. Clem, after being forced to make the difficult decision to kill Lee or let him transform into a zombie, becomes the protagonist of the game herself. After a long journey alone, she meets Alvin Jr. (AJ), an infant she rescues at the end of *The Walking Dead: Season Two*, for whom she will become a figure of protection and a "mentor," as Lee had been for her.

The Walking Dead game series stimulates the player's empathy, both from a cognitive and affective point of view, as described below:

- **Perspective-taking and reflexive thinking:** In this series of video games, there are several elements that can stimulate the players' abilities of perspective-taking and reflexive thinking. First of all, as declared by the game's creative director, Jake Rodkin, and its director and writer, Sean Vanaman, the main characters of *The Walking Dead* game series were purposefully designed to encourage the player to cognitively empathize with them, especially Lee [84]. Lee, in fact, represents a character very far from the typical stereotypes of video game protagonists. Not only is he an African American, a rare fact for a game's main character, but he is neither a hero nor a villain. Instead, he is a relatively ordinary man who is a victim of circumstance [83]. As underlined by the games journalist Ryan Smith:

"In our society, Lee would typically be seen as a "bad guy," the type of character we'd likely be shooting down without mercy in another video game. [...] [However,] Lee is presented as neither sinner nor saint but a complex vessel we pour ourselves into" [85].

Furthermore, *The Walking Dead* game series challenges players to try to put themselves in the main protagonist's shoes through a pragmatic incentive: important parts of their actions and discourse are chosen by the players who control them. Therefore, in a form similar to role play, the players must take actions and make decisions based on what they know about Lee's and Clem's backgrounds, taking their attitudes and values into account [83]. A second element of *The Walking Dead* game series that stimulates players' perspective-taking and reflexive thinking concerns the types of choices that the protagonists must make in the game. In the course of the game, Lee and Clem must continually weigh their individual (and very different) needs against the needs of the group. In this way, the game underlines the complexity of interpersonal negotiations and stimulates the player to reflect on the impossibility of some choices from a moral point of view: sometimes doing the right thing means doing the wrong thing, and vice versa [83]. Clem, and AJ starting from *Season Three: A New*

Frontier, make those decisions even more difficult since their presence forces the player to consider protecting them on another level. As said by the Telltale designer and writer Harrison G. Pink discussing about Clem:

"You have these decisions that are probably the right decisions for the group—she's watching, but then maybe she needs to understand this, but I might scare her because she'll think I'm a crazy person. There's no wrong choice, if you can justify it and it feels properly motivated to you, it's a valid choice" [86].

- **Empathic concern and emotion recognition:** *The Walking Dead* game series elicits empathic concern and intense emotions in the player first of all through the great attention paid to the narrative of the story and to the construction of the characters. As pointed out by the game scholar Sarah Stang:

  "The quality of the writing is such that the feelings of protectiveness and concern for Clementine, as well as the guilt felt for frightening her, are real sensations experienced by many players" [65].

Clementine is considered an emotional centerpiece of *The Walking Dead* game series, and several players have expressed caring about her fate in a way that few other games have been able to capture [87, 88]. Furthermore, a crucial element of the game from an emotional point of view is the relationship between Clementine and Lee, which has been described by the story consultant on the game's first season, Gary Whitta, as "emotionally authentic" [89]. To build this relationship, Clementine was introduced in the first episode of *Season One* in a scene built specifically to highlight her likability, resourcefulness, and vulnerability [90]. Finally, an additional important aspect of *The Walking Dead* game series related to **empathic concern and emotion recognition** is represented by the care for the emotional expression of the characters, in particular facial expressions. In this regard, Sean Vanaman, creative lead of the game series, has declared:

"We spend a ton of time on the facial animations for the characters in the game. After writing the first episode we start to make lists of the type of things characters are going to feel in the story and then start to generate isolated facial animations to convey those moods and emotions. Those are then used throughout the game" [91].

The game represents the emotions of the characters not through hyperrealistic and advanced graphics, but through color theory and framing facial expressions in such a way that they cannot be ignored [91]. As suggested by the psychologist Jamie Madigan:

"It frequently shows us the faces of the characters and lets us see all the work put into creating easily recognizable and convincing facial expressions. And so it's not the zombies that elicit dread in us. Instead, it's things like the face that Kenny makes when Lee tells him to make a hard decision about his family" [91] (Fig.2).

Fig. 2. Lee and Clementine in an episode of *The Walking Dead: Season One* (Telltale and Skybound Games, 2012).

5   Conclusion

With the aim to offer practical applications and principles for the adoption of video games to promote empathy-related abilities, the focus of this chapter has been to highlight the capacity of video games to foster empathy by discussing the potential of two recent best-selling computer games – *Detroit: Become Human* and *The Walking Dead*. These games were selected since they appear particularly interesting with regard to the promotion of empathy-related abilities in players for three main reasons, namely:

- **High focus on storytelling:** Thanks to the central importance of the story and customization features, it is possible to create a wide range of emotional experiences and ways the player can take on another identity in the game [92]. Storytelling helps the players to put themselves in the characters' place, acting and thinking as if they were them, producing a strong effect on empathy elicitation [10, 58].

- **High interactivity:** The interactivity in video games has also been labeled as the "art of failure" because it moves the player to constantly overcome obstacles and to recover from failure [66]. Because of the agency given to players – defined as the perceptive illusion that causes individuals to recognize themselves as the cause of the movement and actions of a virtual body [93] – within the game world, decisions matter [58]. You, as the player, are responsible both for the choices you make and the consequences that follow (Squire, 2011). Therefore, computer games with high interactivity such as *Detroit: Become Human* and *The Walking Dead* can offer "a functional, or pragmatic, way of knowing, because we make meaning through interacting directly with the world and observing our actions' consequences" [94].

- **Embodiment in different avatars:** Avatars constitute an extraordinary tool for improving empathy, since they allow individuals "to step into someone else's shoes" [95]. As pointed out by Gee [96], the immersive narratives of video games are "embodied in the player's own choices and actions" as they play. As a result, the players think and feel as the video game characters. In this way, through video games players are encouraged to learn new values and experience different perspectives through a projective identity [96], integrating both cognitive and emotional empathy [58].

- **High repeatability:** Through encouraging the player to play out the same events multiple times – for example, through the PlayStation Trophy system, which rewards both extremely positive, pacifist outcomes and the utmost violent and tragic outcomes [97] – further exploration of the game's narrative and specific chapters after obtaining one ending is actively encouraged.

The worldwide popularity and characteristics of *Detroit: Become Human* and *The Walking Dead*, as well as other commercial video games – for example, the *Life Is Strange* game series (Square Enix, 2015–2019) – may serve as a starting point for discussions about empathy, ethics, politics, social issues, and more. Future research on this topic could open doors for the adoption of this kind of video game that, if effective, could have a wide effect on promoting a more empathic society.

Author Contributions. FP proposed the study, supervised the scientific asset, and wrote the first draft of the paper. All four authors were involved in the drafting, revising, and completing the manuscript.

References

1. Entertainment Software Assotiation: Essential Facts About the Computer and Video Game Industry 2018, Entertainment Software Assotiation (2018). http://www.theesa.com/wp-content/uploads/2018/05/EF2018_FINAL.pdf/. Accessed 31 Dec 2019
2. Shieber, J.: Video game revenue tops $43 billion in 2018, an 18% jump from 2017. Techcrunch (2018). https://techcrunch.com/2019/01/22/video-game-revenue-tops-43-billion-in-2018-an-18-jump-from-2017/. Accessed 31 Dec 2019
3. Villani, D., Carissoli, C., Triberti, S., Marchetti, A., Gilli, G., Riva, G.: Videogames for emotion regulation: a systematic review. Games Health J. **7**(2), 85–99 (2018)
4. Reichmuth, P., Werning, S.: Pixel pashas, digital Djinns. ISIM Rev. **18**, 46–47 (2006)
5. Jones, C.M., Scholes, L., Johnson, D., Katsikitis, M., Carras, M.C.: Gaming well: links between videogames and flourishing mental health. Front. Psychol. **5**, 260 (2014)
6. Pallavicini, F., Ferrari, A., Mantovani, F.: Video games for well-being: a systematic review on the application of computer games for cognitive and emotional training in the adult population. Front. Psychol. **9**, 2127 (2018)

7. Pallavicini, F., Bouchard, S.: Editorial: assessing the therapeutic uses and effectiveness of virtual reality, augmented reality and video games for emotion regulation and stress management. Front. Psychol. **10**, 2763 (2019)
8. Katsarov, J., Christen, M., Mauerhofer, R., Schmocker, D., Tanner, C.: Training moral sensitivity through video games: a review of suitable game mechanisms. Games Cult. **14**(4), 344–366 (2019)
9. Morganti, L., Pallavicini, F., Cadel, E., Candelieri, A., Archetti, F., Mantovani, F.: Gaming for earth: serious games and gamification to engage consumers in pro-environmental behaviours for energy efficiency. Energy Res. Soc. Sci. **29**(July), 95–102 (2017)
10. Belman, J., Flanagan, M.: Designing games to foster empathy. Int. J. Cogn. Technol. **14**(2), 5–15 (2010)
11. Kral, T.R.A., et al.: Neural correlates of video game empathy training in adolescents: a randomized trial. Npj Sci. Learn. **3**(1), 13 (2018)
12. Lara, E., Rodas-Osollo, J., Ochoa, A., Rivera, G.: Development of a serious games for asperger syndrome based on a bio-inspired algorithm to measure empathy performance. In: Research in Computing Science, vol. 148(6), pp. 111–121. National Polytechnic Institute (2019)
13. de Vignemont, F., Singer, T.: The empathic brain: how, when and why? Trends Cogn. Sci. **10**(10), 435–441 (2006)
14. Blair, R.J.R.: Responding to the emotions of others: dissociating forms of empathy through the study of typical and psychiatric populations. Conscious. Cogn. **14**(4), 698–718 (2005)
15. Preston, S.D., de Waal, F.B.M.: Empathy: Its ultimate and proximate bases. Behav. Brain Sci. **25**(1), 1–20 (2002)
16. Batson, C.D.: These things called empathy: eight related but distinct phenomena. In: The Social Neuroscience of Empathy, pp. 3–16. MIT Press (2009)
17. Cohen, D., Strayer, J.: Empathy in conduct-disordered and comparison youth. Dev. Psychol. **32**(6), 988–998 (1996)
18. Davis, M.H.: Empathy and prosocial behavior. In: The Oxford Handbook of Prosocial Behavior, pp. 282–306. Oxford University Press (2015)
19. Stephan, W.G., Finlay, K.: The role of empathy in improving intergroup relations. J. Soc. Issues **55**(4), 729–743 (1999)
20. Hoffman, M.L.: Empathy and Moral Development. Cambridge University Press, Cambridge (2000)
21. Davis, M.H.: Empathy. In: Encyclopedia of Human Relationships, pp. 515–520. SAGE Publications, Thousand Oaks (2009)
22. Batson, C.D., Early, S., Salvarani, G.: Perspective taking: imagining how another feels versus imaging how you would feel. Pers. Soc. Psychol. Bull. **23**(7), 751–758 (1997)
23. Davis, M.H.: A multidimensional approach to individual difference in empathy. JSAS Catal. Sel. Doc. Psychol. **10**, 85 (1980)
24. Davis, M.H.: Empathy: A Social Psychological Approach. Westview Press, Boulder (1994)
25. Batson, C.D.: Empathy-induced altruism: friend or foe of the common good? In: For the Greater Good of All, pp. 29–47. Palgrave MacMillan, New York (2011)
26. Davis, M.H.: Empathy. In: Stets, J.E., Turner, J.H. (eds.) Handbook of the Sociology of Emotions, pp. 443–466. Springer, Boston (2006). https://doi.org/10.1007/978-0-387-30715-2_20
27. Decety, J.: The neurodevelopment of empathy in humans. Dev. Neurosci. **32**(4), 257–267 (2010)
28. Bernhardt, B.C., Singer, T.: The neural basis of empathy. Ann. Rev. Neurosci. **35**(1), 1–23 (2012)

29. Riess, H.: Empathy in medicine—a neurobiological perspective. JAMA **304**(14), 1604 (2010)
30. Riess, H.: The science of empathy. J. Patient Exp. **4**(2), 74–77 (2017)
31. Goleman, D.: Social Intelligence: The New Science of Human Relationships. Bantam Books, New York (2006)
32. Singer, T., Lamm, C.: The social neuroscience of empathy. Ann. New York Acad. Sci. **1156**(1), 81–96 (2009)
33. Batson, C.D., Eklund, J.H., Chermok, V.L., Hoyt, J.L., Ortiz, B.G.: An additional antecedent of empathic concern: valuing the welfare of the person in need. J. Pers. Soc. Psychol. **93**(1), 65–74 (2007)
34. Baron-Cohen, S., Wheelwright, S.: The empathy quotient: an investigation of adults with Asperger syndrome or high functioning autism, and normal sex differences. J. Autism Dev. Disord. **34**(2), 163–175 (2004)
35. Eisenberg, N., Miller, P.A.: The relation of empathy to prosocial and related behaviors. Psychol. Bull. **101**(1), 91–119 (1987)
36. Darwin, C.R.: Journal of Researches into the Natural History and Geology of the Various Countries Visited by H.M.S. Beagle. John Murray, London (1990)
37. Batson, C.D., Powell, A.A.: Altruism and prosocial behavior. In: Handbook of Psychology, pp. 463–484. Wiley, Hoboken (2003)
38. Tusche, A., Böckler, A., Kanske, P., Trautwein, F.M., Singer, T.: Decoding the charitable brain: empathy, perspective taking, and attention shifts differentially predict altruistic giving. J. Neurosci. **36**(17), 4719–4732 (2016)
39. Davis, M.H.: Empathy: A Social Psychological Approach. Routledge, Abingdon (2018)
40. Nagamine, M., et al.: The relationship between dispositional empathy, psychological distress, and posttraumatic stress responses among Japanese uniformed disaster workers: a cross-sectional study. BMC Psychiatry **18**(1), 328 (2018)
41. de Wied, M., Branje, S.J.T., Meeus, W.H.J.: Empathy and conflict resolution in friendship relations among adolescents. Aggress. Behav. **33**(1), 48–55 (2007)
42. Main, A., Walle, E.A., Kho, C., Halpern, J.: The interpersonal functions of empathy: a relational perspective. Emot. Rev. **9**(4), 358–366 (2017)
43. Mueller, M.A., Waas, G.A.: College students' perceptions of suicide: the role of empathy on attitudes, evaluation, and responsiveness. Death Stud. **26**(4), 325–341 (2002)
44. Litvack-Miller, W., McDougall, D., Romney, D.M.: The structure of empathy during middle childhood and its relationship to prosocial behavior. Genet. Soc. Gen. Psychol. Monogr. **123**(3), 303–324 (1997)
45. Wagner, U., Handke, L., Walter, H.W.: The relationship between trait empathy and memory formation for social vs. non-social information. BMC Psychol. **3**(1), 2 (2015)
46. Batson, C.D., et al.: Is empathic emotion a source of altruistic motivation? J. Pers. Soc. Psychol. **40**(2), 290–302 (1981)
47. Oswald, P.A.: The effects of cognitive and affective perspective taking on empathic concern and altruistic helping. J. Soc. Psychol. **136**(5), 613–623 (1996)
48. Miller, P.A., Eisenberg, N.: The relation of empathy to aggressive and externalizing/antisocial behavior. Psychol. Bull. **103**(3), 324–344 (1988)
49. Moor, A., Silvern, L.: Identifying pathways linking child abuse to psychological outcome. J. Emot. Abuse **6**(4), 91–114 (2006)
50. Wheeler, J.G., George, W.H., Dahl, B.J.: Sexually aggressive college males: empathy as a moderator in the "Confluence Model" of sexual aggression. Pers. Ind. Diff. **33**(5), 759–775 (2002)
51. Giancola, P.R.: The moderating effects of dispositional empathy on alcohol-related aggression in men and women. J. Abnorm. Psychol. **112**(2), 275–281 (2003)

52. Kollmuss, A., Agyeman, J.: Mind the gap: why do people act environmentally and what are the barriers to pro-environmental behavior? Environ. Educ. Res. **8**(3), 239–260 (2002)

53. Brown, K., et al.: Empathy, place and identity interactions for sustainability. Glob. Environ. Change **56**, 11–17 (2019)

54. Tam, K.-P.: Dispositional empathy with nature. J. Environ. Psychol. **35**, 92–104 (2013)

55. Berenguer, J.: The effect of empathy in proenvironmental attitudes and behaviors. Environ. Behav. **39**(2), 269–283 (2007)

56. Konrath, S.H., O'Brien, E.H., Hsing, C.: Changes in dispositional empathy in American college students over time: a meta-analysis. Pers. Soc. Psychol. Rev. **15**(2), 180–198 (2011)

57. Schumann, K., Zaki, J., Dweck, C.S.: Addressing the empathy deficit: beliefs about the malleability of empathy predict effortful responses when empathy is challenging. J. Pers. Soc. Psychol. **107**(3), 475–493 (2014)

58. Henriksen, D.: Embodied thinking as empathy through gaming: perspective taking in a complex world. In: Henriksen, D. (ed.) The 7 Transdisciplinary Cognitive Skills for Creative Education. SECT, pp. 41–50. Springer, Cham (2018). https://doi.org/10.1007/978-3-319-59545-0_6

59. Gagné, F.: The DMGT: changes within, beneath, and beyond. Talent Dev. Excell. **5**(1), 5–19 (2013)

60. Bertrand, P., Guegan, J., Robieux, L., McCall, C.A., Zenasni, F.: Learning empathy through virtual reality: multiple strategies for training empathy-related abilities using body ownership illusions in embodied virtual reality. Front. Robot. AI **5**, 26 (2018)

61. Elias, J., et al.: Promoting Social and Emotional Learning: Guidelines for Educators. Association for Supervision and Curriculum Development, Alexandria (1996)

62. Karagiorgi, Y., Symeou, L.: Translating constructivism into instructional design: potential and limitations. J. Educ. Technol. Soc. **8**(1), 17–27 (2005)

63. Mcmahan, A.: Immersion, Engagement, and Presence A Method for Analyzing 3-D Video Games. Routledge, New York (2003)

64. Michailidis, L., Balaguer-Ballester, E., He, X.: Flow and immersion in video games: the aftermath of a conceptual challenge. Front. Psychol. **9**, 1682 (2018)

65. Stang, S.: This action will have consequences: interactivity and player agency. Game Stud. **19**(1) (2019)

66. Juul, J.: The Art of Failure: An Essay on the Pain of Playing Video Games. MIT Press, Cambridge (2013)

67. Bogost, I., Ferrari, S., Schweizer, B.: Newsgames: Journalism at Play. MIT Press, Cambridge (2010)

68. Plewe, C., Fürsich, E.: Are newsgames better journalism? J. Stud. **19**(16), 2470–2487 (2018)

69. Rollins, A., Morris, D.: Game Architecture and Design. Coriolis Ed. (2000)

70. Rollings, A., Ernest, A.: Fundamentals of Game Design. Prentice-Hall, Upper Saddle River (2006)

71. Chen, A., Hanna, J.J., Manohar, A., Tobia, A.: Teaching empathy: the implementation of a video game into a psychiatry clerkship curriculum. Acad. Psychiatry **42**(3), 362–365 (2018)

72. Gilbert, L.: "Assassin's creed" reminds us that history is human experience": students' senses of empathy while playing a narrative video game. Theory Res. Soc. Educ. **47**(1), 108–137 (2019)

73. Jenkins, H.: Convergence Culture: Where Old and New Media collide. New York University Press, New York (2006)

74. Lebowitz, J., Klug, C.: Interactive Storytelling for Video Games: A Player-Centered Approach to Creating Memorable Characters and Stories. Focal Press, Waltham (2011)

75. Asimov, I.: I, Robot. Gnome Press and Doubleday, New York (1950)
76. Dick, P.K.: Do Androids Dream of Electric Sheep?. Doubleday, New York (1968)
77. Bukatman, S.: Terminal Identity. The Virtual Subject in Postmodern Science Fiction. Duke University Press, London (1993)
78. Khan, Z.: David Cage Opens Up About Detroit Become Human Development. Playstationlifestyle (2019). https://www.playstationlifestyle.net/2019/05/04/cage-on-detroit-become-human-development/. Accessed 31 Dec 2019
79. Seppala, T.J.: PS4 exclusive "Detroit" is a flawed depiction of race in America Engadget (2018). https://www.engadget.com/2018/05/24/detroit-become-human-ps4-review/. Accessed 31 Dec 2019
80. Jones, H.: "Detroit: become human": exploitative and tasteless. Goomba Stomp (2018). https://goombastomp.com/detroit-become-human-exploitative/. Accessed 31 Dec 2019
81. Orland, K.: Quantic dream patches over one of Detroit's most emotional moments. Ars Techica (2018). https://arstechnica.com/gaming/2018/06/quantic-dream-patches-over-one-of-detroits-most-emotional-moments/. Accessed 31 Dec 2019
82. Linneman, J.: Detroit: become human is a different kind of tech showcase Eurogamer (2018). https://www.eurogamer.net/articles/digitalfoundry-2018-detroit-become-human-tech-analysis/. Accessed 31 Dec 2019
83. Smethurst, T., Craps, S.: Playing with trauma: interreactivity, empathy, and complicity in the walking dead video game. Games Cult. **10**(3), 269–290 (2015)
84. Concepcion, M.: GDC 2013: 9 takeaways from "saving doug: empathy, character, and choice in the walking dead". MTV Video Games (2013). http://www.mtv.com/news/2466983/gdc-2013-9-takeaways-from-saving-doug-empathy-character-and-choice-in-the-walking-dead/. Accessed 31 Dec 2019
85. Smith, R.: Empathy games. Gameological Society (2013). http://gameological.com/2013/05/empathy-in-the-walking-dead/index.html/. Accessed 31 Dec 2019
86. Watts, S.: Interview: the walking dead writer on making a game with "no good decisions". Shacknews (2012). https://www.shacknews.com/article/75594/the-walking-dead-is-about-impossible-choices-writer-says. Accessed 31 Dec 2019
87. Bopp, J.A., Müller, L.J., Aeschbach, L.F., Opwis, K., Mekler, E.D.: Exploring emotional attachment to game characters. In: Proceedings of the Annual Symposium on Computer-Human Interaction in Play - CHI Play 2019, pp. 313–324. ACM Press, New York (2019)
88. Taylor, N., Kampe, C., Bell, K.: Me and Lee: identification and the play of attraction in the walking dead. Game Stud. **15**(1) (2015)
89. New York Post: Interview with 'The Walking Dead' video game writer Gary Whitta. New York Post (2012). https://nypost.com/2012/10/01/interview-with-the-walking-dead-video-game-writer-gary-whitta/. Accessed 31 Dec 2019
90. Wallace, K.: Creating clementine. Game Infomer (2012). https://www.gameinformer.com/b/features/archive/2012/12/26/creating-clementine.aspx/. Accessed 31 Dec 2019
91. Madigan, J.: The walking dead, mirror neurons, and empathy. The psychology of video games (2012). https://www.psychologyofgames.com/2012/11/the-walking-dead-mirror-neurons-and-empathy/. Accessed 31 Dec 2019
92. Triberti, S., Villani, D., Riva, G.: Moral positioning in video games and its relation with dispositional traits: the emergence of a social dimension. Comput. Hum. Behav. **50**, 1–8 (2015)
93. Spanlang, B., et al.: How to build an embodiment lab: achieving body representation illusions in virtual reality. Front. Robot. AI **1**, 9 (2014)

94. Squire, K., Jenkins, H.: Video Games and Learning: Teaching and Participatory Culture in the Digital Age. Teachers College Press, New York (2011)
95. Bailenson, J.: Experience on Demand: What Virtual Reality Is, How It Works, and What It Can Do. Norton & Company, New York (2018)
96. Gee, J.P.: What Video Games Have to Teach Us About Learning and Literacy. Palgrave Macmillan, London (2003)
97. Waszkiewicz, A.: The Posthuman Android and the Transhuman player in Detroit: become human. Acta Hum. **9**, 197 (2019)

METUIGA "Methodology for the Design of Systems Based on Tangible User Interfaces and Gamification Techniques"

Case Study: Teaching Geometry in Children with Visual Problems

Luis Roberto Ramos Aguiar[(✉)] [iD]
and Francisco Javier Álvarez Rodríguez[(✉)] [iD]

Universidad Autónoma de Aguascalientes, Ave.
Universidad 940, 20130 Aguascalientes, Mexico
al266432@edu.uaa.mx, fjalvar.uaa@gmail.com

Abstract. From the analysis of methodologies focused on the construction of interactive systems an adaptation is made for the construction of interactive systems based on tangible user interfaces and gamification techniques, through a well-defined process, where they are incorporated Software engineering best practices. This proposal analyzes and describes the phases for the development of interactive systems based on tangible user interfaces and gamification techniques in order to produce quality interactive systems. The use of this methodology ensures that a quality product that meets the characteristics of functionality, usability and reliability, desirable and necessary characteristics for an interactive system is produced from its early stages of development. A software prototype is also developed using the proposed methodology that replicates features of a Tangible Interface-based Application for Teaching Tactual Shape Perception and Spatial Awareness Sub-Concepts to Visually Impaired Children presented by Jafri et al. [24, 25] and includes features proposed by them such as providing the description of the figures instead of their name, the impression of their name on the tangible objects, feedback through audio, among others applying mechanics and dynamics of gamification. The development methodology involved the study of several aspects, among which are user-centered design, tangible user interfaces, gamification techniques.

Keywords: Methodology · Tangible user interface · Gamification · Visual impairment

1 Introduction

The use of technology in education has led to the development of many applications and Web-based solutions aimed at supporting learning in a creative and amusing environment. Many applications have been designed as digital games to encourage and engage students of any age in their learning process. Unfortunately, for students with

---

The original version of this chapter was revised: this paper was updated and the two more references were added. The correction to this chapter is available at https://doi.org/10.1007/978-3-030-49108-6_45

M. Antona and C. Stephanidis (Eds.): HCII 2020, LNCS 12189, pp. 229–245, 2020.
https://doi.org/10.1007/978-3-030-49108-6_17

visual impairments the opportunities are very limited, because there still exists a significant gap in the accessibility of serious games and applications for learning.

In the literature some specific educational games or applications suitable for visually impaired children have been proposed, such as BraillePlay [1], a suite to teach the braille code. However, a visually impaired student has a very limited number of potential applications to consider, and they are for very specific topics. Accessibility guidelines have been proposed in the literature for several years [2] to require the design of applications suitable for all users and not specific for a certain disability. Nevertheless, this field still requires further studies and research to overcome that gap.

Most of the interaction modalities used for educational games greatly exploit the visual channel to present and display educational content in order to allow students to learn them by imitation. Unfortunately, this approach is not suitable for children with visual impairment. Therefore, we must propose equivalent, accessible and adequate alternative solutions for those who cannot see.

This means a great challenge for all those development teams that must develop a system for people with visual disabilities, because in most cases they do not know the tools and techniques appropriate to generate systems that meet the necessary requirements based on the usability and accessibility criteria that these users need.

In this paper we present a methodological proposal to build interactive systems using tangible user interfaces and gamification techniques. Taking as a case study the teaching of geometry concepts to children with visual impairment. The methodology has been designed to be simple and practical for all those development teams that have the responsibility of creating systems in which the blind child can interact in a simple and natural way, therefore, the interaction of the systems must be based primarily on touch and sound.

Our use case is based on the implementation of the proposed methodology to develop a system that meets the necessary quality requirements that is capable of teaching geometric subjects in children with visual problems.

The rest of the paper is organized as follows: Sect. 2 presents some related background. Section 3 describes the methodologies analyzed. Section 4 presents the proposed methodology. Section 5 presents the implementation of the methodology and finally, Sect. 6 presents the conclusions and future work.

2   Background

Since the METUIGA methodology follows the user-centered design principles and aims to develop interactive systems that include tangible interfaces and gamification techniques, concepts of these themes that compose it are shown below.

2.1   Tangible User Interfaces as Learning Tools

A tangible user interface (TUI) can be defined as one in which the user is provided with a physical representation of the digital information, allowing the user to literally grasp the data with their hands. This is possible thanks to the fact that the data is matched with the physical representations. A TUI must provide feedback to the user, either through the touch itself, through the digitized objects we refer to, or in aural or visual way when the interaction with that object has ended [3].

With a TUI we can transcend the common human-computer interaction, which is usually performed with a screen and images in two dimensions. This interaction can move on to the three-dimensional plane, making the user interact with something closer to reality.

Interest in tangible interfaces has been growing since the early nineties. One of the pioneers in the world of tangible interfaces is Hiroshi Ishii, head of the Tangible Media Group at MIT, who began to investigate with this type of person-to-person interaction in the mid-nineties. The new idea of Tangible Bits arose with the aim of joining the physical world with the digital one. The first tangible interfaces were created where objects, surfaces and spaces were used to materialize digital data [4].

Since the emergence of Tangible User Interfaces (TUI), numerous applications with different functionalities have been created, but hardly any of them has been applied in educational settings. Several reasons why TUI can improve the learning framework [5] are the following:

- Use of physical materials. Keeping in mind that perception and knowledge are linked together, then manipulating physical objects will make it much easier to assimilate their nature. For example, three-dimensional objects can be understood more easily if presented physically than in a digital form.
- Possibility of engaging the user. Interacting with TUI is much more natural than any other method of interaction, therefore it can be more engaging and accessible for children with disabilities.
- Very useful for collaborative learning. Applications with a tangible interface can be designed to be collaborative, enabling several users to interact with the same objects at a time, in contrast to conventional software applications in which a single user interacts with a single screen.
- It has a greater potential as a learning method when dealing with certain topics. As for example when studying the structure of molecules in chemistry or in biology. It has been shown that relying on 3D figures is more useful than relying on drawings or illustrations.
- For all these reasons TUI are a promising technique when it comes to educating any child, but for blind children in particular, they contribute with even more benefits. Only the fact of enhancing their tactile capacity is already a giant step, since, as mentioned, this is essential for their further development. In addition, through an application based on TUI they could get to know the aspect and shape of very large objects by recognizing them in a tactile way, as we can put these objects to scale to be manipulated.

For all these reasons TUI are a promising technique when it comes to educating any child, but for blind children in particular, they contribute with even more benefits. Only the fact of enhancing their tactile capacity is already a giant step, since, as mentioned, this is essential for their further development. In addition, through an application based on TUI they could get to know the aspect and shape of very large objects by recognizing them in a tactile way, as we can put these objects to scale to be manipulated.

2.2   Gamification as Learning Tools

Gamification is based on the use of videogame design elements in non-game contexts to make a product, service or application more fun, attractive and motivating [15]. Thus, [16] raises gamification as the use of games' own designs and techniques in non-playful contexts in order to develop development skills and behaviors. In this context, our gamification approach refers to the application of game mechanics to areas that are not properly game, in order to stimulate and motivate both competition and cooperation between players [17, 18].

For the most part, the authors agree to point out gamification as a fundamental factor in increasing user motivation. To motivate is to awaken the passion and enthusiasm of people to contribute their abilities and talents to the collective mission [15]. So, if you want to use gamification techniques, you need to know the keys to motivation to design games that engage different types of players as we will see later [19]. In this way, gamification techniques are breaking into organizations in order to enhance the motivation and commitment of employees and customers. The fields of use range from innovation, marketing, talent management and learning, to the development of healthy and responsible habits [19].

In this context, the fundamentals of gamification according to [20] are dynamics, mechanics and components. The dynamics are the concept, the implicit structure of the game. The mechanics are the processes that cause the development of the game and the components are the specific implementations of the dynamics and mechanics: avatars, badges, collection points, rankings, levels, teams, among others. The interaction of these three elements is what generates the gamified activity as presented in Fig. 1.

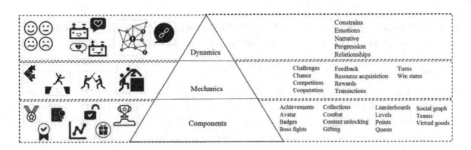

Fig. 1. Pyramid of the gamification elements [20].

In the educational context, gamification is being used both as a learning tool in different areas and subjects, as well as for the development of collaborative attitudes and behaviors and autonomous study [21]. In fact, it should not be seen as much as an institutional process but directly related to a contextualized teaching project, with significance and transforming the teaching-learning process [22].

In this way, gamification can favor all these wishes of the students through the different mechanics and dynamics of the game, but as they point out [23], it is very important that there is a controlled relationship between the challenges shown to the students and the ability of these to carry them out, because if a challenge is too easy, it will cause boredom in the student, while an unattainable challenge will result in frustration, concluding both options in a loss of motivation for learning, being the rewards a very important aspect of Gamification.

2.3 User-Centered Design

The user-centered design (UCD) is an approach that consists of putting the end user at the center of the product design and development process and covering the entire life cycle of the product, that is, from the initial planning stages and analysis of requirements until final validations.

UCD methodologies are based on various international standards, such as: ISO 13407: Human-centered design process, ISO9241-210 standard for the human-centered design of interactive systems, etc.; and define a generic process that includes a series of activities throughout the product development life cycle, but without specifying the methods to be used in each of them.

One of the central ideas proposed by the UCD methodologies is that development processes cannot be resolved as linear processes, but require iterative and agile reviews, which involve constant reviews and evaluation of processes throughout the entire process. Life cycle of solution development.

3   Methodologies Analyzed

There is no formal methodology for interactive system design using tangible interfaces and gamification techniques much less related to children with visual problems, where user aspects are analyzed in a context such as education. For this reason, we carry out an investigation of different methodologies that have been proposed and that have been used for the design of interactive systems, with the purpose of identifying those characteristics that can help in our methodological proposal.

3.1   MPIu+a

The MPIu+a methodology [6] is oriented towards the design of user-centered interactive systems. The proposed model has the following phases: requirements analysis, design, implementation, launch, prototyping and evaluation.

One of the important aspects of the proposal is to integrate software engineering with usability and accessibility engineering principles, providing a methodology capable of guiding development teams during the process of implementing a specific interactive system. The methodology has a color coding oriented to software engineering identified with the color blue, the prototyping includes techniques that will allow the subsequent evaluation phase and is identified with the color green and the evaluation with yellow color, who includes and includes methods of evaluation.

3.2 LEGADEE

In 2012 a methodology called LEGADEE (LEarning GAme DEsign Environment) was proposed [8], it is a useful tool to help design educational games. The objective of the methodology is to facilitate collaboration between the different actors who must intervene during the design of a game.

The methodology is composed of several blocks that correspond to the sequence of the phases that represent the general process of creating the game. In the middle, all the elements external to the project involved in the creation of the game, as domain experts, designers and end users. The Workforce corresponds to the different actors participating in the project, here the different roles to participate (pedagogical experts, psychologists, developers, designers, among others) are described and selected. Teams refers to the computer tools that will support the different actors for the creation of the game. Materials is related to documents, database and any artifact used directly or indirectly as material to create the game.

The methodology includes 7 phases: customer needs, specification of pedagogical objectives, conception, quality control, performance, evaluation with the client and use/maintenance.

3.3 DOODLE

DODDLE (Document-Oriented Design and Development of Experimental Learning), is a methodology proposed [7] for creating serious games focused on documents. This model was influenced by the Analysis, design, development, implementation and evaluation phases of the ADDIE model. The 4 stages involved in the creation of serious games are: Analysis, design proposal, design documentation and production documentation. In turn, each stage is supported with the output of three documents.

To validate the model, the authors proposed new students to use for the conception of a serious game. After the observations obtained, they have noticed that the vocabulary it provides is necessary to be able to communicate between the different roles. In addition, DOODLE has obtained a positive effect on the optimization of production time, educational and playful quality of the game.

3.4 Deficiencies of the Methodologies Analyzed in Relation to the Purpose of the Proposed Methodology

A methodology is important for the design of interactive systems for children with visual problems, since it involves the participation of different experts, such as: students, teachers, programmers, among others with the purpose of defining objectives applied to the context of use. This should take into account two complementary objectives, a tactile objective in order to offer tools that can be manipulated for the child and provide feedback as it progresses, as well as progression scenarios and a recreational objective, with the interest of offering a favorable environment of learning, where different aspects are taken into account, such as: challenges, punctuation, rewards, rules, among others.

Each of the analyzed methodologies (MPIu+a, LEGADEE, DODDLE) has been applied to a context of educational use with a higher education student or researchers. This indicates that user aspects for children with disabilities have not been involved in the initial phase, such as: cognitive, academic, age, gender, learning styles, among others. These aspects may vary, that is, for children with visual impairment, aspects may differ compared to a hearing child. This leads to the importance of a detailed analysis that allows identifying limitations, behaviors, preferences, among others, in such a way that it serves as support to detect the specific needs for each child.

On the other hand, the methodologies analyzed are aimed at a type of user without disabilities, which is why they do not cover the expectations we seek. In addition, there is no methodology for the production of interactive systems that use tangible interfaces and gamification tools, indicating the importance of proposing a methodology that meets these characteristics.

4 Proposed Methodology

Based on this analysis, a methodology called METUIGA (MEthodology for the design of systems based on Tangible User Interfaces and GAmification techniques) is proposed, focused on the development of interactive systems for users with visual problems following the principles of user-centered design and The iterative cascade life cycle will also have tools to use gamification techniques and tangible interfaces in the project.

METUIGA is organized in stages that determine the stage of development in which we are (Fig. 1). The scheme clearly reflects, with a color coding based on the Mplu+a methodology [6], four basic concepts:

- The attached tools for the correct use of gamification techniques and tangible interface tools (Blue).
- Software engineering processes of the iterative cascade life cycle (Red).
- The processes in which tests related to the results obtained in the software process must be implemented (Yellow).
- The processes that must obtain a satisfactory assessment by the development team and end user (Green).

4.1 Considerations of the Elements in the Proposed Methodology

The following elements are part of the development process, but its objective is to support the main phases of the development process (Analysis, Design, Implementation, Launch).

Users
In current development models, designers and/or programmers decide for users, choosing metaphors, organizing information and links, choosing menu options, among others. A User-centered Design process should make it clear that this is the case only

by looking at the scheme the first time. This is what is reflected by having users on the left side covering the rest of the stages of the entire process, in this case, since the user is someone with visual problems it is of great importance that they have contemplated from early stages in the development process.

Gamification

The gamification module works in parallel with the analysis and design phases in order to guide the development teams in the correct selection of the mechanics and dynamics to be implemented based on the needs presented by the user in the project.

Tangible User Interfaces

The tangible user interfaces module provides the necessary tools for the development team to be able to implement this type of technology. Providing a construction scheme for the tangible user interface and advising software tools to facilitate object detection and interactive system development.

Prototyped

This module is involved from the initial phase of methodology, since from the beginning of the development of a system it is necessary to test parts with a multitude of objectives to: Verify functionalities, find out aspects related to the system interface, validate navigation, try new possibilities of techniques, among others.

Evaluation

This module is involved from the initial phase of the methodology, its objective is to test something. So much to know if it works correctly or not, if it meets expectations or not, or simply to know how a certain tool works. Evaluation is a key point for obtaining usable and accessible interactive systems. In this phase, techniques necessary to receive feedback from users are applied. It also relates to usability metrics and evaluation methods.

4.2 Development Process

The objectives of each development phase are presented below, together with a table specifying the activities that were added for the development of interactive systems based on tangible interfaces and gamification and the products that are generated.

4.3 Requirements

Communication with users is a priority aspect for companies that develop software systems. During this stage it is important to make clear the scope and tool of gamification that the system will have based on the user's needs.

The activities defined in this stage and the products generated are presented below (Table 1):

Table 1. Requirements stage activities

Activity	Product
Generation of a document containing the activities carried out at this stage	Document that will contain all the information collected from the activities carried out in this stage
Interview the end users of the application to know the needs of the system	Document with information related to the needs of users in the system
Generation of use cases and actors involved in the system	A list of use cases and system actors
Identify possible risks within the project	A list of initial project risks
Identify the main requirements and restrictions of the system to be developed	A list of the main requirements and restrictions of the system to be developed
Identify functional requirements and not functional	A list of functional requirements and not functional
Identify user interface requirements	A list of user interface requirements
Identify the gamification characteristics of the project	The gamification characteristics of the project
Identify the evaluation tests to be applied at the corresponding stage considering the end users	A table with the tests that will be applied in the application and the end users
Perform the corresponding assessments	A table with the results of the evaluations applied to the system and end users
Analyze the results of the evaluations carried out and identify possible improvements in the corresponding stage	A table with considerations for the corresponding stage

4.4 Design

In this stage the best possible solution is designed, considering that the problem was clearly defined in the requirements stage. Its stages cover different functionalities, activity design, information design, and tangible interface design, as well as the main activities that make up the global interactive systems process.

The activities defined in this stage and the products generated are presented below:

*Note: The evaluations of tangible user interfaces and gamification will be carried out within the evaluations of the design stage within the analysis of evaluation results (Tables 2, 3 and 4).

Table 2. Activities of the software engineering design stage

Activity	Product
Generation of a document containing the activities carried out at this stage	Document that will contain all the information collected from the activities carried out in this stage
Design the system class diagrams	A list with class diagram designs
Design dynamic system flow diagrams	A list with dynamic system flow designs
Build static interface designs involving end users and considering the mechanics and dynamics to implement	A list of static user interface designs
Build dynamic interface designs involving end users	A list of dynamic user interface designs
Perform the modeling and construction of the database design	An initial design of the system database
Perform database security design	A proposal on the system database security design
Identify the evaluation tests to be applied at the corresponding stage considering the end users	A table with the tests that will be applied in the application and the end users
Perform the corresponding assessments	A table with the results of the evaluations applied to the system and end users
Analyze the results of the evaluations carried out and identify possible improvements in the corresponding stage	A table with considerations for the corresponding stage

Table 3. Design stage activities for the use of gamification techniques

Activity	Product
Identify the challenges to be implemented in the gamified system	The challenges to be implemented in the system
Design the gamification structure of the system	A diagram of the gamification structure
Classify common, individual and collective missions	A list of common, individual and collective missions
Design the interface of an avatar for the system	A proposal on the avatar design for the system

Table 4. Design stage activities for the use of tangible user interfaces

Activity	Product
Design tangible objects considering the information of the designed interfaces	A list of tangible object designs
Classify tangible objects based on their characteristics	A classification list of tangible objects
Design and build the tangible interface based on the recommendations of the methodology	A tool to use tangible user interfaces
Design a warehouse for tangible objects	A tool to store objects

4.5 Implementation

Also known as the coding stage, since it is where the necessary software code must be written that will make it possible for the finally implemented system to comply with the specifications established in the requirements analysis stage and respond to the system design (Table 5).

The activities defined in this stage and the products generated are presented below:

Table 5. Implementation stage activities

Activity	Product
Generation of a document containing the activities carried out at this stage	Document that will contain all the information collected from the activities carried out in this stage
Identify a coding standard for system programming	Information about the selected standard
Apply the selected coding standard	Samples of the use of the coding standard in the code
Design an organization diagram of the components and modules in the system	A diagram of the organization of components and modules
Design a directory structure diagram and final system files	A diagram of directory structures and final files
Build a System Folder Content Information table	A table with information on the contents of the folders
Identify the evaluation tests to be applied at the corresponding stage considering the end users	A table with the tests that will be applied in the application and the end users
Perform the corresponding assessments	A table with the results of the evaluations applied to the system and end users
Analyze the results of the evaluations carried out and identify possible improvements in the corresponding stage	A table with considerations for the corresponding stage

4.6   Launch

In this stage it must be verified that the acceptability of the system has been achieved, through a correct combination of social and practical acceptability. In this phase it is important to have user feedback through tests.

The activities defined in this stage and the products generated are presented below (Table 6):

Table 6. Launch stage activities

Activity	Product
Generation of a document containing the activities carried out at this stage	Document that will contain all the information collected from the activities carried out in this stage
Generate a guide to transfer the application to the end user	Document with relevant information for the correct use of the application
Identify the evaluation tests to be applied in the system and to end users to measure social acceptability and practical acceptability	A table with the tests that will be applied in the application and the end users
Perform the corresponding evaluation	A table with the results of the evaluations applied to the system and end users
Analyze the results of the evaluations carried out and identify if the software has the necessary characteristics to be launched to production	A table with program considerations
Generate a final evaluation of the application before launch	Document with information on the status of the application

5   Study Case

Due to the limitations to work with blind students it was decided to make a first interaction of the proposed methodology based on the work of Jafri et al. [24, 25] which presents a tangible user interface application for teaching shape recognition and spatial concepts to visually impaired children utilizing a computer vision based tangible tracking system which employs activities in the form of a game to teach these concepts. They also report interesting suggestions made by experts (i.e., teachers for visually impaired children who evaluated their system) such as providing an audio description of the shape instead of simply naming it, that we applied in our prototype.

For the presentation of the application we replicate the model shown by [24, 25] who divide their system into three components: a tangible tracking system, geometric objects which are used as the tangible objectives, and an application. The details of these components are as follows:

5.1   Tangible Tracking System

To detect and track objects we use ReacTIVision [9] which is an open-source cross-platform computer vision framework for fast and robust tracking of fiducial markers

(Fig. 2) attached to physical objects, as well as for tracking multi-touch fingers It was designed primarily as a toolkit for the rapid development of tangible user interfaces (TUI) based on interactive multi-touch tables and surfaces [24, 25]. This framework has been developed by Martin Kaltenbrunner and Ross Bencina as the underlying sensor component of the Reactable, a tangible modular synthesizer that has set the standards for tangible multitouch applications (Fig. 3).

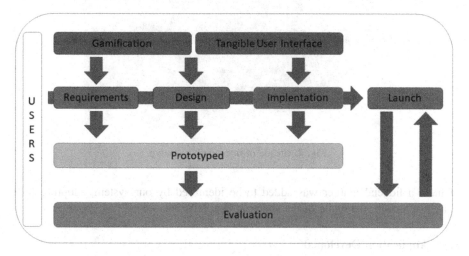

Fig. 2. Stages that make up the proposed methodology.

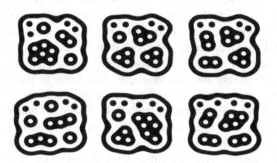

Fig. 3. Fiducial markers [9].

There are several ways to configure the hardware for the tracking system [10]. We have adopted the configuration suggested by the METUIGA (Fig. 4) [24, 25] that consists of a 40 cm × 30 cm acrylic, a 5-v lamp and to detect the objects we mount a high definition camera brand Microsoft.

5.2 Geometric Objects

Since the interaction with the system is through tangible objects, representative figures of the different basic geometric shapes to be used in our system were developed (Triangle, Rectangle, Square, Circle, Pentagon, Hexagon, Rhombus, Oval, Rectangle), which were reviewed and approved by a visually impaired student. Finally, in each one

Fig. 4. Inside of our tangible system.

of them a fiducial marker was added to be identified by our system; adopting Jafri et al.'s approach, the name of the shape in Braille is also added [24, 25].

5.3   Application Developed

An application has been built replicating proposed features by [24, 25] which it is connected to a tangible interface and a tracking system. It has been developed with the objective of allowing the child to learn about geometric objects (Triangle, Rectangle, Square, Circle, Pentagon, Hexagon, Rhombus, Oval, Rectangle) which are available in the application and are identified by means of their corresponding marker.

The child can interact with the application using the tangible interface and receiving feedback through the ear adopting the suggestions made by the experts in [24, 25]. He has two options, in the first one he can put the objects in the acrylic and he will receive feedback of the object that he is putting, in the second option he will be asked questions in the form of riddles so that he responds by putting the figure that he considers is the one we are referring, subsequently the application analyzes if your answer was correct and incorrect informing through audio, the user has three opportunities to respond correctly simulating the lives of a gamma system, when your answer the correct one is awarded a trophy based on its performance as well as a possible medal if it fulfills some specific objective (For example: It uses all the tangible objects).

In comparison with the works presented by [24, 25] who present activities for teaching geometry and spatial themes (teaching tactual shape perception, teaching orientation concepts, teaching spatial relationship concepts) we focus on presenting a different way of identifying geometric objects (Teaching tactual shape perception) through riddles, complementing the user experience with the inclusion of mechanics and dynamics of gamification such as the inclusion of levels according to their performance, the delivery of rewards as they achieve objectives, a scoring system, lives, time and progress.

The following are the questions that the child must answer in case he decides to use the play option.

- I have 6 sides, all the same. Who I am?
- I have 4 sides, 2 short and 2 longer. Who I am?
- I have 3 sides, all are equal. Who I am?
- I have 3 sides, all are equal. Who I am?
- I have 6 different sides. Who I am?
- I am fat and round. Who I am?
- I am long as a building. Who I am?

The following shows the progress made in the construction of the software and the tangible interface following the METUIGA methodology (Fig. 5, Fig. 6).

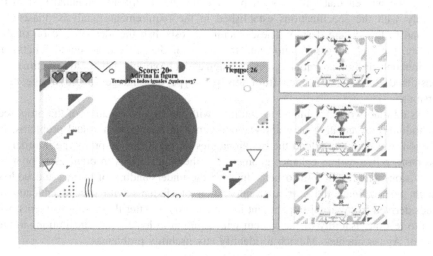

Fig. 5. Implementation of gamification techniques.

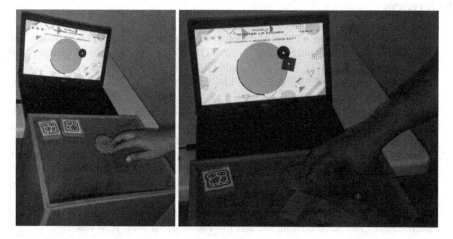

Fig. 6. Application built following the METUIGA methodology using tangible user interfaces and gamification techniques.

6 Conclusions and Future Work

This methodology is a work that is still in process which aims to support the construction of interactive systems using tangible user interfaces and gamification techniques. Modifications were made at the different stages of the user-centered design, to include aspects related to gamification and tangible user interfaces, since it is a methodology specially designed to support the process of building systems that use these techniques.

A functional prototype focused on our case study was carried out, which shows how the first three stages of the proposed methodology are carried out. The prototype is made until the implementation stage. At this stage the necessary software code must already be written that will make it possible for the finally implemented system to comply with the specifications established in the requirements analysis phase and respond to the system design. These documents establish the idea, the vision of the product, the type of gamification and the scope of the project, an initial functional requirements design, an initial dynamic design and a prototype that could sometimes be considered 'disposable', since from this prototype the changes begin in the next versions.

As a future work, we intend to continue with the experimentation of the proposed methodology by creating new applications aimed at people with visual problems, in addition, we intend to extend the functionalities of the presented prototype in order to add more activities that enhance geometric mathematical skills in blind users or with low vision, which will aim to help improve the understanding of figures and bodies which will facilitate the curricular integration of students with special educational needs derived from visual impairment in the classroom. After these improvements, we plan to test the usability of the system with children in local public institutions in the state of Aguascalientes, Mexico to identify any usability problem.

References

1. Milne, L.R., et al.: BraillePlay: educational smartphone games for blind children. In: Proceedings of the 16th International ACM SIGACCESS Conference on Computers and Accessibility. ACM (2014). Author, F., Author, S.: Title of a proceedings paper. In: Editor, F., Editor, S. (eds.) CONFERENCE 2016. LNCS, vol. 9999, pp. 1–13. Springer, Heidelberg (2016)
2. Yuan, Bei, Folmer, Eelke, Harris, Frederick C.: Game accessibility: a survey. Univ. Access Inf. Soc. 10(1), 81–100 (2011). Author, F.: Contribution title. In: 9th International Proceedings on Proceedings, pp. 1–2. Publisher, Location (2010)
3. Shaer, O., Hornecker, E.: Tangible user interfaces: past, present, and future directions. Found. Trends® Trends Hum.–Comput. Interact. 3(1–2), 4–137 (2010)
4. MIT: Tangible Media Group - MIT (2017). https://tangible.media.mit.edu/project/tangible-bits/
5. Marshall, P.: Do tangible interfaces enhance learning? In: Proceedings of the 1st International Conference on Tangible and Embedded Interaction. ACM (2007)

6. i Saltiveri, T.G.: MPIu+a. Una metodología que integra la Ingeniería del Software, la Interacción Persona-Ordenador y la Accesibilidad en el contexto de equipos de desarrollo multidisciplinares. Universitat de Lleida (2007)
7. McMahon, M.: The DODDEL model: a flexible document-oriented model for the design of serious games. In: Games-Based Learning Advancements for Multi-sensory Human Computer Interfaces: Techniques and Effective Practices, pp. 98–118. IGI Global (2009)
8. Marfisi-Schottman, I.: Methodology, models and tools for designing learning games (2012)
9. ReacTIVision Homepage. http://reactivision.sourceforge.net/. Accessed 24 Dec 2019
10. Trackmate: An easy-to-build tangible user interface. http://trackmate.sourceforge.net/codeit. html. Accessed 5 Jan 2019
11. Mor, E., Domingo, M.G., Galofré, M.: Diseño Centrado en el Usuario en Entornos Virtuales de Aprendizaje, de la Usabilidad a la Experiencia del Estudiante. SPDECE (2007)
12. Díaz-Antón, M.G., et al.: Propuesta de una metodología de desarrollo de software educativo bajo un enfoque de calidad sistémica. Univ. Simón Bolívar Caracas Venez 1, 91 (2006)
13. Iso. https://www.iso.org/standard/52075.html. Accessed 28 Dec 2019
14. Gracia Bandrés, M.A., Gracia Murugarren, J., Romero San Martín, D.: TecsMedia: metodologías de diseño centradas en usuarios (2015)
15. Deterding, S.: Gamification: designing for motivation. Interactions 19(4), 14–17 (2012)
16. Burke, B.: Gamification 2020: What is the Future of Gamification. Gartner, Inc. (2012)
17. Kapp, K.M.: Games, gamification, and the quest for learner engagement. T+D 66(6), 64–68 (2012)
18. Kapp, K.M., Latham, W.F., Ford-Latham, H.: Integrated Learning for ERP Success: A Learning Requirements Planning Approach. CRC Press, Boca Raton (2001)
19. Valderrama, B.: Los secretos de la gamificación: 10 motivos para jugar. Capit. Hum. 295, 73–78 (2015)
20. Werbach, K., Hunter, D.: For the Win: How Game Thinking Can Revolutionize Your Business. Wharton Digital Press (2012)
21. Caponetto, I., Earp, J., Ott, M.: Gamification and education: a literature review. In: European Conference on Games Based Learning, vol. 1. Academic Conferences International Limited (2014)
22. Carolei, P., et al.: Gamificação como elemento de uma política pública de formação de professores: vivências mais imersivas e investigativas. Simpósio Brasileiro Games Entretenimento Digit. (SBGames) 15, 1253–1256 (2016)
23. Castellón, L., Jaramillo, Ó.: Educación y videojuegos: Hacia un aprendizaje inmersivo. Homovideoludens 2, 264–281 (2013)
24. Jafri, R., Aljuhani, A.M., Ali, S.A.: A tangible interface-based application for teaching tactual shape perception and spatial awareness sub-concepts to visually impaired children. Procedia Manufact. 3, 5562–5569 (2015)
25. Jafri, R., Aljuhani, A.M., Ali, S.A.: A tangible user interface-based application utilizing 3D-printed manipulatives for teaching tactual shape perception and spatial awareness sub-concepts to visually impaired children. Int. J. Child-Computer Interact. 11, 3–11 (2017)

Makerspaces for Inclusive Education

Cristina G. Reynaga-Peña[1(✉)], Christopher Myers[2],
Juan Manuel Fernández-Cárdenas[1], Azael Jesús Cortés-Capetillo[1],
Leonardo David Glasserman-Morales[1], and Eric Paulos[2]

[1] Tecnologico de Monterrey, Campus Monterrey, Monterrey, NL, Mexico
`cristina.reynaga@tec.mx`
[2] University of California, Berkeley, Berkeley, CA, USA

Abstract. Academic makerspaces have been shown to foster creativity and innovation, as they provide conditions for novel thinking to challenging problems. The capability to foster rich discussions, robust ideas, and unique cross-discipline collaborations and approaches stems directly from the diversity of people, their backgrounds and perspectives, as well as their interests, which become lively in the makerspace. This project leverages the creativity and communities of two makerspaces located in two major higher education institutions, to address the need for educational tools and materials for STEM education of students with visual disabilities. Higher education students who participated in this challenge formed multidisciplinary teams to create novel accessible, affordable devices containing inclusive technology to foster inclusive learning environments. This work is an example of how educational innovation and engineering can merge in a project mediated by makerspaces, culminating not only in the generation of the products expected, but also in valuable outcomes for higher education students who participated in this challenge-based experience.

Keywords: Educational innovation · Higher education · Inclusive education · STEM education

1 Introduction

1.1 Makerspaces in Universities

Makerspaces, also known as fablabs or hackerspaces, serve as gathering points for creation where skills, knowledge, resources, and community merge [1]. They act as platforms to promote creativity and innovation, encouraging the free flow of ideas through hands-on prototyping and open collaboration practices. Such spaces are becoming ever more relevant in the support of engineering and design programs that promote innovation and entrepreneurship [2]. Rooted in its philosophy, a makerspace is a place where anyone can learn about and use digital fabrication technologies to make almost anything [3].

Research carried by Webb [2] suggest that makerspaces are largely student focused, for the promotion of technological skills by showing people how to make things. In particular, universities worldwide have implemented them in a variety of forms to

M. Antona and C. Stephanidis (Eds.): HCII 2020, LNCS 12189, pp. 246–255, 2020.
https://doi.org/10.1007/978-3-030-49108-6_18

support education in STEM fields [4]. In the process of making, students develop STEM skills and knowledge to solve challenges through creative solutions [1].

Users of these spaces are commonly called "makers" and are recognized as being part of the "Maker Movement" [2] and can vary according to the vocation a given makerspace has. For instance, in their study of Norwegian makerspaces, Jensen et al. [5] identified six different categories of makers, varying from children looking for educational experiences to established companies looking for industrial and commercial solutions. They also divided user profiles into two categories based on their expertise level: novel users with limited experience or trying the technological tools for the first time, and extreme users with advanced experience building complex projects.

The maker movement conveys more than lab spaces and tools for creation, it portraits a philosophy in which imagination, creativity, engineering, arts, and an insubordinate mindset merge in the creation of novel functional devices. Hlubinka et al. [1] described a philosophy in which:

- Makers believe that, if it can be imagined, it can be made.
- Makers are more than consumers, they are an active part of a creative process.
- Everyone can be a maker.
- Makers seek out opportunities to learn to do new things, especially through hands-on, DIY interactions.
- Makers surprise and delight with their projects, no matter the state they are (rough-edged, messy and, at times, over-stimulating).
- Makers comprise an open, inclusive, encouraging, and generous community of creative and technical people that help one another do better.
- The economic benefit is not the primary focus of the Maker movement; however, makers are not against it. Entrepreneurship blooms naturally.
- Makers celebrate other makers, their drive, enthusiasm, passion, and skills.

Makerspaces do not operate locally and in isolation, instead they tend to connect to a global network of like minded people and spaces [3]. The concept of community is strongly associated to makerspaces, studies has shown how volunteer contributions by a wide community of enthusiasts are becoming structural to the functioning of the culture and high-tech industries [6].

In academic makerspaces, community members formally and informally learn from one another in a variety of formats: classroom, workshop, or open-studio [7]. Along with this philosophy, inclusion appears as an intrinsic component of makerspaces that are open to an enthusiast community of makers where richer discussions, more robust ideas, and greater interdisciplinary collaborations naturally arise due to the diversity of people, perspectives, and interests. This openness and multi-disciplinary character of makerspaces have also encouraged participation of female students, and thus created inclusive environments in a broader sense.

1.2   Academic Makerspaces in Latin America

In Latin America, several major universities have joined the maker movement in recent years and now have functional academic makerspaces in their facilities. Although the exact number of makerspaces in general is unknown, it is clear that the maker movement is incipient in this region (about 30), and numerically, those in the US (between 240 and 600 registered) surmount at least 10 times those in the entire Latin America, according to Web directories from well-known organizations in this field [8, 9]. Similarly, a recent search for publications about makerspaces in Latin America informed there are few articles that can give us a closer look on how makerspaces perform in the Latin American context. Due to this fact, we extended the search to Iberoamerica, and one of the few reports situated in this context is the paper by Saorín et al. [10], who address the importance of a makerspace as a place to improve the creative competence of engineers in training at a university in Spain. Most recently, de León et al. [11], present ideas on how a classroom can be converted into a makerspace in a school in Tenerife, Spain.

Situated in a setting closer to the Mexican context is a study analyzing the role of 3D printing technology for inclusive innovation in Brazil [12]. In this paper, the authors conclude that "3D printing encourages design thinking in marginalized communities and the open access nature of the technology makes it more accessible to marginalized groups" (p60). In Mexico, the study reported by González-Nieto, Fernández-Cárdenas and Reynaga-Peña [13] details to what extent the sense of belonging, collaborative learning and networking are fundamental aspects for creating an innovative ecosystem in an academic makerspace.

With that into consideration, the work we present in this paper aims to contribute to a general appreciation of how academic makerspaces can foster inclusive STEM education in the Latin American context.

2 Background

2.1 Inclusive STEM Education (Our Project)

A main interest of our work group is to foster inclusive STEM education at the different school levels. For this project, we elected to work with blind and visually impaired (BVI) students as an example of a group in situations of vulnerability. Previous research on the analysis of science education for mainstreamed visually impaired children at the middle school level in Mexico [14] revealed that, even if the implementation of the curriculum is a multi-factorial situation, there are two key aspects where more need is required for improving the educational quality for this population. On one side, there is a noticeable deficit of inclusive STEM educational materials and resources for students with visual disabilities, and on the other, specialized teacher training and teacher professional development is a requisite for successful STEM education. For the work we describe in this paper, we address the first aspect, mainly, the existing deficit of inclusive educational materials. We approached this task in the form of a challenge-based pedagogy with the involvement of higher education students from two major universities, one in Mexico and one in the US, so the process would involve an educational scenario for them too.

In order to achieve that, we developed a novel collaboration between the fields of educational innovation and engineering, mediated by the key participation of the Innovaction Gym at Tecnologico de Monterrey in Mexico and the CITRIS Invention

Lab at UC Berkeley, being both examples of academic makerspaces immersed in leading universities in the field of engineering. Consistently with the concept of an academic makerspace, both laboratories promote invention and innovation by providing each other, mentoring and the infrastructure and/or equipment required for materializing ideas. Everyday processes in a makerspace include iterative prototyping, testing and solving challenges in order to obtain a functional product. A common and flexible thread for both laboratories is that the user range goes from students who are just beginning to explore the processes of making and craftsmanship, to those who are fully immersed in the culture of making as a global movement.

2.2   Inclusive Technologies for STEM Education

Elsewhere, we have elaborated on the shortage of accessible and affordable inclusive technologies for STEM education of students with visual impairments [15], starting from the premise that inclusive educational materials are those that fully support participation of all students, with the same level of engagement and at the same time in a mainstream classroom. Some examples of basic inclusive materials are Braille texts holding color illustrations and regular printed text, or three-dimensional objects with tactile resolution plus attractive visual information.

Technology, used as a support tool, is a potent agent to reduce differences between people with disabilities and without them; technology also helps build up on the autonomy of youth with such condition. However, to the best of our knowledge, few technology-based educational resources utterly comply with the characteristics of being accessible for BVI users, while they are also attractive and inclusive for sighted individuals. Some of those available are multisensory and provide auditory information [16], while others have evolved to be part of more sophisticated contexts, such as museums [17].

In the last decade, 3D printing technology has allowed to materialize three-dimensional representations of objects in a selection of science subjects, including Biology and Astronomy, to support the education of blind learners [18, 19]. Using 3D printed objects is an advancement over the traditional use of 2D tactile thermoformed graphics, and their cost is still affordable; however, simple 3D printed objects usually are single-colored, and do not include interactive technology.

It is well known that Universal Design for Learning (UDL) [20] is the framework of choice for developing inclusive technologies. Implementation of UDL in classrooms benefits students with disabilities who major in STEM fields, as it provides them with alternatives in the materials, content and resources they use for learning [21]. The use of UDL designed educational resources also increase the opportunities for interaction of BVI users with their sighted peers, as both can use the same learning materials. Thus, we proposed that the challenge would be addressed following UDL principles, so the products would be engaging and useful to all learners.

3   Methodological Approach

3.1   Participants

College students who participated in this project belonged to diverse majors, including engineering, mechatronics, biotechnology, business, physics, humanities, technology and computer science, among others. Participants were recruited at both universities through an open call, considering all majors, and the best profiles were invited to join the project, based on their interest in education and their previous experience on projects with social impact, as well as their abilities for making or desire to become makers. Once students were selected, they organized into interdisciplinary teams.

3.2   The Challenge

Explicitly, the call was to create inclusive educational materials based on Universal Design for Learning (UDL) with suitable tactile and auditory features that would also make them multisensorial, through the incorporation of low-cost technology. Technology was considered to support autonomous learning by potential users.

As mentioned in the previous sections, this challenge emerged from a current deficit of STEM educational materials accessible to blind and visually impaired (BVI) learners. The focus on BVI learners was decided under the premise that this group is an example of underserved, vulnerable population. Additionally, the resources to be produced, if complying with the requirements listed below, could be useful for other vulnerable groups as well. This means that the materials to be generated would have the potential to be used by everyone in a mainstream classroom, in equal conditions, in contrast to traditional materials for BVI, which are not attractive for sighted students, and therefore are non-inclusive.

The objective was ambitious, but feasible given the intrinsic resources of both makerspaces, which played a central role in the process. Thus, the challenge for participants was to design and construct prototypes with the following desirable features: the products had to be accessible and inclusive (UDL designed), engaging, scientifically accurate, interactive, multisensorial (with tactile, audio and/or video components), affordable, and reproducible. An ideal product would also have the capability of providing auditory information in various languages. Scientifically precise language would have to be academic, using a horizontal discourse [22], so that marginalization due to social class will be addressed as well.

Maintaining a low production cost is an important feature, as we aimed to produce a repository of files with open licensing, available at no cost, either to print or assemble objects, and therefore, the idea is that they will be available to educators worldwide. The reasoning behind those requisites is that the products could be used in formal and informal environments, and replicated in any place with access to a makerspace (or a digital fabrication lab), or even in a regular fabrication facility.

3.3 Developing Empathy with Target Users

To undertake the task, higher education students were sensitized to the condition of visual impairment through activities that included, among other, conversations with adults with visual impairment, who shared their experiences as blind learners. Some teams also visited local or international associations for the blind, or centers for development of educational resources for students with disabilities, as well as a technology center for the blind. All activities had the intention of creating empathy, but also helping participants understand the needs of the target users and know what was currently available and in use in those places.

3.4 Making Together

A second goal of the project was that participants from each institution interacted with fellow participants at the other university. To facilitate this interaction, communication occurred through remote group meetings and chats, and mutual visits took place in order to exchange ideas and form an extended, bi-national, community of makers. Monterrey students participating in the project visited Berkeley for a week, then Berkeley students visited Monterrey.

Within the first weeks of the project, one activity to build collaboration between participants of both countries and between teams took place. This activity consisted on teams designing a unique chair that would represent an aspect of the culture or context of each of both universities; instructions for building the chair were exchanged between mirror teams at the other university, under the command that the original design could be hacked by the builders. The purpose was that participants would get to know each other, would discover the skills of their teammates, but also to realize what was needed for the instructions to be universal. For example, to take into consideration the differences in measuring systems, availability of materials and clarity of descriptions, in order for the product (in this case, the chair) to be replicated anywhere. Once participants completed the general activities described above, the ideation stage formally began and they focused on the design and development of their educational prototypes.

3.5 International Mentorship

Mentors for the higher education students participating in the project included specialists in engineering, prototyping, technology, programming, educational innovation and inclusive education for the blind. The role of mentors was to offer support and advice, but also to guide participants to do research and build the knowledge needed to materialize their ideas. Mentorship occurred both ways in the international collaboration, and complemented one another. While at Berkeley the major input was on boosting creativity, ideation and problem solving, the group at Monterrey mentored in aspects of science education for BVI students and other vulnerable populations.

Participants from both universities met with mentors on a regular basis throughout the duration of the project, to share advances on their developments and to receive feedback, in order to run several cycles of iteration before functional prototypes were fabricated. The design and development processes also included conversations with end users (blind individuals), with special education teachers, and with accessible technology experts at different stages of the project.

4 Results

Results were tangible in at least two venues: 1) the generation of prototypes of educational materials accessible to blind youth; and 2) valuable learning outcomes for the college participants after the challenge-based experience.

4.1 Prototypes

To date, there are four educational products in the stage of functional prototypes generated by interdisciplinary teams of college students, some of those are in the process of being tested with users.

One team developed a game-like device with sound display designed to help blind students practice math operations through play. A second team produced a device to learn the Braille alphabet, which is suitable and engaging for young learners. A third team developed an educational prototype to learn about the female reproductive system. A fourth team is currently testing an interactive device that provides auditory information on any three-dimensional representation of choice on STEM subjects. This product has the flexibility that the information to be displayed can be recorded and played in any language. A description of this device is available elsewhere [23].

A further goal of this project is the creation of an open repository of the resources generated by participants; this ultimate product will have the potential to benefit an unlimited number of users. To the best of our knowledge, this could be the first repository in Latin America to hold STEM educational materials with technology to foster inclusive education of students with visual disabilities in mainstream classrooms or other formal and non-formal educational settings.

4.2 The Social Part of Innovation Through Making

Students reported that through participation in this project they learned to solve problems in innovative ways, searching for more alternatives than originally thought, in terms of design and use of materials:

"I realized that we are doing a good project in order to help people that are really in need, and to join forces with others who are interested in helping this type of participants" (Log 14-14).

Higher education students also realized the value of collaboration, as they worked in teams to develop solutions for the education of BVI participants. The process of getting to know each other was possible as part of the everyday group work at the makerspaces, but also as a result of the trips they did visiting the other university teaming with them:

"In relation to our interaction as a group, [at the beginning] we didn't know each other well and that made difficult to build trust… after visiting each other, I realize that now we are a team, we know each other's names, likes, jokes, but also we have found the real purpose to continue with this project" (Log 1516-2050).

Teams also were approached by other researchers and makers in different moments when they were presenting their prototypes, who offered help and support to build prototypes:

"We were approached by a scholar from the Faculty of Engineering (Log 7-7), [and] we did networking with Okdo and Arduino, which were very interested in supporting our projects (Log 3-3).

Students also had the opportunity to compare and value strengths in both institutions. Berkeley, located in the Silicon Valley, offered a fertile business atmosphere and Tec de Monterrey was identified as a place for creativity and craftsmanship aimed at the local needs of BVI participants.

Empathy with the needs of users, blind and visually impaired, was crucial: "Talking to them [BVI] helped me to understand aspects that we hadn't considered, that our product needs to have" (Log 2-2). "We learned to become more aware, empathic and humble to accept that we don't know without the sense of sight, and it is our duty to search for information from the right people in order to try our product" (Log 5-5).

Finally, creativity was crucial for developing prototypes that can have a real impact in the life of users: "With this project I have learned that you do not need to be and engineer to be in a makerspace and do things which can help others, everybody, despite your area, age, or interests, you can start learning about the use of tools which make a makerspace a valuable space" (Log 3-3).

4.3   Participant's Engagement and Motivation

Information obtained from observations and student interviews taking place half-way during the project indicate that participants fully engaged in the generation of inclusive STEM education materials accessible to blind youth. They also expressed that the challenge was highly motivating to them and acknowledged that the accompaniment of mentors was crucial to find creative solutions. Within the mentoring process, they appreciated the freedom given to develop their ideas, in contrast to other spaces where they feel they are being limited.

According to the participants themselves, a highlight of the process was the networking of experts who were available to support them on the different stages of their developments. For many of them, this was the first opportunity to apply their knowledge and skills to solve an educational challenge. Some mentioned that they learned how to combine innovation in both fields, their major and education. An excellent example is one participant, majoring in Innovation and Design, who declared that through this experience he found a vocation for his future.

Among the areas that participants identified as most challenging, they mentioned the communication with other participants during the process, understanding disabilities, how to design for teaching/learning at the middle school level, and making ideas tangible.

Most interestingly, participants clearly situated their contribution to solve a pressing challenge in education and understand the social approach of their work.

5 Concluding Remarks

In a process where educational innovation is the main axis of all outcomes, the experience we describe in this work is an example of how a project centered in the use of a makerspace, involved higher education students from different disciplines to contribute to equitable and inclusive STEM education for disadvantaged groups, such as youth with visual disabilities.

The value of craftsmanship in materializing ideas was very relevant to communicate possible solutions and alternatives to different audiences, but also to develop further their own understanding of the challenges faced by BVI youth in school settings and BVI individuals in general.

Finally, the international experience of having students from Mexico and the United States working together in understanding the challenges of BVI educational processes helped university students in both countries to develop a shared community of practice for comparing and testing ideas for STEM education with a UDL perspective.

Acknowledgments. This project was supported by CITRIS-ITESM funds granted to the authors. We thank the advice of Alejandra Díaz de León, from Tecnologico de Monterrey, during early stages of the project.We thank Writing Labs, TecLabs, from Tecnologico de Monterrey for their financial support to present this work at the conference.

References

1. Hlubinka, M., et al.: Makerspace playbook. School edition. Maker Media (2013). www.makerspace.com
2. Webb, K.K.: Makerspaces. In: Publishing, C. (ed.) Development of Creative Spaces in Academic Libraries, Greenville, NC, USA, pp. 37–40 (2018)
3. Hielscher, S., Smith, A.: Community-based digital fabrication workshops: a review of the research literature. SPRU Working Paper Series, SPRU-Science and Technology Policy Research, University of Sussex, Brighton (2014). www.sussex.ac.uk/spru
4. Webb, K.K.: Case studies in the literature. In: Development of Creative Spaces in Academic Libraries, pp. 65–78. Chandos Publishing, Greenville (2018)
5. Jensen, M.B., Semb, C.C.S., Vindal, S., Steinert, M.: State of the art of makerspaces—success criteria when designing makerspaces for norwegian industrial companies. Proc. CIRP **54**(2016), 65–70 (2016)
6. Söderberg, J.: Automating amateurs in the 3D printing community. Work Organ. Lab. Glob. **7**(1), 124–140 (2013)
7. Wilczynski, V.: Academic maker spaces and engineering design. Paper Presented at the 122nd ASEE Annual Conference and Exposition. American Society for Engineering Education, Seattle (2015)
8. The Fab Lab Network web page. https://www.fablabs.io/. Accessed 30 Jan 2020
9. Make Web page. https://makerspaces.make.co/. Accessed 30 Jan 2020
10. Saorín, J.L., Melian-Díaz, D., Bonnet, A., Carbonell Carrera, C., Meier, C., De la Torre-Cantero, J.: Makerspace teaching-learning environment to enhance creative competence in engineering students. Think. Skills Creat. **23**, 188–198 (2017)

11. de León, A.B., Saorín, J.L., De la Torre-Cantero, J., Meier, C.: The classroom as a makerspace: use of tablets and cutting plotter to create pop-up cards in educational environments. Int. J. Emerg. Technol. Learn. (iJET) **14**(10), 116–131 (2019)
12. Woodson, T., Torres-Alcantara, J., do Nascimento, M.S.: Is 3D printing an inclusive innovation?: An examination of 3D printing in Brazil. Technovation **80-81**, 54–62 (2019)
13. González-Nieto, N.A., Fernández-Cárdenas, J.M., Reynaga-Peña, C.G.: Aprendizaje y práctica de la innovación en la universidad: Actores, espacios y comunidades. IE Rev. Invest. Educ. REDIECH **10**(19), 239–256 (2019)
14. Reynaga-Peña, C., Fernández-Cárdenas, J.M.: La educación científica de alumnos con discapacidad visual: un análisis en el contexto mexicano. Sinéctica (53), 1–17 (2019)
15. Reynaga-Peña, C.G., López-Suero, C.D.: Strategies and technology aids for teaching science to blind and visually impaired students. In: Álvarez Robles, T., Álvarez Rodríguez, F., Benítez-Guerrero, E. (eds.) User-Centered Software Development for the Blind and Visually Impaired: Emerging Research and Opportunities, pp. 26–37. IGI Global, Hershey (2020)
16. Landau, S., Wells, L.: Merging tactile sensory input and audio data by means of the talking tactile tablet. In: Proceedings of EuroHaptics 2003, pp. 414–418. IEEE Computer Society (2003)
17. Touch Graphics Homepage. http://touchgraphics.com
18. Grice, N., Christian, C., Nota, A., Greenfield, P.: 3D Printing technology: a unique way of making hubble space telescope images accessible to non-visual learners. J. Blind. Innov. Res. **5**(1) (2015)
19. Horowitz, S.S., Schultz, P.H.: Printing space: using 3D printing of digital terrain models in geosciences, education and research. J. Geosci. Educ. **62**(1), 138–145 (2014)
20. http://www.cast.org
21. Izzo, M.V., Bauer, W.M.: Universal design for learning: enhancing achievement and employment of STEM students with disabilities. Univ. Access Inf. Soc. **14**(1), 17–27 (2015)
22. Bernstein, B.: Vertical and horizontal discourse: an essay. Br. J. Sociol. Educ. **20**(2), 157–173 (1999)
23. Cuellar-Reynaga, D.A., Mendoza-Córdova, M., Ramírez A., Granados U., Santamaría D., Reynaga-Peña, C.G.: Touch and learn: turning simple objects into learning materials. A system that turns simple materials into multisensorial experiences for learning. In: Proceedings of Congreso Internacional de Tecnologías Inclusivas y Educación (CONTIE), pp. 135–140 (2019)

Situated Ability: A Case from Higher Education on Digital Learning Environments

Diana Saplacan[(⊠)] [iD]

Faculty of Mathematics and Natural Sciences, Department of Informatics,
University of Oslo, Gaustadalléen 23B, 0373 Oslo, Norway
diana.saplacan@ifi.uio.no

Abstract. Universal Design (UD) is often associated with disability studies. However, UD is not about disabilities, but about designing for as many people as possible. Traditionally, disability studies are discussed through the lens of medical, relational, social, or socio-relational models. This paper proposes a new salutogenic approach instead, namely the concept of *situated ability*. Based on the work of Aaron Antonovsky and the salutogenic approach of ease/dis-ease model and his Sense-of-Coherence (SOC) theoretical construct, the paper proposes and discusses *situated ability* and the *ability continuum*. Situated ability is sugggested as a form of catalyzing discussions around social equity in a digital society. The proposed concept is supported with examples from an empirical qualitative study on Digital Learning Environments (DLE) used in Higher Education (HE). The empirical data was collected through interviews, and analyzed using Systematic Text Condensation (STC). The findings are discussed through the lens of the proposed concepts. Finally, the paper argues that a such perspective is needed for maintaining the dignity of *others*, i.e., the users who experience lower situated abilities when interacting with digital systems; for fostering *salutogenic* discussions about practice and design that enables users, without focusing on dedicated solutions for the lower abled, such as assistive technologies; and for social equity in a digital society.

Keywords: Universal Design (UD) · Situated ability · Diversity · Digital Learning Environments (DLE) · Higher Education (HE)

1 Introduction

The Universal Declaration of Human Rights (1948), article 26§1, indicates that Higher Education (HE) "shall be equally accessible to all" [1]. At the same time, learning is "a social and cognitive process through which individuals become increasingly able to participate in the activities associated with a particular social context" (Baker and Lattuca 2010, p. 812 in [2], p. 60). New learning barriers are introduced when HE adopts Digital Learning Environments, hereby DLE's that are difficult to use for students and course instructors. A 2018 report from Norway presents a list of such barriers met by the students in HE [3]. Amongst the presented barriers, almost 20% of the respondents encountered difficulties in using DLE's or resources [3] (p. 33). According to another study, circa one third of graduate students deal with mental health issues,

© Springer Nature Switzerland AG 2020
M. Antona and C. Stephanidis (Eds.): HCII 2020, LNCS 12189, pp. 256–274, 2020.
https://doi.org/10.1007/978-3-030-49108-6_19

e.g., depression and anxiety [4]. Psychosocial dimensions triggered by the DLE may scaffold or hinder the students' learning, depending on their ability to cope with challenges.

In the recent years, a high focus has been on strengthening the universities' *diversity*, e.g., see England's "widening participation" agenda [5]. "The diversity among humans is not a failure to be corrected, but *the way* human life is expressed. Consequently, the diversity is also what Universal Design should accommodate." [6] (p. 1346). Scholars say that actions taken with the aim of promoting *diversity*, instead of disrupting them, can even reinforce them [7].

In the folk understanding, *disability* is often associated with *disable bodies,* "so that disability is conceptualized as a property of the individual body rather than as an individual's most salient characteristic" [8] (p. 95). However, disability should be understood as a "transactional relationship involving a person and situation" [8] (p. 95). Disability is not an isolated concept, a constant, but a relational one, that includes a person and a situation. While the majority of the studies touching on UD matters focus on *disability studies* (see [6, 9–11]), and special education [12], Wobbrock, J. has coined within Human Computer Interaction, the notion of *situational impairment.* Moreover, several studies have investigated the idea of *situational impairment* or *situational induced impairment* [13–20]. However, this study presents the notion of *situated ability*, as a salutogenic perspective on understanding and supporting UD, through designing for diversity and social equity in a digital society: a case from Higher Education (HE). The research question addressed in this study is: *what do we talk about when we talk about situated ability when using digital learning environments in Higher Education (HE)?*

The paper continues with giving the background for this study (Sect. 2), by briefly presenting Universal Design (UD), disability studies and some of the current models used in disability studies, for understanding disability. Section 3 presents the related work, introducing the reader to the work of Aaron Antonovsky on the salutogenic approach of ease/dis-ease model and his Sense-of-Coherence (SOC) theoretical construct. The related work presented in Sect. 3 will ground later the discussion. Section 4 presents the theoretical framework. First, we introduce the ability/-disability dichotomic pair of terms. Thereafter we give an account on *ability in design,* supported by some examples from the Human-Computer Interaction (HCI) research where the focus was put on the *abilities* of the individuals instead of their *disabilities*. Thereafter, the section presents *situatedness* and *situational impairments*. Finally, the section ends with framing the newly introduced concept in this paper, namely *situated ability*. Further, Sect. 5 presents briefly the method, whereas Sect. 6 presents the findings. Finally, the Discussion presented in Sect. 7 proposes a new perspective on studying UD and diversity in HE: the *situated ability* perspective, for more social equity in the digital society. Section 8 ends the paper by presenting the contributions and the conclusions.

2 Background

2.1 Universal Design

Historically, Universal Design (UD) originates from the work of Ronald Mace, and his studies in architecture, about designing a physical environment that suits *as many as possible* [21]. However, within disability studies, UD has under a long time been discussed sometimes as Design for All (DfA), sometimes as inclusive design, as inclusion in social computing [22], or as universal access. Ageing is also one of the issues often debated in inclusion studies [23], as well as the concern of digital natives and digital immigrants [24, 25]. UD promotes values such as: "participation, non-discrimination, equality and equal opportunities" [10] (p. 203). The aim of UD, as a political strategy, is to promote equal rights for all. Based on The UN Convention on the Rights for Persons with Disabilities (CRPD), a political and moral document [26], people with *disabilities* should be included in society and regarded as having equal rights. However, UD, although often associated with *disabilities,* and *disability studies,* has as an aim to include the diversity of the human being, represented through a plurality of users [6]. Other similar approaches are: design of assistive technologies, rehabilitation engineering, universal usability, design for all, user interfaces for all, inclusive design, or extra-ordinary human-computer interaction, and nevertheless *ability based design* that have some core concepts in common with the others – albeit with some differences (read a detailed account in [27]).

2.2 Disability Studies

Ferguson and Nusbaum (2012) explain the origins of *disability studies,* together with some of their core themes [28]. *Disability studies* emerged as an academic discipline in early '80's, from the *disability rights* movement [28]. The authors argue that the expression received an ambiguous use lately [28]. From sociology to history, humanities, arts, feminism, and queer studies, to education and special education, psychology, and policy and practices, the field has evolved across-, inter-, and trans-disciplinary [28]. Although with strong traditions in the above named fields, *disability studies* is not a synonym for, "or at least should not be", for special education and rehabilitation studies, community support and inclusive education, or disability rights [28] (p. 72). Disability studies comprise more than these traditions and the disability rights movement [28]. According to Society for Disability studies: *"**Disability studies** recognizes that disability is a key aspect of human experience, and that disability has an important political, social, and economic implications for society as a whole, **including disabled and non-disabled people**."* in [28] (p. 71, emphasizes added). *Disability studies* embrace some core concepts [28]:

(1) Disability is often talked about within the social model, where disability is more than an individual impairment according to the World Health Organization (WHO) (2001): *"**Disability** is **not an attribute of an individual**, but rather a complex collection of conditions, many of which are created by the social environment. Hence the management of the problem requires social action, and it is

the collective responsibility of society at large to make the environmental modifications necessary for the full participation of people with disabilities in all areas of social life. The issue is therefore an attitudinal or ideological one requiring social change, which at the political level becomes a question of human rights. For this model *disability is a political issue*." [29] (p. 20, emphasis added).

(2) Disability studies are best understood when comprehended how disability is experienced in society, and when trying to see ourselves in relation to others, as both the same and different;
(3) Disability studies are interdisciplinary, cross cutting different academic discipline;
(4) Disability studies are participatory, by involving individuals and giving them voices, while the question still remains whether or not it should also be emancipatory;
(5) Disability studies are based on values.

2.3   Medical Model

The medical model is one of the models used in *disability studies.* The model views *disability* as a problem owned by the individual, the disability being located within the individual himself [10]. Disability as understood through this model is "caused by a disease, trauma or health condition, which requires medical care in the form of individual treatment by professionals." [29] (p. 20). The medical model focuses on the diagnoses, on the illness of the individual, and how to *correct* the individual state [10].

2.4   Relational Model

Several *disability studies* use a relational model. Lid argues that UD is a relational and contextual strategy that should be talked about through a relational perspective [6]. The author argues that a relational model looks at UD through the lens of the individual and his/her interaction with the environment [6]. Lid presents the relational model of disability as the Nordic, or GAP model [10]. The author says that disability is a human condition and that disability can emerge in situations or contexts [10]. Lid (2013) agrees with Iwarsson and Ståhl (2003) in [10] that a population cannot be divided within: the abled and the disabled [10]. Disability is recognized as a relation between the social and the material factors, acknowledging human diversity, and individual human experience [10], along with the idea from Martha Nussbaum (2004, p. 341) in [10] (p. 207) that "we all have mortal decaying bodies and are all needy and disabled in varying ways and to varying degrees." Disability as an experience, as the first-person experiences, or as vulnerability of the individual and the embodied situated knowledge are valued in the relational model [10]. Moreover, it is almost imperative to include empirical studies in order to be able to talk about disability [10] (p. 209).

2.5   Social Model

The social model is a third model used in *disability studies.* In this model, UD vis iewed through the social model perspective and refers to a social understanding of disability [6]. This means that UD is understood through the disabling environment and through the environment barriers [6]. Disability in the social model lies within the environment that *oppresses* the individual in some way [10]. Disability in the social model is blamed on the *material environment,* whereas the individual experience, the embodied and tacit knowledge of the individual is nevertheless neglected [6]. However, Lid (2014) criticizes this model, since the individual with disability is not regarded and under-focused in this model [6].

2.6 Socio-Relational Model

Disability can also be regarded through a socio-relational model [6]. Lid (2014) grounds these arguments into the seminal work from Carol Thomas (1999) on *Female forms,* and on theorizing disabilities (2012) [6]. Her work talks about the *experienced disability,* arguing that *disabling mechanisms* from the environment "can be avoided through social, political and physical measures" [6] (p. 1346).

3   Related Work

In the previous section, Background, we gave an account on the existent models talking about disabilities. However, all of these models focus, at some degree, on the individuals' disability. This section introduces the work of Aaron Antonovsky an Israely American sociologist that has studied the relationship between stress, health and well-being. His salutogenic approach to health will be later used in discussion.

3.1   Antonovsky's Salutogenic Ease/Dis-ease Model

A. Antonovsky's academic work was based on the question on what are the origins of health [30]. He argued that too much focus was given to pathogenesis, referring to the origins of disease (patho, referring to disease; genesis, referring to origins). A. Antonosvky coined instead the term salutogenesis, originating from saluto, meaning health, and genesis, meaning origins [30], as opposed to pathogenesis, from the medical pathogenic paradigm.

Moreover, A. Antonovsky (1967) has confirmed that "the impact of a given external situation upon a person is mediated by the psychological, social and cultural resources at his disposal" (Antonovsky & Kats, 1967, p. 16, in [30], p. 29)

Further, A. Antonovsky has developed during the first 15 years of research the Salutogenic Model of Health (SMH), and thereafter, during the next 15 years, the Sense of Coherence (SOC) theoretical construct building upon his earlier SMH [30]. His work addressed, not only sociologists or medical sociologists, but also medical staff working in psychology, psychiatry, physicians, architects, and anyone "who professionally or personally want to understand and enhance the adaptive capacities of human beings" (Antonovsky, 1979, preface, VIII) in [30] (p. 26).

According to Antonovsky, salutogenesis is viewed as a "movement toward the health end of a health continuum" [31]. Throughout his work, Antonovsky, proposed to look away from the medical dichotomy of sickness vs. healthiness, formulating the health/dis-ease continuum [30].

3.2   Antonovsky's Sense-of-Coherence (SOC) Theoretical Construct

The SOC theoretical construct was defined as: *"The sense of coherence is a global orientation that expresses the extent to which one has a pervasive, enduring though dynamic feeling of confidence that (1) the stimuli deriving from one's internal and external environments in the course of living are structured, predictable, and explicable; (2) the resources are available to one to meet the demands posed by these stimuli; and (3) these demands are challenges, worthy of investment and engagement."* (Antonovsky, 1987, p. 19) in [30] (p. 32). SOC theoretical construct is formed out of three elements: (1) comprehensibility; (2) manageability; and (3) meaningfulness [32]. Comprehensibility is the cognitive dimension of the sense of coherence. It refers to how comprehensible, understandable, clear, structured, and coherent the information provided is, as opposed to non-comprehendible, non-understandable, unclear, non-structured, and incoherent (based on Antonovsky, 1991, p. 39 in [32], p. 97). Manageability is an instrumental dimension of SOC. It refers to the degree of manageability of the situation with regard to the resources available [32]. The third element of SOC is meaningfulnes. This last element of SOC refers to how comprehensible and manageable the situation at hands is, in order for the person to be able to cope with it [32].

4   Theory: From *Disability* and *Situatedness* to *Situated Ability*

This section gives an account on *ability* vs. *disability*. Thereafter, we introduce ability in design, *situatedness* and *situational impairment*. This theoretical anchoring into these concepts is necessary in order to be able to frame situated ability. The section ends with the framing of *situated ability*.

4.1   Ability vs. Disability

The term *ability* is defined as one's characteristic, aptitude, proficiency, or capability of being suitable or adaptable for a specific purpose [33]. The term was first introduced in the 14th century, and comes from the old French *ableté,* translated as the ability to inherit something [34]. In its turn, this term comes from the Latin word *habilitatem,* synonym to having an aptitude or ability, being able to manage [34]. In the later 14th century, *unability* antonym was used for a while, with the meaning of *incapability or incompetence* [34]. Later, in the middle of 15th century, today's antonym *inability* was formed, earlier *inhabilite,* from the prefix *in-* and the noun *ability* [34]. However, the term was used to express a legal meaning, of not being suitable for office. Only in the 16th and 17th century, the antonym *disability* took form, with the meaning of *"loss of power"* and *"incapacity in the eyes of the law"* [34].

Disability as experienced by different individuals is manifold. At the same time, in order to understand diversity, disability, and consequently inclusion and UD, a wide range of individual experiences, e.g., first-person and/or situated experiences, is needed: both from individuals with disabilities and without disabilities [6].

E.F. Kittay (2011) argues that not only the *disabled* is subject to some form of dependency, but all people, claiming that even people without disabilities are only "temporary abled" through the course of life [35] (p. 49). A parent of a disabled daughter, Kittay (2011) argues that all persons move in- and out- of dependency relationships at different stages in their lives, due to different health or functioning conditions [35]. She also argues that *the disabled* is not "a special case", but it is an inherent characteristic in human beings [35] (p. 54). She continues: "From this perspective, we reason that our societies should be structured to accommodate inevitable dependency within a dignified, flourishing life – both for he cared for, and for the carer. Finally, if we see ourselves as always selves-in-relation, we understand that our own sense of well-being is tied to the adequate care and well-being of another. Caregiving work is the realization of this conception of self, both when we give care generously and when we receive it graciously." [35] (p. 54).

The contrasting pair of terms: *ability/disability* was used in a number of research studies, either to express the perspective of one or of the other, or their corresponding synonyms. Further, disability studies focusing on the blind was presented in Fuglerud work (2014) [36]. Moreover, several studies on dyslectic students was presented in the work of Berget and Sandnes (2016), see [37, 38]. Other similar studies focused on what the users can do, and created ability-based optimization algorithms, see [39] Further, online learning and *disability* was explored in a literature review from early '00's [40]. The general idea that the study promoted was that online learning accessibility for students with disabilities is beneficial for *all* students, beyond those with disabilities: students with different learning styles or situational preferences [40].

4.2   Ability in Design

A number of HCI studies were made having this *ability* approach, or *designing for ability*. For instance, *capabilities* of older adults were phenomenologically explored in the substantial design work and studies performed by- and presented in Joshi doctoral thesis (2017) [41].

Further, Wobbrock et al. (2017) elevated Ability Based Design (ABD) over disability in a number of publication, see [27, 42, 43]. ABD focuses on the users' abilities throughout the design and use process, rather than on their disabilities [27]. *Ability* is the central focus in this type of design. While assistive technologies focus on what the users cannot do and try to fulfill that gap, ABD focus on what the users can do. Wobbrock et al. (2011) suggested that one cannot have disabilities as one cannot have "dis-height" or "dis-money" [27] (p. 9.1) [42] (p. 5). The question that ability based design answers is *"what can a person do?"* [27] (p. 9.2). An ABD system is a system that is aware, at some degree, about what the user can or cannot do. The focus within ABD is shifted from what the user cannot do to what the user can do, the responsibility being put on the system rather than on the individual: the system should be designed to accommodate or be able to adapt, or be adapted to the user, not the other way around [27] (p. 9.4). However, large variation in individuals' abilities cannot be ignored [27] (p. 9.3). Some of the ABD core principles are: (1) Ability – focusing on ability rather than disability; (2) Accountability – the users are allowed to be whom they are; the responsibility of changing the design of a system to accommodate the users is put on the designers, rather than on the users; (3) Adaptation – the systems' interface may adapt themselves or may be adapted by the users to fit the user's needs; (4) Transparency – the system's property to make aware the user about the adaptations; (5) Performance – the system's property of holding track of the user's performance; (6) Context – the system's property of sensing the users' context; (7) Commodity – low-cost and availability of hardware and software.

Several projects informed ABD, as presented in [27], such as: desktop text entry projects, e.g., the Dynamic Keyboard Model, Invisible Keyguard, TrueKeys, TrackBall Edge Write; mouse pointing studies, e.g., Steady Clicks, Angle Mouse, SUPPLE, Automatic Mouse Pointing Assessment, Voice Draw; mobile devices studies, e.g., Barrier pointing, Walking User Interface, Slide Rule; and web based study, e.g., WebAnywhere (p. 9:10). Other examples of similar ability based projects are: VoiceOver, WalkType, or SwitchBack [43]. Amongst a number of other projects, focusing on the abilities of children, rather than their disabilities, are presented in PLAY-ABLE, such as: Drawing Machines, Voice-in-Tone, Free-Jay, Sketch-Stadion, Bowling-for-All, Rock-Paper-Scissors, and Voice-Box [44].

Moreover, ABD was recently framed as a new design approach focusing on individuals' abilities in a context, i.e. on *"what people can do"* [43] (p. 62). ABD shift the responsibility of accessibility in the interactive systems, from the user, to the system itself [43] (p. 62). The point of departure in ABD is that disabilities reside within disabling environments and situations, rather than on the individual (p. 62).

However, ABD has so far been applied to individual systems [43]. For a larger impact, ABD requires a Global Public Inclusive Infrastructure (GPII) [43]. Critical points on GPII are put out by Vanderheiden and Treviranus (2011) [23] and Vanderheiden et al. (2014) [45]. ABD, as an ideal, sets the grand challenge of anyone, anytime, and anywhere could interact with any system based on what it is suiting him or her best, i.e., based on his or her *"situated abilities"* [43] (p. 70, emphasis added). Along the same lines, others talk about ability-centered design (ACD) [46]. ACD refer to either static or dynamic systems, i.e., system that are "alive" and can develop organically, adapting to the user in real time [46]. ACD is also sometimes defined as the designed for latent potential abilities [46].

4.3   On *"Situatedness"* and *Situational Impairments*

Situated comes from the verb situated and their corresponding Latin terms situate-, situare and scituare [47]. Etymologically, the verb situate dates back to the 13th century in the British resources, and it has the meaning of placing something, something that is put into place, established or set up [47]. The adjective situated was formed within English through derivation, from situate and the suffix –ed [48]. The corresponding Latin term is situates. Situated has the meaning of being "sited in a particular location", or "having a particular location of position" [48]. When the term is used together with practices, experiences or interactions, it has the meaning of being grounded within-, being dependent on-, or being determined by those circumstances of social context [48].

The adjective situational was also formed within English through derivation, from the noun situation and the suffix –al. The term appears to be have been used in the curriculum of the Polytechnic of Vienna, in the middle of the 19th century. It is thought to have its origins from the German situationell, with the meaning of being related to, or determined by (a) situation(s), or circumstances.

The canonic work of L. Suchman (1987) [49] presents the idea of plans and situated actions. Her work refers to how systems are designed according to procedures and routines, however without taking into account the unforeseeable and unpredictable, and yet individuals take actions from without their momentary situations and circumstances. Recently, studies talk about situational induced impairments and disabilities (SIID). The notion was first introduced by Sears and Young (2003), according to [19] (p. 3). Later, situational impairment was used instead. Both notions are used by researchers to denote that a user can be disabled under certain conditions or circumstances, although he or she could be abled under the "right" conditions [43]. A number of studies investigate situational impairments, often application based studies (see [13–20, 50]).

4.4 Framing *Situated Ability*

The notion of *situated ability* was used in the work of Wobbrock et al. (2018): "ability-based design pursues an ambitious vision—that anyone, anywhere, at any time can interact with systems that are ideally suited to their situated abilities, and that the systems do the work to achieve this fit." [43] (p. 64). As the authors [43] indicate, we are all disabled in some situations or under certain circumstances. However, situated ability was not defined or explained, other than in relation to disability. Wobbrock et al. had their focus instead on the earlier described ABD. Based on Antonovsky's work presented in the related work, and on the ability in design presented in the current section, we suggest the following definition for *situated ability: Situated ability is the ability to comprehend, manage, or find the meaning in the interaction with a digital system.*

5 Method

To unveil some of the issues encountered in using multiple DLE in HE, 6 interviews were performed as part of this study. 3 interviews were performed with pedagogical experts, whereas 3 other interviews were performed with academics having their expertise in UD and/or Human-Computer Interaction. The audio-recorded interviews lasted about 6 h in total. All interviews were transcribed verbatim. These were analyzed through systematic text condensation [51]. The study followed the Norwegian ethical guidelines.

6 Findings

This section presents some of our findings regarding the *situated abilities* due to situation, environment, or design of DLE's. Our findings show that students and teaching staff experienced a variation in the abilities of the students in the HE environment due to age and/or lack of experience with DLE and being an international, or being a non-Norwegian speaking student. In general, it seems that the DLE are "*not necessarily difficult, but complex*", as one participant said.

The first three interviewees were involved in teaching a diverse range of students with multicultural backgrounds, native Norwegians to non-Norwegians and international students, to English- and non-English speakers, to other employees at the HE institution, to courses on digitalization for elderly people, and people with- and without known physical or cognitive (dis)abilities. In general, the participants agreed that there is wide range amongst students' experiences with computers and DLE and tools. The next three participants, i.e. the experts in universal design, explained that they did encountered visually impaired, dyslectic students, deaf students, autistic students, hearing impaired, ADHD students, and students with other type of physical limitations, such as having the need of laying down during lectures. We show six examples of low *situated abilities,* in the next paragraphs.

One of the participants confirmed that there is a large variation in the students' abilities regarding their digital literacy. This often depended on the *students' situated abilities* given by their background experiences with DLE's. The participant said: *"It's often that the students, like the natives, they come to the University, first year students and they know they will be using (...) digital learning platforms, because most of them have used it in high school, or even in lower grades, while students coming from other parts of the world, don't have this ingrained experience, or simply experience of using the technology in this way. And I think there is always a gap there that often creates difficulties for the other group, not because they are not good performers, or good learners, or interest or motivated, because they simply need, a different encounter, start encounter with technology".*

One of the participants confirmed that there has been a variation amongst the students' *situated abilities* to use DLE's and the design of these: *"We had both students with dyslexia and ADHD. And of course this makes more stress, makes it more difficult when you have to search for everything, and when it is not consistent the words that you are using, for different buttons in the system. And it can be named this in this area of the system, and that in another, or in the next page you are opening, and in different organizations and so on. I think the overview over site how it can be named, and how you can find things, it's important for everyone, and even more for those with dyslexia, and if you have to read more, it's even more difficult, and how ADHD it's more time consuming, you need to keep your concentration for longer, of course it's difficult. And if you are motor impaired, it's difficult. If you use a joystick only to manipulate, I guess it wouldn't be not possible, not at all".*

Moreover, the participants also noticed a variation in the Norwegian vs. non-Norwegian students' situated abilities on digital literacy. It seems that the design of the DLE's lowered the students' situated abilities: *"I usually had the first course in the semester, of the semester, in the start of the study... so everything was new to the students. And we had a lot of international students. So they had also this language barrier. Because not everything is in English. And you have to open, you have to log into [the old system], before you can choose that you want to have it in English. And with the last version we had in [the old system], it was difficult to find the button for choosing English too. And then you did choose English, not everything was translated. So you suddenly had Norwegian words popping-up".*

One participant that had experience in teaching international students explained how she often encountered some form of *situated abilities* with regard to language.

More precise, language barriers. She also confirmed that students struggled with DLE's and tools. According to her, the students were digital immigrants and therefore were less used with using DLE and tools. However the requirements on using those were the same for all. She had often received emails even after explaining how to use the system, from students with *situated abilities*, about not finding their way around the system.

Two of the participants were concerned about the cultural and social dimension in *situated abilities*, arguing that the HE system and DLE and tools should take into consideration those in their design. One of the participants mentioned that the cultural diversity was earlier seen as problem in schools, whereas now it seen as an opportunity or challenge for learning: a *situated ability*.

Further, one of the participants explained how the DLE and tools are designed for the majority of the students, but not for the exceptions. The same participant revealed a situation where one of the digital systems used for entering a course in HE gave an automatic feedback to someone saying: *"You are not qualified."* and nothing else. The person receiving the feedback from the system had an immigrant background, and yet some *situated abilities*. The participant explained how he was almost ready to give up his studies after one year of hard-work of getting all the necessary preparation work and documentation for entering the HE. The participant also explained that the prospective student felt devasted because of that short message. He interpreted it as: *"You are not worth it of entering the Higher Education."* In the end, the prospective student was indeed qualified to enter the course, but due to his situated abilities, he has not understood the message. However, until they have disentangled the whole situation, the deadline to enter the course was already passed, and he could not start studying that year. Our participant explained then that this had to do, on the one hand, with the design of the system: the system was not designed for individuals with *situated abilities*. The participant thought that the system was rather designed for teenagers, as the main group of users, and less for older students. The teenagers would get help with their application from their teachers that have specific knowledge on how to apply, but it would forget about the other types of participants: adults, immigrants, or people with a lower information technology literacy - individuals with *situated abilities*.

Moreover, according to our participant, the system has introduced an *"invisible social barrier"* through this type of digital feedback. Specifically, she meant that not all the new-comers/immigrants know how exactly the rules are in Norway. If the feedback message does not include details on what is missing and does not know whom to contact, the prospective student can miss out on his/her life plans. According to the participant, of course, this was also a very visible situation of cultural conditioning: where the person expected to interact verbally with someone telling him/her that his/her application is ok, but would need some specification on some papers, but the documentation actually qualifies him/her for the course.

In addition, one participant indicated the need for courses for using the systems, especially for those that are not digital natives: *"But I think also with computer technology, you need some education. Yeah... You go to school to learn to write, but you should also be more qualified to use the technology you are introduced to. So think it's too easy to just say: "here it is a new program". Even if you have used this, and had user tests, and been involved beforehand, you may be need some... some guidance on how to do it... and this you see, especially in the elderly population who is not digital natives. (Laughs) Like me... So they are not used to this like all... so the threshold for using all the new systems are much bigger... it would have been easier if it would have been more arenas for learning those systems".*

However, one of the participants explains how some other students, without any known *situated abilities* are also frustrated about used DLE's and the physical environment: *"Yeah, I can tell. It's not only people with disabilities that are frustrated, have frustrations about the access to ICT, or the amount of different things they have to go into (laughs).. and be logged on to and getting information everywhere from. So it's a bit time-consuming. And that was not only problematic for disabled, but also for other students. And the same with hearing environment, at university colleges, where there were a lot of frustrations about noise, in the overall areas, in the areas of where they get together with people, and in the lectures rooms. It was difficult to hear the teachers: what they were saying. So a lot of complains about that - not only the hearing impaired students!"*

One participant that has taught elderly people taking courses mentioned that many of the elderly are bright and clever people, but they have some situated abilities when it comes to computers: they do not have experience with computers, and therefore it takes time for them to adapt to the digital systems imposed by the society. The participants described a situation when she taught a course for the retired people, on using computers, where the class was two hours: she had them all logged in after 1 h and 15 min. The interviewee explained how elderly people needed a lot of time, and she had to create a space for slow speed, slow learning, and calmness. In her view, these details were essential for enabling them to learn about digitalization.

Another participant explained how in her role as a course instructor, she had to be very mindful when planning and carrying out a course, in terms of choosing DLE and tools, in order to enable students' *situated abilities*, i.e., to use the DLE's: *"And now I am using the regular instructor [new system]. For now, that's what I am using. But again, my participants, my students are not the regular students. So I guess it's not representative. But I know they will be using [the new official system] [stresses on it], when they will come to teach the courses starting with the next semester. I think for most of them, it's going to be [the new official system] - only. And I also know that for many of them - at least those who are in their late years of their career - it's difficult to get to work with [the new official system], because it's new technology, and they have been used to use something else, and it's fairly... not necessarily difficult, but complex, it has a lot of functionalities, and it is really going to.. it makes it necessarily that you think, that you choose, that you think about how you are going to use it, and kind of integrate it, collect your functionalities that you need, and integrate them and make good use of them. Because if you want to use everything, you get overwhelmed".*

7 Discussion

UD addresses the design for all people, or for as many people as possible. However, the question often addressed in UD is *what can all (or the majority) do*, rather than focusing on the individual: *what can the individual do*. Moreover, UD is also often associated with disability studies, although it should not be *only* about disabilities. This section provides a reflective discussion on *situated ability* and the *ability continuum,* based on the earlier presented literature and empirical findings. We propose this perspective with the hope of catalyzing more discussions on social equity in digital society.

7.1   Situated Ability and the Ability Continuum: A Salutogenic Approach to Ability

Many of the disability studies follow one or several of the models presented in Sect. 2: medical-, relational-, social-, or socio-relational model. All of these models focus more or less on the individuals' disability, rather than on his or her *ability.* Inspired by A. Antonovsky's, we proposed a salutogenic perspective when talking about dis-/abilities. We introduce in this paper the concept of *situated abilities,* instead of talking about *disabilities,* as opposed to a pathogenic view. According to Antonovsky, "the impact of a given external situation upon a person is mediated by the psychological, social and cultural resources at his disposal" (Antonovsky & Kats, 1967, p. 16, in [30], p. 29). The ability of an individual is nevertheless seen in relation to the individuals' environment and the lived situation: the ability is *situated,* and one can experience himself or herself as being less or more abled. Ability, viewed on an ability continuum, similarly to Antonovsky's health continuum [31], can move towards a lower- or a greater scale of experienced ability in the situation at hand.

Similarly to Antonovsky's health/dis-ease continuum [30], we have formulated the *situated ability continuum.* While Antonovsky's SOC theoretical construct and its elements refer to one's general health situation, we borrow these terms and repurpose them into a discussion around design and universal design: how *comprehensible* a design is for one, how *manageable* a design is for one, and how *meaningful* a design is for one. We argue that these three elements can serve us to a purposeful discussion and model around ability/disability, and *situated ability.* Inspired by Antonovsky's work and the health continuum, we illustrate in Fig. 1, the *ability continuum.*

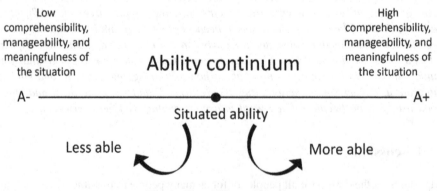

Fig. 1. The ability continuum

7.2   Illustration of Situated Ability and the Ability Continuum

Rather than dividing individuals in abled vs. disabled, we consider that everyone has some abilities under the right circumstances and conditions given a situation. However, we do not neglect the medical diagnoses of someone. What we would like to emphasize on is the relation between design and one's situated abilities. Our findings showed several examples of abilities constrained by given situations, e.g., *situated abilities*. We have encountered several situations of *situated abilities*. Similarly to Wobbrock et al. (2017) [27], we have emphasized the situated abilities of the users. We show-cased several examples where ability based design (see [27]) was not taken into consideration, as the participants experienced a high level of *low situated abilities*. To epitomize the *ability continuum*, we illustrate some concrete situations which we then connect to our findings.

Situation 1. An old adult is asked to find a physical book and read from it. The old adult knows how to find a physical book, to open it and to read it. This is a situation where the old adult shows comprehension on the situation, manages the situation, and the steps he/she follows make sense for him/her, i.e., it is meaningful for the individual. This is an example of an old adult and his/her situated ability on the high end of the ability continuum.

A contrasting example of an old adult being on a low end ability continuum is when the individual is asked to find an e-book in an online library system, borrow it online and read from it. The old adult will perhaps comprehend the task in the semantic or linguistic way. However, the old adult, especially if he/she does not have any previous experience with such a task, will more like not comprehend what steps to take, neither manage it without assistance. Therefore, the task will not be meaningful for the old individual. This is an example of an individual having a situated ability on the low end ability continuum.

Similar to this first example, our findings showed that elderly or old adults that did not have experiences with DLE's and needed more time to interact with these. As confirmed by our participants, this is not because they were not "clever" or "bright people", but because of their low *situated abilities* in the given situation. Similar findings on designing for elderlies' abilities were illustrated in [41].

Situation 2. A blind person is asked to find and read a physical book. The blind person will perhaps manage to find the physical book and to open it at a random page. However, the blind person will not be able to read the book. The person will comprehend the task and will partially manage the task, i.e., by finding a book. However, the task is not meaningful for the person considering his/her situated ability. If we look at this situation, from a situated ability continuum perspective, we can say that the individual has a situated ability on the very low end of the ability continuum.

A contrasting situation to this is when a blind person is asked to find an e-book on an online e-book reader on his/her smartphone and listen to it at a very low volume. The individual will be able to navigate through his/her smartphone, find the right e-book reader application using some form of voice command inputs, and listening carefully to the very fast speaking smartphone audio output. The individual will be able to comprehend the task, to manage the task, and nevertheless will find it meaningful.

The individual will more likely even manage to perform the task in a quite short amount of time, compared to someone that is not blind and has never perform a such task. This shows that the blind person, in the given situation, has his/her situated ability on a very high end on the ability continuum.

Similarly, our findings showed that not only students with diagnosed disabilities, according to the medical model, had encountered difficulties in interacting with DLE's, but also non-diagnosed students. Hence, the empirical data illustrated how one's *situated abilities* can be constrained or hindered by the environment. Regarding the question often posed in ABD, of *what individuals can do* [27, 43] was not posed. Perhaps, only the general question posed usually when talking about UD was asked: *what all (or the majority) can do?* Similarly to the ABD systems and its core principles, we suggest that the responsibility of what a user can do should be put on the system, rather than on the user. Several studies (see [27, 43, 44]) showed that this can be possible.

Situation 3. One example on the low end on the situated abilities is when an international student newly arrived to a new country is asked to use an online digital system that has the country's official language as the default language and that the language cannot be changed unless the user is logged in. Moreover, the official language is not English. The student can speak English, but he/she did not yet learn the language of his new country. The individual will find himself on a lower ability continuum, given the circumstances, compared to a native speaking student. He/she will comprehend the task to navigate the online digital system, will manage the task, and it will become meaningful, however it will be characterized of small challenges on the way, because of the language barrier. This is an example of a low situated ability on the ability continuum. After a while, the student will perhaps learn the language, and the online system, and then he/she will not have the same challenges with navigating the system. In this case, the individual will comprehend the language better, will be able to manage the tasks better, and it will be more meaningful for him/her to navigate the online system. Consequently, his situated ability has moved from a lower end on the ability continuum to a higher end on the ability continuum.

Similarly, our findings showed that students who lacked experience with DLE's, seemed to have a lower situated ability when dealing with DLE's. Nevertheless, the design of the DLE seemed to do not enable or increase students' situated abilities, but to lower them. Several issues seemed to have been encountered by the students: 1) the students had to login on a Norwegian webpage, before being able to change the language of the DLE; and 2) inconsistency in the design of the names of the buttons often confused the students. In this sense, perhaps ability based design should come as beneficial (see [27, 42, 43]). Although ABD is still, for now, limited to individual systems [43], our findings showed that often it is not even present.

8   Conclusion

Universal Design (UD), often associated with disability studies, it is not about disabilities, but about *designing for all* people [21]. In this paper, we proposed a new perspective to study UD – a salutogenic one. Inspired by Antonovsky [52], and his health/dis-ease continuum [30], we proposed an *ability continuum,* with a *low end- and a high end on abilities.* Depending on the situation at hand, we argue that individuals can experience as being less abled, or more abled. We called one's ability in a given situation as *situated ability.* Inspired by the Sense-of-Coherence theoretical construct from Antonovsky, we defined *situated ability* as *the ability to comprehend, manage, or find the meaning in the interaction with a digital system.*

This perspective does not disregard, neglect, or undermine the other existent models often used in disability studies: medical, relational-, social-, or socio-relational models. We argue instead that having this salutogenic approach in mind may contribute to other kind of debates in design: how can we foster discussions, and promote the individual's dignity and independence, without looking at the old, the blind, the deaf, the dyslectic etc. as different, without needing to configure and make special customization, or how to design for enabling as many people as possible, rather than focusing on dedicated tools such as in assistive technologies. Although we framed in this paper the notion of *situated ability,* some of the questions that still remain are: *How can we make design of systems better by focusing and enabling a high degree of situated abilities instead of disabilities? How can we be better designers by shedding light on individuals' situated ability, by creating design conditions for them which enable the users? How can we see ourselves in relations to others in order to understand their situated abilities? How can we make this responsibility ours, the designers, or the researchers in design, without pushing it on the users? How can this perspective of situated abilities become a more natural and salutogenic way of talking about disabilities?*

Finally, we argue that a such perspective is needed: for maintaining the dignity of *others,* i.e., the users who experience lower situated abilities when interacting with digital systems; for fostering *salutogenic* discussions about practice and design that enables users, without focusing on dedicated solutions for the lower abled, such as assistive technologies; for social equity in a digital society; and nevertheless, Universal Design talks about design for all, for as many people as possible, and not design for the disabled. Having this in mind, our intention is through this paper to catalyze discussions that have this *salutogenic* approach, rather than a *pathogenic* one – this without disregarding, neglecting, or not recognizing the benefits of having the other models focusing on *disabilities,* rather than *abilities,* as well. Nevertheless, we wish to increase awareness on the potential benefits such an approach could have!

Acknowledgements. Special thanks to Universell, the participants, and my supervisor Jo Herstad for inspirational readings on Wobbrock, proof-reading, and good discussions.

References

1. United Nations: Universal Declaration of Human Rights. Universal Declaration of Human Rights, 06 October 2015. https://www.un.org/en/universal-declaration-human-rights/index.html. Accessed 19 Nov 2019
2. Posselt, J.R.: Rigor and support in racialized learning environments: the case of graduate education. New Dir. High. Educ. **2018**(181), 59–70 (2018). https://doi.org/10.1002/he.20271
3. PROBA samfunnsanalyse: Barrierer i høyere utdanning for personer med nedsatt funksjonsevne. PROBA Samfunnsanalyse, 2018–02, Project number 17040 (2018)
4. Eisenberg, D., Lipson, S.K., Posselt, J.: Promoting resilience, retention, and mental health. New Dir. Stud. Serv. **2016**(156), 87–95 (2016). https://doi.org/10.1002/ss.20194
5. Dooris, M., Doherty, S., Orme, J.: The application of salutogenesis in Universities. In: Mittelmark, M., et al. (eds.) The Handbook of Salutogenesis, pp. 237–245. Springer, Cham (2017). https://doi.org/10.1007/978-3-319-04600-6_23
6. Lid, I.M.: Universal design and disability: an interdisciplinary perspective. Disabil. Rehabil. **36**(16), 1344–1349 (2014). https://doi.org/10.3109/09638288.2014.931472
7. Posselt, J.R.: The diversity bargain and other dilemmas of race, admissions, and meritocracy at Elite Universities. Political Science Quarterly, 22 March 2018. https://link.galegroup.com/apps/doc/A535995820/AONE?sid=lms. Accessed 19 Nov 2019
8. Stone, S.D.: The situated nature of disability. In: Cutchin, M.P., Dickie, V.A. (eds.) Transactional Perspectives on Occupation, pp. 95–106. Springer, Dordrecht (2013). https://doi.org/10.1007/978-94-007-4429-5_8
9. Grue, J.: Interdependent discourses of disability - a critical analysis of the social/medical model dichotomy. Ph.D. thesis, University of Oslo, Oslo, Norway (2011)
10. Lid, I.M.: Developing the theoretical content in universal design. Scand. J. Disabil. Res. **15**(3), 203–215 (2013). https://doi.org/10.1080/15017419.2012.724445
11. Hamraie, A.: Universal design research as a new materialist practice. Disabil. Stud. Q. **32**(4) (2012)
12. Rao, K., Ok, M.W., Bryant, B.R.: A review of research on universal design educational models. Remedial Spec. Educ. **35**(3), 153–166 (2014). https://doi.org/10.1177/0741932513518980
13. Abdolrahmani, A., Kuber, R., Hurst, A.: An empirical investigation of the situationally-induced impairments experienced by blind mobile device users. In: Proceedings of the 13th Web for All Conference, New York, NY, USA, pp. 21:1–21:8 (2016). https://doi.org/10.1145/2899475.2899482
14. Jupp, J., Langdon, P., Godsill, S.: Mobile computing in maintenance activities: a 'situational induced impairments and disabilities' perspective. In: Stephanidis, C. (ed.) UAHCI 2007. LNCS, vol. 4554, pp. 696–705. Springer, Heidelberg (2007). https://doi.org/10.1007/978-3-540-73279-2_77
15. Macpherson, K., Tigwell, G.W., Menzies, R., Flatla, D.R.: BrightLights: gamifying data capture for situational visual impairments. In: Proceedings of the 20th International ACM SIGACCESS Conference on Computers and Accessibility, New York, NY, USA, pp. 355–357 (2018). https://doi.org/10.1145/3234695.3241030
16. Sarsenbayeva, Z.: Situational impairments during mobile interaction. In: Proceedings of the 2018 ACM International Joint Conference and 2018 International Symposium on Pervasive and Ubiquitous Computing and Wearable Computers, New York, NY, USA, pp. 498–503 (2018). https://doi.org/10.1145/3267305.3267310

17. Sarsenbayeva, Z., van Berkel, N., Luo, C., Kostakos, V., Goncalves, J.: Challenges of situational impairments during interaction with mobile devices. In: Proceedings of the 29th Australian Conference on Computer-Human Interaction, New York, NY, USA, pp. 477–481 (2017). https://doi.org/10.1145/3152771.3156161
18. Tigwell, G.W., Flatla, D.R., Menzies, R.: It's not just the light: understanding the factors causing situational visual impairments during mobile interaction. In: Proceedings of the 10th Nordic Conference on Human-Computer Interaction, New York, NY, USA, pp. 338–351 (2018). https://doi.org/10.1145/3240167.3240207
19. Wobbrock, J.O.: Situationally aware mobile devices for overcoming situational impairments. In: Proceedings of the ACM SIGCHI Symposium on Engineering Interactive Computing Systems, New York, NY, USA, pp. 1:1–1:18 (2019). https://doi.org/10.1145/3319499.3330292
20. Wolf, F., Soni, P., Kuber, R., Pawluk, D., Turnage, B.: Addressing the situational impairments encountered by firefighters through the design of alerts. In: Proceedings of the 16th Web For All 2019 Personalization - Personalizing the Web, New York, NY, USA, pp. 22:1–22:10 (2019). https://doi.org/10.1145/3315002.3317556
21. Center for Universal Design, North Carolina State University: Center for Universal Design NCSU - About the Center - Ronald L. Mace (2008). https://projects.ncsu.edu/design/cud/about_us/usronmace.htm. Accessed 20 Apr 2018
22. Constantinou, V., et al.: Towards the use of social computing for social inclusion: an overview of the literature. In: Zaphiris, P., Ioannou, A. (eds.) LCT 2018. LNCS, vol. 10924, pp. 376–387. Springer, Cham (2018). https://doi.org/10.1007/978-3-319-91743-6_28
23. Vanderheiden, G., Treviranus, J.: Creating a global public inclusive infrastructure. In: Stephanidis, C. (ed.) UAHCI 2011. LNCS, vol. 6765, pp. 517–526. Springer, Heidelberg (2011). https://doi.org/10.1007/978-3-642-21672-5_57
24. Prensky, M.: H. Sapiens digital: from digital immigrants and digital natives to digital wisdom. Innov. J. Online Educ. 5(3) (2009)
25. Prensky, M.: Digital natives, digital immigrants. In: From Digital Natives to Digital Wisdom: Hopeful Essays for 21st Century Learning, pp. 67–85. Corwin Press, Thousand Oaks (2012)
26. United Nations (UN): Convention on the rights of persons with disabilities (2006). http://www.un.org/disabilities/convention/conventionfull.shtml. Accessed 17 Oct 2016
27. Wobbrock, J.O., Kane, S.K., Gajos, K.Z., Harada, S., Froehlich, J.: Ability-based design: concept, principles and examples. ACM Trans. Access. Comput. TACCESS 3(3), 9:1–9:27 (2011). https://doi.org/10.1145/1952383.1952384
28. Ferguson, P.M., Nusbaum, E.: Disability studies: what is it and what difference does it make? Res. Pract. Pers. Sev. Disabil. 37(2), 70–80 (2012). https://doi.org/10.1177/154079691203700202
29. World Health Organization (ed.): International classification of functioning, disability and health: ICF. World Health Organization, Geneva (2001)
30. Vinje, H.F., Langeland, E., Bull, T.: Aaron Antonovsky's development of salutogenesis, 1979 to 1994. In: Mittelmark, M.B., et al. (eds.) The Handbook of Salutogenesis, pp. 25–40. Springer, Cham (2017). https://doi.org/10.1007/978-3-319-04600-6_4
31. Eriksson, M.: The sense of coherence in the salutogenic model of health. In: Mittelmark, M. B., et al. (eds.) The Handbook of Salutogenesis, pp. 91–96. Springer, Cham (2017). https://doi.org/10.1007/978-3-319-04600-6_11
32. Eriksson, M., Mittelmark, M.B.: The sense of coherence and its measurement. In: Mittelmark, M.B., et al. (eds.) The Handbook of Salutogenesis, pp. 97–106. Springer, Cham (2017). https://doi.org/10.1007/978-3-319-04600-6_12
33. ability, n.: Oxford English Dictionary Online. Oxford University Press (2020)

34. ability: Online Etymology Dictionary (2020). https://www.etymonline.com/search?q=ability . Accessed 22 Jan 2020
35. Kittay, E.F.: The ethics of care, dependence, and disability*. Ratio Juris **24**(1), 49–58 (2011). https://doi.org/10.1111/j.1467-9337.2010.00473.x
36. Fuglerud, K.S.: Inclusive design of ICT: the challenge of diversity. Universitet i Oslo, Oslo, Norway (2014)
37. Berget, G., Sandnes, F.E.: Do autocomplete functions reduce the impact of dyslexia on information-searching behavior? The case of Google. J. Assoc. Inf. Sci. Technol. **67**(10), 2320–2328 (2016). https://doi.org/10.1002/asi.23572
38. Berget, G., Herstad, J., Sandnes, F.E.: Search, read and write: an inquiry into web accessibility for people with dyslexia. Stud. Health Technol. Inform. **229**, 450–460 (2016)
39. Sarcar, S.: Ability-based optimization: design and evaluation of touchscreen keyboards for older adults with dyslexia. In: Proceedings of the 31st Australian Conference on Human-Computer-Interaction, Fremantle, WA, Australia, pp. 472–475 (2019). https://doi.org/10.1145/3369457.3369519
40. Kinash, S., Crichton, S., Kim-Rupnow, W.S.: A review of 2000–2003 literature at the intersection of online learning and disability. Am. J. Dist. Educ. **18**(1), 5–19 (2004). https://doi.org/10.1207/s15389286ajde1801_2
41. Joshi, S.G.: Designing for capabilities: a phenomenological approach to the design of enabling technologies for older adults (2017)
42. Wobbrock, J.O.: SIGCHI social impact award talk – ability-based design: elevating ability over disability in accessible computing. In: Proceedings of the 2017 CHI Conference Extended Abstracts on Human Factors in Computing Systems, New York, NY, USA, pp. 5–7 (2017). https://doi.org/10.1145/3027063.3058588
43. Wobbrock, J.O., Gajos, K.Z., Kane, S.K., Vanderheiden, G.C.: Ability-based design. Commun. ACM **61**(6), 62–71 (2018). https://doi.org/10.1145/3148051
44. Umanski, D., Avni, Y.: PLAY-ABLE: developing ability-based play activities for children with special needs. In: Proceedings of the 11th International Convention on Rehabilitation Engineering and Assistive Technology, pp. 1–4. SGP, Midview City (2017)
45. Vanderheiden, G.C., Treviranus, J., Ortega-Moral, M., Peissner, M., de Lera, E.: Creating a global public inclusive infrastructure (GPII). In: Stephanidis, C., Antona, M. (eds.) UAHCI 2014. LNCS, vol. 8516, pp. 506–515. Springer, Cham (2014). https://doi.org/10.1007/978-3-319-07509-9_48
46. Evenson, S., Rheinfrank, J., Dubberly, H.: Ability-centered design: from static to adaptive worlds. Interactions **17**(6), 75–79 (2010). https://doi.org/10.1145/1865245.1865263
47. situate, v.: Oxford English Dictionary Online. Oxford University Press (2020)
48. situated, adj.: Oxford English Dictionary Online. Oxford University Press (2020)
49. Suchman, L.: Plans and situated actions: the problem of human-machine communication. Xerox Corporation Palo Alto Research Centers, Palo Alto, California 94304 (1985)
50. Mott,M.E., Wobbrock, J.O.: Cluster touch: improving touch accuracy on smartphones for people with motor and situational impairments. In: Proceedings of the 2019 CHI Conference on Human Factors in Computing Systems, New York, NY, USA, pp. 27:1–27:14 (2019). https://doi.org/10.1145/3290605.3300257
51. Malterud, K.: Systematic text condensation: a strategy for qualitative analysis. Scand. J. Public Health **40**(8), 795–805 (2012). https://doi.org/10.1177/1403494812465030
52. Antonovsky, A.: The salutogenic model as a theory to guide health promotion. Health Promot. Int. **11**(1), 11–18 (1996)

Digital Skills for People with Disabilities in a Learning and Demonstration Experience Laboratory

The Project, "Emscher-Lippe hoch 4"

Ann Christin Schulz[1]([⊠]) [iD] and Caroline Hirtz[2] [iD]

[1] Sozialforschungsstelle Dortmund - Central Scientific Institute
of the Technische Universität Dortmund, 44339 Dortmund, Germany
annchristin.schulz@tu-dortmund.de
[2] Diakonisches Werk im Ev. Kirchenkreis Gladbeck-Bottrop-Dorsten gGmbH,
46238 Bottrop, Germany
C.Hirtz@diakonisches-werk.de

Abstract. The project "Emscher-Lippe hoch 4" (EL4) faces the challenges of digitalization in the Emscher-Lippe region in Germany. Within the project one issue is the empowerment of people with disabilities' participation through low-threshold learning and demonstrating experience laboratories like MakerSpaces. To do so, EL4 installed a so called "Mini-FabLab" in a sheltered workshop in Bottrop. This Mini-FabLab looks at digital technologies from a social and not just from a technological perspective – it thus does not ask for general technological designs, but rather asks for new social practices like the empowerment of people with disabilities. Furthermore with its location in an old covered storage room, the Mini-FabLab illustrates that every place can become a place for inclusion. Through this, the Mini-FabLab enables people with disabilities the opportunity to develop individualized 3D-printed objects and assistance systems for their workplace as well as for their everyday life. As a result, various objects, like for example twist locks, keychains, toothpaste squeeze and blade stoppers were developed to use it as toys but also as assistive tools. Some of these will be presented in the paper, whereby the process of the idea finding (identification of a problem), development and solution of the object will be described in detail.

Keywords: Emscher-Lippe hoch 4 · Mini-FabLab · People with disabilities

1 Introduction

Digitalization is omnipresent. It hits everyone and touches each area of social and societal life. No matter what age, education or gender – everyone notices digitalization, because social relationships, actions and communications are constantly shifted into digital media. But digitalization is not only a purely technological change. It is a social transformation process [1], which is marked by technological innovation as well as the configuration of new social practices. Digitalization thus triggers social and societal changes which leads to opportunities but also risks. This is the reason why digitalization

M. Antona and C. Stephanidis (Eds.): HCII 2020, LNCS 12189, pp. 275–290, 2020.
https://doi.org/10.1007/978-3-030-49108-6_20

provides on the one hand the opportunity to a self-fulfilled participation and on the other hand also leads to risks of (digital) exclusion. Especially those people, who struggle against already existing dimensions of social and societal inequalities (age, gender, impairment, education), are threatened by dependencies, opportunities for manipulations and (digital) exclusion [2]. Moreover, they do not benefit from the opportunities of digitalization and they cannot design these processes actively. This is the reason why they are threatened by digital exclusion. Through this a "digital divide" arises, which divides people, who benefit from digitalization from those, who do not. In order to counteract this, there are already existing places of digital inclusion as well as social practices. One example is the "Mini-FabLab", the research project "Emscher-Lippe hoch 4" (EL4) [3] has installed.

EL4 discusses the challenges of digitalization in the Emscher-Lippe (EL) region - the northern part of the federal state "North Rhine-Westphalia" in Germany with cities like Bottrop, Gelsenkirchen and Recklinghausen. EL is a severely disadvantaged region in structural change and is thus located there on purpose. With about 1.1 million people living there, it is a region in Germany that is mostly at risk of downward swing [4]. Every fifth person lives in poverty and it has the highest unemployment rate in North Rhine-Westphalia [5]. Apart from these relatively negative aspects, it is at the same time also a location for technological and innovational research. There are universities, research institutions as well as learning and demonstrating experience laboratories, which offer technological and social innovations. These innovations are used by EL4 to handle the introduced challenge of digital exclusion in the EL region. To do so, EL4 organized diverse activities in the practice field "digital inclusion" and focuses especially on learning and demonstrating experience laboratories. Thereby, its emphasis lays on the empowerment of disadvantaged people. Moreover, to support their participation at the workplace as well as in society, EL4 operates with a unique inclusive approach called "Mini-FabLab" - an open space, which is especially designed for people with disabilities in a sheltered workshop in the EL region. For this, already existing experiences made during other projects on which the project partners have worked on, have been incorporated. Examples are the FabLab of the Ruhr West University of Applied Sciences (HRW) in Bottrop [6], PIKSL Laboratories in Düsseldorf, Bielefeld, Kassel and Dortmund [7] and the "SELFMADE" MakerSpace in Dortmund [8]. These experiences were transferred into a new innovative and inclusive approach, whereby the strengths were covered and the weaknesses were improved.

1.1 Analysis of Strong and Weak Points of Places of Digital Inclusion

In the following, strengths and weaknesses of three other places of digital inclusion will be presented. At the same time, the Mini-FabLab will always be in focus to show on the one hand its learnings and on the other hand its improvements from these places. At first the paper refers to Bottrop's FabLab, then to the PIKSL Laboratories and finally to the "SELFMADE" MakerSpace in Dortmund.

Bottrop's FabLab [6] was established in 2012 and is located at the HRW - an university with technological focus in the EL region. It has an area over 600 qm and a co-working space with 150 qm. The FabLab is an open space, where different technological devices and machines are available for everyone - the equipment reaches from computers and tablets over 3D-printers, laser-cutters and vinyl-cutters up to sensors, drones and robots. In the FabLab, visitors find different areas. There is for example one large 3D-printing area with different 3D-printers, an area with a laser-cutter, one with VR-devices and vinyl-cutters and a centralized workplace with computers to convert ideas in 3D-printable and laser-cuttable files. The FabLab offers visitors the chance to use all these devices and machines for free. Thereby they get support by makers if they have any questions in the handling or about the equipment. To do so, the FabLab has over 100 events per year and is therefore one of the most active FabLabs internationally. In "open evenings" and "open project days", visitors have the opportunity to learn about FabLabs in general as well as to work on their own ideas. Supported by makers, everyone can develop their own 3D-printed prototypes and solutions, independent from their (digital) competence level. Thus, this FabLab is open for students, entrepreneurs, citizens as well as for people with disabilities. Because people with disabilities did not visit it as often as others did, EL4 decided to face this missing interest of visiting the FabLab. For this, several events took place in the Mini-FabLab before the actual initiation of it. This started with sensibilizing events for pedagogical personnel, who work in the sheltered workshop. They received information about FabLabs in particular, as well as specific ones, matched to people with disabilities (information about the opportunities of a FabLab for people with disabilities). After the sensibilizing events for pedagogical personnel, workshops for people with disabilities took place. During these workshops, diverse digital devices and machines like vinyl-cutters, 3D-printers, 3D-scanners, VR-devices and 3D-Doodle pens were presented and used in a learning-by-doing approach after a short introduction to basic functionalities and processes. Together with makers being engaged in the project, people with disabilities started to develop first 3D-printed assistive devices. They quickly became enthusiastic about all the opportunities and asked shortly after the events for further workshops. Therefore, it became clear: something like this is needed for people with disabilities. This is the reason why one project partner (Diakonie) got the idea to create a space directly in one of their sheltered workshops, where people with disabilities can develop 3D-printed products and assistance systems on their own for their workplace as well as for their everyday life. Thus, EL4 installed a so called "Mini-FabLab" in a sheltered workshop in Bottrop (in the "Rheinbabenwerkstatt"). Additionally, to the problem of missing interest, the Mini-FabLab also reduces barriers, Bottrop's FabLab has to deal with the university. The arrival, staircases, doors, tables, equipment etc., which are not barrier-free, also hinder people with disabilities from visiting Bottrop's FabLab. With its location directly at people with disabilities' workplace, the Mini-FabLab reduces such barriers and offers people with disabilities the possibility to join the maker environment. Besides this, the Mini-FabLab learned from Bottrop's FabLab in technological aspects about 3D-printing, 3D-scanning, VR-devices etc. These high-level competences were incorporated in the Mini-FabLab. Moreover, Bottrop's FabLab is also locally and internationally networked with other learning and demonstrating experience laboratories and makers. This broad network is also important for the Mini-FabLab. Therefore, the Mini-FabLab can learn about their strategies in networking.

PIKSL[1] Laboratories are open spaces, where people with and without disabilities come together to develop social and digital innovations [7]. In contrast to Bottrop's FabLab, it is not located at an university, but in the center of districts in Germany, e.g. in the federal state North Rhine-Westphalia in big cities like Düsseldorf, Bielefeld and Dortmund as well as in the federal state Hesse in Kassel. Moreover, its provider is "In der Gemeinde leben gGmbH" (IGL). This is a provider which is supported by two social welfare organizations (Diakonie and Bodelschwinghsche Stiftung Bethel). The room itself is colorful and barrier-free. Moreover, PIKSL Laboratories offer technologies like computers, tablets and 3D-printers. In the workplace area, visitors can use their own computers, smartphones, tablets, but also the ones situated by PIKSL. To do so, the room is designed as a big workplace area with barrier-free tables and chairs, workplaces without technologies and workplaces with technologies. The first impression reminds one of an internetcafé, but it is more than this - it is a place to meet each other, to try out digital technologies and to design digital products for free, with the option of support. Thereby, the aim is that people with and without disabilities adapt digital competences and that companies as well as organizations were sensibilized in designing inclusive and barrier-free offerings. To do so, people with disabilities are regarded as experts, because they are the ones, who run courses like using the internet, social media etc. The offerings are therefore user-centralized and less complex. This user-centralized approach, as well as defining people with disabilities as experts, are the biggest strengths of PIKSL Laboratories and acted thus as a model for the Mini-FabLab. This is the reason why people with disabilities were involved in designing the Mini-FabLab, but also in other processes concerning the Mini-FabLab. The challenge of restrictions in the Mini-FabLab can thus only be removed by people with disabilities, because they know best about their needs. In doing so, the barriers that people without disabilities did not see, can be solved. The Mini-FabLab learned in this aspect from PIKSL Laboratories and became what it is now only through their user-centralized approach. Another improvement is the development to an inclusive PIKSL-network. The first PIKSL Laboratory was opened in Düsseldorf [9] and after its success, thanks to a wide public attention, further interchangeable PIKSL Laboratories (in Bielefeld, Kassel, Dortmund) followed. Becoming such a big network is also the aim of the Mini-FabLab, because the Diakonie realized that it is important to integrate such rooms in sheltered workshops. This is the reason why the Mini-FabLab continually works on it, for example with organized events (see Sect. 2.3), to be connected to the maker-scene. But this is in process and therefore not yet a strength. On the other hand, PIKSL Laboratories also face the problem of the journey, as visitors have to come there on their own, whereas in the Mini-FabLab, the visitors are directly on site. As already mentioned above in the part of Bottrop's FabLab, the journey to PIKSL Laboratories can not be as barrier-free as to the Mini-FabLab, so that the Mini-FabLab reduces such barriers and thus opens people with disabilities the opportunity to join the maker environment.

---

[1] Person-centered interaction and communication for more self-determination in life.

The "SELFMADE" MakerSpace in Dortmund was the best practice example for the development of the Mini-FabLab. It is a space that was developed throughout a project (SELFMADE) that was funded by the German Federal Ministry of Education and Research. Moreover, it is also located in an outdoor workplace of a sheltered workshop in the inner city of Dortmund, close to the main railway station [10]. Due to its location in an outdoor workplace of a sheltered workshop, the MakerSpace is not only used as a MakerSpace. It is turned twice a day into a dining room for people with disabilities working there [11]. But as a MakerSpace, it also offers barrier-free technologies like 3D-printers and laptops for free - like the other two places of digital inclusion mentioned above. Thereby the "making" permeates the everyday working tasks of people working there [11]. The room itself is an inclusive space with wheelchair-accessible furniture, moveable IT-stations, shelves with 3D-printed objects and workplaces that are equipped with tables and chairs as well as some with computers. The MakerSpace thus offers a large area, in which primarily 3D-printable assistive tools are developed for people with disabilities together with them. Basis of this is the "Inclusive Participative Action Research" and a design approach [11]. Moreover, the aim is the support of people with disabilities' participation and self-determination [12]. Therefore, the "Design Thinking" approach [13], which centers on problems people with disabilities have, is used to develop 3D-printed solutions to solve their problems. Exactly this idea of a problem-centralized 3D-printing seemed also suitable for the Mini-FabLab, especially when people with disabilities have problems at their workspace or everyday living environment. The Design Thinking approach is thus one of the main best practice examples that the Mini-FabLab integrated in its strategy. On top of this, also the five levels of the self-determination concerning the 3D-printing process that Bosse and Pelka in their article described [12], were integrated into the Mini-FabLab (see Sect. 2.2). The Mini-FabLab thus learned much from strategies of this MakerSpace. To empower people with disabilities, to be more low-threshold and to illustrate that every place can become a place for inclusion, EL4 had to locate the Mini-FabLab at a sheltered workshop.

The Mini-FabLab in Bottrop learned from these three places of inclusion in different aspects. Referring to Bottrop's FabLab, the Mini-FabLab learned about the necessity of *accessibility*. All kinds of barriers make it harder for people with disabilities to visit such a place and use all the digital equipment in there. This is the reason why short distances are as important as barrier-free equipment. In this context, the *usability* became also clear. Especially in the collaboration with people with disabilities, the design of the room and equipment has to be geared to meet their needs. To ensure people with disabilities' usability and accessibility, it is essential to regard them as *experts* - like PIKSL Laboratories did. In contrast to people without disabilities, they know exactly about their needs. They can express what kind of equipment needs to be adjusted so that they can use it. An *user-centralized approach*, like the Design Thinking in the SELFMADE MakerSpace, that integrates people with disabilities is therefore necessary. It focuses on the problems people with disabilities have to deal with in their everyday life and workspace and tries to cure this by developing digital solutions. Thereby it is important that people with disabilities do not only get access to digital devices and machines, but get rather *empowered* to use it. Makers, pedagogical personnel as well as people with disabilities, who can support others, are therefore in foreground to empower people without or less digital competences in developing their own digital solutions. But before this, people with disabilities have to be sensitized about all the opportunities of such a place (see events like "open evenings" and "open project days" in Bottrop's FabLab). *Sensitization* thus improves people with disabilities' interest in digitalization and weakens their fear about it. Especially the illustration of opportunities concerning inclusion, turned out to be particularly useful. Furthermore, the analysis of the three places mentioned above shows that *networking* is very helpful to be connected to other makers and places of digital inclusion. With such a network, it is possible to exchange ideas constantly, to adapt the equipment to new digital developments as well as to gain interest of other visitors. In this context, a continuously exchange to other places can also show, where an establishment of such places is possible. These learnings about accessibility, usability, the role of people with disabilities as experts, the user-centralized approach, empowerment, sensitization and networking, were the main points that influenced the establishment of the Mini-FabLab. As a result of this, the following chapter shows how these were implemented in the Mini-FabLab.

2   Mini-FabLab

Diakonisches Werk Gladbeck-Bottrop-Dorsten was founded in 1929 and acts with its sheltered workshops according to the diaconal guiding principle of "just participation" to enable employees to live as self-determined as possible. The sheltered workshops of the Diakonisches Werk Gladbeck-Bottrop-Dorsten ("Bottroper Werkstätten"), built in 1976 are equipped with over 40 years of experience in the production of contract work and the provision of services. Moreover, "Bottroper Werkstätten" offer jobs and qualifications in various occupational fields, e.g. agriculture, housekeeping, electrical installation or nursing assistants. There, the main task is to coach employees with disabilities to participate in working life and to support their individual path. Thus, people, who are currently unable to work in the free economy due to their disability, maintain a job through the "Bottroper Werkstätten". By doing so, the "Bottroper Werkstätten" try to stabilize the overall personality, to motivate and to maintain people with disabilities' performance and employability.

"Bottroper Werkstätten" have six different sheltered workshops, where people with disabilities get the opportunity to participate in working live. One sheltered workshop is the above mentioned "Rheinbabenwerkstatt", which offers 287 workplaces for people with intellectual disabilities. Its main focus lays on its special offer of workplaces for people with disabilities who are not able, not yet able or not yet able again to be employed in the general labour market. Moreover, the "Rheinbabenwerkstatt" tries to stabilize, expand and maintain the individual abilities and opportunities of people with disabilities. So, the main goal is, to provide vocational education and to support personal development and the empowerment of people with disabilities' participation at work, according to German law (see SGB IX §136 ff.) as well as to the UN Disability Law compliant. One opportunity to do so, is Bottrops' first MakerSpace in a sheltered workshop, the Mini-FabLab in the "Rheinbabenwerkstatt", which was official opened in July 2019.

2.1 The Room

In contrast to the three spaces mentioned in Sect. 1.1, the Mini-FabLab[2] is located in one old, converted storage room of the Rheinbabenwerkstatt in Bottrop. This should show that it is possible to integrate something like this almost everywhere, if some changes are made. Therefore, there are some restrictions, e.g. in the (universal) design of the room, that need to be eliminated. This restriction means that the Mini-FabLab has to design the room in such a way that it can be used by as many people with disabilities as possible without further adjustments. This is a main challenge, because people with disabilities have different kinds of impairment that leads to different demands on the room. The room has to be wheelchair-accessible, as well as designed with equipment that can be used by people with spasticity, visual impairment, hearing impairment and by people with intellectual disabilities. As a result of this, the Mini-FabLab was designed and created together with people with disabilities working at the Rheinbabenwerkstatt. The Mini-FabLab integrated people with disabilities as expertes directly from the beginning. As already mentioned above, this was learned by PIKSL. Therefore, the concept of the room is primarily designed by the wood workshop of the Rheinbabenwerkstatt. To create the Mini-FabLab, the entire equipment of the room had to be removed first. As a second step, it was checked if some of this equipment can still be used. It turned out that the existing old tables, which can be adjusted in height by cranks, only needed new surfaces. Thereby, it was very important that the tables are designed in such a way that they can be used by everyone.

Fig. 1. Workplaces

As in Bottrop's FabLab, in PIKSL Laboratories and in the SELFMADE Maker-Space, the Mini-FabLab also consists of a main workplace. It has three different workplaces, which are marked by characters (A,B,C) to ensure clear identification. The tables of these workplaces are fitted with a table socket, as well as with a screen, a mouse and a keyboard (see Fig. 1). To keep order, a Silhouette Cutter is used to design

---

[2] The total cost for the renovation and the needed equipment was about 3,000 euro, whereby the technical equipment was covered by the EL4 project. In the current equipment state, the Mini-FabLab costs approx. 6,530 euro.

letterings and pictograms. Especially pictograms can be used for people without reading ability and attached to the appropriate places. Besides this, already printed objects are presented in shelves as the SELFMADE MakerSpace did. In contrast to this MakerSpace, the Mini-FabLab uses various height-adjustable shelves. The idea behind is the same - the objects that are presented in the shelves can be used for demonstrations and for hands-on experience.

On the opposite side, a much smaller 3D-printer work area than in Bottrop's FabLab has been set up (see Fig. 2). Three 3D-printers are positioned here. The Mini-FabLab benefited from Bottrop's FabLab weaknesses in terms of lack of accessibility as well as from SELFMADE MakerSpace strength in its wheelchair-friendly furniture environment. This is the reason why the height of the worktop was chosen in such a way that both, wheelchair users and non-wheelchair users, can use it at the same time. To do so, wheelchair users drive under the worktop, whereas non wheelchair users can work while standing. Furthermore, one of the three 3D-printer is located on a rotating plate. This can rotate 360° to point into the working area but also into the entrance area. On top, there is a glass panel to increase employees with disabilities' participation in 3D-printing by viewing the 3D-printing process at any time. The rotating platform makes it possible to follow the 3D-printing process from the outside without any potential danger. This has also the function of advertising the Mini-FabLab for every employee of the Rheinbabenwerkstatt who do not know the Mini-FabLab yet.

Fig. 2. 3D-printer work area with one rotating plate and glass panel

Throughout the entire room, large characters help the users orientating themselves in the Mini-FabLab. Moreover, to support the open space idea, the motto of the Mini-FabLab is always "Do not just look, but try it out!". For this purpose, all objects, which can directly print out without any adjustments are labelled to identify them. To do so, a mobile tablet is used. Using this, people with disabilities can select an object and see directly to which memory card it is assigned. Depending on their state of independence, the desired object can be printed out with or without support. In doing so, the Mini-FabLab uses the concept of PIKSL, who involve people with disabilities as experts. People of disabilities are experts of themselves - they have a precise idea of their needs and barriers they are confronted with. This is the reason why some equipment and strategies have already adjusted, expanded or replaced. Concerning the workplace, the keyboard has changed for visually impaired people to the same one as in Bottrop's FabLab - a keyboard with good legible letters and maximum yellow-black-contrast. Moreover, it turned out that people with disabilities need more support in using the 3D-printer than initially believed. On basis of this experience, instruction booklets about "How to start a 3D-printer" were made together with people with disabilities. In this instruction booklet, nine steps from "choing an object" to "print this chosen object" are described in simple language. To support it visually, also pictures are used for instruction. Beside this, there are some further barriers concerning the 3D-printer. These are the missing safety pane in front of the 3D-printers, for people with disabilities' difficult to handle buttons and too little SD-card slots. To remove these restrictions, solutions from the SELFMADE MakerSpace were used [8]. This is the reason why a safety pane in front of the 3D-printers has been installed to protect users from burnings. Moreover, a rotary bottom and a SD-card holder (both 3D-printed) were purpose-built to make the handling of the 3D-printers easier for people with disabilities. With the aid of these adjustments, especially people with spasticity or missing hand extremities get the chance to use the 3D-printers on their own. This enables people with disabilities to use 3D-printers and thus empowers their autonomy and self-determination.

Fig. 3. The old converted storage room before the reconstruction

With its location in an old covered storage room, the Mini-FabLab became a lighthouse in the maker-scene. It shows, true to the maker-motto, that everything is possible. Figure 3 therefore illustrates that "unusable places" can also be used for such an inclusive place.

2.2 Self-determination in the Mini-FabLab

The Mini-FabLab provides people with disabilities the opportunity to develop new ideas and products for their workplace as well as for their everyday life. While doing so, people with disabilities are always supported by pedagogical personnel, if they have any questions. The pedagogical personnel thus help in developing products and in using the machines. Although pedagogical personnel are always present, people with disabilities should try to develop their products on their own – the pedagogical personnel do not act as a "producer", but rather as supporters of people with disabilities' independence. Moreover, they also act as a "gap closer" between technological interfaces and people with disabilities' digital competences to use these technologies.

As already mentioned in Sect. 1.1, the Mini-FabLab integrated the five levels of the self-determination concerning the 3D-printing process from Bosse and Pelka [12]. These levels range from the need of assistance to the own development of new objects. People with disabilities, who are on the first level, choose given objects out of the shelves on their own, but need assistance to print it. Assistance can be given by other people with disabilities, pedagogical personnel or makers. On the second level, people with disabilities also choose given objects out of the shelves. They do not need as much assistance as people with disabilities on the first level, because they can operate with the 3D-printer totally or partly on their own. For this, they use the above mentioned instruction booklets actively. In contrast to the first two levels, people with disabilities on the third level choose their objects not out of the shelves. They choose them from open source "curated lists", where 3D-printed objects are collected digitally. Moreover, this is the last level, where people with disabilities need some help in printing the objects. The self-determination in these three levels focuses thus on the selection of objects. In contrast to this, the last two levels have more focus on the community-building and modelling of objects. This is the reason why people with disabilities on level four choose objects from communities and sharing platforms like "thingiverse" or "myminifactory" and print them without changes. Printing it with some changes or modelling own projects is the last rank, people with disabilities can reach. On these two levels, people with disabilities gain more autonomy and self-determination than on the other levels. Anyone has the opportunity to print objects – totally independent from their technical competences.

2.3   Events Concerning to the Mini-FabLab

Although the Mini-FabLab embodies the place of developing new ideas and 3D-printed objects, it is also open for other issues around digitalization. This is the reason why different events, which are directly linked to the Mini-FabLab, were organized. Thereby, the Mini-FabLab orientated towards some PIKSL courses (like cyber mobbing) and workshop series. As one workshop series, the "Digital Week" was organized. The idea about it was born during the establishment of the Mini-FabLab, the associated concept as well as of the analysis of PIKSL. The process of idea-finding started with pedagogues, who were asked about topics for the employees. From their results as well as from ideas of the project management, five different topics were scheduled for each day of the week in September 2019. People with disabilities got thereby the opportunity to learn more about topics like safety in social networks, cyber mobbing and robots. For the first mentioned topic, an expert gave a speech on the safety in social networks, whereby people with disabilities discuss actively with the expert about their attitude towards safety as well as about their behavior in social networks. Cyber mobbing, as the second above mentioned example, was also presented actively by an expert in a workshop. Here, the goal was to inform about cyber mobbing in general as well as to answer specific questions like "How can I protect myself against cyber mobbing?" and "How can I help someone, who is affected by cyber mobbing?". After the successful participation in this workshop, people with disabilities got a certificate. Another workshop during the "Digital Week" was about and with robots. This means, that the topic "robots" was on the one hand presented theoretically with a PowerPoint presentation, but also on the other hand presented approachable with the robots itself. With this "hands-on-workshop", people with disabilities became more clear about what robots are and what they are doing. With "Pepper" (humanoid robot) and "Paro" (medical commitment robot), people with disabilities got an idea about how robots work. By speaking, dancing and playing games with Pepper and stroking Paro, people with disabilities learned as close as possible about the functionalities of these robots.

Another event was the module "Embedded Systems" at the HRW in the winter semester 2018/2019 and 2019/2020. It has been launched for students of Applied Computer Science, Human-Technology Interaction, Energy Computer Science and Business Computer Science. In cooperation with the sheltered workshop in Bottrop, students of the HRW developed in one semester electronic assistance systems for people with disabilities through the service-learning approach. In a group of one person with at least one disability, three students and a coach of the HRW-FabLab-Team, students developed prototypes to improve and facilitate people with disabilities' working processes, living situations or mobility. This process was implemented together with the user (people with disability). Moreover, an interactive process with regular user meetings took place. Thus, the person with disability was actively involved in the process of creation and can contribute his own opinion to the respective stage of development. In order to show people with disabilities the development of 3D-printed objects, students had, beside Bottrop's FabLab, the opportunity to use the Mini-FabLab. Through this, people with disabilities' participation in the development process became easier, especially when they did not have the mobility to come to the FabLab at HRW. In the end, the students presented their prototypes to interested visitors. In addition to this, the students created a wiki about their project and made it available to the public - all results are presented on the project website [3].

3   Examples of 3D-Printed Tools in the Mini-FabLab

In general, various objects, like little figures and keychains ("fun objects") as well as toothpaste squeeze and blade stoppers (assistive tools) were developed in the Mini-FabLab. The first mentioned objects were primarily downloaded from an open platform called "thingiverse", where diverse 3D-models are available to print directly without any individual changes. Although the assistive tools were also downloaded from thingiverse, these objects were modified by individual needs, e.g. some blade stoppers were modified for different kitchen knives (meat knives, bread knives).

Besides this, the following three examples will exemplify different objects, which are developed in the Mini-FabLab through a "Design Thinking" [13] approach. It started with problems people with disabilities had in their working space, e.g. holding pens (case A), deflection barrels (case B) and connecting plugs (case C). After understanding each problem, the status quo was observed from an outside-perspective. In case A for example it became clear that the person can not hold pens because of his/her hand impairment. As a result of this, multiple perspectives were discussed together with makers, pedagogical personnel and the people with disability. Together, they brainstormed about solutions, whereby the needs of the target person have always been in foreground. With this user-centralized perspective, makers developed first prototypes. These prototypes were finally tested by the target person, whereby he/she can always pronounce his/her options about it. By doing so, wishes of improvements were told to develop the prototype further. In the end of these Design Thinking process, an assistance tool to cure the problems at work results. Three of them are presented in the following. Although other authors, like Bosse and Pelka [10–12] have already published examples of 3D-printed objects, we decided to do it either, to get a feeling about what is possible in such a small old covered storage room.

3.1   Example A

At the reception of the sheltered workshop, a person with hand impairments had difficulties to hold pens. The skill of holding a pen is essential, because it is his/her daily work to check the list of visitors for correctness as well as to write one's own name abbreviation. This makes clear that there was a need to correct the missing skill by developing a special holder for pens. Together with the person, maker developed a holder. With the help of children's plasticine, they made a hand print. After it hardened for three days, a scan file was created with a 3D-scanner (Shining 3D EinScan Pro 2X Plus), which was processed in the Sculpting Program to smooth surfaces and to correct inequalities (see Fig. 4). Afterwards, the counterpart was created. In this example a fork was used, because the given problem was transferable to forks, spoons and knives. Thereby it was a problem that the fork was sprayed white because of the sensitiveness to reflections of the 3D-scanner. When the object (in this case the fork) had a matt surface, it was also scanned and processed. In order to that, the two parts can become one. They were put together in a further step and the negative of the fork was placed in the hand print. Finally, the last step was the conversion to a printable file in the program "Ultimaker Cura". The cutlery holder was now ready and can be printed (see Fig. 5).

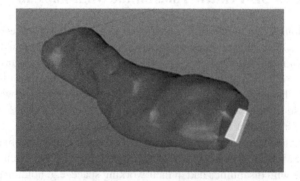

Fig. 4. The file for the cutlery holder

Fig. 5. The 3D-printed cutlery holder

3.2 Example B

A potential customer asked the "Bottroper Werkstätten" if they were able to carry out the order for the assembly of the deflection bins. This meant for the "Bottroper Werkstätten" the following: if they were able to build a good auxiliary device, a new order would be placed. Therefore, the first step was to select all employees who would use the work equipment. In a first round, ideas were collected and possible problems with the assembly were pointed out. Then a first jig was built with paper and adapted to the workpiece. By scanning the individual parts of the workpiece, the jig parts could be created in "Fusion 360" (3D-printing software). With an Ultimaker 2+ (3D-printer), the auxiliary jig was printed and then tested by the users. During the test phase it was noticed that it was still very difficult to remove the parts from the jig. This is the reason why, in the next step of the process a divisible auxiliary fixture was built, which was first equipped with a folding hinge. Problematic was that this auxiliary device could not be used, because the angle did not allow the complete removal of the workpiece from the auxiliary device. Therefore, in the third development step, two plates were inserted above the device. These plates were removable and the workpiece could be removed without any problems. This is the reason why this version (see Fig. 6) is currently in daily use in the Rheinbabenwerkstatt. Moreover, the workstation was supplemented by a clamping aid from the wood area of the "Bottroper Werkstätten", because it was necessary to use an electric screwdriver to fasten the screws. This prevents the workpiece and the auxiliary device from slipping.

Fig. 6. Redirect tons and the self-build auxiliary (FA. Müller & Biermann GmbH & Co.KG)

3.3   Example C

A person who suffers from hemiplegia works in the electrical installation at a test station, where the correct current conduction of switching power supplies for lighting must be checked. For this purpose, it is necessary to connect two plugs on the right and left. Due to the fact that the person is paralyzed on one side, he/she has problems in connecting the two plugs. To enable this employee to carry out this work, a testing device was built (see Fig. 7). First of all, a large wooden plate has been seen, which had bulges for individual plates. These plates in turn were provided with specially created 3D-printed elements to clamp the part to be inspected. To do so, wood, material and 3D-filament were used. The plates can be replaced by screws according to the order. For this employee, this device offers a high added value, because he/she can perform high-quality work with only one hand. Moreover, he/she can participate in the assembly process actively. The panel shows the work of the wood workshop and the individually printed elements from the 3D printer. In addition, the actual work tool, the measuring device and the corresponding piston are also shown here. The plate elements are interchangeable depending on the size of the workpiece. The workpiece is inserted in the center and connected to the power circuit on the right and left. An exchange element can be seen at the top right of the following Fig. 7.

Fig. 7. Test station for switching power for led-illumination

4   Conclusion

The Mini-FabLab established by EL4 is a space to empower people with disabilities through a low-threshold learning and demonstrating experience laboratory. The paper introduces this space and illustrates in the first part how the Mini-FabLab has learned from other places. To do so, the strengths were implemented and the weaknesses were converted into strengths. This is the reason why people with disabilities as well as their accessibility are more on focus than in Bottrop's FabLab. Moreover, the role of people with disabilities as experts was implemented from PIKSL to design and do everything in the Mini-FabLab with regard to their needs. In this context, the user-centralized approach from the SELFMADE MakerSpace became central. Thereby the three examples mentioned above give an insight into the opportunities of the Mini-FabLab. The examples illustrate that people with disabilities can develop more than "just" little figures and keychains in the Mini-FabLab. Although it has the smallest area compared to the other places, a large range of complex 3D-printed objects are still possible (see Sect. 3). The area has thus influence to support people with disabilities as well as to integrate them into the digital world, everyday life and workplace. Furthermore, it came to light that people with disabilities get a better feeling about the opportunities of a Mini-FabLab, if it is directly in their workplace. The solutions are easier than thought and with the help of the Mini-FabLab, no one had to change their workplace due to his/her impairment. This is the reason why the one, who works at the reception, can still work there, thanks to his/her 3D-printed pen holder (see example A). Example B clarified that received working orders from customers were only possible with 3D-printing and therefore with the help of the Mini-FabLab. The last example (C) illustrates that every workplace can be adjusted to employees' impairments. Only some 3D-printed elements are necessary to develop a workplace for people who can basically do not work there without physical efforts. The 3D-printing thus opens an entry to workplaces, people with disabilities did not have before. So the adjustment of workplaces through 3D-printing opens enormous chances in integrating people with complex impairments in the working spaces. Thereby, the closeness to the target group is special in the Mini-FabLab and singular in the EL region right now. This is the reason why it is a role model and lighthouse in inclusion by which others can learn. Especially the location and closeness to people with disabilities can be an important feature that future spaces should take into account, because it does not matter where a Mini-FabLab is set up. It can be everywhere - in a laboratory at an university, in centers of districts or even in an old covered storage room in a sheltered workshop. The main focus lays on the fact that people with disabilities are reached, integrated and empowered.

References

1. Kaletka, C., Pelka, B.: Web 2.0 zwischen technischer und sozialer innovation. Anschluss an die medientheoretische Debatte. In: Howaldt, J., Jacobsen, H. (eds.) Soziale Innovation. Auf dem Weg zu einem postindustriellen Innovationsparadigma, pp. 143–161. VS Verlag, Wiesbaden (2010)
2. Pelka, B.: Digitale Teilhabe: Aufgaben der Verbände und Einrichtungen der Wohlfahrtspflege. In: Kreidenweis, H. (ed.) Digitaler Wandel in der Sozialwirtschaft. Grundlagen - Strategien - Praxis, pp. 57–80. Nomos, Baden-Baden (2018)
3. EL4 Homepage. www.el4.org. Accessed 24 Jan 2020
4. Hüther, M., Südekum, J., Voigtländer, M.: Die Zukunft der Regionen in Deutschland. IW Medien, Köln (2019)
5. G.I.B. (eds.): Arbeitsmarktreport NRW 2017. 4.Quartalsbericht Dezember. Bottrop (2018)
6. HRW FabLab Homepage. http://fablab.hochschule-ruhr-west.de/content/index_ger.html. Accessed 29 Jan 2020
7. PIKSL Homepage. https://piksl.net/ed/. Accessed 29 Jan 2020
8. SELFMADE Homepage. http://selfmadedortmund.de/. Accessed 29 Jan 2020
9. PIKSL Standorte. https://piksl.net/ed/standorte/. Accessed 29 Feb 2020

10. Bosse, I., Krüger, D., Linke, H., Pelka, B.: The maker movement's potential for an inclusive society. In: Howaldt, J., Kaletka, C., Schröder, A., Zirngiebel, M. (eds.) Atlas of Social Innovation. 2nd volume - A World of new Practices, pp. 54–57. oekom, München (2019)
11. Bosse, I., Pelka, B.: Peer production by persons with disabilities - opening 3D-printing aids to everybody in an inclusive MakerSpace. J. Enabl. Technol. (2020). [Peer-reviewed paper]
12. Bosse, I., Pelka, B.: Selbstbestimmte und individualisierte Fertigung von Alltagshilfen per 3D-Druck für Menschen mit Behinderungen. In: Orthopädie Technik 02/20 (2020). [Accepted paper]
13. Brown, T., Wyatt, J.: Design thinking for social innovation. Dev. Outreach 12(1), 29–43 (2010)

Digitally-Supported Inclusive Vocational Education

Conceptual Considerations for the Hotel and Restaurant Industry

Nele Sonnenschein[✉] and Anna-Maria Kamin

Bielefeld University, Universitätsstr. 25, 33615 Bielefeld, Germany
{nele.sonnenschein, anna-maria.kamin}@uni-bielefeld.de

Abstract. In view of current media and societal developments it appears necessary to consider inclusion in vocational education with regard to digital media. Digital media is often referred to as having a great impact on equal and successful participation in education and social life, with particular emphasis on providing access for people with disabilities. However, the central importance of digital media for inclusion in vocational education has neither been given sufficient attention in theory development and empirical studies, nor in design approaches for educational practice. The paper starts from this research gap and attempts to rethink inclusion, vocational education and digital media in a new theoretical and conceptual approach. It deals with the central question of how digital media can support people with disabilities in vocational education and promote inclusive vocational learning in the workplace. For this purpose, it presents first interim results of a research project, in which innovative concepts for digitally-supported inclusive vocational education are currently being developed and tested, using the hotel and restaurant industry as an example. More precisely, conceptual ideas for inclusive vocational learning with digital media tools will be discussed with regard to theoretical approaches on inclusive didactics, vocational education, media didactics and inclusive media education. It has already become clear that it will be essential to find a balance between institutional or professional requirements, didactic principles of inclusive learning and media-related opportunities for support in this context.

Keywords: Inclusion · Vocational education · Inclusive vocational learning · Inclusive media education · Digitally-supported learning environment

1 Introduction

Inclusion, understood as a societal development task and social aspiration, requires to rethink and fundamentally change in all areas of society in order to enable all people to participate equally, irrespective of their individual skills, social or cultural origin, age, gender or health (Zorn et al. 2019). With regard to vocational education – which, in Germany, combines a theoretical part in vocational schools and practical on-the-job training in companies – the objective is not only to create an inclusive (vocational)

M. Antona and C. Stephanidis (Eds.): HCII 2020, LNCS 12189, pp. 291–303, 2020.
https://doi.org/10.1007/978-3-030-49108-6_21

education system, but also equal opportunities for access to the labor market. For this reason, people with disabilities or other disadvantaged groups should be given the same opportunities to obtain qualified vocational education and seek employment in the first labor market instead of being trained and employed in special occupations, as it is currently often the case (Bylinski 2016).

Considering the great impact of digital media on our living environments and everyday life, the realization of inclusion in vocational education, and beyond in all areas of society, seems to be increasingly linked to media infrastructures. Digital media is often referred to as having the potential to create opportunities for education and participation (Zorn et al. 2019). In particular, it can facilitate access to social life, education and employment especially for people with disabilities (Bosse 2016). However, the way in which inclusion through digital media can be successfully implemented in vocational education has hardly been considered yet – neither in theoretical concepts and empirical studies, nor in design approaches for educational practice. For this reason, the discussion on inclusive vocational education seems to be too short-sighted in several ways. On one hand, the barriers people with disabilities often face when using digital media and, relating thereto, when accessing vocational education, are not completely taken into account. On the other hand, the potential of digital media for inclusive vocational learning and participation in the labor market is not sufficiently incorporated. It therefore seems necessary to include these relevant aspects in the discourse on inclusion in vocational education and to (re-)consider the role of digital media both in theoretical models and in design approaches for educational practice.

Against this background, this paper aims to investigate how digital media can support people with disabilities in vocational education and promote inclusive vocational learning in the workplace. It presents first interim results of the collaborative research project *Digitization.Inclusion.Work. (DIA)*[1], in which innovative concepts for digitally-supported inclusive vocational education are currently being developed and tested, using the hotel and restaurant industry as an example. After giving a brief summary of the special features of vocational education in Germany, mainly for people with disabilities, design possibilities for inclusive vocational learning with digital media tools are discussed. Based on theoretical concepts and the results of the needs assessment carried out in the pilot phase of the project, initial conceptual considerations on the organization of digitally-supported inclusive vocational learning have been developed. Key findings of the needs assessment as well as the conceptual ideas resulting from it are given as an insight. Furthermore, developed media-didactical guidelines will be illustrated to point out initial design approaches on inclusive vocational learning with digital media tools in the workplace, which can be used in educational practice.

---

[1] The project *Digitization.Inclusion.Work. – New Ways of Vocational Education in the Hotel and Restaurant Industry (DIA)* is funded by the Federal Ministry of Education and Research of Germany and the European Social Fund of the European Union for a period of three years (2018/08/01–2021/07/31) within the program "Inclusion through digital media in vocational education". As the project is still ongoing, within this paper only first theoretical and conceptual considerations and interim results are presented. These will be revised and validated subsequently in the evaluation of the project.

2 Vocational Education for People with Disabilities

The German vocational education system has some special characteristics that need to be described briefly to better understand the subsequent theoretical and conceptual considerations on inclusive vocational education. In contrast to higher education, with high standards and strict admission requirements, the two forms of vocational education offer low-threshold access to recognized training programs and, therefore, to the labor market. Depending on the occupation, apprentices are either trained in *school-based training* or within the *dual system*. Vocational education in either case is completed both at vocational schools and at companies, where the apprentices gain valuable practical skills and experiences. School-based training is typically supplemented by several (unpaid) internships, whereas apprentices within the dual-system are usually employed by a company. In both cases, this form of organization facilitates access to the labor market by enabling an easy transition from vocational education to working life (BIBB).

At the same time, vocational education within the dual system is organized based on economic demands within companies. With regard to their economic success, companies tend to employ apprentices or trainees whose qualifications and personal skills meet the requirements at best. Consequently, it turns out to be especially difficult for people with disabilities to obtain qualified vocational education (Bylinski 2016). As research findings show, companies that have not employed apprentices with handicaps in the past expect several problems or challenges in doing so in the future, such as higher supervision expenditures or a lack of qualified staff for education and training (Metzler and Seyda 2016). As it is not an attractive or economically efficient option for companies to employ people with disabilities, this entry to the labor market is quite narrow. Therefore, as a last resort, many people with disabilities are trained in special programs or special facilities, where they cannot acquire a qualified vocational qualification (Euler and Severing 2014). For this reason, the German vocational education system is not perceived as an inclusive one in its basic structure at the moment. Actually, it appears to be rather segmented, since it tries to support young people with handicaps through institutional differentiation and is not providing joint training of people with and without disabilities (Baethge 2016).

In contrast though, vocational education in Germany underlies legal conditions which set clear objectives for including people with disabilities. In accordance with the *German Vocational Training Act* for example, people with disabilities are granted the right to be educated in regular and recognized training programs. This means, everyone should theoretically be trained *together* instead of having separate special programs or facilities, as it is currently the norm. Special needs need to be taken into account when designing apprenticeships for people with disabilities in order to adapt content, chronological structure and the use of special assistance to the target group. Only when vocational education in a recognized training program is impossible due to the type and severity of a disability, disabled people should be qualified in a special theory-reduced training program (Bylinski 2015). Considering these legal conditions as well as the *United Nations Convention on the Rights of Persons with Disabilities*, inclusion has been controversially discussed in the field of vocational education in Germany for the last years. In order to meet the legal requirements, initial considerations on a structural reorganization of the German vocational education system have been made.

3 Design Approaches on Inclusive Vocational Education

Design approaches on inclusive vocational education should generally incorporate all levels of the vocational education system – the societal level, the institutions and concrete learning arrangements (Bylinski 2016). Due to institutional differentiation within vocational education and the existence of many diverse special programs and support interventions for people with disabilities in Germany, the approaches discussed so far primarily focus on structural and institutional modifications. From this perspective, the essential objective of inclusive vocational education is to create structures that enable more young people, especially people with disabilities and other disadvantaged groups, to access regular and recognized training programs. Therefore, the basic idea of existing design approaches is the organization of educational processes oriented more towards the individual instead of focusing on specific characteristics, such as disability. Essentially, this demands a departure from previous practices of stigmatization, categorization and institutional differentiation (Bylinski 2015).

In order to achieve this objective, vocational education needs to be organized much more flexible and individualized. Training programs need to be adaptable to a wide range of different life situations and individual needs and, thus, should be addressed to all people instead of specific groups (Bylinski 2015; Oehme 2016). This emphasizes that school-to-work transitions should not be seen as transitions of certain groups, but rather need to be understood as individual educational pathways which need to be supported (Neises 2018). At the same time, inclusive vocational education requires the possibility to connect various training programs in order to allow flexible crossovers and partial qualifications (Bylinski 2015). In this respect, the qualification of the teaching staff in the field of vocational education with regard to inclusive learning, both within vocational schools and within companies, can be seen as one of the decisive factors for implementing inclusion in vocational education. Furthermore, concepts of special training programs for people with disabilities need to be transferred to regular and recognized ones in order to offer more training spots within the dual system to people with disabilities (Baethge 2016). This goes along with the need to acquire further training resources within companies in general (Euler 2016).

Apart from these fundamental considerations on how to organize inclusive vocational education at a structural level, there are only a few approaches that focus on concrete didactic concepts for inclusive vocational learning in the various learning environments, which are vocational schools, companies and external facilities. In this regard, initial design approaches are mainly discussed based on theoretical considerations on inclusive didactics, which have already been elaborated quite extensively for the school sector (for examples see: Reich 2014; Kullmann et al. 2014), but have hardly been used for vocational education yet. The central didactic principles that are debated in the context of inclusive vocational learning arrangements include subject orientation, internal differentiation, as well as cooperative and process-oriented diagnostics. Therefore, inclusive vocational learning should be organized in groups of heterogeneous learners, whereby each learner is generally considered individually and offered individual learning pathways within the group context. At the same time, learning objectives are defined individually and in cooperation with the learners. As further elements of inclusive vocational learning, also multi-professional teamwork and an orientation towards potentials and resources are mentioned (Bylinski 2016). In this respect, not only cooperation among learners is at the core, but also networking among pedagogical staff in order to be able to better meet individual needs and different learning requirements.

4   Inclusion in Vocational Education Through Digital Media

4.1   Social Participation and Digital Media

It could be shown, digital media has not yet been considered within design approaches on inclusive vocational education, although inclusion is increasingly linked to media infrastructures in a mediatized society. These links between digital media and inclusion or social participation can generally be described on three different dimensions. With regard to *media content*, the extent to which diversity is represented and the way how individual social groups are shown in the media are of central importance. This can have a great impact on awareness and perception of disability within a society and associated tendencies of inclusion or exclusion (Bosse et al. 2019). Furthermore, concerning the *use of digital media*, accessibility is considered a fundamental prerequisite for inclusion. Barrier-free digital media can provide access to communication, information and to (educational) media content to all people, regardless of their personal skills and competencies. In this context, accessibility not only refers to technical usability, but also to the perception and comprehension of media content. Thirdly, digital media can help to reduce barriers for various groups of people and, thus, offer them possibilities for *participation* in different areas of (social) life (Zorn et al. 2019). Looking at assistive technologies, digital media can for example help people with disabilities to overcome and compensate for physical impairments, cognitive impairments or sensory deficits (Dirks and Linke 2019).

4.2   Technical and Pedagogical Potentials for Inclusive Learning

Since inclusion and digital media are closely linked in multiple ways, digital media also needs to be looked at with regard to inclusive learning in vocational education more particularly. In general, digital media has great potential for inclusive learning both in technical, as well as in pedagogical terms. Technically, flexible options for the operation of digital media devices through integrated setting options, such as voice overs, assistive touch, zoom and many others, are the basis for access to media content. Supplemented by flexible reception options, which are mainly based on a variety of presentation forms, such as text, (moving) images and audio, as well as the possibility to use digital media independent of location and time, it is adaptable to a wide range of personal needs, skills and preferences (Miesenberger et al. 2012). In view of these technical features, digital media seems to be usable and even very useful within inclusive learning arrangements in pedagogical terms. Digital media can enable access to educational content and potentially facilitate its perception and comprehension especially for people with handicaps, and, therefore, support them individually. Moreover, digital media open up new ways for communication and interaction. Diverse online tools, such as learning management systems or (mobile) learning applications, allow new forms of collaborative and cooperative learning that can be used in inclusive learning arrangements to create shared learning situations within a group of heterogeneous learners. Through the adaption of digital media to personal needs, every learner is given the chance to participate in accordance with his and her individual skills and competencies (for examples see: Bosse et al. 2019).

5   Design Approaches on Digitally-Supported Inclusive Vocational Education in the Hotel and Restaurant Industry

5.1   The Project *Digitization.Inclusion.Work.*

Even though design approaches on inclusive vocational education, as well as the general potential of digital media for inclusion and inclusive learning have already been considered theoretically at least to some extent, concrete didactic concepts for inclusive vocational learning arrangements supported by the use of digital media have hardly been elaborated nor tested in practice. Only a few innovative projects, funded by the *Federal Ministry of Education and Research*, have dealt with questions on the design and realization of digitally-supported inclusive vocational education (for examples see: Fisseler and Schaten 2012; Kunzendorf 2019). With regard to this research gap, within the current research project *DIA,* concepts for inclusive vocational learning with digital media tools in the workplace are being developed and tested for the hotel and restaurant industry. It is examined how digital media can be used in different situations in everyday working life, how it can offer assistance especially for people with disabilities and, thus, support their learning processes. The overall aim of the project is to find new ways to enable people with disabilities to take part in a regular vocational training program, to acquire recognized vocational qualifications and to work together with people without handicaps, which shall offer them new opportunities for social participation. Therefore, in the course of the project a barrier-free digitally-supported learning environment, which will assist people with and without disabilities with their daily tasks and acquiring professional key competencies, is being developed and tested. The research project is a collaborative project which is carried out by a hotel, where people with and without disabilities work and are trained together, a media company and the Bielefeld University.

5.2   Needs Assessment on Support Possibilities Through Digital Media

In order to develop technical solutions and didactical concepts for digitally-supported inclusive vocational learning that is well adapted to the needs of people who are working or being trained in the hotel and restaurant industry, a needs assessment among employees and apprentices of the partner hotel has been carried out at the beginning of the project. This step was taken in line with theoretical approaches on design-based and participatory research (Kamin and Meister 2017; Euler and Sloane 2018), as the implementation of the project is oriented towards this. Thus, mainly based on the results of the evaluation of the needs assessment, the initial design of the digitally-supported learning environment has been developed. At the same time, concepts for the use of digital media in the workplace, with the purpose of facilitating inclusive vocational learning, have been elaborated. These will be tested in the field and refined continuously along with the feedback and experiences of employees and apprentices. In addition, the technical solutions will be redesigned successively.

In the course of the needs assessment, a heterogeneous group of 18 people (with regard to age, gender, educational background, origin and health) has been interviewed. Thus, there were people with different kinds of handicaps and people without disabilities, apprentices, unqualified employees as well as employees with completed vocational training among the respondents. Besides information on their educational background, the main topics of the needs assessment were problems with daily tasks, individual impairments as well as the possession and use of digital media devices. Moreover, the respondents were asked how they think digital media can support them with their daily tasks. The interviews were summarized, interpreted and evaluated systematically using qualitative content analysis (Mayring 2015). The evaluation identified a number of areas where respondents felt that the incorporation of digital media could lead to simplification or improvement.

Explanations of Work Tasks. First of all, many expressed the urgent wish or need for explanations of work tasks, either in general or regarding specific tasks they regularly have problems with. If, in recurring daily situations, employees and apprentices are unsure what to do they would appreciate the opportunity to take a look at explanations and educational content (e.g. in the form of checklists, images or short videos) through digital media. This refers to general information on work tasks, but also to useful tips on alternative processing types. In this context, one can assume that digital media can provide assistance in the work process and in vocational learning by offering flexible access to learning materials.

Reminders. Since many of the respondents mentioned problems with concentration and their memory, reminders also seem useful in assisting with daily tasks and vocational learning. In this regard, participants would like to use digital media for the repetition of important aspects they need to know for doing their job correctly. Furthermore, digital media might help them to remember all steps required for the completion of a work task within a process (e.g. through checklists). Used as reminders, it seems possible that digital media can contribute to the maintenance of the workflow and can help to ensure work tasks are completed properly and on time. This issue seems interesting considering inclusion and participation in vocational education, since apprentices with support needs might become more independent of continuous personal supervision and instruction.

Dealing with Problems. Another thing where respondents wish for support or regularly have difficulties with is dealing with problems or special (unexpected) situations. Therefore, they would appreciate to have access to guidelines on how to behave, react or what to do in certain difficult or challenging situations during the work process. Concerning this matter, digital media could for example be used to collaboratively work on a case collection, where possible solutions and action alternatives for different situations are discussed and documented. Moreover, in this context it also seems to be interesting to train independence, communication skills or social competencies through collaborative, digitally-supported learning tasks according to approaches on *active media work* (Schell 2005). Strengthening independence, communication skills and social competencies might as well help employees and apprentices to (better) deal with challenges at work.

Specific Support Needs. Besides these problems to meet professional requirements, some of the employees and apprentices also expressed specific support needs regarding their personal and individual impairments in the interviews. In this context, one can imagine to use digital media as assistive technology to compensate for different impairments (e.g. physical impairments, cognitive impairments or sensory deficits) and, thus, reduce barriers for participation in the labor market. People with disabilities can be enabled to (better) fulfill certain tasks with the support of digital media and, therefore, can potentially have better chances to be educated in a regular training program and to acquire recognized vocational qualifications.

Communication and Language. In particular, many of the employees and apprentices stated they had problems with or see a need for support regarding communication and language. This not only refers to people with disabilities, but also to people with a migrant background who have not learned to speak German fluently and confidently yet. To address these problems, it seems reasonable to use digital media for practicing language skills (e.g. with language learning applications), for communication (e.g. through a written chat to communicate with people with hearing impairments) or for using (online-)tools for translations. Supporting communication and language skills or using digital media as assistive technology in this specific field might facilitate or even promote the cooperation between employees and apprentices in the workplace.

Specific Technical Requirements. With regard to the development of the digitally-supported learning environment of the project *DIA*, some of the employees and apprentices also pointed out some technical requirements during the interviews. These mainly refer to aspects of accessibility and usability (e.g. zoom options, large buttons or voice control), which need to be taken into account when designing and developing technical solutions. To be supportive with regard to participation in vocational education and at work, technical applications need to be intuitively usable and designed without technical barriers, especially for people with disabilities (Fisseler and Schaten 2012).

Digitization of Work Processes. In addition, some of the employees and apprentices who have been interviewed also expressed requests regarding the digitization of work processes in general. Since the project *DIA* focusses on digitally-supported inclusive vocational learning, this issue has not received further attention. Nevertheless, in the overall context of inclusion in vocational education, the digitization of work processes is of great importance. The use of digital media could simplify workflows and, therefore, create new opportunities for people with disabilities to participate. However, awareness should be given to the fact that as a result of digitization some work tasks might be replaced by digital media, which means especially jobs for low-skilled workers will potentially be eliminated (Kunzendorf 2019).

5.3 A Concept for Digitally-Supported Inclusive Vocational Learning

With regard to the results of the needs assessment during the pilot phase of the project, as well as further theoretical approaches on inclusive didactics, vocational education, media didactics and inclusive media education, conceptual considerations on inclusive vocational learning with digital media tools in the workplace have been developed for the hotel and restaurant industry. Within these initial concepts of the project *DIA*, digital media generally is considered in two different ways. On the one hand, it is seen as an assistive technology in work context or process. On the other hand, it is also used as a didactic tool for (inclusive) vocational learning in the workplace and beyond. According to this basic conceptual idea, the digitally-supported learning environment developed in the project consists of two different parts, which are to be understood as complementary while each focusses on one of these particular issues.

First of all, a *mobile application* which provides employees and apprentices, each with and without disabilities, with flexible access to assistance and explanations via mobile devices is being developed. The application will offer support directly in the work process and will provide learning materials for a complete, correct and proper completion of several work tasks in the hotel (e.g. cleaning the guest rooms, preparing breakfast buffet or working at the reception). According to guidelines for a *Universal Design for Learning* (CAST 2018), these learning materials are prepared using different presentation forms in order to provide options for perception and comprehension. In particular, each work task will be explained by providing texts, (moving) images, audios and if necessary sign language and, thus, can be received adapted to individual skills or personal needs. Furthermore, the mobile application will be designed barrier-free as far as possible and provide several options for operation (e.g. voice control or voice output). It will be accessible for all employees and apprentices of the hotel, irrespective of individual skills or impairments. The content structure, in line with approaches of vocational education and didactics (Becker 2013), is designed based on the work process to ensure an easy orientation and an intuitive user experience on the one hand, as well as clear references to daily tasks. As the application can be used when needed and with the preferred method of data input and output, it also meets requirements for inclusive learning with digital media tools, such as individualization, subject orientation or activity orientation (Bosse 2017). Overall, it also takes the results of the needs assessment into account, since content and presentation forms are consistent with the support needs expressed by the employees and apprentices.

In addition to this mobile application, which can be used as assistive technology in the workplace or within the work process in the first place, a *concept for vocational qualification* that creates extended learning opportunities is being designed within the project. This is based on a broad understanding of vocational education, which not only includes the acquisition of theoretical and practical professional knowledge, but also incorporates personality development (Hensge et al. 2011). Various learning materials and learning tasks will be provided and worked on with the help of digital media (e.g. a learning management system). Consequently, digital media in this part of the project is predominantly used as a didactic tool for (inclusive) vocational learning. Bound to professional knowledge, several digitally-supported exercise units, each with a different thematic focus (e.g. housekeeping, hygiene, event planning or dishes), are designed. Each unit encompasses different learning tasks, which aim at the acquisition or further development of either basic skills, such as calculation, reading, and writing, or soft skills, such as teamwork, communication skills, and dealing with problems. The exercises are predominantly oriented towards daily tasks and designed according to media didactic principles of problem-based learning (Kerres 2018). Thus, they allow different ways of access and various forms of learning. Moreover, they are each supplemented by different forms of assistance to enable everyone to solve the tasks, irrespective of individual skills or prior knowledge. The assistance is prepared using different levels and several presentation forms to meet a wide range of learning requirements and, accordingly, to take basic ideas of inclusive learning with digital media tools into account. In line with these, employees and apprentices with and without disabilities should, furthermore, learn together and support each other in their learning process, which is why there are also exercises that can or need to be worked on collaboratively (Bosse 2017).

Altogether it is the primary goal to combine aspects of inclusive learning, media education and vocational education in the approaches and concepts elaborated in the project *DIA*. People with disabilities are given the chance to participate in vocational education or work through the use of digital media which, on the one hand, can support them to (learn how to) complete work tasks correctly and to manage work processes, or helps them to cooperate with others. On the other hand, digital media also offers them possibilities for extended vocational learning as well as the further development of holistic competencies and their personalities. Subsequent tests at the hotel, as well as an accompanying evaluation, will allow to investigate to what extent the digitally-supported learning environment developed in the project *DIA* can meet the requirements and needs for support in the work process and if it can contribute to vocational qualification, especially for people with disabilities. The learning outcome from this project can be used to define guidelines for digitally-supported inclusive vocational learning in the workplace more detailed and to transfer them to other sectors.

6 Conclusion

In general, digital media has great potential to contribute to inclusion in vocational education, as it can provide people with disabilities with flexible access to learning materials on the basis of individually adaptable options for operation and reception and it can support them to cooperate with others. With regard to the conceptual ideas of the research project *DIA*, in which digital media is used specifically to support and facilitate work processes and to acquire crucial professional competencies, it has become clear that the project aims to allow greater independence both in the acquisition of professional knowledge, as well as in the practical implementation in the workplace or the training facility. In contrast to conventional personal instruction, as it is common in the context of vocational education in the hotel and restaurant industry, the use of digital media creates an extension of vocational learning settings. Digital media can enrich vocational learning in the workplace by using innovative methods, new forms of learning and different ways of presentation that meet various learning requirements and personal needs. For this reason, it can be assumed that digital media will create a more flexible and individualized learning and, thus, can contribute to (better) inclusion in vocational education. Consequently, digital media can potentially foster social participation in general through greater professional involvement.

Nevertheless, some limits of inclusive vocational learning already became clear in the conceptual phase of the project. Vocational education is characterized by high normative demands and standards with regard to a correct and proper completion of work tasks, which contradicts basic principles of inclusive learning. These are based on the idea of offering each learner individual learning pathways in order to achieve individually defined goals instead of predefined ones. In this respect, it needs to be further investigated to what extent various forms of digital media support are suitable to transcend the existing discrepancies. The conceptual drafts presented here have already pointed out that a compensation of individual deficits and impairments, as well as the enrichment of vocational learning settings by digital media can possibly be the basis. However, concrete didactic concepts for digitally-supported inclusive vocational learning in the workplace need to be tested in the field and further developed. In this context, it will be essential to find a balance between institutional and professional requirements, didactic principles of inclusive learning (e.g. individualized learning, cooperative learning or activity orientation) and media-related support possibilities. Overall, learning with digital media tools must not be seen as a substitute for already existing methods and forms of learning in vocational education, but, with regard to inclusion, rather provides a useful and future-oriented extension in the field of vocational education.

References

Baethge, M.: Berufsbildung für Menschen mit Behinderungen: Perspektiven des nationalen Bildungsberichts 2014. In: Zoyke, A., Vollmer, K. (eds.) Inklusion in der Berufsbildung: Befunde - Konzepte – Diskussionen, (Berichte zur beruflichen Bildung), pp. 43–57. W. Bertelsmann Verlag, Bielefeld (2016)

Becker, M.: Arbeitsprozessorientierte Didaktik. bwp@ Berufs- und Wirtschaftspädagogik – online (24) (2013). www.bwpat.de/ausgabe24/becker_bwpat24.pdf. Accessed 07 Feb 2019

Bosse, I.: Teilhabe in einer digitalen Gesellschaft – Wie Medien Inklusionsprozesse befördern können (2016). www.bpb.de/gesellschaft/medien/medienpolitik/172759/medien-und-inklusion. Accessed 20 Sept 2018

Bosse, I.: Gestaltungsprinzipien für digitale Lernmittel im Gemeinsamen Unterricht. Eine explorative Studie am Beispiel der Lernplattform Planet Schule. In: Mayrberger, K., Fromme, J., Grell, P., Hug, T. (eds.) Jahrbuch Medienpädagogik 13: Vernetzt und entgrenzt – Gestaltung von Lernumgebungen mit digitalen Medien. JM, pp. 133–149. Springer, Wiesbaden (2017). https://doi.org/10.1007/978-3-658-16432-4_9

Bosse, I., Kamin, A.-M., Schluchter, J.-R.: Inklusive Medienbildung: Zugehörigkeit und Teilhabe in gegenwärtigen Gemeinschaften. In: Brüggemann, M., Eder, S., Tillmann, A. (eds.) Medienbildung für alle: Digitalisierung. Teilhabe. Vielfalt, (Schriften zur Medienpädagogik), pp. 35–52. kopaed, München (2019)

Bosse, I., Schluchter, J.-R., Zorn, I. (eds.): Handbuch Inklusion und Medienbildung. BeltzJuventa, Weinheim/Basel (2019)

Bundesinstitut für Berufsbildung (BIBB): The German VET System. https://www.bibb.de/en/39.php. Accessed 16 Jan 2020

Bylinski, U.: Inklusive Berufsausbildung: Vielfalt aufgreifen - alle Potenziale nutzen! In: Erdsiek-Rave, U., John-Ohnesorg, M. (eds.) Inklusion in der beruflichen Ausbildung, (Schriftenreihe des Netzwerk Bildung, 34), pp. 47–58. Friedrich-Ebert-Stiftung, Berlin (2015)

Bylinski, U.: Gestaltung individueller Entwicklungsprozesse und inklusiver Lernsettings in der beruflichen Bildung. bwp@ Berufs- und Wirtschaftspädagogik – online (30) (2016). http://www.bwpat.de/ausgabe30/bylinski_bwpat30.pdf. Accessed 14 Aug 2018

CAST: Universal Design for Learning Guidelines. Version 2.2 (2018). http://udlguidelines.cast.org. Accessed 06 Mar 2019

Dirks, S., Linke, H.: Assistive Technologien. In: Bosse, I., Schluchter, J.-R., Zorn, I. (eds.) Handbuch Inklusion und Medienbildung, pp. 241–251. BeltzJuventa, Weinheim/Basel (2019)

Euler, D.: Inklusion in der Berufsausbildung: Bekenntnisse - Erkenntnisse - Herausforderungen - Konsequenzen. In: Zoyke, A., Vollmer, K. (eds.) Inklusion in der Berufsbildung: Befunde – Konzepte – Diskussionen, (Berichte zur beruflichen Bildung), pp. 27–42. W. Bertelsmann Verlag, Bielefeld (2016)

Euler, D., Severing, E.: Inklusion in der beruflichen Bildung: Daten, Fakten, offene Fragen (2014). https://www.bertelsmann-stiftung.de/fileadmin/files/BSt/Publikationen/GrauePublikationen/LL_GP_Inklusion_Hintergrund_150610final.pdf. Accessed 17 Sept 2018

Euler, D., Sloane, P.F.E.: Design-Based-Research. In: Rauner, F., Grollmann, P. (eds.) Handbuch Berufsbildungsforschung, 3rd edn., pp. 782–790. wbv Media GmbH & Co. KG, Bielefeld (2018)

Fisseler, B., Schaten, M.: Barrierefreies E-Learning und Universal Design. In: Biermann, H., Bonz, B. (eds.) Inklusive Berufsbildung: Didaktik beruflicher Teilhabe trotz Behinderung und Benachteiligung, 2nd edn., (Berufsbildung konkret, 11), pp. 208–218. Schneider Verlag Hohengehren, Baltmannsweiler (2012)

Hensge, K., Lorig, B., Schreiber, D.: Kompetenzverständnis und -modelle in der beruflichen Bildung. In: Bethscheider, M., Höhns, G., Münchhausen, G. (eds.) Kompetenzorientierung in der beruflichen Bildung (Berichte zur beruflichen Bildung), pp. 133–157. W. Bertelsmann Verlag, Bielefeld (2011)

Kamin, A.-M., Meister, D.M.: Digital unterstütztes Lernen in Pflegeberufen unter entgrenzten Bedingungen – ein gestaltungs- und entwicklungsorientiertes Forschungsprojekt. In: Mayrberger, K., Fromme, J., Grell, P., Hug, T. (eds.) Jahrbuch Medienpädagogik 13: Vernetzt und entgrenzt – Gestaltung von Lernumgebungen mit digitalen Medien. JM, pp. 213–229. Springer, Wiesbaden (2017). https://doi.org/10.1007/978-3-658-16432-4_14

Kerres, M.: Mediendidaktik: Konzeption und Entwicklung digitaler Lernangebote, 5th edn. Walter de Gruyter GmbH, Berlin/Boston (2018)

Kullmann, H., Lütje-Klose, B., Textor, A.: Eine Allgemeine Didaktik für inklusive Lerngruppen – fünf Leitprinzipien als Grundlage eines Bielefelder Ansatzes der inklusiven Didaktik. In: Amrhein, B., Dziak-Mahler, M. (eds.) Fachdidaktik inklusiv: Auf der Suche nach didaktischen Leitlinien für den Umgang mit Vielfalt in der Schule, (LehrerInnenbildung gestalten, 3), pp. 89–107. Waxmann, Münster Westf (2014)

Kunzendorf, M.: Berufsfeld Arbeit/Beruf. In: Bosse, I., Schluchter, J.-R., Zorn, I. (eds.) Handbuch Inklusion und Medienbildung, pp. 146–156. BeltzJuventa, Weinheim/Basel (2019)

Mayring, P.: Qualitative Inhaltsanalyse: Grundlagen und Techniken. Beltz, Weinheim/Basel (2015)

Metzler, C., Seyda, S.: Erwartete und tatsächliche Hemmnisse und Lösungen für und in der Ausbildung von Menschen mit Behinderung aus Unternehmenssicht. bwp@ Berufs- und Wirtschaftspädagogik – online (30) (2016). http://www.bwpat.de/ausgabe30/metzler_seyda_ bwpat30.pdf. Accessed 07 Feb 2020

Miesenberger, K., Bühler, C., Niesyto, H., Schluchter, J.-R., Bosse, I.: Sieben Fragen zur inklusiven Medienbildung. In: Bosse, I. (ed.) Medienbildung im Zeitalter der Inklusion. Landesanstalt für Medien Nordrhein-Westfalen (LfM), Düsseldorf (LfM-Dokumentation, 45), pp. 27–75 (2012)

Neises, F.: Exklusion überwinden – Zugänge zu und Teilhabe an regulärer Ausbildung und Beschäftigung. In: Arndt, I., Neises, F., Weber, K. (eds.) Inklusion im Übergang von der Schule in Ausbildung und Beruf: Hintergründe, Herausforderungen und Beispiele aus der Praxis (Berichte zur beruflichen Bildung), pp. 55–70. Verlag Barbara Budrich, Bonn (2018)

Oehme, A.: Der sozialpädagogische Blick auf (mehr) Inklusion in der beruflichen Bildung. In: Bylinski, U., Rützel, J. (eds.) Inklusion als Chance und Gewinn für eine differenzierte Berufsbildung, (Berichte zur beruflichen Bildung), pp. 43–56. W. Bertelsmann Verlag, Bielefeld (2016)

Reich, K.: Inklusive Didaktik: Bausteine für eine inklusive Schule. Beltz Juventa, Weinheim/Basel (2014)

Schell, F.: Aktive Medienarbeit. In: Hüther, J., Schorb, B. (eds.) Grundbegriffe Medienpädagogik, pp. 9–16. kopaed, München (2005)

Zorn, I., Schluchter, J.-R., Bosse, I.: Theoretische Grundlagen inklusiver Medienbildung. In: Bosse, I., Schluchter, J.-R., Zorn, I. (eds.) Handbuch Inklusion und Medienbildung, pp. 16–33. BeltzJuventa, Weinheim/Basel (2019)

Design of a Tangible Programming Tool for Students with Visual Impairments and Low Vision

Emmanuel Utreras and Enrico Pontelli$^{(\boxtimes)}$

New Mexico State University, Las Cruces, NM 88003, USA
eutreras@nmsu.edu, epontell@cs.nmsu.edu

Abstract. This article presents the design of a tangible tool for teaching basic programming concepts to students with visual impairments and low vision. Meeting the preliminary requirements of this ongoing project *(Tangible input, cost-efficient, and minimal maintenance)*, the paper describes the design of the hardware of this prototype with inexpensive materials, such as Lego blocks, 3.5 mm stereo audio jack connectors, relays, resistors, and an Arduino Mega microcontroller. To identify the Lego blocks that represent the code instructions, the system provides three different methods of identification; color, 3D printed labels, and braille labels. To acquire feedback and validate this prototype, a preliminary study with nine participants with Visual Impairment and Low Vision has been carried out. All participants completed the task successfully, provided feedback about the prototype, and all recommended this prototype to teach basic programming concepts. Currently, the project is focused on the implementation of music as an output method of programs created by users. The objective is to create a programming tool completely independent of visual graphics or information.

Keywords: Novice students · Tangible · Children · Teaching · Visual impairments · Low vision · Programming concepts

1 Introduction

Studies have proven that learning *programming concepts* in elementary school improves the overall learning process in children, allowing them to develop Computational Thinking (CT) [1] and problem-solving skills. Furthermore, early exposure to CT is a strong motivator in the pursuit of studies in computing. Recognizing the importance of learning programming concepts in the early years, various approaches have been developed. Program visualization environments have been designed to help students, by representing the data control and memory visualization of a program through the use of graphic animations (e.g., Jeliot 3 [10], Virtual-C [12], etc.), even though they use a text-based input method. Visual programming is an approach that has gained popularity with

The authors are supported by NSF 1914635, NSF 1401639, and NSF 1345232.

M. Antona and C. Stephanidis (Eds.): HCII 2020, LNCS 12189, pp. 304–314, 2020.
https://doi.org/10.1007/978-3-030-49108-6_22

children, thanks to the easy syntax and exciting projects that they can create. Most of these environments use a Blocks-based method, whereby programs are built by assembling graphical blocks that represent the different programming concepts. The typical output of these programs are predominantly visual representations, such as movements of robots (e.g., Lego NXT) or graphic animations (e.g., Scratch [8], Alice [4], AppInventor [19]). Another approach used in modern systems to encourage children's learning is through the use of *Tangible User Interfaces (TUI)*. TUI environments allow children to associate concepts through the manipulation of physical objects, such as cubes or bricks (e.g., Tern [5], E-Block [17], T-Maze [16], Robo-Block [11], Playte [3], etc.). However, most of the TUI tools still use graphics as the main output method. The aforementioned tools are designed to motivate children through the use of visual graphics either as input, output, and/or feedback.

Traditional (text-based) programming introduces different obstacles that children with *visual impairments (VI)* and *low vision (LV)* must overcome (Keyboard, screen, and mouse). Designed to aid people with VI accessing visual information, assistive hardware and software have been developed, such as refreshable Braille displays, screen magnifiers, and screen readers. Even though these technologies indeed help people with VI, learning programming concepts can be frustrating, since prior knowledge of programming and software organization are required. In addition, unfortunately, the approaches developed to encourage children into programming classes are not compatible with assistive technologies. This issue might have adverse effects on children with VI and prevent them from pursuing a career as a computer scientist or a related field.

The objectives of this project are to: **A)** develop a tangible interface that does not use visual graphics content as an input or output method, **B)** build a prototype that includes all the basic programming concepts that programs with visual graphics grant to the users, and **C)** provide the children with VI a fun experience allowing them to create exciting projects in introductory programming classes.

2   Related Work

Researchers are working on the accessibility of text-based programming environments to encourage children with VI. *Quorum* [14] is a simplified text-based programming language developed for K-12 education. Quorum is easy to learn by children with VI, since it uses a screen reader technology and an intuitive syntax. *Bonk* [7] is an accessible web page environment with features such as speech-to-text output for the creation of interactive audio games. To help programmers with VI and blindness navigate through Java code, plugins and prototypes have been created. *StructJumper* [2] is a plugin for Eclipse that creates a tree structure, that allows users to jump into different parts of the code. *JavaSpeak* [13] is a prototype that provides audible information to the user about a program, helping them to better understand Java syntax and programming concepts. On the other hand, to make blocks-based accessible, *Blocks4All* [9] is a blocks-based environment that allows users with VI and blindness to develop programs, by providing audio cues to connect virtual blocks. The result of the created code is translated to a Dash robot movements with audible information.

Taking advantage of TUI's new technology and to provide an equal learning opportunity, researchers have been working on the development of tangible programming environments accessible to children with VI. *P-Cube* [6] is a tool with a tangible input that allows the user to program a robot's movement. The users with VI can identify each cube using the sense of touch; each cube contains a 3D printed symbol that represents the direction and duration of the robot's movement. The code is executed by a robot that indicates its position in real-time. On the other hand, *Torino* [15] is a tangible programming language developed by Microsoft researchers to promote collaborative learning between children with VI. Instead of cubes, this environment uses circular and oval objects which are connected by the user to create programs. The output of the created program is executed in an audible form (e.g., audible stories and music). Torino also provides real-time feedback through audio. Even though the mentioned tools are designed for children with VI, many of them use similar inaccessible output media or they do not cover all the basic programming concepts that virtual environments provide to sighted children.

3 Design of Prototype

3.1 Preliminary Requirements

As we started exploring the design of a tangible programming environment that is accessible to students with VI, we identified the following preliminary requirements for the design:

- *Tangible Input.* a Tangible interface is an approach that allows students to associate programming concepts through tactile sense. To replace the traditional input (keyboard and mouse), the best approach is to implement a tangible system that allows users to create a program by physical manipulation.
- *Block Identification.* To identify the blocks that represent instructions of the code, our design should include different ways of identification. By using different methods we can target different VI and include sighted children.
- *Output of the Code.* To avoid the use of visual graphics, an audible output such as music or audible stories are good approaches for children with VI. This first version of the tool is focused on generating melodies.
- *Minimum Maintenance.* An easy-to-deploy system that requires little to no maintenance facilitates the use in classrooms where computers are limited. In addition, the exclusion of batteries in our tool eliminates the expense of buying or charging batteries for each block.
- *Cost Efficient.* The most important preliminary requirement of this project is to maintain a low cost in the production of the prototype. In this way, in the future, we can provide each child with the opportunity to access the tool.

3.2   Prototype Components

Following the mentioned pre-requirements, the design of our prototype consists of three main components: Modified Lego blocks and Lego panel, an Arduino Mega microcontroller, and a computer with speakers. The Lego panel, divided into cells where the blocks will be stacked, an Arduino which will calculate the electrical resistance, and lastly a computer that will save the different values in a matrix and convert them into an audio output. Using modified Lego blocks with an electrical resistor circumvents the necessity of batteries in each block and will allow us to design a tool that supports programming in 3 dimensions. Therefore, the user can stack blocks to represent a different instruction (e.g., a loop that repeats three times will contain a loop block with two stacked blocks). This will help the student with VI count how many times the loop will iterate.

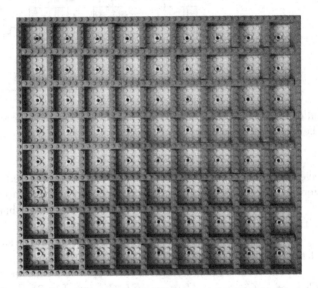

Fig. 1. Modified Lego panel of the prototype. The panel is divided into 8 rows by 9 columns. The cells are divided with 1 × 4 Lego bricks. Each cell contains a 3.5 mm female stereo audio jack connector to read the block's resistance.

3.3   Lego Panel

The modified Lego panel is divided with 1 × 4 Lego bricks forming 8 × 9 cells. The size of each cell was set to fit a 2 × 2 Duplo Lego. At the center of the cells, a female 3.5 mm stereo audio jack connector was placed (see Fig. 1) to calculate the resistance at the male jack connector in the blocks. The height of the cells was adjusted to facilitate the connection of the blocks for VI and LV users. It also helps users to locate a block's specific coordinates on the panel by using touch.

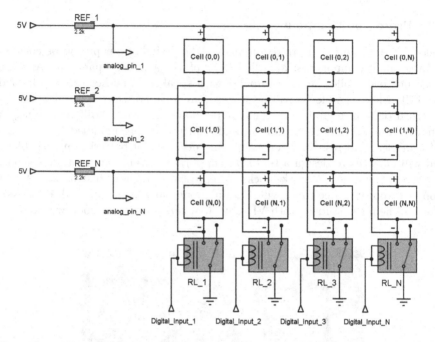

Fig. 2. Internal connection diagram of the Lego panel. The squares represent the cells that contain the female stereo audio jack.

The positive terminals of each cell in the same row are connected together to one of the reference resistor's terminal and the Arduino analog read input. The other resistor's terminal is connected to a 5 V source. Each row has the same circuit at positive terminals. (e.g., $5V \leftarrow R_{ref} \leftarrow Analog_{read} \leftarrow +C_{0,0} \leftarrow +C_{0,1} \leftarrow +C_{0,2} \leftarrow +C_{0,n}$). The negative terminals of each cell in the same column are connected together to a relay (switches that operate electrically) which by default is set to open circuit. Each column is connected to a different relay (e.g., $-C_{0,0} \rightarrow -C_{1,0}, \rightarrow -C_{2,0} \rightarrow -C_{n,0} \rightarrow RELAY$) (see Fig. 2). The advantage of this design is that it allows us to reduce the number of components used in the prototype by controlling relays and analog reads. For example, instead of using one relay per cell, we used one relay per column and one voltage divider circuit (series circuit) per row. The C++ code will iterate through each relay, activate and deactivate them, control the analog pins to measure the reference voltage, and calculate the unknown resistance. To visualize this, suppose we activate relay RL_1 by sending a pulse through Digital_Input_1. Although we will have current flow in all cells in column 0, we only measure the reference voltage at Cell (0, 0) by using the analog_pin_1. Once the voltage is measured, we calculate the unknown resistance, send a pulse to deactivate RL_1 which will open the circuit at Column 0, and activate RL_2. The algorithm will repeat the same steps through all cells reading the blocks from top-down and left-right (see Fig. 3).

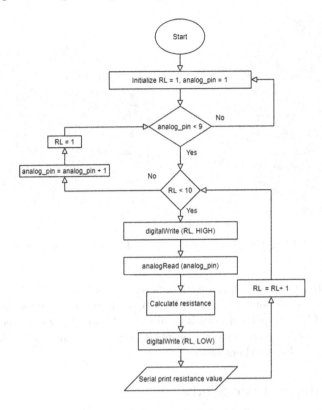

Fig. 3. Algorithm to read the blocks.

3.4   Lego Blocks

The Lego blocks contain an electrical resistor with a specific value welded in a 3.5 mm male audio jack connector. Each block has three methods to be identified. The first method is by the color of the block. Distinct colors represent different instructions in the code and identical colors represent identical instructions. The second method is by the sense of touch. Each block has a 3D printed symbol on top that represents an instruction and can be identified by touch (see Fig. 4). The third method is by braille printing. A braille printed label with the name of the instruction is placed in front of the block for children that are able to read braille (see Fig. 5). Another function of the braille-printed label is to indicate to the user which side is the front of a block. Using 3D printing may create confusion since the shape changes depending on which face of the block is used. To avoid this ambiguity, the user can first locate the front face containing the braille label and identify the correct symbol position.

The prototype supports basic programming concepts such as constants, variables, and loops. During the progress of development, further instructions such as conditional statements and functions call will be implemented to promote collaborative work between students. To add a 3-dimensional programming concept

Fig. 4. Lego block top view.   **Fig. 5.** Lego block front view.

into our prototype, fixed blocks with different heights were included to represent different instructions. For example, a block that represents a loop of three iterations will have four blocks stacked (loop block, and 3 iteration blocks). Currently, we are working on making loop blocks more dynamically by allowing the user to stack the blocks themselves.

4 Preliminary User Study

After assembling the hardware for our prototype which met some of our preliminary requirements, we designed a preliminary user study to acquire feedback and validate the design of our interface. To maximize the feedback, we recruited nine adults (five female and four male) with VI and LV and little or no previous experience in tangible programming tools. The study includes task completion, an interview, and a questionnaire. To analyze the results, we video recorded the hand movements of the participants while using the prototype and audio recorded the answers in the interview.

To validate the connector type (3.5 mm stereo audio jack) in our prototype, we allowed users to perform tasks pertaining to the connection and disconnection of blocks into the modified Lego panel with different cell heights. All the participants were able to complete the tasks after selecting a suitable cell height (mostly three or four 1 × 4 Lego's bricks stacked). Once a comfortable height was set it was an easy task to perform, as demonstrated by the results of the questionnaire. One participant found it neither easy nor hard to perform the task, four participants *Agree* and four *Strongly Agree* that connecting and removing blocks was easy, concluding that the task can be performed easily with a specific cell height which will work as a frame for the blocks (see Fig. 6).

The method of rows and columns (see Fig. 1) helps users to move through the panel. Using touch to count the cells, participants successfully completed the tasks designed to measure the effectiveness of the rows and columns method.

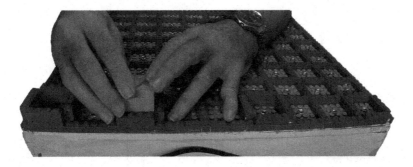

Fig. 6. Example of a user connecting a Lego block.

At the end of the interviews, the participants were able to answer a question-naire about the prototype and provide suggestions for the future. All participants recommend the prototype and audible output as a viable method for teaching novice children with VI basic programming concepts. Some of the recommendations suggested by the users after testing the prototype include the use of buttons to record created music, magnets to connect blocks to the panel, and improvements on the 3D printed symbols.

5   State of the Prototype

Currently, we have completed the design and hardware assembly of our tool. The prototype is able to successfully read blocks and translate them to instructions. In addition, we have carried out a preliminary user study to validate the proto-type and obtain feedback for future improvements that will be implemented in future steps. We are currently working on the connector of the loop blocks to make it dynamic, as well as the coding section to build music.

5.1   Music Environment

The main objective of this project is to translate the tangible block's instructions into audible output for the development of a tool independent of visual graphics. To accomplish this objective we are using an environment called SuperCollider [18] which is an audio synthesis platform that allows users to generate music and sounds through coding. To implement the audio environment to our prototype we divided the codes into three parts. The first is the C++ code uploaded to the Arduino. This code controls the hardware of the Arduino, calculates the resistance, and prints values into the Serial. The interpreter code is written in Python language. It reads the resistance values printed in the Serial and translates them into instructions. Once the blocks are identified, an Open Sound Control (OSC) will send messages to SuperCollider to create the synths and play it through computer speakers (see Fig. 7).

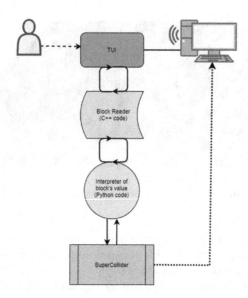

Fig. 7. Prototype system communication. The C++ code is a loop to control the hardware, reading and calculating the resistance values. The Python code will interpret these resistance values into instructions and communicate with SuperCollider to create the audio synths.

5.2   Future Improvements

Although this project is in development stage, there are some improvements that we want to implement for the future. One of these improvements is the connection method of the Lego blocks in the panel. To meet our main objective of maintaining a low cost in the production, we decided to use a 3.5 mm stereo audio jack as a connection method of the Lego blocks and the panel. However, these require precision to connect. To overcome this problem in our prototype we divided the panel into cells with 1 × 4 Lego bricks at a specific height, creating a frame that restricts to a single option of stacking the blocks and facilitating the connection. In the future, we can change the stereo audio jack connectors to magnetic pin connectors to minimize the force applied to the Lego panel and facilitate the block connections. Another improvement is the replacement of relays with transistors. Transistors are electronic components that conduct current in a specific pathway (emitter-collector) when a specific voltage is applied (base). One of the disadvantages of using relays is the clicking noise they generate when they activate and deactivate, which can be distracting for children since our tool works with audio. To solve this problem, in the future we could use transistors instead of relays. Lastly, we are planning the coupling of two tangible tools that can communicate with each other to promote collaborative work among the students. One way to implement this improvement is the addition of two blocks (e.g. Function call and Function answers) where a student can incorporate pieces of music or sounds made by another student in a project.

6   Conclusion

Visual and tangible environments help novice students with programming concepts; however, they are difficult or impossible to use by children with VI and LV. In this paper, we describe the design of a tangible tool prototype to help children with VI to learn programming concepts without the use of visual graphics and text-based input. We are working to cover all the basic programming concepts such as variables, constants, conditions, loops, functions, and function calls. This prototype was designed to minimize the maintenance of the tool (e.g., charging batteries), use no visual graphics, and to be an affordable tool by using Lego bricks, stereo audio jack connectors, resistors, relays and an Arduino Mega. We want a prototype attractive to both students with VI and sighted students. In this way, segregation of students due to their impairments is avoided while the inclusion of collaborative work among students is promoted. A preliminary user study has been carried out to get feedback and validate the prototype. A group of nine adults with VI and LV participated in the study. All of the participants were able to successfully complete the task and recommend this prototype to teach basic programming concepts to children with VI and LV.

Acknowledgments. The authors would like to thank Asociación Puertorriqueña de Ciegos, Inc., its president Ms. Luz Colón, and its coordinator Ms. Wanda Diaz for their collaboration which made this project possible. We would also like to thank electrical engineers Hector M. Carrasco and Gerson Diaz for all their support during the hardware development process.

References

1. Aho, A.V.: Computation and computational thinking. Comput. J. **55**(7), 833–835 (2012). https://doi.org/10.1093/comjnl/bxs074
2. Baker, C.M., Milne, L.R., Ladner, R.E.: StructJumper: a tool to help blind programmers navigate and understand the structure of code (2015). https://doi.org/10.1145/2702123.2702589. http://dx.doi.org/10.1145/2702123.2702589
3. Christensen, D.J., Fogh, R., Lund, H.H.: Playte, a tangible interface for engaging human-robot interaction. In: IEEE RO-MAN 2014–23rd IEEE International Symposium on Robot and Human Interactive Communication: Human-Robot Co-Existence: Adaptive Interfaces and Systems for Daily Life, Therapy, Assistance and Socially Engaging Interactions, pp. 56–62 (2014). https://doi.org/10.1109/ROMAN.2014.6926230
4. Cooper, S., Dann, W., Pausch, R.: Computer science education using animated 3D graphics to prepare novices for CS1 (2010). https://doi.org/10.1076/csed.13.1.3.13540. http://www.tandfonline.com/action/journalInformation?journalCode=ncse20
5. Horn, M.S., Jacob, R.J.K.: Tangible programming in the classroom with tern. In: Proceedings of ACM CHI 2007 Conference on Human Factors in Computing Systems, vol. 2, pp. 1965–1970 (2007). https://doi.org/10.1145/1240866.1240933. http://doi.acm.org/10.1145/1240866.1240933

6. Kakehashi, S., Motoyoshi, T., Koyanagi, K., Ohshima, T., Kawakami, H.: P-CUBE: block type programming tool for visual impairments. In: Proceedings - 2013 Conference on Technologies and Applications of Artificial Intelligence, TAAI 2013, pp. 294–299 (2013). https://doi.org/10.1109/TAAI.2013.65
7. Kane, S.K., Koushik, V., Muehlbradt, A.: Bonk: accessible programming for accessible audio games (2018). https://doi.org/10.1145/3202185.3202754
8. Maloney, J., Resnick, M., Rusk, N., Silverman, B., Eastmond, E.: The scratch programming language and environment. ACM Trans. Comput. Educ. (TOCE) **10**(4), 16 (2010)
9. Milne, L.R., Ladner, R.E.: Blocks4All: overcoming accessibility barriers to blocks programming for children with visual impairments. In: Conference on Human Factors in Computing Systems - Proceedings, vol. 2018-April. Association for Computing Machinery, April 2018. https://doi.org/10.1145/3173574.3173643
10. Moreno, A., Myller, N., Sutinen, E., Ben-Ari, M.: Visualizing programs with Jeliot 3. In: Proceedings of the Working Conference on Advanced Visual Interfaces - AVI 2004, p. 373 (2004). https://doi.org/10.1145/989863.989928. http://dl.acm.org/citation.cfm?id=989863.989928
11. Nusen, N., Sipitakiat, A.: Robo-blocks: a tangible programming system with debugging for children. In: Proceedings of the 11th International Conference on Interaction Design and Children, IDC 2012, pp. 98–105 (2012). https://doi.org/10.1145/2307096.2307108. http://www.nectec.or.th/icce2011/program/proceedings/pdf/C6_S21_216S.pdf
12. Pawelczak, D., Baumann, A.: Virtual-C - a programming environment for teaching C in undergraduate programming courses. In: 2014 IEEE Global Engineering Education Conference (EDUCON), pp. 1142–1148, April 2014. https://doi.org/10.1109/EDUCON.2014.7096836. http://ieeexplore.ieee.org/lpdocs/epic03/wrapper.htm?arnumber=7096836
13. Smith, A.C., Francioni, J.M., Matzek, S.D.: A Java programming tool for students with visual disabilities. In: ACM SIGACCESS Conference on Assistive Technologies: Proceedings of the Fourth International ACM Conference on Assistive Technologies, vol. 13, pp. 142–148 (2000)
14. Stefik, A., Siebert, S.: An empirical investigation into programming language syntax. ACM Trans. Comput. Educ **13**, 1–40 (2013). https://doi.org/10.1145/2534973. http://dx.doi.org/10.1145/2534973
15. Thieme, A., Morrison, C., Villar, N., Grayson, M., Lindley, S.: Enabling collaboration in learning computer programing inclusive of children with vision impairments. In: Proceedings of the 2017 Conference on Designing Interactive Systems - DIS 2017, pp. 739–752 (2017). https://doi.org/10.1145/3064663.3064689. http://dl.acm.org/citation.cfm?doid=3064663.3064689
16. Wang, D., Zhang, C., Wang, H.: T-Maze: a tangible programming tool for children, pp. 127–135 (2011)
17. Wang, D., Zhang, Y., Chen, S.: E-block: a tangible programming tool with graphical blocks. Math. Probl. Eng. **2013** (2013). https://doi.org/10.1155/2013/598547
18. Wilson, S., Cottle, D., Collins, N.: The SuperCollider Book. The MIT Press, Cambridge (2011)
19. Wolber, D., Abelson, H., Spertus, E., Looney, L.: App Inventor. O'Reilly Media, Inc., Newton (2011)

Accessible Learning Management Systems in Higher Education

Leevke Wilkens[1]([✉]) [iD], Christian Bühler[1] [iD], and Ingo Bosse[2] [iD]

[1] TU Dortmund University, Dortmund, Germany
Leevke.wilkens@tu-dortmund.de
[2] Chair of Sociology of Diversity, TUM Department of Sport and Health Sciences, Technical University of Munich, Munich, Germany

Abstract. Within a research project at TU Dortmund University/Germany a new learning management system (LMS) will be developed. This research project "Degree 4.0 – Digital reflexive teacher education 4.0: Video-based - accessible - personalized", particularly works with videos to foster reflexive teacher education – provided via the learning platform.

Due to the increasing diversity of the student body, accessibility and full participation need a greater focus. Even though, technology and digital media have the potential to foster participation in higher education, this potential cannot be exploited, when accessibility is not considered in the development.

In order to gain insights on accessible digital learning platform, in advance of the development, expert interviews were conducted. It became evident that all student interactions on the platform need to be accessible, according to the WCAG guidelines. Additionally, when using videos to initiate reflexive learning, these videos and all related tasks have to be accessible, too. Especially the online editing software and functions need careful considerations.

A learning platform, providing such interactions needs to support different screen modes, e.g. with the option to see the given task and the own progress, simultaneously. Furthermore, the videos must have captions and audio description, which may pose didactical challenges: the audio descriptions need to include all important aspects without giving away possible solutions.

Overall, the learning objective needs to stay in focus; thus, the editing itself should not be too complex and be done step-by-step.

Keywords: Accessible learning management system · Higher education · Inclusion

1 Introduction

"Online learning opens doors to education for everyone who has access to the technology to participate. Or does it?" [9]. Despite the potential digital media can offer for "full and equal participation in [higher] education" [35], the use of digital media by itself is not a guarantee for inclusive higher education. It is not enough to provide university teaching via digital media. Instead, digitization and inclusion must be considered together, respective the accessibility of the media used [39]. In line with the prevalence of digital videos throughout higher education, due to the technological

M. Antona and C. Stephanidis (Eds.): HCII 2020, LNCS 12189, pp. 315–328, 2020.
https://doi.org/10.1007/978-3-030-49108-6_23

development in recent years [12], the research project "Degree 4.0 – Digital teacher education 4.0: video based – accessible – personalized" particularly works with videos to foster reflexive teacher education, which will be provided via the Learning management system (LMS). This LMS will be developed by an external developer.

Four subjects (mathematics, computer sciences, music, German studies) and the rehabilitation sciences from TU Dortmund University and will provide the content for the LMS (Fig. 1).

Reflexive Teacher Education via a Learning Management System

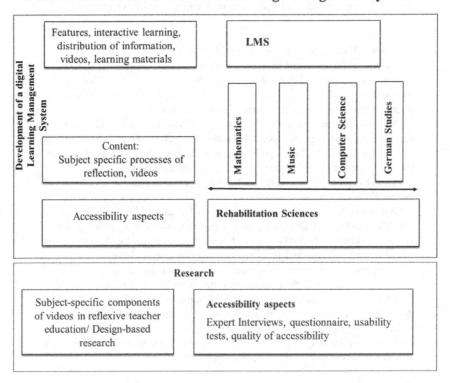

Fig. 1. Structure of the DEGREE 4.0 project (Based on the structure in the grant-proposal (2018))

In order to utilize the potential, which is attributed to digital media for inclusive education, accessibility and Universal Design [11] need to be considered up front in the development process [16]. Therefore, expert interviews were conducted to prepare and support the development process, and to gain insights on accessible LMS, inclusive teaching and usage of videos in higher education. Videos can foster inclusion, but as well create new barriers, if not accessible. Especially, the usage of accessible videos in didactical settings needs to be focused. When creating accessible videos, guidelines for audio description and/or subtitles are usually designed for movies or TV shows and not for videos with corresponding tasks to initiate reflection by students [28, 29].

Therefore, the research question is: "What are accessibility aspects when using videos to foster reflexive teacher education via an inclusive and accessible learning management system?" This article presents and discusses initial findings based on expert interviews and draws conclusions for accessible LMS in higher education. To frame those findings the related work as well as the methodology is presented.

2 Related Work

In order to contextualize the project, related work regarding inclusive university, accessibility and usability of LMS are examined.

2.1 Inclusive University

Within the higher education system, inclusion is increasingly important due to the rising diversity of students regarding living conditions, family background, employment and disability. Findings from a national study in 2017 stated, that 7% have at least one child, 48% come from a nonacademic background, 20% from a migrant background and 11% identified themselves as having a disability [26]. The increasing diversity of students is also stated in international studies [37]. Beyond the necessity of accessible offers in higher education, resulting from the diversity of the students there is a legal obligation in many countries, e.g. UN-CRPD and respective legislation.

Inclusive education "can be defined as an educational approach proposing schools in which all students can participate and all are treated like valuable school members" [27]. It aims at improving learning and participation at all levels of the educational system. Accordingly, the system, in this case universities need to enable anyone to participate, rather than individuals needing to adapt to the current situation [19]. In an inclusive university the diversity of students should be valued and considered when designing the learning environment, attendance teaching as well as digital teaching. One approach for such inclusive higher education is the Universal Design for Instruction, which comprises nine principles:

- Equitable use
- Flexibility in use
- Simple and intuitive
- Perceptible information
- Tolerance for error
- Low physical effort
- Size and space for approach and use
- A community of learners
- Instructional climate [31]

These principles are a framework "to inform faculty planning and practice rather than a rigid procedure or prescription for instruction" [31]. It is a proactive approach to support inclusive education. Several of these principles can be supported by the use of digital media [14]. This is of special interest in the context of higher education, where eLearning is a growing area and becomes more and more important due to the ongoing digitization of education.

Additionally, eLearning holds a great potential to foster the inclusion in higher education, while inaccessible LMS and content (e.g. PDF, videos) pose new barriers instead of removing them [18], which is elaborated in the next section.

2.2 Accessibility and Usability of Learning Management Systems

The development of digitization in the last decade opened up new possibilities for learning, access to information and communication. By now, Web 2.0 technologies – which can be characterized by a high degree of interactivity, self-organization, participation, cooperation or collaboration and user centricity [24] – and the respective learning technologies are omnipresent in higher education. Students engage in various forms of eLearning every day, e.g. course registration, library use and distributed online course materials [21].

In order to meet the needs and abilities of diverse students, technology is often associated with the promise to improve accessibility in education [6, 13], because it allows for flexible locations and times, as well as the possibility of individualized and personalized access. Furthermore, accessible websites are easier to navigate and understand for everyone [7]. Nevertheless, in the discourse on eLearning, the perspective on inclusion is often disregarded. Both perspectives are rarely considered together, although the potential of digital solutions for inclusive education is high [39].

Therefore, in order to exploit this potential and to foster inclusion and participation in Higher Education, all used technology needs to be accessible and LMS need to provide accessible formats, interaction and content [36]. The need for accessible websites and mobile apps offered by public entities, thus universities, is enshrined in the European web directive for the member states of the European Union. But rather often, these technologies are not designed with accessibility in mind [10]. Therefore, students who have problems using the different technologies are disadvantaged in their studies [21].

The first step towards an accessible and inclusive eLearning is an accessible platform and features itself. In the next step all used software and respective material need to be accessible, too.

ELearning consists in a large extent of written communication and online learning material which is made available by the lecturers [15]. The whole learning- and communication process is dominated by writing [1]. Regarding accessibility eLearning has the advantage, that providing accessible documents online is relatively easy.

But for some years the usage of video, not just passive (reception of videos) but also active (editing and annotations), has been predicted as potential for knowledge building [30] as well as to initiate reflection. For instance, annotations can function as anchors for reflection and discussion, especially when they can be shared with peers [20].

Although videos can contribute to inclusive teaching, they can also exclude certain students if accessibility is not considered [33]. The three main accessibility requirements for videos are:

- Accessible video-player
- Subtitles
- Imparting purely visual information for people with visual impairments (e.g. audio description) [5]

In the discussion around the usage of eLearning tools, accessibility and inclusion in higher education it is important to note that the mere digitization of a course does not mean that it is accessible and usable for all [34]. It needs to be kept in mind, that for students with disabilities digitization can become a new barrier in the system of higher education [5]. Thus, considering accessibility upfront is an important aspect when developing or implementing digital teaching – designing an existing LMS accessible subsequently is expensive and difficult [8, 12].

3   Sample and Methodology

Expert interviews were conducted in the run-up to the development of the LMS in order to ensure that accessibility and Universal Design is considered from the beginning. The sample was designed to take the needs of a wide range of students into account.

Therefore, experts for different types of impairments (hearing-, vision-, motor impairments and mental illness) were interviewed. Further interviews were conducted with specialists for digital and/or inclusive higher education. They were identified as experts because of their respective profession – professorship for one of the disability groups of interest or their work place as service providers. Particularly, some of the interviewees were experts on their own behalf [23]. Topics included digital learning platforms, the usage of videos in teaching, different needs of students, digital media and inclusive teaching in higher education. A particular focus within the interviews was the usage of videos, since videos are on the one hand a digital tool which may foster inclusion (time independence, possibility to rerun, listening and seeing rather than reading), but also pose specific challenges for some students (hearing impairment, visual impairment) and on the other hand, are a research focus in Degree 4.0.

The interviews were transcribed and then analyzed using qualitative content analysis [25]. In order to ensure objectivity, the coding process included at least two coders, several comparisons between the coders as well as revisions of the code system and code manual. The final coding system consists of eleven main categories addressing the different needs of students with disabilities (e.g. subtitles, audio description, assistive technology) and – to adopt an inclusive approach – also needs of all students regarding usage of digital media and videos in higher education. This allowed us to identify aspects which may not be specific to disabilities, but nonetheless make (digital)-teaching in higher education more accessible. Furthermore, in reference to the Universal Design for Instruction [31], its nine principles, which can promote accessibility when using eLearning and ICTs [34] were used to code the material. Finally, two coders analyzed the data material separately, and then discussed the differences, so a joint coding of the material took place.

4   Results

The analysis of the interviews highlighted several requirements for the development of the LMS and implications for the usage of videos in inclusive higher education. First, general implications will be outlined before findings differentiated according to key factors, which may pose barriers, are presented.

4.1   General Implications

The importance of using the WCAG guidelines as a baseline and during the whole development process was once more validated.

Another aspect for designing an LMS is the choice of the font, which should be without serifs. At least this is an aspect which is consensus up to now. However, the usage of serifs is discussed, as there are studies stating that fonts with serifs can be as easily read as without serifs [2].

When developing and implementing an LMS, diverse learners must be considered, hence different levels of prior knowledge, different learning types and familiarity with digital tools must be taken into account rather than just focusing upon students with disabilities. Therefore, when designing digital media for education, principles like Universal Design and/or Universal Design for Instruction should be considered. More specifically, one expert defined the UDI principles, as principles which implicate that teaching must be made useful for students with different abilities including previous knowledge levels and learning pace.

A digital learning environment can support the implementation of the UDI principles, as it is relatively easy to present different media. Thus, different learning styles can be supported, e.g. some prefer to learn with videos while others prefer reading. Such preferences do not necessarily have anything to do with an impairment.

Another UDI principle (simple intuitive) is also applicable for lecturers, as the system needs to be learned within a reasonable time, thus relatively easy to use. Additionally, it has to be possible for lecturers to quickly and easily comment on assignments or work-in-progress.

Especially pointed out are two UDI principles "community of learners" and "instructional climate". Also, in a digital learning environment the learning community needs to be supported. Teaching needs to be designed in a way that everyone is included and learners form a community, instead of learning separately. The contact between students, respective lecturers, has to be friendly and appreciative in digital terms. But particularly, the communication between lecturers and students may entail new challenges. As one of the interviewees stated: "Students are happy when lecturers know their names. (...). The closer the contact, the more openly one talks about difficulties" (KS, l. 58). When primarily teaching digital, this personal contact can be different, e.g. it becomes more challenging to remember names and recognize students when one does not see the students as often as in attendance learning.

Especially, when teaching digital, it is important to create a learning climate. In an appreciative environment, one can think freely and under no pressure, which otherwise lowers self-reflection and creativity. One way to create an appreciative environment is transparency. So, that one knows what to expect and what is expected. In such an environment it is more likely, that fears and concerns are expressed towards the lecturer. This is particularly important when working with videos.

As an overarching aspect, lecturers have to signal willingness to adapt certain tasks, materials, etc. if students have special needs.

Nevertheless, to build an accessible, inclusive and digital learning environment, a certain standard of accessibility should be maintained from the outset and then respond to individual needs when those are requested.

Nonetheless, for inclusive education it is important that both virtual and physical environment is accessible.

4.2 Digital Teaching

Digital teaching is a completely different form of teaching. It is associated with a higher effort for the lecturers than within classroom teaching. The proportion of written text which needs to be written by the lecturers and read by the students is much bigger than in traditional teaching.

But digital teaching does not just include the material itself. With regard to Web 2.0 technologies, all student interaction on the platform needs consideration and has to be accessible. Especially when using videos to initiate reflexive learning, these videos and all related tasks (e.g. video editing) have to be accessible.

4.3 Advantages

A great advantage of digital studies is the possibility to compensate the absence from courses. This is particularly relevant for students with disabilities, as they can compensate construction-related barriers or other impairment-related reasons for their absence. Obviously, these advantages apply to students without impairments, too. For example, when they are absent due to family responsibilities, etc.

Another advantage is, that via learning platforms, digital files (e.g. files or presentations) can be easily made accessible for students with visual impairments. For students with visual impairments, eLearning has the advantage that one can take the time needed.

"You can play back the audio description, you can take a break if you are overloaded or the battery is low" (BD, l. 58).

But, despite the advantages of eLearning, it has to be considered, that the use of digital media is always associated with additional time, compared to face-to-face lectures, simply because the operating of the screen reader takes more time, regardless of the accessibility of the website.

Individuals with visual impairments need considerably more time for internet research. Compared to individuals without visual impairments, a significantly higher percentage of individuals with visual impairments give up frustrated at some point, especially when the website is not accessible.

4.4   Become Familiar with Used Media

In particular, when implementing a new LMS and/or new media to learn with, opportunities should be offered to get to know the media and their usage. This facilitates that the students notice that it may make things easier, is communicative and has an added value for the course.

A way to reduce the inhibition threshold to visit a password-secured LMS are implemented news notifications. If such notifications present important information, the LMS is visited more often, thus students become familiar with the LMS.

4.5   Lecturers

Not just for students, but also for lecturers, eLearning pose changes. Therefore, such system has to be relatively easy to use and be learned within a reasonable time. This includes handling the tools, but also facing the problem to give feedback to 50 students in writing instead of reacting to the comments made by students in the classroom, orally. Additionally, lecturers must learn to design accessible materials, so not just the LMS is accessible, but also the content. This enables lecturers to adapt the materials spontaneously if changes are needed. Ideally, lecturers should maintain a certain standard from the outset proactively and then respond to individual needs if requested, reactively.

Additionally, as already pointed out above, also in digital teaching, the learning climate and participation have to be designed, including communication opportunities between students.

4.6   Operability

A learning platform, providing such interactions needs to support different screen modes (full screen, split screen) with the option of watching the video and work on the given task simultaneously.

A platform becomes unattractive for students with visual impairments, if the controls are cumbersome – links have to be clicked several times in order to start a task or when the whole page has to be viewed again and again. Short-cuts and short ways need to be possible. The experts also stressed the importance of the WCAG guidelines, e.g. that headings need to be formatted as such, so the operation by assistive technology is possible. An LMS is attractive if you can orientate yourself easily and find something quickly.

In order to be able to use the LMS, it has to be multifunctional and should be operable with the equipment needed, e.g. assistive technology. This does not just apply to the LMS, but also for the provided video player. One expert further stated, that universities should consider providing necessary equipment for students with motor impairments (different control options, speech recognition software) or at least information on how they can be financed, like social welfare.

4.7 Written Communication

Keeping in mind that eLearning is often associated with a lot of written text, it needs to be considered that for deaf students written language often poses a challenge. Considering that communication via the LMS is an important feature in eLearning, communication via Skype or other forms of verbal communication, poses a barrier for students with hearing impairments. But it is said, that written communication is not as spontaneous as verbal communication. A proposed solution for verbal communication was a sign language interpreter on demand, who can be added in the communication via Skype. At the same time this solution was classified as wishful thinking, due to the financing.

Nevertheless, for students with anxiety or social phobia, discussions via chats or other digital means present a solution to participate in discussions. But because, eLearning can be used as a strategy to avoid social interaction in total, as there is the possibility to work alone at the computer a balance between attendance and digital teaching is preferred by one expert (Interview with CS).

4.8 Videos

Videos are a particularly important element in teacher education. Lessons can be analyzed and children, learning situations or communication behavior can be observed. There is no better medium than videos to convey practical teaching, where eye contact, focus and more is relevant.

Another advantage of videos is, that it is no longer necessary to visit several schools in order to analyze different situations, these situations can be collected and stored in one place and can be watched and analyzed several times. When planning to use videos in lectures, eLearning etc. it has to be kept in mind that these videos have to be accessible for all students (see sections subtitles and audio description). Already in the video producing paying attention to good contrast, e.g. the person in focus wears something striking, can support students with visual impairment, who still work visually.

However, videos also have disadvantages. Especially, when students are supposed to be filmed so they can reflect themselves. But the threat of videos going viral has to be considered as a legitimate reason for fears. Those need to be respected, since one cannot know what might happen and who may gain access to the data. Therefore, if students do not want to be filmed, they should not be pressured to do so.

Additionally, for students with mental illness, watching videos can be an overload. Especially, if they are supposed to be in the video, which will be discussed in the classroom (digital or attendance). There might be students who are afraid of being filmed, which needs to be taken seriously. One idea was to let the students decide whether an image or just sound recording is made. Key factors for using videos are to take fears, even irrational ones, of students seriously and to build a climate of trust. Only in a climate of trust, students dare to communicate fears to their lecturers.

Regarding the value of videos in teacher education, one expert had the hypothesis that especially for students with disabilities seeing oneself in a teaching situation might help to reflect whether difficulties arise due to the impairment or due to yet not acquired competences. This hypothesis has to be evaluated.

Video Editing

Not only the videos, but also all related tasks need to be accessible. For example, in the Degree 4.0 project it is planned that the students edit videos. When designing an editing task, it is important that the learning objective stays in focus. If video editing becomes very complex, the task becomes less attractive. Therefore, when choosing an editing software one criteria should be that the editing can be done in small steps, especially for people who cannot concentrate well. The cognitive load should be laid on the task rather than the technical realization.

Subtitles

When students with hearing impairments use videos as source of information (e.g. recorded lectures) or to initiate reflection, they need subtitles, at least. But in higher education, this evolves the question: "Who does all the subtitling?" (TK, l. 38). Again, financing and time questions arise. As a pragmatic way, the automatic subtitling on YouTube was named, which is relatively good, assuming a high clarity of the speech. When producing such a video it might be helpful to keep that in mind and to try to use the camera angle to clarify who is speaking, like it is often done on television.

Audio Description

Keeping an audio description in mind when producing is helpful, because the amount of information which can be included in the audio description highly depends on the video. The time, which can be used for the audio description depends on the breaks in the audio track, where the audio description can be inserted.

If there are no breaks in the audio track, the time which can be used for the audio description shortens correspondingly. The challenge is to know the important aspects for the task, and what might be important to the students. Therefore, audio description can be didactically challenging when using videos to initiate reflection. It is crucial for the learning process that such an audio description covers all important aspects, in accordance with the task, without giving away the solution.

The central question is: "What is important?" and there is not only one correct answer to this question, only the person giving the task can decide what needs to be included and what already solves the task.

When designing an audio description for students with visual impairments, the setting of the video should be described briefly at the beginning in order to give the same overview about the setting and the people involved as students without a visual impairment might have. Additionally, an interesting and pleasant voice is recommended.

5   Conclusion and Implications

In the analysis, it became obvious that merely an accessible LMS is not enough to ensure that all students can participate in (digital) higher education.

From the expert interviews it can be derived that the accessible technology, in accordance with the WCAG guidelines, are a basic framework. Other studies show that also students without a disability rather than just students with disability are disadvantaged by an inaccessible LMS [21], as an accessible LMS can compensate a poorly-lit workplace, technical issues (e.g. broken touchpad on a Laptop and no available mouse), loud environment or other temporary issues. Additionally, customized accommodations may not be necessary as often as with an LMS, developed without accessibility in mind. Applying Universal Design to an online course can "make a course more flexible, thereby maximizing the learning of all students" [10].

But it is necessary to consider the physical context, integration into teaching, interaction between students and teachers next to the digital context. An accessible LMS is a needed criterion for inclusive education, but not solely. The importance of designing the technical elements accessible, according to the WCAG, is quite obvious. Next to the LMS all materials need to be accessible, too. Thus, all lecturers need to be informed and be able to provide accessible handouts, presentations etc. "Here, working time seems to provide a narrow bottleneck" [8]. To address these issues, workshops for lecturers are considered, together with the Service Office for Students with Disabilities.

But when working with videos, additional didactical and also financial issues arise. Providing accessible videos with subtitles and audio description for reflexive teacher education involves didactical considerations.

A next step in the Degree 4.0-project will be to test a framework for the lecturers in order to support the "descriptor" who creates the audio description. This framework derives from the work of Benecke [3]. Benecke generated a model for audio description, mainly for movies and works with so called "Holons". A holon merges the text information and the individual world knowledge [3] and influences the decision the descriptor makes by the respective holon [4]. One can argue that, if holons can be applied for the audio description for movies, it is also worth a try to make this approach usable for videos for reflexive teacher education. Especially, when the audio description is created by an external descriptor rather than the lecturer itself. Therefore, the framework for lecturers may help to make the holon of the lecturer transparent for the descriptor. Another aspect which will be tested is, derives from an expert-made statement emphasizing the important use of interesting and pleasant voices for audio descriptions. Nevertheless, there are approaches to make Text-to-Speech (TTS) synthesis useful for audio description. However, testing this kind of audio description, the natural voice is preferred rather than the synthetic one [22]. In Degree we still decided to make use of text-to-speech Software in order to ensure a consistent voice throughout all videos and because it is not as expensive as the conventional approach and thus may increase the number of audio descriptions [32].

Although Degree is focusing on video, it is important to note that digital media altogether, can be effective for some students, but they are most effective if they are aligned with the learning objectives and the overall course design [12]. As one expert puts it, "Digital media should be used where its use is really worthwhile" (BR, l. 66).

In the conclusion and implication part some additional considerations were presented. Derived from this, further work includes the actual development of the LMS by an external software developer according to the WCAG and the outlined findings from the expert interviews, conducting a survey with all student teachers to consider their needs in advance and the evaluation of the quality of the accessibility, especially with regard to the audio description via TTS of the LMS with students with and without disabilities.

Often the requirements of accessibility are not fully recognized when designing buildings or internet sites, in this case an LMS. However, retrofitting the product according to accessibility guidelines is expensive, difficult and unpopular [8, 38]. But since, developers cannot be solemnly blamed, if they do not consider accessibility issues – often accessibility is regarded as a feature rather than an incorporated part of the user experience [17]. The presented project is one approach to support developers in designing an accessible LMS, to implement accessibility from the beginning and shows some challenges which can arise when using video and eLearning to foster reflexive learning in teacher education.

Acknowledgements. The project on which this report is based was funded by the BMBF-Bundesministerium für Bildung und Forschung [Federal Ministry of Education and Research] under the funding code 16DHB2130. The responsibility for the content of this publication lies with the authors.

References

1. Bauer, E.: Zur Relevanz literaler Kompetenzen beim online Studieren. In: Griesehop, H.R., Bauer, E. (eds.) Lehren und Lernen online, pp. 149–166. Springer, Wiesbaden (2017). https://doi.org/10.1007/978-3-658-15797-5_8
2. Beck, F.-J.: Lösen von Traditionen! Geben wir den sehbehinderten Schülerinnen und Schülern die Möglichkeit, das Lesen ohne selbst geschaffene Barrieren zu erlernen! blind-sehbehindert **03**, 181–192 (2014)
3. Benecke, B.: Audiodeskription als partielle Translation. Modell und Methode. LIT Verlag, Berlin/Münster (2014)
4. Benecke, B.: Audiodeskription - Methoden und Techniken der Filmbeschreibung. In: Maaß, C., Rink, I. (eds.) Handbuch Barrierefreie Kommunikation, pp. 455–470. Frank & Timme Verlag für wissenschaftliche Literatur, Berlin (2019)
5. BIK für Alle (o.J) Barrierefreies E-Learning - Tipps für E-Learning-Anbieter. http://www.bik-fuer-alle.de/barrierefreies-e-learning.html#Basiswissen
6. Bosse, I., Armstrong, N., Schmeinck, D.: Is cloud computing the silver lining for european schools? Int. J. Digit. Soc. **7**(2), 1171–1176 (2016)
7. Bühler, C.: "Accessibility" über Desktopanwendungen hinaus – Barrierefreiheit. Informatik-Spektrum **40**(6), 501–510 (2017). https://doi.org/10.1007/s00287-017-1075-9
8. Bühler, C., Burgstahler, S., Havel, A., Kaspi-Tsahor, D.: New practices: promoting the role of ICT in the shared space of transition. In: Seale, J. (ed.) Improving Accessible Digital Practices in Higher Education, pp. 117–141. Springer, Cham (2020). https://doi.org/10.1007/978-3-030-37125-8_6
9. Burgstahler, S.: Opening doors or slamming them shut? Online learning practices and students with disabilities. Soc. Incl. **3**(6), 69–79 (2015). https://doi.org/10.17645/si.v3i6.420
10. Burgstahler, S.E.: Equal access: universal design of distance learning programs. In: A Checklist for Making Distance Learning Programs Welcoming and Accessible to All Students (2017)
11. Center for Universal Design About UD (2008). https://projects.ncsu.edu/ncsu/design/cud/about_ud/about_ud.htm
12. Dinmore, S.: Beyond lecture capture: creating digital video content for online learning – a case study. J. Univ. Teach. Learn. Pract. **16**(1), 7 (2019)

13. Fernandez, S.: Making space in higher education: disability, digital technology, and the inclusive prospect of digital collaborative making. Int. J. Inclusive Educ. 1–16 (2019). https://doi.org/10.1080/13603116.2019.1610806
14. Fisseler, B., Markmann, M.: Universal Design als Umgang mit Diversität in der Hochschule. journal hochschuldidaktik **1–2**, 13–16 (2012)
15. Griesehop, H.R.: Wege in die Online-Lehre: Wie lassen sich Lehrende gewinnen und motivieren? In: Griesehop, H.R., Bauer, E. (eds.) Lehren und Lernen online, pp. 67–80. Springer, Wiesbaden (2017). https://doi.org/10.1007/978-3-658-15797-5_4
16. Haage, A., Bühler, C.: Barrierefreiheit. In: Bosse, I., Schluchter, J.-R., Zorn, I. (eds.) Handbuch Inklusion und Medienbildung, 1st edn, pp. 207–215. Beltz Juventa, Basel (2019)
17. Heiman, T., Coughlan, T., Rangin, H., Deimann, M.: New designs or new practices? Multiple perspectives on the ICT and accessibility conundrum. In: Seale, J. (ed.) Improving Accessible Digital Practices in Higher Education, pp. 99–115. Springer, Cham (2020). https://doi.org/10.1007/978-3-030-37125-8_5
18. Kent, M.: Disability and eLearning: opportunities and barriers. Disabil. Stud. Q. **35**(1) (2015). https://doi.org/10.18061/dsq.v35i1.3815
19. Klein, U., Schindler, C.: Inklusion und Hochschule: Eine Einführung. In: Klein, U. (ed.) Inklusive Hochschule. Neue Perspektiven für Praxis und Forschung, pp. 7–18. Beltz Juventa, Basel (2016)
20. Krüger, M., Steffen, R., Vohle, F.: Videos in der Lehre durch Annotationen reflektieren und aktiv diskutieren. In: Csanyi GS, Reichl F, Steiner A (eds) Digitale Medien - Werkzeuge für exzellente Forschung und Lehre. Tagungsband; GMW 2012, Waxmann, Münster, pp. 198–210 (2012)
21. Kumar, K.L., Owston, R.: Evaluating e-learning accessibility by automated and student-centered methods. Education Tech. Research Dev. **64**(2), 263–283 (2016). https://doi.org/10.1007/s11423-015-9413-6
22. Kurch, A.: Produktionsprozesse der Hörgeschädigten-Untertitelungen und Audiodeskription: Potenziale teilautomatisierter Prozessbeschleunigung mittels (Sprach-) Technologien. In: Maaß, C., Rink, I. (eds.) Handbuch Barrierefreie Kommunikation, pp. 437–453. Frank & Timme Verlag für wissenschaftliche Literatur, Berlin (2019)
23. Littig, B.: Interviews, expert. In: Badie, B., Berg-Schlosser, D., Morlino, L. (eds.) International Encyclopedia of Political Science. Sage, Los Angeles (2011)
24. Mayrberger, K.: Web 2.0 in der Hochschule - Überlegungen zu einer (akademischen) Medienbildung für "E-Learning 2.0". In: Herzig, B., Meister, D.M., Moser, H., et al. (eds.) Medienkompetenz und Web 2.0, 1, pp. 309–328. Aufl. VS Verl. für Sozialwiss, Wiesbaden (2010). https://doi.org/10.1007/978-3-531-92135-8_17
25. Mayring, P.: Qualitative Inhaltsanalyse. Grundlagen und Techniken, 12, überarb. Aufl. Beltz Pädagogik. Beltz, Weinheim (2015)
26. Middendorf, E., Apolinarski, B., Becker, K. et al.: Die wirtschaftliche und soziale Lage der Studierenden in Deutschland 2016. 21. Sozialerhebung des Deutschen Studentenwerks durchgeführt vom Deutschen Zentrum für Hochschul- und Wissenschaftsforschung. Bundesministerium für Bildung und Forschung (BMBF), Berlin (2017)
27. Moriña, A.: Inclusive education in higher education: challenges and opportunities. Eur. J. Spec. Needs Educ. **32**(1), 3–17 (2017). https://doi.org/10.1080/08856257.2016.1254964
28. Norddeutscher Rundfunk, Vorgaben für Audiodeskription (2019). https://www.ndr.de/fernsehen/service/audiodeskription/Vorgaben-fuer-Audiodeskriptionen,audiodeskription140.html
29. Ofcom: Ofcom's Code on Television Access Services (2019). https://www.ofcom.org.uk/__data/assets/pdf_file/0035/179954/tv-access-services-code.pdf. Accessed 22 Jan 2020

30. Prantl, D., Wallbaum, C.: Bearbeiten von Unterrichtsvideos durch Studierende in der Lehrerbildung. Darstellung einer Seminarmethode und Kurzbericht einer wissenschaftlichen Begleitforschung zweier Seminare an der Hochschule für Musik und Theater Leipzig. In: Bergert, A., Lehmann, A., Liebscher, M., et al. (eds.) Videocampus Sachsen - Machbarkeitsuntersuchung, 1st edn, pp. 31–44. Technische Universität Bergakademie Freiberg, Freiberg, Sachs (2018)
31. Scott, S., McGuire, J.M., Shaw, S.F.: Universal design for instruction: a new paradigm for adult instruction in postsecondary education. Remedial Spec. Educ. **24**(6), 369–379 (2003)
32. Szarkowska, A.: Text-to-speech audio description: towards wider availability of AD. J. Spec. Trans. **15**, 142–162 (2011)
33. Thompson, T.: Video for all: accessibility of video content and universal design of a media player. In: Burgstahler, S.E. (ed.) Universal Design in Higher Education. From Principles to Practice, 2nd edn., pp. 259–273. Harvard Education Press, Cambridge
34. Thomson, R., Fichten, C.S., Havel, A. et al.: Blending universal design, e-learning, and information and communication technologies. In: Burgstahler, S.E. (ed.) Universal Design in Higher Education. From Principles to Practice, 2nd edn., pp. 275–284. Harvard Education Press, Cambridge (2015)
35. UN-United Nations: Conventions on the Rights of Persons with Disabilities and Optional Protocol, New York (2006)
36. Weber, G., Voegler, J.: Inklusives E-Teaching (2014). https://www.e-teaching.org/etresources/media/pdf/langtext_2014_weber_voegler_inklusives-eteaching.pdf. Accessed 12 Nov 2018
37. Weedon, E., Riddell, S.: Higher Education in Europe. In: Bennett, A., Southgate, E., Shah, M. (eds.) Widening Higher Education Participation. A Global Perspective, pp. 49–61. Chandos Publishing, Waltham (2016)
38. Welti, F.: Die UN-BRK- Welche Bedeutung hat sie für die Hochschulen? In: Klein, U. (ed.) Inklusive Hochschule. Neue Perspektiven für Praxis und Forschung, pp. 60–79. Beltz Juventa, Basel (2016)
39. Zorn, I.: Digitalisierung als Beitrag zu einer inklusiven Hochschuldidaktik. In: Platte, A., Werner, M., Vogt, S., et al. (eds.) Praxishandbuch Inklusive Hochschuldidaktik, 1st edn, pp. 195–202. Beltz Juventa, Basel (2018)

Social Media, Digital Services, eInclusion and Inovation

Open Government Data Through the Lens of Universal Design

Mexhid Ferati[✉], Fisnik Dalipi, and Zenun Kastrati

Linnaeus University, Kalmar, Sweden
{mexhid.ferati,fisnik.dalipi,zenun.kastrati}@lnu.se

Abstract. Open Data are increasingly being used for innovation, developing government strategies, and enhancing the transparency of the public sector. This data is aimed to be available to all people regardless of their abilities, professions and knowledge. Research is showing, however, that open data, besides being physically inaccessible to people with special needs, those are also semantically inaccessible to people who lack data science expertise. In order to identify specific accessibility challenges associated with open government data portals and datasets, we conducted an analysis using seven principles of Universal Design. In total, nine challenges are identified based on issues discovered. Three challenges are identified on the web portal interface level, namely: dataset filtering and categorization, access using a keyboard, and breadcrumb and back navigation. The other six challenges are identified on dataset level: dataset previewing, dataset size, dataset formats, dataset purpose, dataset labelling, and dataset literacy. For each challenge, we propose recommendations as a mean to incite a discussion about the features that open data should possess in order to be widely accessible, including people with disabilities and those lacking data science expertise and knowledge.

Keywords: Open government data · Universal design principles · Open government data principles · Accessibility

1 Introduction

Open Data are increasingly being used as an indispensable source for many governments' strategies associated with enhancing the transparency of the public sector and increasing civil engagement, or when addressing various innovation challenges of the future. For businesses, open data resources can help towards improving the relationship with customers and making more intelligent and strategic moves by performing data analytics on top of open data. Recently, many different countries have started to launch open innovation approaches in public sectors [1–3].

The continuous evolution of open content philosophy and approach highlights the fact that it represents an important field for research and study. Having said that, government data shall be considered open if the data are made public in a way that complies with the several principles [4]. Additionally, in order for the open data portals to empower citizens and meet their needs, they also need to be highly available services that provide reusable data that are universally available and accessible [5–8]. The Open Data Institute defines

© Springer Nature Switzerland AG 2020
M. Antona and C. Stephanidis (Eds.): HCII 2020, LNCS 12189, pp. 331–340, 2020.
https://doi.org/10.1007/978-3-030-49108-6_24

open data as "data that is made available by government, business and individuals fui anyone to access, use and share" [9]. This definition implies that such data is accessible and understandable by anyone regardless of their background and profession.

However, levels of access to these open data contents still remain below the expectations [10]. Open data should empower people to create value independently, nonetheless, these data are usually provided in a cumbersome structure and raw format that could be challenging for the general public without a certain level of technical skills to understand and use properly.

Just a quick browsing of any Open Data Web repository (e.g., the Swedish https:// oppnadata.se) reveals hundreds of data sheets available in various formats and raw data that are difficult to use without a proper knowledge and expertise. Similar situation can be easily identified with other countries worldwide. Countries like Canada, Australia and France, which according to Open Data Barometer [11] are leaders in the field, have taken proactive steps to enhance the availability and user friendliness of data. However, there still remain challenges and barriers revolving around accessibility and usability of open data that prevents their widespread utilization and proliferation. Thus, the question remains whether *open* in the Open Data means that they are just physically accessible, but semantically inaccessible to people who lack data science expertise.

There exist several standards and principles which specify and aid in the development of more accessible online content, such as WCAG [12], and the Human-Centered Design for Interactive Systems [13]. Despite the fact that so many countries have joined the open data initiative by offering open data from various sectors, the main purpose of open content philosophy has not yet been evidenced, whereas the relevance and impact of WCAG has not been fully emphasized. One of the reasons for neglecting WCAG could be the volume of its techniques which is massive and also its complexity [14, 15]. Moreover, it takes quite a significant time and effort to identify particular guidelines, which makes the usability assessment slow and expensive [16].

To the best of our knowledge, universal design principles [17] have not yet been discussed or used for usability assessment purposes on open governmental datasets. And compared to WCAG, universal design principles are more generic and suitable for an initial investigation of open data. Consequently, inspired also by the fact that there is inadequate (or scarce) evidence in scholarly studies that have attempted to evaluate the acceptance and usability of open data through the lens of universal design principles, this paper may contribute to fill this gap. Hence, the main goal behind this position paper is to incite a discussion about the necessary features open data resources should have in order to be truly open, accessible and usable by all users to the greatest extent possible. In this context, universal design principles along with other usability considerations and concerns to investigate the open government datasets are used.

In order to direct the discussion that this paper aims to provoke, we look at the open government data website portals of countries who are leaders in using open data in social inclusion. As part of this evaluation we identify nine challenges and recommendations grouped on a web interface or dataset level.

The remainder of this paper is structured as follows. In the next section we provide a related work where we highlight relevant studies conducted focusing on the open data and their accessibility. We provide then an overview of principles of open government data and universal design. In section four, we describe the challenges and recommendations identified with the datasets evaluated. We finally, conclude this paper with some insights for future directions.

2 Related Work

Over the past few years, an increasing interest has been shown in the study of open government data, with a special focus placed on exploring the openness of these data. Different principles and measures have been used to evaluate the quality and openness of open government data. For instance, study [18] used an evaluation framework which is designed to evaluate the openness of open government datasets from the perspective of ordinary citizens - people who do not possess advanced technical skills. The evaluation framework, which relies on the eight Sebastopol principles [4] explained in the next section, was used to evaluate the extent to which the datasets released by the UK government are open. Four hundred datasets published on the centralized government portal were examined and the findings showed that only 10% of open government data resources contain open data. Around 65% of the open datasets consist of aggregated data rather than raw data.

A similar framework for analyzing open government portals has been presented in [19]. Seven government portals were assessed from the perspective of transparency for public accountability. The results indicate that these portals fail to offer important structural and organizational requirements needed to support ordinary citizens engagement.

There is a body of literature that investigated the open governmental data portals. For instance, the authors in [20] proposed a new framework for usability evaluation of open data portals from the perspective of an ordinary citizen. Principles like data discoverability, accessibility and reusability were used to evaluate the quality of data portals of five countries, namely Australia, Canada, India, UK and USA. The findings indicated that the portals, in general, were evaluated as quite usable. In particular, Australia was ranked as the best performer, whereas USA received the lowest rating score.

Another research work which examines the quality of open government data portals is presented in [21]. Scales such as Open Data Portal Index, Data Content Index, Overall Index, Number of Datasets and Number of Datasets per 100,000 inhabitants were used to assess open data portals in American cities. The findings showed that portals were in a very early stage of development and much work is needed to improve user usability to help ordinary people understand the data. Study [22] presented a similar approach of examining the open government data portals, but for the 28-member states of European Union over a period of three years. The research found that EU countries are very heterogeneous when it comes to open government data portals development and much effort needs to be taken to homogenize them.

Our research work distinguishes from the studies presented above in two aspects: 1) rather than defining and using different indexes and scales to assess open government datasets, we use universal design principles to evaluate these datasets in terms of accessibility, and 2) we examine the datasets of three countries that besides highest ranked engagement of ordinary citizens for public accountability, they also score best with regards to social inclusion.

3   Open Government Data and Universal Design Principles

In 2007, the Open Government Working Group [4] held a meeting in Sebastopol, California, to devise a list of principles for open government data. Eight principles were proposed that open government data should comply with, namely:

- **Data should be complete** and without any limitations in terms of privacy, security or privilege. Additionally, this principle maintains that data should be available in its entirety.
- **Data should be primary** as collected at the source and provided in raw format with proper level of granularity.
- **Data should be timely** and available immediately after those are ready.
- **Data should be accessible** by people with a wide range of abilities as well as a wide range of uses. Being aware of users' disabilities and that they might use various assistive software and hardware devices.
- **Data should be machine readable** to allow automated processing and allow independent analysis of raw data.
- **Data should be non-discriminatory** and available to anyone without any special requirements, e.g., registration or behind wall.
- **Data should be non-proprietary** and no group should have exclusive control over it by imposing a proprietary format.
- **Data should be license-free** and without subject to any copyright, trademark or patent.

Of our particular interest is the fourth principle that considers data accessibility. We expand this principle and investigate more closely by implementing the seven principles of universal design [17]:

- **Equitable use** to ensure that data is usable by all people, including those with disabilities. Moreover, data should be presented and organized well and in an accessible format.
- **Flexibility in use** to accommodate various user ability levels by providing data in multiple and diverse formats as well as supporting various interaction modes, mouse, keyboard, etc.
- **Simple and intuitive use** to help users understand the data regardless of their experience, and language skills. The datasets should also follow consistent design.
- **Perceptible information** that enables users to use the data regardless of context and allow the text to be enlarged.
- **Tolerance for error** meaning that the data should account for user's errors and ability to easily recover in case that happens by guiding the user step by step.
- **Low physical effort** should be the norm to make the data usable comfortably with minimum level of fatigue and by dividing the data into sections to make access easier.
- **Size and space for approach and use** with regard to controls available when using the data, which should be large enough to be easily seen and accessible. Also, all objects, such as buttons, should be accessible by a keyboard in addition to a mouse.

4   Approach

Once we are aware and understand the principles in the previous section, we turn to the portal Open Barometer [11] that maintains an up-to-date status on open data initiatives around the world. The organization of the World Wide Web Foundation, which is behind the portal, continuously produces reports with the most recent being the 4th edition of the global report published in May 2017 [11]. The report shows that only 7% of the data is fully open; 25% of datasets are machine-readable; 25% of datasets have an open license, and only 10% of budget datasets are open. The datasets containing details of budget expenses are particularly important to combat corruption and enable government accountability.

Despite these low percentages, the report shows some indication that open data is contributing to economic growth, but not so much to social inclusion. With regards to open government data, the social inclusion is perceived by the degree the data eases access to public services to marginalized groups or increasing their involvement in policy decisions. Countries that score best with regards to social inclusion are Canada, France and Australia [11].

In order to uncover challenges and propose recommendation, we initially analyze the open government data website portals of these three countries (Canada [23], France [24], Australia [25]) through the principles of universal design. Then, we analyze five randomly selected datasets from portals of these countries using the principles of universal design. The portals and datasets analyzed are organized as challenges and recommendations in the next section.

5   Challenges and Recommendations

This section provides an overview of issues we identified through the process of evaluating datasets found on the portals of three countries with the highest rating for social inclusion. Issues found on different portals and datasets are grouped by their similarity and themed as challenges. In total, nine challenges are identified. For each challenge, we also provide recommendations on how those could be addressed. The challenges and recommendations are organized in two groups: web interface and dataset challenges and recommendations.

5.1   Web Interface Challenges and Recommendations

Access to datasets is typically done via the web interface where those datasets are hosted. Thus, before users can access the datasets, they must be able to access the web interface, which should comply to accessible standards. Hence, we initially evaluated the "landing pages" of open government data website portals of the three countries we are investigating.

Dataset Filtering and Categorization. The Canadian and Australian open government portals provide the ability to browse the data by *subject* or search by *keywords*. The datasets can be browsed by several filters, such as, *organization, location, format,* *subject*, *resource types*, etc. The main page of the French open government portal does not provide any browsing by filters; however, datasets are organized in *categories* (e.g., Agriculture and Food, Education, Research, etc.) and *tags* (employment, budget, etc.).

To adhere to various types of users and ensure equitable use, it is recommended that the main pages of all portals offer the ability to explore data with suitable level of granularity. Hence, ability to browse datasets by *categories*, *filtering*, *facets* and *tags* is a necessary feature of every web interface that hosts datasets to enable users to easily locate the desired datasets.

Access Using a Keyboard. All three website portals are with suitable contrast and responsive design to enable users to zoom in and still be able to navigate the site comfortably. The French and Australian portals provide the ability to browse the site using a keyboard in addition to a mouse. The Canadian portal, however, shows limited functionality using a keyboard; not all objects on the page could be accessed by tab-browsing. For instance, it is not possible to engage the "Access" button using a keyboard, which opens individual datasets.

To ensure equitable and flexibility in use, we recommend that all open government data portals be usable by means of a mouse and a keyboard. Especially, this is essential for users with disabilities who use assistive software when browsing websites only via a keyboard. Moreover, a responsive design should be implemented to accommodate visual impaired users who need to increase the size of objects on the screen and also suitable color contrast to make objects and text more discernible and readable.

Breadcrumb and Back Navigation. The Canadian and Australian websites have a suitable implementation of back navigation, in case users need to browse back. They also have a breadcrumb navigation implemented. The French website, on the other hand, has no implementation of the breadcrumb navigation, which might make it difficult for users to recall the page they are currently on, how they got there, and if they need to browse back. Going back is only possible via browser's back button.

To ensure proper intuitive use and tolerance for errors, in case users navigate forward, but need a way to trace their navigation back, portals should have a back button and breadcrumb navigation implemented.

5.2 Dataset Challenges and Recommendations

Dataset Previewing. Many datasets are provided in multiple formats (docx, csv, xls, json) to accommodate various types of users. For some users, however, it might be difficult to access the datasets that require their download and exploration using third-party applications. This particularly becomes a necessity when dataset files are large and downloading them takes time.

We recommend providing a preview of the datasets on the website interface to help users get a glimpse on the data without downloading the data and opening it via desktop applications. Additionally, data previewed on the website, could be generally more accessible and structured better. Previewing datasets helps users decide whether to download the actual dataset. At least, this is useful for superficial exploration by utilizing the customization functions provided on the website, for example when one needs to exclude certain attributes, e.g., age. It could be sufficient even if a concise level of data is shown on the website, and in case users need more details, they could choose to download and open the actual dataset. An example of such previewing of datasets is shown on the Australian portal, the so-called intellectual property neural open-data visualization and analysis [26]. Users can interact with the data on the website itself and can customize how they want to see the data, e.g., graphs, tables, etc. This could be very useful for users who are intellectually and cognitively challenged, and interactive exploration of the data could help them understand the data better and uncover insights.

Dataset Size. Many datasets are quite large, which makes them difficult to use. In our case, using a MacBook Pro with 3,1 GHz Intel Core i5, 16 GB of RAM, we were unable to open a csv file of 2,7 GB. Moreover, next to the dataset name there was no label indicating the size of the dataset, which is necessary for users to decide whether to download the dataset, especially large ones.

We recommend that next to those large dataset files, websites provide guidance on how to open and use such large files. Another recommendation could be to avoid uploading such large datasets and perhaps splitting them in more manageable sizes. All datasets should have information about their size.

Dataset Formats. Datasets are provided in multiple formats to accommodate a wide range of users. Some datasets, however, are only provided in a single format, such as iCal, which is a calendar structured data. In such cases, users are forced to view the data on a calendar application, which might prove difficult, because it could be challenging and uncomfortable for some users.

We recommend providing such data also in another more generic format (e.g., docx, xlsx, pdf), which could increase the accessibility of such datasets. For example, providing the same data in an excel sheet could be more usable for some users. Additionally, if the dataset is provided in a format that the users are not familiar with, there should be a guide to inform users which application is necessary to explore the dataset and even provide alternatives when users for some reason cannot obtain that particular software. This should contribute to decreasing the physical and mental efforts of users to discover themselves the type of application needed. Alternatives should especially include non-proprietary and open source software, which all users could afford and easily obtain. In general, it is expected that users have an understanding about each format that the datasets are provided. Thus, basic description about each format is necessary.

Dataset Purpose. It is clear that some datasets are suitable for machine-readability and some for human-readability, but this is not always understandable just by looking at the format the datasets are provided.

We recommend that datasets should be categorized by machine- and human-readable. This way, users can direct themselves to the dataset they need, whether they plan to explore the dataset by looking at it personally, or feed it to a software. This information is especially beneficial to users who lack technical understanding.

Dataset Labelling. In our investigation, we identified datasets that are provided in an archived format (e.g., zip), but on the website the dataset is labelled as csv. This could confuse users. Although, datasets are provided in multiple formats, it seems like different formats in some cases serve different purposes based on the label provided that classifies the datasets. For instance, in an occasion, the dataset with formats csv and docx is labelled as a *dataset*, however, the same dataset in other formats, such as, xlsx, json and html is provided with a label *guide* and *website*. This is confusing and perhaps misleading, because the same data should be provided using different formats. Besides this, we noticed cases when datasets contain columns with abbreviations that makes it difficult to understand what the data is about.

We recommend that datasets are correctly labelled. Also for each type of dataset (e.g., guide), it should be clear what its purpose is and how does it complement other datasets. Additionally, dataset columns and rows should be described as clearly as possible to avoid any ambiguities and should not assume any previous knowledge of users.

Dataset Literacy. While exploring the datasets, one gets the impression that most of the data are not understandable to common users who might lack the appropriate knowledge about different types of dataset files and dataset heading labels. Hence, for these users, data literacy competencies are required in order to work with such data. Data literacy, according to Gartner, is the ability to read, write and communicate data in context, including understanding of data sources and constructs [27]. However, reading datasets implies comprehending the data, which represents a key pre-condition for further dataset use and processing in multiple contexts. In this perspective, for the datasets that we have analyzed and which are predominantly in a raw format, it is hard to be easily read, utilized and communicated for any purpose, let alone to derive conclusions. In general, it is expected that users know sufficiently about the technical aspects related to dataset organization and presentation. Moreover, users are required to know how to operate statistical software in order to analyze and understand the data, while their intent might be to just get a basic overview of the data.

We recommend that, besides providing the datasets in a raw format, which is the required level of granularity for data analysis, a simplified version of the data should be provided. This simplified version could offer aggregated level of data aimed at people not possessing technical expertise and knowledge, but may just be interested in understating the overall message of the data. This could be implemented similar to our suggestion in the section of Dataset Previewing.

6 Conclusion and Future Work

With this position paper, we wanted to initiate a discussion about the accessibility of open government data. In order to identify issues and challenges with existing approaches in publishing open government data, we analyzed the portals of three countries scoring highest for social inclusion: Canada, France and Australia. We used Universal Design principles as a guidance when looking at randomly selected datasets from these three countries. The evaluation process we conducted was superficial, because our aim with this paper is not to provide detailed evaluation analysis and findings, but to identify initial patterns and challenges, and provide suitable recommendations.

During the evaluation, we identified three challenges for the web interface where datasets are hosted, namely: dataset filtering and categorization, access using a keyboard, and breadcrumb and back navigation. On the dataset level, we identified six additional challenges: dataset previewing, dataset size, dataset formats, dataset purpose, dataset labelling, and dataset literacy. For each identified challenge, we provided recommendations.

A future direction for us will be to conduct a more comprehensive evaluation of the accessibility of open government data and to confirm the validity of the challenges and recommendations identified in this position paper. Additionally, we aim at conducting a study with the open data supplied by the municipality where we are located and identify any additional challenges. Based on challenges identified, we aim to develop a prototype based on recommendation provided and then evaluate the prototype with stakeholders, both, end users and dataset providers.

References

1. Tate, M., Bongiovanni, I., Kowalkiewicz, M., Townson, P.: Managing the "Fuzzy front end" of open digital service innovation in the public sector: a methodology. Int. J. Inf. Manage. **39**, 186–198 (2018)
2. Kankanhalli, A., Zuiderwijk, A., Tayi, G.K.: Open innovation in the public sector: a research agenda. Gov. Inf. Q. Int. J. Inf. Technol. Manage. Policies Pract. **34**(1), 84–89 (2017)
3. Cheah, S.L.Y., Ho, Y.P.: Effective industrial policy implementation for open innovation: the role of government resources and capabilities. Technol. Forecast. Soc. Chang. **151**, 119845 (2020)
4. Open Government Data Principles. https://public.resource.org/8_principles.html. Accessed 26 Dec 2019
5. Millette, C., Hosein, P.A.: Consumer focused open data platform. In: 2016 3rd MEC International Conference on Big Data and Smart City (ICBDSC), p. 1–6. IEEE (2016)
6. Ruijer, E., Grimmelikhuijsen, S., Hogan, M., Enzerink, S., Ojo, A., Meijer, A.: Connecting societal issues, users and data. Scenario-based design of open data platforms. Gov. Inf. Q. **34** (3), 470–480 (2017)
7. Yang, H.-C., Lin, Cathy S., Yu, P.-H.: Toward automatic assessment of the categorization structure of open data portals. In: Wang, L., Uesugi, S., Ting, I.-H., Okuhara, K., Wang, K. (eds.) MISNC 2015. CCIS, vol. 540, pp. 372–380. Springer, Heidelberg (2015). https://doi.org/10.1007/978-3-662-48319-0_30
8. Ahmed, S.U., Dalipi, F., Aasnæs, S.: Open data based digital platform for regional growth and development in Norway: a heuristic evaluation of the user interface. Int. J. Adv. Softw. **12**(3&4), 239–248 (2019)
9. Open Data Institute. https://theodi.org/. Accessed 26 Dec 2019
10. Ojo, A., et al.: Realizing the innovation potentials from open data: stakeholders' perspectives on the desired affordances of open data environment. In: Working Conference on Virtual Enterprises, pp. 48–59. Springer, Cham (2016)
11. Open Data Barometer. https://opendatabarometer.org/doc/4thEdition/ODB-4thEdition-GlobalReport.pdf. Accessed 26 Dec 2019
12. Web Content Accessibility Guidelines (WCAG). https://www.w3.org/WAI/standards-guidelines/wcag/. Accessed 26 Dec 2019

13. Ergonomics of human-system interaction—Part 210: Human-centred design for interactive systems, ISO 9241-201 (2019). https://www.iso.org/standard/77520.html. Accessed 26 Dec 2019

14. WCAG 2.0, Accessibility, is it an impossible standard that provides the basis for excuses? http://sitemorse.com/news/2016/07/06/wcag-2-accessibility-impossible-standard/. Accessed 26 Dec 2019

15. Ferati, M., Mripa, N., Bunjaku, R.: Accessibility of MOOCs for blind people in developing Non-English speaking countries. In: Di Bucchianico, G., Kercher, P. (eds.) Advances in Design for Inclusion. Advances in Intelligent Systems and Computing, vol 500, pp. 519–528, Springer, Cham (2016). https://doi.org/10.1007/978-3-319-41962-6_46

16. Paddison, C., Englefield, P.: Applying heuristics to accessibility inspections. Interact. Comput. **16**(3), 507–521 (2004)

17. Story, M.F.: Principles of universal design. In: Universal Design Handbook. McGraw-Hill, New York (2001)

18. Wang, V., Shepherd, D.: Exploring the extent of openness of open government data–a critique of open government datasets in the UK. Gov. Inf. Q. **37**, 101405 (2019)

19. Lourenço, R.P.: An analysis of open government portals: A perspective of transparency for accountability. Gov. Inf. Q. **32**(3), 323–332 (2015)

20. Máchová, R., Hub, M., Lnenicka, M.: Usability evaluation of open data portals: evaluating data discoverability, accessibility, and reusability from a stakeholders' perspective. Aslib J. Inf. Manage. **70**(3), 252–268 (2018)

21. Thorsby, J., Stowers, G.N., Wolslegel, K., Tumbuan, E.: Understanding the content and features of open data portals in American cities. Gov. Inf. Q. **34**(1), 53–61 (2017)

22. Espinosa, J., Luján-Mora, S.: Open government data portals in the European Union: considerations, development, and expectations. Technol. Forecast. Soc. Chang. **149**, 119769 (2019)

23. Canadian portal of Open Data. https://open.canada.ca/en/open-data. Accessed 26 Dec 2019

24. French portal of Open Data. https://www.data.gouv.fr/en/. Accessed 26 Dec 2019

25. Australian portal of Open Data. https://data.gov.au/. Accessed 26 Dec 2019

26. Australian Intellectual Property Open Live data. https://ipnova.ipaustralia.gov.au/#/. Accessed 26 Dec 2019

27. Gartner – A Data and Analytics Leader's Guide to Data Literacy. https://www.gartner.com/en/publications/data-analytics-strategy. Accessed 22 Jan 2020

Cultural Inclusion and Access to Technology: Bottom-Up Perspectives on Copyright Law and Policy in Norway

G. Anthony Giannoumis$^{(\boxtimes)}$ (iD)
and Wondwossen Mulualem Beyene (iD)

Oslo Metropolitan University, Oslo, Norway
gagian@oslomet.no

Abstract. The United Nations Convention on the Rights of Persons with Disabilities obligates States Parties to ensure access to information and communications technology and recognizes the right to enjoy cultural products in accessible formats. In 2013, the World Intellectual Property Organization adopted the Marrakesh Access Treaty (MAT), which obligated State Parties ensure the accessibility of cultural products by introducing an exception to copyright law. However, despite these efforts, cultural products remain largely inaccessible for persons with disabilities due to, among other things, copyright laws that limit the production and distribution of accessible books. Research demonstrates that examining policy implementation from a "top-down" perspective provides a useful basis for examining the implementation of the MAT. However, research has yet to examine the implementation of the MAT from a "bottom-up" perspective. This article examines the "bottom-up" mechanisms for ensuring access to culture for persons with disabilities and asks, "How can the implementation of copyright law and policy promote access to culture for persons with disabilities?" The results from a case study in Norway suggest that implementing copyright law involves interdependent networks of policy actors that have adopted a social regulatory approach to promoting the rights of persons with disabilities and publishers.

Keywords: Digital accessibility · Web accessibility · Copyright · Marrakesh Access Treaty · Cultural inclusion · Policy implementation

1 Introduction

The United Nations Convention on the Rights of Persons with Disabilities (CRPD) obligates States Parties to ensure access to information and communications technology (ICT) and in particular recognizes the right to enjoy cultural materials in formats usable by persons with disabilities. However, persons with disabilities continue to experience barriers in using ICT and accessing cultural products. This article refers to cultural products as published literary or artistic works that use ICT as a means for accessing or using the product. The CRPD conceptualizes disability as an evolving concept that results from the interaction between an individual's impairment and social barriers that limit full and effective participation in society on an equal basis with others.

© Springer Nature Switzerland AG 2020
M. Antona and C. Stephanidis (Eds.): HCII 2020, LNCS 12189, pp. 341–355, 2020.
https://doi.org/10.1007/978-3-030-49108-6_25

In order to promote access to cultural products for persons with disabilities, the Marrakesh Treaty to Facilitate Access to Published Works by Visually Impaired Persons and Persons with Print Disabilities (MAT) aims to promote access to literary and artistic works for persons with disabilities. The term print disability is coined to describe "people who cannot effectively read print because of a visual, physical, perceptual, developmental, cognitive, or learning disability" [1]. The MAT obligates States Parties to provide an exception to national copyright law that facilitates access to cultural products for persons with disabilities. This article refers to copyright law and policy as any form of social regulation - i.e., legislative, financial or persuasive policies - aimed at encouraging the creation of cultural products by protecting the reproduction and distribution of those products.

Concurrent with the design of the MAT, technology service providers, government agencies and cultural institutions continue to promote the mass-digitization of cultural products [2]. For example, the European Union (EU) initiated Europeana, a website that aggregates digitized content from museums, archives, libraries and audio-visual collections throughout Europe [2]. To ensure access for persons with disabilities, these cultural products must be provided in formats usable by persons with disabilities. For example, persons with print disabilities may experience barriers accessing and using cultural products that include text-based content. However, in order to realize the objectives of the MAT State and non-State actors must take action to limit copyright law and ensure the removal of barriers in accessing cultural products for persons with disabilities.

Research demonstrates that policy implementation involves translating policy objectives into action. Research differentiates "top-down" and "bottom-up" perspectives on policy implementation. While top-down approaches to policy implementation typically refer to the roles and activities among State actors, bottom-up implementation refer to the relationships and interdependencies among State and non-State actors that evolve over time. Research on the MAT has typically adopted a top-down perspective emphasizing the roles and responsibilities of State actors in adopting, interpreting and drafting or reforming copyright law and policy [3–8].

However, research has yet to examine the implementation of the MAT from a "bottom-up" perspective. This article examines the mechanisms for ensuring access to culture for persons with disabilities through the implementation of the MAT and national copyright law and policy. This article asks, "How can the implementation of national and international copyright law and policy promote access to culture for persons with disabilities?" This article explores different analytic perspectives for examining the implementation of copyright law and policy as a means for ensuring access to culture for persons with disabilities. Specifically, this article examines qualitative data from a case study of Norwegian libraries and examines different perspectives on social regulation of copyright and the role of interdependent networks of policy actors. This article suggests a framework for analyzing the implementation of copyright law and policy as a means for ensuring access to culture for persons with disabilities.

This article proceeds in six sections. First, it presents an analytic framework for examining the implementation of copyright law and policy. Second, this article presents the methods used to explore the implementation of copyright law and policy. Third, it examines the barriers experienced by persons with disabilities in accessing cultural products. Fourth, this article examines the results of the case study including copyright law and policy as a form of social regulation. Fifth, it concludes by summarizing the results and providing further suggestions for research and practice aimed at promoting access to cultural products for persons with disabilities.

2 Analytic Framework

This section provides an overview of research on policy implementation, social regulation, and policy networks. First, it analyses research on policy implementation to frame the top-down and bottom-up perspectives on the implementation of copyright law and policy. Second, this section analyses research on social regulation to frame the variety of approaches for promoting access to cultural products for persons with disabilities through copyright law and policy. Third, it analyses research on policy networks – i.e., interdependent connections among policy actors – to frame the roles and relationships among policy actors involved in implementing copyright law and policy. Together, these three analytic perspectives provide a model for examining the implementation of copyright law and policy as a means for ensuring access to cultural products for persons with disabilities.

2.1 Policy Implementation

Research demonstrates that policy implementation may involve "top-down" and "bottom-up" processes [9–11]. This article conceives of policy implementation as a process that translates policy into action. Research supports this conceptualization and affirms that implementation processes can explain the difference between policy goals and outcomes [9, 12]. According to Hill and Hupe [9] implementation refers to the activities involved in fulfilling policy objectives, which are enacted in response to particular social problems. Research has differentiated top-down from bottom-up perspectives on policy implementation [9–11]. According to Hill and Hupe [9], top-down implementation refers to the series of steps or actions following from the design and enactment of a law or policy. The authors contrast top-down with bottom-up implementation, which refers to the decisions and processes used by State and non-State actors involved in interpreting, sometimes ambiguous, policy goals and translating those goals into practice.

Research on policy implementation suggests that implementing international copyright law involves translating the objectives of the MAT into action. From a top down perspective, implementing the MAT involves a clear series of actions following the MAT's entry into force. However, from a bottom up perspective, implementing the MAT involves a network of interdependent policy actors both within and outside of government whose interrelationships over time may contribute to both policy design and changes in practice. These changes may occur because of both top-down pressures resulting from enactment of the national or international copyright law or bottom-up interactions that promote change within an organization and ensures access to cultural products for persons with disabilities.

This article uses research on policy implementation as an analytic lens to examine the obligations of the MAT from a top-down perspective and the mechanisms for ensuring access to culture for persons with disabilities from a bottom-up perspective. From a bottom-up perspective, State and non-State actors such as libraries and publishers may influence the implementation of copyright law and policy and organizational processes may ensure or limit access to culture for persons with disabilities.

2.2 Social Regulation

Research demonstrates that social regulation aims to influence market actors in an effort to achieve social outcomes [13–16]. This article conceives of social regulation as the use of law and policy to coerce or persuade market actors to promote or achieve a social objective. This conceptualization is supported by Levi-Faur [15] who affirms that social regulation consists of "ex-ante bureaucratic legalization of prescriptive rules and the monitoring and enforcement of these rules by social, business, and political actors on other social, business, and political actors". The author differentiates "second-party" regulation where State actors regulate business or market actors regulate other market actors and "third-party" regulation where "the relations between the regulator and regulate are mediated" by an independent party. The author argues that third-party regulation involves interactions among government actors, businesses and non-governmental organizations. Levi-Faur [15] argues that one form of third-party regulation "co-regulation" involves cooperation among State and non-State actors in designing and implementing regulations.

Töller [17] further explores aspects of third-party regulation and co-regulation by examining voluntary approaches to regulation. The author argues that voluntary approaches to regulation involve rules that aim to persuade actors to incur costs beyond what is required by the law. The author suggests that voluntary approaches to regulation can involve "codes" or standards where market actors agree to adhere to collectively established requirements. The author goes on to examine the relationship between voluntary approaches to regulation and threats of compulsory regulation by the State or the threats of boycotts by other market actors.

Research on social regulation suggests that the implementation of copyright law and policy can act as a voluntary means for ensuring access to culture for persons with disabilities. In the context of the MAT, research on social regulation suggests that State actors may use copyright law and policy to ensure access to culture for persons with disabilities. Essentially, State actors may use exceptions to copyright law and policy to encourage market actors create and distribute accessible cultural products.

This article uses research on social regulation as an analytic lens to examine use of copyright law and policy as a means to ensure access to culture for persons with disabilities. From a social regulation perspective, the implementation of the MAT involves regulating the behavior of organizations such as libraries by providing exceptions in copyright law that encourage libraries to voluntarily create and distribute accessible cultural products.

2.3   Policy Networks

Research demonstrates that networks of interdependent actors influence policy [9, 15, 18, 19]. This article conceives of policy networks as the interdependent relationships among State and non-State actors nationally and internationally. This conceptualization is supported by Rhodes [19] who affirms that policy networks refer to "formal [...] and informal linkages between governmental and other actors structured around shared [...] interests in public policy making and implementation". Djelic and Quack [18] take a top-down perspective to examining policy networks and argue that actors within policy networks contribute to the translation of agreed upon beliefs into public policy. Merry [20] adopts a bottom-up perspective by examining the interpretation of human rights in local settings. According to the author, intermediaries such as community leaders and non-governmental organizations, "translate the discourses and practices from the arena of international law and legal institutions to specific situations of suffering and violation" [20].

Adam and Kriesi [21] stress the interdependencies among policy actors arguing that government agencies, private enterprises and civil society organizations depend on one another to implement regulations effectively. According to the authors, "actors are dependent on each other because they need each other's resources to achieve their goals" [21]. The authors argue that "[g]overnment agents do not occupy a dominant position within these networks, and they are not able to unilaterally impose their will, but they can attempt to manage the interdependent relations to promote joint problem solving in policy making" [21].

Abbott and Snidal [22] argue that participation in policy networks provide opportunities for non-State actors to design regulations. The authors suggest that international organizations such as the OECD and ILO orchestrate policy networks by "mobilizing and working with private actors and institutions to achieve regulatory goals" [22]. According to the authors orchestration processes typically including "catalyzing voluntary and collaborative programs; convening and facilitating private collaborations; persuading and inducing firms and industries to self-regulate; building private capacities; negotiating regulatory targets with firms; and providing incentives for attaining those targets".

Research on policy networks suggests that networks of interdependent policy actors share authority and maintain multiple and overlapping relationships nationally and internationally. In the context of implementing national and international copyright law and policy, interdependent networks of policy actors contribute to the implementation of national and international copyright law and policy. Non-state actors including private enterprises and civil society organizations may depend on and act in collaboration with State actors to ensure access to culture for persons with disabilities in practice.

This article uses research on policy networks as an analytic lens to examine the complex interactions and interdependencies among State and non-State actors involved in ensuring the rights of both copyright holders and persons with disabilities. From a policy network perspective, ensuring access to culture for persons with disabilities involves a complex network of interdependent actors whose relationships, identities and levels of organization (e.g., national or international) influence the implementation of the MAT.

3   Methods

To examine access to culture for persons with disabilities, this article conducted a case study of copyright law and policy in Norway. The case study focused on the bottom-up implementation of national and international law and policy, which provides exceptions to copyright as a means for ensuring access to cultural products for persons with disabilities. Previous research demonstrates that case studies provide a useful approach for examining a current phenomenon in context, where investigators have limited to no control over events [23]. Thus, case studies provide a useful research design to understand policy implementation. George and Bennett [24] describe case studies as an "instance [case] of a class of events [a phenomenon]" [24]. Yin [23] provides a more detailed description of case studies as empirical inquiries that "investigate a contemporary phenomenon in-depth and within its real-life context, especially when the boundaries between the phenomenon and context are not clearly evident" [23]. Thus, case studies provide an in-depth examination of the meaningful characteristics of real-life events and provide a useful research design for understanding complex social phenomena [23].

Case studies can also provide detailed explanations of processes that cause a particular phenomenon [24, 25]. By detailing causal processes, case studies may identify new variables and hypotheses [24, 26]. The results of case studies allow investigators to expand and generalize theories [23–26]. Thus, rather than generalizing statistically by "enumerating frequencies", case studies typically generalize to "theoretical propositions" [23]. Case studies aim to inform theory and models of policy implementation by evaluating theoretical assumptions and extending models of policy implementation by identifying new and potential causal conditions and areas of exploration. A single case study provides an opportunity to conduct an in-depth examination of a phenomenon in a unique context. In this article, the case study of copyright law and policy in Norway provides a basis for confirming or extending causal assumptions within models of policy implementation, social regulation and policy networks.

The bottom-up implementation of the MAT provides a useful case for analysis because an interdependent network of international policy actors contributed to the design of the MAT. Upon ratification and entry into force, States Parties have an obligation to implement the provisions of the Treaty in national law and policy. However, market actors retain the ultimate responsibility for ensuring that the aims of the MAT are realized in practice. Norway provides a useful case for examining the implementation of the MAT as Norwegian copyright law provides exceptions aimed at ensuring access to cultural products for persons with disabilities. In addition, Norway has ratified the CRPD and has signed but not yet ratified the MAT.

Empirical data from policy documents and semi-structured interviews provides a basis for analyzing the implementation of copyright law and policy in Norway. Document data from national and international law and policy provides a useful basis for examining the implementation of copyright law and policy from a top-down perspective. This article uses policy documents including international law and policy, national copyright law and policy in Norway, government documents that discuss the legislative history of relevant Norwegian laws and organizational policies collected from publicly available sources on the web and through interpersonal communications with policy actors involved in implementing national copyright law and policy.

Data from semi-structured interviews with policy actors involved in providing access to cultural products for persons with disabilities provide a useful basis for examining the implementation of copyright law and policy from a bottom-up perspective. Four libraries in the Oslo area, were purposively selected because of their digital services. This article uses qualitative interview data collected from elite interviews with six decision makers. The interviews examined the experiences of library staff in handling copyright issues related to digital resources and their approach to ensuring access to persons with disabilities. The interview data provided a useful basis for examining the perspectives of non-State actors in implementing copyright law and policy.

4 Copyright and Access to Culture for Persons with Disabilities

Research demonstrates that underprivileged groups experience barriers in accessing culture [27]. This article conceives of access to culture as the provision of cultural materials and information in formats and technologies accessible and usable by persons with disabilities. This conceptualization is supported by the CRPD, which affirms in Article 30 that States Parties "recognize the right of persons with disabilities to take part on an equal basis with others in cultural life and shall take all appropriate measures to ensure that persons with disabilities [...] [e]njoy access to cultural materials in accessible formats". In addition, the CRPD recognizes the right to access information in Article 9 stating that "States Parties shall take appropriate measures to ensure to persons with disabilities access, on an equal basis with others, to [...] information and communications technologies and systems". The right to participate in cultural life, in many cases, is intertwined with obligations for accessibility. Barriers to accessing cultural products limit whether and how persons with disabilities can participate in cultural life [28].

The UN CRPD Committee, which is responsible for monitoring the implementation of the CRPD, argues that accessibility is an obligation whenever goods and services are provided to the public. According to the Committee goods and services "must be accessible to all, regardless of whether they are owned [...] or provided by a public authority or a private enterprise". The CRPD Committee reiterates the obligations for State Parties to ensure that cultural products are provided in accessible formats and in particular cites the barriers experienced by persons with intellectual disabilities. According to the Committee, "[p]ersons with intellectual disabilities cannot enjoy a book if there is no easy-to-read version or a version in augmentative and alternative modes".

One of the characteristics of the information society is the proliferation of content in text, audio, video and graphics formats [29]. As the result, persons with disabilities have new opportunities to access electronic books, journals and other print-based cultural products in accessible formats. However, despite an overall increase in digitized cultural products, ensuring the accessibility both of products "born-digital" and those newly digitized materials remains a challenge [30]. Ferri and Giannoumis [2] examined access to culture and digitization efforts in the European Union. The authors argue that "compliance with intellectual property rights (namely copyright) has challenged" efforts to ensure accessible cultural products.

Copyright poses a challenge to ensuring access to cultural products for persons with disabilities because rights holders have a legitimate interest in protecting against the unauthorized reproduction and distribution of their intellectual property. In practice, preserving copyright can limit the production and distribution of materials in alternative formats. This has the potential for hindering access to knowledge and stifling innovative ways of delivering information [31]. For example, Harpur and Suzor [28] cite a conflict in the US where Amazon disabled the text-to-speech feature on their Kindle tablet device, at least in part, because of requests from publishers. As the result, there have been calls for changing, modifying or interpreting copyright laws in order to encourage, not complicate, the distribution of cultural products in alternative formats [32].

Research demonstrates that copyright laws have acted as a barrier for persons with disabilities in accessing cultural products. This article conceives of copyright as a national legal right to use and distribute a cultural product. This conceptualization is supported by the World Intellectual Property Organization (WIPO) who affirms that copyright "is a legal term used to describe the rights that creators have over their literary and artistic works" [33]. According to WIPO copyright may cover cultural products such as "books, music, paintings, sculpture, and films" [33]. Williams [34] similarly posits that copyright law "provides rights holders exclusive rights over written works in order to stimulate innovation". However, the author argues that in some instances copyright law can "restrict dissemination of accessible written works".

Papadopoulou [4] provides a more nuanced explanation of copyright as a barrier to accessing cultural products. According to the author copyright restricts any unauthorized reproduction, adaptation, distribution of a work to the public. The author argues that "any use of the work requires copyright clearance, unless it falls within the scope of an exception" and without an exception persons with disabilities may encounter barriers in accessing works.

The obligations enshrined in the CRPD further recognize the potential barrier that copyright law may have on ensuring access to cultural products for persons with disabilities. In Article 30, the CRPD states "States Parties shall take all appropriate steps [...] to ensure that laws protecting intellectual property rights [e.g., copyright] do not constitute an unreasonable or discriminatory barrier to access by persons with disabilities to cultural materials". The CRPD Committee provides an example where copyright law may act as a barrier accessing cultural products stating "[p]ersons with intellectual disabilities cannot enjoy a book if there is no easy-to-read version of it, augmentative and alternative modes". In other words, copyright law may prevent the reproduction of a book in an easy-to-read format that is accessible for persons with intellectual disabilities.

The concerns over copyright as a barrier to accessing cultural products have however been taken up by in the MAT adopted by the WIPO in 2013 as a means for promoting access to books for persons who are blind, visually impaired and print disabled. The MAT requires its contracting parties to adopt national law provisions that permit the reproduction, distribution and making available of published works in accessible formats through limitations and exceptions to the rights of copyright holders. Harpur and Suzor [28] noted that this law could provide a "baseline exception to global copyright norms to ensure that copyright does not operate as a barrier to accessibility". This entails the need of looking through country-specific situations for striking the balance between the two rights: access and protection. This would initiate examining the laws and the opportunities they provide. For instance, in discussing US copyright law, Cate [31] stated, "Copyright law protects only expression. No matter how original or creative, there is no protection for facts, ideas, procedures, processes, systems, methods of operation, concepts, principles, or discoveries. Even expression will not be protected if it includes one of a limited number of ways of conveying an idea, concept, or fact."

Those "expressions" can be channeled in text and/or multimedia format. Therefore, the argument for promoting accessible cultural products focuses on the channels for which a product is provided in a way that ensures equal access for persons with disabilities.

Several authors have examined the implementation of the MAT from a top-down perspective [3, 5, 6, 8, 34]. Li [3], examined the implementation of the MAT in the context of the "digital era". The author applied the obligations of the MAT to the use of ICT, and argued that national laws used to implement the MAT must consider ICT as a means for reproducing and distributing accessible cultural products.

Zemer and Gaon [8] examine the implementation of the MAT as a means for reforming national copyright exceptions. The authors argue that implementing the MAT aims to promote "the global public interest in accessing and using cultural resources". The authors argue that copyright reforms should take into account the benefits for persons with disabilities in general and resist limiting copyright exceptions only to persons that are blind, visually impaired and otherwise print disabled.

Sganga [6] analyses the implementation of the MAT by examining the tension between copyright and disability policies aimed at promoting social inclusion. The author argues for an approach that "moves beyond the mere provision of ad hoc exceptions and aims at building an international regulatory framework" for ensuring access to among other things, cultural products. The author concludes by stating that the EU and UN have attempted to establish stakeholder platforms for promoting access to cultural products for persons with disabilities. However, despite successful models based in local and national libraries, the EU and UN platforms have yet demonstrate a "positive effect on the percentage of cultural materials available in accessible formats".

5 Implementing Copyright Law in Norway

The Norwegian copyright law Section 16a provides libraries, archives, and museums the right to make copies of published works and make them available to the public. Article 17 of the law also recognizes the need to reproduce literary, scientific or musical works in a form suitable for the blind, visually impaired and others who have difficulty in reading. The Norwegian Library for Braille and Talking Books (NLB) has been responsible for reproducing and loaning books in braille or audio formats to users with impairments depending on their needs. However, the advent of digital content in libraries, antidiscrimination laws coupled with developments in technology set the precedent for all digital contents to be universally accessible wherever they are, either at mainstream or specialized libraries. Technologies to enforce copyright, though, have the potential to complicate the provision of accessible cultural products.

The task of ensuring access of information to all, however, needs to harness the provisions given by law for both parties (rights holders and users). The Norwegian Copyright Act Section 17 states the need for producing literary, scientific, or musical works in a form suitable for the blind, visually impaired and others with disability. Section 17a also states that "specified organizations and libraries, for royalty-free use of the disabled, shall be entitled to [...] make copies of published literary or scientific works by recording on a device which can reproduce it". The Norwegian Copyright Act must nevertheless be reconciled with the obligations enshrined in the Antidiscrimination Accessibility Act, which according to Section 12 states, "[b]reach of the duty to ensure universal design [...] shall constitute discrimination." Similar to the definition used in the CRPD, the Antidiscrimination Accessibility Act refers to universal design as "designing or accommodating the main solution [...] so that it can be used by as many people as possible". In 2013, the Norwegian government adopted regulations for the universal design of ICT solutions. According to the regulations websites must comply with the Web Content Accessibility Guidelines [35].

The analysis proceeds in two sections. First, this article examines copyright law in Norway as a form of social regulation and focuses on the mechanisms for ensuring accessible cultural products. Second, this article examines the interdependencies of non-State actors involved in implementing exceptions to copyright law in practice.

5.1 Copyright Law as Social Regulation

From a social regulation perspective, implementing copyright law and policy in Norway involves the use of legislative, financial and persuasive policies to encourage non-State actors to voluntarily create and distribute accessible cultural products.

The libraries interviewed included the University of Oslo Library, the library of Oslo and Akershus University College of Applied Sciences, the Norwegian Electronic Health Library and the National Library. The four libraries were approached based on the assumption that they have relatively well-developed digital services. The National library is mainly engaged in digitization of Norwegian cultural materials. The digitization process is regulated by the agreement the institution makes with rights holders. The other three libraries are less engaged in digitization and provide access to digital content through subscription licenses. Therefore, those libraries could present a examples for examining the relationship between copyright laws and organizational practices concerning the accessibility of digitized and born-digital cultural resources.

The results from the semi-structured interviews suggest that non-State actors adopt different approaches to promoting access to cultural products depending on the source of the product. For example, some respondents said their approach to ensuring accessibility varies depending on whether they produce or purchase the resource. Respondents mentioned that they have a policy that requires everything they produce (for example, open access journals, research works by students and teachers) to have a creative commons license. Creative commons licensing refers to a suite of licensing schemes that provide for the free distribution of a copyrighted work [36].

The respondents contrasted their approach to creating works with purchasing works stating that "But things we buy, of course we have to hold to the contract we have signed. But there is actually issue with interlibrary loan". The issue with interlibrary loan, as they explained it, was that they are not authorized to send an electronic article to students who request it. The library has to print it out and send it by mail. In other words, if a user of a library requests a copy of an electronic journal article from another library, the library that receives the request has to print that article and send it by mail. The respondents added that the library maintains a webpage that lists their eBook vendors and what those vendors allow users to do (e.g., copy, read only, etc.) the eBooks.

The results also suggested that while non-State actors in Norway are actively digitizing cultural products, agreements between libraries and publishers may limit the extent that libraries can distribute those cultural products in accessible formats. The national library is actively digitizing their entire collection including books, newspapers, photos and media. As a respondent explained, the Legal Deposit Act provides them the right to digitize for preservation purposes. They provide access to digitized works via an electronic service called "bokhylla.no" or "electronic bookshelf". However, as the respondent from the library explained, "dissemination of the digitized objects is [...] restricted to objects that are free, or objects where there is an agreement with the rights holders."

The contract between the national library and representative of the copyright holders affirms the right of the national library to make available published works covered by copyright, including "the necessary reproduction of viewing copies based on the digital storage copies that the National Library of Norway makes pursuant to the regulations issued pursuant to the Norwegian Copyright Act". The contract further states that the materials may be made available on the National Library of Norway webpages for users with Norwegian Internet Protocol (IP) addresses. IP addresses refer to the unique identifier attached to each device connected to the Internet. The contract adds that the library, on concrete requests, may give access to other users for distinct purposes mainly for education and research purposes. However, the material should be available only for viewing on computer screen, no printing and downloading allowed until the copyright protection period of the material expires.

When asked what they have done to make those digitized resources on bokhylla.no accessible for people with disabilities, a respondent from the national library expounded on the mechanisms used to protect documents saying the text is not exposed to users to prevent its download, copying, or modification. The respondent claims that the library has created prototype solutions for activating texts to make it accessible for screen readers but have not yet deployed the solution. In addition, according to publicly available documents, the contract between the national library and the right holders does not contain the provisions necessary for ensuring access to cultural products for persons with disabilities.

The data provides useful insights into the experience of libraries in signing agreements with content providers and the extent to which concerns of universal design are included either in procurement of resources or in digitization of already existing documents. The data suggests that complex barriers mediate access to cultural products, especially for people with disabilities. Nonetheless, the data also suggest that agreements between libraries and rights holders may provide a useful basis for ensuring access to cultural products in practice.

The agreements between libraries and content providers can be signed at institutional level or country level. The advantage of country level agreement could be the freedom they offer users to access the material they want from any institution in the country. National-level access would remove the need of repeated authentication and complications in interlibrary loans that may frustrate some users.

The data also suggest that approaches to ensuring accessibility may differ depending on whether the cultural product is "born-digital" or retroactively digitized. The data suggests that libraries subscribe to electronic journals and eBooks from different vendors who allow different levels of access to the content. Some content could be read, printed or downloaded (and accessible to screen readers) while others could not. The predominant mode of access for cultural products protected under copyright is the "view only" mode. This could make the materials inaccessible for people using text-to-speech tools. The efforts adopted by libraries to create technological solutions to make digitized documents accessible for screen readers and at the same time prevent them from being downloaded shows that there is some recognition for accessibility concerns.

5.2   Interrelations Among Non-state Actors

From a policy network perspective, ensuring access to culture for persons with disabilities involves a complex network of interdependent actors whose relationships, identities and levels of organization (e.g., national or international) influence the implementation of the MAT.

The results from the semi-structured interviews suggest that libraries depend on copyright holders to ensure access to cultural products. One respondent stated, "Copyright is often handled by these companies [i.e., copyright holders]". He explained the existence of different ways companies handle copyright issues which, as the result, requires different types of agreements to be signed between the library and the companies. The respondent added that "sometimes we manage to have good access other times it is not good, it is somehow complicated [...] some allow you only to read and the others allow you to download a chapter of a book". He further stated, "On each agreement, you have different kinds of solutions about access".

The results also suggested that despite the reliance on copyright holders to ensure access to cultural products, libraries sometimes have the opportunity to negotiate for improved access. A respondent said that they make agreements at national level and added,

In most cases we use the standard contracts we get from publishers, I usually browse through the contracts, in some case, for example, if they have paragraphs that puts limitations on how to use the content, I just delete it, and I never had any problem from the publishers. Because when we buy things on a national level, it doesn't really make any sense to have a paragraph about interlibrary loans, you know, because, through our agreement they have access anyway.

The respondent commented that the reason they sign agreements for national access was to make information available and easily accessible to all of their users.

In addition, the majority of the respondents mentioned the NLB as a place where people with disability can have access to cultural products suitable to their needs. While many libraries in Norway have physical facilities equipped with braille printers, magnifying screens, scanner mouse, etc. at the disposal of the user, the respondents mentioned that the needs of persons with disabilities are often better served by the NLB.

The data suggest that the different agreements between libraries and rights holders create a network of interdependencies. Clauses that protect the rights of all individuals to access cultural products could be included in negotiations between libraries and rights holders. These clauses could be part of a subscription service or a digitization program. This in turn would encourage libraries to integrate principles of universal design in organizational processes and identify opportunities for using copyright exceptions to negotiate with copyright holders for improved access.

6 Discussion and Conclusion

This article asked, "How can international copyright agreements promote access to culture for persons with disabilities?" To frame the answer to this question, this article introduced research that relates to policy implementation, social regulation and policy networks. This article demonstrates that, from a bottom-up perspective, implementing copyright law and policy involves an interdependent network of non-State actors that utilize contractual agreements for ensuring access to cultural products and balancing the rights of persons with disabilities and copyright holders.

This article builds on previous research by providing empirical evidence in support of theories on policy implementation. The results demonstrate that from a bottom-up perspective, non-State actors such as libraries and rights holders implement copyright law and policy in practice. The results extend previous research that examined the implementation of the MAT from a top-down perspective. This article argues that future research could usefully examine the role of libraries and publishers both as a comparative case study of national actors and a multilevel case study of regional, national and supranational actors.

The article also builds on previous research by providing empirical evidence in support of theories on social regulation. The results demonstrate that agreements between libraries and rights holders represent a form of social regulation between non-State actors. The results extend previous research on copyright law and policy by arguing that agreements between libraries and rights holders could provide a useful basis for ensuring access to cultural products in practice.

Finally, this article builds on previous research by providing empirical evidence in support of theories on policy networks. The results demonstrate that libraries often depend on rights holders to ensure access to cultural products. The results extend previous research on policy networks by arguing that while libraries may make cultural products openly available for redistribution, libraries rely on contractual agreements with rights holders to stipulate whether and how cultural products can be made accessible for persons with disabilities.

Thus, this article argues that although, exceptions may ensure that copyright does not pose a barrier to accessing cultural products for persons with disabilities, agreements between libraries and publishers may provide a useful basis for ensuring access to cultural products in practice. By providing new data on the mechanisms for ensuring the effective implementation of the MAT, national governments may, in the words of US President Barrack Obama, "[o]pen up a world of knowledge for persons with print disabilities by improving their access to published works" [37].

References

1. Lazar, J., Goldstein, D.F., Taylor, A.: Ensuring Digital Accessibility Through Process and Policy. Elsevier Science, Amsterdam (2015)
2. Ferri, D., Giannoumis, G.A.: A revaluation of the cultural dimension of disability policy in the European Union: the impact of digitization and web accessibility. Behav. Sci. Law 32(1), 33–51 (2014)
3. Li, J.: Facilitating access to digital content for the print disabled: the need to expand exemptions to copyright laws. Intellect. Prop J. 27(3), 355 (2015)
4. Papadopoulou, M.D.: Copyright exceptions and limitations for persons with print disabilities: the innovative Greek legal framework against the background of the international and European developments. Available at SSRN 1874620 (2010)
5. Rekas, A.: Tracking the progress of the proposed WIPO treaty on exceptions and limitations to copyright to benefit persons with print disabilities. In: Waddington, L., Quinn, G., Flynn, E. (eds.) European Yearbook of Disability Law, vol. 4. Intersentia, Cambridge (2013)
6. Sganga, C.: Disability, right to culture and copyright: which regulatory option? Int. Rev. Law Comput. Technol. 29, 88–115 (2015)
7. Williams, S.: Closing in on the light at WIPO: movement towards a copyright treaty for visually impaired persons and intellectual property movements. U. Pa. J. Int'l. L. 33, 1035 (2011)
8. Zemer, L., Gaon, A.: Copyright, disability and social inclusion: the Marrakesh Treaty and the role of non-signatories. J. Intellect. Property Law Pract. 10(11), 836–849 (2015)
9. Hill, M., Hupe, P.: Implementing Public Policy: An Introduction to the Study of Operational Governance. Sage, London (2008)
10. Matland, R.E.: Synthesizing the implementation literature: the ambiguity-conflict model of policy implementation. J. Public Adm. Res. Theor. 5(2), 145–174 (1995)
11. Sabatier, P.A.: Top-down and bottom-up approaches to implementation research: a critical analysis and suggested synthesis. J. Public Policy 6(01), 21–48 (1986)
12. DeGroff, A., Cargo M.: Policy implementation: implications for evaluation. In: Ottoson, J. M., Hawe, P. (eds.) Knowledge Utilization, Diffusion, Implementation, Transfer, and Translation: Implications for Evaluation. Wiley Subscription Services at Jossey-Bass, San Francisco (2009)

13. Ayres, I., Braithwaite, J.: Responsive Regulation Transcending the Deregulation Debate. Oxford University Press, New York (1992)
14. Jordana, J., Levi-Faur, D.: The politics of regulation in the age of governance. In: Jordana, J., Levi-Faur, D. (eds.) The Politics of Regulation Institutions and Regulatory Reforms for the Age of Governance. E. Elgar, Cheltenham (2004)
15. Levi-Faur, D.: Regulation and regulatory governance. In: Levi-Faur, D. (ed.) Handbook on the Politics of Regulation, pp. 3–21. Edward Elgar Pub, Cheltenham (2011)
16. Majone, G.: The European community between social policy and social regulation. JCMS J. Common Mark. Stud. 31(2), 153–170 (1993)
17. Töller, A.E.: Voluntary approaches to regulation - patterns, causes, and effects. In: Levi-Faur, D. (ed.) Handbook on the Politics of Regulation. Edward Elgar Pub., Cheltenham (2011)
18. Djelic, M.-L., Quack, S.: Transnational communities and governance. In: Djelic, M.-L., Quack, S. (eds.) Transnational Communities Shaping Global Economic Governance, pp. 3–36. Cambridge University Press, Cambridge (2010)
19. Rhodes, R.A.W.: Policy network analysis. In: Moran, M., Rein, M., Goodin, R.E. (eds.) The Oxford Handbook of Public Policy, pp. 425–447. Oxford University Press, Oxford (2006)
20. Merry, S.E.: Transnational human rights and local activism: mapping the middle. Am. Anthropol. J. 108, 31–51 (2006). American Anthropological Association
21. Adam, S., Kriesi, H.: The network approach. In: Sabatier, P.A. (ed.) Theories of the Policy Process, pp. 129–154. Westview Press, Boulder (2007)
22. Abbott, K., Snidal, D.: International regulation without international government: improving IO performance through orchestration. Rev. Int. Organ. 5(3), 315–344 (2010)
23. Yin, R.K.: Case Study Research: Design and Methods. Sage Publications, Thousand Oaks (2013)
24. George, A.L., Bennett, A.: Case Studies and Theory Development in the Social Sciences. MIT Press, Cambridge (2005)
25. Boix, C., Stokes, S.C.: Introduction. In: Boix, C., Stokes, S.C. (eds.) The Oxford Handbook of Comparative Politics. Oxford University Press, Oxford (2007)
26. Mitchell, J.C.: Case and situation analysis. Sociol. Rev. 31(2), 187–211 (1983)
27. Bouder-Pailler, D., Urbain, C.: How do the underprivileged access culture? Int. J. Arts Manag. 18(1), 65 (2015)
28. Harpur, P., Suzor, N.: The paradigm shift in realising the right to read: how ebook libraries are enabling in the university sector. Disabil. Soc. 29(10), 1658–1671 (2014)
29. ITU: Measuring the information society report. International Telecommunications Union, Geneva, Switzerland (2014)
30. Southwell, K.L., Slater, J.: An evaluation of finding aid accessibility for screen readers. Inf. Technol. Libr. 32(3), 34 (2013)
31. Cate, F.: Intellectual property and networked health information: issues and principles. Bull. Med. Libr. Assoc. 84(2), 229 (1996)
32. Kelly, B., et al.: From Web accessibility to Web adaptability. Disabil. Rehabil. Assist. Technol. 4(4), 212–226 (2009)
33. WIPO: Copyright (2016). http://www.wipo.int/copyright/en/. Accessed 19 March 2016
34. Williams, P.: Collaboration in Public Policy and Practice: Perspectives on Boundary Spanners. Policy Press, Bristol (2012)
35. Giannoumis, G.A.: Regulating web content: the nexus of legislation and performance standards in the United Kingdom and Norway. Behav. Sci. Law 32(1), 52–75 (2014)
36. Creative Commons: About the Licenses (2016). https://creativecommons.org/licenses/. Accessed 19 March 2016
37. Office of the Press Secretary: Letter to the Senate (2016)

The Information Repertoire
of People with Disabilities

Annegret Haage$^{(\boxtimes)}$ (ID)

Faculty of Rehabilitation Sciences,
TU Dortmund University, Dortmund, Germany
annegret.haage@tu-dortmund.de

Abstract. In a study on the information repertoire of people with disabilities in Germany, 617 people were asked which media they use to obtain information on topics relevant to them. The aim is to investigate participation in public communication and to find out which factors influence the size and diversity of the information repertoire of people with disabilities. The core of the study was a cluster analysis, which identified typical information repertoires. The clusters were compared in their composition according to social and impairment-related characteristics, barriers in the media and the importance of information needs.

As a result, six typical information repertoires were formed, which differ significantly in size and composition. From the clusters, constellations of contextual factors can be derived which particularly hinder or facilitate equal participation in public communication. Four particularly disadvantaged constellations were identified.

Keywords: Participation in public communication · Information repertoire · Disability · Digital disability divide · Accessibility · Media use

1 Introduction

Information has become an essential resource in society and an essential basis for economic value creation. It belongs to the basic functions of media. Equal access to information is of great importance for participation in society. According to the United Nations Convention on the Rights of Persons with Disabilities (UNCRPD), participation in public communications includes the right to freedom of expression and opinion and access to information (Article 21 of the UNCRPD). Article 9 of the UNCRPD (accessibility) establishes the right to equal access "to information and communications, including information and communications technologies and systems" [31].

To examine the participation of people with disabilities in public communication, the aspect of media in today's mediatized society [22] cannot be limited to "mass media". In converging media environments, the boundaries between mass communication and interpersonal communication, between the media-public sphere and the

The study was conducted as part of the author's dissertation at the TU Dortmund University [10].

M. Antona and C. Stephanidis (Eds.): HCII 2020, LNCS 12189, pp. 356–369, 2020.
https://doi.org/10.1007/978-3-030-49108-6_26

personal public sphere are blurred [28]. Previously clearly defined categories of media devices and services, of mass and individual communication can hardly be clearly distinguished today [21].

Social media and all kinds of intermediaries on the Internet have greatly changed the structure of the public sphere in recent decades and created new types of public spheres. Intermediaries include search engines, network platforms, video platforms and instant messenger services. They now represent an important route for accessing information and content [29].

In order to investigate participation in public communication, it is therefore necessary to include the entire range of possible sources and, in addition to online and offline journalistic media, to include numerous non-media Internet sources and intermediaries. The indicator for equal participation is not only the accessibility of media offerings, but also the actual use and perceived barriers to use. The latter is the subject of the present study. The use of media is considered with regard to individual media: How many people use a particular medium? However, the analysis of the audience of the respective media genres says little about how diverse and broad the media repertoire is that people use to inform themselves. The study therefore draws on the approach of information repertoires, a more recent theoretical approach from communication studies that looks at media use from a user-centred and holistic perspective [16, 17].

This study contributes to the identification of barriers and facilitators for the free and equal information in converging media environments in Germany. It examines where technical and social barriers impede their repertoire of information.

2 State of Research

On the one hand, digital media are said to have great potential to promote the equal participation of people with disabilities [4]. On the other hand, research by the digital divide shows that social inequality continues on the Internet [6, 19, 30]. Part of the digital divide research deals with disability, some researchers also speak of a "digital disability divide" [6, 9, 26]. This divide is not per se due to the impairment. Rather, disadvantages arise at different levels, which are closely linked. Impairment is often associated with social inequality. Many studies on impairment and digital inequality show a link between social and digital inequality among people with disabilities (PwD) [6, 8, 23], [32]. In comparative studies the social differences between people with and without disabilities were taken into account and controlled. Even then, differences in access and use were still apparent, indicating an digital *disability* divide [6], [32].

A central problem is the technical barriers in the media - inaccessible websites, complex structures and language, videos without subtitles and audio description, and incompatibility with assistive technologies. The high innovation density of mainstream technologies and applications is a challenge for assistive technologies, especially for assistive software like screen readers [12], [32]. In addition, there is insufficient support from the personal and professional environment for PwD who need assistance [13, 18]. In many countries, such as Germany, legislation does not sufficiently obligate the media and ICT to provide accessibility and does not sufficiently monitor compliance with legal standards. This is why Germany has already been called upon several times by the UN Committee on the Rights of Persons with Disabilities to "explain the strategies and action plans concerning the availability and accessibility of public information, including websites, television and various public and private, as well as social, media for persons with disabilities and their specific timeframes" [5].

Some studies identify little motivation among people with disabilities to use digital technologies. The lack of motivation can result from discouraging barriers in the media and/or a lack of media literacy and experience with the Internet [26], [32]. Lack of experiential knowledge makes it more difficult to learn new skills on the Internet. This creates a vicious circle that hinders the acquisition of media competence [13].

At the same time, a number of empirical studies show that digital media promote the participation of people with disabilities in public and private communication and that these advantages are used intensively by many people. In a comparative study in the USA, PwD used online activities in the area of cultural production such as downloading videos, online games and posting their own content more often than people without disabilities [6]. A study in Germany on the use of Web 2.0 applications showed similar results [1]. The convergent media landscape therefore has the potential to provide suitable formats for the different needs.

The type of impairment determines whether and how media are used and which functions and information needs are satisfied with which media devices and media types. For example, people with hearing impairments use the Internet more often than people with other impairments because they encounter fewer barriers than people with visual impairments, with the exception of audio-visual formats [1, 2, 6]. Television plays still a major role in the media resources of PwD. More PwD regularly watch TV compared to the general population in Germany [11].

It can be assumed that the information repertoire is influenced by the interaction of personal and environmental context factors with the impairments.

3   Research Design

The aim of the present study is to examine the information repertoire of people with disabilities. Therefore, research instruments from two disciplines were combined: the ICF classification system from inclusion research[1] and the information repertoire approach from media studies.

The information repertoire approach is an analytical concept to investigate media use in a time of deep mediatization [15]. While audience research mainly investigates the audiences of individual media genres, repertoire-oriented research records which media a person uses. The approach investigates not only the use of individual media genres, but also the repertoire that people put together to find out about the environmental conditions relevant to them [14, 17].

People compile their repertoire of information by selecting from a variety of sources those that are meaningful, useful and accessible to them. The totality of the

---

[1] There is no clear translation for "Teilhabeforschung" in German-speaking countries.

repertoire shows how manifold the people inform themselves. The relative weight of media genres in the repertoires provides information about preferences, facilitators and barriers. Thus, the composition of the repertoires makes it clear which media genres meet the needs of people with different impairments particularly well. On the other hand, barriers become visible when media offers are not used, although respondents would like to do so.

Due to its three principles of user orientation, wholeness and relativity, the information repertoire approach is a useful tool to investigate the use of information from the perspective of participation in public communication. The ICF is the conceptual interface for examining the information repertoire under the conditions of health problems. The ICF is an instrument to identify disability in activities and involvement in life situations. According to the ICF's understanding, disability is the result of the interaction of impairments and the personal and environmental contextual factors [33]. In order to investigate participation restrictions in the domain of public communication, media activities and relevant context factors must be surveyed. Figure 1 illustrates the operationalization of the research project using the ICF model of the interaction between the ICF components. The environmental and personal factors were derived from the state of research.

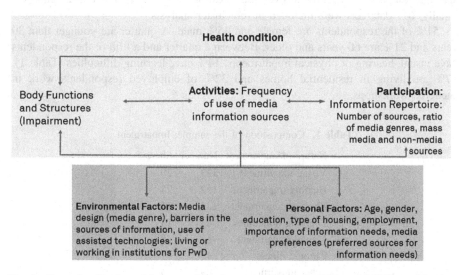

Fig. 1. Operationalization of the research project according to the ICF model [33], modification by the author

In the explorative study, 663 people with disabilities were asked online and in face-to-face interviews how often they use 31 predefined sources of information and which they would use more frequently if they were accessible. The sources are divided into the media genres of television, radio and newspapers, with a distinction being made as to whether they were used via legacy devices or online. In addition, other Internet sources not published by professional media organisations, search engines and social media were queried.

In addition, the participants were asked how important different areas of information needs are to them and which are the preferred sources of information for the different information needs. Finally, the relevant context factors were queried, as shown in Fig. 1 (personal data, the nature of the impairment, the use of assistive technology).

The core of the evaluation was a cluster analysis with which typical information repertoires can be identified. The clusters were compared in their composition according to social and impairment-related characteristics, barriers in the media and the importance of information needs. The assumption was that typical participation constellations can be derived from the types of information repertoires. From this, conclusions can be drawn as to which contextual factors are more likely to facilitate or hinder a broad information repertoire.

4   The Results

4.1   The Sample

A total of 663 PwD answered the survey. 446 answered online, 171 were interviewed face to face. In preparation for the cluster analysis, the sample was adjusted by 46 data sets that did not sufficiently answer the questions relevant to the cluster analysis. Finally, 617 data sets were included in the cluster analysis.

51% of the respondents are female and 45% male. A quarter are younger than 30 years and 21% are 60 years and older. Between a quarter and a fifth of the respondents have visual, hearing or physical impairments, 14% have learning difficulties (Table 1). 17% are living in residential homes and 32% of employed respondents work in sheltered workshops.

Table 1. Composition of the sample: Impairment

Nature of impairment	Number	Share
Visual impairment	123	20
Hearing impairment	152	25
Physical impairment	132	21
Learning difficulties	85	14
Mental impairment	51	8
Chronic illness	45	7
Other impairment	29	5

The sample is not representative for the total of people with disabilities in Germany. Younger and higher educated people are overrepresented. For the exploratory study, however, it was possible to ensure that the important subgroups according to impairment and subgroups such as visual or hearing status or communication orientation are represented in sufficient numbers to be able to make statements about the subgroups.

4.2   The Cluster Analysis

The aim of the cluster analysis is a typology of information repertoires of people with disabilities. The clusters were determined using the ward-procedure. The 31 variables of the information sources were included in the analysis. The analysis was preceded by a factor analysis to reduce outlier values and measurement errors [7, 27].

Six clusters have been identified that can be well described and explained from theory. They comprise between 165 and 75 respondents and differ in the size and diverse composition of the respective information repertoire (Table 2).

Table 2. Overview of the clusters [10]

Name	Number of respondents	Short description
1 Versatilely informed hearing impaired people	112	Highest number of information sources, many newspapers, little radio; political and social focus, high barriers with audiovisual media, very many deaf respondents, high percentage of high school graduates
2 Young social media-oriented, information disadvantaged	165	Smallest information repertoire, focus on social media and personal sources, lowest interest in information, high barrier experience in all genres, many young respondents, many work and/or live in institutions for PwD
3 Older visually impaired Minimal-Onliner	94	Medium repertoire with a lot of radio but few newspapers and Internet, medium interest in information needs, especially in everyday questions and world affairs, highest share of experiences with barriers, especially Internet and newspapers, over 50 s, highest share of visually impaired respondents
4 Younger highly educated Internet users	75	Medium repertoire with a clear focus on internet sources and online media, medium interest in information, especially in special topics, little experience with barriers, most likely barriers with quality newspapers, high percentage of high school graduates, all kinds of impairments
5 Very old user of legacy devices with high interest in local information	75	Below average repertoire with above average use of radio and newspapers, but hardly any use of the Internet, medium interest in information, above average interest in local information, little experience of barriers, very old respondents, all kinds of impairments
6 Versatile informed and Infotainment Oriented	93	Second largest repertoire, varied in all genres, infotainment orientation, high interest in information in all areas, little experience with barriers, only with newspapers and media libraries of professional media organisations, younger to middle-aged respondents of all impairments except hearing, second highest percentage of visual impairments and learning difficulties

The short portraits of the clusters already show that there are different constellations of participation in public communication. On the positive side, all clusters have a repertoire from different media genres and all use both information sources from professional media organisations and other Internet sources.

Basically, the potential of convergent high choice media landscape for various impairments is evident. Certain forms of media are suitable for certain types of impairments, as no disabilities occur. This applies to people with visual impairments for audio media and to people with hearing impairments for text media. In digital media environments, it is also possible to offer accessible media forms that are not initially accessible to people with sensory impairments. Text information can be made accessible through screen readers, videos become usable through subtitles, sign language translation or audio descriptions. This advantage can be seen in the results of the study, the sources of information on the Internet play an important role in all clusters. In almost all clusters, more sources on the Internet are used daily than via legacy devices. An exception is cluster 5 of very old people, who use very few online sources. However, it also shows that not everyone benefits in the same way from the potential of the convergent media landscape as a support factor.

4.3   Disabling Constellations of Context Factors

The cluster analysis showed that the interaction of several contextual factors tends to hinder participation in public communication.

Barriers in the Media, Age and Visual Impairment

Severely visually impaired and blind respondents over the age of 50 are confronted with a particularly high number of barriers in the media. Many of them are therefore to be found in clusters with a medium or rather small information repertoire (No. 3 or 5). In particular, they would make more frequent use of TV stations' media libraries online, local and regional daily newspapers offline and online, as well as websites of other providers and social media. However, they are not or only with difficulty accessible for them. At a high age over 70, most respondents decide against using the Internet and online media. Many do not acquire visual impairment until adulthood. For older people, learning to use digital media and assistive technologies in retirement can be a major hurdle. Respondents over 70 years of age use screen readers significantly less often than younger. Screen readers in particular require users to have good imagination and memory. Mobile media, which offer advantages for many impaired people due to their intuitive operation, also place demands on blind people in these two respects.

As software-based assistive technologies, screen readers, magnification software and voice-overs are dependent on the accessibility of digital media. In Germany, there are major accessibility problems, especially in the websites of print media, media libraries of television and radio stations. In addition, there are updates and relaunches of apps and Internet pages to which screen readers must respond. This discourages older visually impaired people in particular from using online media. If the accessibility and usability of Internet media does not improve, this very generation is in danger of being left behind by digital change (Fig. 2).

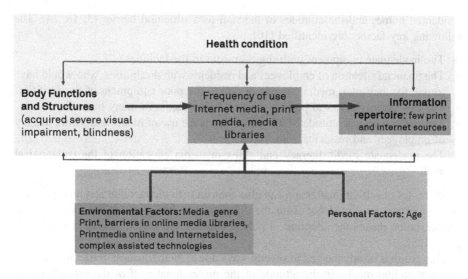

Fig. 2. Disabling constellation of barriers in the media, age and visual impairment [10]

Special Institutions, Usability and Barriers in the Media

Those who work and live in special institutions for PwD are above average in cluster 2 with by far the smallest information repertoire. These are mainly people with learning difficulties, psychological and physical impairments, who have a need for support in everyday life and probably also in the use of digital media. The respondents in this cluster are rather young and use mainly popular social media such as messengers like WhatsApp, video platforms like YouTube and social networks like Facebook. Their interest in general political and social information is relatively low. Their first source of information in most areas such as city and region, topics and groups of interest as well as everyday issues are not media, but family, friends or employees of the special institutions in which they work or live.

Exclusion in work and life apparently also leads to a lower interest in information and a rather small and less diverse repertoire of information. Barriers in the media also contribute to this, because many respondents would use media that report on politics and society more often if they were accessible to them. Most frequently they mention television news online and offline, radio and local newspapers. Barriers therefore occur in all media genres and formats. Taking the need for support as a common feature, the media barriers are likely to be mainly in the complexity on different levels:

- Complex structure of media offerings, which is subject to constant change
- Complex user guidance
- Text heaviness and heavy language
- Insufficiently explained backgrounds.

The influence of living and working in special institutions on the information repertoire is closely related to the type of impairment and the resulting need for support. A number of studies point to the structural conditions in the sheltered workshops and residential homes and the attitudes of the staff as a structural barrier [3, 18, 24]. The following key factors are identified [10]:

- The inadequate equipment with digital media in the facilities
- The financial situation of employees and residents with disabilities, who would have to pay for their own media equipment due to the poor equipment of the facilities.
- The low priority given to participation in digital media in many institutions
- The rather sceptical attitude of the staff towards the use of media and media literacy of employees and residents with impairments
- The inadequate media literacy and skills in media education of the pedagogical staff.

Processes of self-stigmatization can also contribute to the fact that certain topics and media formats are sorted out from the outset as too complex for themselves. Self-stigmatization means the adoption of public stigmata and prejudices about one's own group [25].

This group is disadvantaged in several ways due to their situation in life: in mate-rial access to digital media, in the attitude of the professional staff of the institutions, in motivation and barriers in the media (Fig. 3).

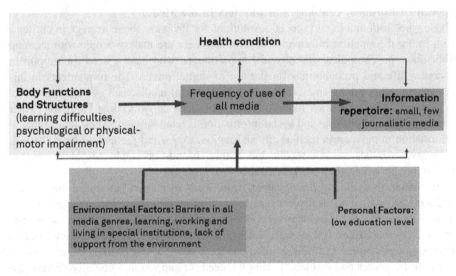

Fig. 3. Disabling constellation of special institutions, usability and barriers in the media [10]

Hearing Impairment and Low Education Level

A large proportion of respondents with hearing impairment belong to clusters with a large and varied repertoire. However, a close connection with a high and middle education level is evident. Younger deaf and hard of hearing respondents with lower education level are often found in cluster 2 with the smallest repertoire. They are particularly disadvantaged by barriers in the media and a limited literacy skills.

Text information plays an important role for hearing impaired respondents. However, this is often too difficult for this group. Learning the written language is more difficult in cases of prelingual deafness or severe hearing loss. In Germany, there is also often a lack of adequate support in schools [20]. Subtitles are often too complex and too fast for information programs. However, sign language translations are still rare on German television. This has serious consequences for the information repertoire, as radio is not an appropriate source of information. Therefore, this group is also disadvantaged in terms of information in Germany (Fig. 4).

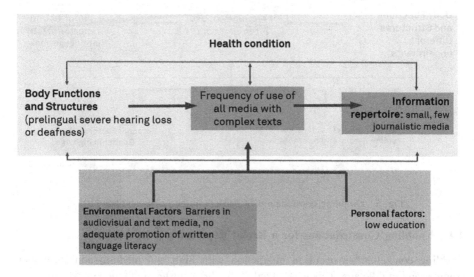

Fig. 4. Disabling constellation of hearing impairment and low education level

Age, Impairment, Barriers and Usability of Internet Resources

People of retirement age use digital media significantly less often than younger people. This difference is even greater for people with disabilities. Other studies have shown a correlation with education [22]. A high level of education facilitates access to the Internet at an advanced age. In the present study, there were no significant correlations with education in the over-70s age group ($p = 0.087$). In combination with an impairment, the entry is apparently so difficult that even older people with a medium and high level of education do not dare to enter the Internet. This applies to all impairments. Only at a high age over 70 years there is still a difference by gender. Women with disabilities over 70 use less often than men in the same age group.

If Internet media were more easily structured and universally accessible, the repertoire of older PwD might be more diverse.

For people with learning difficulties and with physical and motor impairments, this age effect occurs earlier. In these groups, significantly more people over 50 years of age are represented in cluster 5 with few Internet sources than in the other types of impairments. There are correlations with the activity in sheltered workshops ($p = 0.046$). Those who work there are unlikely to come into contact with the Internet through their work. However, for age groups that did not grow up with the Internet, work is an important driver for including the Internet in their media repertoire in the course of adult life (Fig. 5).

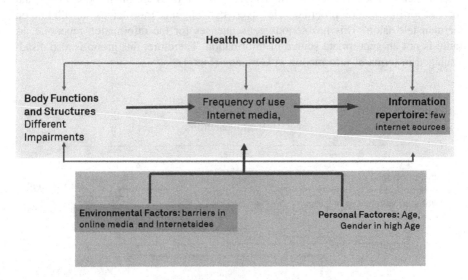

Fig. 5. Disabling constellation of barriers in the media and age [10]

4.4   Enabling Constellations for a Broad Repertoire of Information

Enabling constellations occur in interaction with high and medium education and younger and middle age. This is reflected in the three clusters with the largest and most diverse information repertoires.

The younger the respondents are, the more likely they are to use many social media and Internet sources for information and fewer journalistic media sources. A high level of education increases the probability of belonging to cluster 4, in which the whole range of non-media and journalistic digital media is used. There is no concentration on a particular impairment, so it can be assumed that the Internet resources are well suited to the different needs. The respondents seem to have a high level of competence in dealing with digital media, which also enables them to deal with hurdles and barriers in the media. According to an earlier study on Web 2.0 use, many PwD are developing strategies to access the desired content despite barriers on the Internet [1].

Particularly in the case of sensory impairments, the interplay of younger and middle age and middle and high education promotes a diverse repertoire of information. However, barriers in the media cannot always be compensated by good strategies. Deaf respondents often state that they would watch more television programs if they were accessible. Visually impaired and blind respondents criticize barriers in print media and Internet sources that they cannot overcome. For them, the time of occurrence of the impairment also plays a role. The earlier the impairment was acquired, the greater and more diverse the repertoire of information. They have grown up with digital media and assistive technologies and have probably already learned how to use them in education.

Higher educational qualifications are less common among respondents with physical impairments and learning difficulties. In clusters 1 and 4 with large and diverse information repertoires, hardly any respondents from these groups are to be found. The unequal distribution of educational opportunities also affects the information repertoire.

5 Conclusion

The aim of this exploratory study was to find an approach that goes beyond previous studies on media use by PwDs and examines participation in public communication across all media. In order to develop an indicator for participation, two research approaches were combined: the repertoire-oriented approach of media use research and the classification scheme of the ICF. The information repertoires make it possible to draw conclusions about participation in public communication from the survey of the use of media genres. The ICF provides the interface to analyze the interplay of relevant context factors in the environment and the individual that influence the information repertoire. This allowed the identification of constellations of contextual factors that have a particularly hindering effect on the information repertoire. It can be deduced which groups are particularly disadvantaged and where there are particularly urgent fields of action.

The poor accessibility of many media is one of the most important fields of action. Above all, respondents would use more journalistic sources in all media genres if they were accessible to them. This is a challenge for media organizations, but also for politicians. It is to be hoped that the EU Accessibility Directives, which have currently been transposed into national law in Germany, will have a positive effect. However, the associations for PwD are particularly critical of the laws affecting the journalistic media. There are still no concrete obligations and quota for the media in Germany.

However, the study also shows that equal participation in public communication is related to the level of general inclusion in society. Exclusion in education and work also has a negative impact on the information repertoire.

References

1. Berger, A., Caspers, T., Croll, J., et al.: Web 2.0/barrierefrei. Eine Studie zur Nutzung von Web 2.0 Anwendungen durch Menschen mit Behinderung, Bonn (2010)
2. Bosse, I., Hasebrink, U.: Mediennutzung von Menschen mit Behinderungen. Forschungs-bericht (2016). http://www.kme.tu-dortmund.de/cms/de/Aktuelles/aktuelle-Meldungen/Lang fassung-der-Studie-_Mediennutzung-von-Menschen-mit-Behinderungen_-veroeffentlicht/ Studie-Mediennutzung_Langfassung_final.pdf
3. Bosse, I., Zaynel, N., Lampert, C.: MeKoBe - Medienkompetenz in der Behindertenhilfe in Bremen. Bedarfserfassung und Handlungsempfehlungen für die Gestaltung von Fortbildun-gen zur Medienkompetenzförderung. Abschlussbericht (2018). http://www.bremische-landesmedienanstalt.de/studie-zu-medienkompetenz-der-behindertenhilfe-veroeffentlicht. Accessed 15 Nov 2018
4. Bühler, C.: Sieben Fragen zur inklusiven Medienbildung. In: Bosse, I. (ed.) Medienbildung im Zeitalter der Inklusion, Düsseldorf, pp. 27–57 (2012)

5. Committee on the Rights of Persons with Disabilities. List of issues prior to submission of the combined second and third periodic report of Germany (2018). https://www.gemeinsam-einfach-machen.de/GEM/DE/AS/UN_BRK/Staatenpruefung/Zweite_Staatenpruefung/Bericht_englisch.pdf?__blob=publicationFile&v=2. Accessed 14 Feb 2020
6. Dobransky, K., Hargittai, E.: Unrealized potential. Exploring the digital disability divide. Poetics **58**, 18–28 (2016). https://doi.org/10.1016/j.poetic.2016.08.003
7. Döring, N., Bortz, J. (eds.): Forschungsmethoden und Evaluation in den Sozial- und Humanwissenschaften. Springer-Lehrbuch. Springer, Heidelberg (2016). https://doi.org/10.1007/978-3-642-41089-5
8. Duplaga, M.: Digital divide among people with disabilities: analysis of data from a nationwide study for determinants of Internet use and activities performed online. PLoS ONE **12**(6), e0179825 (2017). https://doi.org/10.1371/journal.pone.0179825
9. Goggin, G.: Disability and digital inequalities. rethinking digital divides with disability theory. In: Ragnedda, M., Muschert, G.W. (eds.) Theorizing Digital Divides, pp. 63–74. Routledge, London (2018)
10. Haage, A.: Das Informationsrepertoire von Menschen mit Beeinträchtigungen. Eine Studie zur Mediennutzung von Menschen mit Beeinträchtigungen. Dissertation, TU Dortmund (2019)
11. Haage, A., Bosse, I.K.: Media use of persons with disabilities. In: Antona, M., Stephanidis, C. (eds.) UAHCI 2017. LNCS, Part III, vol. 10279, pp. 419–435. Springer, Cham (2017). https://doi.org/10.1007/978-3-319-58700-4_34
12. Haage, A., Bühler, C.: Barrierefreiheit. In: Bosse, I., Schluchter, J.-R., Zorn, I. (eds.) Handbuch Inklusion und Medienbildung, pp. 207–215. Beltz Juventa, Weinheim (2019)
13. Haage, A., Zaynel, N.: Medienpädagogische Qualität bedeutet, alle zu berücksichtigen. Erkenntnisse aus der Forschung zur Mediennutzung, Medienkompetenz und -bildung von Menschen mit Beeinträchtigungen. In: Knaus, T., Meister, D., Narr, K. (eds.) Futurelab Medienpädagogik, pp. 167–180. kopaed, München (2018)
14. Hasebrink, U., Domeyer, H.: Zum Wandel von Informationsrepertoires in konvergierenden Medienumgebungen. In: Hartmann, M., Hepp, A. (eds.) Die Mediatisierung der Alltagswelt, pp. 49–64. VS Verlag für Sozialwissenschaften/GWV Fachverlage, Wiesbaden (2010)
15. Hasebrink, U., Hepp, A.: How to research cross-media practices? Investigating media repertoires and media ensembles. Convergence **23**(4), 362–377 (2017). https://doi.org/10.1177/1354856517700384
16. Hasebrink, U., Hölig, S.: Deconstructing audiences in converging media environments. In: Sparviero, S., Peil, C., Balbi, G. (eds.) Media Convergence and Deconvergence, pp. 113–133. Springer International Publishing, Cham (2017)
17. Hasebrink, U., Popp, J.: Media repertoires as a result of selective media use. A conceptual approach to the analysis of patterns of exposure. **31**(3), 369–387 (2006). https://doi.org/10.1515/COMMUN.2006.023
18. Heitplatz, V.N., Bühler, C., Hastall, M.R.: Caregivers' influence on smartphone usage of people with cognitive disabilities: an explorative case study in Germany. In: Antona, M., Stephanidis, C. (eds.) HCII 2019. LNCS, vol. 11573, pp. 98–115. Springer, Cham (2019). https://doi.org/10.1007/978-3-030-23563-5_9
19. Helsper, E.J., Reisdorf, B.C.: The emergence of a "digital underclass" in Great Britain and Sweden: changing reasons for digital exclusion. New Med. Soc. **19**(8), 1253–1270 (2017). https://doi.org/10.1177/1461444816634676
20. Hennies, J.: Prälinguale Hörbehinderung und Schriftsprachkompetenz. In: Maaß, C., Rink, I. (eds.) Handbuch Barrierefreie Kommunikation, pp. 201–220. Frank & Timme Verlag für wissenschaftliche Literatur, Berlin (2019)

21. Hölig, S., Domeyer, H., Hasebrink, U.: Souveräne Bindungen: Zeitliche Bezüge in Medienrepertoires und Kommunikationsmodi. In: Suckfüll, M. (ed.) Rezeption und Wirkung in zeitlicher Perspektive, 1st edn, pp. 70–88. Nomos, Baden-Baden (2011)
22. Krotz, F.: Mediatisierung. Fallstudien zum Wandel von Kommunikation, 1. Aufl. Medien - Kultur - Kommunikation. VS, Verl. für Sozialwiss, Wiesbaden (2007)
23. Macdonald, S.J., Clayton, J.: Back to the future, disability and the digital divide. Disabil. Soc. 28(5), 702–718 (2013). https://doi.org/10.1080/09687599.2012.732538
24. Mayerle, M.: Berufsfeld Tagesförderung/ Wohneinrichtungen. In: Bosse, I., Schluchter, J.-R., Zorn, I. (eds.) Handbuch Inklusion und Medienbildung, pp. 170–180. Beltz Juventa, Weinheim (2019)
25. Röhm, A.: Stigmatisierung und Entstigmatisierung von Menschen mit Behinderungen: Einfluss unterschiedlicher medialer Darstellungen auf Einstellungen und Handlungsintentionen. Dissertation, TU Dortmund (2017)
26. Sachdeva, N., Tuikka, A.-M., Kimppa, K.K., et al.: Digital disability divide in information society. A framework based on a structured literature review. J. Inf. Commun. Ethics Soc. 13 (3/4), 283–298 (2015). https://doi.org/10.1108/jices-10-2014-0050
27. Schendera, C.F.G.: Clusteranalyse mit SPSS. Mit Faktorenanalyse. Wirtschaftsmathematik- und Statistik 8-2011. Oldenbourg, München (2010)
28. Schmidt J-H (2013) Social Media. Medienwissen kompakt. Imprint: Springer VS, Wiesbaden
29. Trültzsch, S., Kouts-Klemm, R., Aroldi, P.: Transforming digital divide in different national contexts. In: Carpentier, N., Schröder, K.C., Hallett, L. (eds.) Audience Transformations Shifting Audience Positions in Late Modernity, pp. 191–209. Routledge, New York (2014)
30. United Nations. Convention on the Rights of Persons with Disabilities (2006). https://www.un.org/development/desa/disabilities/convention-on-the-rights-of-persons-with-disabilities/convention-on-the-rights-of-persons-with-disabilities-2.html. Accessed 10 Feb 2020
31. Vicente, M.R., López, A.J.: A multidimensional analysis of the disability digital divide. Some evidence for internet use. Inf. Soc. 26(1), 48–64 (2010). https://doi.org/10.1080/01615440903423245

Stakeholder Journey
Analysis for Innovation

A Multiparty Analysis Framework for Startups

Jo E. Hannay$^{(\boxtimes)}$ ⓘ, Kristin Skeide Fuglerud ⓘ, and Bjarte M. Østvold ⓘ

Norwegian Computing Center, Postboks 114 Blindern, 0314 Oslo, Norway
{jo.hannay,kristin.skeide.fuglerud,bjarte}@nr.no

Abstract. When analysing how the information-technological innovation of a startup company is perceived to affect the market, we encountered challenges when using existing customer journey analysis frameworks. In particular, we identified a need to express critical events for technology adoption, a need to express universal access principles and a need to express journeys for multiple stakeholders in the same diagram; all in an easily readable manner. To do this, we extended an existing stripped-down customer journey framework with elements for the above aspects. We present this extended framework as a *stakeholder journey framework*. Based on the initial application of this framework on the startup company's innovation product, we conclude that the stakeholder journey framework aided in uncovering issues within technology adoption and universal access that would otherwise not have been addressed.

Keywords: Customer journey analysis · Stakeholder journey framework · Innovation · Technology adoption · Universal access

1 Introduction

Organisations who wish to introduce new IT services into the market face particular challenges regarding needs analysis and requirements engineering. Innovation implies, in many instances, not only the introduction of new services, but also establishing the market's perceived need for those services. Innovation can aim at augmenting existing business processes, as in *value chain innovation*,[1] whereas in *disruptive innovation*, new technological services do not merely meet needs and demands of existing business processes, they change business and societal processes or create new ones altogether [16].

Some disruptive innovations can trigger total discontinuities in the market. Geoffrey A. Moore describes how the exponential growth in computing power (in line with namesake Gordon E. Moore's law [20]) routinely destabilises the entire IT sector, creating instability that unleashes "vortexes" of new market demand [17]. The romantic vision of "unicorn startups" arises perhaps from those companies that strike gold; both when creating vortexes (Facebook) and

---

[1] https://www.gsb.stanford.edu/faculty-research/centers-initiatives/vcii.

© Springer Nature Switzerland AG 2020
M. Antona and C. Stephanidis (Eds.): HCII 2020, LNCS 12189, pp. 370–389, 2020.
https://doi.org/10.1007/978-3-030-49108-6_27

when using their momentum to create successes within a vortex (WhatsApp, Angry Birds). The people behind such chance innovations (which were not meant to be innovations at all) had seemingly no other plan than to fulfil a, perhaps trivial, need for themselves and their friends. Such has become the allure of non-deliberated fortune that organised venture capital initiatives now are referred to as "garages".

However, according to a recent analysis of 1,100 startups, only a little over one percent succeed;[2] the most frequent reason for failure being "no market need".[3] For the vast majority of innovationists, this suggests that a better understanding of what an innovation addresses and in what situations it will be used would reduce the risk of failure. This entails, at least to some degree, that aiming for value chain innovation might more likely lead to success than would an aim to disrupt the market.

Design thinking and customer journey analysis (CJA) [2] are currently in vogue as mind- and toolsets for understanding how customers would use services as a part of their profession or in their lives. This helps to deliberate on the *whole product* [16], not just some technical functionality in isolation. CJA takes many forms and involves variations of process flows in terms of phases, customer actions, touchpoints with technology, emotions, thoughts and more. By now, there is a proliferation of CJA methods and templates offered by consulting companies.

Recently, a stripped-down customer journey framework (CJF) was presented which models customer journeys purely in terms of touchpoints with technology, along with annotations that indicate phases and other process flow elements [10]. Further, the CJF promotes the elicitation and comparison of *planned* versus *actual* customer journeys. Here, we focus on eliciting planned journeys; that is, the intended use of an innovation, as perceived prior to deployment.

Due to its frugality, we are able to apply an extended version of the CJF to a complex case, in which a startup company is running a project to develop digital, AI-supported information services for facilitating property (real estate) buying and selling processes. The complexity arises from the fact that multiple stakeholders are involved who traditionally have conflicting interests and from the fact that these stakeholders have different key technology adopter roles in Rogers' *innovativeness* dimension [18]. For example, if the service offers better and more detailed information on a property's true state, property buyers may be the *early adopters* of the service technology, eager to be equipped with better information for their potential bid. On the other hand, estate agents may take the role of the *late majority*, not willing to use the service during marketing and sales unless everyone else in the business does so; thereby potentially halting the innovation if they are the primary service onboarders.

There is a fundamental challenge as to the nature and amount of information to present through the service. Decision making relies on salient and actionable cues [1,8]. Startups often have an abundance of ideas, and it is essential to

---

[2] https://www.cbinsights.com/research/venture-capital-funnel-2/.

[3] https://www.cbinsights.com/research/startup-failure-reasons-top/.

understand what functionality gives added value rather than produces waste and confusion [5]. Moore proposes that technology adopters look for solutions to only a narrow set of problems [16].

In many countries, there is an increased focus on accessibility for people with disabilities through politics and legislation. Directive (EU) 2016/2102 of the European Parliament on the accessibility of websites and mobile applications requires public bodies to ensure that their websites and apps are accessible to persons with disabilities. The directive refers to the Web Content Accessibility Guidelines (WCAG) 2.1[4]. The aim of these guidelines is to make functionality perceivable, operable, understandable and robust for a wide range of people, without adding extra functionality or a specialised design for certain user groups. In Norway, most of these requirements will apply for private organisations as well. The more a service is digitised, the more dependent its users become on the accessibility, usability and utility of each touchpoint.

In spite of the adoption of accessibility legislation in EU and many countries, the needs and perspectives of people with disabilities are often ignored during service design, and it is rarely mentioned in academic literature on customer journey analysis. At the EU level, about 26.3% of women aged 16 and over, and 21.8% of men of the same age group, declare a disability [9]. This means that it is important to consider their needs and perspectives to avoid design exclusion of this rather large minority.

To illustrate how an innovation can address universal accessibility, there is therefore a focus on universal accessibility in our extended CJF.

2   Stakeholder Journey Framework

We call our extension of the CJF of Halvorsen *et al.* [10], a stakeholder journey framework (SJF).

The CJF of Halvorsen *et al.* [10] has a focus on technology *touchpoints*; that is, integral points of contact and interaction with technology. The CJF operates with two types of touchpoint; namely, those initiated by the service provider (blue circle in Fig. 1) and those initiated by the service consumer (orange circle in Fig. 1).

We think of such an integral point of contact as an interaction with technology that allows a user to perform a well-defined task that can be initiated and concluded as a single event in ones' daily life, but perhaps being a part of a larger sequence of events. A task performed with a mobile app is an example of such a touchpoint.

2.1   Services

The functionality that enables a task to be completed in a touchpoint is often offered as a *service* [4,14]. The service concept embodies a host of principles, but

---

[4] https://www.w3.org/TR/WCAG21/.

central is the principle of loose coupling in the sense that the service consumer owns or provides the data, while the service provider owns or provides the functionality to process that data. Services can also vary in terms of statefullness; in that they may or may not need to maintain portions of system state over a period of time. The degree of statefullness coincides with the need for a service to function in an isolated event or in a sequence of events.

In the SJF, we formulate touchpoints in terms of services. A solid arrow (Fig. 1) between touchpoints indicates that the underlying services share state. This includes sharing data.

2.2 Technology Adoption

The SJF extends the CJF by expressing crucial points for technology adoption. A filled light-green circle (Fig. 1) indicates a touchpoint that exposes or introduces a consumer to a service and which is considered crucial for adoption of the technological innovation in that service. People who do adopt innovations at a stage before the innovation is at all common in the market are the *early adopters* in Rogers' terminology [18]. Rogers characterises an early adopter as an "individual to check with"; that is, someone to whom others who are sitting on the fence waiting to see if an innovation is worth trying, will look to for positive or negative cues. Early adopters are therefore crucial actors for advancing an innovation in the market. A filled dark-green circle (Fig. 1) indicates a touchpoint that is crucial for adoption, and where there is an active push of a service by either the provider or a consumer of the service. People who push innovations in this way sort under what Rogers calls *innovators*. Innovators often have an interest in innovations as such, regardless of their (economic) benefit, or they have a degree of venturesomeness that enables them to take risks in adopting technology not yet subjected to the masses. Innovators are those individuals who launch the new idea into the boundaries of the existing processes [18], where early adopters take up the beat. This transfer between innovators and early adopters is indicated in the SJF with a dashed arrow (Fig. 1). Together, innovators and early adopters constitute the initial 16% of adopters of an innovation [18].

2.3 Universal Accessibility

Further, the SJF extends the CJF to take into account universal accessibility. This can be done at each touchpoint within a user story or in the journey narrative. There are several methods to evaluate universal accessibility. It is important to think about technical accessibility as well as usability for people with disabilities, sometimes referred to as usable accessibility [7]. The former refers to the user's ability to perceive, operate, understand and use the functionality of the service. The latter refers to the user's ability to use the service to achieve his or her goals. Technical accessibility is usually addressed during the implementation phase by ensuring that the code complies with the before-mentioned WCAG 2.1 guidelines. One should be aware that the stakeholder journey can be broken if it is dependent on touchpoints from service providers that have not addressed

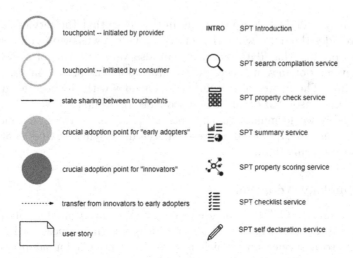

Fig. 1. Symbols for stakeholder journey framework

universal accessibility. In addition to technical accessibility, one should evaluate the stakeholder journey from a usable accessibility point of view. This means to evaluate the usability from the perspectives of people with different types of disabilities. In early design stages, one way to do this, is through a persona walk-through of the stakeholder journey using personas with disabilities [19].

2.4   Multiparty

We find it necessary to express journeys for multiple stakeholders in one diagram. The SJF extends the CJF using swimlanes for stakeholders, with the possibility to express interactions between different stakeholders' touchpoints. Many customer journey formats disable multiple journeys in a single diagram. The SJF, with its succinct notation inherited from the CJF, enables this.

2.5   Symbols

The original CJF uses graphical symbols to indicate a touchpoint's medium (telephone, email, regular mail, customer service desk). In the particular case that we shall use to illustrate the extended framework, the medium is a web application running on a computer or smartphone. We use graphical symbols to indicate the service offered at a touchpoint. These symbols are given in the second column of Fig. 1, and we will return to these below.

2.6   Stories and Narratives

Although the original CJF depicts touchpoints only, the elicitation methods used to arrive at a diagram with touchpoints may involve any number of other notations. Diagrams in terms of touchpoints are therefore a summary of a much larger body of information. In the original CJF, the touchpoint diagrams are annotated with business process phases. To understand technology adoption and universal accessibility, we need to annotate journeys with hypothetical motivations to use the services. In the SJF, we use familiar techniques from requirements engineering to summarise planned functionality and stakeholder motivations and interactions at each touchpoint into the following user story format [11,13]:

> User Story: As ⟨stakeholder⟩, I can ⟨perform functional action in my domain⟩ by using ⟨service S⟩ to ⟨handle and use information⟩.

User stories are depicted by the "note" symbol in Fig. 1.

User stories in this format are subsequently used to write textual narratives for entire journeys to supplement the graphical representation.

2.7   Objectives and Returns

We also find it necessary to relate to the visions that the stakeholders have for the innovation. Visions can be explicit or tacit and formulated at various process levels [13]. Here we distinguish between *solution objectives, functional objectives, project objectives* and *returns*. In our example case, we will only explicate project objectives, but it is useful to hold in mind how these differ from solution and functional objectives.

The user stories are assessed on their estimated contribution to each project objective, using benefit points [11]. This enables the project to prioritise which story, and hence which services to construct first [12].

Solution Objectives are what the system under development should fulfil as a technical solution; for example, to display a simpler technical conditions profile for properties. In the user story format above, these objectives pertain to ⟨service S⟩ enabling stakeholders to ⟨handle and use information⟩.

Functional Objectives are what the system under development should lead to in the stakeholders' business and life processes; for example, to obtain a better understanding of the technical conditions of a property. Here, these objectives pertain to the ⟨perform functional action⟩ in the user story format above.

Project Objectives pertain to effects outside the processes that are directly formed by solution objectives and functional objectives; for example, to reduce the number of buyer-seller conflicts following house sales. Project objectives (also known as *impact goals* or *effect goals*) express a business' (perhaps evolving) reasons for initiating and running a development project [11,12].

Returns express the expected worth of business objectives [11,12]; for example, reduced payments (EUR 10 million) or increased sales (EUR 30 million). Whereas the three types of objective above can have diverse denominations (readability, decision quality, number of conflicts), returns are expressed in monetary terms; even in the case when returns may be non-financial [11,12].

2.8   Work Phases

Inspired by the original CJF, the SJF employs five incremental methodological phases: Phase 1: overview, scope, and delimitation of innovation, Phase 2: identification and design of planned stakeholder journeys, Phase 3: stakeholder recruitment and data collection on actual journeys, Phase 4: analysis of actual journeys. Phase 5: adjustment and refinement of planned journeys.

This paper focuses on, and outlines a methodology for, Phase 2. To meet the exploratory setting of startups planning an innovation, we extend this phase with incremental elicitation and structuring of journeys. We employ practices from agile benefits-driven development, which also allows for explicit consideration of universal accessibility.

3   Example Case – Smart Property Transaction

In this section, we describe a case to illustrate the SJF. A startup company is running a research-driven project to develop smart property transaction (SPT) services to help stakeholders to make better-informed decisions when selling and buying property. Services are developed and deployed incrementally. Stakeholders that are included in the development phases include buyers and sellers of property, property agents, property assessors, insurance companies and the startup.

Phase 1 involved workshops, informal meetings and stakeholders' personal experiences of buying and selling property. A central goal that materialised from this phase was to reduce conflicts after a property is handed over, by informing buyers and sellers better of the technical conditions of the property during the selling and buying process.

Phase 2 is in progress when writing. We show how *planned stakeholder journeys* evolve through a series of stakeholder workshops.

Phase 3 will involve observing how services are used once they are deployed. This gives rise to *actual stakeholder journeys* [10], that are described textually and graphically using the same methods and symbolism as for planned journeys.

Phase 4 will analyse actual journeys with respect to how they deviate from the planned stakeholder journeys. This involves understanding which touchpoints actually occurred, what actually happened at each touchpoint and which other touchpoints actually occurred (instead). This further involves understanding what dynamics of innovation adoption actually happened in actual journeys and how universal accessibility actually played out.

Phase 5 will then use the deviations between planned stakeholder journeys and actual stakeholder journeys to inform further service increments and give rise to adjusted planned journeys.

3.1   Phase 2 Activities

The main activities in Phase 2 were workshops with the startup company, their affiliates and a group of estate brokers, with subsequent structuring and consolidation by the researchers. The work proceeded incrementally on the following activities:

stakeholder mapping, where participants were to brainstorm on what types of individuals and organisations that would have effects on, and be affected by, SPT services. Participants were invited to submit proposals freely on a stakeholder chart on a whiteboard; see Fig. 2. A few salient stakeholder types (seller, buyer, property broker) were then chosen by group discussion for further elaboration in the form of personas. In addition, insurance company and property appraiser were selected as background persona types; that is, entities that have effect on, and are affected by, SPT, and that will appear in stakeholder journeys, but who are not elaborated on further as personas.

persona elaborations, where the salient personas were elaborated upon. The researchers provided templates and example personas, which were then elaborated upon by the workshop participants.

While there is a widespread view that personas should be developed based on extensive user research, we chose to co-create personas with the workshop participants; that is, with people who represent, or are in daily contact with, the persona types in question. Co-creating personas in this way comes at the cost of statistical representativity, but is rapid and eliminates an extra layer of data interpretations. By tapping directly into the experience and knowledge of people that have a broad experience with and knowledge of the persona types in question, we can increase the coherence and realism of the personas, and reveal particularly relevant information that may be lost in a quantitative approach [6].

We therefore included a discussion point for personal challenges and needs in the persona template and encouraged the workshop participants to include some form of impairments or special needs into the persona descriptions.

stakeholder journey elicitation, where participants were to sketch high-level stakeholder journeys from the perspectives of the given personas. The researchers provided examples of high-level stakeholder journeys using a simplistic notation based on Business Process Model and Notation (BPMN) 2.0[5] and an experimental version of SJF for use during the workshop; see Fig. 3. The participants then discussed in groups designated to a given persona and came up with respective stakeholder journeys.

stakeholder journey elaboration, where participants were to detail high-level stakeholder journeys. The researchers provided examples of more detailed stakeholder journeys using the same notation as for the high-level journeys, for use during the workshop. The participants then discussed in groups designated to a given persona and came up with respective stakeholder journeys; see Fig. 4.

stakeholder journey consolidation, where researchers summarised and structured the elaborated stakeholder journeys. From the results of the workshop, we distilled planned stakeholder journeys as shown in Fig. 5 and Fig. 6.

---

[5] http://www.omg.org/spec/BPMN/2.0.

Fig. 2. Stakeholder mapping brainstorming phase

3.2 Personas

So far, we have developed six personas, which includes two sellers, two buyers and two estate agents. Among these, were one elderly female seller persona with arthritis and somewhat reduced vision, a pregnant buyer persona, and a male buyer persona with asthma who is concerned about ground radon values. While these personas can only shed light over a small part of potential universal accessibility issues, it has helped to highlight some concrete needs; see examples in the stakeholder journey descriptions below. We also plan to conduct workshops with people with different types of disabilities to get further insights into universal accessibility issues for SPT services.

3.3 Services

The following SPT services arose in part from the workshops and in part from the startup company's own ideas. They are the current consolidations of functionality formulated as services.

SPT introduction service gives an overview of SPT services; to be used whenever there is an opportunity for sell-ins.

SPT property check service lists recommendations for what a seller can do to increase the value of a property before selling. Based on price estimates for refurbishments.

SPT search compilation service compiles properties of interest based on the user's searches in other search engines. This readies the user for investigating a favourites list further with SPT.

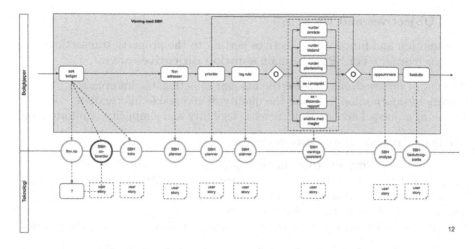

Fig. 3. Example stakeholder journey for buyer persona type

SPT summary service summarises the key characteristics of properties found and tagged during a search, so that a user can compare properties of interest.

SPT property scoring service extracts crucial information regarding the property from its documentation; to be used when investigating a property in depth. The extraction uses a combination of machine learning on property appraisal documents, knowledge of the appraisal process and comparisons with similar properties. Its output is a score reflecting the technical conditions of the property.

SPT checklist service lists crucial items of a property that a potential buyer should check; to be used at home and during a viewing.

SPT self declaration service assists a seller with filling out a self-declaration form on the property, required in order to buy a property sales insurance.

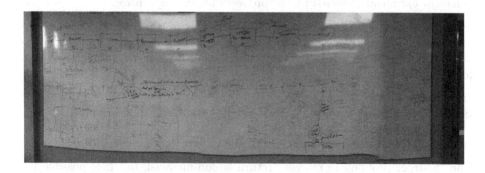

Fig. 4. Stakeholder journey brainstorming for buyer persona "Catarina"

3.4   Objectives and Returns

The solution and functional objectives pertain to the property transaction process (or journey). For SPT, the main **solution objectives** are to:

Amount of information: increase the amount of actionable information
Quality of information: increase the quality of actionable information
Degree of universal accessibility: increase legibility and simplicity of information

The main **functional objectives** are to:

Better understanding: improve the understanding of a property's worth
Higher level of trust: increase levels of trust and security in buyers and sellers
   on the validity and soundness of the property transaction
Simpler tasks: simplify the tasks of the process
Less diverse tasks: reduce the number of tasks or task variations in the process

The main **business objectives** from the point of view of the SPT project and product owners, are to:

Better decisions: induce better-informed decisions
Fewer conflicts: reduce buyer-seller conflicts
More customers: increase the number of customers

It is also useful to express objectives from the point of view of other stakeholders. For example, buyers' objectives might be to:

Short-term optimisation: buy the dream property for as little as possible

while sellers' objective might be to

Short-term optimisation: sell the property for as much as possible, fixing as little as possible

The mission of the SPT project is to give sellers and buyers tools to shift their diverging foci away from short-term optimisation to:

Balanced optimisation: sell/buy the property for the right price,

from the assumption that a common understanding of what the "right" price is, will led to better outcomes for all.

   In turn, the project objectives are expected (or desired) to contribute to the following **returns**:

Increased profits: X million
Sharper profiling in market: At least as important as "Increase profits"; say 1.5*X million
Increased stakeholder investment: Z million

The "Sharper profiling in market" return is non-financial, but it is possible to assess its importance relatively to one of the financial returns and indirectly set a monetary value on it. This enables one to include that return when prioritising user stories according to benefit and cost for realisation and production. We do not pursue this here, and the monetary values are for illustration only.

3.5   Planned Stakeholder Journeys – Initial

Figure 5 shows the initial combined journeys for each stakeholder. We give a short narrative for each journey together with its user stories.

Journey for Buyer: The potential buyer starts by browsing properties using existing search engines, where there is a link to the SPT search compilation service. At this point, it will be useful for the buyer to be able to enter mandatory search criteria based on specific needs, such as wheelchair access, elevator, short distance to public transport, radon level limits, etc. This is perceived to be an important entry point for introducing the service to possible early adopters.

Eventually, the potential buyer starts investigating favourites compiled in this service more thoroughly, perhaps using traditional information sources (including social media), but also using the SPT summary service to structure more detailed information.

Before viewing a particular property, the potential buyer can use the SPT property scoring service to see the basis for the asking price. When viewing the property, the potential buyer can use the SPT checklist service to structure what issues to check. Again, the buyer may want to rank properties according to his or her specific needs.

If ending up buying the property, the buyer can get help from the same SPT checklist again to check issues for the handing-over process.

Since the buyer might now have to sell an existing property, the buyer will be prompted to use the SPT introduction service; but now as a potential seller. This will be triggered by the service provider (blue circle) but also by the insurance company, in the case the buyer purchases a buyer's insurance.

The user stories for buyer are listed below:

Browse properties: As a potential buyer of a property, I can get an overview of interesting properties by using the SPT search compilation service to set up a list of properties based on searches in commercial search engines.

Investigate properties: As a potential buyer of a property, I can build a better basis for decision making by using the SPT summary service to investigate properties by quality and pricing criteria with comparisons to mid-values of the neighbourhood, region, type of house, universal accessibility, etc.

Understand asking price: As a potential buyer of a property, I can understand how the asking price is rooted in facts by using the SPT property scoring service to show me how the technical conditions report affects the price in relation to other comparable properties.

Structure observations: As a potential buyer of a property, I can get help on issues to check and on structuring my observation on a property by using the SPT checklist service to show me a structured list over important issues on the property.

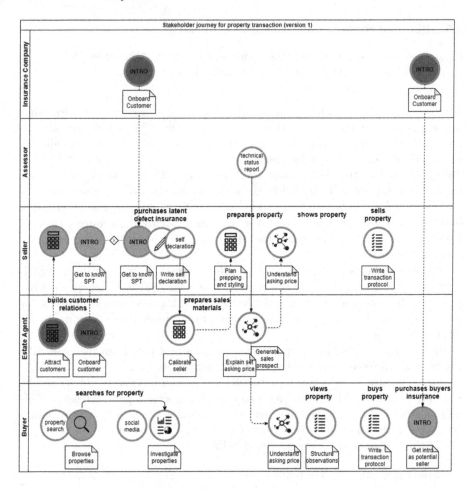

Fig. 5. Planned stakeholder journeys – Initial version

Compose transaction protocol: As a buyer of a property, I can get help on
issues to check during viewing the property before takeover by using the
SPT checklist service to show me a structured list over important issues
on the property.

Get intro to SPT as potential seller: As a buyer of a property, I can get to
know SPT as a potential seller by using the SPT introduction service to see
demos and examples of SPT services and receive a pre-filled user profile.

Journey for Estate Agent: The estate agent is perceived to be one of SPT's
main portals into the property transaction process. The other portal is the insurance company. These portals are where one envisions that SPT is actively introduced into the process. In the case of the estate agent, there is a perceived

dilemma, since estate agents are often, in the outset, geared on marketing and on obtaining the right dynamics in the bidding process for a property, often relying on emotional aspects with potential buyers. SPT is geared toward providing factual information that could be seen as irrelevant or even as undermining the above dynamics. To get estate agents to be the desired innovators for SPT in Rogers' sense would therefore seem challenging. Although estate agents were markedly positive toward SPT during the workshops, it would seem crucial that they see sufficient incentive to push the innovation.

The estate agent starts the journey by attracting new potential property sellers as customers. Using the SPT property check service, the agent tries to bestow confidence with the potential client, and subsequently uses the SPT introduction service to demonstrate the agent's unique selling point. Both of these touchpoints involve an active push of SPT onto the customer. If the agent can demonstrate how SPT structures information on factors that make a property accessible and attractive to people with disabilities, such as wheelchair access, single-floor layout, lift, etc., this can constitute a further unique selling point.

If and when the client contract is signed, the agent can use the SPT property check service to set the client's expectations at an early stage.

When the assessor has reviewed the property and written the technical conditions report, the estate agent can use the SPT property scoring service to document how the asking price is calculated and to auto-generate parts of the sales prospect.

The user stories for estate agent are listed below:

Attract customer: As an estate agent, I can increase a potential seller's trust and sense of security and increase confidence in me as an agent by using the SPT property check service to show how refurbishments may increase the attractiveness of the property and/or estimated sales price.

Onboard customer: As an estate agent, I can create enthusiasm with the seller and promote our unique selling point of SPT by using the SPT introduction service to show examples from the SPT service portfolio.

Calibrate seller: As an estate agent, I can provide a rational base line for sales price expectations early by using the SPT property check service to quickly explain the technical conditions of the property based on the seller's self declaration.

Explain set asking price: As an estate agent, I can get a seller to understand the rationale for my suggestion for asking price by using the SPT property scoring service to show the technical conditions of the property.

Generate sales prospect: As an estate agent, I can generate a sales prospect automatically by using the SPT property scoring service to retrieve key technical information on the property.

Journey for Seller: The seller is, perhaps, the persona type most sceptical to revealing more technical detail of the property. However, new legislation is putting increasing liability on property sellers, and sellers should therefore benefit from an as enlightened process as possible. Sellers would still presumably not be early adopters (unless forced to be by legislation), but rather be in the early or late majority segment in Rogers' terminology; that is, those who use technology when it has become run-of-the-mill.

In this journey, the seller gets prompted by an estate agent to look at the SPT property check service, and subsequently to experience further SPT services via the SPT introduction service.

When the seller chooses an agent and has purchased the (optional) latent defects insurance, the seller is prompted by the service provider or the insurance company to view the SPT introduction service, unless the seller already has done so.

The seller can subsequently get help to fill out the self declaration form using the SPT self declaration service. Here the service can prompt the seller to assess whether the home has accessibility factors that can be highlighted.

When preparing the property for sale, the seller is prompted by the estate agent to use the property check service to decide what to do to the property before putting it on the market. After the technical conditions report has been written, the seller is prompted by the agent to use the SPT property scoring service to come to terms with the agent's suggestion for the asking price. During handover, the seller can use the SPT checklist service as a guide to write the legally binding transaction protocol.

The user stories for seller are listed below:

Get to know SPT: As a seller of a property, I can get an overview of SPT by using the SPT introduction service to see demos and examples of SPT services.

Write self declaration: As a seller of a property, I can get a personalised assistance when filling out the self declaration by using the SPT self-declaration service to give me defaults and pre-filled items in the online form of the sales insurance company.

Plan prepping and styling: As a seller of a property, I can get a personalised to-do list by using the SPT property check service to organise prepping and styling of my property before potential buyers come to see it.

Understand asking price: As a seller of a property, I can understand how the asking price is rooted in facts by using the SPT property scoring service to show me how the technical conditions report affects the price in relation to other comparable properties.

Write transaction protocol: As a seller of a property, I can get help on issues to check during viewing the property before takeover by using the SPT checklist service to show me a structured list over important issues on the property.

Table 1. User stories' contribution to objectives

Objective				
Epics	*Better decisions*	*Fewer conflicts*	*More customers*	Sum
Buyer				
Browse properties	2	1	15	*18*
Investigate properties	7	1	12	*20*
Understand asking price	15	12	1	*28*
Structure observations	8	12	1	*21*
Write transaction protocol	6	10	1	*17*
Get intro to SPT as seller	1	1	15	*17*
Estate agent				
Attract customer	3	1	12	*16*
Onboard customer	4	1	15	*20*
Calibrate seller	10	12	1	*23*
Explain set asking price	15	12	1	*28*
Generate sales prospect	1	5	3	*9*
Seller				
Get to know SPT	1	1	10	*12*
Plan prepping and styling	7	5	1	*13*
Understand asking price	15	12	1	*28*
Write transaction protocol	4	10	1	*15*
Insurance				
Onboard customer	1	4	10	*15*
Sum	*100*	*100*	*100*	

Journey for Assessor: None elicited at the moment.

Journey for Insurance Company: The insurance company has a major incentive to reduce vacuous claims and to reduce (legal) conflicts due to clients (both sellers and buyers) with misguided expectations. In the current journey, the insurance company wishes to onboard clients to SPT whenever clients sign property transaction-related insurance deals.

The user story for insurance company is as follows:

Onboard customer: As an insurance company, I can help clients to have realistic expectations to properties by using the SPT introduction service to show examples from the SPT service portfolio.

3.6   Contribution to Objectives

We tentatively assess the user stories' contribution to project objectives; see Table 1. Following Hannay *et al.* [11], this is done by assessing all users stories relatively to each other on one objective at a time. This ensures that assessment are done with respect to one metric at a time. It has become common to adopt the planning poker use of the Fibonacci sequence also for benefit points, but here we use the so-called *hundred-dollar test*, in which one distributes 100 points on the user stories to indicate their relative contributions. The sum for each user story indicates its relative benefit. The user stories that pertain to explaining and understanding the asking price has the most benefit points in this tentative assessment, and one might consider developing the service(s) needed for those user stories first. This assumes that the three objectives have equal worth with respect to the stipulated returns. Usually, objectives have different worth, which would then give rise to weighted sums in Table 1.

3.7   Planned Stakeholder Journeys – Revised

We then held a third workshop to get feedback on the planned journeys and to get more input as to what functionality should be offered at each touchpoint. This resulted in revised planned stakeholder journeys as shown in Fig. 6.

The value of automatically generating the sales prospect was now seen as negligible, so the user story for that is removed. Further, the importance of using SPT services early for the estate agent to attract customers was now seen as questionable and more of a disturbance to their regular ways of recruiting clients. Hence, the two customer relations touchpoints for the estate agent are omitted.

Instead, emphasis was put on the value of facts-based expectations management of sellers and buyers. The crucial touchpoint for agents to introduce SPT to the process was thus moved to when the technical conditions report is ready, whereupon the estate agent can go into dialogue with the seller and potential buyers to justify the asking price and answer questions regarding the property with a basis on a property score relative to similar properties.

The property scoring service was therefore seen as more to the point, and was perceived to cover the needs in a wider range of touchpoints. In particular, the user story Calibrate seller is reformulated in terms of this service:

Calibrate seller (revised): As an estate agent, I can provide a rational base line for sales price expectations early by using the SPT property scoring service to explain how the property compares to other relevant properties, based on the seller's self declaration.

Plan prepping and styling (revised): As a seller of a property, I can get a personalised to-do list by using the SPT property scoring service to understand what can be gained by prepping and styling my property, based on comparisons with other relevant properties.

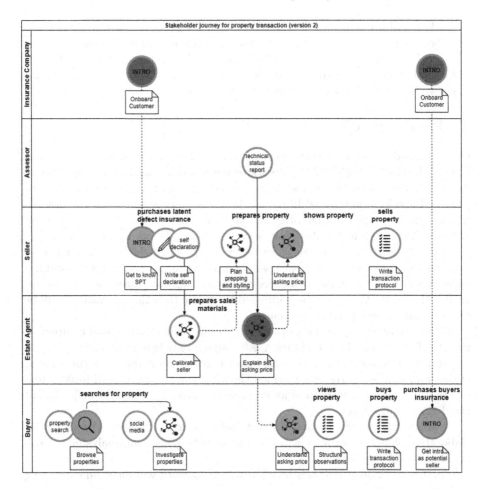

Fig. 6. Planned stakeholder journeys – Revised version

In fact, as more insight is gained on these journeys via walk-throughs and discussions, the required diversity and number of services seems to diminish, in line with the remark earlier that one need look for solutions to only a narrow set of problems. It is not unlikely that the SPT property scoring service might turn out to cover the demands in most of the touchpoints.

In the first version of the stakeholder journeys, the universal accessibility issues were not addressed through the SPT property scoring service. One question that arises with the increased focus on this service, is therefor whether universal accessibility factors somehow can be included, for example in the basis for calculating the property score.

In line with incremental development, the SPT property scoring service will be refined according to the above analyses and released in a bare-bones version as a *minimal viable product* [3,15]. This will enable the first increment of eliciting actual stakeholder journeys. We will then analyse deviations from planned journeys in terms of touchpoints and service content.

4   Final Remarks

Our extended customer framework, the stakeholder journey framework, retains the simplicity of the original framework by design. Empirically, the possibility to express dependencies between stakeholder touchpoints revealed issues with the proposed services that would likely not have been addressed using the original framework. The explicit technology adopter roles helped the startup to localise and prioritise the functionality that is key to getting traction in the market.

Our extended methodology for eliciting planned stakeholder journeys employs practices from agile benefits-driven development, with explicit business objectives. The focus on universal accessibility during the process uncovered particular challenges that must be addressed to ensure that the innovations will be useful to the widest possible audiences.

Current customer journey methodology promotes a strong visual component in both elicitation and representation. Although highly beneficial for brainstorming and rapid summarising, we found that textual summaries in terms of user stories and journey narratives clarified the journeys and uncovered inconsistencies in touchpoints, services and journeys as perceived (perhaps superficially) at the diagrammatic level.

We conclude tentatively that the stakeholder journey framework, with a more elaborative planned journey elicitation phase, is beneficial for analysing innovation needs and requirements.

Further work on the stakeholder journey framework will focus on expressing and resolving conflicting interests, as expressed in objectives. Moreover, work is in progress on expressing and resolving points where journeys may break; both in terms of universal accessibility and in terms of technology adoption. We hold that universal accessibility represents a "stress test" for whether services and touchpoints provide coherent and continuous journeys, rather than a heap of discontinuous functionality. For technology adoption, a single point of disappointment may kill an innovation's chance of getting admitted into an existing process.

We also emphasise universal accessibility of the framework itself. For example, for the visually impaired, stories and narratives are essential for complementing purely visual elements. We shall also optimise the symbolism in terms of form and colour.

Acknowledgements. This research is funded by the Norwegian Research Council under project number 296256 *Smart real estate transactions*. The authors are grateful to Vendu AS for providing the case, to Uppercase AS for hosting the workshops and to the workshop participants who represented estate agents, sellers and buyers.

References

1. Armstrong, J.S. (ed.): Principles of Forecasting: A Handbook for Researchers and Practitioners. Kluwer Academic Publishers, Norwell (2001)
2. Brown, T.: Change by Design: How Design Thinking Transforms Organizations and Inspires Innovation. Morgan Kaufmann, Burlington (2004)
3. Denne, M., Cleland-Huang, J.: The incremental funding method: data-driven software development. IEEE Softw. **21**(3), 39–47 (2004)
4. Erl, T.: SOA Principles of Service Design. Prentice Hall, Upper Saddle River (2007)
5. Erlandson, R.: Universal and Accessible Design for Products, Services, and Processes. CRC Press, Boca Raton (2008)
6. Fuglerud, K.S., Schulz, T., Janson, A.L., Moen, A.: Co-creating persona scenarios with diverse users enriching inclusive design. In: Proceedings of the 22nd International Conference on Human Comupter Interaction (HCI International 2020). Lecture Notes in Computer Science. Springer (2020, to appear)
7. Fuglerud, K.S.: Inclusive design of ICT: the challenge of diversity. Ph.D. thesis, University of Oslo, Faculty of humanities (2014)
8. Gigerenzer, G., Todd, P.M. (eds.): Simple Heuristics that Make Us Smart. Oxford University Press, Oxford (1999)
9. Grammenos, S.: European comparative data on Europe 2020 & people with disabilities: summary. Technical report, The European network of academic experts in the field of disability (ANED) (2018)
10. Halvorsrud, R., Kvale, K., Følstad, A.: Improving service quality through customer journey analysis. J. Serv. Theory Pract. **26**(6), 840–867 (2016)
11. Hannay, J.E., Benestad, H.C., Strand, K.: Benefit points—the best part of the story. IEEE Softw. **34**(3), 73–85 (2017)
12. Hannay, J.E., Benestad, H.C., Strand, K.: Earned business value management—see that you deliver value to your customer. IEEE Softw. **34**(4), 58–70 (2017)
13. Hannay, J.E., Brathen, K., Mevassvik, O.M.: Agile requirements handling in a service-oriented taxonomy of capabilities. Requir. Eng. **22**(2), 289–314 (2016). https://doi.org/10.1007/s00766-016-0244-8
14. Kratzke, N., Quint, P.C.: Understanding cloud-native applications after 10 years of cloud computing - a systematic mapping study. J. Syst. Softw. **126**, 1–16 (2017)
15. Lenarduzzi, V., Taibi, D.: MVP explained: a systematic mapping study on the definitions of minimal viable product. In: 42th Euromicro Conference on Software Engineering and Advanced Applications (SEAA), pp. 112–119, August 2016
16. Moore, G.A.: Crossing the Chasm, Revised edn. Harper Business, New York (2002)
17. Moore, G.A.: Inside the Tornado, Revised edn. Harper Business, New York (2004)
18. Rogers, E.M.: Diffusion of Innovations, 5th edn. Free Press, New York (2003)
19. Schulz, T., Skeide Fuglerud, K.: Creating personas with disabilities. In: Miesenberger, K., Karshmer, A., Penaz, P., Zagler, W. (eds.) ICCHP 2012. LNCS, vol. 7383, pp. 145–152. Springer, Heidelberg (2012). https://doi.org/10.1007/978-3-642-31534-3_22
20. Thackray, A., Brock, D.C., Jones, R.: Moore's Law: The Life of Gordon Moore, Silicon Valley's Quiet Revolutionary. Basic Books, New York (2015)

I Can't Do It, They Say! – Perceived Stigmatization Experiences of People with Intellectual Disabilities When Using and Accessing the Internet

Vanessa N. Heitplatz[1]([✉]) [iD], Christian Bühler[1] [iD],
and Matthias R. Hastall[2] [iD]

[1] Department of Rehabilitation Technology, TU Dortmund University,
Dortmund, Germany
{vanessa.heitplatz, christian.buehler}@tu-dortmund.de
[2] Department of Qualitative Research Methods and Strategic Communication
for Health, Inclusion and Participation, TU Dortmund University,
Dortmund, Germany
matthias.hastall@tu-dortmund.de

Abstract. Stigmatization is a complex process that emerges in manifold forms in a variety of social contexts. This paper sheds light on people with intellectual disabilities (ID) who are often affected by numerous negative prejudices which can lead to restrictions of human rights and various forms of social discrimination. This qualitative focus group study aims to examine perceived stigmatization experiences by people with ID when using and accessing the Internet. Besides, this study focuses on respondents' behavior and coping strategies to deal with perceived stigmatizations. Therefore, data from a focus group study with 50 participants with ID (23 males, 27 females, aged between 18 and 35) conducted in 2018 was secondary analyzed for this paper. Findings show that participants are well aware of stigmatization by their social environment (e.g., parents, caregivers). Issues include incompetence, lack of media literacy, weak cognitive skills and low decision making abilities. The results also indicate that participants react in different ways to perceived stigmatization. In this paper, we analyze behavior characteristics and arrange them into three different user types: "the Anxious Avoider, "the Help-Seeking-Realist", and "the Confident All-Rounder". The three different types differ in terms of Internet usage and coping strategies.

Keywords: People with intellectual disability · Internet usage · Stigmatization experiences

1 Introduction

Stigmatization is a complex process that emerges in manifold forms in a variety of social contexts [1]. The process is present "when elements of labeling, stereotyping, separation, status loss, and discrimination occur together in a power situation" [2]. As a result, participation in almost all areas of daily living (e.g., education, work, health or

M. Antona and C. Stephanidis (Eds.): HCII 2020, LNCS 12189, pp. 390–408, 2020.
https://doi.org/10.1007/978-3-030-49108-6_28

Internet usage) is restricted [3]. Stigmatization often affects vulnerable groups in our society. People with ID are one of those groups among many others (e.g., ethnic minorities, homosexuals, and people with physical or mental health problems) who experience stigmatization, e.g., in forms of violence, "verbal insults or more subtle forms that place restrictions on their lives and lead to difficulties gaining employment or developing personal relationships" [4]. Heitplatz, Bühler & Hastall (2019) were able to show that people with ID might develop intentions for smartphone usage but are prevent from using digital technologies solely due to caregivers' negative attitudes that: "Caregivers need to be constantly aware of their important role in supporting their clients in enhancing media competences and accessing the Internet [...]. Because of strong bonds between caregivers and people with cognitive disabilities, caregivers transfer their own attitudes, experiences and fears to their clients" [5]. Furthermore, there is evidence that stigmatizations can harm psychological well-being of effected persons, lowering their self-esteem and affecting their opportunities to gain life goals [4]. Current research suggests that people with ID are aware of the stigma attached to the label itself and that they may "distance themselves from it instead of cope" [4]. Löfgren-Mårtenson (2008) found that especially young people with ID seem to use the Internet to escape the perceived stigmatizations by their environment: "They feel that through the Net they escape the control of the surrounding world. Without having to ask permission, they are all by themselves, capable of deciding which sites they want to visit and with whom they want to communicate" [6]. Several studies have shown that access to the Internet opens up new opportunities of destigmatization but also goes along with risks of stigmatization for these people [7].

This study deals with the perceived stigmatization experiences of people with ID, which are often related to partly unconscious expressions from the social environment. The following sections will give an overview of the current state of research, describe stigmatization in more detail and examine its effects on people with ID concerning Internet access and usage.

1.1 People with Intellectual Disabilities

The construct of disability has changed from "focusing on pathology or a defect within the person to a socio-ecological person-environment fit conception that focuses on understanding human functioning and disability based on the interaction between personal and environment characteristics" [8]. In this context, the perception of ID has also changed and is now viewed as a condition of an individual in his or her life situation. The disability impacts health, community participation, and the roles an individual plays in the society. Thus, disability in general, but also ID, is seen as a holistic problem with multi-faceted characteristics in an environmental setting [8]. With this understanding, models such as the Human-Activity-Context-Technology-Model [9] or the Human-Activity-Assistive-Technology-Model [10] have been developed for a better understanding of a person's conditions in a social and environmental context.

Whereas the terms "mental retardation", "learning disabilities", or "developmental disabilities" existed during the last 25 years, the term ID is nowadays getting increased acceptance in research and practice. This can be seen in the fact that two international organizations (Section Psychiatry of Mental Retardation and European Association for

Mental Health in Mental Retardation) opened a debate on the term ID and adopted the name in 2005. Several other organizations and also scientific journals did the same although recognizing that terms change over time [11].

The International Model of Functioning, Disability and Health (ICF) describes disability as a multidimensional phenomenon [12]. According to the this Model, disability is analyzed on three levels: body function and structure, activities within an individual context and activities in the social context [8, 11]. Thus, ID is related to mental and intellectual functioning (body structure and functioning) and can be caused by genetic, congenital or environmental factors. In addition to the medical evaluation of body function and structure, the ICF model also emphasizes the importance of activities and participation. Our study follows a widely accepted definition of ID defined by the American Association on Intellectual and Developmental Disabilities: "Intellectual disability is a disability characterized by significant limitations in both intellectual functioning and in adaptive behavior, which covers many every day and practical skills. This disability originates before the age of 18" [13]. The definition refers to mental capacities (e.g., reasoning, memorizing, learning, problem-solving) and adaptive behavior which becomes present in social contexts or practical skills (e.g., activities of daily living, occupational skills, and schedules) [14]. Therefore, ID includes quite different conditions such as Alzheimer's disease, traumatic brain injury, and Down-Syndrome or autism spectrum disorder.

1.2 Stigmatization of People with (Intellectual) Disabilities

Stigmatization is routinely manifested in forms of negative attitudes, discrimination, exclusion, and inequalities of treatment that often goes along with separating or status loss [3, 15]. The **Labeling Theory** [2] describes stigmatization as the definition of a person's characteristic that is associated with prejudices and results in a demarcation or status loss of the concerned persons. Whereas stereotypes are harmful beliefs about groups of people, having prejudices means agreeing with those stereotypes. Discrimination occurs as a behavioral response to prejudices [16] and always includes action consequences (e.g., avoiding those people). Thus, discrimination is an integral part of the stigmatization processes [3]. Three types of stigmatization are described in literature: public stigma [17], structural stigma [18], and self-stigma [16, 19].

Since our qualitative study mainly analyses the opinions and feelings of participants with ID, we have chosen to concentrate and analyze self-stigma and its behavioral consequences in this paper. **Self-stigma** [16, 19] is a three-step process in which devaluations and discriminations are internalized in a person's mindset. First, a person must be aware of public stigmatization by the environment (Awareness). Second, this person then might agree that these negative public stereotypes are true about the group (Agreement). At least, the person concurs that the stereotypes apply to him/herself (Application). Self-stigma is often associated with the belief that a stigmatized person is not able to achieve life goals and it goes along with decreased self-esteem and self-confidence for affected people [19]. Corrigan & Rao (2012) described the **Why Try Effect** as a related negative consequence of self-stigma and thus one opportunity of individuals to react to perceived stigma. Diminished self-esteem leads to senses of opportunities that undermine life goals and independence and often results in a "why try outcome" e.g.: "Why should I attempt to live on my own? I am not able to do such independence. I do not have the skills to manage my own home." [19]. The Why Try Effect is a variant of the labeling theory that states that "the social reaction linked to stigmatization contributes to low self-esteem" [19]. Thus, stigma challenges many people and recent studies indicated that it harms individuals' sense of hope and self-esteem [15, 16, 20]. Another way to react to stigmatization is described by the **Rejection-Identification-Model (RIM)** [20]. It argues that negative impacts of stigma may be mitigated when "members of the stigmatized group reject a stigmatization culture and choose to identify with each other rather than with the majority group" [20]. Thus, RIM is about comparisons with peer groups or other groups in the society, which can have a positive or even negative influence on self-esteem. According to **Social Comparison Theory** [21] individuals strive to evaluate themselves with others. The theory argues that group membership often plays an important and essential role in determining individuals' self-esteem. This is important for people with ID because Chadwick, Wesson & Fullwood (2013) indicated that the "[d]iagnosis with the label intellectual disability can result in life-long labeling, stigma and societal discrimination and restriction of human rights. The label ID is so visible and strong that it often is the primary identity a person has, overriding consideration of other social identities, for example, gender, sexuality and ethnicity" [22]. Social Comparison Theory postulates that individuals try to maintain a positive concept about themselves and that in many social context people with ID derive self-esteem from social group memberships. Research into social comparison concerning people with ID suggests that they generally make comparisons with those who are not being labeled as intellectual disabled [15]. The comparison with lower-status groups may highlight the possibility that their situation could get worse. Crabtree & Haslam (2010) indicated that the perceptions of stigma and social comparison have a significant influence on people with ID: Higher perceptions of stigma lead to more negative feelings about themselves. The authors assumed that positive self-esteem can be achieved when favorable comparisons are made between the individuals' groups and relevant out-groups. The **Social Identity Theory** (Stets and Burke, 2000) explains how identity is created. According to the theory, an individual feels a sense of belonging to a social category (e.g., nationality, ethnic, sports team) which defines the individual. Many people display different social identities that become present in different contexts. At least, most people have one social identity for which negative stereotypes exist. This identity is considered to be marked or stigmatized if it is associated with failure or shame (e.g., the label intellectual disability). The evaluation of a person according to his social affiliation is called social markedness (Fig. 1).

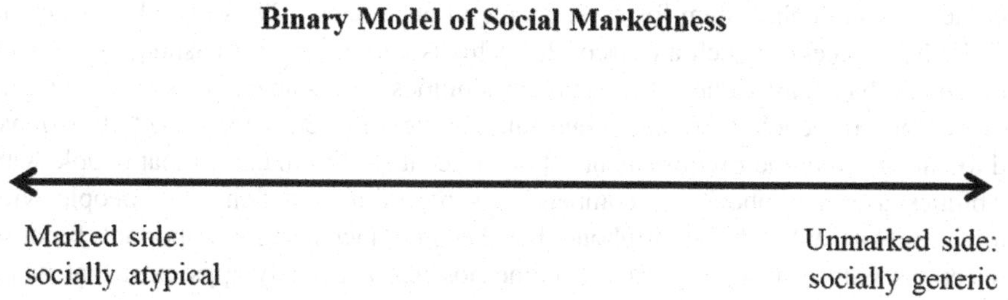

Binary Model of Social Markedness

| Marked side: | Unmarked side: |
| socially atypical | socially generic |

Fig. 1. Binary model of social markedness [23]

Pethig & Kroenung (2019) transferred the Social Identity Theory to the digital divide context. Individuals who are marked as "technology-have-nots" or "offliners" [24] on the left side of the binary model continuum (marked side) are branded as atypical in comparison to those who are on the other side of the continuum. The "digitally advantaged" [25] or "onliner" [24] on the unmarked side are seen as socially generic and as having "a choice between using or not using a particular technology, whereas digitally disadvantaged people do not have that choice, as many have trouble accessing relevant technology" [23]. Due to several factors (e.g., housing conditions, legal guardians, and low socio-economic status) it is still difficult for people with ID to gain access to the Internet and new technologies which often prevents digital participation for this group [5, 26]. Pethig & Kroenung (2019) were able to show that the extent to which disability is perceived as affecting everyday activities has an important psychological and social consequence for people with disabilities. For people with ID, the authors stated that stigma consciousness significantly inhibits the behavioral intention to adopt technologies.

In summary, different forms of stigmatization exist, which usually result in low self-esteem and other negative feelings for affected persons. The reactions to the perceived stigmatization can be very different and range from a mindset of "why try" to a "now more than ever" attitude. In today's world, the Internet is increasingly important for almost all people in our society, since a variety of online services has been developed to make life easier. People with disabilities also access the Internet and use it, among other things, to compensate for their disability. With new opportunities, however, there are also new challenges for this group of people, which will be presented in the following section.

1.3   Current Research on Internet Usage and Stigmatization Processes

Even though the Internet plays an increasingly important role in everyday life for people, not everyone has equal chances to profit from these opportunities. The unequal opportunities in using and accessing the Internet are generally discussed under the term "digital divide": "The differing use of digital media often results in different participation opportunities within important and scarce social resources. Wealth, education, (social) security, health as well as individual autonomy can be assigned to these resources. These social inequalities have far-reaching consequences which affect the social participation of each individual" [27]. People with ID are – among other groups of people (e.g., people with physical, sensory or hearing impairments, older people) – those who experience most barriers (e.g., financial and economic barriers) and are least likely to gain access to the Internet [22, 28]. Whereas smartphones, for example, have become a commonplace item for most people in our society [29], only 34% of people with ID have access to such a device [26]. This is particularly astonishing against the background that smartphones offer many possibilities to facilitate access to the Internet for this group of people (e.g. read-aloud function, text reader, autocomplete functions) and to "fit perfectly their requirements" [14]. Recent studies indicated that people with disabilities use smartphones to compensate some of their deficits. For people with hearing impairments, the smartphone has become increasingly important because connections with hearing aids have become possible and many apps exist that make everyday life easier [30, 31]. Also, people with visual impairments benefit from numerous apps and assistive technologies, such as navigation systems for the smartphone or screen readers and text-to-speech functions to assist online activities [32]. For people with ID, the Internet seems to be an appropriate place for maintaining social relationships, expressing identity and reducing stigma. Furthermore, enhancing self-determination and advocacy are some opportunities for people with ID to participate in the online world [22]. So far, socio-economic factors (e.g., age, gender, education or employment) as well as lack of media literacy have been researched as reasons for digital divides within people with and without disabilities [22, 33]. Moreover, "[t]he increasing usability of generic technology may lead to important benefits for people with disabilities; products designed for mass markets tend to be more easily available, less expensive, and less stigmatizing than specialized technology" [34].

Recent studies examined the Internet usage of people with ID and established that especially young people with ID, who have grown up with the Internet, use it daily [6, 7, 35] for various online activities (i.e., developing romantic relationships, using Social Network Sites (SNS). Even though, people with disabilities are still underrepresented in social networks [7], more and more people with ID interact frequently via social networks, especially Facebook. The Internet provides opportunities to join blogs, groups on SNS or presenting their identity. However, risks are also discussed, which affect not only people with disabilities but all people who use SNS. There is much discussion in research if overexploitation of SNS can significantly alter subjective well-being and perceived life satisfaction [36, 37]. It has been argued that these negative effects might appear due to the vast opportunities of unflattering social comparison on SNS (Rosenthal-von der Pütten et al., 2019). As discussed earlier in this section, also people with ID are engaged in social comparisons and current research suggest that they – as well as the general population – use Facebook and Instagram as a digital platform for this [5, 7]. Risks (e.g., cyberbullying, data disclosure, contact with strangers) are mentioned by all caregivers surveyed [5, 35, 38]. Molin, Sorbring & Löfgren-Mårtenson (2015) indicated in a more recent study that people with ID "claim the right to participate in society" by accessing the Internet. For those people, the Internet creates a secret parallel world where they can have a private life and appreciate the anonymity, where the label of intellectual disability is not as strong as in the "offline world" and where people with ID can build a new social identity.

Finally, it can be summarized that despite existing barriers, especially younger people with ID increasingly find their way to the Internet and use it on a daily basis. It was found that the Internet offers these people an opportunity to escape the perceived stigmatization and to form their own social identity, especially in SNS.

2 Sample and Methodology

Little is known about perceived stigmatization experiences of people with ID when using and accessing the Internet. This study aims to shed light on the perspectives of people with ID and analyzes how they react and cope with the perceived stigmatizations of their social environment. Two research questions guided this analysis: 1) What kinds of attitudes perceive people with ID by their social environment if they use or want to use the Internet? 2) What are the consequences of the perceived stigmatizations to self-esteem and behavior of people with ID when using and accessing the Internet? To answer these research questions, data from a focus group study with 50 participants with ID (23 males, 27 females, aged between 18 and 35) conducted in 2018 was secondary analyzed. In a first inductive content analysis [39] of the interview transcripts, it became clear that some of the participants' statements referred to perceived stigmatization experiences when using and accessing the Internet. For this reason, the authors decided to conduct a second deductive analysis [40] of the interview material to answer the research questions of this study.

The participants with ID have been recruited in their living environments in Germany. Today, almost 40,9% of people with ID are still living in residential housing facilities in Germany [41] which are often associated with limited self-determination, infantilization, and fewer opportunities for participation [42]. Following the definition by Link & Phelan (2001), this study assumes that various characteristics of stigma (e.g., status loss, structural stigmatization) appear in the studied setting (living situation), which is characterized by power and caregivers control [5, 42]. The following section describes the methodological approach to answer the research questions. Previous studies indicated that people with ID are difficult to survey with conventional questionnaires and interviews [43]. In our study, we decided to interview people with ID in eleven focus groups of three to six persons in a combination with the Talking Mats Method: "[it] has been argued that focus groups have important advantages both in the dynamic present and the outcomes that can be achieved when attempting to gain insights into the views of people for whom the use of a questionnaire would be difficult if not impossible" [44]. To give all participants the opportunity to participate regardless of their type and severity of ID, the interview questions were supported by self-developed Talking Mats. Originally, this is a method used for people with reduced communication skills or intellectual disability to express opinions more easily [45]. We used printed images (i.e., smartphones, tablet computers or labels of SNS) with subtitles and symbols to support the questions of the interviewer. Furthermore, all questions were asked in easy language. Before starting the focus groups, all participants were given a consent form based on German standards for conduction scientific studies [46]. The consent form was filled by the participants themselves or their legal guardians.

The focus groups' agendas were divided into three parts. The **first part** aimed to familiarize the participants with the format of the focus group. In a short introduction of a general topic (e.g., the weather), pictures and ratings were used to check the extent of needed support to understand the interviewers' questions and to give the participants the opportunity to get to know each other. In the **second part,** participants were asked about their a) usage of digital devices, b) usage of digital applications, c) perceived support when using and accessing the Internet, and c) problems in the usage of the digital devices. The selection of interview questions and topics of the usage of digital devices and applications was based on the D-21-Digital-Index [24], a German survey instrument used to assess the degree of digitalization of the German population. The **final part** of the focus groups consisted of a final round in which the participants could express their wishes regarding the use of their digital devices and evaluate the discussion. Altogether, each focus group lasted about 45 to 60 min.

After conducting the focus groups, the interview material was fully transcribed [47]. At the end of this process, all identifying personal data were replaced by general placeholders [48]. All participants got their anonymized transcript afterward to give them the opportunity to inform the authors about any modification needs (e.g. further anonymizations). The software Atlas.ti 8 was used for inductive content analysis [39]. In an open coding process [49] quotes were derived from the interview material and joined together into keywords and main topics. After finishing the content analysis, eleven main categories were identified from the interview material. An overview of all identified man topics and subtopics can be found in Heitplatz, Bühler & Hastall (2019). The identified topics indicated that stigmatization can also play an important role in the use of the Internet by people with ID, so the interview material will be examined again with this respect. The results are presented in the following section.

3 Findings

The presentation of the results addresses the perceived stigmatization of the participants from their social environment (e.g., caregivers, parents). In addition, the findings show that assessments of own abilities differ partly among the participants regarding digital media usage which leads to different behavioral consequences. For the following presentation, some text passages are supplemented by quotations, which were translated from German into English. Direct quotations are put in brackets, which include the number of the focus group and the participant.

3.1 Perceived Stigmatizations by Social Environment

Participants perceived quite different attitudes by their social environment about their disability when using and accessing the Internet. The social environment refers to the persons named by the participants: parents, siblings, and caregivers. According to the participants' statements, one of these social attitudes is the attributed **lack of competences**. Respondents in our study noticed that their environment often does not trust them to use an expensive smartphone. They seem to hold prejudices against the handling capabilities of people with ID. One participant reported: "caregivers think I can't handle an expensive phone" because they might think that "I will quickly destroy it anyway" (F8, participant C). Here the prejudice is based on the attitude that people with ID cannot handle their devices responsibly.

The participants also noticed that they are apparently **not trusted to choose a smartphone** by themselves. Instead, they would often receive a smartphone as a gift from their parents, which the parents have chosen. For the participants, however, the smartphone seems to be an important status symbol, which is why they want a modern and stylish smartphone like their friends: "I also wanted a smartphone like my friend. A Samsung Galaxy" (F3, participant B). Another participant states: "I got a smartphone for Christmas from my parents. It had a touchscreen. But it was an older phone, so it didn't work as well. I wanted a phone like my sister." (F4, participant D). This quote expresses the disappointment of the participant, who is apparently annoyed that she is not getting the same smartphone as her sister. Furthermore, the participants reported that the social environment often does not have the **time or patience** to show them how to use the smartphone or to answer their questions although the participants ask for help and support: "I can't do it on my own. I need constant help!" (F8, participant C). Another participant stated: "I would like to learn how to set up the smartphone. My friends don't always have time and my brother lives so far away" (F3, participant C). Due to time concerns by the social environment of people with ID, participants experienced some kind of paternalism "Just let me do this for you" without showing them how to solve participants' issues.

As a further point, the participants revealed that caregivers **do not see the need** for them to use a smartphone: "I have to ask my caregiver to buy a smartphone. And she is not happy if I say I need money for a smartphone" (F8, participant A). Another participant reported a similar situation: "Mom and Dad weren't so excited at first when I said I wanted a smartphone. What do you need a mobile phone for, they asked? You can also call from the [telephone in the] kitchen" (F4, participant D). Considering these quotes and the previously mentioned point that the social environment has little trust in the participants' use, access and use of the smartphone depends to a large extent on the attitude of legal guardians or parents. Therefore, it is not surprising that the participants report about **controls of their smartphone use** by parents and caregivers. While some participants said that parents only check their smartphone once in a while, other participants reported that parents check their smartphone twice a day: "Yes, my Dad checks my smartphone from time to time" (F9, participant D). Another participant stated: "My father rarely checks my smartphone. Only twice a day." (F9, participant B). For the majority of the participants, however, it seems not to be a problem that the parents control their smartphone.

In summary, participants are well aware of the opinions and attitudes of their social environment regarding their Internet use. Ascribed limitations referred to a lack of confidence in people with IDs' technical skills and media literacy, and a lack of patience to answer questions about the usage of digital devices. They also perceived that their use is sometimes strongly controlled by parents or guardians. Some participants also mentioned that their parents see no need for them to own or use a smartphone.

Awareness of prejudice against oneself is the first step in the three-step process of self-stigma (see Sect. 1.2). Now that it is clear that the persons in our sample are aware of prejudices and stigmatizations, the question arises whether they agree with them or disagree with them. The interview material was analyzed to find clues on how the participants perceive their own competences and whether they agree or not agree with the attributions described here, which primarily refer to missing competences. This question will guide the following results of the following section.

3.2 Self-assessment of Own Competences and Behavioral Consequences

Participants' assessment of one's own competences ranges on a continuum from "I have no competences" to "I know everything I need to know". It is important, however, that the majority of participants place themselves in the middle of the continuum.

Starting on the left side of the continuum, there are participants who classify their media literacy as non-existent. Here, for example, you find statements such as "I can't use that [smartphone]. This is too complicated for me" (F8, participant D) or "How do I use the [smartphone]. I don't know how to use it" (F1. Participant C). The participants who classify themselves on the left side have very low self-confidence in their own skills and believe that it would be better if they do not own and use a smartphone (F10, participant B). They describe themselves as "too stupid" (F7, participant D) to use the smartphone or to learn how to use it and are even afraid to try it out (F1, participant D).

As already mentioned, most participants place themselves in the middle of the continuum. Here, they are well aware of their deficits (cognitive, linguistic): "I can a) not read, and b) not write without mistakes" (F8, participant C). Thus, they often ask for help and support. They mentioned that they use the smartphone to compensate for these deficits. For example, they compensate their reading deficits by operating smartphones' voice control to communicate with others or to start information research. Participants are willing to learn and express a desire for more educational opportunities and support. Unfortunately, participants also report that some of their questions cannot be answered because either the parents or legal guardians have no media literacy skills or do not have time to answer them (see Sect. 3.1).

Finally, a few participants are on the right side of the continuum. Characteristic statements are "I don't have to learn anything more. I know all of this "(F10, participant A) or "I don't need any help. I usually help others with their questions" (F11, participant B). Participants on this side are self-confident and reject any help by their social environment.

The results show that the participants assess their skills differently, with most of them assessing their own knowledge and media literacy in the middle of the continuum. However, it can also be seen in the statements that the participants' own assessments may imply different behavior. A person with very low self-confidence on the left side of the continuum, who is often told from the social environment that he or she is not capable of operating a smartphone, might react with fear when using digital media. One participant on this side of the continuum even said that "it would be better not to have a smartphone" because he would be "too stupid" to use it (F10, participant B). Contrary, people on the right side of the continuum are very self-confident and often do not want to be explained or shown anything. The consequences could be aggressive behavior when trying to explain or tell someone that he or she has done something wrong: "If anybody touches my phone he will get a black eye!" (F2, participant D). Some participants reported that they secretly use the Internet because they knew that their caregivers or parents would not approve of it. From these different statements and behaviors, an attempt was made to develop a user typology, which is described in the following section.

3.3 User Typology for Media Behavior

On the basis of the results and statements, participants could be divided into different categorical groups with certain characteristics, namely "The Help-Seeking Realist", "The Anxious Avoider" and "The Confident All-Rounder" (see Fig. 2). The creation of different user types was based on the findings of Molin, Sorbring & Löfgren-Mårtenson (2017) who identified three different types of Internet users among young people with ID. For the differentiation of user types in our study, participants interview quotes were analyzed, keywords were assigned and, finally, main topics were identified. Examples of those main topics are: "Fear", "Reflection" and "Subjectively Competent". The first main topic **fear** includes quotations which obviously show that the participants are afraid of using new technologies, e.g., "They told me that it (using the smartphone) is not that difficult. But they say it's too difficult for me. So I'm afraid to use it." (F1, participant A). The second main theme was given the title **reflection**, as it contains quotations that show that the participants are aware of their deficits and strengths, e.g., "I cannot a) read and cannot b) write without mistakes. Thus, I use voice messages on WhatsApp to communicate with others" (F8, participant D). Finally, citations were assigned to the main topic **subjectively competent**. This topic includes quotes from people who stated that they already know everything about Internet use and behavior and do not need any help or education programs, e.g., "I don't need your help. I often show others how to deal with the Internet" (F5, participant D). The numbers of quotations within the different main topics were used to form three different types of behavior (see Fig. 2).

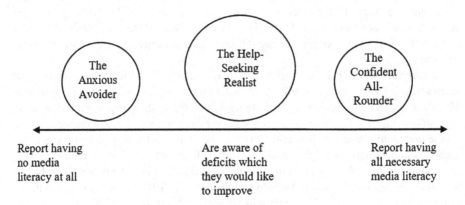

Fig. 2. Three types of behavior

The circles in the figure vary in size, as the largest circle (The Help-Seeking Realist) was the type in the sample that was most commonly represented. The other two types were the respective extremes on the two outer sides of the continuum (see Sect. 3.2).

First, the vast majority of the participants are characterized as "**The Help-Seeking Realist**" (n = 32). This type is identified by a medium degree of self-confidence and reflects one's abilities and competences. People of this type are good at assessing which skills and resources they posses and which they do not. In the sample it is mainly the lack of reading and writing skills, lack of English skills (e.g., for using Instagram or Twitter) and the assessment that help is needed for subjectively perceived complex activities (e.g., initial setup of the smartphone, downloading of apps). Here, the persons of this type can therefore do many things independently, but still lack certain facets of media literacy. However, the group of people wants to learn these skills and therefore expresses an explicit wish for education and support. They are well aware of the social environment" attitudes towards their disability, but do not always agree with them. As an example, they agree with the general attitude that they lack reading and writing skills. However, they do not agree that this makes it difficult for them to use digital media. Instead they show that they use smartphones to compensate for these deficits (e.g., voice control or using specific apps).

The second type, located on the left side of the continuum, has been named **"Anxious Avoider"** (n = 8). The name shows that people of this type have low self-confidence and are very fearful. The results of this study show that this fear and low self-confidence is often a result of perceived attitudes from the social environment of the participants such as "you can't do this" or "I'm doing this for you" (see Sect. 3.2). These perceived attitudes seem to make people feel that they are not competent enough to use a smartphone or the Internet. These people trust very much what caregivers or parents tell them and, as a result, do not dare to use new media and technologies and react very anxiously when trying to familiarize. However, the results of the focus groups also showed that there is a basic interest among these people in using new technologies and getting to know the smartphone. When designing pedagogical offers for people of this type, it must therefore be taken into account that a lot of time and relationship work is needed to introduce them to digital media and offers.

The third and last type can be placed on the right side of the continuum and was called "**The Confident All-Rounder**" (n = 10). Persons of this type showed a very high level of self-confidence in dealing with new media and technologies and felt that they did not need any further offers to improve their media literacy. Persons of this type often reported very intensive Internet use and that other people (e.g., friends, parents) would describe them as addicted to their smartphone. In particular, some people report that they quickly exchange telephone numbers, send friend requests on Facebook and generally handle their data very openly. Persons of this type perceive attitudes of the environment and react mostly with defiance or defensiveness and sometimes with aggressiveness to the help of others. This type is a challenge for the design of pedagogical offers, because on the one hand the persons believe that they have media literacy, but on the other hand they are often the persons who, due to their open attitude towards data protection, may have problems with possible consequences (e.g., cyber bullying) and need intensive pedagogical education and support.

In the following chapter, the results of the study will be further discussed and implications for research and practice are outlined.

4 Discussion

In our study we asked people with ID about their usage of digital media and the Internet. For this paper, we conducted a more in-depth analysis of the interview material to find out about perceived stigmatization experiences of this group of people and to answer the following research questions: 1) What kinds of attitudes perceive people with ID by their social environment if they use or want to use the Internet? 2)

What are the consequences of perceived stigmatizations to self-esteem and behavior of people with ID when using and accessing the Internet? Before answering the research questions, the results should be discussed in the context of other studies and current research.

According to the Labeling Theory (see Sect. 1.2), certain characteristics of people are associated with prejudice and can lead to discrimination and stigmatization. Some studies have already dealt with stigmatization towards people with ID. Findings of recent studies indicated that people with ID are labeled as dangerous and incompetent and that such negative prejudices hinder people with ID from achieving their life goals [50]. Studies have also shown that people with ID are aware of these stigmatizations and perceive different treatments (e.g., control, paternalism) [51, 52]. Although studies have shown that these perceived stigmatizations can lead to low self-confidence and self-esteem or even anxiety, it is rarely discussed in detail what kinds of anxieties these people have or which consequences of reduced self-esteem may occur. Our study attempts to address this research gap. Based on a current topic, namely Internet use, we were able to ask the opinions of people with ID themselves in focus groups and derive indications of perceived stigmatizations. We were able not only to find out that the respondents perceived stigmatizations by their social environment, but we were also able to show that the perceived stigmatizations lead to different behaviors among the respondents, which we have summarized in three user types. The self-statements of the respondents show that perceived prejudices refer primarily to incompetence regarding the use of the Internet and digital media. This goes in line with current research [19, 50]. Furthermore, the respondents report about the following perceived prejudices:

- Not being able to make their own decisions (e.g., choosing a smartphone)
- Being slow in thinking and understanding

As a consequence, the respondents perceive that decisions are taken from them, their opinions are ignored and they are controlled often. According to the Why-Try Effect (see Sect. 2.1), people agree with the negative prejudices, which leads to low self-confidence among these people. Our study shows that the most common type of user among the respondents, the "Help-Seeking Realist", only partially agrees with the perceived prejudices. For example, the respondents admit that they often have problems in reading and writing skills, but would still like to learn how to use digital media and wish that their social environment would take the time to explain questions and show how to operate their smartphone. The lack of initiative from the social environment can be explained by the fact that formal caregivers often have no time for such matters, and also are often not familiar with new media and digital applications [5, 26, 53]. Referring to the stigma reactions described in the Sect. 1.2, the Help-Seeking Realist compares himself or herself with its peer groups and therefore comes to the conclusion that problems/limited skills exist in certain activities (e.g., reading and writing skills). Since there is sometimes a rejection, but also an agreement with the perceived opinions of their social environment, the RIM model can be used to explain that self-confidence among the people of this type is mediocre in relation to the other two types.

In contrast to the "Help-Seeking Realist", the "Anxious Avoiders" agree with the perceived prejudices. As a result, they express fears of using digital media and the Internet and that they believe it would be better that they do not have access to such opportunities. Their self-confidence is considerably damaged and one gets the impression that they blame themselves for not being able to participate in the digital world because of their impairment. Here a why-try outcome (see Sect. 2.1) becomes apparent, which is associated with a low self-confidence of the persons of this types. In contrast to "The Help-Seeking Realist", the "Anxious Avoider" seems to suffer much more from the perceived stigmatization and consequently becomes very insecure in dealing with new technologies, but also in the assessment of his or her own competences and skills. The "Confident All-Rounder" reacts in a similarly extreme way, only that he or she does not agree with the prejudices against his person. As a result, he or she does not avoid the use of digital media, but tries to show himself or herself and the social environment that he or she can find his or her way in the digital world. Persons of this type reject the perceived stigmatizations, i.e. they do not agree with them and often act with a "now more than ever" attitude. Taking the RIM model as an explanation, the high self-confidence can be explained by the rejection of the perceived stigmatization and by the fact that this type probably compares himself or herself with his or her peers and finds that he or she has claimed to have a high Internet usage rate. Furthermore, this is often shown by the fact that people of this type claim to have many friends in social media and can be found on all social networks with one or more profiles. The social network Facebook plays an important role for these people, as it allows them to network and get in touch with people outside their peer group. Shpigelman (2018) was also able to show that Facebook is popular among people with ID, as they can get the confirmation they lack in the real world through likes and comments. Even if this is, apart from all chances, connected with risks [28, 54, 55], social media seem to be a possibility for people with ID to compare themselves with others and, above all, to communicate with other people outside their peer group.

Interestingly, recent studies show that those who interview people with ID directly come to a similar conclusion as this study: people with ID are often aware of their strengths and weaknesses when using the Internet and therefore ask for help when problems occur [6]. On the other hand, the studies that surveyed caregivers of people with ID found that they describe their clients' competencies as being expandable [35, 55] and that the Internet is partly not considered to be "an appropriate place where adolescents should try out different aspects of their identity and use more favorable self-presentations. They [parents] stated that their children do not have any need for alternative self-presentations and, furthermore, that their self-presentations do not vary according to an arena" [35]. At this point, it should be noted that comparatively few studies still survey this group of people, and that many results are therefore available that take formal caregivers into account. Thus, this study contributes to a deeper understanding of the reasons for using or not using the Internet, which include perceived stigmatization experiences among almost all participants of this study but different consequences and behavior strategies. Keeping in mind the living situation of people with ID in our study, who mostly live in residential facilities where they have little contact with people without disabilities, contact to the outside world can play a major role. The research questions for our study can therefore be answered as follows:

- The respondents in our study perceive that they are not considered as competent and that they are slow in understanding and learning about digital media. As a result, their opinions and wishes are often ignored by their social environment.
- As a consequence, the respondents react with different behavior patterns, which are expressed in the three user types described. Consequences on self-confidence can be found in our study, in line with the results of other studies. However, our study explains to a certain extent that stigmatization could be a reason for digital divides within this group of people.

The next chapter summarizes some of the implications that may arise from the results of our study.

5   Implications

Based on our examination, implications arise on the three levels "people with ID", "environment", and "research" to fight stigmatization against people with ID when using and accessing the Internet.

Many studies have shown that providing contact opportunities with stigmatized groups is more often associated with positive attitudes of the general population [51]. Contacts are therefore important at the intersection between people with ID and their environment. In this paper it was discussed that the respondents often live in residential institutions, which are often located far outside the community. Even though the UN-CRPD [56] and other legal measures in Germany attempted to change this, the contact of people with ID to the society is still relatively rare. However, McManus (2010) found that simply having contact with other groups or people may not always have positive outcomes. Not the quantity but the quality of the contacts helps to reduce prejudices against stigmatized groups. But not only the contact, but also the knowledge about these groups of people is important to counteract prejudices as described in this paper. In Germany, it is mainly the large welfare organizations that spread information about people with ID on posters, through flyers or on TV to inform about the disability and to reduce prejudices. This also means that society must be sensitized to the stigmatizations of people with ID. Heitplatz, Bühler & Hastall (2019) showed recently that formal caregivers are often not even aware of their prejudices and do not know about possible effects on people with ID's self-esteem. At the intersection between people with ID and environment it is also important that there are opportunities to try out and use new media and technologies. Consequently, both people with ID and social environment (e.g., parents, teachers, caregivers) need offers to train their media literacy to give each other the support they need. More research is needed to draw attention to the stigmatizations of people with ID in the use of digital media. Further research should examine whether people with other forms of disability experience similar or different stigmatizations experiences, and how they deal with this. Since the present study is concerned with the perspective of people with ID, it would also be useful to conduct inclusive research with different stakeholder groups to ask, for example parents, formal caregivers or teachers together with persons with disabilities about their perceived stigmatization experiences when using and accessing digital media and the

Internet. The approach of asking people with ID themselves about their experiences has proved to be particularly informative and therefore valuable for research. Thus, the focus group methodology used in this study was therefore well suited to explore the perspective of the participants.

In summary, more education and awareness-raising of the social environment is needed. However, the conditions must also be created to enable people with ID and people from the social environment to build up their media literacy. An overarching approach can be the work in tandems of people with and without disabilities, which has proved valuable in several projects, both in inclusive research and in practical work with digital media [57, 58]. The inclusive cooperation of people with and without disabilities offers the possibility to reduce contact fears, establish relationships and reduce prejudices.

References

1. Corrigan, P.W., Wassel, A.: Understanding and influencing the stigma of mental illness. J. Psychosoc. Nurs. Ment. Health Serv. **46**(1), 42–48 (2008)
2. Link, B.G., Phelan, J.C.: Conceptualizing stigma. Ann. Rev. Sociol. **27**, 363–385 (2001)
3. Röhm, A.: Stigmatisierung und Entstigmatisierung von Menschen mit Behinderungen: Einfluss unterschiedlicher medialer Darstellungen auf Einstellungen und Handlungsintentionen, Dissertation Technische Universität Dortmund (2017). http://dx.doi.org/10.17877/DE290R-18180
4. Paterson, L., McKenzie, K., Lindsay, B.: Stigma, social comparison and self-esteem in adults with an intellectual disability. J. Appl. Res. Intellect. Disabil. **25**(2), 166–176 (2012)
5. Heitplatz, V.N., Bühler, C., Hastall, M.R.: Caregivers' influence on smartphone usage of people with cognitive disabilities: an explorative case study in germany. In: Antona, M., Stephanidis, C. (eds.) HCII 2019. LNCS, vol. 11573, pp. 98–115. Springer, Cham (2019). https://doi.org/10.1007/978-3-030-23563-5_9
6. Löfgren-Mårtenson, L.: Love in cyberspace: swedish young people with intellectual disabilities and the internet. Scand. J. Disabil. Res. **10**(2), 125–138 (2008)
7. Shpigelman, C.-N.: Leveraging social capital of individuals with intellectual disabilities through participation on Facebook. J. Appl. Res. Intellect. Disabil. **31**(1), 79–91 (2018)
8. Buntinx, W.H.E., Schalock, R.L.: Models of disability, quality of life, and individualized supports: implications for professional practice in intellectual disability. J. Policy Pract. Intell. Disabil. **7**(4), 283–294 (2010)
9. Hersh, M.A., Johnson, M.A.: On modelling assistive technology systems – part I: modelling framework. Technol. Disabil. **20**, 193–215 (2007)
10. Cook, A.M., Polgar, J.M.: Assistive Technologies. Principles and Practice, 4th edn. Elsevier Inc., Missouri (2010)
11. Salvador-Carulla, L., Bertelli, M.: 'Mental retardation' or 'intellectual disability': time for a conceptual change. Psychopathology **41**(1), 10–16 (2008)
12. German Institute of Medical Documentation and Information. https://www.dimdi.de/dynamic/en/classifications/icf/index.html. Accessed 30 Jan 2020
13. American Association of Intellectual and Developmental Disabilities. https://www.aaidd.org/intellectual-disability/definition. Accessed 30 Jan 2020

14. Gomez, J.C., Torrado, J.C., Montoro, G.: Using smartphones to assist people with down syndrom in their labour training and integration: a case study. Wirl. Commun. Mob. Comput. (2017). https://doi.org/10.1155/2017/5062371
15. Crabtree, J.W., Haslam, S.A., Postmes, T., Haslam, C.: Mental health support groups, stigma, and self-esteem: positive and negative implications of group identification. J. Soc. Issues 66(3), 553–569 (2010)
16. Corrigan, P.W., Rafacz, J., Rüsch, N.: Examining a progressive model of self-stigma and its impact on people with serious mental illness. Psychiatry Res. (2011). https://doi.org/10.1016/j.psychres.2011.05.024
17. Corrigan, P.W., Watson, A.C.: Understanding the impact of stigma on people with mental illness. World Psychiatry 1(1), 16–20 (2002)
18. Link, B.G., Phelan, J.C.: Stigma power. Soc. Sci. Med. 103, 24–32 (2014)
19. Corrigan, P.W., Rao, D.: On the self-stigma of mental illness: stages, disclosure, and strategies for change. Can. J. Psychiatry 57(8), 464–469 (2012)
20. Bogart, K.R., Rottenstein, A.: Disability pride protects self-esteem through the rejection-identification model. Rehabil. Psychol. (2018). https://doi.org/10.1037/rep0000166
21. Festinger, L.: A theory of social comparison processes. Hum. Relat. 7(2), 117–140 (1954)
22. Pethig, F., Krönung, J.: Specialized information systems for the digitally disadvantaged. J. Assoc. Inf. Syst. 20, 1412–1446 (2019)
23. Des Power, M., Power, R., Rehling, B.: German deaf people using text communication on JSTOR. Am. Ann. Deaf 152(3), 291–301 (2007)
24. Initiative D21 e.V.: D21 Digital Index 2018/2019. Jährliches Lagebild zur Digitalen Gesellschaft. Stoba Druck GmbH, Lampertswalde (2018/2019)
25. Grimme Institut. https://imblickpunkt.grimme-institut.de/digitale-teilhabe/. Accessed 30 Jan 2020
26. Haage, A., Bosse, I.K.: Media use of persons with disabilities. In: Antona, M., Stephanidis, C. (eds.) UAHCI 2017. LNCS, vol. 10279, pp. 419–435. Springer, Cham (2017). https://doi.org/10.1007/978-3-319-58700-4_34
27. Becker, M., et al.: How to design an intervention to raise digital competences: ALL DIGITAL week – Dortmund 2018. In: Antona, M., Stephanidis, C. (eds.) HCII 2019. LNCS, vol. 11572, pp. 389–407. Springer, Cham (2019). https://doi.org/10.1007/978-3-030-23560-4_29
28. Hoppestad, B.S.: Current perspetive regarding adults with intellectual and developmental disabilities accessing computer technology. Disabil. Rehabil. Assist. Technol. 8(3), 190–194 (2013)
29. Chadwick, D., Wesson, C., Fullwood, C.: Internet access by people with intellectual disabilities: inequalities and opportunities. Future Internet 5, 376–397 (2013)
30. Müller, T.: Habitualisierte Mobilnutzung – Smartphones und Tablets gehören zum Medienalltag. Ergebnisse der ARD-Mobilstudie. Media Perspektiven 60(9), 410–422 (2013)
31. Maidment, D.W., Barker, A.B., Xia, J., Ferguson, M.A.: Effectiveness of alternative listening devices to conventional hearing aids for adults with hearing loss: a systematic review protocol. BMJ J. (2016). https://doi.org/10.1136/bmjopen-2016-011683
32. Panahi, I., Kehtarnavaz, N., Thibodeau, L.: Smartphone-based noise adaptive speech enhancement for hearing aid applications (2016). https://doi.org/10.1109/EMBC.2016.7590646
33. Shiri, A., Ladner, R.E., Wobbrock, J.O.: Smartphone haptic feedback for nonvisual wayfinding. In: Proceedings of the 13th International ACM SIAGACCESS Conference on Computers and Accessibility, pp. 281–282 (2016)

34. Lancioni, G.E., et al.: Using smartphones to help people with intellectual and sensory disabilities perform daily activities. Front. Public Health (2017). https://doi.org/10.3389/fpubh.2017.00282
35. Allison, C.C., Friedman, M.G., Bryan, D.N.: Use of electronic technologies by people with intellectual disabilities. Ment. Retard. **43**(5), 322–333 (2005)
36. Molin, M., Sorbring, E., Löfgren-Mårtenson, L.: Teachers' and parents' views on the Internet and social media usage by pupils with intellectual disabilities. J. Intell. Disabil. **19** (1), 22–33 (2015)
37. Rosenthal-von der Pütten, A.M., et al.: "Likes" as social rewards: their role in online social comparison and decisions to like other people's selfies. Comput. Hum. Behav. **92**(1), 76–86 (2019)
38. Alhassan, A.A., Alqadhib, E.M., Taha, N.W., Alahmari, R.A., Salam, M., Almutairi, A.F.: The relationship between addiction to smartphone usage and depression among adults: a cross sectional study. BMC Psychiatry **18**(1), 148 (2018). https://doi.org/10.1186/s12888-018-1745-4
39. Seale, J., Nind, M., Simmons, B.: Transforming positive risk taking practices: the possibilities of creativity and resilience in learning disability contexts. Scand. J. Disabil. **15** (3), 233–348 (2012)
40. Elo, S., Kääriainen, M., Kanste, O., Pölkki, T., Utriainen, K., Kyngäs, H.: Qualitative content analysis: a focus on trustworthiness. Int. J. Qual. Methods **4**(1), 1–10 (2014)
41. Mayer, T., Lutz, M.: Geistige Behinderung: Nomenklatur, Klassifikation und die Beziehung zu Epilepsien. Zeitschrift für Epileptologie **30**(4), 251–257 (2017). https://doi.org/10.1007/s10309-017-0133-2
42. Thimm, A., Dieckmann, F., Haßler, T., Thimm, A., Dieckmann, F.: In welchen Wohnsettings leben ältere Menschen mit geistiger Behinderung? Ein quantitativer Vergleich von Altersgruppen für Westfalen-Lippe. Z Gerontol Geriatr. **52**(3), 220–227 (2017). https://doi.org/10.1007/s00391-019-01533-3
43. Park, J.: Selbstbestimmtes Leben für Menschen mit geistiger Behinderung im betreuten Wohnen. https://d-nb.info/1050817036/34. Accessed 30 Jan 2020
44. Trescher, H.: Wohnräume als pädagogische Herausforderung. Springer Fachmedien Wiesbaden, Wiesbaden (2017)
45. Barr, O., McConkey, R., McConaghie, J.: Views of people with learning difficulties about current and future accommodation: the use of focus groups to promote discussion. Disabil. Soc. **18**(5), 577–597 (2010)
46. Bunning, K., Alder, R., Proudman, L., Wyborn, H.: Co-production and pilot of a structured interview using Talking Mats® to survey the television viewing habits and preferences of adults and young people with learning disabilities. Br. J. Learn. Disabil. (2016). https://doi.org/10.1111/bld.12167
47. Deutsche Gesellschaft für Psychologie: Berufsethische Richtlinien (2020). https://zwpd.transmit.de/images/zwpd/dienstleistungen/ethikkommission/ethik-richtlinien-2016.pdf
48. Dresing, T., Pehl, T.: Praxisbuch Interview, Transkription & Analyse Anleitungen und Regelsysteme für qualitativ Forschende, 6th edn. Eigenverlag, Marburg (2015)
49. Meyermann, A., Porzelt, M.: Hinweise zur Anonymisierung von qualitativen Daten. https://www.forschungsdaten-bildung.de/files/fdb-informiert-nr-1.pdf. Accessed 30 Jan 2020
50. Zaynel, N.: Prozessorientierte Auswertung von qualitativen Interviews mit Atlas.ti und der Groundet Theory. In: Scheu, A.M. (ed.) Auswertung qualitativer Daten, pp. 59–68. Springer, Wiesbaden (2017). https://doi.org/10.1007/978-3-658-18405-6_5
51. Corrigan, P.W., Larson, J.E., Rüsch, N.: Self-stigma and the "why try" effect: impact on life goals and evidence-based practices. World Psychiatry **8**(2), 75–81 (2009)

52. McManus, J.L., Feyes, K.J., Saucier, D.A.: Contact and knowledge as predictors of attitudes toward individuals with intellectual disabilities. J. Soc. Pers. Relatsh. **28**(5), 579–590 (2011)
53. Nazar, A., Bo, E., Malin, C., Sonnander, K.: Classical and modern prejudice: attitudes toward people with intellectual disabilities. Res. Dev. Disabil. **27**, 605–617 (2006)
54. Pelka, B.: Digitale Teilhabe: Aufgaben der Verbände und Einrichtungen der Wohlfahrtspflege. In: Kreidenweis, H. (ed.) Digitaler Wandel in der Sozialwirtschaft, pp. 57–80. Nomos, Baden-Baden (2017)
55. Caton, S., Chapman, M.: The use of social media and people with intellectual disability: a systematic review and thematic analysis. J. Intell. Dev. Disabil. **41**(2), 125–139 (2016)
56. Chiner, E., Gómez-Puerta, M., Cardona-Moltó, M.C.: Internet use, risks and online behaviour: the view of internet users with intellectual disabilities and their caregivers. Br. J. Learn. Disabil. **45**(3), 190–197 (2017)
57. Beauftragte der Bundesregierung für die Belange von Menschen mit Behinderungen: Die UN-Behindertenrechtskonvention. https://www.behindertenbeauftragte.de/SharedDocs/ Publikationen/UN_Konvention_deutsch.pdf?__blob=publicationFile&v=2. Accessed 30 Jan 2020
58. In der Gemeinde leben gGmbH: Willkommen bei PIKSL. https://piksl.net. Accessed 30 Jan 2020

Service Design for Accessible Tourism

Hans-Peter Hutter[1]([⊠]), Alireza Darvishy[1], Stephan Roth[1],
Susanne Gäumann[2], Heidi Kaspar[3], Tatjana Thimm[4],
Maksym Gaiduk[5], Sandra Evans[6], and Martin Rosenberg[7]

[1] InIT Institute of Applied Information Technology, ZHAW Zurich University
of Applied Sciences, Winterthur, Switzerland
hans-peter.hutter@zhaw.ch
[2] Claire & George Stiftung, Berne, Switzerland
kontakt@claireundgeorge.ch
[3] Careum Hochschule Gesundheit, Fachhochschule Kalaidos,
Zürich, Switzerland
heidi.kaspar@careum-hochschule.ch
[4] Fakultät Wirtschafts-, Kultur- und Rechtswissenschaften, HTWG Konstanz,
Konstanz, Germany
tthimm@htwg-konstanz.de
[5] Ubiquitous Computing Lab, HTWG Konstanz, Konstanz, Germany
maksym.gaiduk@htwg-konstanz.de
[6] LebensPhasenHaus, Eberhard Karls Universität Tübingen, Tübingen, Germany
sandra.evans@ipc.uni-tuebingen.de
[7] NESTOR Intl. Corp. AG, Appenzell, Switzerland
martin.rosenberg@nestor-swiss.ch

Abstract. This paper presents the goals, service design approach, and the results of the project "Accessible Tourism around Lake Constance", which is currently run by different universities, industrial partners and selected hotels in Switzerland, Germany and Austria. In the 1st phase, interviews with different persons with disabilities and elderly persons have been conducted to identify the barriers and pains faced by tourists who want to spend their holidays in the region of Lake Constance as well as possible assistive technologies that help to overcome these barriers. The analysis of the interviews shows that one third of the pains and barriers are due to missing, insufficient, wrong or inaccessible information about the accessibility of the accommodation, surroundings, and points of interests during the planning phase of the holidays. Digital assistive technologies hence play a major role in bridging this information gap. In the 2nd phase so-called Hotel-Living-Labs (HLL) have been established where the identified assistive technologies can be evaluated. Based on these HLLs an overall service for accessible holidays has been designed and developed. In the last phase, this service has been implemented based on the HLLs as well as the identified assistive technologies and is currently field tested with tourists with disabilities from the three participated countries.

Keywords: Accessible Tourism · Service Design

© Springer Nature Switzerland AG 2020
M. Antona and C. Stephanidis (Eds.): HCII 2020, LNCS 12189, pp. 409–419, 2020.
https://doi.org/10.1007/978-3-030-49108-6_29

1 Introduction

1.1 Accessible Tourism

For more than 30 years, accessible tourism has been discussed in many countries and international organizations are working on global standards for accessible tourism for all [1, 2]. Different associations have developed guidelines for hotels and other service providers in tourism on how to best deal with tourists with disabilities, e.g. [3–6]. These guidelines are written from the perspective of hotel service providers and therefore mainly focus on the holiday journey steps from the arrival of the guests until their departure. Tourists with disabilities and elderly tourists, however, face many additional pains and barriers while planning and booking their holidays and while travelling to the hotel destination and back home. The Project "Accessible Tourism around Lake Constance" (in German, Barrierefreier Tourismusraum Bodensee, or BTB) presented in this paper took the perspective of guests with disabilities from the very beginning and also considered the journey steps before and after the actual holiday trip.

1.2 Project BTB

The project BTB started in March 2018 and lasts until October 2020. It is part of the IBH Living Labs AAL and has a specific focus on lowering the barriers for tourists with disabilities, specifically in the Lake Constance region. The main goals of this project are

- to identify the barriers tourists with disabilities still face when they want to spend holidays in general and specifically in the region of Lake of Constance.
- to identify possible assistive technologies and services to overcome these barriers.
- to develop a holistic service for accessible holidays based on so-called Hotel-Living-Labs (HLLs). HLL are guestrooms in generally accessible hotels that are equipped with specific assistive technologies.

The service for accessible holidays was developed according to the new service development process ISDP proposed in [7] and depicted in Fig. 1.

The remaining sections of the paper will present and discuss mainly the results of the first two phases "Customer and Context Analysis>" and "Service Innovation" as well as first insights of the other phases.

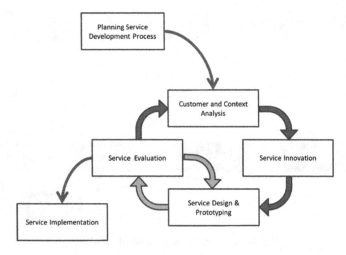

Fig. 1. InIT service development process (ISDP)

2 Customer and Context Analysis

In this user research phase, 32 semi-structured interviews were conducted in Switzerland and Germany with people from the following tourist groups:

- Tourists using wheelchairs or with impaired mobility (10)
- Tourists with visual impairments (5)
- Tourists with hearing impairments (2)
- Tourists with cognitive disabilities (7)
- Elderly tourists with assistive needs (8)

In addition, one group of tourists was interviewed together with their care givers who organize the holiday trips for the whole group. Almost one third of all interviewed persons are retired and more than one third need or prefer to have an accompanying person with them during their holidays.

Nearly all participants stated that a very detailed planning, organization, and validation of all aspects of their holidays is very crucial to them as an adaptation of the plan during the holidays is normally very arduous.

The first part of the interviews comprised general questions about the persons and their holidays, the second part of the interviews was structured along the Customer Journey Map for holiday trips depicted in Fig. 2. This Customer Journey Map was developed by the project partners based on the Universal Job Map from [8].

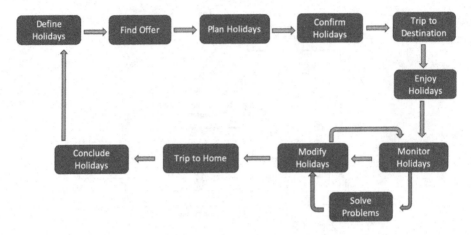

Fig. 2. Customer journey map of holidays

3 Service Innovation

In this phase, the entire customer journeys of the above tourist groups were scrutinized based on the interviews, starting with the determination of the goal and destination of the holidays, through the planning, the journey to the destination and back, the stay at the destination (including indoor and outdoor activities) until the conclusion of the holidays and the reimbursement by the health insurance providers.

3.1 Pains and Barriers Guests with Disabilities Face on Their Holidays

The interviewed tourists with disabilities mentioned 203 barriers or pains they face during their holidays (Fig. 3). With 36% the majority of barriers mentioned in the interviews are related to information that is missing, insufficient, wrong or not accessible to them. 25% of the mentioned barriers or pains are related to the travel from home to the destination and back, most of them occurring with public transportation. 21% of the barriers concern the accommodation itself whereas 16% of the barriers mentioned are occurring during activities outside the accommodation, mainly inaccessible points of interests or inaccessible toilets, but also inaccessible way signs. Among the 2% remaining pains is the price the most prominent aspect which may become a barrier in some cases.

The first step in the customer journey of the tourists is to define what the goals of their holidays should be. The motivation for holidays was in nearly 20% of the cases to get to know new things (regions, people, culture), to enjoy the warm climate, and recreation or doing sporting activities. 10% of the interviewed tourists mentioned "good food" as an important aspect of their holidays.

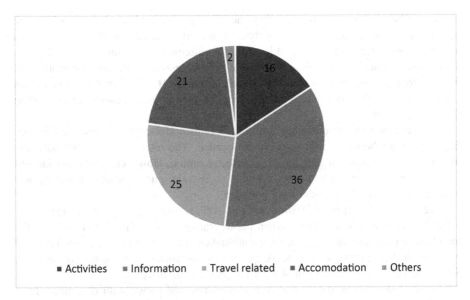

Fig. 3. Major barriers during holiday trips

The next step in the customer journey is to find a suitable offer that meets the tourist's goals and requirements, taking into consideration their specific needs and those of the accompanying persons. In this phase, a lot of detailed information about the accessibility of the accommodation and the surroundings is needed. This information is collected from various sources: 90% of the interviewed tourists with disabilities rely on the internet to get this information and about 38% organize their holidays together with a travel agency. 18% of the interviewed persons rely on recommendations from other persons and less than 10% use a catalog.

Once suitable offers have been identified, the holiday must be planned in detail (e.g. transport of people, luggage, equipment to the destination, organization of assistive technologies and services needed at the destination, planning of activities and many more things). In this stage, a lot of detailed information about accessibility of the accommodation itself, the surroundings as well as the point of interests is needed. Different associations have developed detailed accessibility checklists for hotels, as e.g. [3–6], and accessible hotels should provide accessibility information on that level of detail. In addition, pictures of the accessible rooms showing the important details regarding accessibility or even a floor plan with the most important measures would be very helpful during planning.

Still too often this information is missing or not detailed enough so that the prospective guests have to clarify these issues with a phone call to the hotel or through the travel agency they booked their holidays, which is a big pain for these guests that can become a barrier. Another big pain in this phase is outdated or wrong accessibility information which becomes a problem only later when the guest is at the hotel and realizes that the provided information is not true.

As can be seen from the accessibility checklists in [3–6], wheel chair users have the most requirements regarding accessibility of an accommodation. Guests with other than mobility impairments have less and less strict requirements regarding accessibility. As a consequence, hotels normally only provide very general accessibility information for these tourist groups. For guests with visual impairments, additional barriers in this stage arise when the information on the websites itself is not accessible or difficult to find and navigate.

The next step in the customer journey, "Confirm Holidays", comprises the confirmation of all bookings and reservations needed. The interviewed people normally like to do the booking of their holidays directly online. However, online booking of accessible hotel rooms is often not possible so that the guests or their travel agency have to call the hotel to do the final booking.

The next step, "Trip to Destination," as well as the step "Trip to Home", may involve many barriers, especially when public transportation is used. One third of the travels to the holiday destination were undertaken with private car and another third with public transportation means. A quarter of the travels were done by airplane. Sometimes also taxis were used at least for parts of the travel.

Figure 4 shows that the major pains the interviewed guests with disabilities have regarding their travel to the destination of their holidays and back are emergency situations with the assistive technologies, services or the accompanying person (e.g. no assistance available for changing trains, loss/defect of assistive technologies or luggage), followed by accessibility issues of public transportation means and delays or even cancellations of them. These issues jeopardize the original travel plan and need immediate adaptation of the rest of the travel. The major pain of travelers with their private car is the lack of accessible toilets on their way.

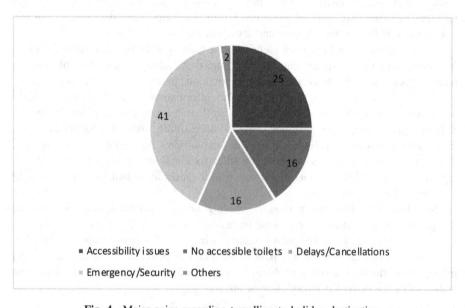

Fig. 4. Major pains regarding travelling to holiday destination

The main step of the whole customer journey is to enjoy the holidays, which comprises not only the standard activities of daily living but also using all indoor and outdoor facilities and services offered by the hotel as well as visits of the surrounding places, points of interests, and events.

Tourists with disability normally choose their accommodation according to accessibility criteria and their special needs. Nevertheless, the most frequently mentioned pains during the holiday stay are accessibility issues with the accommodation (Fig. 5), e.g. too narrow bath rooms or stairs. These accessibility issues normally arise when the corresponding information during planning was missing, inaccurate or wrong, or when the assistive technology provided was not usable, which was mentioned 17% of the times. Other notable issues were no or not available accessible parking lots, problems with the communication in the hotel (for tourists with hearing impairment), or that the hotel was accessible but not family friendly.

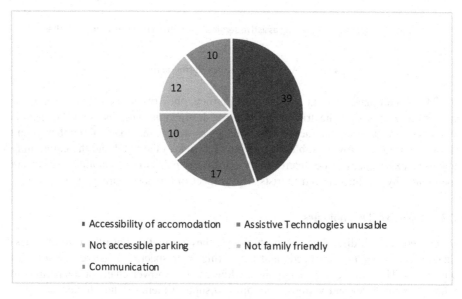

Fig. 5. Major pains regarding the holiday stay

These accessibility issues with the accommodation mean in the best case that the guests have to solve the problem themselves or have to ask the hotel staff for help, e.g., regarding an assistive technology or other facilities in the hotel. In the worst case, these issues require modifications of the holidays, e.g., guests have to change their rooms or even their hotels because it is not accessible for them or is otherwise inadequate.

As can be seen in Fig. 3 16% of the accessibility issues during holidays that were mentioned were related to activities during the holidays. More than half of these issues concern inaccessible points of interests. 2nd most mentions refer to missing assistive services like audio guides or sign language translators, followed by non-barrier-free paths (Fig. 6).

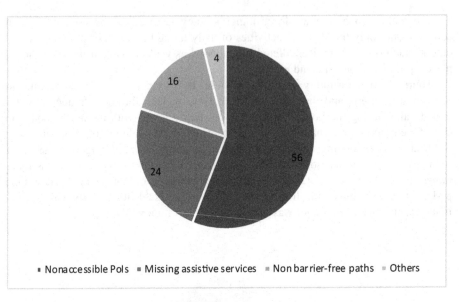

Fig. 6. Accessibility issues during activities

The penultimate step in the holiday journey, the trip to home, has the same accessibility issues as the trip to the holiday destination. The last step, "Conclude Holidays", includes the payment of the holidays as well as the financial reimbursement through insurance providers, but also giving feedback to the hotel and the community about the experiences made. Interestingly, hardly any pains or accessibility issues were mentioned by the interviewed tourists with respect to this last journey step.

3.2   Assistive Technologies

When people with disabilities go on holidays, they normally chose their holiday destination according to their needs and they bring their specific assistive technologies with them. This can be a wheel chair, a white cane, a shower chair, or a smartphone with a screen reader and various other apps to support them on their holidays.

As most of the pains and barriers during holidays are due to missing, inaccurate, or inaccessible information in the planning phase of the holidays and on site, the most important assistive technologies for holidays are digital assistive technologies that allow the guests with special needs to find, access and read all information they need in an accessible way for them. Therefore, accessible websites with detailed, accurate and up to date information about the accessibility of accommodations and their infrastructure, their surroundings, nearby points of interest, and activities offered are key for guests with disabilities. Our interviews revealed that most of the pains and barriers occurring during the holidays of guests with disabilities could be avoided if the corresponding information had been available in the planning phase. During their holiday trip guests with disabilities normally rely on their smartphones to find and access information about their trip, the infrastructure, the surroundings or points of interests in an accessible way for them.

Based on these insights, the project BTB concentrates on digital assistive technologies to find, access and read accessibility related (and other relevant) information about the accommodation, the infrastructure, the surroundings and the points of interest in an accessible way. On the one hand, these are accessible and easy to use websites of accommodations and other holiday service providers that provide detailed, accurate and up-to-date information for planning the holidays. On the other hand, these are assistive technologies based on smartphones and smartwatches that allow to provide location-based up-to-date information about infrastructure, activities, points of interest but also about public transportation in an individually accessible way. They also allow for immediate help in emergency situations which is another major pain for tourists with disabilities.

4 Service Design

The design of a holistic service for accessible holidays developed within the project BTB is based on so-called Hotel-Living-Labs (HLLs) and covers all steps of a holiday journey (see Fig. 2). HLLs are hotel rooms in generally accessible hotels that are equipped with additional digital assistive technologies in order to address the pains and barriers identified in Sect. 3.1.

The participating hotels with HLLs are advertised on a specifically designed platform run by a partner of the project. The platform provides detailed information about all accessibility aspects of the accommodations and its surroundings that are needed for a detailed planning of the holiday and this in an accessible way.

The prospective guests also enter all booking details as far as possible on this platform. The booking and confirmation as well as the clarification of remaining questions is done by the booking service run by the same project partner who runs the platform.

Once the booking of the holidays is confirmed, the guest gets a digital documentation of the booked holidays with detailed information about the accommodation, the booked services as well as information about the travel from their home to the booked accommodation.

The guests are provided with a special "Accessible Holidays App" where they can browse the digital holiday information in an accessible way. The app also informs the guests about any updates related to their travel, their accommodation, or booked services. Last but not least, the app offers an emergency button which directly connects the guests to their travel agency which exactly knows what they have booked, their assistance needs, and where they currently are. With this information, the travel agency can organize adequate help for the guests as soon as possible.

The guests are also invited to download the ginto app [9] where they can find information about the accessibility of the points of interest in their surroundings.

They are also provided with a smartwatch with GPS and phone call functionality developed by one of the partners of the project BTB. In case of an emergency, the guests can easily call one of the predefined numbers by pressing a button on the smartwatch. If the smartwatch detects a fall or an unconsciousness of the guest the stored numbers are called automatically in the order they have been stored. The called persons also get the GPS coordinates of the smartwatch so that they can easily localize the guest.

Finally, some of the HLLs will be equipped with a voice assistant in the hotel room where the guests can easily ask by voice for information about the accommodation as well as the services offered and the surroundings.

The developed service for accessible holidays will be field tested in April-May 2020 with volunteering guests with different disabilities. First results of this field test are expected to be available at the conference.

5 Conclusion and Outlook

This paper has summarized the service design approach and results of the project "Accessible Tourism around Lake Constance" who's goals were to identify todays pains and barriers tourists with disabilities experience when they want to spend holidays in the area of Lake Constance. The results so far have shown that the majority of barriers and pains are related to information that is missing, inaccurate, outdated, or not accessible to the guests during their decision making and planning, but also during their holiday stay. The service design for accessible holidays developed in this project therefore concentrates on digital assistive technologies that provide the needed information detailed enough and in an accessible manner in the planning and booking phase as well as during the stay. The designed service is currently field tested based on Hotel-Living-Labs equipped with these digital assistive technologies. The developed service for accessible holidays will be offered by one of the project partners beyond the end of the project.

Funding. This project is funded in the context of the IBH Living Lab AAL by Interreg, EU EFRE, and the Swiss Confederation.

References

1. World Tourism Organization (UNWTO): Accessible Tourism for All: An Opportunity within Our Reach. World Tourism Organization (UNWTO) (2016)
2. Zero Project | For a world without barriers: Zero Project. https://zeroproject.org/. Accessed 13 Feb 2019
3. Prüfsystem zur Barrierefreiheit, Version 3.0, Qualitätskriterien. Deutsches Seminar für Tourismus (DSFT) Berlin e. V., January 2019
4. Barrierefreier Tourismus für Alle. ADAC, 2003
5. Gäumann, S., hotelleriesuisse, et al.: Barrierefreiheit in der Hotellerie. Claire & George Stiftung (2018)
6. Peter, H.-K.: BKB_Handbuch_barrierefrei_komplett.pdf. BKB Bundeskompetenzzentrum Barrierefreiheit e. V, October 2010
7. Hutter, H.-P., Ahlenstorf, A.: New mobile service development process. In: Marcus, A., Wang, W. (eds.) DUXU 2017. LNCS, vol. 10289, pp. 221–232. Springer, Cham (2017). https://doi.org/10.1007/978-3-319-58637-3_17

8. Bettencourt, L.A.: Service Innovation. How to Go from Customer Needs to Breakthrough Services. Mc Graw Hill, New York (2010)
9. ginto: Deine zugänglichen Orte. ginto. https://www.ginto.guide. Accessed 21 Jan 2020

Homebased Telework as a Tool for Inclusion? A Literature Review of Telework, Disabilities and Work-Life Balance

Anne Igeltjørn and Laurence Habib[(⊠)]

OsloMet – Oslo Metropolitan University, Oslo, Norway
{s315696,laurence.habib}@oslomet.no

Abstract. This paper presents a review of the existing literature on the subject of home-based telework from an inclusion and diversity perspective, with a particular focus on workers with disabilities and workers who have family members with disabilities. The review aimed to map research articles that provide insights into the issues of work-life balance, work-life conflict and work-life enhancement. The articles were screened based on publication date, relevance and research contribution. The selected articles after the screening were synthesized, and their main themes organized in five groups: 1) employment; 2) work patterns and accommodations; 3) performance, 4) policy, and 5) work-life balance and enhancement. The article concludes with an overview of the implications of the findings of the survey for future research directions and highlights the need for a greater focus on diversity and inclusion when studying home-based teleworking and issues of work-life balance, work-family conflict and work-life enhancement. Suggestions as to how this can be achieved are presented, for example in considering new research designs that would include more diverse populations of teleworkers among informants or respondents.

Keywords: Telework · Work-life balance · Disability · Inclusion · Diversity

1 Introduction

The world of work has witnessed several waves of changes and upheavals, often as the result of new technologies. The diffusion of internet technology, especially during the last thirty years, has enabled new ways of working such as home telework. As many work tasks that traditionally were confined to being performed in a traditional office evolved both in form and content, the individuals that were carrying them out experienced being less constrained spatially. As Blake [1] puts it, telework is characterized by "moving the work to the workers, instead of the workers to work" (p. 1).

Concurrently, there has been an increased awareness around issues of work-life balance, as well as access to employment and inclusion at the workplace. However, there seems to be little empirical knowledge on whether and to what extent home and family life is enhanced or rendered more complicated by carrying out parts or all of one's work from home. An additional element of uncertainty arises regarding issues of inclusion and diversity. In particular, little is known about how individuals with family members with a disability and individuals who have themselves a disability experience

© Springer Nature Switzerland AG 2020
M. Antona and C. Stephanidis (Eds.): HCII 2020, LNCS 12189, pp. 420–436, 2020.
https://doi.org/10.1007/978-3-030-49108-6_30

work-life balance in relation to teleworking. This article therefore aims to examine the literature that deals with telework, disabilities and work-life balance.

2   Overview of the Main Concepts

In this section, we provide a short overview of the main concepts used in this paper, namely a) work-life balance and related notions such as work-life conflict, work-life interface, work-life enrichment; b) telework and related terms such as telecommuting and virtual work; and c) disability and inclusion.

2.1   Work-Life Balance, Conflict, Interface and Enrichment

One traditional outlook on work-life balance has consisted of defining it as a lack or a low level of conflict between roles [2]. However, an increased awareness of the existence of conflict has contributed to shifting the focus away from a somewhat unrealistic belief that harmony between the different roles played by individuals is both possible and preferable.

Greenhaus and Beutell [3] define work-family conflict as "a form of interrole conflict in which the role pressures from the work and family domains are mutually incompatible in some respect" (p. 77). They distinguish three types of work-family conflicts: 1) time-based conflict, whereby the different roles that a person has are competing with each other with relation to this person's time; 2) strain-based conflict, where the strain incurred by one or more roles than a person has affects negatively this person's ability to perform in another role; 3) behavior-based conflict, where the type of behavior that is required to fulfil one role (for example in the workplace) differs greatly from the type of behavior expected in another role (for example as a family member) [3]. Later works [4] have distinguished between "family-work conflict", whereby the pressure from work interferes with the demands of family life and "work-family conflict", where the pressure from family life interferes with work.

Another outlook on work-life balance has been to understand it as a high level of work-life enrichment. Work-life enrichment has been defined [5] as: "the extent to which experiences in one role improve the quality of life in the other role" (p. 72). For example, schedule flexibility has been found to empower workers as it acts as a resource that spans boundaries and increases thereby their agency [6].

Other scholars consider the concept of resources as inherent of work-family balance. For example, Voydanoff [7] suggests that "a global assessment that work resources meet family demands, and family resources meet work demands such that participation is effective in both domains" (p. 825) is required. Whereas Valcour [8] presented work-life balance as more an attitude that included affective elements as well as cognitive elements, other authors have argued for taking into account alternative factors in the study of work-life balance. For example, Grzywacz and Carlson [9] have described work-family balance as "accomplishment of role-related expectations that are negotiated and shared between an individual and his or her role-related partners in the work and family domains" (p. 466). They underline that the focus on accomplishment means that satisfaction is left out. Their approach to work–family balance is mainly based on the social aspects of the concept, thereby leaving out the psychological aspects of it. This, they explain "minimizes the potential of reducing work–family balance to an individual problem resulting from poor choices" (p. 466).

2.2 Home-Based Telework and Telecommuting

The literature on telework appears to stem from a large variety of research areas, including information systems, management, transportation, psychology and communication. The terms that are used to refer to telework in the literature also seem to vary depending on the academic discipline of the authors. For example, the concept of telework is often referred to as telecommuting, in particular in works by scholars from the field of sustainable transportation [10, 11], reflecting a societal interest in leveraging the potential of location-independent work to reduce the length and frequency of commuting. In the management and human resources literature, telework is also conceptualized from the point of view of virtual teams [12]. Teleworking as a concept refers to various forms of working involving the use of information technology, including working from home, working from locations outside traditional offices, as well as working in a traditional office but without or with less face-to-face interaction than usual with co-workers and customers [13].

The advantages of teleworking have been described as flexibility both for the workers and for their organizations. For workers, increased autonomy [14], flexible hours and the possibility to save time due to less or no commuting [15] have been highlighted as major advantages. For organizations, the advantages of teleworking include cost reduction due to a reduction in office space and productivity increase. In particular, teleworking has enabled "offshoring", i.e. the process of outsourcing activities to distant locations [16]. However, a number of disadvantages have also surfaced in research, including social isolation [17], increased stress [18], overworking [19], reduced influence, and the limitation of career advancement options [20].

2.3 Disabilities, Inclusion and Diversity in Organizations

Inspired by the work of Cameron and Valentine [21], Jenks [22] presents a historical timeline of disability where four periods can be distinguished: an institutionalization period from 1600 to 1900 where people with various forms of impairment were gathered in institutions run either by the state or by the Church; a medicalization period from 1900 to 1945 that was contemporary to the eugenics movement; a rehabilitation period from 1945 to 1970 where the focus was on rehabilitating veterans from the Second World War; and a post-medicalization period since 1970 where persons with disabilities have started social movements that have had large-scale effects on society.

Humpage [23] describes discourses around disability as embedded in the reigning power structures in a society. In particular, while religious leaders had traditionally represented disability through an explanatory framework permeated with religious beliefs, the rise of scientific thinking and medical knowledge has shifted the discursive power away from religion and towards science. The Medical Model's narrative has emphasized disability as a medical problem that needs to be treated, and ideally cured. This focus on "fixing a problem" has significantly limited the extent to which persons with disabilities have had a say in whether they wanted to participate in the "fixing" process [24].

The emancipatory movements have historically embraced a new understanding of disability generally referred to as the Social Model of disability, which emphasized the distinction between impairment, i.e. the functional limitations of an individual, and disability, which happens when impaired bodies have inadequate access to their environment and can therefore best be understood as a social construct. The Social Model is in many ways a response to the shortcomings of the Medical Model, in particular its role in legitimizing the exclusion or persons with disabilities from the labour market [25].

The Social Model highlights the need to find societal solutions to problems related to disability instead of focusing on fixing individual bodies. Within this model, a physical impairment will only affect a person's well-being negatively if society has failed to make the necessary physical and organizational accommodations that would enable this person to participate fully in social activities [26].

The Relational Model of disability [27] has been described as bringing together both the social and the medical approaches [28], with a focus on the interaction between those two models [29]. According to the Relational Model as described in Lid [29], disability emerges "in the interaction between individuals and the environment, encompassing both social and material factors" (p. 205). The mismatch that surfaces between a person and their environment is referred to as a "gap" [29].

Other models of disability have been suggested, such as the Affirmation Model [30], or Affirmative Model, which focuses on the benefits that are brought about by impairments. This model offers an alternative conception of disability and impairment, in that it promotes a perspective whereby disability and impairment are not considered tragic. It also challenges the idea that disability is undesirable and advocates that diversity in bodies and minds is something that needs to be embraced and celebrated rather than problematized [31].

3   Method

The review conducted in this study was performed during the month of January 2020. The first phase of the process consisted in carrying out a number of searches including keywords that we identified as relevant in order to shed light on the topics under investigation.

3.1   Search Process

The authors of this paper performed a series of searches on the EBSCOhost platform covering the following databases: CINAHL with Full Text; Business Source Elite; CINAHL; EconLit; ERIC (Education Resource Information Center); Library, Information Science & Technology Abstracts; MEDLINE; SPORTDiscus with Full Text; Regional Business News; GreenFILE; SocINDEX; MLA International Bibliography; Food Science Source; eBook Collection (EBSCOhost); Library & Information Science Source; MathSciNet via EBSCOhost; Educations Source; International Bibliography or

Table 1. Shows the different combinations of keywords used during the search process

Searches	Keywords used
Search no. 1	Work-life balance or work-family balance or work-family conflict or work-family enhancement
Search no. 2	Telework or teleworking or telecommuting
Search no. 3	Disability or disabilities AND employment or work life or workplace
Search no. 4	Disability or disabilities AND telework or teleworking or telecommuting

Theatre & Dance with Full Text; Academic Search Ultimate; and Teacher Reference Center. The searches were conducted using four different combinations of keywords shown in Table 1.

3.2 Inclusion and Exclusion Criteria

Papers were included if all three of the following conditions were fulfilled:

1. the paper was published in a peer-reviewed journal or magazine or as part of the proceedings from a peer-reviewed conference or workshop;
2. the language of the paper was English;
3. the paper was published in the timeframe 2000–2020.

Papers were excluded if one or more of the following was true:

1. the paper was not based on empirical research or on a systematic literature review
2. the language of the paper was poor or opaque, making it difficult to understand the contribution of the paper.

4 Findings

4.1 Yearly Spread

By looking at each topic and related keywords, we gained insight into how the individual fields have evolved over that past two decades. The topics of work-life balance, work-family balance, work-family conflict, and work-family enhancement have received an increased amount attention in the academic literature over the past twenty years (Fig. 1). In the year 2000, our search resulted in 32 articles, whereas in 2018, it was a total of 1909 articles, which also returned the highest numbers of articles. In total, our search using those keywords uncovered a total of 16536 articles over the past twenty years.

The same trend can be observed when conducting a search using words related to disability/disabilities in employment, work-life, and workplace perspective (Fig. 2).

Even though the increase in yearly publications over the period is not as substantial as with the topic of work-life balance, it is the search that has resulted in the highest number of publications (37624 results in total over the last 20 years).

The number of publications related to the topic of telework or telecommuting seems to have remained relatively unchanged over the past twenty years, with the highest result numbers of 144 and 141 in the years 2003 and 2012, and the lowest result number in 2011 with 45 publications retrieved from the databases used for the purpose of this study (Fig. 3). In total, searches for this topic resulted in 2184 publications in those databases.

Lastly, the topic of disability/disabilities and teleworking, telework, and telecommuting has relatively few results over the period (Fig. 4). The two years that stand out are 2006 and 2014, with respectively 8 and 10 results. The other years have between 0 to 3 results, with a total of 48 results over the past 20 years. After our inclusion and exclusion criteria was applied to the results generated through the searches, we ended up with a total of 17 papers, where the yearly spread is shown in Fig. 5. It is interesting to see that the most recent of the selected papers is from 2017, which indicates that interest for scholarly work on this topic is currently declining, which is in sharp contrast with the increased interest for issues surrounding work-life balance in general terms.

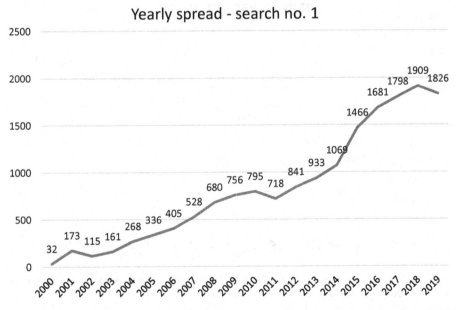

Fig. 1. Yearly spread of the search results, where following keywords were used, work-life balance or work-family balance or work-family conflict or work-family enhancement.

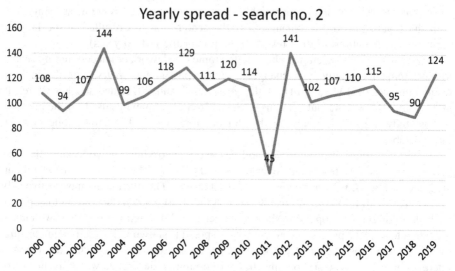

Fig. 2. Yearly spread of the search results, where following keywords were used: telework or teleworking or telecommuting

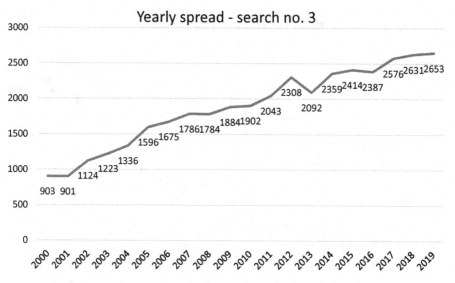

Fig. 3. Yearly spread of the search results, where following keywords were used: disability or disabilities AND employment or work life or workplace

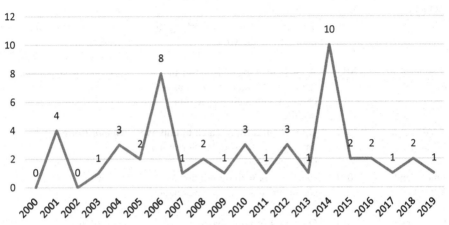

Fig. 4. Yearly spread of the search results, where following keywords were used, disability or disabilities AND telework or teleworking or telecommuting

4.2 Overview of the Selected Articles

See Table 2.

Table 2. Overview of the articles after exclusion of articles that did not meet the criteria

Authors	Year	Article title	Journal
Anderson, Bricout and West [32]	2001	Telecommuting: Meeting the needs of businesses and employees with disabilities	*Journal of Vocational Rehabilitation*
Bricout [33]	2004	Using telework to enhance return to work outcomes for individuals with spinal cord injuries	*NeuroRehabilitation*
West and Anderson [34]	2005	Telework and employees with disabilities: Accommodation and funding options	*Journal of Vocational Rehabilitation*
Baker, Moon, and Ward [35]	2006	Virtual exclusion and telework: Barriers and opportunities of technocentric workplace accommodation policy	*Work*
Kaplan et al. [36]	2006	A framework for providing telecommuting as a reasonable accommodation: some considerations on a comparative case study	*Work*

(continued)

Table 2. (*continued*)

Authors	Year	Article title	Journal
Tennant [37]	2009	The reasonableness of working from home in the digital age	*Review of Disability Studies: An International Journal*
Matthews et al. [38]	2011	A qualitative examination of the work–family interface: Parents of children with autism spectrum disorder	*Journal of Vocational Behavior*
Frieden and Winnegar [39]	2012	Opportunities for research to improve employment for people with spinal cord injuries	*Spinal Cord*
Linden and Milchus [40]	2014	Teleworkers with disabilities: Characteristics and accommodation use	*Work*
Lin, Huang and Wang [41]	2014	Outcomes of home-based employment service programs for people with disabilities and their related factors - a preliminary study in Taiwan	*Disability & Rehabilitation*
McNaughton et al. [42]	2014	"Home is at work and work is at home": telework and individuals who use augmentative and alternative communication	*Work*
Moon et al. [43]	2014	Telework rationale and implementation for people with disabilities: considerations for employer policymaking	*Work*
Rivas-Costa et al. [44]	2014	An accessible platform for people with disabilities	*International Journal of Human-Computer Interaction*
Yeh and Yang [45]	2014	Assisting the visually impaired to deal with telephone interview jobs using information and commutation technology	*Research in Developmental Disabilities*
Ekberg et al. [46]	2016	New Business Structures Creating Organizational Opportunities and Challenges for Work Disability Prevention	*Journal of Occupational Rehabilitation*
Gnanasekaran et al. [47]	2016	Impact of employee benefits on families with children with autism spectrum disorders	*Autism: The International Journal of Research and Practice*
Padkapayeva et al. [48]	2017	Workplace accommodations for persons with physical disabilities: Evidence synthesis of the peer-reviewed literature	*Disability and Rehabilitation*

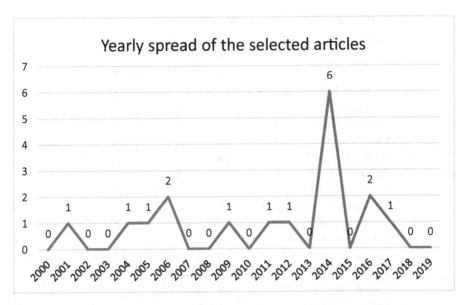

Fig. 5. Yearly spread of the selected articles after exclusion of articles that did not meet the criteria

5 Overview of the Main Topics Covered in the Selected Articles

See Table 3.

Table 3. Overview of the main categories identified in the articles

T1: Employment	T4: Work-Life balance	T7: Policy
T2: Performance	T5: Parenting	
T3: Accommodation	T6: Disability	

6 Discussion

In this section, the results from the mapping exercise are presented using a structure inspired from the categories identified above. The thematic headings in this section mirror the categories in Table 4, with some interrelated categories being merged into the same subsection for the purpose of clarity.

Table 4. Overview of the main topics identified in each of the selected articles

Articles	Main topics covered in the articles						
	T1	T2	T3	T4	T5	T6	T7
Anderson, Bricout and West [32]	X	X	X			X	X
Bricout [33]	X		X			X	
West and Anderson [34]	X		X			X	
Baker, Moon, and Ward [35]	X		X			X	X
Kaplan et al. [36]	X		X			X	
Tennant [37]	X		X			X	
Matthews et al. [38]	X			X	X	X	X
Frieden and Winnegar [39]	X			X		X	
Linden and Milchus [40]	X	X	X			X	X
Lin, Huang and Wang [41]	X		X	X		X	X
McNaughton et al. [42]	X	X	X	X		X	
Moon et al. [43]	X		X	X		X	X
Rivas-Costa et al. [44]	X	X				X	
Yeh and Yang [45]	X	X				X	X
Ekberg et al. [46]	X	X	X			X	X
Gnanasekaran et al. [47]	X			X	X	X	X
Padkapayeva et al. [48]	X	X	X			X	X

6.1   Employment

The first published article included in this review is Anderson et al. [32]. This paper provides an overview of how telecommuting can be a suitable work arrangement for persons with disabilities and aims to map out concerns that employers might have regarding the work arrangement for employees with disabilities.

In a literature review article that focuses on workers with spinal cord injuries (SCI), Frieden and Winnegar [39] reveal that workers with SCI have a low employment rates compared to persons without disabilities in the US, 35% to 64%. In addition, the article indicates that persons with disabilities over forty years of age tend to discontinue paid employment faster than persons without disabilities. Although the article does not provide a definite answer as to what could be the underlying reason for those numbers, it argues that the lack of knowledge on that topic calls for research into methods to stimulate the creations of jobs that are accessible to diverse populations. McNaughton et al. [42] echo those concerns and emphasize the need for companies to be more creative in how they approach the issue of accessible job creation.

The challenge of keeping a job appears to be a major obstruction to the well-being not only workers with disabilities, but also for workers who care for relatives with a disability. The result of an email survey described in Gnanasekaran et al. [47] show that 43% of the respondents either had to find another job, or had to reduce the number of hours in their current job, or had to quit paid employment entirely in order to be able to perform their care duties towards one or more children with disabilities.

Bricout [33] examines how telework can be vital in improving the chance of persons with spinal cord injuries getting back to work and identifies three elements that may play a role in whether a worker will benefit from this work arrangement: personal traits, environmental circumstances, and timing. This type of work often needs some level of technical skills and independence from the worker. In addition, environmental and contextual factors like the work market and the company's views on teleworking may affect the chance of positive teleworking experience. Timing refers to the fact that working in a company with already established telework routines and frameworks will increase the chance of a positive telework experience. How these elements affect each other is uncertain, but teleworking can for this group of workers reduce some of the experienced barriers of returning to work.

In contrast, Lin et al. [41], in a preliminary study of the efficiency of home-based employment service programs for persons with disabilities, find that 36,5% of the participants had an increase in employment status. However, because of the limitations of the study, the authors recommend a longitudinal study to get a better understanding of the long-term impacts of these types of programs and of other possible factors that may affect future job possibilities.

6.2 Focus on Work Patterns and Accommodation

Most of the selected articles refer to work patterns. A survey described in Linden and Milchus [40] uncovers that flexible scheduling is widely used among teleworkers with disabilities and suggest that this is linked to issues of pain and fatigue, which in a traditional work environment could affect a worker negatively. However, although 20% of their survey respondents use telework in some capacity, less than half of them (9% of the total) view home-based telework as an accommodation for their job, which suggests that they might telework for other reasons than their disability.

Kaplan et al. [36] presents teleworking as a possible accommodation to workers with disabilities which can be used as a supplement to other accommodations. They emphasize the suitability of teleworking as an accommodation for employees whose degree of disability fluctuates over time and unpredictably and its potential to enable them to remain employed.

Padkapayeva et al. [48] review the accommodation options that are available in companies to reduce or remove physical, social and attitudinal barriers to gaining and maintaining employment. They identify the need to increase workplace flexibility and worker autonomy in addition to making physical, architectural or technological mod-ifications. Accommodation of work location included working from home for the purpose of reducing work-related travel time and mitigating the effects of physical or architectural limitations in office buildings. This work can be related to the work of West and Anderson (2005), which list potential barriers to the use of telework as an accommodation and outlines a number of funding sources for the acquisition of technology, which are mostly relevant to a US readership.

Tennant [37] reports that access to jobs for persons with disabilities improved in the ten-year period between 1990 and 2000 in the USA and argues that this improvement is likely due to the combined effect of the Americans with Disabilities Act and improvements in technology. However, new employees were offered onsite jobs, and not work-from-home arrangements. The article reveals that work-from-home arrangements are available as an accommodation but are not used to their full potential.

6.3 Focus on Performance

Some of the selected articles focus on the issue of work-related performance. Yeh and Yang [45] examine how a new technical system can increase the efficiency of persons with visual disabilities to conduct their job as a telephone interviewer. The results suggest that the right type of equipment, properly designed software, and a functioning work process will enable workers with visual disabilities to be self-sufficient and to achieve high levels of work performance. This type of system can be used in similar working environments opening up the number of work opportunities for persons with visual impairments. The study had a small number of participants - a total of seven users – but indicated that there are possibilities to find efficient solutions that can improve both worker satisfaction and work efficiency with the right setup.

Another study that delves into the topic of performance is Rivas-Costa et al. [44], which presents an accessible platform created for persons with disabilities. One of the features of the system described in this article is a smart job advisor that would make it easier to find and locate relevant jobs suited to the user's abilities—also reducing the user group's dependence on external help when looking for work. The article describes different control devices that aim to ensure that the system is usable by a wide range of users. Although the research described in this article was a pilot study and therefore did not provide statistically significant results, there was a "consensus on the platform being perceived as useful, convenient, accessible, and simple to use" (p. 492).

6.4 Focus on Policy

Moon et al. [43] suggest a policy framework that takes into account both employer considerations and employee considerations, along technological feasibility and social learning in order to achieve successful outcomes of telework. Ekberg et al. [46] describe virtual workplaces not only as providing increased employment opportunities for persons with disabilities, but also as a way to prevent disability and return to work schemes.

Baker et al. [35] examine how policy can enhance teleworkers' experience of being included in the workspace while reducing feelings of isolation with a special emphasis on the barriers and opportunities that are brought about in teleworking situations. The authors argue for a new outlook on policy that gives more weight to the employees' perspective and focus less on the employer's point of view.

6.5 Focus on Work-Life Balance

The potential benefits of avoiding long commuting time have been outlined in the telework literature as conducive to a higher degree of work-life balance. Moon et al. [43] suggest that this could be an even more important factor for persons with mobility or dexterity impairments. The study described in McNaughton et al. [42] points to similar results, as their participants expressed that the reduction in time spent on commuting was one of the major advantages of teleworking. The study also found that work-from-home agreements offered the participants an increased degree of time and space flexibility, which allowed them to fit necessary non-work activities, such as medical visits, into their schedule. Lastly, for the group of workers using augmentative and alternative communication (ACC) with complex communication needs (CNN), telework is better suited for most of the participants' favored style of communicating. Since direct dialogue can be a challenge for the users of ACC, because of the fast pace, communicating through alternative methods appeared to be beneficial. Isolation from the workplace and the struggle of maintaining a healthy work-life balance seemed to be the disadvantages that the participants experienced most acutely while teleworking. The authors also state that "telework is developed as a choice for individuals with CCN, and not presented as the only available option because of poor infrastructure support (e.g., deficient public transportation, inaccessible buildings)" (p. 124).

Matthews et al. [38] is one of the few works from our search that treats the issue of work-life balance and work-family conflicts in telecommuting households where parents have the responsibility for a child with autism. They suggest that parents of children with a disability typically are in situations where they need to maintain a high level of flexibility in the boundary between work and family.

The email survey that is reported in Gnanasekaran et al. [47] aimed at mapping the lives of families with children with autism. Among the 161 respondents, 91% had used flexible work arrangements, and 86% had used some form of teleworking. One of the main causes for changing or quitting a job was a lack of work flexibility.

7 Limitations of the Review

The limitations of this literature review are twofold. First, the number of articles that satisfied the criteria for the search is relatively low, which suggests that a broader investigation of the literature, including a larger number of scholarly-work databases might be warranted. Second, the lack of clear-cut definitions for the terms used for the search (telework, work-life balance and disability) appears to be a non-negligible hurdle when attempting to carry out a systematic investigation of those topics. However, as the number of academic works on those topics continues to increase, it is probable that those definitions will become clearer over time, and future literature searches might consequently be easier to perform, with fewer articles being excluded due to lack of relevance.

8 Conclusion and Avenues for Future Research

In this article, we have provided an overview of the literature covering directly or indirectly the topics of work-life balance, work-life conflict and work-life enhancement for home-based teleworkers with disabilities or who care for relatives with disabilities.

Although much of the recent research describes telework as a possible accommodation for persons with disabilities as well as workers who have care responsibilities for family members with disabilities, there is generally little focus in the literature on the consequences of telework practices on their work-life balance. The significant surge in interest for work-life balance in the literature does not seem to have resulted in more attention towards its implications for teleworkers with disabilities and teleworkers with family members with disabilities. While several of the articles selected for this review imply that policies could have positive effects on the work environment and work-life balance of home-based teleworkers, none of them describes in any detail how this can be achieved and whether already established policies have yielded satisfactory results or have had unintended consequences.

It is also interesting to note that none of the selected articles (and, to our knowledge none of the non-selected articles either) proposed to study teleworkers with disabilities and teleworkers caring for relatives with a disability using the same analytical lens. In addition, this will allow to get insights in the experiences of individuals who both have a disability and care for a relative with a disability, which seems to be largely absent from the current literature. This gap could potentially be addressed by challenging existing research designs that are limited in scope. Including both groups of teleworkers in the same study might provide new insights into the issue of workplace diversity and access to work for diverse worker populations. More generally, our survey has revealed a relative scarcity of empirical data that can provide an in-depth understanding of the lived experience of those two groups of home-based teleworkers. Future research may include both quantitative and qualitative studies of aimed at uncovering how teleworking practices affect the work-life balance of diverse groups of teleworkers.

References

1. Blake, M.: Teleworking for Library and Information Professionals. Routledge, London (1999)
2. Duxbury, L., Higgins, C.: Work-life balance in the new millennium: where are we? Where do we need to go? CPRN, Ottawa, Canada (2001)
3. Greenhaus, J., Beutell, N.J.: Sources of conflicts between work and family roles. Acad. Manag. Rev. 10(1), 76–88 (1985)
4. Netemeyer, R.G., Boles, J., Mcmurrian, R.C.: Development and validation of work-family and family-work conflict scales. J. Appl. Psychol. 81(4), 400–410 (1996)
5. Greenhaus, J., Powell, G.N.: When work and family are allies: a theory of work-family enrichment. Acad. Manag. Rev. 31(1), 72–92 (2006)
6. Pedersen, V.B., Jeppesen, H.J.: Contagious flexibility? A study on whether schedule flexibility facilitates work-life enrichment. Scand. J. Psychol. 53(4), 347–359 (2012)
7. Voydanoff, P.: Toward a conceptualization of perceived work-family fit and balance: a demands and resources approach. J. Marriage Fam. 67(4), 822–836 (2005)
8. Valcour, M.: Work-based resources as moderators of the relationship between work hours and satisfaction with work-family balance. J. Appl. Psychol. 92(6), 1512–1523 (2007)
9. Grzywacz, J.G., Carlson, D.S.: Conceptualizing work-family balance: implications for practice and research. Adv. Dev. Hum. Resour. 9(4), 455–471 (2007)
10. Kim, S.-N.: Is telecommuting sustainable? An alternative approach to estimating the impact of home-based telecommuting on household travel. Int. J. Sustain. Transp. 11(2), 72–85 (2017)

11. Lachapelle, U., Tanguay, G.A., Neumark-Gaudet, L.: Telecommuting and sustainable travel: reduction of overall travel time, increases in non-motorised travel and congestion relief? Urban Stud. **55**(10), 2226–2244 (2018)
12. Ruppel, C.P., Gong, B., Tworoger, L.C.: Using communication choices as a boundary-management strategy: how choices of communication media affect the work–life balance of teleworkers in a global virtual team. J. Bus. Tech. Commun. **27**(4), 436–471 (2013)
13. Allen, T.D., Golden, T.D., Shockley, K.M.: How effective is telecommuting? Assessing the status of our scientific findings. Psychol. Sci. Public Interest **16**(2), 40–68 (2015)
14. Sardeshmukh, S.R., Sharma, D., Golden, T.D.: Impact of telework on exhaustion and job engagement: a job demands and job resources model. New Technol. Work Employ. **27**(3), 193–207 (2012)
15. Klopotek, M.: The advantages and disadvantages of remote working from the perspective of young employees. Organ. Manag. Q. **40**(4), 39–49 (2017)
16. Kumar, K., van Fenema, P.C., von Glinow, M.A.: Offshoring and the global distribution of work: implications for task interdependence theory and practice. J. Int. Bus. Stud. **40**(4), 642–667 (2009). https://doi.org/10.1057/jibs.2008.77
17. Gajendran, R.S., Harrison, D.A.: The good, the bad, and the unknown about telecommuting: a meta-analysis of the psychological mediators and individual consequences. J. Appl. Psychol. **92**(6), 1524–1541 (2007)
18. Fonner, K., Roloff, M.: Testing the connectivity paradox: linking teleworkers' communication media use to social presence, stress from interruptions, and organizational identification. Commun. Monogr. **79**(2), 205–231 (2012)
19. Grant, C.A., Wallace, L.M., Spurgeon, P.C.: An exploration of the psychological factors affecting remote e-worker's job effectiveness, well-being and work-life balance. Empl. Relat. **35**(5), 527–546 (2013)
20. Golden, T., Eddleston, K.A., Powell, G.N.: The impact of teleworking on career success: a signaling-based view. In: Academy of Management Annual Meeting Proceedings, vol. 2017, no. 1, p. 1 (2017)
21. Cameron, D., Valentine, F.: Disability and Federalism: Comparing Different Approaches to Full Participation. Mc Gill-Queen's University Press, Montreal and Kingston (2001)
22. Jenks, A.: Crip theory and the disabled identity: why disability politics needs impairment. Disabil. Soc. **34**(3), 449–469 (2019)
23. Humpage, L.: Models of disability, work and welfare in Australia. Soc. Policy Adm. **41**(3), 215–231 (2007)
24. Roush, S.E., Sharby, N.: Disability reconsidered: the paradox of physical therapy. Phys. Ther. **91**(12), 1715–1727 (2011)
25. Barnes, C., Mercer, G., Shakespeare, T.: Exploring Disability - A Sociological Introduction. Blackwell, Oxford (1999)
26. Blustein, J.: Philosophical and ethical issues in disability. J. Moral Philos. **9**(4), 573–587 (2012)
27. Linton, S.: Claiming Disability: Knowledge and Identity. New York University Press, New York (1998)
28. Kavanagh, C.: What contemporary models of disability miss - the case for a phenomenological hermeneutic analysis. Int. J. Feminist Approaches Bioeth. **11**(2), 63–82 (2018)
29. Lid, I.M.: Developing the theoretical content in Universal Design. Scand. J. Disabil. Res. **15**(3), 203–215 (2013)
30. Swain, J., French, S.: Towards an affirmation model of disability. Disabil. Soc. **15**(4), 569–582 (2000)
31. McCormack, C., Collins, B.: The affirmative model of disability: a means to include disability orientation in occupational therapy? Brit. J. Occup. Ther. **75**(3), 156–158 (2012)

32. Anderson, J., Bricout, J.C., West, M.D.: Telecommuting - meeting the needs of businesses and employees with disabilities. J. Vocat. Rehabil. **16**(2), 97–104 (2001)
33. Bricout, J.C.: Using telework to enhance return to work outcomes for individuals with spinal cord injuries. NeuroRehabilitation **19**(2), 147–159 (2004)
34. West, M.D., Anderson, J.: Telework and employees with disabilities - accommodation and funding options. J. Vocat. Rehabil. **23**(2), 115–122 (2005)
35. Baker, P.M.A., Moon, N.W., Ward, A.C.: Virtual exclusion and telework - barriers and opportunities of technocentric workplace accommodation policy. Work **27**(4), 421–430 (2006)
36. Kaplan, S., Weiss, S., Moon, N.W., Baker, P.: A framework for providing telecommuting as a reasonable accommodation: some considerations on a comparative case study. Work **27**(4), 431–440 (2006)
37. Tennant, J.: The reasonableness of working from home in the digital age. Rev. Disabil. Stud. Int. J. **5**(4), 10–21 (2009)
38. Matthews, R.A., Booth, S.M., Taylor, C.F., Martin, T.: A qualitative examination of the work–family interface: parents of children with autism spectrum disorder. J. Vocat. Behav. **79**(3), 625–639 (2011)
39. Frieden, L., Winnegar, A.J.: Opportunities for research to improve employment for people with spinal cord injuries. Spinal Cord **50**(5), 379–381 (2012)
40. Linden, M., Milchus, K.: Teleworkers with disabilities: characteristics and accommodation use. Work **47**(4), 473–483 (2014)
41. Lin, Y.-J., Huang, I.-C., Wang, Y.-T.: Outcomes of home-based employment service programs for people with disabilities and their related factors - a preliminary study in Taiwan. Disabil. Rehabil. **36**(17), 1457–1463 (2014)
42. McNaughton, D., Rackensperger, T., Dorn, D., Wilson, N.: "Home is at work and work is at home": telework and individuals who use augmentative and alternative communication. Work **48**(1), 117–126 (2014)
43. Moon, N.W., Linden, M.A., Bricout, J.C., Baker, P.M.A.: Telework rationale and implementation for people with disabilities - considerations for employer policymaking. Work **48**(1), 105–115 (2014)
44. Rivas-Costa, C., Anido-Rifón, L., Fernández-Iglesias, M.J., Gómez-Carballa, M.A., Valladares-Rodríguez, S., Soto-Barreiros, R.: An accessible platform for people with disabilities. Int. J. Hum.-Comput. Interact. **30**(6), 480–494 (2014)
45. Yeh, F.-H., Yang, C.-C.: Assisting the visually impaired to deal with telephone interview jobs using information and commutation technology. Res. Dev. Disabil. **35**(12), 3462–3468 (2014)
46. Ekberg, K., et al.: New business structures creating organizational opportunities and challenges for work disability prevention. J. Occup. Rehabil. **26**(4), 480–489 (2016). https://doi.org/10.1007/s10926-016-9671-0
47. Gnanasekaran, S., Choueiri, R., Neumeyer, A., Ajari, O., Shui, A., Kuhlthau, K.: Impact of employee benefits on families with children with autism spectrum disorders. Autism Int. J. Res. Pract. **20**(5), 616–622 (2016)
48. Padkapayeva, K., Posen, A., Yazdani, A., Buettgen, A., Mahood, Q., Tompa, E.: Workplace accommodations for persons with physical disabilities: evidence synthesis of the peer-reviewed literature. Disabil. Rehabil. **39**(21), 2134–2147 (2017)

Travel Service Design for the Visually Impaired: User Experience from Combining Real Human Assistants and AI Devices in an Appropriate Proportion

Linghong Li[(✉)]

Soochow University, Suzhou 215123, Jiangsu, China
lilinghongchina@hotmail.com

Abstract. Visual impairment in this paper comprises two categories blindness and low vision. China has the largest visually impaired population in the world. They have a lower social status and suffer discrimination. Due to various reasons, they can hardly go out without assistance and live a boring life. Travel is regarded as a way to regain dignity and equality and confidence in life by them. Since 2018, the travel service for visually impaired starts. However, this travel service is in a dilemma. The limited staff and volunteers are unable to meet the increasing demand of visually impaired for travel. The travel agency intends to increase the proportion of AI intelligent devices services and reduce the proportion of human services. On the other hand, although most visually impaired people accept AI devices to avoid seeking help from others in daily living, they do not show the same eager for travel. For them, travel distinguishes from simply going out. They long for social integration when travel. In order to better user experience for the travel service, this paper studies the user experiences it would bring to visually impaired if combining AI devices and real human assistants in an appropriate proportion in a travel service. And, what kind of proportion it would be. By fully considering the financial condition of visually impaired users in China, this paper aims to make the visually impaired travel service design more effective, more adaptable, and get better user experiences in the existing travel environment in China.

Keywords: Travel service design · Visually impaired · User experience

1 Introduction

The definition of "visual impairment" used in this paper follows the categories of the International Classification of Diseases ICD-11 (WHO) [1] and the *GLOBAL DATA ON VISUAL IMPAIRMENTS 2010 (WHO)* [2]. Visual impairment comprises categories 1 to 5, in which blindness, categories 3 to 5. The two categories of moderate and severe visual impairment (<6/18> 6/60 and <6/60> 3/60) are combined (<6/18> 3/60) and they are referred to as "low vision" [2]. Visual impairment in this paper comprises two categories blindness and low vision.

© Springer Nature Switzerland AG 2020
M. Antona and C. Stephanidis (Eds.): HCII 2020, LNCS 12189, pp. 437–450, 2020.
https://doi.org/10.1007/978-3-030-49108-6_31

China has the largest visually impaired population in the world. According to the data in the Visual Impairment and Blindness 2010 (WHO) [3] and the *GLOBAL DATA ON VISUAL IMPAIRMENTS 2010 (WHO)*, the visually impaired population was 75.512 million in China, including 8.248 million blind and 67.274 million low vision [2]. However, it's convinced the visually impaired population has increased rapidly through the years according to the China Disabled Persons' Federation (CDPF), e.g. the current number of the blind is estimated to be over 13 million at present [4], which means there is one in every 107 Chinese people is blind, not to mention the low vision.

Due to various reasons including the city planning and other social factors, visually impaired people in China can hardly go out without assistance. Although China has the world's largest visually impaired population, they are rare to see around every neighborhood. Learned from survey interviews of this research, among all events related to going out, travel is the most desired but most difficult to achieve for visually impaired. They are eager and actively willing to seek every possible opportunity to travel. But for a long time, no agency or any organization other than their family was able to provide them with travel services.

Since the year 2018, a phenomenon worthy of attention is the emergence of visually impaired tour groups in China, which are organized by the travel agency Zhisu-Ronghe, which was founded by the Suzhou Zhisu Charity Service Center and locates in Suzhou China. It is by far the only travel agency in China that only offers tours for visually impaired. In 2019, China's CCTV has reported on the travel service for visually impaired offered by this travel agency.

However, this travel service is in a dilemma. As the travel satisfaction of visually impaired users is less related to the various beauty and the appearance of traveling attractions, but it is fully related to the guidance efficiency of the entire travel service. As the increasing demand of visually impaired who involved in the travel service, the limited staff and volunteers are unable to meet diverse service needs on every trip. On the other hand, this travel service must be implemented in the existing travel environment in China, for example it includes the use of the existing airports, train stations, hotels, the streets and other places. As an alternative, this travel agency intends to increase the proportion of AI intelligent devices services and reduce the proportion of human services that were originally required. Prior to this, all travel services were provided by real people including travel agency staff and a large number of volunteers. There are vary differences in terms of service efficiency and quality, and complaints from visually impaired users abound in the process.

On the other hand, there is a notable phenomenon from visually impaired: although most visually impaired people accept spontaneously AI devices to avoid seeking help from others when they go out in daily living, they do not show the same eager in a journey. For them, travel distinguishes from simply going out. The travel experience is definitely different from the going out experience. Therefore, as they rarely go out and have social activities, they long for more face-to-face conversation and social integration when travel than for AI devices.

With the development of artificial intelligence (AI) technology, the personal AI devices are in optimistic hypothesis that may become one main go-out assistant to the visually impaired people, of which are currently widely used in navigation and screen reading, etc. It is sane to use the artificial intelligence (AI) technology for the travel of visually impaired and it may be the mainstream of the future.

So when considering this case, in order to better user experience for the travel service, it should be necessary to study what kind of user experience it would bring to visually impaired if combining AI devices and real human assistants in an appropriate proportion in a travel service. And, what kind of proportion it would be.

This paper aims to make the travel service design for visually impaired people more effective, more adaptable, and get better user experiences. For this aim, this paper does interview surveys and user experience tests on the travel service of visually impaired. It also proposes travel service design concept as part of the research induction and the conceptual AI devices designed with services for study. Furthermore, there is a constructive discussion towards research in the future for visually impaired.

2 Visually Impaired in China as the User in Travel Service

2.1 Strong Desire for Face-to-Face Conversation and Social Integration in Travel Services

As mentioned in previous section, visual impairment in this paper comprises two categories blindness and low vision. In order to understand their strong desire for face-to-face conversation and social integration in travel services, surveys have been done to study their social role and going out problems in China.

Living and Social Status. The living standards and the income of the visually impaired people in China are below the average income level of this country. According to the statistics of the China Association of the Blind (CAB), only 30% of visually impaired people have stable jobs, of which 95% are engaged in blind massage work and the average monthly income is only around 2,000 RMB (250 EUR) [5, 6]. They suffer much from low social status, discrimination, and live in a boring routine. They tend to stay indoors to avoid self-esteem hurting.

This was mentioned by all visually impaired people in the interviews and could be considered the extremely strong and very general needs that travel is regarded as a way to regain dignity and equality and confidence in life by them. Meanwhile they believe that while traveling, they can regain self-esteem and temporarily get rid of the negative reactions, such as depression, feeling abandoned by society, etc. It can be considered that the needs of visually impaired in China for travel services are more emotional. They put two desires, strong social needs and the elimination of their negative emotions, into their expectations for travel services.

Difficulties in Going Out. Because most the street planning and public space environmental planning in the city planning of China are not applicable to the visually impaired (see Fig. 1), and nearly all the public transport systems are also not applicable to the visually impaired, all these comprehensive factors cause up to 30% of the visually impaired in China never go out even once in one year [7]. According to the Survey of Basic Information for the Visually Impaired of China, there are only 9% the visually impaired in China have the ability to go outdoors unaccompanied but limited to 4–6 times per week [7]. Others must be assisted if they go out in order to avoid unpredictable accidents on the road.

This helps to understand although most visually impaired people are willing to use AI devices to avoid seeking help from others when they go out, they do not show the same eager in a journey. Instead, they long for more conversation and social integration during travel. Because in their daily lives, they can only realize this wish by using the Internet in home. The Internet is in their imagination similar to AI devices.

Fig. 1. Some status of the blind roads (the yellow ones) in China. The planning is not always applicable to visually impaired. There are up to 30% of the visually impaired people in China never go out even once in one year. (Color figure online)

Fig. 2. Signs that prohibit dogs everywhere in China. Dogs are prohibited in nearly all public area and on all the public transport system in China. Moreover, the guide dogs are large dogs, they are banned in most large cities in China. These situations have blocked visually impaired individuals employ guide dogs to help navigate complex environments.

Guide Dogs and Problems Encountered in Use. The number of the guide dogs in China is less than 200 [8]. The current number of the guide dogs is very insufficient compared to the 13 million blind people in China at present. It makes it extremely difficult for the visually impaired people in China to adopt the guide dogs. Moreover, the guide dogs are large dogs, they are banned in most large cities in China, and dogs are prohibited in nearly all public area such as shopping mall and parks etc. and on all the public transport system in China, such as subways and buses, etc. (see Fig. 2).

Therefore, as they rarely go out and have social activities, the visually impaired people in China long for more face-to-face conversation and social integration when travel than for AI devices.

2.2   Preferring Group Tours

Based on the long cooperation of this research with the travel agency Zhisu-Ronghe that offers tour group for the visually impaired people, visually impaired in China prefer travel in groups (see Fig. 3). It could be summarized as followings:

- Affected by the customs of China to travel as a team;
- It is one of the few ways to live their social life;
- It is one of the few ways they can have real interaction with non-family members;
- They really dare not travel independently in China.

Till so far and in the future, group tours would continue to be the only form of travel service offered for the visually impaired.

Fig. 3. The group tour service offered for visually impaired

2.3   Intelligent Guiding Devices in Current Use and Selection Criteria

Intelligent Guiding Devices in Current Use. There are two types of intelligent guide devices being widely used by visually impaired in China, which are the guide map App and the ultrasonic electronic guide cane. Normally, the guide map App are used quite more widely than the ultrasonic electronic guide cane.

Selection Criteria. The low income of visually impaired in China makes price the principal reason when they decide which AI guide device to buy. It is the reason why the guide map App is quite more widely used than the ultrasonic electronic guide cane-because the guide map App is much cheaper to afford. The following tables (see Table 1 and Table 2) is statistics of the use of intelligent guide devices for 50 visually impaired persons, including 25 male and 25 female, who once participated in the travel service offered by the travel agency Zhisu-Ronghe. In these statistics, there is no significant difference in the selection results between male and female visually impaired.

Table 1. The use of intelligent guide devices for 50 visually impaired persons.

AI guide devices in use or purchased	Male (in number)	Female (in number)
Guide map app	25	25
Electronic guide cane	5	7
Others	0	0

Table 2. Potential purchase desire of AI devices affected by prices.

AI guide devices price range (Currency Unit: RMB)	Male (in number)	Female (in number)
0–100 RMB	25	25
101–300 RMB	25	25
301–500 RMB	25	25
501–1000 RMB	13	14
1001–3000 RMB	5	7
3000–RMB	1	2

According to the surveys, the price is an element that must be considered in order to better user experience when designing the travel service, because all the AI devices provided in the travel service are added to the travel service price. This should be taken in consideration that the income of the visually impaired people in China are below the average income level of this country. The price factor is likely to be one reason for them to evaluate their experiences of travel services.

3   Conceptual AI Devices Designed with Human Services for User Experience Tests in This Research

In real life, currently there are only two types of AI devices for visually impaired, the guide map App and the ultra-sonic electronic guide cane, are usually available on the market in China. These types are far from meeting the needs of travel services for visually impaired. According to the problems encountered by actual group tours and the interviews survey with travel agency Zhisu-Ronghe, we designed some conceptual AI devices along with services for testing in order to better study the user experience of combining real human assistants and AI devices in different proportion in travel services (see Fig. 4). At present, these services rely entirely on human assistants to achieve that has caused many complaints from users because of the long waiting hours and service oversight.

Fig. 4. Conceptual AI devices design process of this research.

The premise of all these conceptual designs and services is that they do not change any of the existing travel conditions in China, and the service price would be controlled as low as possible so as not to increase much travel service charges. We take into fully account of the low-income situation of visually impaired in China.

Before we used these design prototypes for actual tour group user experience tests, we performed part tests on real visually impaired individual users to determine the feasibility (see Fig. 5). Such tests provide experiences for subsequent tests in order to control the time process.

Fig. 5. Real visually impaired user test workshop for conceptual AI devices designed along with services.

3.1 Conceptual AI Devices for Check-In and Check-Out of a Hotel Along with Human Service

In China, hotel check-in and check-out require manual operations at the front desk. Only few check-out services are simple procedures. The hotel check-in and check-out processes are tedious for a tour group. It is most tedious for the visually impaired tour group. Because after checking in, the travel agency staff need to guide each visually impaired person of the tour group to find their own rooms. When checking out, the staff also need to guide visually impaired person of the tour group from the hotel rooms one by one to the hotel reception. There are usually 30–40 visually impaired people in one tour group. This causes that after checking in, visually impaired member of the tour group can only wait long time in the hotel lobby, waiting for the staff to send them to the room one by one. When checking out, the process is the same.

This conceptual design along with human service is to solve this problem. It consists of the smart navigation room card, the Bluetooth earphone, the charging panel and an App. In order to reduce the service cost for visually impaired, the smart navigation room card has the same appearance as hotel room card and functioned as a room key.

Fig. 6. The storyboard of how the smart navigation room card works

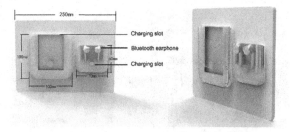

Fig. 7. The smart navigation room card and the Bluetooth earphone in the charging panel

The smart navigation room card has already stored the hotel's room lines. After checking in, visually impaired person can install the App manually, and wears the Bluetooth earphone. Then the navigation to the hotel room starts. The information in the smart navigation room card will be transmitted to the Bluetooth earphone through the App to accurately guide visually impaired to find the room, such as when entering the elevator and walking in the corridor (see Fig. 6).

Fig. 8. The App

After entering the room, put the smart navigation room card and the Bluetooth headset into the charging panel for charging (see Fig. 7). The function of the smart navigation room card is the same as that of the ordinary room card. The main switch of the room power is turned on by inserting this card to the panel. In addition, hotel check-in and check-out requirements can be completed in advance through this App (see Fig. 8).

Throughout the process, visually impaired person needs to manually install Apps at reception. This is the only time that uses human service throughout the process.

3.2 Conceptual AI Devices for Sharing One Hotel Twin Room with Human Service

In China, it is very common for two strangers the same gender to share one hotel twin room during the journey. This is one way to save costs for users who participate in group tours, and to avoid booking difficulties during peak tourist seasons. In the tour group for visually impaired, because the average income of visually impaired is lower in China, they always share one hotel twin room to save costs.

However, when two visually impaired persons as strangers share one twin rooms, it is difficult to identify objects in the hotel room. This is because in one twin room, the two sets of hotel supplies provided are the same. This conceptual design along with human service is to solve this problem. It includes three kinds items, small clips, intelligent touch maps, and an App.

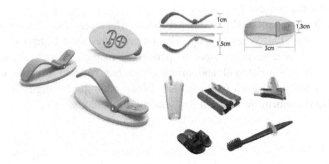

Fig. 9. The small clips used to guide visually impaired to correctly identify hotel objects.

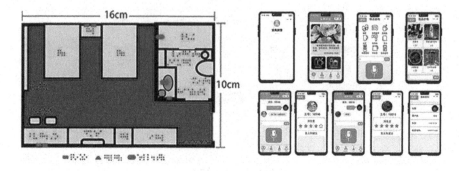

Fig. 10. The intelligent touch maps (left) and the App (right).

The small clips are made of the cheapest plastic to reduce the cost of room fee for visually impaired (see Fig. 9). The text of the intelligent touch maps uses Braille. One of the intelligent touch maps is hung near the switch of the room light at the entrance, and another two on each of the two beds in the room (see Fig. 10). The intelligent touch maps help visually impaired know the orientation of the furniture and hotel supplies in the room. And they can be converted into voice prompts through the App connected to the cell phone. The App program is installed by manual service upon check-in (see Fig. 10). It is used to call the room service and send for other requirements, such as changing sheets, cleaning the room, etc. And the service can be rated on it.

In this process, the human service intervention only helps visually impaired to install the app when check-in, and the others are completed by visually impaired through the app and the room's intelligent touch map.

3.3   Conceptual AI Devices for Airport Baggage Check-In and Claim with Human Service

China's airports are crowded, which makes baggage check-in and claim baggage the most difficult things for visually impaired. As visually impaired cannot discern their luggage from the luggage conveyor belt, they rely entirely on staff and volunteers to help. This process is very tedious. It takes average 1.5–4 h to get everyone's luggage for one visually impaired tour group. It also happens in the baggage pickup of tour buses. This conceptual design along with human service is to solve this problem to improve user experience.

It uses a low-cost smart Bluetooth wristband, which can also be used as a wireless earphone (see Fig. 11). When luggage checking-in, the smart Bluetooth wristband is put on the wrist of a visually impaired person by manual service. A smart barcode scanner records this wristband and prints out a bar code to stick to the Checked baggage of visually impaired (see Fig. 12). When claiming luggage, the smart Bluetooth wristband confirm the luggage by sensing the barcode.

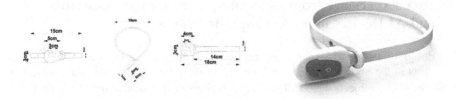

Fig. 11. The smart Bluetooth wristband

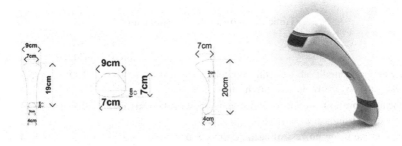

Fig. 12. The smart barcode scanner

Fig. 13. The App

In order to reduce the service cost of visually impaired, an app is designed to connect with the mobile phone of visually impaired, thereby reducing the use of other smart devices (see Fig. 13). The app helps visually impaired people to know the exact location of the luggage conveyor belt. When their luggage pass by, the app sounds alarms to remind visually impaired person know.

Throughout the process, the manual service is to help visually impaired to wear the smart Bluetooth wristbands, print and paste barcodes when checking-in luggage. Real human service may also be available to assist visually impaired in finding and removing luggage from the luggage carousel.

4   User Experience from Combining Real Human Assistants and AI Devices in an Appropriate Proportion

We do questionnaire to visually impaired users to answer questions according to the user tests in the above section. A total of 50 visually impaired people participated in these tests. The subjects were still the exact 50 people mentioned in the above Sect. 2.3 Intelligent Guiding Devices in Current Use and Selection Criteria, 25 males and 25 females. They should score 1–5 points for each question. If it fits his/her mind, score 5 points. If it doesn't fit his/her mind, score 1 point. Then we take the average score for each answer. The Table 3 presents part of the results.

Table 3. Scores from questionnaire

Question	Total score	Score (Male)	Score (Female)
(a) After experiencing the above artificial intelligence devices, I still willing to rely solely on the current manual service	1.5	1.88	1.12
(b) In the using process of each AI device, only one-time human service is used. I think it is enough	1.92	2.4	1.44
(c) I hope in the using process of each AI device, one more human service will be added	3.72	3.2	4.24
(d) I hope in the using process of each AI device, two or more human service will be added	2.64	2.4	2.88
(e) I hope to increase the proportion of human service participation that in the three AI devices up to 50% or more	1.38	1.2	1.56
(f) I think the use of these smart devices improves the quality of travel	4.54	4.6	4.48
(g) I think using these smart devices has affected my expectations for travel	1.18	1.2	1.16

According to the statistics, we obtain the following enlightenment toward user experience:

- The visually impaired users are willing to accept AI devices in travel services;
- Relying solely on real human assistants in the user travel experience does not get a high user experience score;
- Although before the research began, user needs showed that they had a strong social communication desire for travel service and expected face-to-face communication, these intelligent guidance devices (conceptual) have not caused them to resent;
- Users obviously expect one or more manual help or human services in the process of using the AI devices;
- The appropriate proportion of combining real human assistants and AI devices might be: 30%–40% for real human assistants, and 70%–60% for AI devices. But this proportion might vary depending on test content;
- Neither full human services nor full AI device services will lead to real satisfaction of visually impaired users.

5   Conclusion and Further Discussion

The premise of user experience of visually impaired discussed in this paper is based on China's travel environment. In this environment, there are two factors that affect. First, since the income of visually impaired people in China is generally lower than the national average, the function and the final price of AI devices for travel services of visually impaired need to be considered comprehensively. Therefore, this paper proposes a solution to satisfy the various stakeholders involved in travel services for visually impaired to reasonably combine the real human assistants and AI devices in an appropriate proportion.

The research in this paper relates to the common experience such as check-in in group tourism, because the travel service experiences are influenced by these processes when designing travel service for visually impaired. The results of this research can also be applied to understand the balance needed for using AI technologies in real life needs.

There is still more research related to travel service for visually impaired. In the future, such user experience research will be carried out in the following areas:

- Better tactile experiences on a group tour for visually impaired by combining real human assistants and AI devices in an appropriate proportion (see Fig. 14);

Fig. 14. One visually impaired person of the tour group touches the ice to understand the winter scenery.

- Better hearing experiences on a group tour for visually impaired by combining real human assistants and AI devices in an appropriate proportion (see Fig. 15);

Fig. 15. One visually impaired person of the tour group hears sound of the river to understand the scenery.

Fig. 16. The visually impaired tour group share one table Chinese dishes with help of staff.

- Better eating experiences on a group tour for visually impaired by combining real human assistants and AI devices in an appropriate proportion. This may be the hardest part of the entire research because Chinese dishes are "shared" on one table, which is also a group meal form for Chinese group travel (see Fig. 16). There are usually 10 persons share one table dishes. At present this is done entirely by real human services, and each staff can only serve at most 1–2 visually impaired people for dining at one time.

Acknowledgments. Thanks to the students who participated in all the studies and workshops of this research. Thanks to the visually impaired who voluntarily participated in this research. Thanks to the volunteers who assisted visually impaired for test. Special thanks to the Suzhou Zhisu-Ronghe Travel Agency and the Suzhou Zhisu Charity Service Center for their cooperation in this research.

References

1. International Classification of Diseases ICD-11 (WHO). https://icd.who.int/browse11/l-m/en
2. Global Data on Visual Impairments 2010 (WHO). https://www.who.int/blindness/GLOBALDATAFINALforweb.pdf
3. Visual Impairment and Blindness 2010 (WHO). https://www.who.int/blindness/data_maps/VIFACTSHEETGLODAT2010full.pdf
4. The Total Number of People with Disabilities and with Different Types of Disability at the End of 2010 (CDPF). http://www.cdpf.org.cn/sjzx/cjrgk/201206/
5. China Internet Visually Impaired Users Basic Situation Report. http://www.199it.com/archives/460010.html. Accessed 08 Apr 2016
6. Sample Survey Report on Insurance Needs of Visually Impaired (CDPF). http://www.cdp.net.cn/channel_/VisualImpairment/2017-12/18-16668.html
7. Survey of Basic Information for the Visually Impaired. http://www.time-weekly.com/post/268111
8. China Guide Dog South Demonstration Base. http://www.time-weekly.com/post/268111

The Influence of Social Networking Technology on Centennials Purchase Intent

Célia M. Q. Ramos[1](✉) and João M. F. Rodrigues[2]

[1] ESGHT, CinTurs and CEFAGE,
Universidade do Algarve, 8005-139 Faro, Portugal
cmramos@ualg.pt
[2] LARSyS (ISR-Lisbon) and ISE,
Universidade do Algarve, 8005-139 Faro, Portugal
jrodrig@ualg.pt

Abstract. Centennials are the young consumers born into the Internet age who regard social networks as the prime means of communicating with friends, searching for product and brand information. Social networks enable this type of consumer to become a brand agent when they share their opinions through comments and ratings about their products, which contributes to building a brand's online reputation. This study focuses on the youngest population (under 21 years of age) and its use of social media, as a way to find commercial information about products and understand how these platforms can contribute to increased sales and encourage preference for a particular product type. A survey based on the experience economy theory was disseminated online through Facebook to gauge users' behavior, and a Social Networks User Experience (SNUX) model was considered to study the youngest user experience associated with the use of these platforms as medium to find and purchase online products. The SNUX model was analyzed through structural equations modeling using SmartPLS 2.0. From the results obtained, it was concluded that social networks can contribute to increase the personal value of the centennials generation, mainly from the technological experience associated with the use of these platforms, which contributes to the education of these users.

Keywords: Social networks · Consumer behavior · Internet marketing · Technological experience · Information and communication technology · Centennials · Experience economy

1 Introduction

The connection between humans and society, even for those who have physical limitations, is becoming increasingly technology enabled. The use of sensors, Internet-of-Things (IoT), big data, cloud computing, mobile technologies, among other technological pillars of the industry 4.0 [1], are contributing to the leverage of the human–computer interaction.

The whole environment provided by information and communication technologies (ICT) has caused behavioral changes in users, in general, and particularly in the younger generation, which are "internet dependent". They use this medium to

© Springer Nature Switzerland AG 2020
M. Antona and C. Stephanidis (Eds.): HCII 2020, LNCS 12189, pp. 451–465, 2020.
https://doi.org/10.1007/978-3-030-49108-6_32

communicate with friends as a way of keeping in touch with others, while at the same time, to have acceptance among peers [2].

On the other hand, social networks help to connect people who have common interests and friends, which leads to the current need of brands sought to be present in these privileged means of communication, where their potential consumers are, coupled with the fact that the costs associated with advertising campaigns are lower compared to traditional media, which are losing general viewership and do not arouse the interest of the younger population [2].

The focus is based, not from the point of view of the consumption of economic goods influenced by the consumer's behavior, but by the consumption of information in the social networks and how this information influences the purchase intention, with the objective to determine whether or not it contributes to the personal valuation of the youngest population (born after 1999, 16–20 years old). The study takes into account the dimensions associated with the economy of experience: evasion, education, entertainment and aesthetics [3].

The contribution of the article is to identify trends in the behavior of these future adult consumers, who belong to the centennial generation, by focusing on the contribution of the definition of strategies needed to reach this segment.

This article is structured in four sections, in addition to the introduction and conclusion. The first section clarifies how social networks have contributed to change consumer's behavior and how this environment conditions the youngest adult – the centennials – followed by the concepts of the consumer journey and experience economy that have emerged associated to the social networks technological experience. The second section presents the conceptual research model and the research hypotheses associated with the study. The third section defines the methodology used, which considers concepts of structural equation models. The fourth section analyzes and presents the results. In the final section, conclusions are drawn with implications, limitations, and future work.

2   Centennials Purchase Intention

Centennials is a term that refers to people born from the year 2000, inclusive, until our days [4], also known as the Generation Z [2], and is considered more active than previous generations, called Millennials. This generation is very (extremely) connected to social media [5], completely connected to friends, also via social media, have grown up with smartphones and are more selective about their audiences in these platforms [6].

To help marketers understand this generation, McGorry and McGorry [6] developed a study to investigate the implications of Centennials social media use and preferences. They concluded that Centennials prefer to use video to communicate, use social media to communicate with friends and to entertain themselves, prefer Snapchat and Instagram to socialize and YouTube to search for new products and services. McGorry and McGorry [6] also suggest that marketers should create content that is shared in an entertaining and informative way (infomercial style).

With the Internet and all the associated social media platforms, a new kind of economy appeared that contributed to consumer behavior changes and the need to develop new marketing strategies [7]. However, this kind of generation has a way of being in society that goes on, as they are connected 24/7 looking for information. To attract consumers, such as the Centennials who were born in the era of social networks, it is necessary to include digital experiences for these digital natives that meet their emotional needs, search for authenticity and personal preferences. This adds challenges to the organizations to satisfy these consumers who are more demanding in terms of products and service quality [8].

Social networks not only enable the communication of informative and entertaining content, but are also the tool that can get closer to the consumers of this generation since it is possible to create interest groups that "meet the family" created in the social networks, allowing to create collaborative content with interactive information [2] that contributes to the sense of belonging [9].

The importance of this segment is becoming increasingly relevant to marketers, as future adults will be consumers whose purchasing power will increase, additionally considering that they will impact the world. For Williams and Page [9] there are aspects that marketers must keep in mind: seek immediate gratification, believe success will be guaranteed, have liberal social values and high digital skills.

Due to the youth of Centennials, in which only the elders are reaching adulthood, and consequently acquiring the ability to make their independent consumption decisions, studies are scarce. However, due to the relevance of the investigation of the influence of the use of social networks, it has already been analyzed in studies, such as: Duffet [10] examined the influence of interactive social media marketing on teenagers' cognitive, affective and behavioral attitude components; in Herrando, Jimenez-Martinez, and Martin-De-Hoyos [11] study, the information provided by users (in social networks) has been considered more trustworthy than the information shared by companies, which has a great impact on the youngest users. On the other hand, Llopis-Amorós, Gil-Saura, Ruiz-Molina, and Fuentes-Blasco. [12] investigates the behavior associated with different ages and the moderating role of the generational cohort in the influence of social media communications on brand equity creation. Ramos and Matos [13] also found that the Centennials attach greater importance to the information shared about events in social networks.

Although there is no consensus regarding the start and end year of each generation, as noted by Llopis-Amorós et al. [12], consider the start year for Centennials the year 2000, as considered by the authors Jones, Jo, and Martin [14] and Twenge, Campbell, Hoffman, and Lance [4].

The Centennials represent the consumers of the future, which means that they start to attract attention and it becomes relevant to analyze their behavior and purchase intentions in digital environments, as technological natives who are always connected and communicate on social networks. These technological users are always online, on any device, are practical, less competitive but more impatient and more agile than their predecessors and are continually looking for new challenges and impulses [12].

In this context, the first hypothesis of this research is to validate whether the use of social networks is motivated by the personal valuation of the acquisition of knowledge and technological experience associated with their use.

Hypothesis #1 (H_1): Increase personal valuation through the acquisition of knowledge acquired through social networks?

In addition, Xiang and Gretzel [15] point out that these platforms serve as a means to learn about products, brands and services, since they include a large variety of information sources, produced and shared by the users themselves, which increases credibility and trust in the shared content, contributing to the development of the social media experience and consumer engagement in this medium.

The social media experience is associated to the technological experience in the context of the social media platforms, which has emerged as an important tool in identifying and creating opportunities to discover consumer's needs [16], at the same time providing a new way to introduce brand-associated content and develop customer exchanges, engaging with customer interactions.

The social media marketing has a great role as it attracts and retains consumers born in the social networks' era. Digital natives require a complete and more incisive customer knowledge; therefore, stakeholders need to reshape and adapt their strategies to meet this generation's habits and characteristics [16].

The Centennials expect digital customer experience associated to the social networks though all the stages of the customer journey. The customer experience process flows from a pre-consumption phase or pre-purchase to a consumption phase or purchase to an after-consumption phase or post-purchase, in a dynamic and iterative way [17]. In the context of the customer journey, two more phases can be considered: previous experience and future experience. The previous experience is related to feelings and memories created by past consumer experiences, while the future experience is related to the sum of all the experiences that occurred in previous purchases and the one being experienced. The latter is crucial because it is the last, meaning that it is more fresh and present in memory, as presented in Fig. 1.

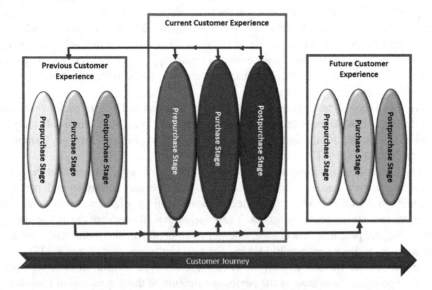

Fig. 1. Customer journey and experience (Source: Adapted from [17]).

Figure 1 shows the customer journey that the previous experience affects, the experience being lived (present) and the future experience. In terms of customer experience, the experience being lived will add value to the previous experience after ending. The pre-consumption phase includes the pre-purchase touch points, such as: brand/product owned, partner owned, customer owned and Social Networks. In this stage, the customer interacts with the brands, recognizes the need or the necessity of the product, service and initiates the search for information [17].

The consumption (or Purchase phase) includes the Purchase Touch Points, which is when the customer interacts with the product/brand and when he/she takes the purchase decision, ordering and doing the payment of the product or service elected. In the after-consumption (or Post-purchase phase), which includes the Post-purchase touch points, customers may engage with the tourism destination and or tourism experiences they consumed, thus promoting and sharing their experience (positive or negative). The customer experience contributes to create memories that can be shared in social networks, complemented with photos and videos. In addition, the user can evaluate all the consumer experience and commenting and sharing on social networks becomes a brand or product agent.

All the stages associated with the customer journey and the customer experience are supported by information, so it is fundamental to reflect on the appropriate communication channels to reach all potential stakeholders and age groups. In the case of Centennials, the communication channel per excellence is social networks. Although the social networks technological experience associated with customer experience is not analyzed from the experience economics concept of Pine and Gilmore [3], i.e., the point of view of the information consumption can contribute to the business. These authors considered that consumers seek to be involved and absorbed in the experience [18, 19].

Aluri [20] applied the economics of the experience theory to the use of the Pokémon GO app to investigate the factors that influence travelers to use the application and its influence on the experience of each individual. Radder and Han [21] examined the experience of visiting a museum through the theory of the "experience economy." On the other hand, Ramos and Rodrigues [22] studied the effect of technological experience, taking into account the concepts of experience economics to investigate how information consumption through social networks contributes to the well-being of the older population, mainly from the technological experience associated with the use of these platforms.

The experience economy by Pine and Gilmore [3] is a concept that unites the dimensions: educational, entertainment, aesthetics and evasion, on a scale from passive to active participation, and feelings of immersion to absorption. In terms of the use of social networks, and taking into account the concepts of the experience economy from an information-consumption perspective (in different formats: text, photographs, videos), the dimension of entertainment can be considered in the viewing of videos and photos, communication with others, the sharing of comments, and more. The educational dimension is revealed by searches for information regarding products, services and news. The dimension of evasion can be observed while the user is viewing photos and videos. The dimension of aesthetics can be measured in terms of the environment provided by the social media interface, i.e., whether it is pleasant, beautiful or intuitive.

In this context, we intend to analyze the contribution of the four dimensions of the experience economy to the social networks technological experience by the Centennial's users. For this analysis, the following four research hypotheses are considered:

1) **Hypothesis #2 (H_2):** Does the social networks technological experience contribute to the brand consumer education of the centennial's users?
2) **Hypothesis #3 (H_3):** Does the social networks technological experience contribute to the brand consumer evasion (and dreaming) of the centennial's users?
3) **Hypothesis #4 (H_4):** Does the social networks technological experience contribute to the brand consumer entertainment of the centennial's users?
4) **Hypothesis #5 (H_5):** Does the social networks technological experience contribute to the brand aesthetics valorization of the centennial's users?

All four dimensions (entertainment, educational, aesthetic and evasion) contribute to the overall experience [3]. The overall experience is associated with the motivation that prompted the use of social networks: entertainment, dreaming, beauty and education. It also contributes to the personal valuation of the youngest user, as presented in H1.

In this context, and in the present study, taking into account information consumption, consumer involvement and the characteristics of the centennial's users, we intend to investigate the impact that the four dimensions of social network technological experience [3] has on centennials, and consequently how the social networks technological experience contributes to increasing the Centennial's personal valuation, considering how this influences their consumer behavior and purchase intentions.

3   Conceptual Research Model and Hypotheses

As already mentioned, the aim of the study is to analyze the Centennials contribution to the social networks technological experience (user experience) as well as the concepts associated with the experience economy.

3.1   Research Hypothesis

In order to investigate the objectives presented and the hypotheses formulated, a set of questions associated with the concept of the experience economy was considered to assess the experience associated with the use of social networks, taking into account the profile of the respondent.

To investigate these hypotheses, a research model was considered to evaluate the user's experience with the use of the social networks, called the Social Networks User Experience Model (SNUX) [22], as presented in Fig. 2.

3.2   Research Model

The SNUX model [22] evaluates the experience economy dimensions of the *Social Networks Technological Experience* (SNTE), where the concepts of the experience economy were considered in the context of the consumption of information and its contribution to the added personal value of the user measured by the variable *Add Value to the User* (AVU), which contributes to increase the consumer and the purchase intention of the Centennials.

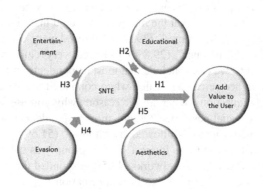

Fig. 2. Research model. (Source: Adapted from [22]).

4 Methodology

After the identification of the research hypotheses, the literature review and delimitation of the research problem, the proposed study methodology was based on the following steps: 1) construction of the survey; 2) data collection; 3) selection and codification of data; 4) selection of methods and techniques of data analysis; and, 5) analysis of the results.

The survey was released in December 2018. Of 131 survey responses, 124 valid responses were obtained. The base sample was social network users below 21 years old, using the probabilistic method of "convenience sampling," in which the sample is selected based on the availability and accessibility of the elements of the population. After data collection, responses were codified to make possible the analysis of the data by descriptive statistics to characterize the sample, and the structural equation model was applied to evaluate the SNUX research model. The interpretation of results was elaborated, and the conclusions presented, along with the limitations and future work.

5 Results

5.1 Characterization of the Sample

Of the 124 respondents, the sample characterization is defined by an average age of 17 years old, a majority of women (55.0%) and student (91.9%). In terms of the education level, the majority were high school students (77.4%), followed by university students (14.5%). Most of the respondents prefer to use smartphones (84.7%), followed by computers (12.1%) and tablets (3.2%).

The users interviewed had a Facebook profile (99.2%), followed by 91.9% on Instagram, and a very close 89.5% on Snapchat and 86.3% on YouTube. Twitter (68.6%), Pinterest (34.7%) and LinkedIn (7.3%) are the social networks that had the lowest value, probably because they did not arouse the interest of this age group.

In response to the question "What kind of content do you share on social networks?," our analysis concluded that the majority answered that they share texts a "few times" (38.7%), images "often times" (39.5%) followed very close by "sometimes" (35.5%), and videos "sometimes" (29.8%) followed very close by a "few times" (28.2%). In these results, we can conclude that most respondents prefer content, such as images, as it has a higher percentage value when compared to others.

In response to the question "What are the reasons why you use social networks?," among those who use social networks "Often", most respondents (84.76%) replied "to communicate with their friends," followed by "hobby" (51.6%) and "discover new trends" (33.1%). What aroused less interest for this group was the "find new". In the group that "sometimes" use social networks: 43.5% responded that they use it to "find new", followed by 41.1% who use it "to find information."

5.2   Evaluation of the SNUX Measurement Model

Following the selection and codification of data, methods and techniques were identified to analyze the data. The structural equation model (SEM) was considered since it is the model indicated to overcome the need to measure multidimensional and not-directly-observable concepts, also called constructs or latent variables [23]. According to the work of Gefen, Straub and Boudreau [24], the SEM "has become the rigueur in validating instruments and testing linkages between constructs".

The structural equation model considered is variance based SEM or partial least squares path SEM [25], which permits the construction of the model in an exploratory phase, with a little portion of the sample that can be without normal distribution [26, 27].

It is necessary to analyze the adjustment quality of the model through three steps: 1) evaluation of the measurement model to guarantee the convergent validity; 2) observation of internal consistency values; and 3) discrimination quality assessment [27]. The evaluation of the measurement model to guarantee the convergent validity is evaluated by observation of the average variance extracted (AVE) [28, 29], where all the AVE values should be more than 0.5, which is a condition to guarantee that the model converges to a satisfactory result.

Observation of internal consistency values take into consideration the values the Cronbach's alpha (CA) and composite reliability (CR), expressed by the rho of Dillon-Goldstein, which makes it possible to ascertain whether the sample is free of biases and whether, on the whole, it is reliable. The values of CA should be higher than 0.6, and values of 0.7 are considered adequate. Values of CR should be higher than 0.7, and values of 0.9 are considered satisfactory [26, 27].

Table 1 presents the estimated values of the adjustment quality of the SNUX model. By using the AVE values, it is possible to conclude that the SNUX model will converge to a satisfactory result, as all the values are higher than 0.5 [30]. Table 1 also permits an analysis of the internal consistency of the model through the values of CA and CR. CA values higher than 0.6 and 0.7 and CR values higher than 0.7 and 0.9 indicate that the model is satisfactory.

Table 1. Values of the adjustment quality of the SNUX model.

	AVE	Composite reliability (CR)	Cronbachs alpha (CA)
AVU	0.5101	0.8779	0.8411
Aesthetic	0.6884	0.8979	0.8499
Education	0.8319	0.9368	0.8997
Entertainment	0.7008	0.8754	0.8018
Evasion	0.5723	0.8401	0.8065
SNTE	0.5277	0.8169	0.7027

In the third step, the discriminant validity assessment permits investigation of the independence between latent variables and other variables. This analysis can be done by observing cross loading, which should be the indicators with the highest factor loading in their respective latent variables, when compared with the observed variables, or by the criterion of Fornell and Larcker [28], which compares the square roots of the AVE values of each latent variable with the Pearson's correlations between the latent variables. The square roots of AVEs should be larger than correlations between those of latent variables.

In the first process, and taking into consideration the values presented in Table 2, the cross loadings of the observed variables in one latent variable is always higher than the cross loadings of the observed variables in another latent variable; these are not the variables that help measure, which shows that the model has discriminant validity, in accordance with the work of Chin [26].

In the second process and taking into consideration the values presented in Table 3, the variance identified in the AVE must exceed the variance that the observed variables share with other latent variables of the model. In practice, discriminant validity exists when the squared root of the AVE of each construct is greater than the correlation values between the latent variables and the observed variables [31]. Table 4 shows that the SNUX model has discriminant validity, as confirmed by the first process, as the values of the square roots of the AVE values, presented in the main diagonal, are higher than the correlation between the latent variables, in accordance to the work of Fornell and Larcker [32].

After guaranteeing discriminant validity in the evaluation of the measurement model (meaning that the adjustments in the measurement model have ended), the next step is the evaluation of the structural model.

Table 2. Values of cross loadings of the observed variables in the latent variables

	AVU	Aesthetics	Educational	Entertainment	Evasion	SNTE
KA	**0.715791**	0.289515	0.178722	0.220468	−0.002875	0.22657
KE	**0.559084**	0.244842	0.246529	0.240481	0.099454	0.391838
KG	**0.816582**	0.214037	0.278001	0.179027	0.092107	0.412
KH	**0.752164**	0.250785	0.337744	0.219192	0.096912	0.394913
KM	**0.77783**	0.264041	0.327287	0.26229	0.029335	0.49246
KR	**0.641311**	0.140296	0.172606	0.191351	0.079917	0.207821
KT	**0.704747**	0.209912	0.283368	0.167557	−0.001024	0.326376
EE_1	0.263285	**0.790219**	0.312779	0.396571	0.217653	0.297911
EE_2	0.255877	**0.750302**	0.322514	0.39435	0.148383	0.213367
EE_3	0.317276	**0.899529**	0.361745	0.518156	0.261722	0.376695
EE_4	0.250302	**0.870169**	0.303444	0.488261	0.283056	0.35242
EN_1	0.324431	0.501143	0.440169	**0.840322**	0.285678	0.416646
EN_3	0.21695	0.435329	0.353429	**0.829662**	0.31961	0.239958
EV_1	0.11434	0.219224	0.326384	0.348003	**0.86007**	0.200442
EV_2	0.077733	0.195456	0.385013	0.234979	**0.601487**	−0.026475
EV_3	0.012648	0.281024	0.198263	0.291955	**0.831521**	0.153302
EV_4	0.071777	0.168134	0.128439	0.237727	**0.704537**	0.045458
ED_1	0.369394	0.360766	**0.917088**	0.435548	0.281417	0.465748
ED_2	0.372655	0.378608	**0.948223**	0.503724	0.269915	0.465756
ED_3	0.295179	0.32009	**0.869263**	0.386045	0.236	0.340018
MC	0.316244	0.31322	0.289685	0.435526	0.211345	**0.682781**
MF	0.470895	0.293321	0.406173	0.202907	0.089862	**0.73745**
MS	0.346926	0.274341	0.382576	0.285334	0.250471	**0.743057**
MT	0.369468	0.231527	0.272062	0.218133	0.063294	**0.740732**

5.3 Evaluation of the Structural Model

In the evaluation of the structural model, the first step is the evaluation of the Pearson's correlations coefficient (R^2) of the endogenous latent variables. In this study there are two endogenous latent variables: AVU with an $R^2 = 0.275$ and SNTE with a $R^2 = 0.279$. These values are moderate and represent the portion of the variance of the endogenous variables that is explained by the structural model [31].

Another aspect to analyze is the model's capacity to predict, which requires the calculation of the Stone-Geisser indicator (Q^2) and the Cohen indicator (f^2) associated to the effect size [29]. The Stone-Geisser indicator (Q^2) evaluates how close the model is to what was expected; the Cohen indicator (f^2) evaluates how useful each construct is for the model. The Q^2 associated with the endogenous latent variables presents a value higher than zero, which means that both variables have predictive power, and the structural model has predictive relevance, as presented in Table 3.

Table 3. Indicators values of the predictive validity and effect size.

		Q^2	F^2
AVU	ENLV	0.226	0.297
Aesthetic	EXLV		0.510
Education	EXLV		0.257
Entertainment	EXLV		0.300
Evasion	EXLV		0.365
SNTE	ENLV	0.142	0.234

Legend: *EXLV* – Exogeneous Latent Variable; *ENLV* – Endogeneous Latent Variable

Table 4. Values of the correlations between the latent variables and the square roots of the AVE values (on the main diagonal)

	AVU	Aesthetics	Educational	Entertainment	Evasion	SNTE
AVU	**0.7141**					
Aesthetics	0.3273	**0.8297**				
Educational	0.3830	0.3892	**0.9121**			
Entertainment	0.2998	0.5471	0.4884	**0.8371**		
Evasion	0.0824	0.2832	0.2894	0.3769	**0.7565**	
SNTE	0.5240	0.3846	0.4719	0.3877	0.2102	**0.7264**

The structural model analyses ends with the individual analysis of the coefficients of the respective model (path coefficients) [30, 31], where it is necessary to analyze the sign, the value and the statistical significance, which should be more than 1.96 (bilateral and with a 5% significance level).

The model can also be analyzed by its direct effects. Table 5 presents the direct effect, which indicates, by the t-test value of 1.5125, that the H_0 should be accepted and the direct coefficient should be zero. This means that the aesthetic dimension does not have an effect on the social network technological experience. Also, the evasion and the entertainment dimensions, which have a t-test lower than the 1.96, means that these dimensions do not have an effect on the social network technological experience. However, as the educational dimension has an effect on the SNTE, which increases the AVU, it can be concluded that the utilization of social networks contributes added value to the Centennials (personal value) if the content educational contents related to the brands and products.

Table 5. Direct effects in the structural relationships between the latent variables

	Structural coefficient	Standard deviation (STDEV)	T-value
Aesthetic → SNTE	0.1852	0.1225	**1.5125**
Education → SNTE	0.3390	0.1033	3.2837
Entertainment → SNTE	0.1145	0.1087	**1.0531**
Evasion → SNTE	0.0164	0.1159	**0.1423**
SNTE → AVU	0.5240	0.0754	6.9488

6   Conclusions

Companies have changed the way they communicate their products by building these networks into their business strategies. The Centennials population will be the new consumer in the future, having different behavior patterns. Consequently, all the stakeholders need to understand their behavior and their characteristics to achieve their interest and potentiate their purchase intention to increase or maintain the sales volume of the company.

It is relevant to analyze the Centennial users' perceptions of the technological experience of using social networks and study how social networks contribute to a sense of well-being and personal valuation by present contents with educational formats, preferring the images format. This study investigated this issue by considering the concepts associated with the experience economy in an information acquisition perspective that added value to the users, and contributed to increasing their purchase intentions, which led to considering the research model called Social Networks User Experience (SNUX) [22] which was analyzed through a structural equations system.

The analysis of the research data allowed the development of a model of the involvement of Centennial users in social networks, which helps us understand the technological experience associated with the adoption and use of social networks, as well as develop strategies that should be considered to communicate products and brands in these platforms, always with an educational message and with the possibility to offer rewards to this generation.

In terms of the technological experience associated with the concepts of the experience economy and the use of social networks by the Centennial generation, this research model found no empirical evidence to support a structural relationship between the aesthetic, entertainment and evasion dimensions and the SNTE. On the other hand, the educational dimension contributes to the SNTE, and the effect of the SNTE in Centennials contributes to an increase in added value to these users.

With the SNUX model, considered in the Centennial's generation, it is possible to conclude that with respect to the SNTE, education contribute to added personal value for Centennials users. Taking into consideration the research hypotheses, H_1 proved that the use of social networks increases personal valuation through the acquisition of knowledge. H_2 proved that the technological experience contributes to the education of the Centennial's user of social networks. However, H_3, H_4 and H_5 were rejected based on the responses of the interviewed, which showed that the technological experience does not contribute to the evasion, entertainment and aesthetic dimension of the Centennial user of social networks.

The limitations with the present study include the fact that the members of the age group that use social networks have a secondary or lower education qualification level. The majority who have not yet reached adulthood have neither consumer power nor, sometimes, decision-making power.

In terms of future work, the analysis of the relationship between the reasons and the dimensions of the technological experience provided by social networks will be considered for the Millennials and the results will be compared with the present generation in the study.

Acknowledgments. This paper is financed by National Funds provided by FCT - Foundation for Science and Technology through project CinTurs (UID/SOC/04020/2019), project CEFAGE (PEst-C/EGE/UI4007/2019) and project LARSyS - FCT Plurianual funding 2020–2023.

Appendix A.

List of the Latent Variables and Their Constructs

Add Value to the User (AVU) – reflective	
KA	Adquiring knowledge about Accomodation
KE	Adquiring knowledge about Events
KG	Adquiring knowledge about Gastronomy
KH	Adquiring knowledge about Health
KM	Adquiring knowledge about Movies
KR	Adquiring knowledge about Restaurants
KT	Adquiring knowledge about Transports
Social Networks Technological Experience (SNTE) – reflective – single item	
MC	The experience is relevant to communicate wth family and friends
MF	The experience is relevant to find for information
MS	The experience is relevant to share information
MT	The experience is relevant to discover new trends
Education dimension- reflective	
ED_1	Stimulates the curiosity to learn about new subjects
ED_2	Learning new experiences
ED_3	Increases the skills
Aesthetic dimension – reflective	
EE_1	A harmonious experience
EE_2	A very attractive experience
EE_3	The interface design is careful
EE_4	The interface design is appealing

(continued)

(continued)

Add Value to the User (AVU) – reflective	
Entertainment dimension – reflective	
EN_1	A captivating experience
EN_2	My friend's publications are fun
EN_3	My friend's publications are interesting
Evasion dimension – reflective	
EV_1	The feeling that the user plays a different role when he/she use social networks
EV_2	The feeling that the user lives in a different place when use social networks
EV_3	The use of social networks distracts completely
EV_4	The social networks use help to forget the daily routine

References

1. Saturno, M., Pertel, V.M., Deschamps, F., Loures, E.D.F.: Proposal of an automation solutions architecture for industry 4.0. In: Proceedings of the 24th International Conference on Production Research, Poznan, ICPR (2017)
2. Aggarwal, V., Yadav, P., Kumari, R.: The effect of social media communication on centennials Purchase Intention. In: Shukla, S., Gupta, K., Bhardwaj, P. (eds.) Marketing to Centennials in Digital World, pp. 1–13. Bazooka, Greater Noida (2019)
3. Pine, J., Gilmore, J.: The Experience Economy. Harvard Business School Press, Boston (1999)
4. Twenge, J.M., Campbell, S.M., Hoffman, B.J., Lance, C.E.: Generational differences in work values: leisure and extrinsic values increasing, social and intrinsic values decreasing. J. Manag. **36**(5), 1117–1142 (2010)
5. Fromm, J.: What Marketers Need to Know About Social Media and Gen Z Forbes December. https://www.forbes.com/sites/jefffromm/2016/12/19/what-marketers-need-to-know-about-social-media-and-gen-z/. Accessed 30 Nov 2020
6. McGorry, S.Y., McGorry, M.R.: Who are the Centennials: Marketing Implications of Social Media Use and Preferences, pp. 179–181 (2017)
7. Sharma, A.: Consumer behaviour and centennials. In: Shukla, S., Gupta, K., Bhardwaj, P. (eds.) Marketing to Centennials in Digital World, pp. 37–49. Bazooka, Greater Noida (2019)
8. Stojanović, M., Projović, M., Živojinović, L., Barać, D., Bogdanović, Z.: A survey on centennials' expectations of mobile operators. In: Rocha, Á., Reis, J.L., Peter, Marc K., Bogdanović, Z. (eds.) Marketing and Smart Technologies. SIST, vol. 167, pp. 178–189. Springer, Singapore (2020). https://doi.org/10.1007/978-981-15-1564-4_18
9. Williams, K.C., Page, R.A.: Marketing to the generations. J. Behav. Stud. Bus. **3**(1), 37–53 (2011)
10. Duffett, R.G.: Influence of social media marketing communications on young consumers' attitudes. Young Consum. **18**(1), 19–39 (2017)
11. Herrando, C., Jimenez-Martinez, J., Martin-De Hoyos, M.J.: Tell me your age and I tell you what you trust: the moderating effect of generations. Internet Res. (2019)

12. Llopis-Amorós, M.P., Gil-Saura, I., Ruiz-Molina, M.E., Fuentes-Blasco, M.: Social media communications and festival brand equity: Millennials vs Centennials. J. Hosp. Tour. Manag. **40**, 134–144 (2019)
13. Ramos, C.M.Q., Matos, N.: Customer experience journey in social networks – analysis of cohorts' behavior. In: Monteiro, J., et al. (eds.) INCREaSE 2019, pp. 1180–1195. Springer, Cham (2020). https://doi.org/10.1007/978-3-030-30938-1_93
14. Jones, V., Jo, J., Martin, P.: Future schools and how technology can be used to support millennial and generation-Z students. In: Paper Presentation at the 1st International Conference Ubiquitous Information Technology (ICUT), pp. 886–891 (2007)
15. Xiang, Z., Gretzel, U.: Role of social media in online travel information search. Tour. Manag. **31**(2), 179–188 (2010)
16. Mohamad, M., Zawawi, Z.A., Hanafi, W.N.W.: The influences of social network marketing on student purchase intention in the digital era: the mediating role of consumer engagement. Glob. Bus. Manag. Res. **10**, 938–947 (2018)
17. Lemon, K.N., Verhoef, P.C.: Understanding customer experience throughout the customer journey. J. Mark. **80**(6), 69–96 (2016)
18. Moutinho, L.: Consumer behaviour in tourism. Eur. J. Mark. **21**(10), 5–44 (1987)
19. Schmitt, B.: Experiential marketing. J. Mark. Manag. **15**(1–3), 53–67 (1999)
20. Aluri, A.: Mobile augmented reality (MAR) game as a travel guide: insights from Pokémon Go. J. Hosp. Tour. Technol. **8**(1), 55–72 (2017)
21. Radder, L., Han, X.: An examination of the museum experience based on Pine and Gilmore's experience economy realms. J. Appl. Bus. Res. **31**(2), 455–470 (2015)
22. Ramos, C.M.Q., Rodrigues, J.M.F.: The contribution of social networks to the technological experience of elderly users. In: Antona, M., Stephanidis, C. (eds.) HCII 2019. LNCS, vol. 11573, pp. 538–555. Springer, Cham (2019). https://doi.org/10.1007/978-3-030-23563-5_43
23. Hoyle, R.H.: The structural equation modeling approach: basic concepts and fundamental issues. In: Hoylw, R.H. (eds.) Structural Equation Modeling: Concepts, Issues, and Applications, pp. 1–15. Sage, Thousand Oaks (1995)
24. Gefen, D., Straub, D., Boudreau, M.C.: Structural equation modeling and regression: guidelines for research practice. Commun. Assoc. Inf. Syst. **4**(1), 7 (2000)
25. Reinartz, W., Haenlein, M., Henseler, J.: An empirical comparison of the efficacy of covariance-based and variance-based SEM. Int. J. Res. Mark. **26**(4), 332–344 (2009)
26. Chin, W.W.: How to write up and report PLS analyses. In: Esposito Vinzi, V., Chin, W., Henseler, J., Wang, H. (eds.) Handbook of Partial Least Squares, pp. 655–690. Springer, Heidelberg (2010). https://doi.org/10.1007/978-3-540-32827-8_29
27. Ringle, C.M., Silva, D., Bido, D.D.S.: Modelagem de equações estruturais com utilização do SmartPLS. REMark **13**(2), 54 (2014)
28. Fornell, C., Larcker, D.F.: Evaluating structural equation models with unobservable variables and measurement error. J. Mark. Res. **18**(1), 39–50 (1981)
29. Hair, J.F., Hult, T.M., Ringle, C.M., Sarstedt, M.: A Primer on Partial Least Squares Structural Equation Modeling (PLS-SEM). SAGE Publications, Los Angeles (2014)
30. Henseler, J., Ringle, C.M., Sinkovics, R.R.: The use of partial least squares path modeling in international marketing. Adv. Int. Mark. **20**, 277–319 (2009)
31. Pinto, P.: Modelos de equações estruturais com variáveis latentes, fundamentos da abordagem Partial Least Squares. Bnomics, Lisboa (2016)
32. Henseler, J., Sarstedt, M.: Goodness-of-fit indices for partial least squares path mod-eling. Comput. Stat. **28**, 565–580 (2012)

Effects of Cognitive Consistency in Microtask Design with only Auditory Information

Ying Zhong[1]([⊠]), Masaki Matsubara[1], Makoto Kobayashi[2],
and Atsuyuki Morishima[1]

[1] University of Tsukuba, Tennodai 1-1, Tsukuba, Ibaraki, Japan
ying.zhong.2018d@mlab.info, masaki@slis.tsukuba.ac.jp,
morishima-office@ml.cc.tsukuba.ac.jp
[2] Tsukuba University of Technology, Kasuga 4-12, Tsukuba, Ibaraki, Japan
koba@cs.k.tsukuba-tech.ac.jp

Abstract. Microtasks expand ways for people to work, which we could not imagine in the past. When people have pockets of time, they can perform microtasks. This paper pursues this approach further by exploring the design of microtasks that interact with workers with audio and physical means only, without any visual representation. Such a task can be performed in situations where workers cannot use display devices. This paper shows that consistency in navigation is an important factor and proposes a principled framework that develops consistent non-visual microtasks. The experimental results with real-world workers show that the resultant task design allows them to produce better results than tasks without consistency.

Keywords: Crowdsourcing · No visual representation · Consistency

1 Introduction

Crowdsourcing has provided a way to solve previously unresolved problems; moreover, it has expanded the ways in which people can work. One of the key concepts used in a particular type of crowdsourcing is microtasks; they can be performed in a short period of time, without requesting the workers having to communicate with the requester to obtain further information than the task instruction.

An interesting effect of microtasks is that they allow people to work in situations where they have not worked before. When they are free for a short period of time, they can perform microtasks. In typical microtasks, both of the task instructions and the result entry form are provided in some visual representation on the screen, and workers type the task result in the result entry form.

This study explores a different modality of microtasks, in an attempt to broaden the situations in which people can work, by addressing the design of microtasks without any visual representations. We assume that the task instruction and any data related to the task are given in *an audio matrix*, which is an N-dimensional space with coordinates, where an audio clip can exist at each

© Springer Nature Switzerland AG 2020
M. Antona and C. Stephanidis (Eds.): HCII 2020, LNCS 12189, pp. 466–476, 2020.
https://doi.org/10.1007/978-3-030-49108-6_33

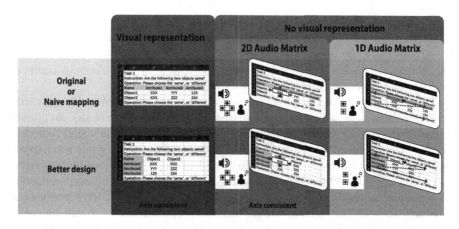

Fig. 1. Example of six task representations used in our experiment. (top-left) Original visual task. (top-middle) Naive mapping 2D audio matrix of the original. (top-right) Naive mapping 1D audio matrix of the original. (bottom-left) axis consistently converted from the original. (bottom-middle) 2D audio matrix of axis consistent structure. (bottom-right) 1D audio matrix of axis consistent structure. In these 2D audio matrix tasks, the user can navigate locations in vertical and horizontal ways with up-down arrow keys and left-right arrow keys, respectively.

	Name	City	Age
t_1	Dave Smith	New York	18

	Name	City	Age
t_2	David Smith	New York	18

(a) structured

	Description
t_1	Kingston 133x high-speed 4GB compact flash card ts4gcf133, 21.5 MB per sec data transfer rate, dual-channel support, multi-platform compatibility.

	Description
t_2	Kingston ts4gcf133 4GB compactflash memory card (133x).

(b) textual

	Name	Brand	Price
t_1	Adobe Acrobat 8		299.99

	Name	Brand	Price
t_2	Acrobat 8	Adobe	299.99

(c) dirty

Fig. 2. Tuple pair examples for the three types of data structure that use human-powered join operation [21].

location. Given an audio matrix task (AM task[1]), the worker can navigate in the matrix in some physical ways, such as by pressing arrow keys, hear the audio matrix at each location, and submitting the task result.

Such an interface allows people to perform tasks in a situation where they do not want to see a display, such as in the bed or while sitting on the beach.

An interesting class of workers is blind people. Our experience of working with many blind people was that most of them could use spreadsheets with tabs efficiently, with the help of screen readers. Theoretically, such a spreadsheet can be modeled as a 2D audio matrix. An N-dimensional audio matrix is a natural mathematical abstraction for such a tool.

This study focuses on a particular class of microtasks, i.e., object comparison tasks, which appear in many real-world applications and are widely seen in online tasks on crowdsourcing platforms, because the proposed method assumes that the tasks are associated with tabular data and object comparison tasks

---

[1] AM Task Demo Video: https://bit.ly/2XrJnQf.

often require them. For example, the entity resolution task is a frequently used object comparison task and is critical in data cleaning and integration [21]. In our experiments, we used one type of object comparison tasks, which is product comparison tasks. The product comparison task asks workers to compare products and choose a product that is more cost-effective.

The contributions of this paper are as follows. First, we empirically show that the *axis consistency*, which is the consistency of the meanings of the navigation in the interface is an important factor in the microtasks with no visual representation. Without visual information, the workers need to *predict* what will happen when they execute actions. This is illustrated in Fig. 1, where an audio matrix task is conceptually represented in a worker's mind as an Excel-like spreadsheet. For example, in the bottom-middle task in Fig. 1, when the worker presses the same key, such as the right arrow key on the keyboard, the task will be easier to understand if it *always* means to compare the values of the same attribute of different objects. However, the task in Fig. 1 top-middle does not guarantee that consistency. The worker needs to press the down arrow key to not only compare the values but also to read the task instruction as well.

Second, we show that the axis-consistent audio matrix microtasks output the results whose quality is comparable with those of microtasks with visual representation.

The important findings are as follows. First, we empirically confirmed that axis consistency is an important factor for microtask design without visual representations. Second, we found that appropriately designed microtasks without visual representations outputs task results whose quality is comparable with those of microtasks with visual representation.

The remainder of this paper is organized as follows. Section 2 describes the related work. Sections 3 and 4 describe the experiment design and its results. Section 5 gives the discussion. Section 6 concludes the paper and presents future work.

2   Related Work

2.1   Microtasks

In crowdsourcing systems, microtasks enable ordinary online workers to work together on tasks that they cannot accomplish alone.

Microtasks on Different Occasions. Microtasks are small tasks, such as categorizing images and writing articles, which can be performed on crowdsourcing platforms such as Amazon Mechanical Turk (MTurk). Crowdsourcing has become a growing market in the current Internet space [16]. Most microtasks are visual tasks and can be run on a personal computer.

There are also some microtask designs for other occasions. Some studies have focused on the passby crowdsourcing approach [17]. In their approach, people can get the task done effortlessly by projecting task images onto the floor and diving into people's personal spaces.

Some researchers focused on the task design and user interface to enhance the worker performance. Sampath et al. [27] claimed that the use of cognitively inspired features for task design is a powerful technique to maximize the performance of crowd workers. Rahmanian et al. [25] studied the effects of difference user interface designs on the performance of crowdsourcing systems.

Our research also aims to expand microtask to visual-impaired users.

Object Comparison. Object comparison is a type of microtask in crowdsourcing. It is a key component in the human-powered join, which is the human-in-the-loop version of the database join operator [20]. Human-powered join is used for problems like entity matching, which plays a key role in many areas such as information integration, natural language understanding, and semantic web [29]. Tasks that use such operations compare entities to check whether the two are the same or choose one entity based on instructions.

There are three different types of data structures that use human-powered join operation (see Fig. 2) [21]:

1. Structured: Data are structured. i.e., tabular data (see Fig. 2(a)).
2. Textual: Data are not structured. (includes text entries) (see Fig. 2(b)).
3. Dirty: Data are structured. However, the attribute values may include missing value (see Fig. 2(c)).

Tasks that use human-powered join operation have received considerable attention [5,9,11]. Crowdsourcing is a way to solve these problems. Corleone is a hands-off crowdsourcing solution that uses the crowd in all major steps [12]. A hybrid human-machine method is proposed in which the machine is used to make an initial rough match for all data, while only the most likely matched ingested pairs are used to verify it [31]. A crowdsourced framework was proposed to address the challenge of emerging entities in social media [18].

An object comparison task is a key component of human-powered join, we can incorporate our framework in many human-powered join operators. Our tasks are also designed according to these structures and contain structured and dirty data.

2.2 Auditory Display Interface

Many systems employ clocks to enhance the auditory display. The system does not rely solely on visual displays to convey information. An auditory display also has its effects, such as guiding attention, and the form of an alarm appears [28].

Voice guidance is a type of auditory display interface. It is widely used in interactive voice response (IVR), which is a telephone technology. By listening to the recorded sound, people can provide answers by pressing the touch phone key [6].

There are many studies on IVR. Some studies have focused on visual display and keyword search and found that telephone voice-menu navigation can be significantly improved with a visual representation [32]. Some studies focused on the use of blind people [2].

A sound interface is more important for the blind people. Some studies have focused on auditory design for the blind people; for example, the use of webpage [8], mobility [7], and virtual environment [19].

This study explores the application of voice guidance on the crowdsourcing platform and aims to design understandable microtasks with no visual representation.

2.3   Cognitive Consistency

Cognitive consistency theories, which flourished between the 1940s and 1960s, constituted a field of research that attempted to explore processing in tasks involving multiple variables. These theories were based primarily on Fritz Heider's balance theory [14,15] and also included cognitive dissonance theory [3,10], congruity theory [24], symmetry theory [23], and numerous neobalance theories [1,4,26].

Cognitive consistency theories were based by four principles of structural dynamics. First, cognitive states are determined holistically rather than elementally. Second, structural properties are dynamic. Third, the dynamic character of mental processes is such that they tend to settle at the states of distinct structural properties. Fourth, and most pertinent to the current experimental project, these dynamic changes that occur at the structural level involve changes, or "reconstructions" [30].

Cognitive consistency theory is the development of general cognitive theory and is often designed as a relatively small structure. The principle of cognitive consistency is widely discussed in social psychology and influences a wide range of psychosocial structures, including cognition, emotional connection, and behavior [13].

People tend to think consistently. Therefore, this research is also based on consistent thinking as the starting point for the task design.

3   Experiment—Product Comparison

We conduct our experiment to find a better task design for understanding entity comparison tasks and to test whether the audio matrix tasks can be understood.

3.1   Recruitment

One-hundred eighty sighted workers (30 workers for each type of task) participated in the experiment through Amazon Mechanical Turk[2].

The workers received a reward of $0.01 when they completed a visual task (total 12 tasks) and a reward of $0.05 when they completed an audio task (total 12 tasks). We assigned visual and audio tasks at random.

---

[2] Amazon Mechanical Turk: https://www.mturk.com.

Task12							
Instruction: Which product is more cost-effective based on the prices and ratings of the following products?							
Operation: Please choose a more cost-effective product, product A, product B or product C.							
Name	Price	Rating					
Product A	60	5					
Product B	60	3					
Product C	60	4					
Operation: Please choose a more cost-effective product, product A, product B or product C.							

Fig. 3. Example of original visual task in experiment 2

Task1							
Instruction: Which product is more cost-effective based on the prices and ratings of the following products?							
Operation: Please choose a more cost-effective product, product A or product B.							
Name	Product A	Product B					
Price	34	24					
Rating	4	5					
Operation: Please choose a more cost-effective product, product A or product B.							

Fig. 4. Example of axis consistent visual task in experiment 2

3.2 Data Set

The data set pertains to public data of shop products on Kaggle.[3] It contains information on the price and the rating of products used in this study.

3.3 Task Design

Price and rating of two or three products were shown to crowd workers. One product in each task is obviously more cost-effective than the others. Based on the price and rating, the crowd workers chose a more cost-effective product. (A lower price and higher rating mean more cost-effective.)

We examined six types of tasks, as shown in Fig. 1; two visual tasks and four audio tasks.

1. Original visual task (Fig. 3)
2. Axis consistent visual task (Fig. 4)
   Axis consistent visual task is converted from original visual tasks. This conversion is an information capacity preserving mapping.
3. Naive mapping 2D audio matrix task
   The task schema of this task is the same as that of the original visual tasks. However, there is no visual information for this task, and crowd workers can answer questions by listening to the content. Crowd workers can also navigate the location of the audio matrix by pressing up, down, left and right arrow keys.
4. Axis consistent 2D audio matrix task
   The task schema of this task is the same as that of 2D visual tasks. Similar to the previous task design, there is no visual information for this task.

---

[3] Kaggle: https://www.kaggle.com.

Crowd workers answer the question by navigating the location of the audio matrix by pressing up, down, left and right arrow keys.

5. Naive mapping 1D audio matrix task

   The task schema of this task is the same as that of original visual tasks. According to the location navigation, this task plays the audio matrix in one way; from left to right and from top to bottom. Crowd workers can navigate by pressing up and down keys. As shown in Fig. 3, the playback order is "Task 1", "Instruction", "Operation", "Name", "Price", "Rating", "Product A", "60", "5"...

6. Axis consistent 1D audio matrix task (We call it axis consistent task, because it is transformed from Axis consistent 2D audio matrix task. However, it has no consistency in this task)

   The task schema of this task is the same as that for 2D visual tasks. According to the location navigation, this task plays the audio matrix in one way; from left to right and from top to bottom. Crowd workers can navigate by pressing the up and down keys. As shown in Fig. 4, the playback order is "Task 1", "Instruction", "Operation", "Name", "Product A", "Product B", "Price", "34"...

3.4 Procedure

Crowd workers were asked to perform 12 microtasks. There was a practice task before the real audio tasks. In the practice task, crowd workers can practice how to use our interface which is simulated from screen reader. Screen reader, which is a software application which can read the information on the screen [22].

4 Results

4.1 Experiment

Figure 5 shows the accuracy rate of each task design in experiment. To find a cost-effective product, the workers need to compare two attributes at the same time. The accuracy rate of visual tasks was higher than that of audio tasks. In audio tasks, the accuracy rate of the axis consistent audio matrix task is the highest.

We conducted a paired t-test to compare the accuracy rate for different task designs. As a result, there were no significant effects from task design between the original structure and axis consistent structure (for visual tasks ($t_{22} = 3.793$, $p = 0.643$), for 2D audio matrix tasks ($t_{22} = 0.574$, $p = 0.457$), and for 1D audio matrix tasks ($t_{22} = 0.029$, $p = 0.867$)).

Table 1 shows the average of total answer time of audio tasks in experiment. The average time taken in the 1D audio matrix task was longer than that in 2D audio matrix tasks. However, the time in the axis consistent 1D audio matrix task was comparable than the other 2D audio matrix tasks, while the time in naive mapping 1D audio matrix task was much longer.

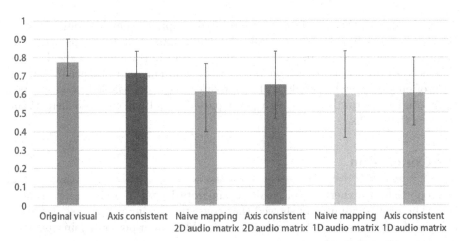

Fig. 5. Accuracy rate of six task designs in experiment. The accuracy rate of visual tasks is higher than that for audio tasks.

Table 1. The average time of each audio task design in experiment

	Audio (2D)	Audio (1D)
Naive mapping	3 m 10 s	5 m 54 s
Axis consistent	3 m 18 s	3 m 34 s

5   Discussion

The result of two experiments and a case study showed that axis consistency is an important factor for microtask design without visual representations. Without visual information, the workers need to *predict* what will happen when they execute actions.

The online sighted crowd workers performed the tasks. Experiment was conducted to choose the answer based on the information the workers heard. This experiment mainly involved a comparison of the numbers (Price and Rating). Crowd workers were required to compare the price and rating of two or three products by listening to the audios. The result shows that tasks with axis consistency had higher accuracy rate.

We also found that there is a case where the 1D audio matrix task is comparable with the 2D audio matrix task in terms of its result quality, which suggests that workers can understand and perform the 1D audio matrix task. It does not conform to the general trend and requires more time to be performed.

In the future, this interface can help blind people to complete online tasks. Increase in home-based work opportunities will be important for people with disabilities, enabling people to work regardless of transportation or medical issues that necessitate people to stay at home. Crowdsourcing can potentially offer a form of employment to people with disabilities [33]. For disabled people, especially students, crowdworking is a good part-time job. It can also help them improve their skills.

6   Conclusion

We reported our experimental results on microtasks with no visual representation. The results empirically showed that consistent audio matrix task design is effective for understanding microtasks using the human-powered join operator with no visual representation.

Our findings are as follows:

- We empirically confirmed that axis consistency is an important factor for microtask design without visual representations.
- We found that the axis-consistent audio matrix microtasks outputs the results whose quality is comparable with those of microtasks with visual representation.

In future work, we shall explore the transformed method. We shall also explore more additional datasets or other languages.

Acknowledgments. This work was partially supported by JST CREST Grant Number JPMJCR16E3 and JSPS KAKENHI Grant Number 17K20022, Japan.

References

1. Abelson, R.P., Rosenberg, M.: Symbolic psycho-logic: a model of attitudinal cognition. Behav. Sci. **3**, 1–8 (1958)
2. Aggarwal, P., et al.: A case study on the use of IVR systems by visually impaired people. In: The 3rd ACM Symposium on Computing for Development (2013)
3. Brehm, J.W., Cohen, A.R.: Explorations in Cognitive Dissonance. Wiley, New York (1962)
4. Cartwright, D., Harary, F.: Structural balance: a generalization of Heider's theory. Psychol. Rev. **63**, 277–293 (1956)
5. Christen, P.: Data Matching. Springer, Heidelberg (2012). https://doi.org/10.1007/978-3-642-31164-2
6. Corkrey, R., Parkinson, L.: Interactive voice response: review of studies 1989–2000. Behav. Res. Methods Instrum. Comput. **34**, 342–353 (2002). https://doi.org/10.3758/BF03195462
7. D'Atri, E., Medaglia, C., Serbanati, A., Ceipidor, U.B., Panizzi, E., D'Atri, A.: A system to aid blind people in the mobility: a usability test and its results. In: 2nd International Conference on Systems (2007)

8. Donker, H., Klante, P., Gorny, P.: The design of auditory user interfaces for blind users. In: Proceedings of the Second Nordic Conference on Human-Computer Interaction (2002)
9. Elmagarmid, A.K., Ipeirotis, P.G., Verykios, V.S.: Duplicate record detection: a survey. TKDE **19**, 1–16 (2007)
10. Festinger, L.: A Theory of Cognitive Dissonance. Row, Peterson, Evanston (1957)
11. Getoor, L., Machanavajjhala, A.: Entity resolution: theory, practice & open challenges. In: Proceedings of the VLDB Endowment (2012)
12. Gokhale, C., et al.: Corleone: hands-off crowdsourcing for entity matching. In: SIGMOD, pp. 601–612 (2014)
13. Heberlein, T.A., Black, J.S.: Cognitive consistency and environmental action. Environ. Behav. **13**, 717–734 (1981)
14. Heider, F.: Attitudes and cognitive organization. J. Psychol. **21**, 107–111 (1946)
15. Heider, F.: The Psychology of Interpersonal Relations. Wiley, New York (1958)
16. Hirth, M., HoBfeld, T., Tran-Gia, P.: Anatomy of a crowdsourcing platform - using the example of microworkers.com. In: Workshop on Future Internet and Next Generation Networks (2011)
17. Iwamoto, E., et al.: Passerby crowdsoucing: workers' behavior and data quality management. In: Proceedings of the ACM on Interactive, Mobile, Wearable and Ubiquitous Technologies, no. 4 (2018)
18. Jiang, L., Wang, Y., Hoffart, J., Weikum, G.: Crowdsourced entity markup. In: CrowdSem (2013)
19. Lahav, O., Schloerb, D., Kumar, S., Srinivasan, M.: A virtual environment for people who are blind - a usability study. J. Assist. Technol. **6**(1), 38–52 (2012). https://doi.org/10.1108/17549451211214346
20. Marcus, A., Wu, E., Karger, D., Madden, S., Miller, R.: Human-powered sorts and joins. PVLDB **5**, 13–24 (2011)
21. Mudgal, S., et al.: Deep learning for entity matching: a design space exploration. In: SIGMOD 2018 (2018)
22. Nengroo, A.S., Kuppusamy, K.S.: Accessible images (AIMS): a model to build self-describing images for assisting screen reader users. Univers. Access Inf. Soc. **17**, 607–619 (2017). https://doi.org/10.1007/s10209-017-0607-z
23. Newcomb, T.M.: An approach to the study of communicative acts. Psychol. Rev. **60**, 393–404 (1953)
24. Osgood, C.E., Tannenbaum, P.H.: The principle of congruity in the prediction of attitude change. Psychol. Rev. **62**, 42–55 (1955)
25. Rahmanian, B., D.J.G.: User interface design for crowdsourcing systems. In: AVI (2014)
26. Rosenberg, M.J.: An Analysis of Affective-Cognitive Consistency. Yale University Press, New Haven (1960)
27. Sampath, H. A., R.R.I.B.: Conititively inspired task design to improve user performance on crowdsourcing platforms. In: CHI (2014)
28. Sanderson, P.M., Anderson, J., Watson, M.: Extending ecological interface design to auditory displays. In: Proceedings of the 2000 Annual Conference of the Computer-Human Interaction Special Interest Group (CHISIG) of the Ergonomics Society of Australia (OzCHI2000) (2000)
29. Shen, W., Li, X., Doan, A.: Constraint-based entity matching. In: AAAI 2005 (2005)
30. Simon, D., Snow, C.J., Read, S.J.: The redux of cognitive consistency theories: evidence judgments by constraint satisfaction. J. Pers. Soc. Psychol. **86**, 814–837 (2004)

31. Wang, J., Kraska, T., Franklin, M.J., Feng, J.: Crowder: crowdsourcing entity resolution. In: VLDB, pp. 1483–1494 (2012)
32. Yin, M., Zhai, S.: The benefits of augmenting telephone voice menu navigation with visual browsing and search. In: CHI 2006, pp. 319–328 (2006)
33. Zyskowski, K., Morris, M., Bigham, J., Gray, M., Kane, S.: Accessible crowdwork? Understanding the value in and challenge of microtask employment for people with disabilities. In: Proceedings of the 18th ACM Conference on Computer-Supported Cooperative Work & Social Computing, CSCW 2015, pp. 1682–1693 (2015)

Intelligent Assistive Environments

Assistive Technology for the Visually Impaired: Optimizing Frame Rate (Freshness) to Improve the Performance of Real-Time Objects Detection Application

Basel Barakat[1]([⊠]) [iD], Aiste Steponenaite[2] [iD], Gurprit S. Lall[2] [iD],
Kamran Arshad[3] [iD], Ian J. Wassell[4] [iD], and Simeon Keates[5]

[1] School of Engineering, University of Greenwich, Kent ME4 4TB, UK
b.barakat@gre.ac.uk
[2] Medway School of Pharmacy, University of Kent, Chatham, UK
[3] Faculty of Engineering, Ajman University, Ajman, United Arab Emirates
[4] Computer Laboratory, University of Cambridge, Cambridge CB2 1TN, UK
[5] School of Engineering and the Built Environment, Edinburgh Napier University, Edinburgh EH10 5DT, UK

Abstract. It has been 100+ years since the world's first commercial radio station started. This century witnessed several astonishing inventions (e.g. the computer, internet and mobiles) that have shaped the way we work and socialize. With the start of a new decade, it is evident that we are becoming more reliant on these new technologies as the majority of the world population relies on the new technology on a daily basis. As world's population is becoming reliant on new technologies and we are shaping our lives around it, it is of paramount importance to consider those people who struggle in using the new technologies and inventions. In this paper, we are presenting an algorithm and a framework that helps partially sighted people to locate their essential belongings. The framework integrates state-of-the-art technologies from computer vision, speech recognition and communication queueing theory to create a framework that can be implemented on low computing power platforms. The framework verbally communicates with the users to identify the object they are aiming to find and then notify them when it is within the range.

Keywords: Assistive technologies · Visual impaired · Artificial intelligence · Machine learning · Real-time objects detection · Information freshness

1 Introduction

The advances in healthcare and vaccines have significantly increased life expectancy in most of the world. For instance, for England and Wales, if a female was born in 1906, her life expectancy was less than 60 years, on the other hand, if she was born in 2016, her life expectancy is 94 years [1]. With such improvements in healthcare, it very important to consider its implications. Vision impairment is currently affecting more than 2.2 billion people worldwide [2], with the majority of the affected people aged

© Springer Nature Switzerland AG 2020
M. Antona and C. Stephanidis (Eds.): HCII 2020, LNCS 12189, pp. 479–492, 2020.
https://doi.org/10.1007/978-3-030-49108-6_34

over 50. Hence, it is predicted that in the future more people will be visually impaired. For these people some of their daily activities (such as locating their essentials) might be challenging. Consequently, it is of paramount importance to design technologies assist the visually impaired.

Alongside the advances in healthcare, the last decade has seen an extraordinary innovation in technologies, such as telecommunication networks, robots and artificial intelligence. One of the main effects, is the vast spread of smartphones, tablets, wearable devices and virtual assistants (such as Amazon Alexa and Google Echo). The spread of these technologies has changed the methods people use to communicate and acquire information. On the other hand, the use of these technologies is challenging for the visually impaired. Most of these technologies depend on graphical interfaces to operate and many offer applications that can be used by the visually impaired.

Advances in artificial intelligence have developed several algorithms that help the computers to identify objects in images [3–6]. One of the main challenges faced deploying such algorithms is the computing complexity that is reflected in the time required to process the images [7]. Hence, Graphics Processing Units (GPUs) are typically used to minimize the processing time. However, GPUs are expensive and so can be beyond the reach of many visually impaired users. Thus, in this paper we proposed a framework to use the Central Processing Unit (CPU) that exists in a conventional low-cost computer.

In this paper, the proposed algorithm is aimed to empower visually impaired users. When the framework is initiated the smartphone verbally asks the user what the object, he/she is looking for, using the smartphone speakers. Afterwards, the user answers with the object they are interested in finding. The user then moves the smartphone around so that the camera captures the surrounding scene. At the moment, the camera 'sees' the object of interest, the smart phone declare that it has 'found your object'.

This paper is organized as follows; Sect. 2 presents the main components of the eye and vision mechanism. Section 3 – presents the effect of visual loss on the economy. Section 4 shows the proposed solution, which utilizes a smartphone and a computer. Section 5 presents the framework optimization and Sect. 6 shows the achieved results and the performance of the proposed framework. Section 7 concludes this paper.

2   The Eye and Human Vision

The eye is an optical instrument allowing us to interpret light and generate images of the world surrounding us. Eyes are adapted to the visible part of the light spectrum; therefore, they can detect wavelengths from 380 to 700 nm. Light reflecting off an object located in the vision field is decoded by the eye in a complex series of events. Firstly, light is refracted by the cornea which helps to focus the light. The total refractive power of the eye is 60 diopters, and cornea alone provides 40 diopters [8]. The light then travels through aqueous humor and passes through the pupil. The pupil is the opening in the center of the colored part of the eye called the iris. Pupil size can be changed through the muscular contraction of the iris which controls the amount of light reaching the retina – the photoreceptive part of the eye. After passing through the pupil, light reaches the crystalline lens. The lens, through changes in shape, is able to focus the light onto a single defined point of the retina. After passing through the lens, light travels through the center of the eyeball filled with jelly like vitreous body until it reaches the retina. A diagram showing the eye main parts is shown in Fig. 1.

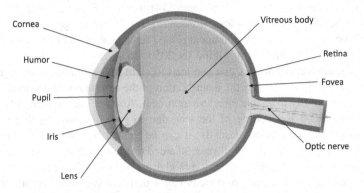

Fig. 1. Diagram of a human eye showing its structures.

The retina is a thin tissue lining the inside of the eyeball. It decodes the image and sends the information to the brain. At the back of it is a layer of photoreceptors known as rods and cones. The human retina has approximately 120 million rods and 6 million cones [8]. Rods are very sensitive photoreceptors; they function in dim light and their image integration time is about 10 ms. Cones, on the other hand, start working at higher light intensities and they can detect rapid light fluctuations, with an integration time approximately 10 times shorter than in rods. For example, when watching a tennis game, it is cones that allow you to see the flying tennis ball. The photoreceptors convert light information to electrical signals traveling through the optic nerve to the visual center at the back of the brain known as the visual cortex [9, 10].

One of the remarkable features of human vision is being able to perceive visual flicker artefacts at rates over 500 Hz when high frequency spatial edges are present [11]. In contrast, traditional movie theatres and televisions present images at a rate of 48–60 Hz and a frame rate of 72 Hz was believed to be sufficient to avoid flicker. This proves that retina has incredibly rapid image processing rate that could also potentially help in memory retention of fast changing images. Indeed, work by [12] has shown that after seeing a series of pictures, viewers can detect and retain information about named targets they have never seen before at a rapid serial presentation of 13 ms per image.

3   Visual Impairment in the World and the Associated Economic Impact

Visual recognition of objects is an important part of the behavioral survival instinct for most animals. As humans, we rely heavily on identification of a wide range of visual objects, with the ability to identify them even in unusual orientations, different illumination and in visually complex environments [13]. However, with age or in presence of certain diseases, vision can be affected resulting in difficulties in generating high resolution images with declines in spatial acuity.

A report published by the World Health Association has stated that the estimated number of visually impaired people in the world is approximately 285 million, with the majority of people being 50 years and older [14]. In the UK alone, there are almost 2 million people living with sight loss, accounting for 3% of the population. It is estimated that because of demographic ageing, the prevalence of sight loss and blindness will increase to approximately 4 million by 2050 [15].

There are several conditions that can lead to sight loss and blindness. Age-related macular degeneration (AMD) is the deterioration of the central retina resulting in vision loss, with no currently available effective treatment. Another common condition is that of a cataract, which is clouding of the lens due to protein clumping that can cause blurry vision and faded colors. Luckily, it can be treated by surgical intervention. In diabetic retinopathy, retinal blood vessels are damaged leading to the vision loss. Another common disease affecting vision is glaucoma, raised fluid pressure within the eye, where damage to the optic nerve can cause partial and eventually full blindness. These are just a few the most prevalent visual impairment causes, and most of them are age related.

In 2017 the global population of aged 60 years and over was 962 million, which is more than twice compared with the 1980 demographics. It is expected that by 2050 the number of older people will double again reaching nearly 2.1 billion [16]. According to World Bank Population Estimates and Projections data, the proportion of population aged 60 years and older increased by 7.2% in the last 59 years. Another 7.5% increase is predicted to happen by 2050 (Fig. 2). Considering the rapid rate of aged population increase in the world, it is certain that the prevalence of age-related visual impairment conditions will continue to rise which will further increase the economic burden.

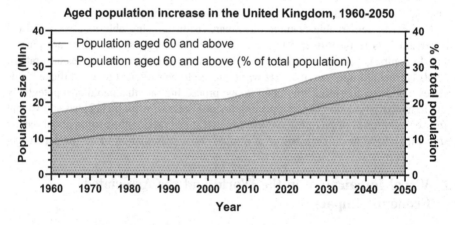

Fig. 2. Aged population data in the UK. Data collected since 1960 shows linear increase in people population aged 60 and above. Future predictions suggest continuous aged population growth, with another nearly 8 million people will be older than 60 years old than it was in 2019 [17].

In the US, the economic burden of eye disorders and vision loss was estimated to be $139 billion, based on the 2011 expenditure adjusted to 2013 using Consumer Price Index [18]. Whereas in the UK, sight loss and blindness in the adult population cost £28.1 billion to the government. Out of that, £410 million were spent on devices and modifications for visually impaired people [5]. The most common ones include mobility and communication devices, optical aids and home modifications [28]. Often the specialized equipment or software adapted to people's needs is costly and it might be difficult to get, therefore cost-effective, easy to use and reliable tools to assist in day to day life would be of great benefit to the users.

4 Proposed Framework

The proposed system consists of two main elements. The first one, is the smartphone and the second is the personal computer (pc). The smartphone is the first point of contact, that users communicate with, while the pc is the server, where object detection occurs, since it has the necessary computing power. Separating the two nodes minimizes the smartphone energy consumption and gives the developers flexibility when updating the system.

To assist visually impaired users, it is necessary to minimize the dependences on a graphical interface. Hence, in the proposed framework, the users interact with the system verbally. The smartphone asks the user what the object he/she is looking for and the user replays naming the object they are interested in finding. Table 1 contains the list of all the currently recognized objects [19]. The user then moves the smartphone around so that the camera captures the surrounding environment. At the moment the camera 'sees' the object of interest, the smart phone says 'found your object'.

Table 1. List of objects recognized by the proposed system [19]

Person	Elephant	Wine Glass	Dining table	Fire Hydrant
Bicycle	Bear	Cup	Toilet	Stop Sign
Car	Zebra	Fork	Tv monitor	Parking Meter
Motorbike	Giraffe	Knife	Laptop	Bench
Aeroplan	Backpack	Spoon	Mouse	Bird
Bus	Umbrella	Bowl	Remote	Cat
Train	Handbag	Banana	Keyboard	Dog
Truck	Tie	Apple	Cell Phone	Horse
Boat	Suitcase	Sandwich	Microwave	Sheep
Traffic Light	Frisbee	Orange	Oven	Cow
Broccoli	Toaster	Hot Dog	Refrigerator	Donut
Carrot	Sink	Pizza	Book	Cake
Chair	Scissors	Sofa	Teddy Bear	Potted plant
Bed	Toothbrush	Hair Drier	Vase	Surfboard
Skis	Clock	Bottle	Tennis Racket	Skateboard
Snowboard	Baseball Glove	Baseball Bat	Kite	Sports Ball

When the application starts the smartphone uses the text to speech functionality that exists on most smart phones to inform the user that the application is running and is ready to start searching for the object of interest by announcing 'What are you looking for?'. The users replay by saying the name of the object (such as a Book). The smartphone then recognizes the user's input using its speech recognition function and then transmitting it to the pc via the network. The computer then initiates the receiving of the video from the smartphone and recognizing the objects in each frame. It is worth mentioning that the streamed video would not be saved anywhere to ensure the privacy of the users.

After receiving the name of the object, the pc begins detection objects on the frames. The objects detection algorithm used is the 'You Only Look Once' (YOLO V3) object detection algorithm using the 'Tiny' weights [6] implemented in Python using

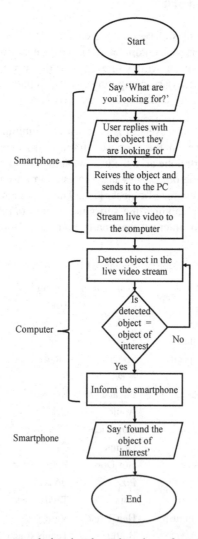

Fig. 3. Flowchart of the framework showing the main tasks performed by the smartphone and the computer.

Pytorch [27] that was pretrained on the objects of Common objects in context (COCO) dataset [19] shown in Table 1. As soon as the object is detected by the algorithm it sends a message back to the smartphone. The smartphone then informs the user that the object has been found. The flowchart of the system is presented in Fig. 3.

5   Optimizing the Proposed Framework Response Performance

To optimize the performance of the objects detection, we have modeled the framework as a queue were the video frames per second (fps) represent inter-arrivals rate (λ) of the queue and the object detection time represents the service time as shown in Fig. 4. Using this model, we derived an optimal expression for the number of fps to maximize the freshness of the frames at the destination (computer) and hence the performance of the framework [20].

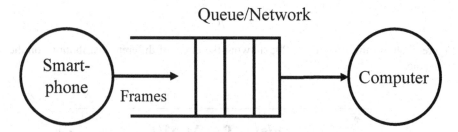

Fig. 4. Queueing system shows the frames generated from the smartphone and received by the computer. The service time of the destination represents the duration required to detect the objects and the inter-arrival time represents the number of frames generated per second.

To evaluate the frames freshness, we use the Information Peak Age (PA) as a metric. PA was introduced in [21–23], as a metric representing the information freshness. It is defined as the maximum time elapsed since the preceding piece of information was generated. In other words, PA (P) is:

$$P = E\{X_n + T_n\}, \forall n, \tag{1}$$

where X_n represents the inter-arrival time of frame n or

$$X_n = \frac{1}{\lambda_n}, \tag{2}$$

where λ is the interarrival rate or the number of fps. T_n represents the delay time of a frame or

$$T_n = W_n + S_n, \tag{3}$$

where W_n is the waiting time (queueing time) and S_n is the service time of frame n.

To optimize the fps rate, it is necessary to accurately model the service time and interarrival time. Hence, the PA value depends on the distribution. For instance, if the inter-arrival time and service time follow an exponential distributions with means $\frac{1}{\lambda}$ and $\frac{1}{\mu}$ respectively, the PA is

$$P^{M/M/1} = \frac{1}{\mu}\left(1 + \frac{1}{\rho} + \frac{\rho}{1-\rho}\right), \tag{4}$$

where the server utilization $\rho = \frac{\lambda}{\mu}$ [23]. For exponential distribution interarrival time and deterministic service time PA is

$$P^{M/D/1} = \frac{1}{\mu}\left(1 + \frac{1}{\rho} + \frac{\rho}{2(1-\rho)}\right). \tag{5}$$

The PA for deterministic service time and inter-arrival time is,

$$P^{D/D/1} = \frac{1}{\mu} + \frac{1}{\lambda}. \tag{6}$$

Figure 5, shows the PA for $\mu = 20$; showing the effect of different distributions on the PA value.

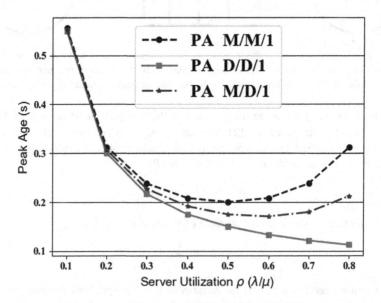

Fig. 5. Peak Age versus Server utilization for M/M/1, D/D/1 and M/D/1 queues for service rate (μ) equals to 20 frames per second (fps).

From Fig. 5, it is notable that the distribution of the service time and inter-arrival time plays a critical role in the PA. Thus, we started the optimization procedure by measuring the service time (i.e., the object's detection time) to optimize the number of fps to have the system responsive as shown in the next section.

6 Experiment Results

In this section, the performance of the proposed system is presented. We used a 'low' video resolution of 160 × 120 to minimize the duration of the communication. The object recognized from the user voice input is communicated to the pc through the network using the Python Socket module [24] and [25]. Initially, we started measuring the time the PC takes to recognize the objects, i.e., the service time. Table 2, presents the measured service time statistics. Although the statistics are insightful, the service time behavior with time can help us to optimize performance. For instance, if we consider the time series of the first 1000 frames presented Fig. 6; it is notable that the service time is stabilizing and decreasing with time.

Table 2. Service time statistics

Parameter	Time (s)
Mean	0.31
Median	0.3
Standard division	0.06
Maximum value	1.75
Minimum value	0.3

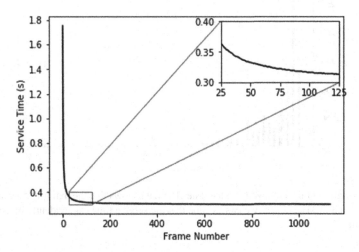

Fig. 6. The service time representing the time for processing and recognizing the objects in each frame.

After identifying the behavior of the service time, it is necessary to identify its distribution. To find the distribution that best fits the service time, we used the Fitter package [26]. The Fitter package tests the data against 80 distributions to identify the best representation. Table 3 shows the best five fitting distributions obtained from the fitting. However, it was found that conducting with more tests, the best fitting distribution changes, hence in Fig. 7 we have plotted the histogram of the achieved service times. We see that most of the frames were served in 0.3–0.31 s. Thus, although the service time is not constant, the variation is not significant, and we can assume that the service time is constant and deterministic.

Table 3. The service time data fitting results

Distribution	Sum square error	Akaike Information Criterion (AIC)	Bayesian Information Criterion (BIC)
Generalized pareto	223.661544	5225.025898	−1817.183655
Exponential	256.870603	13496.455939	−1667.365434
Generalized exponential	257.189093	13607.637665	−1644.863641
Exponentially modified normal	258.963944	13501.576277	−1651.136959
Generalized Half-logistic	270.562111	16640.298840	−1601.497004

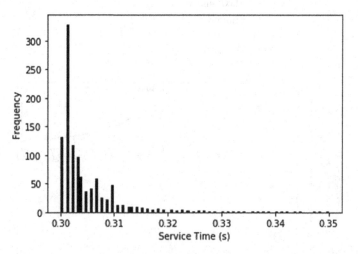

Fig. 7. Histogram of the achieved service time. The data shows that the majority of frames were processed in 0.3–0.31 s, hence, we can assume that the service time can evidently be considered deterministic.

Since, the service time is evidently deterministic, we can minimize the PA by using the PA M/D/1 queue as shown in Fig. 5. The interarrivals time was assumed to follow exponential distribution hence the frames will be communicated through the network and the delays time can be considered to be following exponential distribution. Thus, we have optimized the fps rate to achieve the minimize the PA. Figure 8 presents an experiment where the smartphone was capturing a video of a clock on the computer screen before and after optimizing the frames freshness. We can observe that the difference in the two clocks is approximately 1532 ms. After optimizing the fps, the difference was less than 130 ms as shown in Fig. 9.

Fig. 8. The difference between the captured time and the actual time before optimizing the frames per second rate.

Fig. 9. The difference between the captured time and the actual time after optimizing the frames per second rate.

After optimizing the system response time, we have tested it on several objects to ensure the usability of the proposed system. Figure 10 presents some the captured objects with different backgrounds and lighting. The proposed framework source code and instructions can be found in [29].

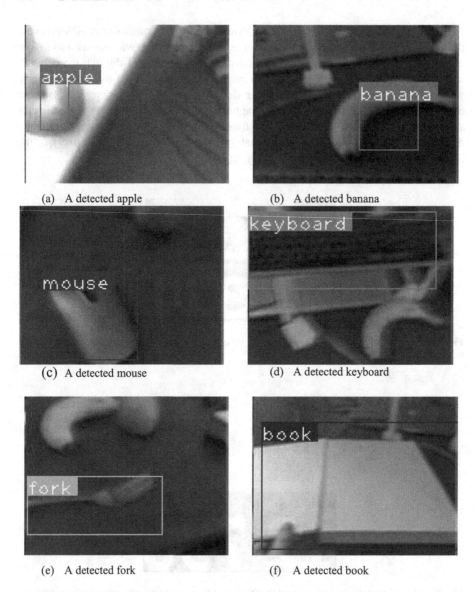

(a)   A detected apple   (b)   A detected banana

(c)   A detected mouse   (d)   A detected keyboard

(e)   A detected fork   (f)   A detected book

Fig. 10. Examples of detected objects using the proposed system

7   Conclusions

In this paper, we have presented a system that can help visually impaired users in navigating their surroundings. The system runs on a smartphone and a computer. The smartphone is used for communicating with the users and the computer is used for the object's detection for each frame. The system is able to identify 82 objects that users use in their everyday life. We optimized the number of frames captured from the camera to optimize the performance of the system. In the future work, the system would be able to adapt its frames rate according to the network and processing power of the pc.

References

1. Office for National Statistics, What is my life expectancy? And how might it change? https://www.ons.gov.uk/peoplepopulationandcommunity/healthandsocialcare/healthandlifeexpectancies/articles/whatismylifeexpectancyandhowmightitchange/2017-12-01. Accessed 27 Feb 2020
2. World Health Organization, Blindness and vision impairment (2019). https://www.who.int/news-room/fact-sheets/detail/blindness-and-visual-impairment
3. Szegedy, C., Vanhoucke, V., Ioffe, S., Shlens, J. and Wojna, Z.: Rethinking the inception architecture for computer vision. In: Proceedings of the IEEE Conference on Computer Vision and Pattern Recognition, pp. 2818–2826 (2016)
4. Redmon, J., Divvala, S., Girshick, R., Farhadi, A.:. You only look once: unified, real-time object detection. In: Proceedings of the IEEE Conference on Computer Vision and Pattern Recognition, pp. 779–788 (2016)
5. Guo, Y., Liu, Y., Oerlemans, A., Lao, S., Wu, S., Lew, M.S.: Deep learning for visual understanding: a review. Neurocomputing **187**, 27–48 (2016)
6. Redmon, J., Farhadi, A.: Yolov3: an incremental improvement. arXiv pre-print arXiv:1804.02767 (2018)
7. Huang, R., Pedoeem, J., Chen, C.: YOLO-LITE: a real-time object detection algorithm optimized for non-GPU computers. In: 2018 IEEE International Conference on Big Data (Big Data), Seattle, WA, USA, 2018, pp. 2503–2510 (2018)
8. Schwartz, S.H.: Visual Perception: A Clinical Orientation, 4th edn. (2009)
9. Artal, P.: Image formation in the living human eye. Annu. Rev. Vis. Sci. **1**(1), 1–17 (2015). https://doi.org/10.1146/annurev-vision-082114-035905
10. Kolb, H.: How the retina works. Am. Sci. **91**(1), 28–35 (2003)
11. Davis, J., Hsieh, Y.H., Lee, H.C.: Humans perceive flicker artifacts at 500 Hz. Sci. Rep. **5**, 7861 (2015). https://doi.org/10.1038/srep07861
12. Potter, M.C., Wyble, B., Hagmann, C.E., McCourt, E.S.: Detecting meaning in RSVP at 13 ms per picture. Attention Percept. Psychophys. **76**(2), 270–279 (2014). https://doi.org/10.3758/s13414-013-0605-z
13. Logothetis, N.K.: Visual object recognition. Annu. Rev. Neurosci. **19**(1), 577–621 (1996). https://doi.org/10.1146/annurev.neuro.19.1.577
14. World Health Organization: Global data on visual impairments 2010 (2010)
15. Pezzullo, L., Streatfeild, J., Simkiss, P., Shickle, D.: The economic impact of sight loss and blindness in the UK adult population. BMC Health Serv. Res. **18**(1), 1–13 (2018). https://doi.org/10.1186/s12913-018-2836-0
16. U.N. Department of Economic and Social Affairs, Population Division, World Population Ageing 2017 - Highlights (ST/ESA/SER.A/397), (2017)
17. World Bank: Population Estimates and Projections data (2019). https://datacatalog.worldbank.org/dataset/population-estimates-and-projections
18. Wittenborn, J., Rein, D.: Cost of Vision Problems The Economic Burden of Vision Loss and Eye Disorders in the United States (2013)

19. Lin, T.-Y., et al.: Microsoft COCO: Common Objects in Context. In: Fleet, D., Pajdla, T., Schiele, B., Tuytelaars, T. (eds.) ECCV 2014. LNCS, vol. 8693, pp. 740–755. Springer, Cham (2014). https://doi.org/10.1007/978-3-319-10602-1_48

20. Barakat, B., Keates, S., Wassell, I., Arshad, K.: Adaptive status arrivals policy (ASAP) delivering fresh information (Minimise Peak Age) in real world scenarios. In: Antona, M., Stephanidis, C. (eds.) HCII 2019. LNCS, vol. 11573, pp. 419–430. Springer, Cham (2019). https://doi.org/10.1007/978-3-030-23563-5_33

21. Huang, L., Modiano, E.: Optimizing age-of-information in a multi-class queueing system. In: 2015 IEEE International Symposium on Information Theory (ISIT), pp. 1681–1685. IEEE (2015)

22. Costa, M., Codreanu, M., Ephremides, A.: On the age of information in status update systems with packet management. IEEE Trans. Inf. Theory 62(4), 1897–1910 (2016)

23. Barakat, B., Yassine, H., Keates, S., Wassell, I., Arshad, K.: How to measure the average and peak age of information in real networks? In: European Wireless 2019; 25th European Wireless Conference, pp. 1–5 (2019)

24. Sarker, M.F.: Python Network Programming Cookbook. Packt Publishing Ltd. (2014)

25. Ferrill, P., Grammens, J.: Pro Android Python with SL4A. Apress, Berkeley (2011)

26. {fitter}, fit data to many distributions. https://github.com/cokelaer/fitter

27. Ketkar, N.: Introduction to pytorch. In: Deep Learning with Python, pp. 195–208. Apress, Berkeley (2017)

28. Lafuma, A., et al.: Evaluation of non-medical costs associated with visual impairment in four European countries: France, Italy, Germany and the UK. Pharmacoeconomics 24(2), 193–205 (2006). https://doi.org/10.2165/00019053-200624020-00007

29. BaselBarakat/Assistive-Technology-for-the-Visually-Impaired-Optimizing-the-Frames-Freshness-of-Real-time-Objects. https://github.com/BaselBarakat/Assistive-Technology-for-the-Visually-Impaired-Optimizing-the-Frames-Freshness-of-Real-time-Objects. Accessed 1 Mar 2020

Affective Computing and Loneliness: How This Approach Could Improve a Support System

Laura Burzagli[1](✉) and Simone Naldini[2]

[1] Consiglio Nazionale delle Ricerche, Istituto di Fisica Applicata
"Nello Carrara", Via Madonna del Piano, 10, 50019 Sesto Fiorentino (FI), Italy
l.burzagli@ifac.cnr.it
[2] MATHEMA, Via Torcicoda 29, 50100 Florence, Italy

Abstract. Affective computing is an emerging research field, which turns out particularly important in a number of applications. In principle, it is supposed to allow the knowledge of the emotional condition of people (through an identification of their feelings) as an input aimed to help computer systems in deciding what information is convenient to provide people as a support to their present activities and to choose the most appropriate interface with the environment. This approach may present remarkable advantages in several application fields, such as e.g. independent living, e-learning, marketing or security. The aim of this contribution is to identify the present technical feasibility of this approach, meant to assess, describe and take care of the general psychological status of people, in connection with the new concepts of health and well-being. In order to test the possible impact of the approach, the integration of available technology and concepts about well-being in a support system is under development in the IFAC laboratory to deal with the loneliness status. Loneliness is not a pathology, but, according to scientific literature, can favour a large number of diseases. That's why the development of a support system which is able to recognize the situation and to provide appropriate recommendations to mitigate possible risks is an activity of particular interest.

Keywords: Support systems · Loneliness · Ambient active living

1 Introduction

In the technical literature, affective computing is described as an emerging field of research "which conjoined sentiment analysis and emotion recognition" [1]. This research activity turns out to be particularly important in a number of application fields in order to: i) recognize the emotional condition of a person (through an analysis of her feelings) as an input to a computer-based system, in addition to text or vocal messages; ii) react with recommendations aimed to support people, if necessary, through the most appropriate interfaces.

This approach, which involve an emotional level within the communication process (as shown in Fig. 1), is supposed to provide remarkable benefits in several application field, such as art, e-learning, marketing or security [2].

© Springer Nature Switzerland AG 2020
M. Antona and C. Stephanidis (Eds.): HCII 2020, LNCS 12189, pp. 493–503, 2020.
https://doi.org/10.1007/978-3-030-49108-6_35

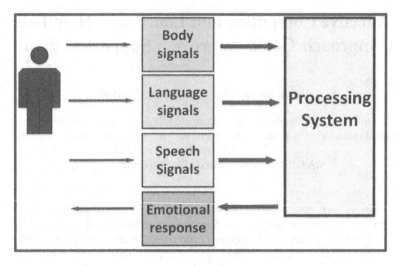

Fig. 1. General interaction

Among the identified application fields, this contribution discusses the value that the knowledge about the emotional conditions of people may have in relation to well-being [3]. Well-being is a concept that is presently being developed at the international level to characterize the possible human condition, at a level more general than the assessment of the absence of pathologies. The promotion of well-being also needs the development of support services to promote it.

In order to describe the procedure for the identification of problems connected to well-being and the corresponding support, an example is presented: a support service to deal with the loneliness status. This condition does not represent a pathology, but, according to scientific literature, can favour a large number of diseases. This is the reason why the development of a support system able to recognize the problem and to provide appropriate recommendations to reduce it is an activity of particular interest. In Sect. 2 a short review of relevant aspects of affective computing is presented. In Sect. 3 a short description of a new concept of health and well-being is introduced. In Sect. 4 the technical feasibility of the recommendation system aimed to reduce the loneliness of elderly people under development is briefly described, and in Sect. 5 aspects related to the affective computing approach are discussed.

2   Affective Computing

The advent of simpler and quicker communication using computers (Computer Mediated Communication - CMC), both at the level of interpersonal communication (communication among people) and of access to information (communication among people and machines) is a reality of daily life. Most research in this field dealt with the rational part of it (particularly at the level of the semantics of text or equivalent pictures), thus neglecting other important components of human communication.

To clarify this assertion, the model of communication of the psychologist Albert Mehrabian can be cited [4]. Three elements of communication were identified as components used to extract the complete meaning of a message: content (word), body language, vocal expression (para verbal aspects). In this model (see Fig. 2) words account for 7% only of the message meaning, tone of voice accounts for 38%, and body language accounts for 55%.

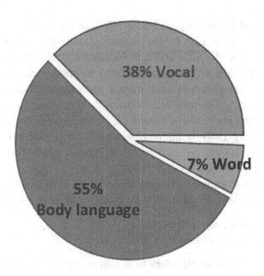

Fig. 2. Mehrabian's communication model

Even if other models could be considered, where different percentage come up, they highlight that an efficient design of new interaction systems must include the study of components of the communication, which are closer to the emotional level. Affective computing takes in consideration this different level of communication.

Two distinct level of affective computing can be considered: sentiment analysis, which is defined as "*a type of data mining that measures the inclination of people's opinions through natural language processing (NLP)*" [5] and emotion recognition, as the process to detect and measure human emotions. While at level of sentiment analysis it is possible to identify only three different levels: positive, negative and neutral, for emotion recognition, the analysis is much more complex, because there is a larger number of possibilities. In the past the number of recognized human emotions was limited (four for Latin Stoic people: metus (fear), aegritudo (pain), libido (lust), and laetitia (pleasure), and more recently six (Ekmann, 1970). Anyway, a multidimensional analysis was recently introduced at the psychological level. In [6] the emotions are grouped into four dimensions. For each of them, anger, anticipation, joy, and trust (as positive feelings), and fear, surprise, sadness and disgust (as negative feelings) are considered.

After the classification of emotions, another important element for affective computing is the modality through which emotions are analysed. As mentioned before, for a complete recognition, features from visual modality, audio modality and textual modality have to be analysed. Since the application considered in the paper does not include any technologies able to record images, such as cameras, in the described experiments analysis is mainly based on audio modality [7].

3 Support Services: From Health to Well-Being

In order to understand better why and how affective computing can give a positive contribution in setting up systems for the support of daily-life activities of people, it is useful to introduce a few elements about the concepts of health and well-being.

The accepted definition of health is provided by the World Health Organization (WHO) as "a state of complete physical, mental and social well-being and not merely the absence of disease or infirmity", as written in "Preamble to the Constitution of WHO as adopted by the International Health Conference, New York, 19 June – 22 July 1946; signed on 22 July 1946 by the representatives of 61 States (Official Records of WHO, no. 2, p. 100) and entered into force on 7 April 1948. The definition has not been amended since 1948" [8].

This definition was extremely visionary when it was introduced, more than 70 years ago. Nowadays a complex situation must be faced, at least due to two elements

- Increase in the average age of people.
- Chronicization of several diseases.

A more recent publication [9] refers to health as "the ability to adapt and to self-manage".

A number of diseases often characterizes the health condition of most elderly people, even if not particularly serious, but which require the adoption of therapies: diabetes, cholesterol, high pressure. In most cases, the therapies allow them a good quality of life, even if in presence of pathologies. However, the general condition of the person also assumes a great importance and it is not only related to the presence or the absence of diseases. Many abilities may decrease, and the general condition (for example, for the autonomy of life) can also depends on the network of human relationships which surround the person.

This principle is valid also for chronic disease, where a pathology is not completely cured, but is controlled with appropriate therapies.

According to this wider concept of living human condition, support services are changing their goal too, because, considering well-being in general, much more attention is paid not only to diseases but also to a number of potentially dangerous conditions, such as loneliness. The prevention of these conditions can be promoted with a correct technological monitoring, supported by an intelligent system able to spot critical situations and to suggest appropriate recommendation to the user. If, for example, the document HEALTH 2020, produced by World Health Organization [10] in 2013 is considered, the *Priority area 1. Investing in health through a life-course approach and empowering people* states that "… Strengthening mental health promotion programmes is highly relevant… One in four people in the European Region experience some type of mental health problem during their lives. A particular challenge is to promote the early diagnosis of depression and prevent suicide... Research is leading to a better under-standing of the damaging association between mental health problems and social marginalization ...".

4   Loneliness Services

According to the previous description of the importance of evaluation of well-being of human being in general, and specifically of elderly people, an application to reduce loneliness is under development.

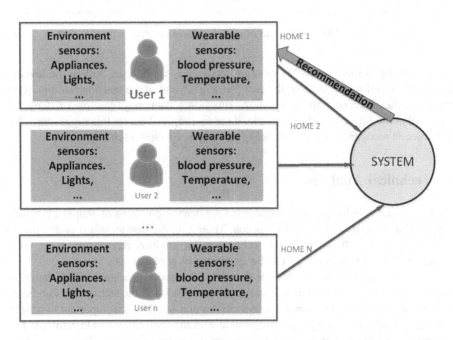

Fig. 3. A general representation of the system

A first level of sensors (Fig. 3) acquires a set of information about user's condition. These signals can come from both the environment, such as the frequency of use of an appliance, or from the detection of specific parameters coming from wearable devices. All these signals are processed and, also on the basis of the state of other people living close to the user, the application provides a recommendation to the user, who can react to the suggestion in different ways: she can accept or ask for a new suggestion which the system provides after a new processing cycle. In order to improve the quality of the next suggestion, a machine learning is used to optimize the processing as shown in Fig. 4.

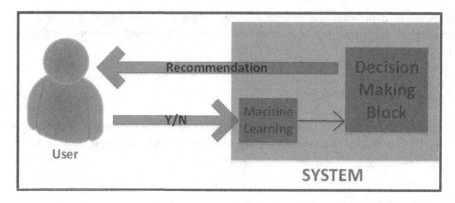

Fig. 4. Diagram of main blocks of the system

According to this process, an emotion recognizer can be used both at the level of acquisition of information about the user (see Fig. 3) and of the reaction (see Fig. 4) of the user after receiving the suggestion. Emotional data may confirm or deny the approval of the suggestion. For example, if the user reply "I accept this suggestion", but the voice is recognized as sad, probably she will not follow such suggestion.

5 Technical Analysis

As already stated before, in the implemented application emotions of people are mainly supposed to be extracted analysing speech. Therefore, the first technical problem is to investigate what is the state of the technology for emotion recognition using vocal signal and how this technology can be integrated in applications.

The first element to consider is the set of emotions, whose identification is important within the context under analysis (loneliness), and the technology to be used for their identification. From an implementation point of view, it is important to adopt a working model with a complexity compatible with the level of current technology. It is obviously possible to hypothesize development of technologies in the future, but, at the moment, it is crucial to integrate existing approaches and technologies in order to set up useful services. In order to do that, the complexities of the context, the emotion model and the features of already available technologies must find a good balance.

The vast majority of available tools for emotion analysis works only on a limited set of emotions, which include the following:

- Neutral
- Happiness
- Anger
- Fear
- Sadness

Even if some of them also consider:

- Disgust
- Surprise
- Frustration
- Amusement.

5.1 Modelling the Application

In the application under development two levels have been identified, on which an emotion recognition analysis can have an impact. The first is the identification of the user's status, in order to produce recommendations. The second is the reaction to the recommendation, which has been provided by the system. For both levels, the first four emotions are sufficient. In fact, the combination of happiness, sadness, anger and fear is able to show a positive or a negative status.

5.2 Information Processing

An analysis of existing tools for emotion analysis has been carried out, in order to insert this processing element into the application.

Unfortunately, most of these tools require the use of proprietary servers for data processing. This does not represent a possible solution, since problems of privacy and security must be considered. Anyway, three open source products have been identified and analysed, which are sufficient to investigate how a block related to emotions recognition can be introduced in the application under development and to test it. In Fig. 5 a synthesis of the products has been introduced, together with a fourth product which is an example of a tool that requires the use of proprietary servers.

Vokaturi
The first analysed product is Vokaturi [11].

The classifier in OpenVokaturi starts by measuring 9 cues related to speech, which, are associated with emotion classes. These emotions are:

- Neutral
- Happy
- Sad
- Angry
- Fear

With the adoption of a neural network with three level of linear connections, the classifier produces a value to the probabilities of each emotion with the sum of all scores equal to 1.

In order to integrate the tool in the system under development the following steps have been identified:

1. To read the audio from a mobile device and send it to the server
2. To create a file in wav format on the server
3. To run the available python script on that file

4. To obtain a classification
5. To use this classification in the application.

Opensmile

Opensmile (SMILE stands for Speech & Music Interpretation by Large-space Extraction), is a software for audio analysis which extracts features, not directly related to emotions, but useful for further analysis, through which information about emotions can be extract. [12] The product provides internal libraries for the extraction of features for the Speech Emotion Recognition (SER) analysis. It provides 993 features, which, however, do not provide directly the identification of an emotion with a corresponding probability. In order to obtain a value that is directly related to emotion, the output file (presented in ARFF format: Attribution Relation File Format, an ASCII text file describing a list of instances sharing a set of attributes) must be processed with a tool such as WEKA (https://it.wikipedia.org/wiki/Weka), an automatic learning and classification tool, which uses .arff data. An example, which is provided at https://iopscience.iop.org/article/10.1088/1742-6596/450/1/012053/pdf, shows how an audio file is classified in six different emotion categories, plus the neutral state:

- Anger
- Boredom
- Disgust
- Fear
- Happiness
- Sadness
- Neutral.

Moreover, Opensmile is natively connected to OpenCV (https://en.wikipedia.org/wiki/OpenCV), a C++ library which deals with image and video processing, oriented to the recognition and the classification of these components. It is very often utilized for facial recognition, as a Machine Learning element for images classification, and in HCI too. Anyway, in the application under development this feature is not utilized, since only audio components are used to recognize emotions.

Tool Python

The third product is Python Mini Project – Speech Emotion Recognition with LibROSA, which is a python library for audio and music analysis, in particular for reading audio files and the extraction of the feature of each sample. It mainly considers and analyses:

- Mel-Frequency Cepstral Coefficient, which represents the short-term power spectrum of a sound
- Chroma, which pertains to the 12 different pitch classes
- Frequency: it comes from Mel Spectrogram Frequency.

For the classification, a neural network, implemented in Python, is used for a multi-level classification. The network is initialized with a large sample of audio files, coming from 24 different users. These samples are in English, 4–7 s. long, and classified on the basis of the emotion that they should communicate. A number of tests with Italian samples are under development.

These samples are classified on the basis of eight emotions:

- Neutral
- Calm
- Happy
- Sad
- Angry
- Fearful
- Disgust
- Surprised.

The tool classifies the specific user samples on the basis of the emotions presented in the samples used for initialization.

Tool	Distribution	Functionality	Analysis and classification details	External API Required	Recognized emotions
OpenVokaturi	Open	SER (Voice analysis and emotion classification)	Voice analysis (pitch,chroma, frequency) and classification based on 9 features plus three-layer network	NO	- Neutral - Happy - Sad - Angry - Fear
OpenSmile	Open	Voice analysis tool only. For emotion classification required external operations (eg. using Weka)	Voice analysis and extraction of 993 feature. Eg: - pitch voice contour - signal energy - voice frequency	NO	- Anger - Boredom - Disgust - Fear - Happy - Sad - Neutral
Python Project	Open	SER (Voice analysis and emotion classification)	Voice analysis and extraction of feature, eg: -power spectrum of voice -voice chroma (pitch class) -voice frequency Classification with a MLP Classificator[4]	NO	The emotions are based on the corpus used to instruct the MLP. In the case in example: -neutral -calm -happy -sad -angry -fearful -disgust -surprised
Beyond Verbal	Closed	SER (Voice analysis and emotion classification)	Voice analysis and classification of -temper -arousal -valence No detail about classification method	YES	Classification of mood in ~400 different emotions

Fig. 5. Products review

It has been interesting and encouraging to see that emotion recognition is apparently of interest in many application fields and open source resources are available to be used in applications aiming to favour well-being of people.

As a result of the previous analysis, Vokaturi has been considered as the most appropriate product to be used in the application under development, in order to start a set of tests. At the moment the process of integration of the product in the system in at the end, and a number of preliminary tests are starting. With these tests an evaluation of the ability of the system to recognize the correct emotions will be carried out and experiments to evaluate the relevance of this information to support people will be started.

6   Ethics in Emotions

An additional aspect to be considered in the design of the application is represented by its ethical implications. With the introduction of the European Union's General Data Protection Regulation (GDPR), a number of problems have appeared for technologies such as emotion recognition. Since the vast majority of these processing applications is based on AI, the document "ETHICS GUIDELINES FOR TRUSTWORTHY AI", published by the High-Level Expert Group on Artificial Intelligence of European Commission [13], must be consider as a reference. This document emphasizes that it is necessary to consider legal concerns since the beginning of any project, in order to avoid heavy modifications at the end of the process. This is particularly important in the case of emotions, for all the connections with privacy [14, 15]. At the moment, two different aspects have been considered in the development of the application: i) if emotion are recognized in a public space. This is not the case of the presented work, since the application is supposed to be used at home; ii) if the processing is carried out on commercial server. At the moment the evaluation is limited to open source products that work either on the client side or on the lab server. The problem still exists, but with a lower level of severity.

7   Conclusions

Affective computing represents a useful approach for new applications aimed to provide support to people in their daily life activities. An analysis is presented, aimed to its efficient integration in an application under development to help people in a condition of loneliness. In this activity, a few notes on an ethical perspective have been also introduced, on the basis of the last documents about an ethical use of Artificial Intelligence, produced by the European Commission.

References

1. Poria, S., Cambria, E., Bajpai, R., Hussain, A.: A review of affective computing: from unimodal analysis to multimodal fusion. Inf. Fusion **37**, 98–125 (2017)
2. Picard, R.W.: Affective computing: from laughter to IEEE. IEEE Trans. Affect. Comput. **1** (1), 11–17 (2010)
3. Ead1e_well_being.pdf. https://standards.ieee.org/content/dam/ieee-standards/standards/web/documents/other/ead1e_well_being.pdf. Accessed 25 Feb 2020
4. Mehrabian, A.: Silent Messages: Implicit Communication of Emotions and Attitudes, 2nd edn. Wadsworth Publishing Company, Belmont (1980)
5. What is Sentiment Analysis? - Definition from Technopedia. https://www.techopedia.com/definition/29695/sentiment-analysis. Accessed 31 Jan 2020
6. Emotion classification Wikipedia. https://en.wikipedia.org/wiki/Emotion_classification#The_Hourglass_of_Emotions. Accessed 25 Feb 2020
7. Schuller, B.W.: Speech emotion recognition: two decades in a nutshell, benchmarks, and ongoing trends. Commun. ACM **61**(5), 90–99 (2018)
8. WHO Frequently asked question. https://www.who.int/about/who-we-are/frequently-asked-questions. Accessed 31 Jan 2020
9. Huber, M., et al.: How should we define health? BMJ 2011 **343**, d4163 (2011)
10. Health2020 (short). http://www.euro.who.int/__data/assets/pdf_file/0006/199536/Health2020-Short.pdf. Accessed 31 Jan 2020
11. Vokaturi emotion recognition software. https://vokaturi.com/. Accessed 25 Feb 2020
12. Tickle, A., Raghu, S., Elshaw, M.: Emotional recognition from the speech signal for a virtual education agent. J. Phys. Conf. Ser. **450**, 012053 (2013)
13. EU High Level Expert Group Ethics Guidelines for Trustworthy AI. https://ec.europa.eu/digital-single-market/en/news/ethics-guidelines-trustworthy-ai. Accessed 31 Jan 2020
14. McStay, A.: The right to privacy in the age of emotional AI report (for The Office of the United Nations High Commissioner for Human Rights) (2018)
15. Furey, E., Blue, J.: Alexa, emotions, privacy and GDPR. In: Proceedings of the 32nd International BCS Human Computer Interaction Conference (HCI), pp. 1–5, Belfast (2018)

A Preliminary Investigation Towards the Application of Facial Expression Analysis to Enable an Emotion-Aware Car Interface

Silvia Ceccacci[1](✉), Maura Mengoni[1], Generosi Andrea[1],
Luca Giraldi[2], Giuseppe Carbonara[3], Andrea Castellano[3],
and Roberto Montanari[3]

[1] Department of Industrial Engineering and Mathematical Sciences, Università
Politecnica delle Marche, Ancona, Italy
{s.ceccacci,m.mengoni,a.generosi}@univpm.it
[2] Emoj Srl, Ancona, Italy
info@emojlab.com
[3] RE:Lab Srl, Reggio Emilia, Italy
{giuseppe.carbonara,andrea.castellano,
roberto.montanari}@re-lab.it

Abstract. The paper describes the conceptual model of an emotion-aware car interface able to: map both the driver's cognitive and emotional states with the vehicle dynamics; adapt the level of automation or support the decision-making process if emotions negatively affecting the driving performance are detected; ensure emotion regulation and provide a unique user experience creating a more engaging atmosphere (e.g. music, LED lighting) in the car cabin. To enable emotion detection, it implements a low-cost emotion recognition able to recognize Ekman's universal emotions by analyzing the driver's facial expression from stream video.

A preliminary test was conducted in order to determine the effectiveness of the proposed emotion recognition system in a driving context. Results evidenced that the proposed system is capable to correctly qualify the drivers' emotion in a driving simulation context.

Keywords: Emotion recognition · Facial expression recognition · Driver Monitoring System

1 Introduction

Nowadays, driver monitoring is a topic of paramount importance, because distraction and inattention are a relevant safety concern, as well as leading factors in car crashes [1]. For example, being distracted can make drivers less aware of other road users such as pedestrians, cyclists and road workers, as well as less observant of road rules such as speed limits and junction controls. Therefore, among driver assistance systems and autonomous driving system, the detection of driver's states has especial importance, since such a status may affect (less benefits) the effectiveness of these systems, e.g. driver is not ready to take back the control, or to responds to a given warning [2, 3].

© Springer Nature Switzerland AG 2020
M. Antona and C. Stephanidis (Eds.): HCII 2020, LNCS 12189, pp. 504–517, 2020.
https://doi.org/10.1007/978-3-030-49108-6_36

Currently, several Driver Monitoring Systems (DMSs) offered by carmakers are based on:

- The vehicle dynamic data to detect "abnormal behavior" and so identify tiredness or drowsiness;
- The use of internal camera, which considers where the driver is looking at, to determine visual distraction (e.g., eyes off the road) and drowsiness.

However, they neglect to consider driver emotional states, despite research demonstrated precisely that emotion and attention are linked, and both have an impact on performances [4]. In particular, driving tasks strongly vary based on emotional state [4], and it is well known that aggressive driving due to inability to manage one's emotions represents a major cause of accidents [5, 6]. In fact, negative emotions – such as anger, frustration, anxiety, fear, and stress - can alter perception and decision-making, leading to the misinterpretation of events and even affect physical capabilities [7, 8].

To improve driving safety, it is therefore necessary to equip cars with emotion-aware system based on AI technologies able to detect and monitoring human emotions and to react in case of hazard, e.g. providing warning and proper stimuli for emotion regulation and even acting on the dynamics of the vehicle.

In this context, this paper proposes to equip the car with a DMS, which thanks to a multimedia sensing network and an affective intelligent interface is able to:

- Monitor the emotional state and degree of attention of driver and passengers, by respectively analyzing the persons' facial expressions and eye gaze;
- Mapping both the cognitive and emotional states with the car interface features in a responsive way, in order to increase human wellbeing and safety.

The paper presents an overall description of the proposed system and focuses on a preliminary experiment aimed at assessing the feasibility of using a low-cost emotion detection system based on facial expression analysis in a car simulator context.

2 Research Background

Induced emotions may affect subjective judgment, driving performance, and perceived workload during car driving. In particular, it seems that induced anger reduces deriver's subjective safety level and lead to degraded driving performance compared to neutral and fear. Happiness also showed degraded driving performance compared to neutral and fear. Fear did not have any significant effect on subjective judgment, driving performance, or perceived workload [9].

As it is well known, a number of environmental factors may arouse emotions (e.g., road traffic condition, driving concurrent tasks such as phone conversation, etc.). For example, people actually spend most of their driving time listening music on their radio or CD player, and this affect the driving attention because of its emotional nature. It has been observed that, while a neutral music does not seem to influence driving attention, sad music would lead to no-risk driving whereas happy music would be associated with a more dangerous driving [4].

However, despite the importance and prevalence of affective states in driving, no systematic approach has yet been developed in order to relate the driver's emotional state and driving performance [10]. Moreover, results of empirical studies seems to evidence that the traditional influence mechanisms (e.g., the one based on valence and arousal dimensions) may not be able to explain the affective effects on driving. In fact, affective states in the same valence or arousal dimension (e.g., both anger and fear belong to negative valence and high arousal) showed different performance results [9]. Consequently, to explain complicated phenomena such as the effects of emotions on driving, a more elaborate framework needs to be defined.

Today several methods and technologies allow the recognition of human emotions, which differ in level of intrusiveness. Obviously, the use of invasive instruments based on biofeedback sensors, (e.g., ECG or EEG, other biometric sensors) can affect the subjects' behavior and in particular it may adulterate his/her spontaneity and consequently the emotions experienced by them [11]. Consequently, in the last years, several efforts have been made to improve non-intrusive emotion recognition systems, based on speech recognition analysis and facial emotion analysis. In particular, facial emotion analysis aims to recognize patterns form facial expressions and to connect them to emotions, based on a certain theoretical model. Most of these systems implements Deep Learning algorithms based on Convolutional Neural Networks (CNN), which take in input different kind of pictures and make predictions based on a trained model [12, 13]. The most robust algorithms developed until now allow to recognize only Ekman & Fresner's primary emotions (i.e., anger, fear, dis-gust, surprise, joy and sadness) [14]. In fact, most of the databases of facial expressions currently available are based on these emotions.

In the past, several emotion-aware car interfaces have been proposed, which uses bio-signals collected through wearable devices [15, 16] or audio signal analysis, e.g., detection vocal inflection changes [17]. Based on the best of our knowledge, only [10] attempted to combine facial expression and speech analysis only at a conceptual level, while no study has actually tested the effectiveness of facial expression recognition systems in a motor vehicle context to enable emotion recognition.

3   The Proposed System

The scheme in Fig. 1 describes the proposed overall system architecture. It is characterized by the following subsystems:

- The Driver Attention Detection (DAD) system: it acquires data (e.g., eye gaze) through the eye tracking system just embedded in the car simulator and processes it by using the machine learning algorithms described in [18] and [19].
- The Emotion Recognition (ER) system: it is a software capable of recognizing Ekman's universal emotions by mean of a convolutional neural network based on the Keras and Tensowflow frameworks, trained merging three different public datasets (i.e., the lab generated CK+ , FER+ and AffectNet) and based on one of the most popular CNN architectures (i.e., VGG13). This trained network has been evaluated on EmotioNet 2018 challenge dataset [20]. Results reported in [21] evidenced high recognition accuracy especially for happiness, anger and neutral emotions.

- The DMS system: it takes the data from the ER and DAD systems as input and reworks them according to rules, in order to determine the prevailing emotion and degree of attention in a given inter-valley of time. It then makes a holistic assessment of the risk associated with the cognitive and emotional state of the driver, using appropriate decisional algorithms (e.g., based on Bayesian Belief Networks as suggested in [22]). For example, it associates a high risk when it releaves strong states of excitement due to anger or happiness, which as has been demonstrated in previous studies may alter driving skills and a low level of attention, while it associates a medium level of risk when it detects an altered emotional state but a high level of attention.

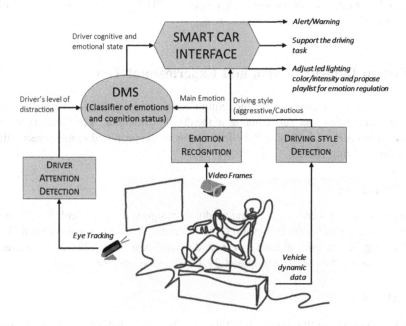

Fig. 1. The proposed system architecture

- The Driving Style Detection Module: it is based on the sensing of driving behavior, based on the acquisition of the CAN network from the vehicle/simulated vehicle. Several researches [23, 24] indicate that driving-related parameters are significant and objective indicators of driver's impairment. For example, steering frequency (e.g. expressed in Steering wheel Reversal Rate) is considered as a relevant indicator to measure driving task demand [25], while Standard Deviation from Lateral Position (SDLP), i.e. the results of the vehicle's movement induced by driver steering actions with respect to the road environment (in specific, the position from the center of the lane), is considered as a direct indicator of driving performance [26].

Safety-related insights can be also measured with the calculation of the Time to Collision (TTC), i.e. the time required for two vehicles to collide at their present speed and on the same path [27]. Nowadays, in-vehicle DMS are often designed to exploit this data, and the topic of Driver Monitoring and Assistance Systems (DMAS), based on system intervention depending on the driver's monitored status, is raising [28].

- Smart Car Interface): it behaves as a Smart Car Agent, interacting with the driver to adapt the level of automation or support the decision-making process or providing audio and video alerts, when an affective state that could compromise the driving performance is revealed. Moreover, it can ensure emotion regulation and provide a unique user experience, e.g. thorough the selection of a proper music playlist according to the emotional state, activation of LED lighting to change cabin colors or creating a more engaging atmosphere.

4   System Implementation and Experimental Test

A first step for the investigation of the requirements of this system has been developed, by integrating 4k full spectrum cameras in the driving simulator. A preliminary test was conducted in order to determine the effectiveness of the proposed emotion recognition system in a driving context.

4.1   Participants

Twenty participants were involved and randomly assigned to the control (5 males and 5 females) or to the experimental group (6 males and 4 females). All participants had a valid driving license since at least 3 years and normal hearing capabilities. The average age was 26.6 for the control group and 29.4 for the experimental group.

4.2   Materials

The RE:Lab simulator that was used in this study is a static driving simulator composed of a complete automobile, fully functional pedals and dashboard, and a large screen showing a highway scenario. The simulation engine is SCANeR Studio 1.8 [19]. Simulated highway scenarios were designed using actual European geometric route design standards and consisted in a simple long O-shape path without any crossroad. During the simulation, several possible driving parameters were monitored: in particular the simulator was able to record the steering wheel movements, the force applied to the pedals and the real-time position of the vehicle in the simulation scenario. These raw data were used to evaluate the driving performance indicators used as independent variables.

Furthermore, the images of a 4k camera installed on the simulator was used as input for the emotion recognition system, while the acoustic stimuli were conveyed through a high-performance headset system.

4.3   Experimental Procedure

Each trial lasted approximately 20 min for the control group and 15 min for the experimental group, all participants firstly drove for a 5-min period in order to familiarize themselves with the simulator; after that, both groups were asked to complete a 6-min driving task during which, only for the experimental group, the six acoustic stimuli of approximately 5-s each were provided and delivered with a delay of 45 s among each one.

Additional to the driving task, the control group received also a listening task with the same stimuli used during the driving task of the experimental group.

At the end of the tasks all participants were asked to compile a NASA-TLX survey to rate the perceived workload.

4.4   The Task

The driving task was the same for the two 6-min driving periods (experimental and control group). The subjects were required to drive on an high-way setting without traffic and to respect the code of the road as they would in a natural setting, information of the speed limit were provided directly within the scenario as road signs and the subjects could see their speed on the dashboard speedometer.

The listening task was performed by the participants of the control group while sitting on the simulator station through a pair of headsets, but in this case without driving and with the simulator switched off, only the camera information for the emotion recognition system were processed.

4.5   Dependent Variables

Firstly, in this study was explored the effect of acoustic stimulations on emotion both in driving and no-driving context, by using a convolutional Neural network model to recognize the six Ekman's universal emotions [21]. The data of classification of each of the six universal emotions have been combined to create an engagement index as metric for emotional involvement opposed to the absence of emotions.

Furthermore, the emotions indexes have been combined in order to generate a differentiation of the emotional engagement in accord with the arousal-valence model [29]. On this base, four new indexes were created:

- Engagement classified on the arousal axis;
  - Active engagement (Surprise, Fear, Anger, Happiness);
  - Passive engagement (Sad and disgust);
- Engagement classified on the valence axis;
  - Positive engagement (Happiness and surprise);
  - Negative engagement (Anger, Disgust, Sadness, Fear).

All these indexes were compared for the different experimental scenarios: driving task with and without stimuli, exposition to stimuli with and without driving task.

Secondly, the effects of the emotional state and engagement on driving performance have been analyzed. To this end, the standard deviation of the Lane position (SDLP), and the standard deviation of the steering wheel angle (SDSTW) have been taken into consideration as indicators for later control performance metrics. While the standard deviation of speed, and the standard deviation of pressure on the gas pedal have been considered as indicators of longitudinal control performance.

Finally, the cognitive workload was assessed for each participant through the NASA-TLX survey [30].

5   Results

5.1   Classification of the Acoustic Stimuli

Seven different sounds were used to elicit emotions on participants while the emotion recognition system was used to classify the participants' reaction to such stimuli both in driving and no-driving context in accord with the Ekman theory of fundamental Emotions.

The stimuli have been chosen taking as inspiration the International affective digital sounds (IADS) [31] from other datasets available online and freely accessible; however, the sounds were not already standardized or categorized.

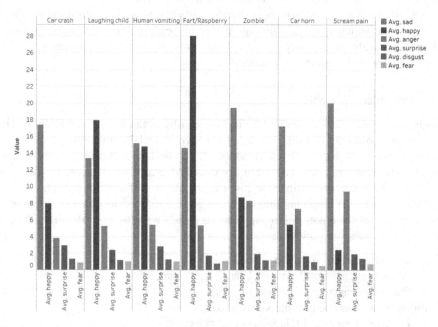

Fig. 2. Fundamental emotions recorded after emotion induction through stimuli in all participants

Among all the stimuli the neutral indicator (namely the absence of emotions) showed the highest value: this may be explained by the nature of the acoustic stimuli, which may not be sufficiently engaging to trigger a strong emotional reaction. However, the emotion recognition system was able to detect the presence of the six fundamental emotions in different percentage associated with each stimulus (Fig. 2). Apart from the neutral indicator, the second main emotion monitored was sadness which was associated with 5 stimuli (car crash, human vomiting, zombie, car horn and scream pain) followed by happiness which showed a higher level in 2 stimuli (laughing child and fart/raspberry).

5.2   Engagement

Together with the Ekman fundamental emotions, the sum of the percentage values associated to the probability of occurrence of each Ekman's emotions (i.e., Joy, Sadness, Anger, Fear, Disgust and Surprise) has been recorded for each tenth of second. This value may be described as a representation of the engagement level of each participant, which is specular to the "neutral/not revealed value" of emotion (Fig. 3).

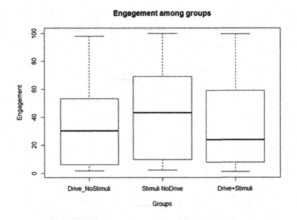

Fig. 3. Differences in engagement among groups

The level of engagement was compared among the different groups using the nonparametric Wilcoxon test due to the lack of normality of the distribution. As result the group engaged in the primary driving task while listening at the auditory stimuli (Mdn = 23.92) showed a significant lower level of engagement, $Z = 12157669$, $p < 0.001$, compared with the group associated with the acoustic stimuli without driving task (Mdn = 43.53). Also the comparison between the group engaged in the driving task with acoustic stimuli (Mdn = 23.92) and without stimuli (Mdn = 30.26) showed a statistically significant difference ($Z = 10501813$, $p < 0.001$) and a lower level of emotional engagement for participants whom drove without acoustic stimuli.

Engagement and Arousal

When we consider the level of engagement as distributed on the arousal continuum, we find a significant higher level of active engagement (anger, happiness, surprise and fear) (Z = 7235033, p < 0.001) for the group exposed to acoustic stimuli while driving (Mdn = 12.2) compared with the group not exposed to stimuli while driving (Mdn = 6.12). The passive engagement (Sadness and disgust) on the other hand, resulted to be significantly higher (Z = 13898945, p < 0.001) in the group not exposed to stimuli (Mdn = 3.52) than in the group exposed to stimuli while driving (Mdn = 0.74) (Fig. 4).

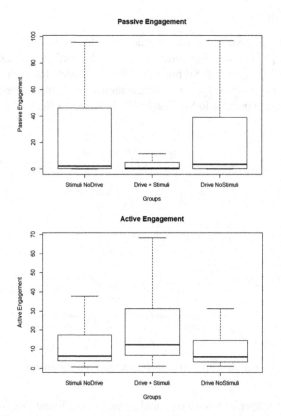

Fig. 4. Differences between groups in terms of passive and active engagement.

Regarding the comparison of the groups exposed to acoustic stimuli with and without driving task, we can observe a significantly higher level of active engagement (Z = 7792699, p < 0.001) in the group with the task (Mdn = 12.2) compared with the group without the driving task (Mdn = 6.38). At the same time, a statistically significant lower level of passive engagement (Z = 12981028, p < 0.001) was shown for the group exposed to stimuli while driving (Mdn = 2.2) than for the group without driving task (Mdn = 0.74).

Engagement and Valence

When we compare the engagement of opposite valence between the groups engaged in the driving task with and without stimuli, we find a statistically significant difference of positive engagement (Z = 7379057, p < 0.001) for the group exposed to stimuli (Mdn = 3.22) compared with the group non exposed to stimuli during the driving task (Mdn = 1.35); conversely, if we compare the Negative engagement between the same groups, we find a significantly higher level of negative engagement in the group non exposed to stimuli (Mdn = 26.51) compared with the group exposed to stimuli while driving (Fig. 5).

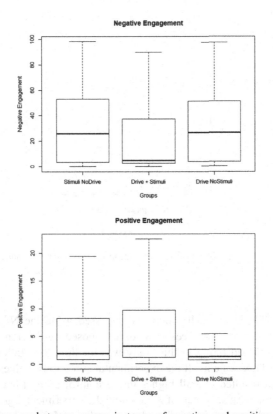

Fig. 5. Differences between groups in terms of negative and positive engagement.

Similarly, the positive engagement appears to be significantly higher (Z = 9193588, p < 0.001) in the group exposed to stimuli while driving (Mdn = 3.22) compared with the group exposed to stimuli without driving task (Mdn = 1.92); while the negative engagement appears significantly higher (Z = 12741859, p < 0.001) in the group without driving task (Mdn = 25.89) compared with the group exposed to stimuli during the driving task (Mdn = 4.74).

5.3 Driving Performance

Assessments of the driving performance were conducted between the group driving with acoustic stimuli and the one driving without stimuli. Of the four performance indicators considered, only the standard deviation of the lane position (SDLP) was found to be statistically different and normally distributed. Indeed, comparing the means through a t test, it showed a statistically higher level $t(15.9) = 4.3043, p < 0.001$ in the group not exposed to acoustic stimuli ($M = 0.53$, $SD = 0.13$) than the group exposed to stimuli while driving ($M = 0.31$, $SD = 0.09$) (Fig. 6).

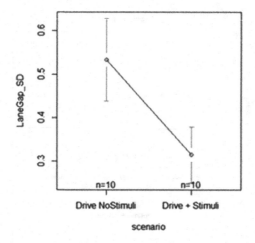

Fig. 6. Effect of emotion stimulation on driving performance.

5.4 Workload

The cognitive workload for each group was assessed using the NASA-TLX, which defines the workload as "the sources of loading imposed by different tasks." [30].

The overall workload rating in this study was medium-low, falling in the bottom half of the NASA-TLX scale in all the experimental conditions (values range from 0 to 20). The workload resulted overall higher in the control group (driving task without acoustic stimuli) with a mean value of 8.18, while the experimental group (driving task with acoustic stimuli) reported a workload mean value of 5.3, for both the groups the item with the highest rating was Effort, respectively 11 in the experimental condition and 6.5 in the control group.

6   Conclusion

The paper introduced at a conceptual level an emotion-aware DMS, which exploits a low-cost emotion recognition system based on facial expression analysis. A preliminary experiment has been carried out in order to assess the feasibility of the proposed system in a driving context.

Results evidenced that the considered emotion recognition system is capable to correctly qualify the drivers' emotion in a driving simulation context: it associate negative emotion (sadness, anger) to stimuli labeled with negative valence (e.g., car crash, human vomiting, car horn, etc.), while it associated a positive emotion (happiness) to stimuli labeled with positive valence (e.g., laughing child).

However, a high percentage of neutral indicator has been collected for all the stimuli, whereas the detected levels of engagement are overall low. This can be due to the nature of stimuli used to induce emotion: the induction of emotions by means of sound stimuli is not as effective as that carried out by means of audiovisual stimuli or other techniques, such as autobiographical recall [32]. Future studies should be conducted using other methods to induce emotions while driving.

The exposition to the auditory stimuli increased the participant active engagement during the driving tasks. The same auditory stimuli involved participants in a more positively (or less negatively) way during driving, if compared with a no-driving situation. In addition, the driving task with emotional stimulation resulted in a lower perception of mental workload and a better performance in terms of lateral control of the driving trajectory.

This may be due to the fact that the driving route was very quiet and repetitive and therefore participants may have found it boring. In fact, boredom can be representative of low-activation of affective states while driving [10]. As a result, the sounds, regardless of their nature, may have contributed to increasing the enjoyment, and consequently the positive affective engagement, of the participants during the driving task. However, future studies should be carried out to better investigate the effect of induced emotions on more realistic driving tasks.

References

1. Stephens, A.N., Groeger, J.A.: Situational specificity of trait influences on drivers' evaluations and driving behaviour. Transp. Res. Part F: Ttraff. Psychol. Behaviour 12(1), 29–39 (2009)
2. Walch, M., Lange, K., Baumann, M., Weber, M.: Autonomous driving: investigating the feasibility of car-driver handover assistance. In: Proceedings of the 7th International Conference on Automotive User Interfaces and Interactive Vehicular Applications, pp. 11–18, September 2015
3. Bimbraw, K.: Autonomous cars: past, present and future a review of the developments in the last century, the present scenario and the expected future of autonomous vehicle technology. In: 2015 12th International Conference on Informatics in Control, Automation and Robotics (ICINCO), vol. 1, pp. 191–198. IEEE, July 2015

4. Pêcher, C., Lemercier, C., Cellier, J.M.: Emotions drive attention: effects on driver's behaviour. Saf. Sci. **47**(9), 1254–1259 (2009)
5. Özkan, T., Lajunen, T., Parker, D., Sümer, N., Summala, H.: Aggressive driving among british, dutch, finnish and turkish drivers. Int. J. Crashworthiness **16**(3), 233–238 (2011)
6. Sârbescu, P.: Aggressive driving in Romania: psychometric properties of the driving anger expression inventory. Transp. Res. Part F Traffic Psychol. Behav. **15**(5), 556–564 (2012)
7. Lisetti, C.L., Nasoz, F.: Affective intelligent car interfaces with emotion recognition. In: Proceedings of 11th International Conference on Human Computer Interaction, Las Vegas, NV, USA, July 2005
8. Matthews, G.: Towards a transactional ergonomics for driver stress and fatigue. Theor. Issues Ergon. Sci. **3**(2), 195–211 (2002)
9. Jeon, M., Walker, B.N., Yim, J.B.: Effects of specific emotions on subjective judgment, driving performance, and perceived workload. Transp. Res. Part F: Traffic Psychol. Behav. **24**, 197–209 (2014)
10. Jeon, M.: Emotions in driving. In: Emotions and Affect in Human Factors and Human-Computer Interaction, pp. 437–474. Academic Press (2017)
11. Ceccacci, S., Generosi, A., Giraldi, L., Mengoni, M.: Tool to make shopping experience responsive to customer emotions. Int. J. Autom. Technol. **12**(3), 319–326 (2018)
12. Generosi, A., et al.: MoBeTrack: a toolkit to analyze user experience of mobile apps in the wild. In: 2019 IEEE International Conference on Consumer Electronics (ICCE), pp. 1–2. IEEE, January 2019
13. Generosi, A., Ceccacci, S., Mengoni, M.: A deep learning-based system to track and analyze customer behavior in retail store. In: 2018 IEEE 8th International Conference on Consumer Electronics-Berlin (ICCE-Berlin), pp. 1–6. IEEE, September 2018
14. Ekman, P., Friesen, W.V.: Manual for the Facial Action Coding System. Consulting Psychologists Press, Ekman, P., Friesen, W.V.: Manual for the Facial Action Coding System. Consulting Psychologists Press, Palo Alto (1978)
15. Nasoz, F., Lisetti, C.L., Vasilakos, A.V.: Affectively intelligent and adaptive car interfaces. Inf. Sci. **180**(20), 3817–3836 (2010)
16. Katsis, C.D., Katertsidis, N., Ganiatsas, G., Fotiadis, D.I.: Toward emotion recognition in car-racing drivers: a biosignal processing approach. IEEE Trans. Syst. Man Cybern. Part A Syst. Hum. **38**(3), 502–512 (2008)
17. Jones, C.M., Jonsson, I.-M.: Performance analysis of acoustic emotion recognition for in-car conversational interfaces. In: Stephanidis, C. (ed.) UAHCI 2007. LNCS, vol. 4555, pp. 411–420. Springer, Heidelberg (2007). https://doi.org/10.1007/978-3-540-73281-5_44
18. Tango, F., Botta, M., Minin, L., Montanari, R.: Non-intrusive detection of driver distraction using machine learning algorithms. In: ECAI, pp. 157–162, August 2010
19. Benedetto, S., Pedrotti, M., Minin, L., Baccino, T., Re, A., Montanari, R.: Driver workload and eye blink duration. Trans. Res. Part F Traffic Psychol. Behav. **14**(3), 199–208 (2011)
20. Benitez-Quiroz, C.F., Srinivasan, R., Feng, Q., Wang, Y., Martinez, A.M.: EmotioNet challenge: recognition of facial expressions of emotion in the wild (2017)
21. Talipu, A., Generosi, A., Mengoni, M., Giraldi, L.: Evaluation of deep convolutional neural network architectures for emotion recognition in the wild. In: 2019 IEEE 23rd International Symposium on Consumer Technologies (ISCT), pp. 25–27. IEEE, June 2019
22. Gullà, F., Cavalieri, L., Ceccacci, S., Germani, M.: A BBN-based method to manage adaptive behavior of a smart user interface. Procedia CIRP **50**, 535–540 (2016)
23. Toledo, T., Lotan, T.: In-vehicle data recorder for evaluation of driving behavior and safety, transportation research record: Journal of the Transportation Research Board, No. 1953, Transportation Research Board of the National Academies, Washington, D.C., 2006, pp. 112–119 (2006)

24. The Royal Society for the Prevention of Accidents: Road Safety and In-Vehicle Monitoring (Black Box) Technology, Policy Paper, February 2013 (2013)
25. Macdonald, W.A., Hoffmann, E.R.: Review of relationships between steering wheel reversal rate and driving task demand. Hum. Factors **22**(6), 733–739 (1980)
26. Verster, J.C., Roth, T.: Standard operation procedures for conducting the on-the-road driving test, and measurement of the standard deviation of lateral position (SDLP). Int. J. Gen. Med. **4**, 359 (2011)
27. Van Der Horst, R., Hogema, J.: Time-to-collision and collision avoidance systems. In: Proceedings of the 6th ICTCT Workshop (1993)
28. Saulino, G., Persaud, B., Bassani, M.: Calibration and application of crash prediction models for safety assessment of roundabouts based on simulated conflicts. In: Proceedings of the 94th Transportation Research Board (TRB) Annual Meeting, Washington, DC, USA, pp. 11–15 (2015)
29. Henia, W.M.B., Lachiri, Z.: Emotion classification in arousal-valence dimension using discrete affective keywords tagging. In: 2017 International Conference on Engineering & MIS (ICEMIS), pp. 1–6. IEEE, May 2017
30. Hart, S.G.: NASA-task load index (NASA-TLX); 20 years later. In: Proceedings of the Human Factors and Ergonomics Society Annual Meeting, vol. 50, no. 9, pp. 904–908. Sage Publications, Los Angeles, October 2006
31. Bradley, M.M., Lang, P.J.: The International Affective Digitized Sounds (; IADS-2): Affective ratings of sounds and instruction manual. University of Florida, Gainesville, FL, Technical Rep. B-3 (2007)
32. Siedlecka, E., Denson, T.F.: Experimental methods for inducing basic emotions: a qualitative review. Emot. Rev. **11**(1), 87–97 (2019)

Research on the Visually Impaired Individuals Shopping with Artificial Intelligence Image Recognition Assistance

Chia-Hui Feng[1,2](✉), Ju-Yen Hsieh[2], Yu-Hsiu Hung[1],
Chung-Jen Chen[3], and Cheng-Hung Chen[4]

[1] Department of Industrial Design, National Cheng Kung University,
No. 1, University Road, Tainan City, Taiwan R.O.C.
p38041075@ncku.edu.tw
[2] Department of Creative Product Design, Southern Taiwan University
of Science and Technology, No. 1, Nan-Tai Street, Yung Kang District,
Tainan City, Taiwan R.O.C.
[3] Department of Visual Communication Design, Southern Taiwan University
of Science and Technology, No. 1, Nan-Tai Street, Yung Kang District,
Tainan City, Taiwan R.O.C.
[4] Innovative Solutions, Acer Incorporated, New Taipei City, Taiwan R.O.C.

Abstract. Shopping is an indispensable part of daily life. It is an easy task for people with healthy eyes. However, it remains a big problem for the visually impaired individuals. Today, the visually impaired individuals have to be accompanied by their family or guided by the store escort when shopping. It is difficult for them to shop alone. This research develops an artificial intelligence image recognition auxiliary device utilizing the artificial intelligence technology Convolutional Neural Network (CNN), providing smart image recognition modules to assist the visually impaired individuals while shopping. CNN is the most effective deep learning algorithm in the field of machine vision, its ability to compare details of product exterior features makes product recognition more efficient via accurate model training.

This study experiments task-oriented shopping in three shopping models, (1) self-shopping, (2) accompanied shopping, (3) device assisted shopping. It measures through three indicators: shopping time, accuracy in choosing the correct product, and device satisfaction. The research subjects are 18 college students, 8 male students and 10 female students. The subjects are blindfolded, simulating the visually impaired individuals to perform experiments in a state without any vision. one-way repeated-measures ANOVA is used to explore the differences among the three shopping models. Surveys are collected at the end of the experiment to analyze the degrees of satisfaction for the AIoT device. The results of this study are: (1) task operation time of the three shopping models are significantly different p = .000, and gender difference has no significant impact. (2) the task operation accuracy rate of the three shopping models are significantly different p = .000, gender difference also has significant impact p = .000. The accuracy rate for self-shopping is 39%, 12.5% for men and 60% for women. The accuracy rate for companied shopping is 97.25%, 93.75% for men and 100% for women. The accuracy rate for device assisted shopping is 90.25%, 87.5% for men and 92.5% for women. (3) highest score in satisfactory rating is

© Springer Nature Switzerland AG 2020
M. Antona and C. Stephanidis (Eds.): HCII 2020, LNCS 12189, pp. 518–531, 2020.
https://doi.org/10.1007/978-3-030-49108-6_37

the extensiveness of product information audio at an average at 4.5. Satisfactory rating of product information audio accurateness averages at 4.44 points. As to device effective for shopping assistance, the average satisfactory rating is 4.17. And the average satisfactory rating for device operation usability is 4.00.

Keywords: The visually impaired individuals · Machine learning · Computer vision · Product recognition

1 Introduction

According to statistics from the World Health Organization (WHO) in 2019, at least 220 million people worldwide suffer from visual impairment [1]. Most people rely on vision in their lives, whereas visually impaired people face various difficulties in their daily lives. Shopping is a basic human behavior to meet the physiological needs. It is a breeze for the people with healthy eyes, but the visually impaired individuals face many frustrations and restrictions in daily shopping because of visual defects. The visually impaired cannot obtain information through ways such as visual observation, reading text and images. They can only rely on touch and hearing, but these conditions are not sufficient in correctly recognizing the product. Shopping thus poses a major problem for the visually impaired individuals.

Visually impaired individuals usually have to rely on friends, family members or shopping guides in the store to make shopping runs. Availability of an accompany is a major issue for the visually impaired individuals. The visually impaired individuals must ask about product information, and such repeated request may cause impatience from the accompanying person on top of not being able to meet the needs of the visually impaired individuals, [2] inevitably causing the physical and mental burden. If the shopping guide of the store encounters a situation of limited manpower, the visually impaired individuals must wait patiently. The store may even decline to provide the visually impaired individuals with shopping guide service. The visually impaired individuals risk having misguided information as the many varieties of products made it difficult for them to read the contents of the goods. As a result, the visually impaired individual may not be able to gather important nutrition facts from the products, or they ended up purchasing the wrong product [3]. Research on the daily shopping behaviors of severely visually impaired people also points out that the visually impaired people are most worried not being able to compare product information in details while shopping. They need to rely on the assistance of others [4]. After shopping, the visually impaired individuals must use memory to evoke relevant information about the product they purchased, such as touching the material and packaging size of the product, shaking the product to hear the sound and smell the package to identify the product [5]. The visually impaired individuals must also remember the placement of various items at home. The family members cannot move said items. It increases burden in their lives during communications between the visually impaired individuals and the family members.

With the advent of Artificial Intelligence (AI), the development and application of artificial intelligence technology take root in all areas of human society, contributing to technology advancement in areas of transportation, finance, medical treatment, entertainment, education, and so on. Image recognition has notably flourished in recent years, resulting in unmanned stores, face recognition, etc. AI is also used in the development of image recognition for mobile devices, such as Aipoly Vision, VocalEyes AI, SeeingAI, using mobile phone lenses to capture people, events, and objects around them, and describing the captured contents through audio to the visually impaired individuals. These innovations increase the visual impaired individuals' efficiency with daily chores. Through providing AIoT device product image recognition, this study aims to assist visually impaired people when shopping, and to improve the independent and autonomous life of the said individuals.

Due to limitations of impaired vision, visually impaired people are unable to obtain product information while shopping. They worry about asking others for assistance, which may cause psychological pressure and real life difficulties. In order to help the visually impaired individuals to become more independent, the research will assist the visually impaired in areas of not being able to differentiate products and not being able to read product information while shopping. The study develops a device combining artificial intelligence technology with hardware and software of AIoT, so that the visually impaired can use this device to identify the product by name, product composition, price, and expiration date. The purpose of the study is to explore visually impaired people and different gender in using artificial intelligence combined with the Internet of Things device while making purchase. The actual measurement is conducted with three indicators: shopping time, accuracy in choosing the correct product, and device satisfaction.

2   Literature Review

2.1   Convolutional Neural Network

Convolutional neural network (CNN) is a kind of feedforward neural network. It is most commonly seen and most suitable for image recognition. Convolutional neural network is composed of three neural layers, which are the convolution layer, the pooling layer and the fully connected layers. The convolution layer uses the convolution kernel to capture picture features, calculating the weights based on the numeral values to generate feature map. Due to the huge amount of feature parameter data after convolution, the most important features are left through the pooling layer, which reduces the inference complexity. After multi-layer convolution and pooling operations, it finally enters the fully connected layer to combine and classify the features, and eventually outputs. Convolutional neural networks have developed vigorously in the vision field, such as image classification [7] and super-resolution imaging [8]. All of these are moving towards high accuracy and high efficiency.

2.2   AIOT (The Artificial Intelligence of Things)

The Internet of Things (IoT) was proposed by Kevin Ashton of the Automatic Identification Center at the Massachusetts Institute of Technology in 1999 [9]. It is an idea of connecting an object to the Internet so that the item can sense, detect, and respond, and communicate data with other objects. While using the collected information as big data analysis and inference, it can fulfill intelligent identification and management through the Internet of Things technology. The three-level infrastructure of the Internet of Things is divided into the Perception Layer (Sensors & Actuators), the Network Layer (Interconnection) and the Application Layer (Models & Analytics). The perception layer has sense and recognition. The network layer passes the data collected by the perception layer to the network and data storage. The application layer integrates technology for real world applications. The diversity nature of the Internet of Things enables it to be used in many areas, man to object, object to object, facilitating different aspects of human society. The combination of AI and IoT is AIoT (The Artificial Intelligence of Things, AIoT). Through the Internet of Everything, the IoT collects and accumulates a large amount of data stored in the cloud through sensors, and then uses AI to perform big data analysis. The combination of strengths of AI and IoT has become the hottest topic and trend today, such as unmanned storage, drone delivery, and unmanned stores. In 2018, the Amazon Go smart retail store officially operated in Seattle, USA. Through artificial Computer Vision and Just Walk Out Technology, a dense camera system was installed on the ceiling to track each customer. It identifies whether the consumer takes out or places the goods, before checking out with the customer's linked credit card. AIoT applications will greatly affect human shopping behavior and bring convenience to human life.

This study will use Google AutoML Vision machine to learn product identification, to integrate with IoT devices by generating a product image dataset through a large number of product images to achieve accurate product predictions, to build a model that is unique to the visually impaired shopping, and to integrate with AIoT hardware devices to help identify prototype designs.

2.3   The Shopping Model for the Visually Impaired Individuals

The visually impaired individuals need to have the ability to take care of themselves independently, including shopping skills. Due to limited vision, shopping alone is a difficult challenge. Facing a wide range of products in the store, the visually impaired individuals have no way of knowing the product information unless relying on the assistance of others to complete shopping. The visually impaired individuals may be able to obtain the necessary supplies, such as food or daily necessities, with the help of family or friends. However, they encounter inevitable psychological burden and distress in purchasing more personal products. The visually impaired individuals may also be afraid of bothering others, and they usually choose to buy same products over and over, depriving them of the option to find alternative. When the visually impaired people shop in actual stores, they need to draw up a shopping list, memorize it with recording equipment or braille, reserve the date and time of store service in advance, and go to the store where the store assistant is available. The assistant may help the visually impaired individuals to get the designated goods directly, or accompany the visually impaired individuals through the entire shopping process, potentially causing many inconveniences.

2.4   The Current Shopping Assistance for the Visually Impaired Individual

Stores today do not provide the visually impaired individuals with an optimized shopping environment, nor can stores offer them appropriate assistance. The NextVPU company launched a smart eyewear Angel Eye in 2017 using computer vision and artificial intelligence technology, and having visual recognition, navigation and positioning functions. In 2004, the RoboCart, a robot shopping cart, was equipped with a computer and rangefinder to guide the visually impaired individuals to find the product location and obtain product information with a handheld RFID barcode scanner [10]. ShopTalk wearable devices use a barcode scanner to scan the barcode on the product, and use headphones for voice feedback to inform the visually impaired of product information [11]. The Lin (2019) research on the three shopping models for the visually impaired individuals with smart wearable devices indicates that the average accuracy rates of the three modes reach a significant level. The accuracy rate of device shopping is 95%, significantly higher than 75% for shopping alone and 75% for accompanied shopping. Time involved in effective performance carries no prominent differences [12]. This study explores the effectiveness of the device by implementing the three shopping models. The handheld mobile devices have developed ever increasing Apps that can help visually impaired identify products. Such Apps, including Be My Eyes, Aipoly Vision, Envision, Visualize, VocalEyes AI, Seeing AI, etc., can all assist blind people in recognizing the surroundings.

Based on the current situation of the visually impaired individuals, this research develops AIoT shopping devices to assist the visually impaired individuals with a goal of improving their shopping experience.

3   Research Method

This study conducts the research of assisting the visually impaired individuals with artificial intelligence image recognition by having test subjects perform task-oriented shopping in three different models: self-shopping, accompanied shopping, and device assisted shopping. IBM SPSS Statistics Version 26 analysis software is used for data analysis, operation time, product acquisition accuracy, and device satisfaction. The research methods such as research subjects, research tools and research design are described as follows:

3.1   Research Subjects

The research subjects of this study are college students, aged between 18 to 21 years old, a total of 18 students, 8 male and 10 female. Students are to sign the experiment consent before participating in the experiment. The purpose and the experiment procedures are explained to them. During the test, they are blindfolded. The task designation test is performed in order to simulate the visually impaired individuals. The task verification is performed in the simulation store.

3.2   Research Tools

This study uses AIoT-assisted shopping device to conduct device shopping experiment, and simulates the store by displaying 17 commercial products from the market to carry out the experiment.

Establish the AIoT Product Training Dataset:

Machine learning training dataset requires a large number of images to train product models. It uses Github open source software written in Python and image search download tool (google images download) to download Google images in batches. This tool supports cross-platform, shortening the time used to collect products. chromedriver is used in situations where the number of downloaded pictures exceeds 100. After collecting pictures, the program checks whether the pictures match the products. In situation where the pictures are not enough for an effective recognition, photos are manually taken from various angles to increase the recognition rate. The image file format is converted to csv format and stored in the Google AutoML cloud dataset.

Use Google AutoML Vision to develop product graphics training, use image search and download tools to collect training images to a computer, build a product dataset, train a machine learning model, and simulate product definition labels in the store accordingly to classify images. In order to improve the model accuracy, the trained model is continuously iterative to optimize the model exact precision and recall. Select the training model with the highest accuracy rate to connect with the AutoML API. The confusion matrix is the performance list of the visualization algorithm for the AI device product module. Observe the error rate of the product image. The data table can help understand which classification errors occur. Then use the specific labels to train and enhance the accuracy rate. The threshold tool affects the model accuracy and average recall precision. The closer this score approaches 1.0, the better the model performs during the test. Finally, write a Python program to connect the trained modules, the camera lens of the Internet of Things with Acer Cloud Professor.

Shopping Device with AIoT Assistance:

Push the button to trigger the autofocus camera lens. Send the captured product to the product dataset for identification. Then use the Bluetooth headset to play the recognition result of products by name, price, product composition, and expiration date through voice to the visually impaired individual. It allows the visually impaired individual to confirm the products purchased.

AIoT hardwares: Professor Acer CloudProfessor Windows 10, Ardunio Leonardo, expansion board module, Logitech autofocus camera, USB Hub, trigger button and wireless Bluetooth headset, as in Fig. 1.

Fig. 1. AIoT device hardware equipment.

(1) Product Label Voice Dataset:

Select 17 items on the market, record the product name, price, composition, and expiration date. Adjust speed and volume, and save it in wav format.

(2) Product Shelf Installment:

The experiment is to simulate a real store. The shelf is based on research of the relevant stores. The best vision and display range is from 60 cm to 150 cm [13]. This study sets the display height of the product at 80 cm to 150 cm. There is one item on each rack with a total of 17 items, as in Fig. 2.

Fig. 2. Product shelf display.

3.3   Test Design

This experiment selects 17 commercial products, mainly snacks, beverages and daily commodities. This research carries out the experimental tasks through three shopping modes: A) shopping alone, B) accompanied shopping, C) device assistance shopping. The location of the goods is changed according to different tasks to avoid learning. Each task must find four designated commodities in the simulation store set up in the experiment. The experiment will evaluate by recording time required for the task, product identification rate and device satisfaction rate. It uses Questionnaire of Likert five-level scale for satisfaction verification.

(1) Task A. Shopping Alone

The subject conducts experiment on product specified by the designator. The visually impaired individual enter the simulation store to shop for the specified product.

(2) Task B. Accompanied Shopping

The subject conducts experiment on product specified by the designator. The visually impaired individual and the accompanying person enter the simulation store to shop for designated product.

(3) Task C. Device Assistance Shopping

The subject conducts experiment on product specified by the designator. The visually impaired individual wearing device enters the simulation store shopping. The subject must use the device to identify product, listen to product information and find the product.

4 Results

4.1 Research Subjects Results of Establishing AIoT Product Training Dataset

This research uses Google AutoML Vision to build a dataset of 1,329 products. Optimize the model after four iterations, the final model has an average accuracy rate of 0.976 and a recall rate of 0.920, as in Fig. 3.

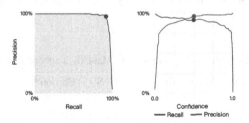

Fig. 3. Accuracy and recall rates of model threshold.

After confusion matrix, the accuracy rate for commodities such as Uni-President Black Tea is 67%. The error rate for Uni-President Milk Tea is 22%. The error rate for Apple Cidra is 11%. The accuracy rate for Kinder Chocolate Maxi is 14%. The error rate for toothpaste reaches 14% and the error rate for fruit candy is 14%.

4.2   Analysis Result for Time Operation Effectiveness Record

A total of 18 college students wear blindfolds, 8 males account for 44% of the total sample, and 10 females account for 56% of the total sample.

Task one is shopping alone. The average operation time is 204.709 s, standard deviation 159.909. Male shopping time 159.941 s, standard deviation 113.303. Female shopping time 240.524 s, standard deviation 187.375. The second task is accompanied shopping. The average operation time is 208.946 s, standard deviation 69.500. Male 225.963 s, standard deviation 76.104. Female 195.332 s, standard deviation 64.465. Task three is device assistance shopping. The average operation time is 377.858 s, standard deviation 203.964. Male 456.771 s, standard deviation 191.260. Female 377.858 s, standard deviation 200.412. As shown in Table 1.

Table 1. AIoT task operation time analysis table.

Mode	Item	Gender	Mean	SD	Number
A	Shopping Alone	Male	159.941	113.303	8
		Female	240.524	187.375	10
		Total	204.709	159.909	18
B	Accompanied Shopping	Male	225.963	76.104	8
		Female	195.332	64.465	10
		Total	208.946	69.500	18
C	Device Assistance Shopping	Male	456.771	191.260	8
		Female	314.728	200.412	10
		Total	377.858	203.964	18

As Table 2 shows, the single-factor variation analysis of repeated quantities meets the homogeneity hypothesis of variation, and it meets the spherical test hypothesis. The Mauchly's W coefficient is .697 ($x2 = 5.415$, $p = .067 > .05$), so no correction tool is required.

Table 2. AIoT task operation time Mauchly's spherical test table.

Within subjects effect	Mauchly's W	Approx. Chi-Square	df	Sig.	Epsilon[b]		
					Greenhouse-Geisser	Huynh-Feldt	Lower-bound
Factor	.697	5.415	2	.067	.767	.886	.500

The data complies with the sphericity test hypothesis. The sum of squares for group effect and independent variable effect is 386285.378. The mean square value is 193142.689. $F (2,32) = 11.344$, $p < .001$. This indicates that under different shopping modes, the task operation time of the subjects has significant differences.

Taking gender as the inter-subject factor, the sum of squared deviations from the mean of the effect for the independent variable is 110138.553, the mean square value is

55069.276, and F (2,32) = 3.234, p > .001, indicating that in different shopping modes, gender has no significant difference in the subjects' task operation time. As in Table 3.

Table 3. AIoT task operation time within subjects effect test.

Source		Type III sum of squares	df	Mean square	F	Sig.
Factor	Sphericity assumed	386285.378	2	193142.689	11.344	.000
	Greenhouse-Geisser	386285.378	1.535	251668.435	11.344	.001
	Huynh-Feldt	386285.378	1.772	218028.002	11.344	.000
	Lower-bound	386285.378	1.000	386285.378	11.344	.004
Factor* gender	Sphericity assumed	110138.553	2	55069.276	3.234	.053
	Greenhouse-Geisser	110138.553	1.535	71756.268	3.234	.068
	Huynh-Feldt	110138.553	1.772	62164.633	3.234	.060
	Lower-bound	110138.553	1.000	110138.553	3.234	.091
Error (Factor)	Sphericity assumed	544838.719	32	17026.210		
	Greenhouse-Geisser	544838.719	24.558	22185.461		
	Huynh-Feldt	544838.719	28.348	19219.938		
	Lower-bound	544838.719	16.000	34052.420		

Through pairwise comparison of dependent single-factor variation numbers, the results show that the subjects' task operation time in the three different shopping modes C > B > A, as in Table 4.

Table 4. Pairwise comparison of the subjects' AIoT task operation time.

(I)factor	(J)factor	Mean difference (I-J)	Std. error	Sig	95% confidence interval for difference 95%	
					Lower bound	Upper bound
A	B	−10.415	43.621	.814	−102.887	82.056
	C	−185.517*	31.760	.000	−252.846	−118.188
B	A	10.415	43.621	.814	−82.056	102.887
	C	−175.102*	53.243	.005	−287.973	−62.231
C	A	185.517*	31.760	.000	118.188	252.846
	B	175.102*	53.243	.005	62.231	287.973

Note: A. Shopping Along, B. Accompanied Shopping, C. Device Assistance Shopping

4.3 Analysis Result for Task Correction Rate

Task one is shopping alone. The average correct operation rate is 39%, standard deviation 28.725. Male 12.5%, standard deviation 18.9. Female 60%, standard deviation 12.9. The second task is accompanied shopping. The average correct operation rate is 97.25%, standard deviation 8.075. Male 93.75%, standard deviation .000. Female 100%, standard deviation .000. Task three is device assistance shopping. The average operation accuracy rate is 90.25%, standard deviation 12.55. Male 87.5%, standard deviation 13.375 s. Female 92.5%, standard deviation 12.075, as in Table 5.

Table 5. AIoT task operation accuracy rate analysis table.

Mode	Item	Gender	Mean	SD	Number
A	Shopping Alone	Male	12.5%	18.9	8
		Female	60%	12.9	10
		Total	39%	28.725	18
B	Accompanied Shopping	Male	93.75%	11.575	8
		Female	100%	.000	10
		Total	97.25%	8.075	18
C	Device Assistance Shopping	Male	87.5%	13.375	8
		Female	92.5%	12.075	10
		Total	90.25%	12.55	18

As shown in Table 6, the analysis of the single factor variation of repeated quantity meets the homogeneity assumption of the variation number, and reaches the spherical test hypothesis. The Mauchly's W coefficient is .891 (x2 = 1.733, p = .420 > .05), so the use of correction tool is not required.

Table 6. AIot task operation accuracy rate Mauchly's sphericity test table.

Within subjects effect	Mauchly's W	Approx. Chi-Square	df	Sig.	Epsilon[b]		
					Greenhouse-Geisser	Huynh-Feldt	Lower-bound
factor	.891	1.733	2	.420	.902	1.000	.500

The data complies with the spherical test assumption. The sum of squared deviations from the mean of the independent variable effect is 62.689. The mean square value is 31.344, and F (2,32) = 127.503, p < .001. It indicates that in different shopping modes, the subjects' task operation accuracy rates are significantly different.

Taking gender as the inter-subject factor, the sum of squared deviations from the mean of the independent variable effect is 8.319, the mean square value is 4.159, and F (2,32) = 16.919, p < .001. It indicates that in different shopping modes, the gender has a significant difference in task operation accuracy. Table 7.

Table 7. AIot task operation accuracy rate within subjects effect test.

Source		Type III sum of squares	df	Mean square	F	Sig.
Factor	Sphericity assumed	62.689	2	31.344	127.503	.000
	Greenhouse-Geisser	62.689	1.803	34.764	127.503	.000
	Huynh-Feldt	62.689	2.000	31.344	127.503	.000
	Lower-bound	62.689	1.000	62.689	127.503	.000
Factor* gender	Sphericity assumed	8.319	2	4.159	16.919	.000
	Greenhouse-Geisser	8.319	1.803	4.613	16.919	.000
	Huynh-Feldt	8.319	2.000	4.159	16.919	.000
	Lower-bound	8.319	1.000	8.319	16.919	.001
Error (Factor)	Sphericity assumed	7.867	32	.246		
	Greenhouse-Geisser	7.867	28.852	.273		
	Huynh-Feldt	7.867	32.000	.246		
	Lower-bound	7.867	16.000	.492		

Through the pairwise comparison of the dependent single factor variation analysis, the results show that the subjects' task operation accuracy rate is B > C > A in three different shopping modes, as in Table 8.

Table 8. AIot task operation accuracy rate pairwise comparison.

(I)factor	(J)factor	Mean difference (I-J)	Std. error	Sig.	95% Confidence interval for difference 95% Lower bound	Upper bound
A	B	−2.487*	.149	.000	−2.802	−2.173
	C	−2.212*	.157	.000	−2.544	−1.881
B	A	2.488*	.149	.000	2.173	2.802
	C	.275	.140	.068	−.022	.572
C	A	2.212*	.157	.000	1.881	2.544
	B	−.275	.140	.068	−.572	.022

4.4 Analysis Result for Device Satisfaction

The highest score in satisfactory rating is the extensiveness of the product information audio at an average at 4.5. And product information audio accurateness averages at 4.44 points. As to device effective for shopping assistance, the average score is 4.17. And the average score for device operation usability is 4.00.

5 Conclusion and Discussion

The result of experiment indicates that the task operation time of the three models significantly differs. The device assisted shopping model took longer to complete as the input and output of the device took time. Handheld camera lens may not be able to confirm that the product is captured. Lighting or angles may also limit the device accuracy in terms of product recognition. When the device fails to recognize the product, notification takes times to make audible cues. The operation time lengthens as a result of repeated recognition process. Time for the accompanied shopping model varies depending on the personality and lifestyle of the test subject. The experiment discovers that some test subjects rely entirely on the companion while other test subjects tend to judge on their own with touch and smell before relying on their respective companion. When test subjects shop alone without any help, the subjects resort to shopping experiences in the past to identify package. They recognize product via smell and guess via intuition. The test time for this model is short, but the accuracy rate is relatively lower relative to other shopping models.

The result of task operation accuracy rate carries significant differences in three shopping modes. Different gender also contributes to prominent disparity. If device assistance shopping recognizes the products in the confusion matrix, such as Uni-President black tea and milk tea, it is easy to pick the wrong product due to likely recognition mistakes. Accompanied shopping is highly accurate because it is assisted by a companion. As to shopping alone, the accuracy rate for women is higher than that for men. The research notices that women are more familiar with the products. Sunscreen lotion, for instance, is a product frequently acquired by women. Men seldom purchase it. For this particular item, sunscreen lotion, the accuracy rate is lower for men.

This study stresses to probe if the device is efficient to assist the visually impaired individual in shopping. The experimental results show that device assistance shopping broadcasting voiced product information can effectively enhance shopping ability of the visually impaired individual while shopping alone. It is expected that system recognition will speed up in the future. Lighting restriction and enlarged vision field are expected to effectively heighten the level of accompanying shopping, and solve the problem of insufficient accompanying manpower. The subjects in this experiment are blindfolded. Due to certain discrepancies of daily habits between the sighted and the visually impaired individual, this research is just a preliminary attempt. The future experiment will invite the visually impaired individual to test the actual device. As more and more handheld mobile devices are used by the visually impaired individual, our future experiment scheme includes the development of multi-platform concept for handheld mobile device software.

References

1. Journal 2(5), 99–110 (2016). World Health Organization, https://www.who.int/publications-detail/world-report-on-vision. Accessed 17 Jan 2019

2. Kulyukin, V., Kutiyanawala, A.: Accessible shopping systems for blind and visually impaired individuals: design requirements and the state of the art. Open Rehabil. J. **3**, 158–168 (2010)
3. Kostyra, E., Zakowska-Biemans, S., Sniegocka, K., Piotrowska, A.: Food shopping, sensory determinants of food choice and meal preparation by visually impaired people. Obstacles and expectations in daily food experiences. Appetite **113**, 14–22 (2017)
4. Chuang, Y.: A Study of People with Severe Visual Impairments regarding their daily shopping behaviors (2013)
5. Lin, C.: A study of the effect of wearable assistive shopping device on visual impaired shoppers (2019)
6. Li, K.F., Wang Y.K.: Artificial Intelligence is Coming. Commonwealth (2018)
7. Krizhevsky, A., Sutskever, I., Hinton, G.E.: ImageNet classification with deep convolutional neural networks. Commun. ACM **60**(6), 84–90 (2017)
8. Dong, C., Loy, C.C., He, K., Tang, X.: Image super-resolution using deep convolutional networks. IEEE Trans. Pattern Anal. Mach. Intell. **38**(2), 295–307 (2016)
9. Ashton, K.: That 'Internet of Things' thing. RFID J. **22**, 97–114 (2009)
10. Gharpure, C.P., Kulyukin, V.A.: Robot-assisted shopping for the blind: issues in spatial cognition and product selection. Intel. Serv. Robot. **1**(3), 237–251 (2008)
11. Nicholson, J., Kulyukin, V., Coster, D.: ShopTalk: independent blind shopping through verbal route directions and barcode Scans. Open Rehabil. J. **2**, 11–23 (2009)
12. Hung, Y.-H., Feng, C.-H., Lin, C.-T., Chen, C.-J.: Research on wearable shopping aid device for visually impaired people. In: Antona, M., Stephanidis, C. (eds.) HCII 2019. LNCS, vol. 11572, pp. 244–257. Springer, Cham (2019). https://doi.org/10.1007/978-3-030-23560-4_18
13. Lin, C.S., Huang, Y. J.: Success Operation of Shopping Mall. Tiaoho Culture Co. (1999)

Single Image-Based Food Volume Estimation Using Monocular Depth-Prediction Networks

Alexandros Graikos[1], Vasileios Charisis[1(✉)], Dimitrios Iakovakis[1],
Stelios Hadjidimitriou[1], and Leontios Hadjileontiadis[1,2]

[1] Department of Electrical and Computer Engineering,
Aristotle University of Thessaloniki, Thessaloniki, Greece
`vcharisis@ee.auth.gr`
[2] Department of Electrical and Computer Engineering,
Khalifa University of Science and Technology, Abu Dhabi, United Arab Emirates

Abstract. In this work, we present a system that can estimate food volume from a single input image, by utilizing the latest advancements in monocular depth estimation. We employ a state-of-the-art, monocular depth prediction network architecture, trained exclusively on videos, which we obtain from the publicly available EPIC-KITCHENS and our own collected *food videos* datasets. Alongside it, an instance segmentation network is trained on the UNIMIB2016 food-image dataset, to detect and produce segmentation masks for each of the different foods depicted in the given image. Combining the predicted depth map, segmentation masks and known camera intrinsic parameters, we generate three-dimensional (3D) point cloud representations of the target food objects and approximate their volumes with our point cloud-to-volume algorithm. We evaluate our system on a test set, consisting of images portraying various foods and their respective measured volumes, as well as combinations of foods placed in a single image.

Keywords: Food volume estimation · Monocular depth estimation · Food image processing · Deep learning

1 Introduction

People's nutritional concerns are on a rising trend over the last few years, as they become more and more involved with the health benefits, safety and environmental sustainability of the foods they consume [18]. Consequently the need for automated dietary assistants, which help users monitor their daily nutritional intake, has emerged, as they have the potential to facilitate the assessment and maintenance of a pursued diet. In order to boost adherence, a desired feature of such assistants, apart from accuracy, is requiring minimal user engagement, as users are prone to making errors when asked to estimate their own food intake [23] and giving up on using applications that require heavy interaction [7].

© Springer Nature Switzerland AG 2020
M. Antona and C. Stephanidis (Eds.): HCII 2020, LNCS 12189, pp. 532–543, 2020.
https://doi.org/10.1007/978-3-030-49108-6_38

To satisfy the minimal user-interaction requirement, a suggested approach is to ask users to take pictures of their meals [6], from which the nutritional information can be extracted in an automated fashion. In order to automate this process, both the different food types and their volumes must be first determined and used in conjunction with food density and nutrition databases [1,24], to approximate the total nutritional value of the meal. Whilst the food type detection has been adequately solved using widely-applied classification networks, trained on food-image datasets [3,15,21], estimating the volume remains a complex issue with varied proposed solutions.

The majority of existing works, employ well-established computer vision methodologies to estimate the target food volume. However, these approaches, for the most part, cannot be generalized and applied in complex environments, which is necessary since the assistant is expected to operate, most of the time, in non-ideal conditions. They also usually involve extra effort on the users' side, in the form of requiring them to take images from multiple views or to calibrate the camera, which contradicts the ease-of-use target originally set. On the contrary, learning-based methods may be able to surpass both the generalization and wearisome user input requirement problems, but rely heavily on the quantity and quality of the training data, which in most cases are scarce.

We aim to contribute towards a user-friendly, image-based dietary assistant, by introducing a system for estimating the volumes of the foods present in an image, using deep convolutional neural networks (CNNs). First, we train a depth prediction network, using easily obtained monocular video sequences related to food and an instance segmentation network on a labeled food-image dataset. During inference, the user provides a single image of his meal and combined with the predicted depth map, a 3D point cloud projection is created. The segmentation network identifies the different foods in the given image and by applying our point cloud-to-volume algorithm on each, we approximate the individual food volumes.

Our method incorporates the advantages of learning-based approaches, while avoiding the pitfalls related to the availability of high-quality training data. We demonstrate this property by showing how the fine-tuning of the depth prediction network, on smartphone-captured food videos, can significantly improve the volume estimations with relatively minimal effort. We finally present the performance of our system on a collected test set, where we compare the volumes estimated from images taken to ground truth volume measurements.

2   Related Work

2.1   Image-Based Food Volume Estimation

Color image-based food volume estimation approaches can be separated into two groups, depending on the underlying methodology used. The first group utilizes computer vision techniques, which require calibrating the camera and taking one or more images of the target food object, while in the second and more recent group, works are based on training deep convolutional networks to process the images and estimate the volume either directly or indirectly. It should be noted, that all methods to be discussed in this section also entail locating the food in the input images. However, we will not go into detail regarding the segmentation methods used, since authors either employ well-established algorithms or omit it altogether.

Among the first group, [2,19] use common everyday items with known sizes, such as a coin or the user's thumb, to define a pixel-to-metric distance scaling factor and combine the top and side view of the food object to approximate the volume. In [26], a food shape dictionary was composed and during inference, the user is asked to take an image, having placed a calibration checkerboard in the scene, in order to fit one of the pre-defined shapes, of known volumes, to the food object.

Other methods in this group attempt to reconstruct a 3D model of the food object from multiple images and use it to approximate the volume. Hassanne-jad et al. [16] ask the user to take a short video of his meal, from which certain key frames are automatically extracted and combined to create a 3D point cloud representation. Similarly, in [26], authors also propose reconstructing the food object from multiple views, taken individually by the user, while in [9] they present a method to produce a point cloud, but this time only requiring two separate images. However, for all the reconstruction methodologies mentioned, a calibration checkerboard must be present in the scene at all times, to allow for proper scaling and the detection of the camera pose transformations between views.

This restriction also highlights the main issue with approaches based on computer vision techniques; the demand for multiple actions by the user. Having to constantly carry and place a certain item for calibration or taking multiple images from various views, can place a significant burden on users and potentially lead to drop-outs from using diet-monitoring applications.

Aiming to overcome these limitations, Myers et al. [22] proposed training a deep convolutional network to predict the depth of a user-provided image and, given the camera intrinsic parameters, project each pixel to a point in 3D space. From this projection, similarly to methods discussed above, a rough reconstruction of the food object is created and used to estimate the food volume. In [11], the authors move a step further and propose training a multi-task CNN to simultaneously predict food calories, category, ingredients and cooking instructions, ignoring the need for estimating the volume completely. However, the downside of both methodologies is that the result ultimately depends on having enough quality ground truth data, which in each case are hard to collect. Food depth images need to be captured with a high-fidelity depth sensor, whereas gathering a dataset that annotates food images with calories, type, ingredients and cooking instructions is a time-consuming process.

2.2 Self-Supervised Depth Estimation

Recent research on monocular depth estimation has bypassed the obstacle of ground truth depth data scarcity, by training the network in a self-supervised manner [25]. This translates to utilizing the depth predictions in reconstructing other available views of the input scene and computing the training loss on these images instead of the depth. For example, [13,25] process an image from a stereoscopic pair to predict a disparity map and reconstruct the other view,

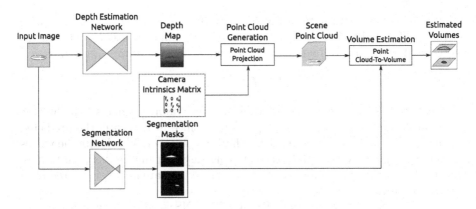

Fig. 1. Proposed system architecture.

on which the loss is computed. More recently, [14, 27] reconstruct for each frame in a video, the previous and next frames, using the predicted depth map and camera pose transformations, eliminating the need for calibrated images at input. Formulating the loss for self-supervised training enables the gathering of training data with regular camera sensors and therefore, reduces the overall cost and complexity of training the depth prediction network.

3 Method

The proposed food volume estimation system can be separated into three distinct parts: (a) the depth estimation network (b) the segmentation network and (c) the point cloud-to-volume algorithm. An overall illustration of the system is shown in Fig. 1.

3.1 Depth Estimation Network

The depth network architecture used in the proposed system is the one presented in the work of Godard et al. [14], in which they demonstrate training a depth estimation network using only monocular video sequences. In each training step, three consecutive frames I_{t-1}, I_t, I_{t+1} of the video are used. The depth prediction network infers a depth map D_t of the input frame I_t, while a pose estimation network generates the camera pose transformations $T_{t \to t-1}$, $T_{t \to t+1}$ between the current and its adjacent frames. The predicted depth map, pose transformations and known camera intrinsic matrix K are used to synthesize the center frame by sampling from the previous and next as

$$
\begin{aligned}
I_{t-1 \to t} &= I_{t-1} \langle proj(D_t, T_{t \to t-1}, K) \rangle \\
I_{t+1 \to t} &= I_{t+1} \langle proj(D_t, T_{t \to t+1}, K) \rangle,
\end{aligned}
\tag{1}
$$

where *proj* is the coordinate projection described in [27] and $\langle \ \rangle$ the sampling operator. The final training loss is the sum of a photometric loss L_p between the synthesized and original images and a depth smoothness error L_s, given as

$$L = L_p + \lambda L_s. \tag{2}$$

This approach fails to generate a meaningful training signal when the true pose transformations $T^{gt}_{t \to t-1}$, $T^{gt}_{t \to t+1}$ are zero, since in this case, the predicted depth values do not affect the image synthesis whatsoever. This limits the videos we can train the network with to those having sufficient motion between frames, which is not as common among food videos, since they are mostly captured from stationary cameras.

We train the network on the EPIC-KITCHENS dataset [8], which includes more than fifty hours of egocentric food-handling videos. The selected cooking and meal preparation sequences were taken from six different kitchens, with the consideration of incorporating variations in the environment, actions and lighting conditions. This dataset, despite being sub-optimal for the task, with it focusing around the miscellaneous actions of preparing food in a kitchen, was chosen in lieu of other food-specific video datasets, due to being the only one to satisfy the camera motion limiation. For instance, in the Pittsburgh fast-food image dataset [4], the authors employ a stationary camera and a rotating platter to capture their videos, which would not be suitable for training with this architecture.

To further improve the depth predictions, we fine-tune the network weights on a dataset of food-specific videos we collected, which we will refer to as *food videos*. In total, 38 videos were captured on daily occasions, using commercial smartphone cameras and portray a number of different food types and environments. Training with this dataset further backs the argument on the ease of training depth estimation networks in a self-supervised manner, considering that gathering an equivalent dataset of food-image depth data would require substantially more resources and time.

3.2 Food Segmentation Network

In order to be able to locate the food objects present in a given image, we train an instance segmentation network on a dataset of labeled food images. The model utilized for this purpose is the Mask R-CNN [17], which extends the object detection Fast Region-based CNN [12] architecture, by additionally predicting individual segmentation masks for each object found. With this approach, we are able to discern between the different foods present in the input, including multiple instances of the same food type and produce a segmentation mask for each, to estimate their volume separately.

We initialize the network using weights pre-trained on the COCO dataset [20] and fine-tune for food object segmentation on the UNIMIB2016 dataset [5]. The later, is composed of 1,027 meal tray images, labeled with bounding boxes, food types and segmentation masks for the food objects depicted. Since we are not interested in predicting the specific food types, we ignore the food-type labels.

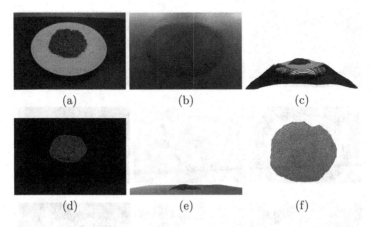

Fig. 2. System stages of estimating the volume of a food object. (a) Input image. (b) Depth prediction. (c) Point cloud representation of the input. (d) Generated segmentation mask. (e) Base plane estimation. (f) Triangulation.

3.3 Volume Estimation

Having inferred the depth map D of the input image and given the camera intrinsic matrix K, we project each pixel (x, y) to a corresponding point in 3D space, using its homogeneous coordinates and the inverse projection model

$$P_{xy} = K^{-1} \begin{bmatrix} x & y & 1 \end{bmatrix}^T D_{xy}, \tag{3}$$

to form a point cloud representation P. In turn, the segmentation masks generated by the instance segmentation network, are applied onto the image to distinguish between the different foods depicted and split P into subsets of food object points.

For each of these sets of points, we first remove any outliers using a statistical outlier removal (SOR) filter and then determine the base plane on which the food is placed upon by applying principal component analysis. The eigenvector of the least important component is set as the plane normal vector, while the plane is also adjusted to be at the bottom of the object. The final step for approximating the volume contained between the base and food is projecting the food points onto the plane and partitioning the covered area into triangles by computing an α-complex from the Delaunay triangulation [10]. The total volume is made up of the triangular prisms, defined by each triangle and the average distance of its vertices from their corresponding food points. The stages of estimating the volume of a food object in an image, as described above, are portrayed in Fig. 2.

This approach, only works in cases where the food is placed on top of a planar plate. We cannot estimate the volume of foods that are inside containers, such as a bowl, in which case the volume is not defined by the food object but instead by the container itself.

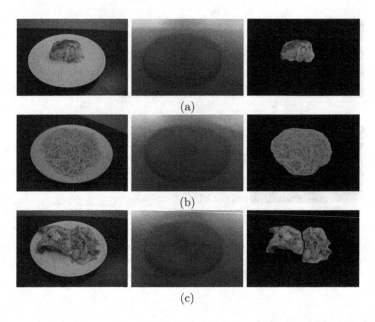

Fig. 3. Samples from the test set used for evaluation, along with the depth and segmentation mask predictions. (a) Sample from the *Souffle* food type. (b) Sample from the *Spaghetti* food type. (c) Sample from the *Potatoes2/Chicken2* food type.

4   Evaluation

4.1   Implementation Details

In our experiments, we trained the depth estimation network on an input resolution of 128×224 and a batch size of eight-frame triplets per step. We set the depth outputs to be in the range of 0.01 to 10 units and the smoothness term λ to 10^{-2}. We performed the data augmentations suggested by [14] on brightness, contrast, saturation, hue and left-right image flipping.

Training on the EPIC-Kitchens dataset, we used the sequences P01_10, P05_08, P10_04, P15_12, P20_01, P30_10, selecting frames from the original recordings with a stride of 10, to produce a total 42,066 frames to train on. We trained the network for 20 epochs with a learning rate of 10^{-4}, halved at epoch 15.

For our own *food videos* dataset, we extracted four frames per second for all 38 sequences, generating 1,712 frames to fine-tune the depth estimation network on. As before, we trained for 20 epochs, with the same initial learning rate and scheduling.

The depth predictions of the network are not on a metric scale, since there is no ground truth depth value fed to it during training with monocular videos. To overcome this, we apply the median ground truth rescaling proposed by [27], where the predicted depth map D is multiplied by a scalar

$$s = \frac{median(D^{gt})}{median(D)}. \tag{4}$$

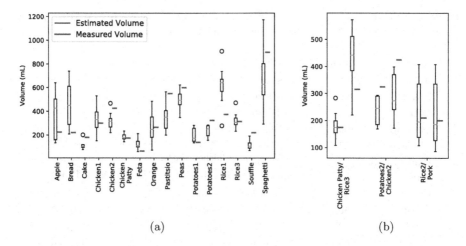

(a)   (b)

Fig. 4. Measured volume and distribution of system estimations on (a) the 16 test foods (b) the combined meals.

The median ground truth depth value $median(D^{gt})$ used for our experiments, is set as the estimated distance between the camera sensor and the food object, which we defined for all test cases at 0.35 m.

To train the Mask R-CNN network, we set the input batch size to 2, learning rate to 10^{-3} and performed data augmentations in brightness, contrast, saturation and hue, uniformly, in the ranges of ± 40, ± 0.2, ± 40, ± 20, respectively, as well as left-right and up-down flipping, with a probability 0.5. We initialized the network with pre-trained weights on the COCO dataset and trained on a split of 925 training and 102 validation inputs, with all non-packaged food classes aggregated into a single *food* class. The network was trained for eight epochs in total, freezing all but the top layers for the first three, allowing for steady adaptation of weights.

During volume inference, the camera intrinsic matrix is generated from the field-of-view angle of the camera sensor used, which we set at an estimated average value of $70°$. The Z-Score for the SOR filter was computed from the maximum distance of each point to its neighbors and the α value for constructing the α-complex was set at 0.01.

4.2 Results and Discussion

To evaluate our system, we measured the volumes of 16 foods, using the water displacement method and captured eight images of each, from varying angles. The distributions of our system volume estimations, grouped by food type, are demonstrated, alongside the measured volumes, in Fig. 4 (a). In addition to that, we also present the mean absolute percentage errors (MAPE) of our estimations, per food, in Table 1 (a). Due to the low resolution of our measurement setup, we add a ± 20 mL measurement error to the ground truth volumes we present.

Table 1. Volume measurements and mean absolute percentage error (MAPE) of estimations for (a) the 16 test foods (b) the combined meals.

Food	Volume (mL)	MAPE
Apple	225	89.094
Bread	220	108.30
Cake	180	39.030
Chicken1	300	29.285
Chicken2	425	27.677
Chicken Patty	175	13.737
Feta	65	99.798
Orange	265	40.362
Pastitsio	550	37.283
Peas	600	18.512
Potatoes1	140	42.661
Potatoes2	325	26.925
Rice1	375	71.288
Rice3	315	15.852
Souffle	220	47.019
Spaghetti	900	35.395

(a)

Food	Volume (mL)	MAPE
Chicken Patty	175	21.235
Rice3	315	45.380
Potatoes2	325	26.790
Chicken2	425	30.766
Rice2	210	45.119
Pork	200	52.160

(b)

In cases where the segmentation network partitioned a single food object into portions that the object is made up of, we compensated by simply adding up the individual predicted volumes.

We also tested the ability of our system to estimate multiple volumes simultaneously, by arranging two different foods in a single plate and predicting their individual volumes from a single image of the combined meal. For this scenario, we evaluate our system on three meals of eight images each, with results presented in the same format in Fig. 4 (b) and Table 1 (b). Concerning the *Rice2* and *Pork* meal, we mixed the two foods together beforehand, to intentionally stress the segmentation network, and recorded any results where the foods were not separated, as having estimated the same volume for both. Therefore, their estimation distributions are similar. We present samples from our test set, along with the depth and segmentation mask predictions in Fig. 3.

In Fig. 5, we showcase the benefits gained when fine-tuning the depth prediction network on our own collected *food videos*. If we were to use the original prediction, we would struggle to create an adequate point cloud representation of the scene and subsequently estimate the volume, since it has reduced precision in the areas of peak interest, i.e., on and around the food object, and portrays several depth inaccuracies.

Although the depth network manages to infer accurate depth unit maps, the volume estimation algorithm also depends on applying the correct median distance rescaling, since it operates on metric depth values. We acknowledge this

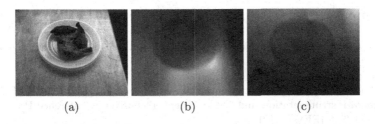

Fig. 5. Comparison of predictions, before and after fine-tuning the depth network on the *food videos* dataset. (a) Input image. (b) Predicted depth before fine-tuning. (c) Predicted depth after fine-tuning.

weakness of our system and demonstrate it in the volume predictions for *Rice1*, where all but one images used were taken from a much closer distance than the one set for scaling. This resulted in noticeably larger volume estimations and exhibits the need to communicate effectively the camera to food object distance to the user, or bypass it completely by finding a way to extract the median depth automatically.

Our point cloud-to-volume algorithm is mostly hindered by its limitation to generalize, as we previously mentioned for most computer vision-based methodologies. The algorithm was designed for and operates best, when the target food object is stacked on top of a plate and most of it is visible from the angle the image is taken from. If this is not the case, the predicted base plane can be incorrectly placed and results in computing a volume that does not properly represent the depicted object. As an example, when estimating the volumes of *Apple* and *Orange*, the images that portray only a side of the objects will lead the algorithm to place the base plane perpendicular to the plate and therefore, only compute a slice of the total volume.

5   Conclusion

In this work, we presented our approach for image-based food volume estimation, aiming to contribute towards the development of a burden-free and accurate dietary assistant application. We capitalize on the latest advancements in monocular depth estimation, to show that using both the publicly available and our easily collected data, we are able to train a depth prediction network and employ it in estimating food volumes, requiring only a single image at inference. Nevertheless, there are still a plethora of issues to resolve before claiming success, but we firmly believe that following in the direction of learning-based methods paves the way for fruitful results.

Acknowledgment. This project has received funding from the European Union's Horizon 2020 research and innovation programme under grant agreement No 817732.

References

1. U.S. Department of Agriculture, A.R.S.: FoodData central (2019). https://fdc.nal. usda.gov/
2. Almaghrabi, R., Villalobos, G., Pouladzadeh, P., Shirmohammadi, S.: A novel method for measuring nutrition intake based on food image. In: 2012 IEEE International Instrumentation and Measurement Technology Conference Proceedings, pp. 366–370. IEEE (2012)
3. Bossard, L., Guillaumin, M., Van Gool, L.: Food-101 – mining discriminative components with random forests. In: Fleet, D., Pajdla, T., Schiele, B., Tuytelaars, T. (eds.) ECCV 2014. LNCS, vol. 8694, pp. 446–461. Springer, Cham (2014). https:// doi.org/10.1007/978-3-319-10599-4_29
4. Chen, M., Dhingra, K., Wu, W., Yang, L., Sukthankar, R., Yang, J.: PFID: pittsburgh fast-food image dataset. In: 2009 16th IEEE International Conference on Image Processing (ICIP), pp. 289–292. IEEE (2009)
5. Ciocca, G., Napoletano, P., Schettini, R.: Food recognition: a new dataset, experiments, and results. IEEE J. Biomed. Health Inform. **21**(3), 588–598 (2016)
6. Cordeiro, F., Bales, E., Cherry, E., Fogarty, J.: Rethinking the mobile food journal: exploring opportunities for lightweight photo-based capture. In: Proceedings of the 33rd Annual ACM Conference on Human Factors in Computing Systems, pp. 3207–3216 (2015)
7. Cordeiro, F., et al.: Barriers and negative nudges: Exploring challenges in food journaling. In: Proceedings of the 33rd Annual ACM Conference on Human Factors in Computing Systems, pp. 1159–1162 (2015)
8. Damen, D., et al.: Scaling egocentric vision: the epic-kitchens dataset. In: Ferrari, V., Hebert, M., Sminchisescu, C., Weiss, Y. (eds.) ECCV 2018. LNCS, vol. 11208, pp. 753–771. Springer, Cham (2018). https://doi.org/10.1007/978-3-030-01225-0_44
9. Dehais, J., Anthimopoulos, M., Shevchik, S., Mougiakakou, S.: Two-view 3D reconstruction for food volume estimation. IEEE Trans. Multimedia **19**(5), 1090–1099 (2016)
10. Edelsbrunner, H., Harer, J.: Computational Topology: An Introduction. American Mathematical Society, Providence (2010)
11. Ege, T., Yanai, K.: Image-based food calorie estimation using recipe information. IEICE Tran. Inf. Syst. **101**(5), 1333–1341 (2018)
12. Girshick, R.: Fast R-CNN. In: Proceedings of the IEEE International Conference on Computer Vision, pp. 1440–1448 (2015)
13. Godard, C., Mac Aodha, O., Brostow, G.J.: Unsupervised monocular depth estimation with left-right consistency. In: Proceedings of the IEEE Conference on Computer Vision and Pattern Recognition, pp. 270–279 (2017)
14. Godard, C., Mac Aodha, O., Firman, M., Brostow, G.J.: Digging into self-supervised monocular depth estimation. In: Proceedings of the IEEE International Conference on Computer Vision, pp. 3828–3838 (2019)
15. Hassannejad, H., Matrella, G., Ciampolini, P., De Munari, I., Mordonini, M., Cagnoni, S.: Food image recognition using very deep convolutional networks. In: Proceedings of the 2nd International Workshop on Multimedia Assisted Dietary Management, pp. 41–49 (2016)
16. Hassannejad, H., Matrella, G., Ciampolini, P., Munari, I.D., Mordonini, M., Cagnoni, S.: A new approach to image-based estimation of food volume. Algorithms **10**(2), 66 (2017)

17. He, K., Gkioxari, G., Dollár, P., Girshick, R.: Mask R-CNN. In: Proceedings of the IEEE International Conference on Computer Vision, pp. 2961–2969 (2017)
18. International Food Information Council (IFIC) Foundation: 2019 Food and Health Survey (2019). https://foodinsight.org/wp-content/uploads/2019/05/IFIC-Foun dation-2019-Food-and-Health-Report-FINAL.pdf
19. Liang, Y., Li, J.: Deep learning-based food calorie estimation method in dietary assessment. arXiv preprint arXiv:1706.04062 (2017)
20. Lin, T.-Y., et al.: Microsoft COCO: common objects in context. In: Fleet, D., Pajdla, T., Schiele, B., Tuytelaars, T. (eds.) ECCV 2014. LNCS, vol. 8693, pp. 740–755. Springer, Cham (2014). https://doi.org/10.1007/978-3-319-10602-1_48
21. Martinel, N., Foresti, G.L., Micheloni, C.: Wide-slice residual networks for food recognition. In: 2018 IEEE Winter Conference on Applications of Computer Vision (WACV), pp. 567–576. IEEE (2018)
22. Myers, A., et al.: Im2calories: towards an automated mobile vision food diary. In: Proceedings of the IEEE International Conference on Computer Vision, pp. 1233–1241 (2015)
23. Schoeller, D.A., Bandini, L.G., Dietz, W.H.: Inaccuracies in self-reported intake identified by comparison with the doubly labelled water method. Can. J. Physiol. Pharmacol. **68**(7), 941–949 (1990)
24. U. Ruth Charrondiere, D.H., Stadlmayr, B.: FAO/INFOODS databases, density database version 2.0 (2012) http://www.fao.org/3/ap815e/ap815e.pdf
25. Xie, J., Girshick, R., Farhadi, A.: Deep3D: fully automatic 2D-to-3D video conversion with deep convolutional neural networks. In: Leibe, B., Matas, J., Sebe, N., Welling, M. (eds.) ECCV 2016. LNCS, vol. 9908, pp. 842–857. Springer, Cham (2016). https://doi.org/10.1007/978-3-319-46493-0_51
26. Xu, C., He, Y., Khannan, N., Parra, A., Boushey, C., Delp, E.: Image-based food volume estimation. In: Proceedings of the 5th International Workshop on Multimedia for Cooking & Eating Activities, pp. 75–80 (2013)
27. Zhou, T., Brown, M., Snavely, N., Lowe, D.G.: Unsupervised learning of depth and ego-motion from video. In: Proceedings of the IEEE Conference on Computer Vision and Pattern Recognition, pp. 1851–1858 (2017)

On the Allocation of Resources in Sensor Clouds Under the Se-aaS Paradigm

Joel Guerreiro$^{(\boxtimes)}$ (ID), Luis Rodrigues$^{(\boxtimes)}$ (ID), and Noelia Correia$^{(\boxtimes)}$ (ID)

CEOT & FCT, University of the Algarve, 8005-139 Faro, Portugal
{jdguerreiro,lrodrig,ncorreia}@ualg.pt

Abstract. As the number of smart Things grows in the Internet of Things, so does the focus on Cloud-based Sensing as a Service for sensors and data sharing. Under this paradigm, a resource allocation model for the assignment of both sensors and Cloud resources to consumers/applications is proposed. This semantics-based resource allocation model is adequate for many emerging IoT Se-aaS business models, like the ones supporting multi-sensing applications and/or integration of data from multiple domains. A heuristic algorithm is also proposed having this model as a basis. Results show that the approach is able to incorporate strategies that lead to a more efficient use of devices and Cloud resources.

Keywords: Internet of Things · Cloud · Sensing as a Service

1 Introduction

The *Internet of Things* (IoT) is becoming a reality and trillions of smart Things are expected to be connected to the Internet in a near future. As more and more Things become available, large amounts of data with processing needs emerge meaning that new challenges arise in terms of storage and processing. The *Sensing as a Service* (Se-aaS) model, relying on Cloud infrastructures for storage and processing, emerges from this reality [1,2].

Many Cloud-based "as a service" models have emerged over the last years. The *Everything as a Service* (XaaS) is the term used for this set of service models that aim to concentrate software and hardware resources, offering them as services to a large number of users and, therefore, leveraging utility and consumption of computing resources [3]. The most relevant are: *i) Infrastructure as a Service* (IaaS), providing computing resources (e.g., virtual machines); *ii) Platform as a Service* (PaaS), providing computing platforms that may include operating system, database, Web server, and other; *iii) Software as a Service* (SaaS), where the Cloud takes over the infrastructure and platform while scaling automatically. All these models promote the "pay only for what you use". The Se-aaS model emerged more recently and the idea is for sensing devices and their data to be shared at the Cloud. That is, there is a multi-supplier

© Springer Nature Switzerland AG 2020
M. Antona and C. Stephanidis (Eds.): HCII 2020, LNCS 12189, pp. 544–556, 2020.
https://doi.org/10.1007/978-3-030-49108-6_39

deployment of sensors and multi-client access to sensor resources. Besides service selection frameworks, Se-aaS systems may provide storage, visualization and management facilities [4]. Naturally, Cloud service providers must compensate the device owners for their contribution, or find some incentive mechanism for them to participate [5,6]. Secure user-centric service provisioning in also a critical issue to be considered [7].

In this article, sensor Clouds under the Se-aaS paradigm are considered and a resource allocation model is developed. This semantics-based resource allocation model is adequate for many emerging IoT Se-aaS business models, like the ones supporting multi-sensing applications and/or integrating data from multiple domains, allowing for the orchestration of both sensor and Cloud resources to face client requests. A heuristic algorithm is proposed having this model as a basis. As far as known, no similar models have been proposed in the literature.

The remainder of this article is organized as follows. In Sect. 2 the Se-aaS architecture is discussed, together with design/planning of such architectures. Related work is also presented. Section 4 formalizes the resource allocation model, and a heuristic algorithm is developed having this model as a basis. Performance results are analysed in Sect. 5, while Sect. 6 concludes the article.

2   Sensing-as-a-Service

Similarly to the just mentioned Cloud-based "as a service" models, the resources in Se-aaS systems should be dynamically provisioned and de-provisioned on demand. Figure 1 shows the service architecture of a Se-aaS system where sensors and data are accessed by multiple users/applications in real time, through service subscription. The main challenges when planning and designing such systems are the following:

- Underlying complexity should be hidden, so that services and applications can be launched without much overhead;
- Scalability while avoiding infrastructure upgrade, and ensuring a low cost-of-service per consumer;
- Dynamic service provisioning for pools of resources to be efficiently used by consumers.

Se-aaS have been applied to *Wireless Sensor Networks* (WSNs) and IoT [19,22]. The general idea when using Se-aaS for the virtualization of WSNs is that the Cloud should abstract different physical device platforms in order to give the impression of an homogeneous network, enhancing user experience when configuring devices. For IoT there is virtualization of sensing services provided by the devices. In the most simple case, a virtual sensor ends up being responsible for passing user's specifications to device(s) and for processing the sensed data before delivering it to users. IoT Se-aaS systems are the focus of this article.

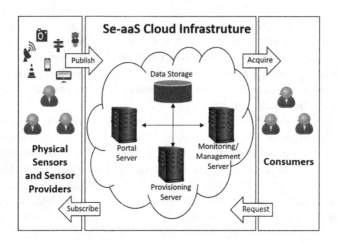

Fig. 1. Se-aaS architecture.

IoT Se-aaS systems end up having multiple functionalities in its design, which may include [1]:

- Virtualization of sensors;
- Dynamic provisioning;
- Multi-tenancy.

Virtualization is used to enable the management and customization of devices by clients/applications/consumers, eventually allowing for the mapping of a single device to multiple consumers. Dynamic provisioning allows consumers to leverage the vast pool of resources on demand. A virtual workspace (e.g., virtual machine) is usually created for the provisioning of a virtual sensor group (one or more virtual sensors), which is under the control of one or more consumers. Multi-tenancy allows the sharing of sensors and data, while providing dedicated instances for each sensor provider. Issues like scaling according to policies, load balancing and security, need to be considered. Figure 2 illustrates the virtualization layers of Se-aaS systems.

3   Related Work

In [6,8], Cloud-based sensing services using mobile phones (crowd sensing) are discussed. The general idea is to utilize the sensors of mobile devices to fulfill some need. In the context of smart cities, Se-aaS is discussed in [2] and [9]. The former addresses technological, economical and social perspectives, while the latter proposes the abstraction of physical Things through semantics, so that these can be integrated by neglecting their underlying architecture. In [10] and [11], the semantic selection of sensors is also addressed. Multimedia Se-aaS have been explored in [12–15]. These mainly focus on real-type communication requirements, and [14] explores Cloud edges and fogs.

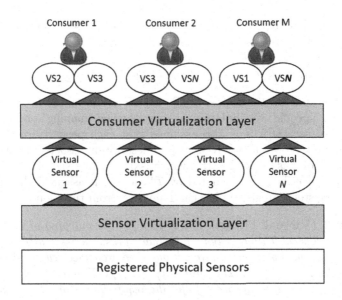

Fig. 2. Virtualization layers in Se-aaS.

The integration of WSNs with the Cloud is addressed in [4,16,17], where data storage and/or device assignment to tasks is addressed for a uniform and widespread use of WSNs. In [4], a WSN virtualization model is discussed. Service-centric models in [18–20] focus on the services provided by a WSN acting as a service provider.

Models more focused on IoT-related functionalities appeared more recently in [21,22]. Physical resources are abstracted, virtualized, and presented as a service to the end users. This way, the access and interaction with physical Things becomes uniform and in compliance with IoT/WoT goals. Specific platforms providing efficient sharing mechanisms for data (among multiple applications) have been proposed in [1,23].

In this article, a semantic-based resource allocation model is developed, suitable for many emerging IoT Se-aaS business models, which supports multi-sensing applications and data integration from multiple domains, managing sensor and Cloud resources, responding to client requests. As far as known, no similar models have been proposed in the literature. A heuristic algorithm is also proposed having this model as a basis.

4   Resource Allocation Model

4.1   Definitions and Assumptions

Definition 1 (Physical Thing). *A sensor detecting events/changes, or an actuator receiving commands for the control of a mechanism. The model of a physical Thing i includes all properties necessary to describe it, denoted by*

$\mathcal{P}_i$, and all its functionalities, denoted by $\mathcal{F}_i$. That is, $\mathcal{P}_i = \{p : p \in \mathcal{P}\}$ and $\mathcal{F}_i = \{f : f \in \mathcal{F}\}$, where $\mathcal{P}$ is the overall set of properties (e.g., sensing range, communication facility, location), and $\mathcal{F}$ the overall set of functionalities (e.g., image sensor), from all devices registered at the Cloud.

Properties and functionalities, at $\mathcal{P}$ and $\mathcal{F}$, are assumed to be semantic-based. Thus, specific vocabularies are used when naming properties and functionalities (see [24]). It is also assumed that each property $p_i \in \mathcal{P}_i$ has a "subject/predicate/object" (or RDF triple) description associated with it (e.g., cameraResolution hasValue 12.1MP), which is denoted by $spo(p_i)$. The set of all registered physical Things is denoted by $\mathcal{T}^P$, and it is assumed that providers voluntarily register/unregister physical Things to/from the Cloud.

Definition 2 (Virtual Thing). *Entity used for the mapping of multiple consumers onto physical Things, having a virtual workspace associated to it. A virtual Thing j can be materialized through one or more concerted physical Things, denoted by $\mathcal{M}_j$, $\mathcal{M}_j \subset \mathcal{T}^P$. Therefore[1], $f_j \triangleq \cup_{i \in \mathcal{M}_j} \mathcal{F}_i$ and $\mathcal{P}_j = \cup_{i \in \mathcal{M}_j} \mathcal{P}_i$. A virtual Thing materialization must fulfill the requirements of all its consumers.*

In other words, a virtual Thing has in background one or more physical Things working together to provide the requested functionality, producing data that reaches the Cloud using standard communication. The set of virtual Things created by the Cloud is denoted by $\mathcal{T}^V$.

Clients/applications specify Thing requests (to the Cloud) using Web templates. Each request r has a functionality requirement and a set of minimum/maximum property requirements, denoted by $\bar{f}_r$ and $\bar{\mathcal{P}}_r$, respectively. The functionality and minimum/maximum property requirements are also semantic-based, each $p_r \in \bar{\mathcal{P}}_r$ having a "subject/predicate/object" description of the condition/requirement that is being defined (e.g., cameraResolution greaterThan 12.1MP; frequency Sampling equal To 10 s), denoted by $spo(p_r)$. The overall population of requests (from all clients/applications) is denoted by $\mathcal{R}$.

Virtual Things, to be created at the Cloud, are the ones to be materialized into physical Things. Then, each request $r \in \mathcal{R}$ must be binded to a single virtual Thing, while a virtual Thing can be binded to multiple requests (with same functionality and compatible property requirements). With such approach, data generated by a virtual Thing can be consumed by multiple application requests, reducing data collection/storage and increasing the usefulness of data. The right set of virtual Things to be created at the Cloud, their bindings to requests and their materialization into physical Things should be determined while using resources efficiently, which is discussed next.

---

[1] The symbol $\triangleq$ means equal by definition, in our case logically/semantically equivalent.

The goal of Cloud virtualization is for users to remain unaware of physical devices involved in the process. This way, physical Things can be dynamically allocated to virtual Things used by applications. On the other hand, the client ends up having no deployment and maintenance costs, while having an on-demand fault tolerant service because virtual Things can always use other available physical Things. Clients should not be aware of such change due to virtualization.

4.2 Problem Formalization

Let us assume a particular partition of $\mathcal{R}$ (population of requests), denoted by $\eta^i = \{\mathcal{R}_1^i, \mathcal{R}_2^i, ...\}$, where all elements in a $\mathcal{R}_j^i$ have the same functionality requirement. A virtual Thing $k \in \mathcal{T}^V$ binded to $\mathcal{R}_j^i$ must provide the requested functionality, which is the same for all requests in $\mathcal{R}_j^i$. The following allocation function $f : \eta^i \rightarrow \mathcal{T}^V$ can be defined:

$$f(\mathcal{R}_j^i) = \{\exists! k \in \mathcal{T}^V : \bar{f}_k = f_r, \forall r \in \mathcal{R}_j^i\}. \tag{1}$$

One or more physical Things materialize one virtual Thing. Assuming $\tau^i = \{T_1^{P,i}, T_2^{P,i}, ...\}$ to be a specific partition of $\mathcal{T}^P$, each $T_j^{P,i}$ making sense from a functional point of view, the function $g : \tau^i \rightarrow \mathcal{T}^V$ is defined for virtual Thing materialization:

$$g(T_j^{P,i}) = \{\exists! k \in \mathcal{T}^V : f_k \triangleq \cup_{l \in T_j^{P,i}} \mathcal{F}_l\}. \tag{2}$$

This states that a virtual Thing $k \in \mathcal{T}^V$ is materialized by $T_j^{P,i}$, including one or more physical Things, if they are functionally similar.

Different partitions, and allocations done by f and g, have different impacts on the use of resources (Cloud and physical Things) and provide different accomplishment levels for property requirements (more or less tight). Therefore, the best partitions should be determined. Let us assume that η^U is the universe set including all feasible partitions of requests, $\mathcal{R}$. That is, $\eta^U = \{\eta^1, \eta^2, ..., \eta^{|\eta^U|}\}$ and $\eta^i = \{\mathcal{R}_1^i, \mathcal{R}_2^i, ..., \mathcal{R}_{|\mathcal{T}^V|}^i\}$, $\forall i \in \{1, ..., |\eta^U|\}$. Assume also τ^U to be the universe set including all feasible partitions of physical Things, $\mathcal{T}^P$. That is, $\tau^U = \{\tau^1, \tau^2, ..., \tau^{|\tau^U|}\}$ and $\tau^i = \{T_1^{P,i}, T_2^{P,i}, ..., T_{|\mathcal{T}^V|}^{P,i}\}$, $\forall i \in \{1, ..., |\tau^U|\}$. The impact of f and g allocations, regarding to the gap between requirements and properties of physical Things, can be described by the following cost function $h : \eta^U \times \tau^U \rightarrow \Re^+$:

$$h(\eta^i, \tau^j) = \sum_{\{\mathcal{R}_k^i \in \eta^i\}} \sum_{\{p \in \chi\}} min_{r \in \mathcal{R}_k^i} \{\Delta_{r,p}^{GAP}(f(\mathcal{R}_k^i), \tau^j)\} \tag{3}$$

where $\chi = \cup_{r \in \mathcal{R}_k^i} \bar{\mathcal{P}}_r$ includes all minimum/maximum property requirements from requests in $\mathcal{R}_k^i$. For each property $p \in \chi$, the min is used to capture the lowest gap between requirements and physical Things regarding property p

(e.g., if two requests in $\mathcal{R}_k^i$ request for 12.1MP and 24.2MP camera resolutions, respectively, and the materialization of $\mathcal{R}_k^i$'s virtual Thing is a physical Thing providing 48.4MP, then the 24.2 to 48.4MP gap is the request-supply gap to be considered; the other request is considered to be fulfilled). Note that, $f(\mathcal{R}_k^i)$ returns the virtual Thing assigned to $\mathcal{R}_k^i$. Since multiple physical Things can be associated with a virtual Thing materialization, the $\Delta_{r,p}^{GAP}$ at expression (3) must be defined by:

$$\Delta_{r,p}^{GAP}(l,\tau^j) = \begin{cases} max_{t \in \mathcal{T}_k^{P,j}:\exists p_t = p, p_t \in \mathcal{P}_t}\{\Delta^{GAP}(spo(p), spo(p_t))\}, \\ \text{if } \exists \mathcal{T}_k^{P,j} \in \tau^j : g(\mathcal{T}_k^{P,j}) = l \\ \\ \infty, \text{otherwise} \end{cases} \tag{4}$$

where Δ^{GAP} provides the gap between the property requirement and property value at one of the physical Things enrolled in materialization. Since there might be more than one physical Thing, from all physical Things enrolled in a specific materialization, including a certain property then max is used to capture the highest gap value, avoiding virtual Thing materialization from having physical Things with property values far above the requirements. The best resource allocation will be:

$$(\eta^i, \tau^j)^* = argmin_{\eta^i \in \eta^U, \tau^j \in \tau^U}\{h(\eta^i, \tau^j)\} \tag{5}$$

The previously mentioned gaps can be determined using SPARQL which is a language designed to query data across diverse data sources, whether the data is stored natively as RDF or viewed as RDF via middleware. A variety of SPARQL processors are available for running queries against both local and remote data [25].

4.3   Resource Allocation Algorithm

Based on the previous model, a resource allocation algorithm is proposed in Algorithm 1. This is based on the following assumptions:

- As physical Things are registered at the Cloud, possible materializations are computed using SPARQL. Therefore, there is a pool of materializations for a functionality f, denoted by $\mathcal{M}(f)$, each materialization involving one or more physical Things. A physical Thing may be at multiple pools.
- As consumer/application requests are inserted at the Cloud, an auxiliary graph $\mathcal{G}(\mathcal{R}, \mathcal{L})$ is updated. The $\mathcal{R}$ includes all requests, while $\mathcal{L}$ denotes a set of links. A link between r_i and $r_j \in \mathcal{R}$ exists if: i) requests have the same functionality requirement; ii) property requirements are compatible. SPARQL is used to determine compatibility.

The first step initializes cost vectors, one per resource request r, denoted by $\mathbf{c}_r$. Since different materializations may exist, resulting into different materializations costs, these vectors have size $|\mathcal{M}(f_r)|$. The set of other requests joining r in a specific materialization (partition), to which a specific cost is associated with, will be stored in $\mathbf{v}_r$. When searching for feasible solutions, clique subgraphs are extracted from $\mathcal{G}(\mathcal{R}, \mathcal{L})$ and their possibility of materialization is analyzed. Regarding the last step, where virtual Things are built based on materialization cost vectors, different selection criteria have been considered:

– Cheapest materialization cost (CMC) first;
– Cheapest materialization, of the request with less materialization choices (LMC), first;
– Cheapest materialization, of the request with highest cost variance (HCV), first.

The impact of these choices have been analysed and compared in the following section.

5   Performance Analysis

5.1   Scenario Setup

To carry out evaluation a pool of functionalities was created, each with its own pool of properties. Based on these, physical Things and requests were generated as follows:

– Physical Things have a randomly generated functionality with 50% of its properties (extracted from corresponding pool).
– The functionality required by each request is randomly selected from the pool of functionalities, together with 50% of its properties. Each (r_i, r_j) pair, $r_i, r_j \in \mathcal{R}$, sharing the same functionality requirement is assumed to be compatible with probability δ (see Sect. 4.3).
– The cost gap between a property requirement and a supplied device property is randomly selected from $\{\Delta_1, ..., \Delta_5\}$, where Δ_1 is the lowest cost and Δ_5 is the highest (moderate and extreme cost levels).

Table 1 shows the parameter values adopted for the performance evaluation of CMC, LMC and HCV strategies. The following section discusses results on the total resource allocation cost and on the total number of materializations (virtual Things).

Algorithm 1: Resource allocation heuristic.

1 /* *Initialization step* */;
2 **for** *each* $r \in \mathcal{R}$ **do**
3   Create cost vector $\mathbf{c}_r$ of size $|\mathcal{M}(f_r)|$;
4   Create aggregation vector $\mathbf{v}_r$ of size $|\mathcal{M}(f_r)|$;
5   **for** *each* $m \in \mathcal{M}(f_r)$ **do**
6   /* *Initialize cost of possible materialization* */;
7          $\mathbf{c}_r(m) = \infty$;
8   /* *Requests joining r in possible materialization* */;
9          $\mathbf{v}_r(m) = \emptyset$;
10   **end**
11 **end**
12 /* *Searching for feasible solutions* */;
13 **for** *each* $r_i \in \mathcal{R}$ **do**
14   /* *pick clique subgraphs including r_i* */;
15     $\bar{\mathcal{R}} = \{\mathcal{Z} \subseteq \mathcal{R} : r_i \in \mathcal{Z} \wedge (r_j, r_k) \in \mathcal{L}, \forall r_j, r_k \in \mathcal{Z}\}$;
16   /* *pick maximum clique for which there is at least one feasible materialization* */;
17     $\bar{\mathcal{R}}^{\mathrm{MAX}} = argmax_{\mathcal{Z} \in \bar{\mathcal{R}}:\exists feasible \; m \in \mathcal{M}(f_{n_i})}\{\omega(\mathcal{Z})\}$;
18   **for** *each* $r_j \in \bar{\mathcal{R}}^{MAX}$ **do**
19   /* *for each possible materialization of f_{r_i}* */;
20   **for** *each* $m \in \mathcal{M}(f_{r_i})$ **do**
21   /* *see best materialization cost for r_j* */;
22             $cost =$internal sum of Eq. (3), using $\mathcal{R}_k^i = \bar{\mathcal{R}}^{\mathrm{MAX}}$;
23   **if** $\mathbf{c}_{r_j}(m) > cost$ **then**
24                 $\mathbf{c}_{r_j}(m) = cost$;
25                 $\mathbf{v}_{r_j}(m) = \bar{\mathcal{R}}^{\mathrm{MAX}}$;
26   **end**
27   **end**
28   **end**
29 **end**
30 /* *choose best resource allocations* */;
31 Build virtual Things based on materialization cost vectors until all requests are fulfilled or no more devices exist;

Table 1. Parameter values.

Functionality pool size	10
Avg size of property pools	10
Total number of devices	80
Device's properties (from pool)	50%
Request's properties (from pool)	50%
δ	0.5
$\{\Delta_1, ..., \Delta_5\}$	$\{1, ..., 5\}$

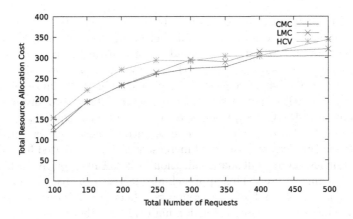

Fig. 3. Total resource allocation cost.

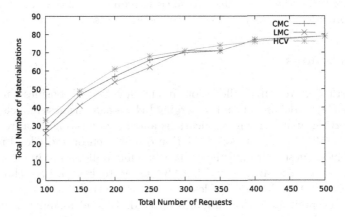

Fig. 4. Total number of materializations (virtual Things).

5.2   Analysis of Results

The plot in Fig. 3 shows the total resource allocation cost for CMC, LMC and HCV strategies. Results show that CMC and LMC strategies present the lowest overall resource allocation costs, meaning that the request-supply gap is lower than in HCV. That is, devices with properties closer to requests are being used for materialization, releasing devices with capabilities above what is required for future requests. The relatively high resource allocation costs presented by strategy HCV means that choosing first the requests with highest cost variance leads to an increase in the overall materialization cost. Relatively high costs may end up being selected.

The plot in Fig. 4 shows the total number of materializations for CMC, LMC and HCV strategies. This corresponds to the number of virtual Things or devices under utilization. From CMC and LMC strategies, the one requiring less devices is LMC. That is, the LMC is the most effective strategy since it requires less devices and assigns devices more adequate to the requirements of requests. Strategy HCV presents a relatively higher number of materializations, meaning that more virtual spaces (virtual Things) and devices are being used for a specific set of requests. The results also show that the number of materializations stabilizes when the number of requests is high, meaning that almost all physical Things are under utilization (assigned to client requests). More physical Things are registered into the Cloud to better respond the client requests.

In summary, choosing first the requests with highest cost variance, which means that materialization cost could increase more if not treated first, does not improve by itself the overall materialization cost because relatively high costs may end up being selected. This approach also leads to the use of more devices, avoiding their availability for future requests. Therefore, this criteria should not be considered alone when searching for high quality allocation solutions, and must integrate with other parameters. Among the strategies under analysis, the LMC seems to be the most effective since it requires less devices and assigns devices more adequate to the requirements of requests.

6   Conclusions

In this article a resource allocation model for Se-aaS business models is addressed. The model fits multiple emerging IoT Se-aaS business models, like the ones supporting multi-sensing applications and/or integrating data from multiple domains, allowing for the orchestration of both sensor and Cloud resources to face client requests. Results show that the model allows the implementation of multiple strategies, among which LMC seems to be the best choice. This strategy leads to the allocation of less devices, while the most adequate devices for consumer/application needs are also selected. This adequability is measured through a semantics-based resource allocation cost. Strategies considering multiple parameters, when searching for high quality allocation solutions, may be explored in the development of future Se-aaS resource allocation heuristics.

Acknowledgements. This work was supported by FCT (Foundation for Science and Technology) from Portugal within CEOT (Center for Electronic, Optoelectronic and Telecommunications) and UID/MULTI/00631/2019 project.

References

1. Kim, M., Asthana, M., Bhargava, S., Iyyer, K.K., Tangadpalliwar, R., Gao, J.: Developing an on-demand cloud-based sensing-as-a-service system for internet of things. J. Comput. Netw. Commun. **2016**, 1–17 (2016)
2. Perera, C., Zaslavsky, A., Christen, P., Georgakopoulos, D.: Sensing as a service model for smart cities supported by internet of things. Trans. Emerg. Telecommun. Technol. **25**, 81–93 (2014)
3. Duan, Y., et al.: Everything as a service (XaaS) on the cloud: origins, current and future trends. In: IEEE 8th International Conference on Cloud Computing (2015)

 4. Misra, S., Chatterjee, S., Obaidat, M.S.: On theoretical modeling of sensor cloud: a paradigm shift from wireless sensor network. IEEE Syst. J. **11**(2), 1084–1093 (2017)
 5. Pouryazdan, M., et al.: Quantifying user reputation scores, data trustworthiness, and user incentives in mobile crowd-sensing. IEEE Access **5**, 1382–1397 (2017)
 6. Sheng, X., Tang, J., Xiao, X., Xue, G.: Sensing as a service: challenges, solutions and future directions. IEEE Sens. J. **13**(10), 3733–3741 (2013)
 7. Madria, S.: Sensor cloud: sensing-as-service paradigm. In: IEEE International Conference on Mobile Data Management (2018)
 8. Al-Fagih, M.A.E., Al-Turjman, F.M., Alsalih, W.M., Hassanein, H.S.: Priced public sensing framework for heterogeneous IoT architectures. IEEE Trans. Emerg. Topics Comput. **1**(1), 133–147 (2013)
 9. Petrolo, R., Loscrì, V., Mitton, N.: Towards a smart city based on cloud of things, a survey on the smart city vision and paradigms. Trans. Emerg. Telecommun. Technol. **28**, e2931 (2015)
10. Misra, S., et al.: Optimal gateway selection in sensor-cloud framework for health monitoring. IET Wirel. Sens. Syst. **4**(2), 61–68 (2014)
11. Hsu, Y.-C., Lin, C.-H., Chen, W.-T.: Design of a sensing service architecture for internet of things with semantic sensor selection. In: International Conference UTC-ATC-ScalCom (2014)
12. Lai, C.-F., Chao, H.-C., Lai, Y.-X., Wan, J.: Cloud-assisted real-time transrating for HTTP live streaming. IEEE Wirel. Commun. **20**(3), 62–70 (2013)
13. Lai, C.-F., Wang, H., Chao, H.-C., Nan, G.: A network and device aware QoS approach for cloud-based mobile streaming. IEEE Trans. Multimedia **15**(4), 747–757 (2013)
14. Wang, W., Wang, Q., Sohraby, K.: Multimedia sensing as a service (MSaaS): exploring resource saving potentials of at cloud-edge IoTs and Fogs. IEEE Int. Things J. **4**(2), 487–495 (2017)
15. Xu, Y., Mao, S.: A survey of mobile cloud computing for rich media applications. IEEE Wirel. Commun. **20**(3), 46–53 (2013)
16. Kumar, L.D., et al.: Data filtering in wireless sensor networks using neural networks for storage in cloud. In: International Conference ICRTIT (2012)
17. Zhu, C., Li, X., Ji, H., Leung, V.C.M.: Towards integration of wireless sensor networks and cloud computing. In: International Conference CloudCom (2015)
18. Deshwal, A., Kohli, S., Chethan, K.P.: Information as a service based architectural solution for WSN. In: IEEE International Conference on Communications in China (ICCC 2012) (2012)
19. Distefano, S., Merlino, G., Puliafito, A.: Sensing and actuation as a service: a new development for clouds. In: IEEE 11th International Symposium on Network Computing and Applications (2012)
20. Zaslavsky, A., Perera, C., Georgakopoulos, D.: Sensing as a service and big data. In: International Conference on Advances in Cloud Computing (2012)
21. Dinh, T., Kim, Y.: An efficient sensor-cloud interactive model for on-demand latency requirement guarantee. In: IEEE International Conference on Communications (ICC) (2017)
22. Distefano, S., Merlino, G., Puliafito, A.: A utility paradigm for IoT: the sensing cloud. Perv. Mob. Comput. **20**, 127–144 (2015)

23. Ishi, Y., Kawakami, T., Yoshihisa, T., Teranishi, Y., Nakauchi, K., Nishinaga, N.: Design and implementation of sensor data sharing platform for virtualized wide area sensor networks. In: International Conference on P2P, Parallel, Grid, Cloud and Internet Computing (2012)
24. Compton, M., et al.: The SSN ontology of the W3C semantic sensor network incubator group. J. Web Semant. Sci. Serv. Agents World Wide Web **17**, 25–32 (2012)
25. W3C: SPARQL Query Language for RDF

Applications of Speaker Identification for Universal Access

Saritha Kinkiri[1]([⊠]) and Simeon Keates[2]

[1] University of Greenwich, Chatham ME71PQ, UK
s.kinkiri@gre.ac.uk
[2] Edinburgh Napier University, Edinburgh EH11 4DY, UK
s.keates@napier.ac.uk

Abstract. Speaker Identification is the process of a machine identifying who is speaking automatically based solely on the voice of the person speaking. Recognising a person in a meeting room or on telephone, purely from their voice is an important and interesting research challenge. The voice is one of the human biometric properties. Recognition of a particular person's voice can be used in different applications such as: unlocking an office door, marking student or employee attendance, monitoring elderly people's health, online banking services, or helping people with dementia to be able to identify a who is speaking. This paper explores a range of such applications and discusses how emerging technologies can be used to support a variety of users in a series of different contexts of use.

Keywords: Human speech · Speaker identification · Biometric · Applications

1 Introduction

Generally, the human brain retrieves information from its "memory", described in neurological terms as a set of interconnected neurons. While neurons are quite slow in comparison to the transistors used in modern computers, their functionality is quite different too [1, 6]. For example, if you want to catch a ball, you need to estimate the trajectory of the ball in order to catch it, estimated automatically in the brain through a derivative pattern that aligns with previously learned patterns, influenced by certain parameters such as the estimated weight of the ball, force of throwing and environmental conditions, such as the wind etc. [2, 3]. On the other hand, computers would need to calculate each and every step analytically to ensure that a robot catches the same ball. An additional difference between computers and the human brain lies in the fact that a computer has a separate memory in the form of memory cards and hard drives, and it does not store automatically, whereas the human brain seems to be one large pattern-focused memory device that stores and adjusts its contents continuously [5, 10].

1.1 Voice Recognition

Verbal speech one of the most common ways used for communication. It uses words to convey information to others [7, 8]. The nature of the sounds produced as part of that speech assists in the identification of who is speaking too, but it is not always

M. Antona and C. Stephanidis (Eds.): HCII 2020, LNCS 12189, pp. 557–567, 2020.
https://doi.org/10.1007/978-3-030-49108-6_40

straightforward to recognize the identity of the person. Verbal speech constitutes a speaker's accent, speaking style, and pronunciation, etc. [4, 9], but our ability to recognize who is speaking can be affected by background noise, the emotional state of the person and even something as simple as whether they have a common cold or a blocked nose. Typically, as people, we can identify a speaker with a comparatively high degree of accuracy if they are sufficiently familiar to us [10]. We use a combination of parameters to identify a person such as speaking accent, speaking style, and pronunciation etc. However, we may not always use the same parameters every time. If someone has a particularly distinctive characteristic, such as a lisp or a very particular way of saying a common word, we can use that information to speed up the process of recognizing who is talking. However, training a computer to use identify and use such shortcuts is not easy. Consequently, we need to explore more systematic approaches to recognizing who is talking.

Automated voice/speaker recognition typically comes in two different types of task: speaker identification and speaker verification [3]. Speaker identification is the task of identifying who a speaker is from a field of possible candidates, usually by either trying to match the speaker to the closest stored speech template or by trying to iteratively eliminate possible candidates until only a single potential candidate remains.

Speaker identification can be further subdivided into two types, namely: closed set and open set. The closed set is where the possible range of candidate speakers is defined and the voice to be recognized is from within that set. The open set includes the possibility that the speaker may not be from within the existing set of stored speaker templates.

It is possible to subdivide the recognition one step further into text dependent or text independent. Text dependent is where the speaker is uttering a known (defined) phrase or set of phrases, whereas text independent is basically any possible spoken content. Figure 1 summarizes these different approaches to identifying the particular person who is speaking.

2   Example Case Studies of Speaker Recognition in Use

The purpose of this paper is to explore a range of different potential uses of this new technology to examine how it can support the principles of universal access. Universal Access is typically taken to focus on addressing the needs of those with some form of impairment or functional limitation that may either be innate, e.g. arising from a medical condition or injury, or situational, i.e. where the impairment or limitation arises from the circumstances that someone finds themselves in. Examples of the latter can include while driving or in a very busy environment [e.g. 11]. Here we will consider examples that address both causes of impairments.

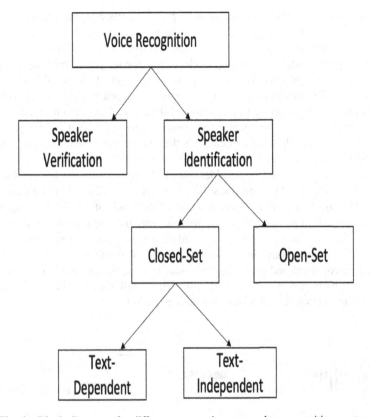

Fig. 1. Block diagram of a different approaches to speaker recognition systems

2.1   Security Applications

The most commonly cited example of speaker identification is its use for identifying a particular person for security reasons, such as for telephone banking. Typically a person is enrolled for this security service and is asked to utter a particular phrase. The person's utterance is then compared with a stored reference, which is an example of closed-set text-dependent recognition. If the match is within a pre-determined threshold, the caller is permitted to access the banking services. If the match is not made, the caller is passed to an alternative authentication service, as shown in Fig. 2.

The ability to use speaker recognition, once is has been demonstrated to meet the necessary security requirements in terms of its ability to recognize an individual person uniquely, would mean that someone who finds it difficult to remember PINs and passcodes may be able to access such services more easily.

Beyond the obvious banking applications, it is straightforward to think of situations where someone who is older or has severe functional impairments may wish to benefit from such technology, such as additional security at home. Imagine a door locking system that required both a key and a stored passphrase for a carer or cleaner to be able to enter the house. Such a system would increase the physical security of a potential vulnerable person.

Similarly there have been numerous newspaper reports over the years of scammers targeting older adults by posing as representatives of financial institutions, such as banks, to obtain log-on information to banking services. A layer of speaker recognition technology would render such an approach useless for telephone banking services.

It is possible to go even further with the technology. It is possible to picture a system where all representatives of agencies that supported a potentially vulnerable person had their voices stored in a centralized database. That person could phone the database service and ask the agency representative to speak into the telephone. The database service could then authenticate whether the person who spoke was a genuine representative.

A simple example would be an older woman living on her own has the front door bell ring. She opens the door and finds there is a large man claiming to be from the gas company. He says that there has been a report of the smell of gas from a neighbor and he needs to come into the house to check to make sure that there is no leak in the house. Before allowing him into the house, she could phone the gas company's voice checking service and ask him to speak into the telephone. If the database services tells her that the voice is recognized and gives the same name as the ID tag on his suit, she can be reassured that he is genuine. Should the voice check fail, though, she would know not to let him into her house and to call the police instead.

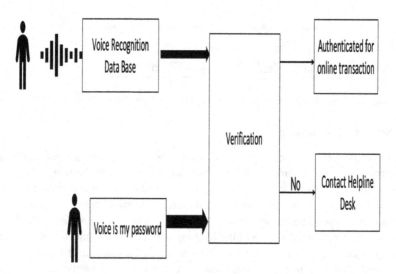

Fig. 2. Speaker authentication for telephone banking services

2.2   Forensic Speaker Recognition

Unfortunately, criminals will find a way past even the best security. Even then, though, speaker recognition technology can help through the identification of an unknown speaker(s). However, there is still no source providing a 100% confirmation of speaker recognition at the moment due to the differences in speech sample environments.

However many criminals end up thinking that committing crimes using voice-related tricks such as ransom calls, harassment calls, or blackmail threats will mask their crimes. With the help of speaker identification, this is no longer true. In fact, speaker recognition for surveillance could stop such crimes from taking place by monitoring speech via mobiles, telephones, computers, etc., which are constantly listening for certain words related to terrorism or criminal activity.

Voice samples of suspects could be compared with the unknown (criminal) speaker. Speaker identification requires comparison of one unknown speaker to a database of stored samples/suspects, from which, a set of suspects are separated whose voice is within the range of the criminal voice. Speaker identification comes down to analyzing the acoustic parameters off voice closely related to voice characteristics, as shown in Fig. 3.

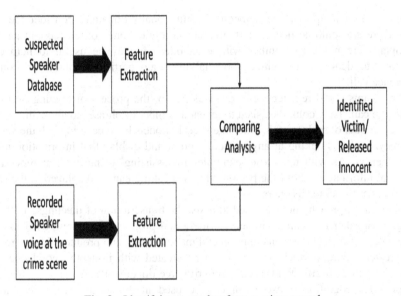

Fig. 3. Identifying a speaker from a crime record

2.3   Assisting People with Memory Loss or Dementia

Aside from crime and crime prevention, another obvious are of potential applications for this technology is in healthcare.

Dementia is a condition associated with slow, long-term progressive loss of memory. It can restrict quality of life quite severely. People with advanced dementia often cannot remember names or recognize people and this can be distressing both for them and for those with whom they are trying to communicate. For example, people cannot say their friends/family names when they talk/see to them.

In such cases, a speaker recognition device can be produced to help people to recognize the names of those they are talking to by listening to their voice. For example, for a given patient, close relatives and friends of the patient can be enrolled into a speaker identification system. Once they are in the system, reference models/templates can be created from the voices of each individual, which is compared to the speech of the person to be identified.

For the person with dementia, when listening to these individuals (whether present in the same room or over a telephone, for example), the system will identify and suggest the name of the individual, thereby, assisting the person in recalling the correct name. The system could easily be augmented to also include more detail about the person, such as their relationship to the person with dementia. The information could remain on the display/screen of the device to ensure that even if the person with dementia or memory loss begins to forget to whom they are talking, they can refer back to the display for a reminder at any time.

2.4   Identifying a Speaker from Multiple Speakers

Moving to an example where someone is situationally-impaired, consider the case where there are multiple people participating on a telephone conference call and the participants are not very familiar with each other. It may be useful to help each participant to identify or recognize who is talking at any particular point in time on the conference call.

Participants could register their voices as part of the process of logging on to the conference call. They could be asked to repeat a number of phrases to allow the system to build a model of their speech. Once the speech models have been logged, the system can analyze who is talking at any particular point and display that information to the other listeners. As with the earlier examples for assisting people with memory loss, additional information about the person who is speaking can be displayed at the same time to assist the other listeners.

The same approach could be used to assist the transcription of meetings, as shown in Fig. 4. Speaker recognition is being widely and progressively being used to transcribe data. It reduces time-consumption and manual work, and produces higher results with greater accuracy. Such programs can be created with in-depth knowledge, and terminology in a specific field, producing error-free documents.

Speaker recognition transcription can be used in numerous places such as in interviews, where the interviewer is constantly taking down the answers provided by the interviewee. Here, a speaker recognition device can be used, which can differentiate between the interviewer and interviewee and take down all information instead of manually writing, and breaking the flow of the interview [12].

Another example is legal transcription, where attending depositions, or hearings can lead to accumulation of important data left to be transcribed. Instead, the use of a speaker recognition program in such cases, designed to differentiate between the jury, the judge, the witnesses, and the lawyers and transcribe multiple-voice recordings, can save huge amounts of time.

Medical transcription is one of the most important areas where the use of a speaker identification device can reduce the time taken in the treatment, or diagnosis of patient. For example, in the emergency ward, where trauma is incoming 24/7, and patient treatment is number one priority, the use of a speech recognition device to transcribe emergency room reports can save time for authorized professionals; that is, time taken to write down the reports. Instead, they can use that time to treat, diagnose, operate, or discharge a patient as soon as possible.

Fig. 4. Simultaneous multiple speaker detection and recognition

2.5   Military Activities and Air Force

Speech recognition in these areas needs to be specialized and requires high performance to eliminate poor signals in remote areas, communicate through long distances and limited band-width channels, cancel background noise, and assist in maximizing hands-and-eyes operations so that the entire focus can be casted on the task on hand.

The key in these operations is to activate voice operated tasks, only by officials. In terms of fighter cockpit applications, speaker recognition programs are already installed into fighter aircrafts with voices of certain commanders, authorized to fly the specialised aircrafts. Before flight, this program identifies the commander, and activates the aircraft, ready to fly and accept future commands during the flight. During flight, speaker recognition will allow the pilot to give speech commands such as release of weapons parameters, setting radio frequencies, and commanding auto-pilot system.

2.6   Personal Digital Assistant

The most common, modern, and up to date applications of speech recognition are digital assistants such as Siri (Apple), and Alexa (Amazon). A combination of speaker identification, and verification, can allow secure and personal use of these digital assistants, not only at home but at work, in the car, and even during outdoor activities.

Considering the example of a smart phone, if the users hands are occupied but he/she needs to access the phone, speaking to the phone wakes up the voice recognition program and moves on to identifying the user. Once, verified, the system allows the user to make further commands such as set reminders/alarms, call/message contacts, browse the Internet, and so on, using voice identification. This is also beneficial to save time and multitask, thereby reducing screen time and increasing productivity.

The in-car system provides access to information without physically distracting the driver. For instance, if the driver forgets the way to their destination, they can activate the speech recognition system with the push off a button and ask for directions via speech. The sole purpose of introducing speech identification in this case would be that if the system realizes that an unknown person is asking for information like directions to home, the system can activate an alarm indicating an intruder while simultaneously sending the location of the vehicle to the police &/or car-owner(s) (Fig. 5).

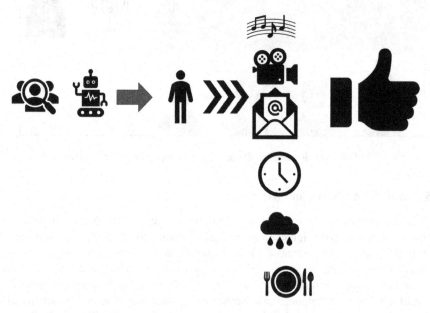

Fig. 5. User interfaces for a personal digital assistant

2.7   Helping Patients in Hospital

The process of recognizing who is speaking involves the collection and analysis of many facets of the speech. This includes general features, such the frequency, phase, amplitude and rate of speech, as well as analysis of more specific contents of the speech, such as individual phonemes.

It is possible to combine the speaker recognition system with other technologies, such as a voice stress analyzer to give a snapshot of someone's emotional state. Insurance companies sometimes use such technology to determine whether a caller to their call center is likely to be telling the truth or not.

Combining such technologies in a healthcare setting offer new opportunities for monitoring the wellbeing of patients. For example, in a hospital environment, it is not easy to monitor older adults 24 h a day, 7 days a week. Technological aids, such as using a camera can assist with monitoring activity, but are typically not much use at keeping track of daily activities and health-related issues. An observer is required to keep an eye on the person under observation at all times. Setting up cameras in rooms is also costly and causes obvious privacy issues.

An alternative would if voice samples could be collected from the microphone and can be used to identify who is speaking and also run basic analysis of the voice for signs of distress, such as a change in frequencies, rate of speech or other indicators.

Most of the time, saving every tiny bit of information is not required to make a decision on patient's health. One can collect voice samples from a patient through microphone and store them on database. Listening to a person voice, one can predict their needs such as: hungry, sick in terms of cold or tired, emotional state such as whether they are in pain, sad, angry etc. Figure 6 gives an example of the design of such a system.

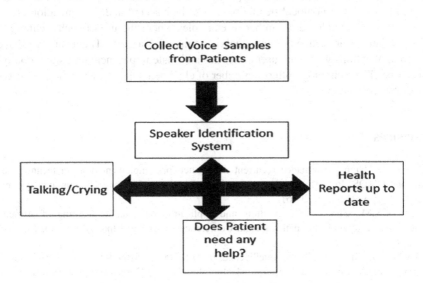

Fig. 6. Block diagram of a speaker identification system

3 Summary

The human brain consists of several systems and subsystems that have proven to be particularly challenging to discover and understand. So far, research has shown that the brain has different layers with different functionalities that process information from sensory organs and thus from the surrounding environment. The brain receives input from these sensory organs to learn information and improve overall intelligence. Basically, the human brain does not need these sensory organs to be intelligent on their own. For example, Helen Keller had no sight or no hearing, yet she managed to learn and become one of the best writers in the world. The human brain does not know the difference between hearing, feeling or vision, because it takes information directly from these sensory organs as patterns.

Everything in the world around us is based on patterns. For example, language is a combination of patterns at various levels, such as, letters combine to form syllables; syllables combine to form words; words combine to form clauses and sentences and then these are all stored in sequential order. So, the question then becomes how the information is presented as patterns and how those patterns are stored possibly including sequential/timing information. For example, if someone wanted to explain their house to a friend then normally the explanation starts from the entrance moving on to e.g. the kitchen or living area and then to the playroom. Even though someone's house is well known to them, still there is a priority to the order in which they tell their friend. This is since all information patterns are associated with one another through a massive network.

As humans, we use combination of parameters to be able to identify a speaker. Parameters could be varied based on applications and persons as well. For example, we can identify local and nonlocal people based on their accent and pronunciation etc.

This paper has explored a number of examples where the use of such technology can be of benefit in achieving the goals of universal access. The examples have included applications where the user either has an innate impairment or a situationally-induced one. The technology offers a number of clear benefits for a wide range of users in a number of contexts.

References

1. Ansari, S.: High performance recurrent neural network implementations in technologies beyond CMOS. In: 2016 3rd International Conference on Devices, Circuits and Systems (ICDCS), pp. 212–216 (2016)
2. Xue, M.X.M., Zhu, C.Z.C.: A study and application on machine learning of artificial intelligence. In: 2009 International Joint Conference on Artificial Intelligence, pp. 272–274 (2009)
3. Hawkins, J., Blakeslee, S.: On Intelligence, p. 272 (2004). ISBN: 978-0805074567
4. Li, C., Liu, Z., Liu, L.: Elicitation of Machine Learning to Human Learning from Iterative Error Correcting, pp. 14–17 (2013)
5. Wolff, J.G.: The SP Theory of Intelligence and the Representation and Processing of Knowledge in the Brain, vol. 44, pp. 1–56 (2016)
6. Wolff, J.G.: The SP theory of intelligence: distinctive features and advantages. IEEE Access 4, 216–246 (2016)
7. He, X., Deng, L.: Speech recognition, machine translation, and speech translation-a unified discriminative learning paradigm. IEEE Signal Process. Mag. 28(5), 126–133 (2011)
8. Surampudi, S.G., Pal, R.: Speech Signal Processing Using Neural Networks, pp. 660–665 (2015)
9. Rajput, N., Verma, S.K.: Back propagation feed forward neural network approach for speech recognition. In: Proceedings of 2014 3rd International Conference on Reliability, Infocom Technologies and Optimization (Trends and Future Directions), ICRITO 2014 (2015)

10. Liu, Y., Xu, M., Cai, L.: Improved keyword spotting system by optimizing posterior confidence measure vector using feed-forward neural network. In: Proceedings of the International Joint Conference on Neural Networks, no. 61171116, pp. 2036–2041 (2014)
11. Kinkiri, S., Keates, S.: Identification of a speaker from familiar and unfamiliar voices. In: Proceedings of the 2019 5th International Conference on Robotics and Artificial Intelligence, pp. 94–97, November 2019. ACM (2019)
12. Keates, S.: Designing user interfaces for ordinary users in extraordinary circumstances: a keyboard-only web-based application for use in airports. Int. J. Univ. Access Inf. Soc. **12**(2), 205–216 (2013). https://doi.org/10.1007/s10209-012-0276-x

Smartphone Navigation Support for Blind and Visually Impaired People - A Comprehensive Analysis of Potentials and Opportunities

Bineeth Kuriakose$^{(\boxtimes)}$ (iD), Raju Shrestha (iD), and Frode Eika Sandnes (iD)

Department of Computer Science, Oslo Metropolitan University, Oslo, Norway
bineethk@oslomet.no

Abstract. Smartphones are indispensable tools for many people for various assistive tasks. They are equipped with different sensors that provide data on motion, location and the environment. This paper explores the various sensors and output modalities existing in a smartphone to make it useful as a navigation support device for blind and visually impaired users. In addition, different usecase scenarios were also scrutinized where the potential of a smartphone as a navigation device can be explored further. The technology holds potential for the implementation of successful navigation support system by utilizing the various sensors and features existing in a smartphone. This in-depth analysis of the various possibilities with a smartphone in the navigation support system design might become useful in the further research in the domain.

Keywords: Smartphone · Blind · Visually impaired · Navigation support

1 Introduction

The invention of the mobile phone was a notable achievement. When the mobile phone turned to become *smartphone*, the features and different possibilities to explore them more were also enhanced. Esmaeili Kelishomi *et al.* [18] states that one of the most significant technology trends in the current decade is an enormous proliferation of smartphone devices. People use smartphones for various needs ranging from making a simple call to using it for computing purposes. The extensive use of smartphones makes them an important platform that serves the sensing and communication needs of people [31]. Due to its diverse functionality, the smartphone is transforming into an assistive technology capable device with better features for all kinds of users.

As the trends have been changing and the smartphone manufacturers are expanding their consumer markets, many features have become available for people who are blind and visually impaired. The accessibility option in almost all types of smartphones shows the support given to the community and can

© Springer Nature Switzerland AG 2020
M. Antona and C. Stephanidis (Eds.): HCII 2020, LNCS 12189, pp. 568–583, 2020.
https://doi.org/10.1007/978-3-030-49108-6_41

be considered as a business expansion motive in attracting customers from various domains. The Global Accessibility Reporting Initiative (GARI)[1] is a project implemented to help various clients to acquire knowledge about the accessibility traits of different mobile devices and help them to identify a most suitable one that can assist their specific needs. Years back, a Braille smartphone was introduced by Sumit Dagar targeted specifically for visually impaired people, which was claimed to be first of its kind around the world [15]. Similar to smartphones existing today, Braille phone provides access to many of the features existing in a regular smartphone. Instead of using visual display, it relies on a tactile display as an interface.

There are many reasons for which visually impaired people use a smartphone [24]. A survey on the use of smartphone among visually impaired persons in Japan shows that the navigation requirement is on the high priority list [57]. There are many smartphone apps and portable systems that have been developed to support the navigation of blind and visually impaired people. It should also be noted that they did not try to make use of the different smartphone sensors and features, and utilize them well in the the design of navigation support system for blind and visually impaired people.

It is a known fact from the recent developments that smartphones are becoming more like personal assistants [30]. Besides its existing features, it can be also used to monitor the behaviour, to track movements and also to help in the navigation of the user. A large part of this evolution is enabled by sensor technologies. A sensor is a device that detects and measures the changes in the nearby environment. Sensors are used to bring intelligence and awareness to smartphones, thus enhancing its usability [38]. Today's smartphones are equipped with more than 15 sensors that capture data on motion, location and the environment around the user [53]. The sensors existing in a smartphone can be categorised into three major groups: motion sensors, environment sensors and position sensors [17,53]. Motion sensors measures axis-based motion sensing, like acceleration forces and rotational forces along with three axes. Sensors belonging to this category include accelerometer, gravity sensors, and gyroscopes sensors. Environmental sensors measure environmental parameters such as temperature, pressure, light and humidity etc. This category includes thermometers, barometers, photometers etc. Position sensors measure the physical position of a device. That is it identifies whether the device is in landscape mode or portrait mode and also the direction of its orientation. Sensors belonging to this category are orientation sensors and magnetometers.

This paper analyzes different possibilities and opportunities in today's smartphones for their use as a navigation support device by blind and visually impaired people. The features existing in the latest smartphone like different high quality sensors, faster network connectivity and higher computational capability of hardware can be investigated further to develop assistive systems for navigational support with relevant facilities and features for their effective and practical use. There were previous related attempts to explore the smartphone

---

[1] https://www.gari.info.

computing possibilities for assisting visually impaired people [14,58]. In both of these studies, the authors mentioned the different assistive technologies possible for visually impaired users using smartphones in a broader sense. The first study mainly focussed on audio and tactile feedback based assistive systems. And the second study mainly discussed on the different features of assistive tools and some technical details regarding machine learning methods that can be used in the navigation context. Moreover, the papers did not give any detailed coverage on the different possible options available with the smartphone sensors and technologies in the navigation support system design.

This paper is organised as follows. Section 2 discusses some important sensors, connectivity options and other hardware features available in a smartphone and how it can be used in designing a navigation support device. Section 3 discusses the common output modalities available in a smartphone. Section 4 deals with an analysis of some common smartphone apps and how different sensors are used for various functions. Section 5 proceeds with some usecases and scenarios where we can apply the smartphone features in assisting navigation of blind and visually impaired people.

2   Sensors and Related Technologies

With a variety of sensors, different connectivity technologies and other hardware features like memory, graphical processor, storage capacity etc., the capabilities of current smartphones have already transcended beyond running the standard phone applications [29]. This section discusses some of the important sensors and technologies available in a smartphone and how it can be utilised in designing a navigation support device for visually impaired people. The section is divided into three subsections based on the categorisation of the total possible options in the smartphone. The subsections includes smartphone sensors, connectivity technologies and the computational capability of hardware which can be explored further.

2.1   Smartphone Sensors

Different smartphone sensors that were already used or have the possibility to use in the future for the navigation support of blind and visually impaired people are discussed here.

Accelerometer: The accelerometer is an electromechanical device that is used to measure the force of acceleration caused by movement or by vibration or by gravity. These forces can be static like gravity force, dynamic senses movement or vibrations [5,49]. The accelerometer sensor in a smartphone can be used in the navigation context mainly for two different purposes. The first one is for motion input where it can be used to track the movement of the user. In this way, it can be used as a pedometer to count steps which can be used to check how long the user is away from the destination point by comparing it with the actual distance. The second use of accelerometer is for orientation sensing. It is also used to adjust the orientation of content and presentation of an app to make it user-friendly. This feature can mainly be used in navigation apps to get a wider viewing angle of the surroundings to capture the scene in a camera in real-time and use it for further processing like object and other obstacle identification. Also, the landscape orientations can be made useful to create a better user interface with large buttons for visually impaired users.

Gyroscope: Gyro sensors are also known as angular rate sensors or angular velocity sensors which can sense angular velocity. Gyroscope can provides orientation details and different directional information like left/right/top/bottom with great accuracy. This property will help the users to get informed on how much the smartphone is rotated and also regarding its direction in which it is tilted [13]. Gyro sensors have mainly been used for four applications in a navigation system design. (1) It can be used for sensing the angular velocity and in measuring the amount of motion itself. This is useful in checking the movement of a pedestrian who is visually impaired. (2) It can be used for sensing the angles produced by the sensor's own movement. The angle moved is fed to and reflected in a navigation application which can be used the direction the user points the smartphone. (3) It can sense vibration produced by external factors. (4) It can be used to correct the orientation or balance of an object. This feature is useful when the user who is visually impaired wants to initiate the navigation application in his phone just by shaking it. It reduces the complexity in the interface design of the application adaptable for a blind or visually impaired user.

Magnetometer: A magnetometer is used to embed the function of a compass in a smartphone. This sensor can be used to point at the earth's magnetic north pole via detecting magnetic fields [45]. A magnetometer is mainly used in location-based apps such as Google Maps or Apple Maps to determine correct orientation. This feature may be useful in detecting the direction of navigation and help to identify the movement in which the user is moving. If its the wrong direction which is not actually intended for, the smartphone application can notify the user with a certain type of warning signal. In addition to this feature, a magnetometer sensor can also be used in metal detector apps since it can detect the presence of metal. If we install small metals in an indoor building in guiding the user to a room, it opens another possibility in indoor navigation. By sensing the presence of metals, an indoor navigation application can be designed which can direct the user in reaching the correct room [41].

Proximity Sensor: A proximity sensor can detect the distance from a object located infront of it. This feature can be used to give information about the distance of an object from the user in navigation. The main limitation of this sensor is it can only used when the objects are very close. It is unable to provide distance measurement for distant objects [45]. For example, if the user wishes to see the bus timings board in a bus stop this sensor might be useful after the bus timing board is identified by a camera through object detection.

Global Positioning System (GPS): This sensor in the smartphone communicates with the satellites to determine the precise location on Earth [45]. GPS is used in all location-based apps such as Google Maps, Apple Maps etc. GPS is highly useful in detecting user location during outdoor navigation. GPS could not be useful when the user is in an indoor because of signal restrictions. The GPS technology does not actually use the mobile data network to sense the location. This could be the reason why the GPS sensor can work in an area where there is no mobile signal. But the internet is required initially to load the map and to commence the location identification. Modern-day GPS units inside smartphones actually combine GPS signals with cell signal strength to get more accurate location readings [41,55]. A survey on navigation systems for visually impaired people using GPS is provided in [37].

Microphone: Smartphones generally use micro-sized microphone sensors for capturing sound [45]. Apart from making and receiving calls, microphones are also used for voice search and voice commands for navigation assistant apps. It can detect the user's voice to authenticate the app and also the get to know the destination which the user wants to travel.

Barometer: The barometer measures the air pressure which is useful in identifying the changes in the weather and also in calculating the altitude in which the user is located. It can give the user notification in the outdoor climate during the navigation. This helps the user to get prepared before the weather condition changes during the navigation. Barometers are best used in combination with other sensors such as GPS, Wi-Fi and beacons which helps in navigation [5,45].

Cameras: Some advanced camera phones have optical image stabilisation (OIS), larger sensors, bright lenses, and even optical zoom options. The cameras in a smartphone can be made useful in navigation for detecting objects or persons along the walking path. Another application area of smartphone cameras are there in detecting barcodes and QR codes. Barcode or QR codes have different possibilities in the indoor navigation context [45]. The QR codes placed in the indoors can be detected using the smartphone which can help the user in the navigation as well as identifying a room or venue inside a building. Some of the systems which use QR codes as navigation choices are [2,3,28].

Time of Flight (ToF) Sensor: This sensor uses infrared light to determine depth information. The sensor emits a light signal, which hits the subject and returns to the sensor. The time it takes to bounce back is then measured and provides depth-mapping capabilities [43]. A ToF sensor can be used to measure distance and volume, as well as for object scanning, indoor navigation, obstacle detection and avoidance.

2.2   Connectivity Technologies

There are different technologies in which a smartphone can be used to get connected to a network wirelessly. This section provides a brief description on different connectivity technologies available in a smartphone which can be used in the navigation support design.

WiFi: Wi-Fi may be used to provide local network and Internet access to devices. Using Wi-Fi to connect to the Internet drains less battery life and cheaper than using a smartphone network, especially in situations where the cellular coverage fluctuates [7]. This can be used for connecting the navigation app with the internet during indoors (as well as outdoors) and helps the user to access features in the app.

Bluetooth: Bluetooth is designed to allow devices to communicate wirelessly with each other over relatively short distances. Bluetooth technology allows for hands-free smartphone use. It typically works over a range of fewer than 100 meters. Bluetooth Low Energy (BLE) beacons have become the superior technology in indoor navigation systems because of the long battery life it can offer [33]. The signal send by a beacon can be read by any external device that has a Bluetooth signal receiver with a requirement of being in a close proximity. Many systems [1,40] were proposed with Bluetooth beacons as the major component in the indoor navigation systems for visually impaired people. Pairing the smartphone with a Bluetooth headset or other device increases the phone's usability especially when the user needs to travel around and receive the audio notifications via headset to clear the obstacles. The Bluetooth Special Interest Group (SIG) had announced a new Bluetooth standard called Bluetooth LE during CES 2020[2]. In addition to good audio quality offered to headphones, the new standard can also provides better battery efficiency. Also, it supports audio multi-stream and broadcast features [59]. Multi-stream feature enables a single source device to broadcast to multiple devices. One of the application of these features is in the design of indoor navigation system. Suppose the user wants to get guidance in directions to move inside a building. A remote human or machine assistant can guide the user using the multi-stream Bluetooth feature and helps to reach the destination.

Near Field Communication (NFC): NFC is used in a smartphone to interact with something in close proximity. It operates within a radius of about 4 cm and provides a wireless connection between the device and another. This allows for two-way communication with both devices involved being able to send and receive information. NFC transmits or receives data via radio waves. Each smartphone has an NFC reciever which follows certain protocols which helps them to communicate with another NFC enabled device. It functions through

---

[2] https://www.ces.tech.

electromagnetic induction. So there can be a passive device, such as a poster or sticker which requires no power source of its own and also that can transmit data when an active device, like a smartphone, comes into contact with it. NFCs are used to track the user and thus guide to reach a destination during navigation [23]. Different NFC based navigation systems for visually impaired were also proposed [4].

Cellular Connectivity: When the smartphone application is being connected to the internet, it gives more options to get real-time assistance and also processing. The increased densification of high-speed 5G networks provides enriched location identification services and navigation support for blind or visually impaired people in making a comfortable and safe navigation [21]. If there is high-speed network connectivity like as 5G, the navigation assistance and processing of real-time data such as videos/images/sounds can be done in the cloud. This will give an option to make use of an extensive dataset for testing real-time. Also, an alert system can be designed in a remote server in case of emergencies during the navigation. The fast processing will helps in communications with nearby stations to help the users in case of a need for an assistance.

2.3   Computational Capability of Hardware

Over the past years, the computational capability of smartphones has been proliferated to an extent of an average desktop computer or even more [54]. Smartphones with good storage and RAM capacity are getting introduced to the market widely. Modern smartphones are integrated with the latest embedded chipsets which can do many different tasks. GPUs (Graphics Processing Units) are one of the essential parts of those chipsets and their performance is becoming useful in testing and designing various application in a smartphone.

The GPUs in a smartphone can be used in different ways in the design of navigation for visually impaired people. Data from different sensors can be combined together and can be used for assisting in the navigation. The non-visual information such as location, orientation from different smartphone sensors and also other visual information from cameras can be integrated together to design a navigation support system for visually impaired people. Deep learning-based object detection models can be embedded in smartphones and used in identifying obstacles during the navigation.

Different light weight deep learning based libraries are available today exclusively for operations in mobile and embedded devices. TensorFlow Lite[3] is a neural network library for mobile devices from Google. It lets the users run machine-learned models on mobile devices with low latency which can be used in classification, regression etc. MobileNet [25], SqueezeNet [27], ShuffleNet [60], CondenseNet [26] are some of other examples of similar kind. The reduced model size and increased accuracy in upgraded versions of each model open opportunities to have navigation support systems with enhanced features. In addition

---

[3] https://www.tensorflow.org/lite.

to that, many mobile device-based object detection models were also proposed such as Peleenet [56]. Lin and Wang proposed a convolutional neural network named KrNet [35] for navigational assistance which can be able to execute scene classification on mobile devices in real-time.

3 Smartphone Output Modalities

Three output modalities are possible using a smartphone: Aural, Visual and Haptic. In case of navigation system design for visually impaired people, both aural and haptic can be more useful than visual based feedback notification to the user. The two modalities are discussed below. In addition, almost all smartphones existing today have been designed to enable concurrent vibration and audio stimulation, or audio-haptics [10].

3.1 Audio Feedback

Audio feedback is generally provided to smartphone users via audio output typically headphones, specifically in the noisy environments associated with navigation, where a smartphone's speaker may be masked by surrounding noises. When someone is wearing headphones, it actually reduces the ability of the user to hear sounds from the environment [8]. Wireless airpods which got popular recently can be a feasible and convenient option for the visually impaired users during to receive real-time feedback during the navigation.

3.2 Haptic Feedback

Haptic devices interact with the sense of touch. Vibrotactile feedback from eccentric mass motors has been the modality of choice for the majority of prototype mobile haptic interfaces [51,52]. Haptic feedback can give stimuli to the visually impaired users in various situations during navigation. Such as, to stop at some point, move slowly, some obstacle ahead of the user etc. The system can be designed to give various vibration stimuli in different instances. Most vibrotactile stimuli used in smartphones are transmitted in very simple information, such as alerts [20]. Also, the addition of complex vibrotactile stimuli to smartphones allows improved communication using the sense of touch to compensate or even substitute for deficiencies in other senses [14,46]. This could be a useful feature in the navigation support design when there exist situations which cannot depend on audio modality such as in a noisy environment.

4 Smartphone Apps for Navigation Support

Several smartphone applications were proposed for the navigation support of blind and visually impaired people. And each of them works either indoor, outdoor or both environments. The applications try to exploit various smartphone sensors and features. Some of the most widely used smartphone applications are discussed here. Also, we have tried to analyse how smartphone sensors and technologies are used these apps to serve their purpose.

Be My Eyes [6] is an app which allows a visually impaired person in moving through an unfamiliar environment with the help of a sighted individual. The app will work both indoors and outdoors using a live video connection. The app uses GPS to detect the user location. Blind users can request help from a sighted person during the navigation, and the sighted users will then be called for help. As soon as the first sighted volunteer accepts the request for help, a live audio-video connection is established between them. The connected sighted user can help the blind person what they see when the user points their phone at something using the rear-facing camera. The camera and microphone sensors are used for communication between the visually impaired and the sighted volunteer. A data network should also be established between the two entities for the communication.

Ariadne GPS [11] offers the possibility to know the position of the user and to get information about the street, its number, etc. and explore the map of what is around. The app is accessible using voice over and also the user can be alerted via vibration and sound. In addition, the app has the following main features: letting the user to explore a specific zone, letting the user to add and list favourite points, alerting when the user is near to one of the favourite points. The app uses the GPS of the phone and also works in several languages. But it uses remote services from Google. Hence, some information may be inaccurate or unavailable at certain times, depending on the GPS signal, the network and server availability.

BlindSquare [42] uses GPS and the internal compass in a smartphone to locate the user and then it collects information about the surrounding environment from the Foursquare website and OpenStreetMap. BlindSquare uses algorithms to decide the most relevant information and then speaks it to the user with a synthesized voice. BlindSquare uses Acapela voices in various languages to give information about the user's location even when the smartphone is inside a bag or a pocket. The app claims to works in both indoor and outdoor environments.

GetThere [32] assists the user by giving information about their current location and also guides them to reach a specific destination. The app can convey the users about their current location simply by shaking the smartphone. It can also recognize when the user is moved away from the route which was planned prior and also assists to move back into the right track. A notification alarm can be set to indicate when a person is close to their destination, which can be a useful feature during travel by bus or train. GetThere is a conversational app which gives the user to choose either audio or touch based input modality. Most of the functionalities in the app does not require an Internet connection. GetThere uses OpenStreetMap for navigation.

Low Viz Guide [19] is an indoor navigation app enables users to find their way around large meeting spaces and always to take the shortest route between two places. The user is guided by a combination of positioning algorithms, Bluetooth low-energy beacons, and a free app on a smartphone. Routing-by-voice is available through the use of the smartphone's accessibility feature.

The Seeing Eye GPS [12] is an accessible turn-by-turn GPS app with all the navigation features plus features unique to blind users. Instead of multiple layers of menus, the three important navigation elements are on the lower portion of every screen: Route, Point of Interests and Location. At intersections, the cross street and its orientation are announced. Seeing Eye GPS uses VoiceOver feature for audio voice output and does not contain its own voice synthesizer.

By analysing the features and functions in all these smartphone applications, we found that the voice based input is the main source from users to know the destination and thus to initiate the navigation guidance. Some of the applications use camera to get visual information about the location and surroundings during the navigation and then send them to a remote facility to get assistance. The main disadvantage in this case is regarding the time delay in processing the visual information and also the mandatory requirement of a data network. So an app which depends on data network may fail when the network is unavailable. All of the devices use GPS as the user location identification for outdoors. The output modality in most of the applications is audio based and some have a haptic feedback option in addition. The availability of a multiple feedback is always a good option in the navigation support system design. This will enable users to have various options for output modalities incase one is not available.

5   Usecases

After exploring different sensors and output modalities in a smartphone, we present here three potential usecase scenarios where the smartphone can be used in the context of a navigation support.

5.1   Usecase 1: Object Detection and Obstacle Avoidance

If there is a portable navigational solution for visually impaired users, it will be practicable. Suppose the user is walking along with a smartphone in which the depth camera is projected to face straight in the walking direction. The camera captures the real-time videos and identifies the object and its distance from the user. The information is passed to the user via audio output. Object detection may be possible by having a pre-trained deep learning model such as YoloV3 [47] or MobileNet+SSDv2 [22] in the smartphone itself. The depth camera can be utilised to determine the distance of the object from the user from the video frames itself. After object detection, the result with the identified object and its distance can be retrieved back to the user in the form of audio feedback. The similar idea was explored in several works [34,44]. But in a majority of them, the neural computation is done at a system backpacked with the user or cloud-based services where the data needs to be transferred via a data network. This approach has several disadvantages. It includes the cost of implementation, a requirement of a data network to send data and also delay in processing in sending and retrieving back the results. But all these limitations can be reduced if the computation is done is on the smartphone itself while capturing the input data from the same smartphone itself. Possibilities are existing for such an option with the hardware features available with a present smartphone as discussed in Sect. 2.3 In the real case scenario where blind and visually impaired people needs to navigate, both speed and accuracy are important constraints. Data processing and feedback to the user needs to happen without any delay. It is crucial since the external and internal factors contribute to the safe navigation of the person.

Because of all these, it is better if the object recognition model is integrated in the smartphone itself. As a preliminary work in this direction, we have done an experiment with an object detection and recognition model based on MobileNet+SSDv2. The model was pre-trained using the COCO dataset [36] which is a large-scale dataset used for object detection, segmentation and captioning. An android application is developed which uses a smartphone camera to capture the scene in front. The objects are detected in real time and can inform the user what it is. Figure 1 illustrates detected and recognized objects using the model. This model can be further extended by integrating voice feedback about the type and distance to the object back to the user, which can be a useful navigation support solution.

Fig. 1. An illustration of object detection and recognition using smartphone with MobileNet+SSDv2.

5.2   Usecase 2: Intersection Crossing

Pedestrians who are visually impaired often travel in unfamiliar areas and cross at intersections. It is considered as one of the most difficult and risky aspects of independent navigation [50]. Some important tasks that are involved in crossing a street includes the following [9]. First is locating the street where the pedestrians must determine when they reach a street. This is accomplished by using the GPS and also the network which gives the precise location of the street. Second is intersection assessment where the pedestrians need to obtain some important information about intersection environment, including the crosswalk location, the direction of the opposite corner, the number of intersecting roads, the width of the street to be crossed, and whether there are any junctions or islands in the crosswalk. The camera on the smartphone can identify the traffic junctions and also the crosswalks. Directional sensors in the smartphone can be used to aid the directions for crosswalks. And the third is crossing the roadway. After determining the geometry of the intersection, aligning to face towards the destination curb, determining that the intersection is signalized, the audio feedback in the smartphone can be used to help the users to give instructions. There were some works such as CrossNavi [48] done in the area of intersection crossing. As stated by authors of the paper, the ranging and localization accuracy is still undesirable in CrossNavi. Also, there is a scope in furthur enhancements by exploring different possible options available in a smartphone presently [58].

5.3   Usecase 3: Remote Alert in Emergency Situations

Situations can come when blind or visually impaired people require support from a second person when there is an emergency. Consider the situation when there is a medical emergency happened for a person who is visually impaired when he is in an unknown place. The first thing usually people can do is dialling an emergency contact saved in the phone. But there might be a chance while the person on the other end may not be available or in worse some other situations which the user could not get connected to that person. If there is an emergency notification system integrated with the navigation system in the smartphone itself, within a simple voice command or touch, messages and calls can go to the nearest support centre. The support centre can access the user location using smartphone GPS and can provide necessary assistance to the user immediately. The same thing can be applied if the user got lost in the middle of someplace and got stuck. In that case also, the same support system can be used.

  If there is an environmental emergency during the navigation or an emergency announcement from the concerned authorities, the visually impaired person in navigation can also get alerts from the navigation system. The system can be designed in such a way to alert the users in such situations too. This can be made possible by integrating various sensors and features on the smartphone itself. Some similar applications were already done earlier [16, 39].

6 Conclusion

Today's smartphones are integrated with a wide variety of sensors which hold potential for sensing, detecting, and recognizing different things useful in many different applications. The three different output modalities, visual, aural, and haptic existing in a smartphone, the latter two in particular, also open different possibilities for effective user interaction during the navigation of blind and visually impaired people. Moreover, from the analysis of various existing mobile apps currently available for navigation support, it has been clear that there are still rooms for improvement on feature additions by utilizing various other sensors/hardware features in the smartphone. By combining various sensors and using them efficiently and with added features and functionalities, better systems can be designed and developed to support the navigation of the blind and visually impaired people. The three specific usecases discussed provide insights into some potential scenarios where the smartphone can be used for the navigational support of visually impaired people. We believe that this in-depth analysis of the existing features in a smartphone and possibilities for using them for navigation assistance of blind and visually impaired might become useful for further research in the area.

References

1. Ahmetovic, D., Gleason, C., Kitani, K.M., Takagi, H., Asakawa, C.: NavCog: turn-by-turn smartphone navigation assistant for people with visual impairments or blindness. In: Proceedings of the 13th Web for All Conference, p. 9. ACM (2016)
2. Al-Khalifa, S., Al-Razgan, M.: Ebsar: indoor guidance for the visually impaired. Comput. Electri. Eng. **54**, 26–39 (2016)
3. Alghamdi, S., Van Schyndel, R., Alahmadi, A.: Indoor navigational aid using active RFID and QR-code for sighted and blind people. In: 2013 IEEE Eighth International Conference on Intelligent Sensors, Sensor Networks and Information Processing, pp. 18–22. IEEE (2013)
4. AlZuhair, M.S., Najjar, A.B., Kanjo, E.: NFC based applications for visually impaired people - a review. In: 2014 IEEE International Conference on Multimedia and Expo Workshops (ICMEW), pp. 1–6. IEEE (2014)
5. Batt, S.: How an accelerometer in a smartphone works to track your movement? April 2019. https://www.maketecheasier.com/how-accelerometer-works/. Accessed Jan 2020
6. BeMyEyes: Bringing sight to blind and low-vision people, September 2003. https://www.bemyeyes.com/. Accessed Jan 2020
7. Bolton, N.: The Advantages of Using Wi-Fi on Your Smartphone, October 2016. https://smallbusiness.chron.com/advantages-using-wifi-smartphone-71651.html. Accessed Jan 2020
8. Botzer, A., Shvalb, N., et al.: Using sound feedback to help blind people navigate. In: Proceedings of the 36th European Conference on Cognitive Ergonomics, p. 23. ACM (2018)
9. Carter, D., Barlow, J.: Understanding how blind pedestrians cross at signalized intersections, March 2009. http://www.apsguide.org/appendix_d_understanding.cfm. Accessed Jan 2020

10. Chang, A., O'Sullivan, C.: Audio-haptic feedback in mobile phones. In: CHI 2005 Extended Abstracts on Human Factors in Computing Systems, pp. 1264–1267. ACM (2005)
11. Ciaffoni, L.: An innovative app for your mobility, June 2011. https://www.ariadnegps.eu/. Accessed Jan 2020
12. Corp, A.T.: Seeing Eye GPS, June 2013. https://apps.apple.com/us/app/seeing-eye-gps/id668624446. Accessed January 2020
13. Corp, S.E.: Gyro sensors - How they work and what's ahead: about Gyro sensor: Technical Information: other Information, May 2010. https://www5.epsondevice.com/en/information/technical_info/gyro/. Accessed Jan 2020
14. Csapó, Á., Wersényi, G., Nagy, H., Stockman, T.: A survey of assistive technologies and applications for blind users on mobile platforms: a review and foundation for research. J. Multimodal User Interfaces 9(4), 275–286 (2015)
15. Dagar, S.: Braille Phone, August 2018. https://dagar.me/braille-phone. Accessed Jan 2020
16. Das, R.C., Alam, T.: Location based emergency medical assistance system using OpenstreetMap. In: 2014 International Conference on Informatics, Electronics & Vision (ICIEV), pp. 1–5. IEEE (2014)
17. Developers, A.: Sensors Overview : Android Developers, December 2011. https://developer.android.com/guide/topics/sensors/sensors_overview. Accessed Jan 2020
18. Esmaeili Kelishomi, A., Garmabaki, A., Bahaghighat, M., Dong, J.: Mobile user indoor-outdoor detection through physical daily activities. Sensors 19(3), 511 (2019)
19. GmbH: LowViz Guide Indoor Navigation, May 2015. https://apps.apple.com/us/app/lowviz-guide-indoor-navigation/id987917857. Accessed Jan 2020
20. González-Cañete, F., Rodríguez, J.L., Galdón, P., Díaz-Estrella, A.: Improvements in the learnability of smartphone haptic interfaces for visually impaired users. PLoS One 14(11), e0225053 (2019)
21. Graves, K.: 5G Will Spur New Opportunities for Americans with Disabilities, May 2018. https://www.ctia.org/news/5g-will-spur-new-opportunities-for-americans-with-disabilities. Accessed Jan 2020
22. Heredia, A., Barros-Gavilanes, G.: Video processing inside embedded devices using SSD-MobileNet to count mobility actors. In: 2019 IEEE Colombian Conference on Applications in Computational Intelligence (ColCACI), pp. 1–6. IEEE (2019)
23. Hoffman, C.: What is NFC (Near Field Communication), and What Can I Use It For, May 2018. https://www.howtogeek.com/137979/htg-explains-what-is-nfc-and-what-can-i-use-it-for/. Accessed Jan 2020
24. Holly: How do blind and visually impaired people use a mobile phone?, February 2019. https://lifeofablindgirl.com/2019/02/03/how-do-blind-and-visually-impaired-people-use-a-mobile-phone/. Accessed Jan 2020
25. Howard, A.G., et al.: MobileNets: efficient convolutional neural networks for mobile vision applications. arXiv preprint arXiv:1704.04861 (2017)
26. Huang, G., Liu, S., Van der Maaten, L., Weinberger, K.Q.: CondenseNet: an efficient densenet using learned group convolutions. In: Proceedings of the IEEE Conference on Computer Vision and Pattern Recognition, pp. 2752–2761 (2018)
27. Iandola, F.N., Han, S., Moskewicz, M.W., Ashraf, K., Dally, W.J., Keutzer, K.: SqueezeNet: alexNet-level accuracy with 50x fewer parameters and ¡ 0.5 MB model size. arXiv preprint arXiv:1602.07360 (2016)
28. Idrees, A., Iqbal, Z., Ishfaq, M.: An efficient indoor navigation technique to find optimal route for blinds using QR codes. In: 2015 IEEE 10th Conference on Industrial Electronics and Applications (ICIEA), pp. 690–695. IEEE (2015)

29. Ignatov, A., et al.: AI benchmark: running deep neural networks on Android smartphones. In: Proceedings of the European Conference on Computer Vision (ECCV) (2018)
30. Islam, N., Want, R.: Smartphones: past, present, and future. IEEE Pervasive Comput. **13**(4), 89–92 (2014)
31. Lane, N.D., Miluzzo, E., Lu, H., Peebles, D., Choudhury, T., Campbell, A.T.: A survey of mobile phone sensing. IEEE Commun. Magazine **48**(9), 140–150 (2010)
32. Lasher, L.: GetThere GPS nav for blind - apps on Google Play, November 2016. https://play.google.com/store/apps/details?id=com.LewLasher.getthere&hl=en Accessed Jan 2020
33. Ligero, R.: Beacons: the cornerstone of indoor positioning, September 2019. https://accent-systems.com/blog/beacons-the-cornerstone-of-indoor-positioning/. Accessed Jan 2020
34. Lin, B.S., Lee, C.C., Chiang, P.Y.: Simple smartphone-based guiding system for visually impaired people. Sensors **17**(6), 1371 (2017)
35. Lin, S., Wang, K., Yang, K., Cheng, R.: KrNet: a kinetic real-time convolutional neural network for navigational assistance. In: Miesenberger, K., Kouroupetroglou, G. (eds.) ICCHP 2018. LNCS, vol. 10897, pp. 55–62. Springer, Cham (2018). https://doi.org/10.1007/978-3-319-94274-2_9
36. Lin, T.-Y., et al.: Microsoft COCO: common objects in context. In: Fleet, D., Pajdla, T., Schiele, B., Tuytelaars, T. (eds.) ECCV 2014. LNCS, vol. 8693, pp. 740–755. Springer, Cham (2014). https://doi.org/10.1007/978-3-319-10602-1_48
37. Loomis, J., Golledge, R., Klatzky, R.: GPS-based navigation systems for the visually impaired. Fundamentals of Wearable Computers and Augmented Reality, January 2001
38. Masoud, M., Jaradat, Y., Manasrah, A., Jannoud, I.: Sensors of smart devices in the internet of everything (IOE) era: big opportunities and massive doubts. J. Sensors **2019**, 1–9 (2019)
39. Meliones, A., Filios, C.: Blindhelper: a pedestrian navigation system for blinds and visually impaired. In: Proceedings of the 9th ACM International Conference on PErvasive Technologies Related to Assistive Environments, p. 26. ACM (2016)
40. Murata, M., Ahmetovic, D., Sato, D., Takagi, H., Kitani, K.M., Asakawa, C.: Smartphone-based indoor localization for blind navigation across building complexes. In: 2018 IEEE International Conference on Pervasive Computing and Communications (PerCom), pp. 1–10. IEEE (2018)
41. Nield, D.: All the sensors in your smartphone, and how they work, August 2018. https://gizmodo.com/all-the-sensors-in-your-smartphone-and-how-they-work-1797121002. Accessed Jan 2020
42. Pirttimaa, I.: What is BlindSquare? September 2012. https://www.blindsquare.com/about/. Accessed Jan 2020
43. Pocket-lint: what is a ToF camera and which phones have one? March 2019. https://www.pocket-lint.com/phones/news/147024-what-is-a-time-of-flight-camera-and-which-phones-have-it. Accessed Jan 2020
44. Poggi, M., Mattoccia, S.: A wearable mobility aid for the visually impaired based on embedded 3D vision and deep learning. In: 2016 IEEE Symposium on Computers and Communication (ISCC), pp. 208–213. IEEE (2016)
45. Priyadarshini, M.: Which sensors do i have in my smartphone? how do they work? April 2019. https://fossbytes.com/which-smartphone-sensors-how-work/. Accessed Jan 2020
46. Rantala, J., et al.: Methods for presenting braille characters on a mobile device with a touchscreen and tactile feedback. IEEE Trans. Haptics **2**(1), 28–39 (2009)

47. Redmon, J., Farhadi, A.: Yolov3: an incremental improvement. arXiv preprint arXiv:1804.02767 (2018)
48. Shangguan, L., Yang, Z., Zhou, Z., Zheng, X., Wu, C., Liu, Y.: Crossnavi: enabling real-time crossroad navigation for the blind with commodity phones. In: Proceedings of the 2014 ACM International Joint Conference on Pervasive and Ubiquitous Computing, pp. 787–798. ACM (2014)
49. Sharma, S., SharmaSagar, S.: What is the use of accelerometer in mobile devices? October 2019. https://www.credencys.com/blog/accelerometer/. Accessed Jan 2020
50. Shen, H., Chan, K.Y., Coughlan, J., Brabyn, J.: A mobile phone system to find crosswalks for visually impaired pedestrians. Technol. Disabil. 20(3), 217–224 (2008)
51. Spiers, A.J., Dollar, A.M.: Design and evaluation of shape-changing haptic interfaces for pedestrian navigation assistance. IEEE Trans. Haptics 10(1), 17–28 (2016)
52. Spiers, A.J., Van Der Linden, J., Wiseman, S., Oshodi, M.: Testing a shape-changing haptic navigation device with vision-impaired and sighted audiences in an immersive theater setting. IEEE Trans. Hum. Mach. Syst. 48(6), 614–625 (2018)
53. Tillu, J.: Mobile sensors: the components that make our smartphones smarter, June 2019. https://medium.com/jay-tillu/mobile-sensors-the-components-that-make-our-smartphones-smarter-4174a7a2bfc3. Accessed Jan 2020
54. Ventola, C.L.: Mobile devices and apps for health care professionals: uses and benefits. Pharm. Therapeutics 39(5), 356 (2014)
55. Walkhighlands: Use of GPS and Smartphones as navigation aids, August 2012. https://www.walkhighlands.co.uk/safety/gps-smartphones.shtml. Accessed Jan 2020
56. Wang, R.J., Li, X., Ling, C.X.: Pelee: a real-time object detection system on mobile devices. In: Advances in Neural Information Processing Systems, pp. 1963–1972 (2018)
57. Watanabe, T., Miyagi, M., Minatani, K., Nagaoka, H.: A survey on the use of mobile phones by visually impaired persons in Japan. In: Miesenberger, K., Klaus, J., Zagler, W., Karshmer, A. (eds.) ICCHP 2008. LNCS, vol. 5105, pp. 1081–1084. Springer, Heidelberg (2008). https://doi.org/10.1007/978-3-540-70540-6_162
58. Weiss, M., Luck, M., Girgis, R., Pal, C.J., Cohen, J.P.: A survey of mobile computing for the visually impaired. ArXiv abs/1811.10120 (2018)
59. Yeo, K.: Bluetooth LE: a new standard that could enable smaller true wireless headphones, January 2020. https://www.hardwarezone.com.sg/tech-news-bluetooth-le-new-wireless-standard. Accessed Jan 2020
60. Zhang, X., Zhou, X., Lin, M., Sun, J.: ShuffleNet: an extremely efficient convolutional neural network for mobile devices. In: Proceedings of the IEEE Conference on Computer Vision and Pattern Recognition, pp. 6848–6856 (2018)

Designing System Architecture for the Catering Management System of Chang Gung Health and Culture Village

Ellie Li[1,3], Alice M. Wong[2,3(✉)], and Kevin C. Tseng[3,4(✉)]

[1] National Taiwan Normal University, Taipei, Taiwan
[2] Chang Gung Memorial Hospital, Taoyuan, Taiwan
walice@cgmh.org.tw
[3] Product Design and Development Lab, Taoyuan, Taiwan
ktseng@pddlab.org
[4] National Taipei University of Technology, Taipei, Taiwan

Abstract. In the past, due to the traditional diet service model in the long-term care institutes lack of information exchange between the dining service providers and the residents, it is difficult to understand the dietary needs and preferences of the residents accordingly so that reducing the satisfaction of meals and the diet healthcare of the residents. This study aims to design the architecture of an intelligent catering management system to assist institute manager, health professional nutritionist and cafeteria operator to resolve the data inconsistency problems of diet management. This study uses a systematic innovative product design and development approach (IPDD) to guide data collection and analysis, and build the interaction structure of the user behaviour model and complete the service system architecture. A tangible contribution of this study is to propose the architecture of an intelligent cantering management system to aid institute manager, health professional nutritionist and cafeteria operator to provide meal services, as well as to improve the satisfaction of the dining and to advance the diet healthcare of the residents.

Keywords: Catering service system · The elderly and health care

1 Introduction

With a rapidly ageing population, "the age-friendly health care service for the elderly" has become an essential issue in promoting older people's health [1]. Many studies have shown that an unhealthy diet is one of the leading causes of noncommunicable diseases. Besides, the risk of hypertension, hyperglycemia, hyperlipidemia, kidney disease and metabolic syndrome can increase with age [2]. Therefore, "the age-friendly health care service for the elderly" has become a significant issue that should be highly concerned. However, In Taiwan, 1.5% of the elderly over 60 years old live in senior communities. Their dietary health is mainly influenced by the meals provided by the canteens in the institutes. Most foods are served by the canteens in the senior communities, while the menu planning is limited by the food materials in season after referring to the health professional nutritionists' suggestions. However, some older

© Springer Nature Switzerland AG 2020
M. Antona and C. Stephanidis (Eds.): HCII 2020, LNCS 12189, pp. 584–596, 2020.
https://doi.org/10.1007/978-3-030-49108-6_42

people do not satisfy with the food provided due to the poor design of the menu planning, or they do not get used to the taste [3], or the dining environment lacks consideration of psychological and social needs [4], so they refuse to have meals in the canteen. But, from the manger's perspective of the senior community and the out-sourcing company of the cafeterias, how to save food preparation time, effectively use human resources, and control the cost are the most critical concerns in cafeteria management. Furthermore, the efficiency of nutritionists is often the biggest obstacle in improving the catering service [3].

A previous study [5] investigates 35 nutritionists through an open type semi-structured questionnaire to find out the problems and causes of the catering service in senior communities, as well as the improvement strategies as nutritionists suggest. In this study, nutritionists agree that enough calories and balanced nutrition can reduce the probability of illness, the discharge rate, the hospitalization rate, and the death rate of the residents. However, in nursing practice, the residents often complain about the poor design of the menu planning, or they do not get used to the dishes provided, or family members reflect that the elders do not eat the meal provided by the cafeterias. These are the most common problems that happen in senior communities and lead to malnutrition-caused health problems. However, the above issues related to senior communities' health care service are caused by not only meal problems, but also the institute's management, for instance, how to motivate the institute in developing catering service. Several issues need to be considered including cost and budget in the institute's oper-ation, so it is worth discussing the meal preparation time, the workforce for meal service, cost control, and the work efficiency of the nutritionists in future studies.

In addition, previous studies also suggest that for the elderly who lives in senior communities, the meal is not only a dietary activity providing nutrition, but also a social activity which shows the elderly's mental status, which should be highly con-cerned. If the elderly feel satisfied with the foods, they will be pleasant and full of expectation. If cafeteria owners can investigate the menu that the residents are inter-ested in, and serve these menus smarter, it is expected that the residents can enhance their life enjoyment and satisfaction [3]. Researchers [6] suggest that the team of professional chefs and nutritionists should change menus regularly. To achieve ideal long-term care, institutes must provide meals which are familiar to older people so that they can choose meals freely as they used to in their daily life [7]. In the future, the meal service for the elderly should consider their psychological needs in addition to the food itself [4]. Health Promotion Administration (HPA) suggests that tools should be designed for professionals to implement health assessment or investigation to improve the efficiency of health promotion and nursing [8]. The critical content and information about health promotion should be simplified to make users understand. A clear and understandable calory and nutrition facts should be popularized while encouraging cafeterias to provide healthy food with a menu indicated calories. The senior com-munity should provide a healthy diet course. The above research perspectives can be used as a reference for the design of this study.

In recent years, with the rapid development and perfection of information and communications technology (ICT), intelligent health care for the elderly is given more opportunities. Smart service can provide new integrated health care services through smart technology [9, 10, 11]. Because of this, it is a necessity to design an intelligent catering management system that applies to senior communities to assist institute managers, nutritionist and canteen operators to provide catering services.

2 Current Situation of Dietary Management in Chang Gung Health and Culture Village

This study chooses Chang Gung Health and Culture Village's (CGHCV) canteen as the experimental field. CGHCV is affiliated to Chang Gung Medical Foundation. In January 2005, Building A was officially opened and the central kitchen started to come into use. In 2015, the canteen in Building A was renovated, with the catering service method being changed. The vision of CGHCV is to provide the residents with a comfortable and safe environment, comprehensive health care, and diversified choices for relaxing. In terms of physical activity, mental cognition, productivity, and life satisfaction, CGHCV expects the elderly can enjoy a healthy and joyful living environment [12]. In terms of catering management, the researchers [6] find that when the elderly choose residence, they attach the greatest importance to health. However, most institutes of the senior community or retirement village rely on outsourcing meal service, which makes it difficult to control food nutrition or change menu in a short period, so that the resident's need to have decent meals is hard to be met.

Besides, in terms of technology-assisted catering management, by comparing the case in this study with the catering service situation in similar senior communities for the elderly (see Table 1), it can be found that intelligent services are still not applied in the catering sector even in large-scale senior communities in Taiwan. Therefore, the following problems can happen easily: untimely understanding of residents' needs results in low satisfaction; residents have various and convenient ways to buy food materials for cooking by themselves, which reduces the number of people eating in the canteen so that the senior communities' dietary care for the residents is affected.

Table 1. Meal service situation in similar senior communities

	CGHCV canteen	Ruenfu canteen
Cafeteria type	Set meal, lunch box, vegetarian food, noodles, banquet restaurant	Soft food, vegetarian food, noodles, stir-fry, banquet restaurant
Distinguishing feature	Healthcare image	Private service
Payment methods	Monthly settlement based on actual consumption	The total price of three meals per person per month is about NT$6,900, calculate the amount based on the actual number of meals
Indoor kitchen	Each household has an induction cooker and range hood available	Induction cooker can be used, each household is equipped with a range hood for use
Shopping method	7/11, Carrefour free shuttle	Shopping cart (accompanied by employees, picking up and out shopping)
Intellectual	No	No

In addition, the researchers found out through field research in CGHCV that the canteen has been in a poor operation since it was opened. CGHCV has more than 800 residents, but only 50% of the number of residents have meals in the canteen—about 450 diners for each meal, among them two-thirds are residents, one-third are employees. The failure to estimate the number of diners in the canteen results in a large number of leftovers and food waste.

Based on the interview data, this study sorts out CGHCV's catering management system (see Fig. 1) and its related problems. The current operating systems in the field of dietary care still needs to be improved. It cannot help staff to understand the needs of residents timely or change the menu regularly according to the preferences of residents, leading residents to complain that the menu never changes for years. Therefore, some of them prefer to take a shuttle bus to buy chicken, fish, and vegetables in the market, instead of having meals in the cafeteria, which affects the senior communities' dietary care for the residents. The residents are picky about the food taste, and also ask for an affordable price. When they have meals in the cafeteria, they concern about the dining environment and also have social needs. CGHCV arranges two health professional nutritionists to take care of the dietary health of more than 800 residents, which is a heavy workload. The cafeteria staff decides the amount of food during food preparation according to their experience, which can cause the problem of insufficient food or waste. Besides, the operator also bears the operating cost pressure, such as the cost for manual calculation of money. In the background that only 50% of residents having meals in the cafeteria and the cafeteria does not have a stable customer base, the operator lacks the database of the menu and food quantity. Therefore, it is effortful for them to collect the nutrition intake situation of residents and control the budget.

One of the current operating systems that CGHCV uses is the U-Care system (see Table 2), including personal health management, activity management, positioning system and personnel dispatch, notification of special health condition, and emergency medical system. This system has not involved an intelligent catering management system through which information can be exchanged between residents and the

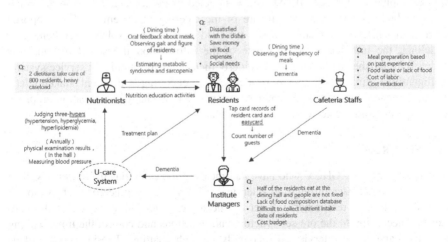

Fig. 1. CGHCV's catering management system.

cafeteria. Therefore, this study focuses on the design of an intelligent catering management system. Its purpose is to provide residents with meals which meet their expectation and have better taste and to assist institute manager, health professional nutritionist and cafeteria operator to provide residents with dietary and health services.

Table 2. U-Care System of CGHCV (sorted by the research of this study; information provided by the staff of CGHCV)

System	Function
Personal health management	Physiological data collection system, health data input system, health status analysis system, life reminder and information inquiry, health education system, personal multimedia centre, a dietary suggestion reminder system, and built-in hardware
Activity management	Indoor activity recording system, activity arrangement and suggestion system, and visitor and telephone recording system
Positioning system and personnel dispatch	Positioning system and medical personnel dispatch system
Notification of special health condition	Abnormal condition notification function, event tracking function, telemedicine consultation function, and special health condition identification system
Emergency medical system	Personal nursing data integration, and high-speed data transmission for the ambulance

3 The Proposed Architecture of the Catering Management System

The architecture of an intelligent catering management system is proposed to assist institute manager, health professional nutritionist and cafeteria operator to resolve the data inconsistency problems of the catering management. An innovative product design and development approach (IPDD) was conducted to guide data collection and analysis, and build the interaction structure of the catering management. The proposed catering management system is based on field research to explore user behaviour modelling, the intelligent service mode of the information flows and the business model. It establishes a comprehensive elderly dietary health intelligent service system, intelligent the dining process of residents, and encourages different stakeholders, including institute managers and cafeteria operators, to exchange information, improve service quality and create service value together.

3.1 Field Research

Recruit residents of CGHCV who have had meals in the cafeterias in Building A, then confirm the target user through an interview. The interview time for each person is about 0.5–1 h. The researcher will set up the topic, guide the direction of the conversation according to the pre-set structure and questions and control the time, making the participants to be interviewed relaxingly through chatting. The interview will be recorded and typed into verbatim transcriptions. The researcher will then summarize and analyze the interview records through Affinity Diagram, classify the key points, find out the common pattern from interviewees' experience to complete the classification and name them, conclude the theme and specific structure through user experience, and present the user experience by a visual diagram. The user behaviour model is established through Persona, that the residents of CGHCV are divided into information exploration type (target user), information acceptance type (potential user), and passive type towards information. Use the user journey map to present user experience of using the scenario design of the service flowchart of the system, and evaluate them in stages (Table 3).

The semi-structured interview is used to collect the experience, habits, needs, and expectations about catering service of 10 residents, including one male and nine females, aged between 63 and 81, with an average age of 72.9 years old. Two stakeholders are interviewed, including a staff of CGHCV and a health professional nutritionist. Both have worked in CGHCV for more than one year. They are familiar with the lifestyle, eating habits, dietary needs of residents, and the possible improvement in the future (see Table 4).

Table 3. Interviewee information.

No.	Gender	Age (years)	Education	Residence/Working time (years)	Smartphone experience	Identity
R1	Female	73	College degree	2	Yes	Resident
R2	Female	63	University degree	3	Yes	Resident
R3	Male	70	University degree	5	Yes	Resident
R4	Female	68	High school	5	Yes	Resident
R5	Female	75	College degree	2	Yes	Resident
R6	Female	68	University degree	5	Yes	Resident
R7	Female	78	High school	2	Yes	Resident
R8	Female	81	Primary school	5	Yes	Resident
R9	Female	76	Primary school	3.5	Yes	Resident
R10	Female	77	Primary school	3	Yes	Resident
S1	Male	42	University degree	1.5	Yes	Staff
N1	Female	39	University degree	7	Yes	Nutritionist

Questions for residents (see Appendix 1) include personal information, lifestyle, Internet use and information needs, commonly used information sources, and dietary situation. Questions for stakeholders include residents, cafeteria, and the intelligent service system. According to the interview result, the primary needs and problems can be summarized from four aspects as follows: (1) Most of the residents come from different regions. Their living backgrounds lead to diverse tastes. (2) Their ages are between 60 to more than 100 years old. The elder ones' teeth have degraded faster. Their different biting force results in a significant gap in requirements for the hardness of feed. (3) The residents require good heat preservation of dishes. (4) The menu repeats frequently. The main problem the managers encounter is that they cannot track the nutrition intake of the residents accurately. The problems that the health professional nutritionists encounter are that they have many kinds of work, and cafeteria food quality control occupies too many working hours, which results in a limited time to focus on health care for residents. Besides, the number of residents they are responsible for taking care of is too large. The main problems that the cafeteria encounters are that the chef cannot determine the number of residents who have meals in the cafeteria every day, resulting in insufficient food or an excessive amount of leftovers, as well as long food preparation time and high labour cost. The details are shown in the table below (see Table 4).

Table 4. Key words in interview results

	Before the meal	During the meal	After the meal	Cost
Residents	The dining time specified by the cafeteria does not match the circadian rhythm of the residents No food is served if coming to the cafeteria late Expect for special dishes in holidays to recommend to family and friends Get used to western breakfast Expect to slow down their eating speed, but it is hard to integrate into social groups if not eating in cafeterias often Get used to fixed seats The dishes are the same for lunch and dinner; unwilling to have dinner in the cafeteria	Bland/salty taste (region difference) Soft/hard taste (teeth degeneration due to age difference) The high repetition rate of dishes The unattractive outward appearance of the dishes No change in the cooking method of meat Expect new dishes would be developed regularly Dishes turn cold (served in small saucers) A small amount of food (served in small saucers) Dishes do not taste good (taste degradation) Expect the dishes and taste can be changed Tables are not clean; people speak loudly and throw down the dinner plate after eating (residents' quality)	Lack of security in electronic bookkeeping Malnutrition (satisfying with anything served. No requirement in taste) Meat can be a little more expensive. The amount of meat should be enough A large number of dumplings in the dish "dumplings in the soup" Small appetite; take lunch away for dinner	Expensive (shrewd in money matters)
Institute manager	Establish a food database, including prices and nutrients		Dine-in tableware is taken away (residents' quality) Unable to collect the data of nutrients resident intake	Water/electricity/gas subsidy for the cafeteria operator High as fee (to agree with residents' biting force, heat or steam the food materials first before frying)

(continued)

Table 4. (*continued*)

	Before the meal	During the meal	After the meal	Cost
Health professional nutritionist	Spend quite a long time to supervise kitchen/test dishes Balance the cafeteria operator's purchasing cost and the menu price	Observe the gait and stature of residents	Nutrition and health education activities	
Cafeteria staff	An uncertain number of diners		Insufficient dishes/a large amount of leftover (an uncertain number of diners)	Workforce cost Low efficiency of bill-paying in cash

3.2 System Framework

Figure 2 displays the system framework of the proposed catering management system. The user roles of the proposed system include the residents of CGHCV, institute managers, and cafeteria operators. The proposed system has its database to store the basic health data of the residents and the system required data and been able to retrieve the U-Care system data. Four user interfaces are designed and the flowchart (see Fig. 3) is established based on the needs of end-users. The functional design is divided into three aspects, including food management, social contact, and health management.

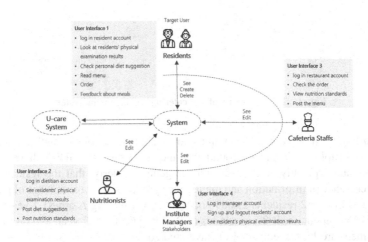

Fig. 2. System framework

4 Discussions

This study proposes the architecture of an intelligent catering management system to aid dieticians and cafeteria managers to resolve the data inconsistency problems of the catering management, as well as to improve the satisfaction of the dining and to advance the diet healthcare of the residents. The proposed system architecture intends to involve the perspectives from technology and user experience to design an intelligent catering management system, which encourages CGHCV managers, cafeteria operators and residents to exchange information actively to improve the quality of diet service. Therefore, persona-based journal maps were created and served as a research and design tool to understand the current catering journey of core user segments and to find opportunities to make improvements that add value for those groups. A user journey map (see Appendix 3) shows the problems that the core user may encounter when they first use the designed scenario of the catering services of the system and divides the residents' using process into three stages. The first stage is before having the meals; the second stage is the dining process in the cafeteria; the third stage is after having the meals, then analyze the users' touchpoints with the system, as well as their behaviours, thoughts and emotional changes.

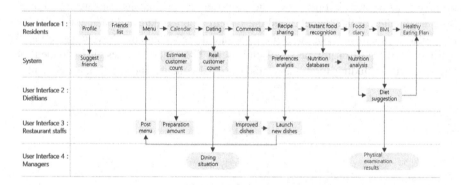

Fig. 3. The flowchart of the catering management system

According to the secondary data and semi-structured interviews with ten residents and two stakeholders, it can be found that the residents of CGHCV have obvious differences and typicality compared with the general elderly, that the residents have higher acceptance of information and intelligence products. The average age of residents is 79.7 years old (742 residents in 609 households of Building A are 81.1 years old on average; 121 residents in 108 households of Building C are 70.7 years old on average). Most of them are highly educated or have studied abroad. Many residents are mainlanders, which leads to a great diversity in dietary habits, more demands, and higher requirements. For the convenience of research and design, Persona (see Appendix 2) was created for the information exploration type and analyzes their character characteristics, dining characteristics, information acquisition channels, and the degree of intelligent product usage. In this study, three Personas of the residents of CGHCV were suggested according to their technology acceptance: information exploration type, information acceptance type, and the passive type towards information, and focuses on information exploration type as the main object of the study.

This study summarizes the reasons why residents do not want to have meals in the cafeteria, which can be divided into three aspects, including resident factors, cafeteria factors, and external factors. The resident factors include the difficulty to integrate into social groups unless having meals in the cafeteria frequently. The residents' taste preferences are different; the demand for the hardness of food is different. The diverse quality of residents' results in the dining environment needs to be improved. Residents expect the menu to be changed more often.

Cafeteria factors include: the dining time specified by the cafeteria does not match the circadian rhythm of the residents. No food is served if coming to the cafeteria late. No special dishes can be recommended to family and friends during the Spring Festival or holidays. The dishes are all Chinese style, with no dish they get used to in the past. To save costs and food preparation time, dishes for lunch and dinner are the same. Dishes in different cafeterias are the same. The menu changes once a quarter, resulting in a high repetition rate of dishes. The dishes' outward appearance is not attractive. No change in the cooking method of the main course. The food amount of the course is inappropriate. The heat preservation effect is quite unsatisfactory.

External factors include: the cafeteria of the nursing home, which locates opposite to CGHCV, is more attractive in taste. Free shuttle bus to Carrefour and Taipei are quite convenient. Family members bring a lot of food and 7–11 gift coupons while visiting the residents. The cafeteria and fruit store monopoly the market inside CGHCV, while the market price outside is more competitive. The above finding and perspectives can be used as a reference for the design of this study.

In this study, a tangible contribution of this study is to propose the architecture of an intelligent cantering management system to aid institute manager, health professional nutritionist and cafeteria operator to provide meal services, as well as to improve the satisfaction of the dining and to advance the diet healthcare of the residents.

Acknowledgements. The author(s) disclosed receipt of the following financial support for the research, authorship, and/or publication of this article: This work was supported in part by the Ministry of Science and Technology of Taiwan, ROC under Contracts MOST 108-2410-H-027-024-MY3, MOST 106-2628-H-027-001-MY3 and MOST 108-2622-8-027-007-TM1, by the Chang Gung Medical Foundation (grant nos. CMRPD3E0373, CMRPG5E0083, CMRPD2F0211, CMRPG5F0143, and CMRPD2F0213). The funders had no role in the study design, data collection and analysis, decision to publish, or preparation of the manuscript.

Appendix 1: Interview Outline

Interview Outline (Resident).

Item	Questions
Characteristics	1. What is your age? 2. Are you still working? If you are not working, what kind of work do you do before entering CGHCV? 3. What is the highest educational qualification that you have completed? The name of the school and department that graduated? 4. Does anyone come to visit you? How often? Do you have a meal together? Where would you choose to have a meal? What is the reason to choose?
Lifestyle	1. What are the activities of daily life? 2. Is there any goal or wish?
Digital product and internet usage	1. What smart products are used in daily life? 2. Have you used the Internet? What is the purpose of using the Internet? What difficulties have you encountered? 3. What are the common sources of information?
Meal situation	1. Do you have any dietary preferences or special needs? 2. When will you come to the cafeteria? How much time will it take? What is the process? 3. Who did you meet during the meal? How to communicate? 4. What factors influence your dining experience? What do you feel about these experiences? 5. Any suggestions for meal service? about dishes, quality, surrounding, process, etc.

Interview Outline (Stakeholder).

Item	Questions
Resident	1. What are the characteristics of the residents? 2. What dining habits do residents have? 3. What are the dietary health needs of residents?
Cafeteria	1. What is the status of cafeteria operations? 2. What difficulties did you encounter during the meal service? Is there any possibility of improvement in the future? 3. How to collect the dining needs and feedback of residents?
Intelligent service system	1. What information service systems are there? Where to provide services through smart technology? 2. What databases are available for residents' diets and health? What methods are used for data collection?

Appendix 2: Persona

JING-YA YANG

Gender	Female
Age	80
Provincial	Mainlander
Belief	Taoism
Family	Single, 2 daughters
Occupation	Retired Teacher

Description

- 156cm/56kg, silver short hair, fair and wrinkled skin with a little freckles on her hands;
- neat and tidy, dresses herself up, likes elegant clothing with flowers;
- speaks slowly and gently, optimistic, warm-hearted, takes the initiative to greet others;
- Rich but careful with money

Lifestyle

- The gentle pace of living, often watches TV, read books, seats on the massage chair, workouts in the morning, goes to the market or hospital

Digital product and internet usage

- Has smart phone, can use LINE/GOOGLE/iPad basic functions and take UBER to the airport

Learning ability

- Bachelor's degree, can speak English, likes to learn new things, gets information from friends/staffs/TV/newspaper

Eating habits and behaviors

- Has some special nutritional needs
- Likes dumplings,
- Likes light and delicate food

Appendix 3: User Journey Map

Journey	Before meal						During meal		After meal		
Activity	Make an appointment	View menu	See nutritional advice	Order	Electronic payment	View calendar	Feedback	Share	View health information	View bill	Get Gift Certificate
Emotion	No matching friends found	No satisfactory dishes	Have an easy-to-follow diet plan	Ordering is complicated	Insecure electronic checkout	Calendar with reminder function	Forget what ate before	Complex evaluation method / Enjoy to share with friends	Visualizing nutritional intake	Clear bill	Get coupon
Pain Point	Lack of meal friends	Dish satisfaction		Complicated operation	Sense of security		Poor memory, Operational ability				
Chance	Friend recommended	Recipe sharing		Simplified operation	Interactive design of e-payment		Simplify the evaluation system				

References

1. Health Promotion Administration: Senior Friendly Health Care Agency Certification 2.0 (Long-Term Care Agency Version) Operating Instructions. Health Promotion Administration, Taipei (2017). (in Chinese)
2. Health Promotion Administration: 2015 Taiwan Longitudinal Study in Aging. Health Promotion Administration Taiwan Aging Studies Series, 13 (2018). (in Chinese)
3. Mei-Ya, H., Yi-Chen, H., Chin-Hua, L., Ching-Chuan, H.: Using a PDCA cycle to improve residents' dietary satisfaction at a long-term care facility. J. Healthcare Manage. **15**(4), 327–341 (2014). (in Chinese)

4. Yu-Yun, W., Ben-Jeng, W.: Community for long - term care for elderly people dining innovative service model - take NP catering group as an example. In: Tunghai University, Executive Master of Business Administration Program (2017). (in Chinese)

5. Grace, Y., Chiu-Min, C., Ya-Fen, C., Frances Chang, M.: Survey on food service problems and solutions in long-term care institutions. J. Long-term Care **18**(3), 313–320 (2014)

6. Ye-Chuen, L., Chia-Ju, L.: Discuss new leisure living environment of the aged-service consideration factors of nursing home. J. Sport Leisure Hosp. Res. **7**(2), 65–84 (2012). (in Chinese)

7. Kuei-Mei, S., Chun-Mei, F.: Degree of satisfaction with happy meals served to residents of a nursing home. Nutri. Sci. J. **36**(2), 35–41 (2011). (in Chinese)

8. Health Promotion Administration: 2018 Health Promotion Administration Annual Report. Taipei: Health Promotion Administration (2018). (in Chinese)

9. Maglio, P.P.: Editorial Column-Smart Service Systems. Service. Science **6**(1), 1–2 (2014)

10. Wünderlich, N.V., Wangenheim, F.V., Bitner, M.J.: High tech and high touch: a framework for understanding user attitudes and behaviors related to smart interactive services. J. Serv. Res. **16**(1), 3–20 (2013)

11. Anttiroiko, A.V., Valkama, P., Bailey, S.J.: Smart cities in the new service economy: building platforms for smart services. AI Soc. **29**(3), 323–334 (2014)

12. Chang, H.-K., Chen, K.-W., Shih, T.-W., Ma, C.-M., Chou, Y.-M.: Design of a healthcare service flow management system-a case study of culture and health promotion village. Sun Yat-Sen Manage. Rev. **12**(6), 119–139 (2004)

Efficient Small-Scale Network for Room Layout Estimation

Ricardo J. M. Veiga$^{(\boxtimes)}$ ⓘ, Pedro J. S. Cardoso$^{(\boxtimes)}$ ⓘ,
and João M. F. Rodrigues$^{(\boxtimes)}$ ⓘ

LARSyS & ISE, University of the Algarve, 8005-139 Faro, Portugal
{rjveiga,pcardoso,jrodrig}@ualg.pt

Abstract. Retrieving the layout of different cluttered indoor scenes from monocular images is a challenging task, using a smaller deep neural network than the existing proposals. Previous geometric solutions are prone to failure in the presence of cluttered scenes because they depend strongly on hand-engineering features and the expectation of the possibility of the vanishing points' calculation. With the growth of neural networks, the geometric methods were either replaced or fused within the emerging area of deep learning. The more recent solutions rely on dense neural networks with additional adjustments, either by the calculation of the vanishing points, position based, or by layout ranking. All these methods presented valid solutions to this challenge with the flaw of being computationally demanding. Here, we present a more lightweight solution, running the segmentation on a smaller neural network and introducing a discriminative classifier for the posterior layout ranking and optimization. Our proposed method is evaluated by two standard dataset benchmarks, achieving near state of the art results even with a fraction of the required parameters than the available state of the art methods.

Keywords: Semantic segmentation · Layout estimation · Light-weight architecture

1 Introduction

The indoor layout estimation is an important task which allows us to predict an indoor environment's geometric limits, which as applications in the fields of augmented reality, indoor modeling [25,29,40], indoor navigation [1,41], robotics [2], virtual reality, and visual cognition [17,30].

The conventional geometrical form present on the vast majority of our day-to-day indoor environments is similar to a three-dimensional (3D) box or cuboid. Our main task, presented in this paper, is the delimitation and segmentation of an indoor environment's limits: walls, floor and ceiling, into corners and edges using only a single monocular image.

When we are inside any room, our viewpoint orientation and position defines the captured layout, which carries 3D information about the indoor scene.

© Springer Nature Switzerland AG 2020
M. Antona and C. Stephanidis (Eds.): HCII 2020, LNCS 12189, pp. 597–610, 2020.
https://doi.org/10.1007/978-3-030-49108-6_43

Fig. 1. LSUN dataset example. Left to right: input image, segmentation map, super-imposed segmentation map, superimposed edge map.

This is a challenge for monocular images due to the lack of a depth channel. These parametric rooms, where we consider the planes' boundaries to be perpendicular between each other, is normally referred as the Manhattan assumption [6]. Although it seems trivial for our eyes to find any common room's layout, it is a challenging task in the field of computer vision to estimate its boundaries. The complexity of this case increases exponentially when the indoor scene is cluttered with furniture and/or other objects.

Most of the challenges for monocular indoor layout estimation are not related to the rooms' architecture but to the additional amount of information distributed through the image. Although, in a cuboid room its boundaries converge to three mutually orthogonal vanishing points [34], which can be found by finding the 'Manhattan lines' [31] and their intersections points, indoor scenes are usually filled with additional expected or unexpected objects, whose nature and shape can influence the retrieval of the present environment's lines and corners. Due to the aleatory distribution of the clustered objects, we know that in most rooms, their boundary could be partially or completely occluded. Nonetheless, the same tridimensional shapes are present on most man-made constructions, which allows us to anticipate the presence of edges across the planes' intersections. Prior work, until the introduction of fully convolutional networks (FCN) to achieve pixelwise labelling [28], focused on obtaining the room's geometry through similar methods based on the location of the vanishing points.

Recent methods focus on the use of FCN or deep convolutional neural networks (DCNN), with encoder-decoder, iterative or double refinement architectures, either for the retrieval of edges, or segmentation of the present layout, room's points and type, or points and edges. There is normally present a posteriori refinement processing over the convolutional network result, which adjusts the layout reconstruction based on layout ranking, or position based. All the existing state-of-the-art methods already present significant results comparing with the ground-truth, either by corner or pixel error. Our presented approach introduces a novel implementation of the room layout estimation, which replaces the previous heavy backbones of VGG16, ResNet50, and ResNet101 for a more small-scale network aimed for mobile use, the MobileNetv2 for backbone network plus DeepLabV3 for semantic segmentation model, followed by a discriminative classifier and a sliding window for layout ranking and refinement. We used an input image resolution of 224 × 224, which is the default for MobileNetV2 and also, coincidentally, the same size used on one of the top three state-of-the-art methods [42].

The proposed method is an important step towards a cloudless indoor layout estimation due to its lightweight performance, aimed to edge or mobile devices implementations, which would benefit the human and robot interaction with our surroundings, being the main contributions of this paper: (a) the proposal of lightweight solution for indoor scenes layout estimation and (b) a novelty method for layout ranking refinement.

This paper is structured as follows. Related works and state of the art are reviewed in Sect. 2, followed by the description of the proposed method in Sect. 3. Experimental results are presented in Sect. 4. The concluding remarks and future work are drawn in Sect. 5.

2   Related Work

The main turning point for the indoor layout estimation was its reformulation as a structuring learning problem, firstly introduced by Hedau et al. [16], which also presented the first benchmark dataset for this kind of estimation. The idea to approximate a cuboid to a three-dimensional indoor scene was also presented and is derived from the Manhattan assumption [32]. Pixelwise geometric labels were also introduced: *left wall, middle wall, right wall, floor, ceiling, object*. The authors adapted techniques from Hoiem et al. [19] and divided their methodology in two stages. First, a large number of layout hypotheses are generated by multiple rays from three vanishing points [34], which were obtained by the Manhattan Lines [31]. Some of these hypothesis presented low accuracy due to the amount of clutter and were impossible to be recovered on the second stage. Afterwards, every hypothesis was scored and ranked using a structured regressor and the features from the labels to find the fitting cuboid with the highest ranking.

Similar layout hypothesis ranking were presented by Lee et al. [22], which associated the layouts to orientation maps generated by line segments that represented the different regions orientation. Gupta et al. [14] and Hedau et al. [17] introduced 3D object reasoning and estimation to refine the structured predictions. Wang et al. [39] used the indoor clutter to model the room layout. Del Pero et al. [9,10] used Markov Chain Monte Carlo (MCMC) [13] to search for the generative model parameters to extract the spatial layout of both the room as the cluttered objects. Similarly, Schwing et al. [36,37], also applied a dense sampling and introduced the integral geometry decomposition method for a efficient structure estimation [39]. Chao et al. [3] presented a different concept which uses human detections to estimate the vanishing points more accurately, improving highly cluttered indoor scenes 3D interpretation.

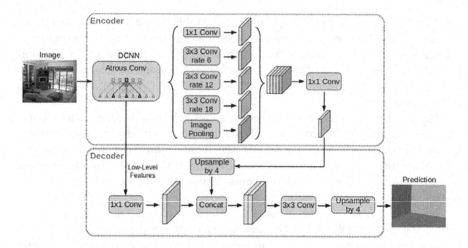

Fig. 2. DeepLabV3+ encoder-decoder architecture [5].

The evolution of convolutional neural networks (CNN) and the birth of the FCNs [27] started a new age of state of the art achievements in multiple computer vision topics, including semantic segmentation, scene classification and object detection. Mallya et al. [28] was the first proposed method exploring the FCNs to predict the informative edge maps, obtaining rough contours that were afterwards added as new features to the layout hypothesis ranking, together with the line membership [16] and geometric context [18]. Zhang et al. [43] continued this path exploring the deconvolutional networks, with and without fully connected layers. Afterwards, Dasgupta et al. [8], instead of learning edges, the authors used FCNs to predict semantic labels. Although the post-processing still relied on the vanishing lines to refine the results, the used previous edge map was replaced by a heat map of semantic surfaces. Ren et al. [33] proposed a refinement from the coarse result obtained by the a multi-task convolutional neural network (MFCN) [7] combining the layout contours and the surfaces properties.

Lee et al. [21] presented RoomNet, a novel formulation to the indoor layout problem, with an end-to-end network that estimates the locations of the room's layout keypoints instead of its edges. Also, Zhao et al. [45] introduced an unique solution estimating the edges through semantic segmentation and proposing a physics inspired optimization scheme. Zou et al. [46] and Sun et al. [38] explored retrieving the room spatial layout from single panoramic images, using similar methods to RoomNet [21] and also recurrent neural networks (RNN), like the long short-term memory (LSTM) architecture. Lin et al. [23] proposed the use of a deep fully convolutional neural network with a layout-degeneration method to remove the need for post-processing refinements. The Manhattan assumption [32] is also used in the Flat2Layout method [20], combining a pre-processing of vanishing points to a Resnet50 [15] to post-process into a flat room layout representation. Zhang et al. [42] presented a dual decoder network that is fed by the same encoder, obtaining simultaneously and edge and segmentation maps, which are then combined into the scoring function for ranking and refinement of the layout hypothesis estimation.

3   Method

3.1   Overview

As mentioned in the introduction, see Sect. 1, our objective is the delineation and segmentation of an indoor environment's limits walls, floor, and ceiling, see Fig. 1, from left to right: the input image, segmentation map, superimposed segmentation map, superimposed edge map.

In the context of indoor spatial layout estimation, most research methods proposed are based o the 'Manhattan World' assumption [32], where any room in an image contains three orthogonal directions coinciding on three vanishing points [34]. Hedau et al. [16] represented its layout model using the rays from the outside vanishing points and the inside frame vanishing point. Our proposed method doesn't rely on the vanishing points for training or refinement, but still follows the Manhattan assumption indirectly.

The estimation of a room layout can be divided in tree type of maps: edges, keypoints, and segmentation. Each of these heat maps have their advantages and disadvantages, according to the complexity of the input image: amount of clutter, type of room, occlusion of important spatial edges or corners, randomness of unusual objects. All the obtained results are pixelwise, or pixel-independent, and so each pixel of these maps contains the probability of belonging to a class. Edges maps consist of three layers to distinguish between the boundaries edges: wall-wall, wall-floor, wall-ceiling; or they only contain a single layer without differentiating the labels. The keypoints map consists of multiple layers for each keypoint that are scored afterwards. The segmentation heat map is formed by five layers, one for each label: left wall, center wall, right wall, floor, and ceiling.

Type 0   Type 1   Type 2   Type 3   Type 4   Type 5   Type 6   Type 7   Type 8   Type 9   Type 10

Fig. 3. Different type of room layouts available on LSUN. From left to right, each room type is indexed from 0 to 10 as in introduced by Zhang et al. [44]. On top we see the images, on the middle the segmentation maps, and on the bottom the edge maps.

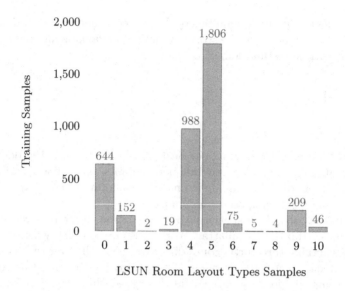

Fig. 4. Distribution of the amount of samples per type of the training images from the LSUN dataset.

Our proposed method adopts a semantic segmentation approach in conjugation with a discriminative classifier and layout refinement by a sliding window. The pipeline follows as described on Fig. 2, with the input image being fed into the MobileNetV2 network inside the DeepLabV3 semantic segmentation model, the coarsed layout result type is then classified by a support vectoring machine (SVM), and a type corresponding layout is slided vertically and horizontally over the previous obtained coarsed layout.

3.2   Network Architecture

An indoor scene can be captured from different viewpoints; the geometric layout present in that view can be approximated to one of the eleven types of layout present on the Large-scale Understanding Challenge (LSUN) dataset [44], as can be seen in Fig. 3. The ground truth of any room layout, either in a cluttered room or a open indoor scene, will coincide with some of the features that can be extracted from an image, such as the Manhattan lines. With the introduction of deep convolutional neural networks (DCNN) to tackle the room layout estimation, most of these low-level features and context clues were merged in end-to-end pipelines.

Similar to some previously proposed methods, we also used a encoder-decoder for semantic segmentation of the labels: *wall left, wall center, wall right, floor, ceiling.* With most of the state of the art results on the PASCAL VOC segmentation challenge [12] being achieved through the use of DCNN, it was a natural transition from the prior methods to the age of deep learning.

Table 1. Room layout estimation performance on Hedau [16] dataset.

Method	Year	Pixel error (%)	Training dataset
Hedau *et al.* [16]	2009	21.20	Hedau
Del Pero *et al.* [9]	2012	16.30	Hedau
DeLay [14]	2010	16.20	Hedau
Zhang *et al.* [43]	2016	14.50	Hedau
Ramalingam *et al.* [32]	2013	13.34	Hedau
Mallya *et al.* [28]	2015	12.83	Hedau+
Schwing *et al.* [37]	2012	12.80	Hedau
Del Pero *et al.* [10]	2013	12.70	Hedau
DeLay [8]	2016	9.73	Hedau
LayoutNet [46]	2018	9.69	LSUN
CFILE [33]	2016	8.67	Hedau
RoomNet [21]	2017	8.36	Hedau+LSUN
Edge Semantic [42]	2019	7.94	Hedau
Ours	**2020**	**7.63**	**LSUN**
Lin *et al.* [23]	2018	7.41	LSUN
Edge Semantic [42]	2019	7.36	LSUN
ST-PIO [45]	2017	6.60	SUNRGBD+LSUN
Flat2Layout [20]	2019	5.01	LSUN

Our proposed method was developed aimed to edge and mobile devices. Therefore, we chose a more lightweight implementation, replacing the common VGG16, ResNet101, and ResNet50 previously used with the MobileNetV2 as backbone and DeepLabV3 as the semantic segmentation model of our network. In Fig. 2 is possible to observe the DeepLabV3 architecture, as introduced in Chen et al. [4]. The first block, the DCNN, is where the MobileNetV2 lies. As was proposed by Sandler et al. [35], the use of shortcut connections between the bottlenecked layers allowed for a better preservation of relevant information throughout the network. Where the lightweight depthwise convolutions on the intermediate expansion layers allowed the filtering of non-linear features, which in this precise problem, is a benefit. With this framework as backbone, we are able to use only 4.52 million parameters, compared to the 138 millions of the VGG16. The DeepLabV3 model, with the proposed atrous spatial pyramid pooling module, which is a peculiar case of dilated residual networks, allows for a better probe of the convolutional features at multiple scales.

We fine-tuned a DeepLabV3 [4] model pre-trained on the PASCAL VOC 2012 dataset [12] with the network backbone of a MobileNetV2 [35] pre-trained on the MS-COCO dataset [24]. The information fed during the training to the network was the image and its semantic segmentation map, as can be seen on top and middle in Fig. 3.

Table 2. Room layout estimation performance on LSUN [44] dataset.

Method	Year	Pixel error (%)	Corner error (%)
Hedau *et al.* [16]	2009	24.23	15.48
Mallya *et al.* [28]	2015	16.71	11.02
DeLay [8]	2016	10.63	8.20
RoomNet [21]	2017	9.86	6.30
CFILE [33]	2016	9.31	7.95
Ours	**2020**	**6.94**	**5.46**
Flat2Layout [20]	2019	6.68	4.92
Edge Semantic [42]	2019	6.58	5.17
Lin *et al.* [23]	2018	6.25	–
ST-PIO [45]	2017	5.29	3.84

4 Experimental Results

4.1 Layout Refinement

During the training of the network, we also trained a discriminative classifier. Inspired by the famous MNIST digits handwritten recognition [11], we trained a supporting vector machine (SVM) with the edges layouts, as the ones present on the bottom of Fig. 3.

After we obtained a coarse semantic segmentation from the DeepLabV3 model, we isolated its edges to became a binary image and fed it to the SVM to classify the room type, performing a layout hypothesis ranking. With the obtained result, we use randomly the original corresponding layout types. We called this stage the sliding window, as inspired by the single shot detectors (SSD) method [26]. Starting in the middle, with an additional margin of 5 pixels to each side, we move the image left and right, up and down, creating a heat map based on the coinciding edges between the neural network and the multiple layout templates. Afterwards, when the heat map coincides, or we pass of a maximum of 100 layout estimations, we assume the pixelwise maximum values across the heat map as the estimated layout. Is important to note that the LSUN dataset has unbalanced room layout types, which can be further analysed on Table 2. Therefore, when a room layout type, limited to a lower sampling, if the heat map obtained by the sliding window does not coincide, the next in the ranking obtained by the SVM is considered as a possibility.

4.2 Datasets

Our network was trained on the LSUN room layout dataset [44], which contains a diverse collection of indoor scenes organized in: *bedroom, classroom, conference room, dinette home, dining room, hotel room, living room, and office.* All the

Fig. 5. Examples of room layout estimations using our method on the LSUN dataset. From left to right: input image, semantic segmentation ground truth, our network prediction, final estimation after refinement.

provided layouts can be approximated to cuboids and are also divided in 11 different types of layouts, as can be seen in Fig. 3. The dataset is composed of 4000 training images, 394 validation images, and 1000 testing images, but since there are no public ground truth labels for testing, we split the whole dataset, not using only the validating set, as in previous work [33]. This dataset is unbalanced in terms of type distribution, as is shown in Fig. 4, which influences its ability to properly generalize and predict the under-sampled room layout types. We also performed tests on the Hedau [16] dataset, which is consisted of 209 training images and 104 testing images, using our LSUN pretrained model. Mallya et al. [28] also introduced an augmentation of the Hedau dataset [16] called Hedau+, but we didn't use it in our benchmarks.

4.3 Accuracy

The performance evaluation is measured by two standard metrics: pixel error, and corner error. On the Hedau [16] dataset, only the pixel error was measured.

The pixel error consists on measuring the pixelwise accuracy of the obtained layout with the ground truth, across all images, and average it. The corner error is relative to the Euclidean distances between the obtained corners and their associated ground truth, averaged across all images. The LSUN room layout challenge dataset [44] provides a toolkit to measure this evaluations.

4.4 Experimental Results

We trained the network only on the LSUN dataset [44], but also performed the evaluation measuring on the Hedau [16] dataset. The LSUN dataset presents a wide range of resolutions, therefore, we rescaled to 224 × 224 using bi-cubic interpolation prior to training. We also performed image augmentation while training by colour shifts, cropping, horizontal flipping, and jittering. Vertical flipping wasn't considered due to the nature of the room's orientation.

Table 1 compares the efficiency of the different available methods on the Hedau dataset, since the Hedau et al. [16] publication. This benchmark only has pixelwise error evaluation. Note that the state of the art present in this benchmark was achieved using a different dataset for training. Even though our method was trained only on the LSUN dataset, we were still able to obtain good results and generalization, although there were some peculiar cases where we obtained divergent results, some of this results are demonstrated in Fig. 6.

On Table 2, we compare the obtained results using the LSUN toolkit. Here we have a pixelwise error rate and also a corner error. Although our results seem average, it is important to notice that we are achieving results over the average with a more smaller neural network. Some of the obtained room layout results are demonstrated in Fig. 5.

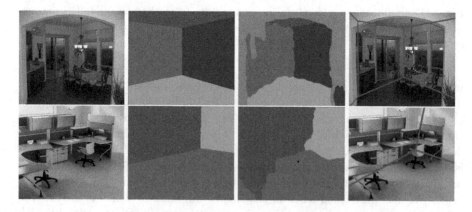

Fig. 6. Examples of some failures in the room layout estimation using our method on the LSUN dataset. From left to right: input image, semantic segmentation ground truth, our network prediction, final estimation after refinement.

The proposed algorithm was implemented using tensorflow on a PC with an Intel i9-9900K CPU and a Nvidia GTX 2070 Super, with the semantic segmentation being obtained in 12 ms, and the posterior refinement in 9 ms. While these results are achieved on a personal computer (PC), the authors are already developing an implementation on a mobile device.

5   Conclusions and Future Work

We presented an efficient room layout estimation method based on a smaller neural network, with MobileNetV2 as backbone and DeepLabv3 as the semantic segmentation model, with a posterior process of layout ranking based on a discriminative classifier of the edges and a sliding window method to refine the layout estimation. Our method is the first to implement a MobileNetV2 plus DeepLabv3 network for room layout estimation, with only a fraction of the parameters used on previous methods: VGG16 has 138 million, ResNet101 has 44.5 million, ResNet50 has 25.6 million, MobileNetV2 has 4.52 million. Even that our proposed method doesn't outperform the current state of the art, we demonstrated that a network with a fraction of the parameters can achieve near state of the art results in either the Hedau, as the LSUN, datasets.

Future work will focus on implementing our method on edge and mobile devices, improving the sliding window method, and also transitioning and evaluating our method with a backbone of MobileNetV3, small and large, plus DeepLabV3+.

Acknowledgements. This work was supported by the Portuguese Foundation for Science and Technology (FCT), project LARSyS - FCT Plurianual funding 2020–2023.

References

1. Boniardi, F., Caselitz, T., Kümmerle, R., Burgard, W.: A pose graph-based localization system for long-term navigation in CAD floor plans. Robot. Auton. Syst. **112**, 84–97 (2019)
2. Boniardi, F., Valada, A., Mohan, R., Caselitz, T., Burgard, W.: Robot localization in floor plans using a room layout edge extraction network. arXiv preprint arXiv:1903.01804 (2019)
3. Chao, Y.-W., Choi, W., Pantofaru, C., Savarese, S.: Layout estimation of highly cluttered indoor scenes using geometric and semantic cues. In: Petrosino, A. (ed.) ICIAP 2013. LNCS, vol. 8157, pp. 489–499. Springer, Heidelberg (2013). https://doi.org/10.1007/978-3-642-41184-7_50
4. Chen, L.-C., Papandreou, G., Schroff, F., Adam, H.: Rethinking atrous convolution for semantic image segmentation. arXiv:1706.05587 (2017)
5. Chen, L.-C., Zhu, Y., Papandreou, G., Schroff, F., Adam, H.: Encoder-decoder with atrous separable convolution for semantic image segmentation. In: Proceedings of the European conference on computer vision (ECCV), pp. 801–818 (2018)
6. Coughlan, J.M., Yuille, A.L.: The Manhattan world assumption: Regularities in scene statistics which enable Bayesian inference. In: Advances in Neural Information Processing Systems, pp. 845–851 (2001)

7. Dai, J., He, K., Sun, J.: Instance-aware semantic segmentation via multi-task network cascades. In: Proceedings of the IEEE Conference on Computer Vision and Pattern Recognition, pp. 3150–3158 (2016)

8. Dasgupta, S., Fang, K., Chen, K., Savarese, S.: Delay: robust spatial layout estimation for cluttered indoor scenes. In: Proceedings of the IEEE Conference on Computer Vision and Pattern Recognition, pp. 616–624 (2016)

9. Del Pero, L., Bowdish, J., Fried, D., Kermgard, B., Hartley, E., Barnard, K.: Bayesian geometric modeling of indoor scenes. In: 2012 IEEE Conference on Computer Vision and Pattern Recognition, pp. 2719–2726. IEEE (2012)

10. Del Pero, L., Bowdish, J., Kermgard, B., Hartley, E., Barnard, K.: Understanding Bayesian rooms using composite 3D object models. In: Proceedings of the IEEE Conference on Computer Vision and Pattern Recognition, pp. 153–160 (2013)

11. Deng, L.: The MNIST database of handwritten digit images for machine learning research [best of the web]. IEEE Signal Process. Mag. **29**(6), 141–142 (2012)

12. Everingham, M., Van Gool, L., Williams, C.K.I., Winn, J., Zisserman, A.: The pascal visual object classes challenge 2012 (voc2012) results (2012). http://www.pascal-network.org/challenges/VOC/voc2011/workshop/index.html (2011)

13. Gilks, W.R., Richardson, S., Spiegelhalter, D.: Markov Chain Monte Carlo in Practice. Chapman and Hall/CRC, Boca Raton (1995)

14. Gupta, A., Hebert, M., Kanade, T., Blei, D.M.: Estimating spatial layout of rooms using volumetric reasoning about objects and surfaces. In: Advances in Neural Information Processing Systems, pp. 1288–1296 (2010)

15. He, K., Zhang, X., Ren, S., Sun, J.: Deep residual learning for image recognition. In: Proceedings of the IEEE Conference on Computer Vision and Pattern Recognition, pp. 770–778 (2016)

16. Hedau, V., Hoiem, D., Forsyth, D.: Recovering the spatial layout of cluttered rooms. In: 2009 IEEE 12th International Conference on Computer Vision, pp. 1849–1856. IEEE (2009)

17. Hedau, V., Hoiem, D., Forsyth, D.: Thinking inside the box: using appearance models and context based on room geometry. In: Daniilidis, K., Maragos, P., Paragios, N. (eds.) ECCV 2010. LNCS, vol. 6316, pp. 224–237. Springer, Heidelberg (2010). https://doi.org/10.1007/978-3-642-15567-3_17

18. Hoiem, D., Efros, A.A., Hebert, M.: Geometric context from a single image. In: Tenth IEEE International Conference on Computer Vision (ICCV 2005), vol. 1, pp. 654–661. IEEE (2005)

19. Hoiem, D., Efros, A.A., Hebert, M.: Recovering surface layout from an image. Int. J. Comput. Vis. **75**(1), 151–172 (2007)

20. Hsiao, C.-W., Sun, C., Sun, M., Chen, H.-T.: Flat2Layout: flat representation for estimating layout of general room types. arXiv:1905.12571 (2019)

21. Lee, C.-Y., Badrinarayanan, V., Malisiewicz, T., Rabinovich, A.: RoomNet: end-to-end room layout estimation. In: Proceedings of the IEEE International Conference on Computer Vision, pp. 4865–4874 (2017)

22. Lee, D.C., Hebert, M., Kanade, T.: Geometric reasoning for single image structure recovery. In: 2009 IEEE Conference on Computer Vision and Pattern Recognition, pp. 2136–2143. IEEE (2009)

23. Lin, H.J., Huang, S.-W., Lai, S.-H., Chiang, C.-K.: Indoor scene layout estimation from a single image. In: 2018 24th International Conference on Pattern Recognition (ICPR), pp. 842–847. IEEE (2018)

24. Lin, T.-Y., et al.: Microsoft COCO: common objects in context. In: Fleet, D., Pajdla, T., Schiele, B., Tuytelaars, T. (eds.) ECCV 2014. LNCS, vol. 8693, pp. 740–755. Springer, Cham (2014). https://doi.org/10.1007/978-3-319-10602-1_48

25. Liu, C., Schwing, A.G., Kundu, K., Urtasun, R., Fidler, S.: Rent3D: floor-plan priors for monocular layout estimation. In: Proceedings of the IEEE Conference on Computer Vision and Pattern Recognition, pp. 3413–3421 (2015)
26. Liu, W., et al.: SSD: single shot multibox detector. In: Leibe, B., Matas, J., Sebe, N., Welling, M. (eds.) ECCV 2016. LNCS, vol. 9905, pp. 21–37. Springer, Cham (2016). https://doi.org/10.1007/978-3-319-46448-0_2
27. Long, J., Shelhamer, E., Darrell, T.: Fully convolutional networks for semantic segmentation. In: Proceedings of the IEEE Conference on Computer Vision and Pattern Recognition, pp. 3431–3440 (2015)
28. Mallya, A., Lazebnik, S.: Learning informative edge maps for indoor scene layout prediction. In: Proceedings of the IEEE International Conference on Computer Vision, pp. 936–944 (2015)
29. Martin-Brualla, R., He, Y., Russell, B.C., Seitz, S.M.: The 3D Jigsaw puzzle: mapping large indoor spaces. In: Fleet, D., Pajdla, T., Schiele, B., Tuytelaars, T. (eds.) ECCV 2014. LNCS, vol. 8691, pp. 1–16. Springer, Cham (2014). https://doi.org/10.1007/978-3-319-10578-9_1
30. Qiao, H., Li, Y., Li, F., Xi, X., Wu, W.: Biologically inspired model for visual cognition achieving unsupervised episodic and semantic feature learning. IEEE Trans. Cybern. **46**(10), 2335–2347 (2015)
31. Ramalingam, S., Brand, M.: Lifting 3D Manhattan lines from a single image. In: Proceedings of the IEEE International Conference on Computer Vision, pp. 497–504 (2013)
32. Ramalingam, S., Pillai, J.K., Jain, A., Taguchi, Y.: Manhattan junction catalogue for spatial reasoning of indoor scenes. In: Proceedings of the IEEE Conference on Computer Vision and Pattern Recognition, pp. 3065–3072 (2013)
33. Ren, Y., Li, S., Chen, C., Kuo, C.-C.J.: A coarse-to-fine indoor layout estimation (CFILE) method. In: Lai, S.-H., Lepetit, V., Nishino, K., Sato, Y. (eds.) ACCV 2016. LNCS, vol. 10115, pp. 36–51. Springer, Cham (2017). https://doi.org/10.1007/978-3-319-54193-8_3
34. Rother, C.: A new approach to vanishing point detection in architectural environments. Image Vis. Comput. **20**(9–10), 647–655 (2002)
35. Sandler, M., Howard, A., Zhu, M., Zhmoginov, A., Chen, L.C.: MobileNetv2: inverted residuals and linear bottlenecks. In: Proceedings of the IEEE Conference on Computer Vision and Pattern Recognition, pp. 4510–4520 (2018)
36. Schwing, A.G., Fidler, S., Pollefeys, M., Urtasun, R.: Box in the box: joint 3D layout and object reasoning from single images. In: Proceedings of the IEEE International Conference on Computer Vision, pp. 353–360 (2013)
37. Schwing, A.G., Hazan, T., Pollefeys, M., Urtasun, R.: Efficient structured prediction for 3D indoor scene understanding. In: 2012 IEEE Conference on Computer Vision and Pattern Recognition, pp. 2815–2822. IEEE (2012)
38. Sun, C., Hsiao, C.-W., Sun, M., Chen, H.-T.: HorizonNet: learning room layout with 1D representation and pano stretch data augmentation. In: Proceedings of the IEEE Conference on Computer Vision and Pattern Recognition, pp. 1047–1056 (2019)
39. Wang, H., Gould, S., Koller, D.: Discriminative learning with latent variables for cluttered indoor scene understanding. In: Daniilidis, K., Maragos, P., Paragios, N. (eds.) ECCV 2010. LNCS, vol. 6314, pp. 497–510. Springer, Heidelberg (2010). https://doi.org/10.1007/978-3-642-15561-1_36
40. Xiao, J., Furukawa, Y.: Reconstructing the world's museums. Int. J. Comput. Vis. **110**(3), 243–258 (2014)

41. Xu, Q., Li, L., Lim, J.H., Tan, C.Y.C., Mukawa, M., Wang, G.: A wearable virtual guide for context-aware cognitive indoor navigation. In: Proceedings of the 16th International Conference on Human-Computer Interaction with Mobile Devices & Services, pp. 111–120. ACM (2014)

42. Zhang, W., Zhang, W., Gu, J.: Edge-semantic learning strategy for layout estimation in indoor environment. IEEE Trans. Cybern. **50**, 2730–2739 (2019)

43. Zhang, W., Zhang, W., Liu, K., Gu, J.: Learning to predict high-quality edge maps for room layout estimation. IEEE Trans. Multimed. **19**(5), 935–943 (2016)

44. Zhang, Y., Yu, F., Song, S., Xu, P., Seff, A., Xiao, J.: Large-scale scene understanding challenge: room layout estimation. In: CVPR Workshop (2015)

45. Zhao, H., Lu, M., Yao, A., Guo, Y., Chen, Y., Zhang, L.: Physics inspired optimization on semantic transfer features: an alternative method for room layout estimation. In: Proceedings of the IEEE Conference on Computer Vision and Pattern Recognition, pp. 10–18 (2017)

46. Zou, C., Colburn, A., Shan, Q., Hoiem, D.: LayoutNet: reconstructing the 3D room layout from a single RGB image. In: Proceedings of the IEEE Conference on Computer Vision and Pattern Recognition, pp. 2051–2059 (2018)

Low-Resolution Retinal Image Vessel Segmentation

Hasan Zengin[1]📷, José Camara[2], Paulo Coelho[3,6(✉)]📷,
João M. F. Rodrigues[4]📷, and António Cunha[5,6]📷

[1] Mehmet Akif Ersoy University, Burdur, Turkey
[2] Universidade Aberta, Porto, Portugal
[3] Polytechnic Institute of Leiria, Leiria, Portugal
paulo.coelho@ipleiria.pt
[4] LARSyS and ISE, Universidade do Algarve, Faro, Portugal
[5] University of Trás-os-Montes and Alto Douro, Vila Real, Portugal
acunha@utad.pt
[6] INESC TEC - Institute for Systems and Computer Engineering,
Technology and Science, Porto, Portugal

Abstract. Segmentation process serves to aid the pathology diagnosing process since segmentation filters the interference from other anatomical structures and helps focus on the posterior segment structures of the eye, highlighting a set of signals that will serve for diagnosis of various retinal pathologies. Automatic retinal vessel segmentation can lead to a more accurate diagnosis. This paper presents a framework for automatic vessel segmentation of lower-resolution retinal images taken with a smartphone equipped with D-EYE lens. The framework is evaluated and the attained results were presented. A dataset was assembled and annotated of train models for automatic localisation retinal areas and for vessel segmentation. For the framework, two CNN based models were successfully trained, a Faster R-CNN that achieved a 96% correct detected of all regions with an MAE of 39 pixels, and a U-Net that achieved a DICE of 0.7547.

Keywords: Faster R-CNN · U-Net · Low-resolution retinal images · Segmentation · Screening

1 Introduction

Advances in science, especially in technological field, have improved the computing power of devices, and have enabled the development of information in medical imaging and medical diagnostics, the called Computer-Aided Diagnosis (CAD) systems, that can assist physicians in various tasks such as measuring anatomical structures, monitoring changes by comparing sequential images, diagnosing and planning treatment. They also prevent fatigue errors and increase work efficiency. In the ophthalmological field, such advances have enabled the primary

© Springer Nature Switzerland AG 2020
M. Antona and C. Stephanidis (Eds.): HCII 2020, LNCS 12189, pp. 611–627, 2020.
https://doi.org/10.1007/978-3-030-49108-6_44

prevention and early detection of pathologies that evolve asymptomatically and whose treatment may delay the deleterious effects of visual function. Many CAD systems are not yet used in clinical practice for several reasons. Claro et al. [5] discuss that retinal images that may have very different qualities due to various types of lesions and artefacts that make it difficult to design an image processing algorithm that is capable of handling a large number of retinal images. There are several algorithms for retinal image processing in the literature and different groups of researchers use different image bank metrics to track the performance of these algorithms, making it difficult to compare methods.

Retinal image became an important topic for the diagnosis serving as a diagnostic parameter for early and late retinal diseases as well as follow the evolution of numerous diseases such as diabetic retinopathy, hypertension, vascular diseases (arterial and venous occlusions), autoimmune diseases, glaucoma, senile macular degeneration, tumours, retinal detachment, among others.

In clinical practice, retinal structures may be visualized under myosis (undilated pupil) or mydriasis (artificially dilated pupil using anticholinergic and adrenergic drugs). The pupil represents a natural diaphragm of the eye that regulates the amount of external light and its diameter may vary from one individual to another. Viewing the retina under myosis allows for greater patient comfort but viewing a smaller fundus field. Visualization under mydriasis allows for a larger field of retinal visualization but may result in greater patient discomfort due to photophobia (increased sensitivity to external light) until the effect of instilled mydriatic drug decreases. To minimize and prevent the effects and pathology progression, laser therapy in the earliest stages of diabetic retinopathy is often recommended, although the success of such intervention depends on precocious detection and regular checkup/follow up by an ophthalmologist. Several methods have been proposed for early diagnosis of this disease [14] such as scanning laser ophthalmoscope, angiography, optical coherence tomography and fundus camera [13,15], which has been known as one of the primary methods for retinopathy screening [26]. Also, recent advances in image processing have promoted the diffusion of their application to several fields, including the areas of medical sciences, in particular, ophthalmology. A reliable procedure to evaluate retinopathies early is the structural analysis of retinal vessel network - the only blood vessel network of the body that is visible in a non-invasive imaging method [6]. Retinal images are taken with fundus cameras that produce high-quality and high-resolution retinal images for this analysis. Then, with vessel segmentation, interference from other anatomical structures are filtered, helping to obtain the focus of interest on posterior segment structures of the eye. This highlights a set of signals that will serve for diagnosis of various pathologies, such as, early changes in diabetic retinopathy (microaneurysms, microhemorrhages, cotton wool exudates), glaucoma (optic disc haemorrhages, delineation of the excavation and the outer limit of the optic papilla), and senile macular degeneration (coalescent druses, vascularization in the macular region). Manually segment retinal veins is a burdening task, highly time- and cost-consuming, therefore, investigations of automatic or semi-automatic methods for vessel segmentation have been evolving to assist specialists [2,20].

For treatment, early diagnosis has high-importance value. Detection needs regular retinal imaging, and this is a sort of process which is followed by taking high-resolution photos taken by expensive machines like fundus cameras, Optos UWF and Centervue's Eidon. However, the use of low-cost lenses using non-mydriatic pupils can bring several advantages besides economy, greater portability and ease of use and greater patient comfort, on the other hand, decreasing the quality of the photos obtained.

The latest trends in research show the extensive use of convolution neural networks (CNN) for the segmentation of retinal vessels and detection of the disease [7], beyond many other methods [20]. Nevertheless, a mutual aspect of the methods is that all focused on segmenting vessels with high-resolution retina images. The appearance of low-resolution retinal images obtained with low-cost devices suitable for the observation of retinal lesions is an opportunity to promote the dissemination of eye disease screening tests. The produced images have a small aperture and low quality. Although studies have already been published to prove the usefulness of these images, there is still a lack of studies to evaluate the effectiveness of automatic methods to segment retinal vessels in this type of image. These low-resolution and low-quality retinal images create extra difficulties in the use of traditional vessel segmentation methods [28].

This paper presents a framework focused on the vessels segmenting on lower-resolution retinal images taken with a smartphone equipped with D-EYE lens. The D-EYE [1] is a low-cost lens that can be attached to the lens of a smartphone to get undisturbed pupil background photos and videos with the added advantage of bringing more comfort to the patient with the disadvantage of not having the necessary sharpness when used in eyes with small pupils, in eyes with opacity of media (keratitis, cataract), in very bright environments, with the patient not collaborating. It is able to capture up to 20° under miosis at the posterior pole of the eye depending on individual pupil size.

A dataset was created with 26 retina videos around the optic disc, with lower-resolution images, and annotated two subsets, one with the localization of the retinal visible area and other with vessel segmentation. Here, a framework is proposed to provide the first step for a mobile solution to segment retinal vessels around the optic disc. The framework has two main steps: (a) The detection of the optic disc region using a Faster R-CNN and (b) visible vessel segmentation made by U-Net, trained with the mentioned dataset.

The main contributions of the paper are: (i) a low-resolution dataset created using D-EYE vessel annotation, (ii) a low-cost retinal vessel segmentation framework.

Section 2 presents and discusses the related work; Sect. 3 describes and illustrated the created dataset. Section 4 describes in detail the framework for low-resolution vessel segmentation, Sect. 5 presents the tests and attained results, and Sect. 6 finalizes the paper with discussion and conclusions.

2 Related Works

Image segmentation is the process of partitioning a digital image into multiple sets of pixels, in order to change its representation into something more meaningful and easier to analyze. Due to its wide range of applications, this process has become an attractive process in the image processing research area and, thus, a high number of algorithms have been developed over the years, including for the retinal vessel segmentation purpose.

Images used in published retinal vessel segmentation studies are taken with fundus cameras, that are expensive equipment that produces high-quality and high-resolution retinal images. The emergence of low-cost solutions, such as the taken from smartphones equipped with D-EYE [1], has given rise to evaluation and publications of their clinical employment. For example, in [28], a preference study was made between the use of a smartphone equipped with D-EYE lens and the use of the direct ophthalmoscope. 92% of the medical students that participated claimed their preference for use D-EYE. In [16], ophthalmologists deduced that smartphone captured fundus images are readable by experts, with an average between 86% and 100%, and they have an acceptable quality in 93%–100% for cataract patients. Vilela et al. [25] presented a meta-analysis study to check the agreement between retinal images obtained via smartphones and images obtained with retinal cameras or fundoscopic exams, claiming a very strong agreement between smartphone-based fundoscopic images and clinical examinations gold standards, so this resource can facilitate medical student learning and can also be an assessment for unprivileged or remote populations.

To the best of our knowledge, no studies have been published to evaluate vessel segmentation methods in low-resolution fundus images such as the taken from smartphones equipped with D-EYE.

The published methods for vessel segmentation of retinal images with high-quality and high-resolution retinal images use both supervised and unsupervised methods [2,10]. Supervised methods, such as support vector machine (SVM) and artificial neural network (ANN), have been used with a great impact on medical imaging segmentation and classification due to their increased performance. The unsupervised methods are used to discover hidden patterns from blood vessel from the retinal images [2]; they are out of the scope of this work.

Tuba et al. [23] proposed an overlapping block-based method characterised by SVM classification, whose features were obtained from discrete cosine transform (DCT) coefficients and chromaticity. Although this algorithm presents the advantage to classify large retinal vessels accurately, it is limited to classify thinner vessels. Wang et al. [27] proposed an algorithm where a vector containing 30 features of every pixel of the retinal image was formed containing features in Gaussian scale space, multiscale Gabor filter, and the vector field divergence. These feature vectors were then used as input to an SVM classifier. The authors claimed an improved segmentation performance and a reduced running time.

Jiang et al. [11] proposed a method that applies a deep fully convolutional neural networks (FCN), which integrate novel methods of data preprocessing, data augmentation, and full convolutional neural networks. The authors claim that the proposed framework achieves state-of-the-art vessel segmentation performance in all three public benchmark tests, the datasets DRIVE [21], STARE [9] and CHASE_DB1 [17].

Some works are presented by applying the well-known U-Net [19] network and its modifications. Jin et al. [12] proposed deformable U-Net (DUNet) using U-shape structures and local features to perform retinal vessel segmentation in an end-to-end method. The up-sampling operators used in DUNet improve the output resolution, capture the contextual information, and to facilitate specific localization by combining both high- and low-level features. Another approach is LadderNet [29], which can be considered as a chain of multiple U-Nets and benefits from multiple paths of information flow, which provides the potential to capture more complicated features and produce a higher accuracy. Other authors proposed methods based on U-Net, both a Recurrent Convolutional Neural Network (RCNN) – RU-Net [3], where recurrent convolutions are applied before down-sampling, before up-sampling and before outputting the segmentation map, and also a Recurrent Residual Convolutional Neural Network (RRCNN) – R2U-Net [3], where residual learning is added to the convolutional unit.

3 Dataset

To train and evaluate the proposed platform, three datasets were used: dataset 1 (DS1), dataset 2 (DS2) and dataset 3 (DS3) - see Table 1.

Table 1. Image datasets used to train and evaluate the framework.

	DS1	DS2	DS3
Resolution (pixels)	1920×1080	320×320	80×80
Train	18 videos; 3,881 images (64%)	2 videos; 252 images (73%)	14 images; 1,967 patches (70%)
Validation	3 videos; 776 (13%)	1 video; 40 images (11%)	3 images; 421 patches (15%)
Test	5 videos; 1,375 images (23%)	1 video; 55 images (16%)	3 images; 422 patches (15%)
Total	26 videos; 6,060 images	4 videos; 347 images	20 images; 2,810 patches

A dataset of 26 low-resolution videos of the optic papilla under myosis (undilated pupil) was captured from the left and right eyes of 19 volunteers to train and evaluate this framework. The videos have an average of 15–20 s, were captured with an iPhone S6 with a D-EYE lens attached to the camera, present 1920×1080 pixels resolution at 15 frames per second. The videos obtained have low quality due to factors such as light diffraction according to pupil size, media opacity, optical axis alignment, physiological eye intrinsic movements, and eyelid ptosis.

The videos were split into single images and organized in two different datasets, dataset1 (DS1) to be used in the detection of the retinal visible area, and the dataset2 (DS2) to be used in the segmentation of the retinal veins.

For the dataset1, the video-images were manually separated into two folders: "good images" when the retinal area and their veins are visible; and "bad images" for the remain. 4,657 images were selected and their retinal region labelled with the LabelImg software [24]. For the dataset2, 347 images were selected and manually segmented their veins with the labelling software Sensarea [4]. A square patched image was created based on the predicted outbox centre with 320×320 pixels and zeroing the out pixels of the image, as can be seen in Fig. 1.

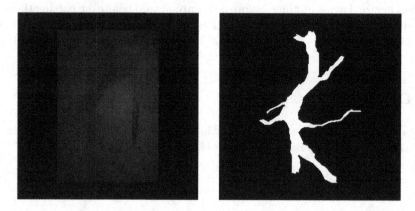

Fig. 1. At left, a high-resolution retina image with the zoomed optic-disk; At right, a low-resolution retina image with a zoomed area of the retina, both from the same eye.

Additionally, as dataset3 (DS3), a training set of retina public dataset DRIVE: Digital Retinal Images for Vessel [21] was used for pre-training a segmentation CNN. It is composed of 20 colour images with 565×584 pixels acquired using a Canon CR5 non-mydriatic 3CCD camera with a 45-degree field of view (FOV) and their manual segmentation of the vasculature mask. Dataset2 images have larger dimensions than those in the DRIVE dataset. To adjust veins dimensions between both datasets, it was decided to obtain dataset2 patches subsample images with 80×80 pixels, as shown in Fig. 2.

Fourteen images were used for the train set (producing 1,967 patches), 3 for the validation (producing 421 patches), and 3 for the test set (producing 422 patches).

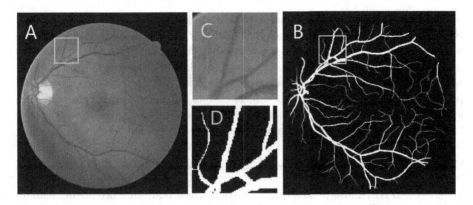

Fig. 2. Example of DRIVE dataset and patches created for dataset3: (A) retina image; (B) veins mask; (C) image patch; and (D) veins patch mask.

4 Framework for Low-Resolution Vessel Segmentation

The proposed framework for low-resolution vessel segmentation has two main steps (see Fig. 3): the (A) detection of the retinal visible area and the (B) vessel segmentation.

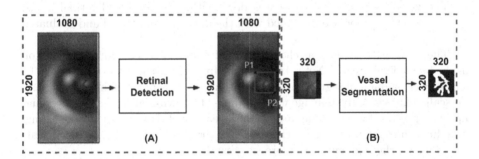

Fig. 3. Pipeline diagram for the proposed low-resolution vessel segmentation framework.

The detection of the retinal visible area (A) consists in to compute the location of a rectangle defined by P1 and P2, that encloses the visible area in the image (the area of interest). In this case, input images have 1920×1080 pixels, due to the D-EYE low lens aperture the area of interest has up to 320×320 pixels.

In this work, it was used a Faster R-CNN model although there is an enormous amount of object/region detection methods applied to computer science. Specifically, the Fast R-CNN [8] and the Faster R-CNN [18] were considered due to its low system requirements and fast computation for classifying object characteristics. Both models extract feature maps from the input image using CNN.

After this operation instead of selective search like in Fast R-CNN [8], in Faster R-CNN it takes region proposal network (RPN), that making this approach more advanced to feature extraction. Conceptually, Faster R-CNN is composed of 3 independent neural networks: the feature network (FN), the region proposal network (RPN) and the detection network (DN). The FN is applied to extract and produce relevant features from the images, so its output maintains the structure and shape of the original image. The RPN is usually constituted by a 3 convolutional layer network, where there is a common layer that feeds the following ones. One is used for classification purposes and the other for bounding box regression. The RPN main purpose is to generate a certain number of bounding boxes, with a high probability of containing an object. The DN takes input from both FN and RPN, and produces the final class and bounding box, being usually composed of 4 Fully Connected layers.

To evaluate the model, the Mean Absolute Error (MAE) defined in the Eq. 1 is a commonly used metric since it permits to measure the accuracy for continuous variables.

$$MAE = \frac{1}{N} \sum_{i=1}^{N} |y_i - \widehat{y_i}|, \tag{1}$$

where N is the number of variables, y_i is the ground truth value and $\widehat{y_i}$ is the predicted variable. In this case, it was used four variables, two for the coordinates of the upper left corner and the other two for the lower right corner.

The vessels segmentation (B) was done within the detected retinal areas, with a U-Net [19] model pre-trained with the dataset3 and tuned and evaluated with dataset2.

The U-Net [19] model was chosen due to its proven success for segmentation in the biomedical area. U-Net takes its name from the architecture shaped as 'U' letter. It is common in segmentation operations because of matching pooling and up-scaling layers. A given image will be applied to down-scaling for few-layer and up-scaling again for the same amount of layers which is used for down-scaling. Matching the output of 2 layers that are size partners of up-scale and down-scale layers makes the segmentation more successful.

To measure the success of the model, it was used the Dice Coefficient (DICE). The DICE is a relative metric that provides a similarity measure between predicted and ground truth segmentations, as defined in Eq. 2:

$$DICE = \frac{2 \cdot tp}{2 \cdot tp + fp + fn}, \tag{2}$$

where the tp are the total number of pixels belonging to the veins in both masks: predicted and ground truth, the tn are the total number of pixels that mutually don't belong to predicted and ground truth masks. The fp are the total number of pixels predicted as veins but are not present in the ground truth mask. The tn are the total number of pixels predicted as not belonging to veins but are present in the ground truth mask.

5 Tests and Results

The framework was evaluated for the retinal visible area detection and for vessels segmentation test sets described in Sect. 3.

Retinal Visible Area Detection

Faster R-CNN model was used to detect retinal visible area detection. It was implemented in TensorFlow, with features pre-trained with Inception Resnet V2 and fine-tuned with the private dataset1. For augmenting dataset1 were applied rotations with 90-degree steps. The model was trained with default parametrization: l2_regularizer of 0.01, truncated_normal_initilalizer of 0.01, maxpool_kernel_size of 2, maxpool_stride of 2, localization_loss_weight of 2, objectness_loss_weigh of 1, score_converter Softmax, momentum optimizer with learning rate 0.0002, momentum_optimizer_value of 0.9.

The Faster R-CNN obtained results for retinal visible area detection can be seen in Table 2.

Table 2. Testset evaluation of the Faster R-CNN model for retinal visible area detection.

Classification score	Frequency	P1 MAE (pixels)*	P2 MAE (pixels)*	P1 and P2 MAE (pixels)*
0.0	30 (2%)	311 (414)	252 (321)	281 (371)
0.1	4 (0%)	46 (28)	41 (20)	43 (25)
0.2	12 (1%)	63 (41)	40 (31)	51 (38)
0.3	6 (0%)	47 (27)	30 (8)	38 (22)
0.4	7 (1%)	37 (23)	41 (26)	39 (24)
0.5	11 (1%)	76 (69)	50 (37)	63 (57)
0.6	11 (1%)	91 (60)	37 (20)	64 (52)
0.7	14 (1%)	61 (62)	35 (26)	48 (49)
0.8	29 (2%)	67 (50)	36 (20)	52 (41)
0.9	1,251 (91%)	47 (49)	28 (13)	37 (37)
Total images	1,375			

* MAE: mean (standard deviation)

The results are organized in 10 classification scores with intervals of 0.1. The detection was very successful as 91% of the test images were detected with the classification score equal to or greater than 0.9. As the confidence score decrease, the MAE errors keep approximately constant until it reaches the score interval 0.0, where it increases for the mean of 281 and a standard deviation of 371. A closer look at the data (not in Table 2) showed that interval 0.8 has 29 images all with a score greater than 0.85.

In Figs. 4 and 5, it can be seen examples of the predicted areas (green boxes) and the ground truth areas (yellow boxes) in the best and the worst sum of error P1 and P2 in each interval.

In all the intervals the predicted area include the visible retinal area, with the exception of confidence interval 0.0 for the worst sum of error P1 and P2 (Fig. 4, last row), where the prediction selection is in the upper left corner of the image. However, even the best error P1 and P2 in interval 0.0 include the retinal area. All the best error prediction are very accurate when compared with ground truth. The worst cases include the retinal and some other retinal areas (that is, a retinal area not selected in the ground truth probably due to the variability of the observer who annotated the images). So on the one hand, it can be concluded that the detection area was very accurate. On the other hand, the confidence score seems to be related to the quality of the retinal area, and in the lower interval, the areas appear less good particularly in interval 0.0.

We considered reasonable to use a threshold above 0.5 to accept the areas as valid-regions, that in this case achieved 96% of correct detected for all regions, with MAE of 39 pixels.

Retinal Vessel Segmentation

The U-Net model was implemented using Keras, with a TensorFlow backend. For training the U-Net model, it was used the binary cross-entropy as loss function and Adam's optimiser with 10^{-3} learning rate based on Ange Tato and Roger Nkambou's work [22] used to achieve faster a stable convergence. ReLU function was used for the nine layers and in the output layer, the sigmoid activation function has applied.

The model was trained first with DS3 (Model 1), then trained on the join of DS2 and DS3 testsets (Model 2) and later retrained Model 1 with DS2 (Model 3) to tune the network with D-EYE retinal data. The attained results are summarized in Table 3.

Table 3. Results of the Model 1, Model 2 and Model 3.

	Model 1	Model 2	Model 3
(DS3) testset	0.7824	–	0.5784
(DS2 & DS3) testset	0.7474	0.7312	–
(DS2) testset	0.4797	0.7547	0.5580

Model 1 is has a reasonable Dice coefficient that seems adequate for the task (0.7824). Observing Fig. 6, it can be seen that the best result (first column) was achieved a DICE of 0.935 in a patch where vessels are wide and well visible. The model predictions (row 3) have the same structure but seems wider than the ground truth (row 2).

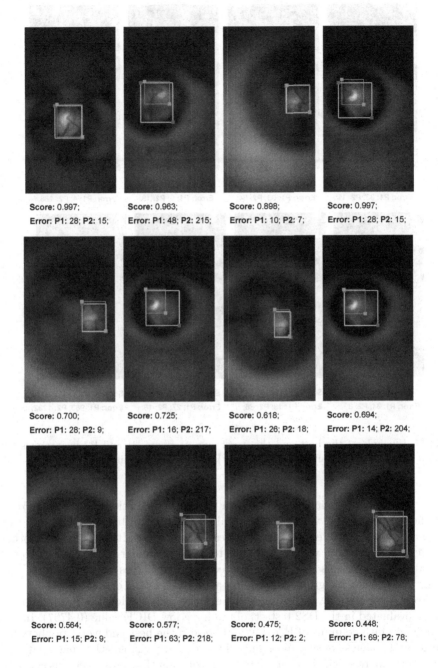

Fig. 4. Example of the best and the worst sum of errors P1 and P2 in intervals 0.9 and 0.8 (first row), 0.7 and 0.6 (second row) and 0.5 and 0.4 (third row). (Color figure online)

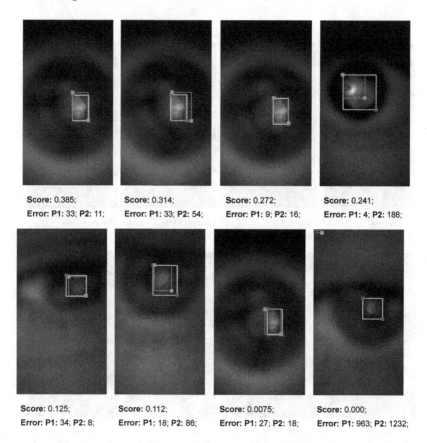

Fig. 5. Example of the best and the worst sum of errors P1 and P2 in intervals 0.3 and 0.2 (first row), 0.1 and 0.0 (second row). (Color figure online)

At the second column, it can be seen the worst prediction (DICE of 0.0512). At the original image, vessels are thin, almost imperceptible and quite different from the vessels expected to find in low-resolution images. It was selected another image patch with thin veins that seems to us more similar to the ones expected (third column). In this case, the predicted image preserves the structure, it also seems wider than the ground-truth and achieved a DICE of 0.8571.

To observe how the model Model 1 performs with the low-resolution images, it was evaluated in the DS2 testset, obtaining a low DICE value (0.4797). In the fourth and fifth columns of Fig. 6, it can be seen the best and worst predictions. Both patch images are very dark and veins are poorly visible - the image-patch of fifth is the poorest. The best-predicted segmentation (DICE of 0.8009) is actually very good, considering the visibility of the veins and though the difficulty of manually creating the ground-truth.

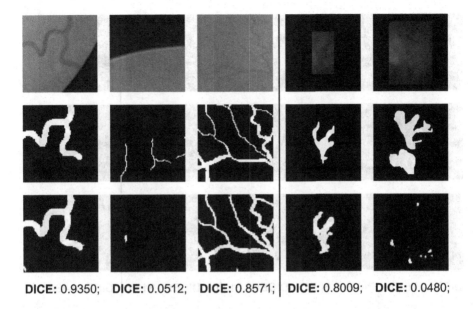

DICE: 0.9350;   **DICE:** 0.0512;   **DICE:** 0.8571;   **DICE:** 0.8009;   **DICE:** 0.0480;

Fig. 6. Example of image patches predicted with U-Net Model 1. The first row, original patches: the first three are from DS3 testset, respectively best, worst and reasonable predictions; and the last two from DS2 testset, respectively best and worst predictions. The second row, ground truth patches, and the third row, Model 1 predictions. (Color figure online)

The Model 2 achieved a DICE of 0.7312 on the join of DS2 and DS3 testsets that is lower than the obtained for Model 1 (DICE of 0.7474), but it achieved better on the DS2 testset (DICE of 0.7547). Examples of predicted images of Model 2 can be seen in Fig. 7.

To illustrate the Model 2 predictions of dataset DS2 testset, were chosen four images: the best prediction (DICE: 0.7510), two in-between predictions (DICE: 0.6054, DICE: 0.5100) and the worst prediction (DICE: 0.4304). For comparison with Model 1, column 5 has the predict results of the worst-patch image predicted by Model 1 (see Fig. 6, column 5). It can be seen that segmentations are much better: in the first two cases, the structure is all connected as in ground-truth, the other two (where veins are less visible in patch images) have several discontinuities in the structure. In column 5, ones can see that the Model 2 produces a much better segmentation (DICE: 0.4304) than the produced by Model 1 (see Fig. 6, lower right image).

The last tests made were for Model 3, by doing a posterior train of Model 1 with DS2, but the results were worse than with Model 1.

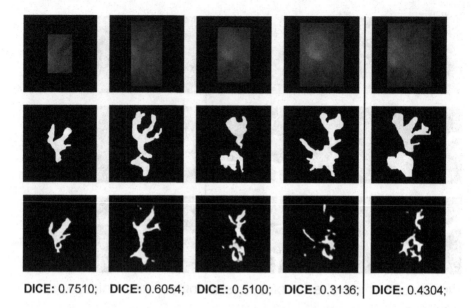

DICE: 0.7510;   DICE: 0.6054;   DICE: 0.5100;   DICE: 0.3136;   DICE: 0.4304;

Fig. 7. Example of image patches predicted with U-Net Model 2. The first row, original patches: the first four are from DS2 testset, respectively best, two in-between, and worst predictions; and for comparison, the worst case of Model 1 low-resolution prediction, is presented in the last column. The second row, ground truth patches, and the third row, Model 2 predictions.

6   Discussion and Conclusions

In this paper, a framework for vessels segmenting on lower-resolution retinal images was proposed, evaluated and the attained results were presented. A dataset of train models was assembled and annotated for automatic localization of retinal areas and for vessel segmentation. For the framework, two CNN-based models were successfully trained, a Faster R-CNN that achieved a 96% correct detection of all regions with an MAE of 39 pixels, and a U-Net that achieved a DICE of 0.7547. This study is precursor to future works to the determination of eye diseases, such as glaucoma and diabetes, applied to low-resolution images.

Acknowledgments. This project was financed by the Portuguese funding agency, FCT - Fundação para a Ciência e a Tecnologia, through national funds, and co-funded by the FEDER, where applicable.

This paper is financed by LARSyS - FCT Plurianual funding 2020–2023.

References

1. D-Eye Web Site. https://www.d-eyecare.com/en_PT/product
2. Almotiri, J., Elleithy, K., Elleithy, A.: Retinal vessels segmentation techniques and algorithms: a survey. Appl. Sci. **8**(2), 155 (2018). https://doi.org/10.3390/app8020155. http://www.mdpi.com/2076-3417/8/2/155
3. Alom, M.Z., Hasan, M., Yakopcic, C., Taha, T.M., Asari, V.K.: Recurrent residual convolutional neural network based on U-Net (R2U-Net) for medical image segmentation (February 2018). http://arxiv.org/abs/1802.06955
4. Bertolino, P.: SENSAREA, a general public video editing application. In: 21st IEEE International Conference on Image Processing (ICIP 2014). IEEE, Paris (October 2014). https://hal.archives-ouvertes.fr/hal-01080565
5. Claro, M., Veras, R., Santos, L., Frazão, M., Carvalho Filho, A., Leite, D.: Métodos computacionais para segmentação do disco óptico em imagens de retina: uma revisão. Revista Brasileira de Computação Aplicada **10**(2), 29–43 (2018). https://doi.org/10.5335/rbca.v10i2.7661. http://seer.upf.br/index.php/rbca/article/view/7661
6. Fraz, M.M., Rudnicka, A.R., Owen, C.G., Strachan, D.P., Barman, S.A.: Automated arteriole and venule recognition in retinal images using ensemble classification. In: Proceedings of the 9th International Conference on Computer Vision Theory and Applications, vol. 3, pp. 194–202. SCITEPRESS - Science and and Technology Publications (2014). https://doi.org/10.5220/0004733701940202
7. Gargeya, R., Leng, T.: Automated identification of diabetic retinopathy using deep learning. Ophthalmology **124**(7), 962–969 (2017). https://doi.org/10.1016/j.ophtha.2017.02.008. https://linkinghub.elsevier.com/retrieve/pii/S0161642016317742
8. Girshick, R.: Fast R-CNN. In: 2015 IEEE International Conference on Computer Vision (ICCV), vol. 2015 Inter, pp. 1440–1448. IEEE (December 2015). https://doi.org/10.1109/ICCV.2015.169. http://ieeexplore.ieee.org/document/7410526/
9. Hoover, A., Kouznetsova, V., Goldbaum, M.: Locating blood vessels in retinal images by piecewise threshold probing of a matched filter response. IEEE Trans. Med. Imaging **19**(3), 203–210 (2000). https://doi.org/10.1109/42.845178. http://ieeexplore.ieee.org/document/845178/
10. Imran, A., Li, J., Pei, Y., Yang, J.J., Wang, Q.: Comparative analysis of vessel segmentation techniques in retinal images. IEEE Access **7**, 114862–114887 (2019). https://doi.org/10.1109/ACCESS.2019.2935912. https://ieeexplore.ieee.org/document/8804190/
11. Jiang, Y., Zhang, H., Tan, N., Chen, L.: Automatic retinal blood vessel segmentation based on fully convolutional neural networks. Symmetry **11**(9), 1112 (2019). https://doi.org/10.3390/sym11091112. https://www.mdpi.com/2073-8994/11/9/1112
12. Jin, Q., Meng, Z., Pham, T.D., Chen, Q., Wei, L., Su, R.: DUNet: a deformable network for retinal vessel segmentation. Knowl.-Based Syst. **178**(8), 149–162 (2019). https://doi.org/10.1016/j.knosys.2019.04.025. https://linkinghub.elsevier.com/retrieve/pii/S0950705119301984
13. Jones, N.P., Sala-Puigdollers, A., Stanga, P.E.: Ultra-widefield fundus fluorescein angiography in the diagnosis and management of retinal vasculitis. Eye **31**(11), 1546–1549 (2017). https://doi.org/10.1038/eye.2017.93. http://www.nature.com/articles/eye201793

14. MacGillivray, T.J., Trucco, E., Cameron, J.R., Dhillon, B., Houston, J.G., van Beek, E.J.R.: Retinal imaging as a source of biomarkers for diagnosis, characterization and prognosis of chronic illness or long-term conditions. Br. J. Radiol. **87**(1040), 20130832 (2014). https://doi.org/10.1259/bjr.20130832. http://www.birpublications.org/doi/10.1259/bjr.20130832

15. McGrory, S., et al.: The application of retinal fundus camera imaging in dementia: a systematic review. Alzheimer's Dement.: Diagn. Assess. Dis. Monit. **6**, 91–107 (2017). https://doi.org/10.1016/j.dadm.2016.11.001

16. Mohammadpour, M., Heidari, Z., Mirghorbani, M., Hashemi, H.: Smartphones, tele-ophthalmology, and VISION 2020. Int. J. Ophthalmol. **10**(12), 1909–1918 (2017). https://doi.org/10.18240/ijo.2017.12.19. http://www.ijo.cn/gjyken/ch/reader/viewabstract.aspx?fileno=20171219&flag=1

17. Owen, C.G., et al.: Measuring retinal vessel tortuosity in 10-year-old children: validation of the computer-assisted image analysis of the retina (CAIAR) program. Investig. Opthalmol. Vis. Sci. **50**(5), 2004 (2009). https://doi.org/10.1167/iovs.08-3018. http://iovs.arvojournals.org/article.aspx?doi=10.1167/iovs.08-3018

18. Ren, S., He, K., Girshick, R., Sun, J.: Faster R-CNN: towards real-time object detection with region proposal networks. IEEE Trans. Pattern Anal. Mach. Intell. **39**(6), 1137–1149 (2017). https://doi.org/10.1109/TPAMI.2016.2577031. http://ieeexplore.ieee.org/document/7485869/

19. Ronneberger, O., Fischer, P., Brox, T.: U-Net: Convolutional networks for biomedical image segmentation. In: Navab, N., Hornegger, J., Wells, W.M., Frangi, A.F. (eds.) MICCAI 2015. LNCS, vol. 9351, pp. 234–241. Springer, Cham (2015). https://doi.org/10.1007/978-3-319-24574-4_28

20. Singh, N., Kaur, L.: A survey on blood vessel segmentation methods in retinal images. In: 2015 International Conference on Electronic Design, Computer Networks & Automated Verification (EDCAV), pp. 23–28. IEEE (January 2015). https://doi.org/10.1109/EDCAV.2015.7060532. http://ieeexplore.ieee.org/document/7060532/

21. Staal, J., Abramoff, M., Niemeijer, M., Viergever, M., van Ginneken, B.: Ridge-based vessel segmentation in color images of the retina. IEEE Trans. Med. Imaging **23**(4), 501–509 (2004). https://doi.org/10.1109/TMI.2004.825627. http://ieeexplore.ieee.org/document/1282003/

22. Tato, A., Nkambou, R.: Workshop track -ICLR 2018 Improving Adam Optimizer, pp. 1–4 (2018)

23. Tuba, E., Mrkela, L., Tuba, M.: Retinal blood vessel segmentation by support vector machine classification. In: 2017 27th International Conference Radioelektronika (RADIOELEKTRONIKA), pp. 1–6. IEEE (April2017). https://doi.org/10.1109/RADIOELEK.2017.7936649. http://ieeexplore.ieee.org/document/7936649/

24. Tzutalin, D.: LabelImg (2015). https://github.com/tzutalin/labelImg

25. Vilela, M.A.P., Valença, F.M., Barreto, P.K.M., Amaral, C.E.V., Pellanda, L.C.: Agreement between retinal images obtained via smartphones and images obtained with retinal cameras or fundoscopic exams – systematic review and meta-analysis. Clin. Ophthalmol. **12**, 2581–2589 (2018). https://doi.org/10.2147/OPTH.S182022. https://www.dovepress.com/agreement-between-retinal-images-obtained-via-smartphones-and-images-o-peer-reviewed-article-OPTH

26. Viswanath, K., McGavin, D.D.M.: Diabetic retinopathy: clinical findings and management. Community Eye Health **16**(46), 21–4 (2003). http://www.ncbi.nlm.nih.gov/pubmed/17491851

27. Wang, Y.B., Zhu, C.Z., Yan, Q.F., Liu, L.Q.: A novel vessel segmentation in fundus images based on SVM. In: 2016 International Conference on Information System and Artificial Intelligence (ISAI), pp. 390–394. IEEE (June 2016). https://doi.org/10.1109/ISAI.2016.0089. http://ieeexplore.ieee.org/document/7816742/

28. Wu, A.R., Fouzdar-Jain, S., Suh, D.W.: Comparison study of funduscopic examination using a smartphone-based digital ophthalmoscope and the direct ophthalmoscope. J. Pediatr. Ophthalmol. Strabismus **55**(3), 201–206 (2018). https://doi.org/10.3928/01913913-20180220-01

29. Zhuang, J.: LadderNet: multi-path networks based on U-Net for medical image segmentation, pp. 2–5 (October 2018). http://arxiv.org/abs/1810.07810

Correction to: METUIGA "Methodology for the Design of Systems Based on Tangible User Interfaces and Gamification Techniques"

Case Study: Teaching Geometry in Children with Visual Problems

Luis Roberto Ramos Aguiar🆔
and Francisco Javier Álvarez Rodríguez🆔

Correction to:
Chapter "METUIGA "Methodology for the Design of Systems Based on Tangible User Interfaces and Gamification Techniques": Case Study: Teaching Geometry in Children with Visual Problems" in: M. Antona and C. Stephanidis (Eds.): *Universal Access in Human-Computer Interaction. Applications and Practice*, LNCS 12189, https://doi.org/10.1007/978-3-030-49108-6_17

In the version of this paper that was originally published, it was not mentioned that the basic idea and requirements of the application for teaching visually impaired children about shapes, presented in the case study, had been taken from the Jafri et al.'s work (see below). Therefore the following references have been added:

- Jafri, R., Aljuhani, A.M., Ali, S.A.: A tangible interface-based application for teaching tactual shape perception and spatial awareness sub-concepts to visually impaired children." Procedia Manufact. **3**, 5562–5569 (2015)
- Jafri, R., Aljuhani, A.M., Ali, S.A.: A tangible user interface-based application utilizing 3D-printed manipulatives for teaching tactual shape perception and spatial awareness sub-concepts to visually impaired children. Int. J. Child-Computer Interact. **11**, 3–11 (2017)

The updated version of this chapter can be found at
https://doi.org/10.1007/978-3-030-49108-6_17

© Springer Nature Switzerland AG 2020
M. Antona and C. Stephanidis (Eds.): HCII 2020, LNCS 12189, p. C1, 2020.
https://doi.org/10.1007/978-3-030-49108-6_45

Author Index

...ated in the United States
...Bookmasters